SCOTT FORESMAN
Reading Street

Let's Practice It!

Custom Edition for Jersey City

GRADE 5

PEARSON

Taken from:

Scott Foresman Reading Street Teacher Resource DVD-ROM, Grade 5
Copyright © 2011 by Pearson Education, Inc.
Published by Scott Foresman
Upper Saddle River, New Jersey 07458

Pearson Learning Solutions, 501 Boylston Street, Suite 900, Boston, MA 02116
A Pearson Education Company
www.pearsoned.com

Printed in the United States of America

8 19

000200010271666752

CF

ISBN 10: 1-256-73976-6
ISBN 13: 978-1-256-73976-0

Content

Grade 5

Name ____________________

Short Vowels VCCV, VCV

- **Generalization** Short vowels are often spelled **a: channel**, **e: method**, **i: distance**, **o: problem**, **u: butter**.

Word Sort Sort words by short vowel patterns VCCV or VCV.

VCCV

1. ____________
2. ____________
3. ____________
4. ____________
5. ____________
6. ____________
7. ____________
8. ____________
9. ____________
10. ____________
11. ____________
12. ____________
13. ____________
14. ____________
15. ____________

VCV

16. ____________
17. ____________
18. ____________
19. ____________
20. ____________

Spelling Words

1. distance
2. method
3. anger
4. problem
5. butter
6. petals
7. enjoy
8. perhaps
9. figure
10. channel
11. admire
12. comedy
13. husband
14. tissue
15. mustard
16. shuttle
17. advance
18. drummer
19. regular
20. denim

Home Activity Your child is learning about words that have the short vowel sounds *a*, *e*, *i*, *o*, and *u*. Have your child name three words from the list and tell you what the short vowel sound is in each word.

Name

Family Times

Summary

Red Kayak

On a cold spring day, 13-year-old Brady Parks helps search for two people who are missing after they went for a canoe ride in a creek near the Corsica River. Brady takes his dog, Tilly, in his father's motorboat to search for the mother and her three-year-old boy. He needs to stay calm and remember what he learned about rescuing people. Lives may depend on him.

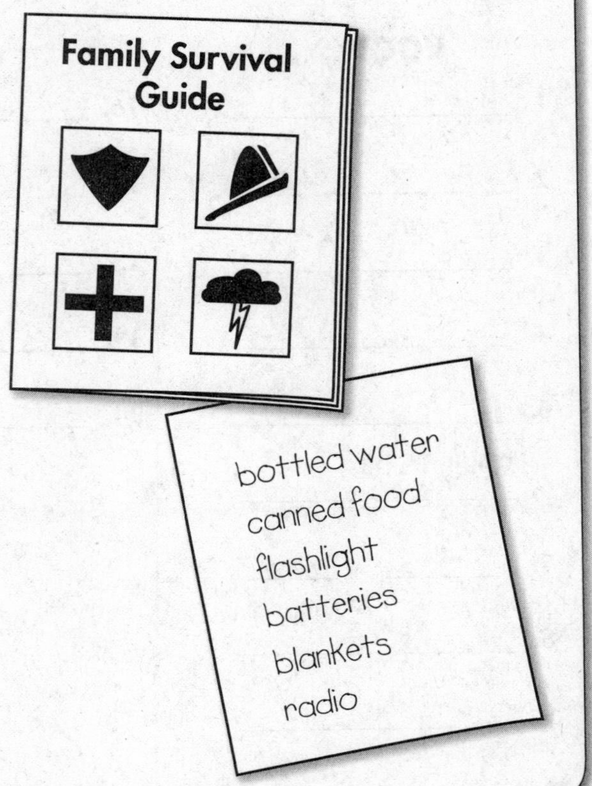

Family Survival Guide
bottled water
canned food
flashlight
batteries
blankets
radio

Activity

Survival Guide Brady was nervous about rescuing Ben, but he was effective. He knew ahead of time what had to be done. With a family member, prepare for how you should handle different types of emergencies that could happen. Write down these plans in a booklet made out of two or more pieces of paper folded in half.

Comprehension Skill

Plot and Character

The **plot** is what happens in a story. **Characters** are the people or animals in a story. Characters show you what they are like by what they say and do and how they treat each other.

Activity

Family Stories Make up an adventure story involving yourself or someone you know and tell it to a member of your family. Try to make the story full of action, and make sure to describe the main character with details you know about the person in real life.

Lesson Vocabulary

Words to Know

Knowing the meanings of these words is important to reading *Red Kayak*. Practice using these words.

Vocabulary Words

intentionally on purpose

insistently repeatedly or with persistence

grumbled complained in a low voice

compressions applications of pressure

minute extremely small

neutral a position of gears in which no motion goes from an engine to other working parts

normally usually

Conventions

Four Kinds of Sentences

Sentences can be classified in four different ways. **Declarative** sentences tell something and end with a period. *For example: I forgot to eat breakfast this morning.* **Interrogative** sentences ask something and end in a question mark. *For example: Would you like something to eat?* **Imperative** sentences give a command or make a request and end with a period. *For example: Sit down.* **Exclamatory** sentences express strong feelings and often end with an exclamation mark. *For example: I'm starving!*

Activity

What Did You Say? With a family member, cut up eight strips of paper. Write *I say* on two strips, *I ask* on two strips, *I command* on two strips, and *I believe* on two strips. Put the strips in a hat, and pick one out of the hat. Make up a sentence that goes with the words on the strip of paper you picked. Say it out loud. Take turns picking out strips one at a time. Your sentences can be as funny or as silly as you like.

Practice Tested Spelling Words

______	______	______	______
______	______	______	______
______	______	______	______
______	______	______	______
______	______	______	______

Name ______________________________

Character and Plot

- A **character** is a person or animal that takes part in the events of a story.
- The **plot** is the pattern of events in a story and includes (1) a problem or **conflict,** (2) **rising action,** as the conflict builds, (3) a **climax,** when the problem or conflict is faced, and (4) a **resolution,** when the problem or conflict is solved.

Directions Read the following passage. Then answer the questions below.

Larry was excited about lunch. For the first time, he had made his own triple-decker sandwich, just the way he liked it. Plus, his mom had added one of his favorite snacks to the bag. Usually Larry just gobbled up his sandwich at lunch and ran out to the playground. But not today—he was going to take his time.

When the lunch bell rang, he grabbed his bag and rushed to the cafeteria. He was so excited he didn't see the backpack someone had left on the floor. SPLAT! Larry tumbled to the floor, landing flat on his lunch bag. When he took his prized sandwich out, it was flat. But Larry didn't mind—he knew it would still be delicious!

1. Why was Larry excited about lunch?

____

2. How do you think Larry felt about making his own sandwich?

____

3. Why was Larry in such a hurry to get to the cafeteria?

____

____

4. What about Larry's character makes you think Larry didn't mind what happened to his sandwich?

____

____

5. On a separate sheet of paper, describe something that you did for yourself for the first time. How was that experience similar to Larry's?

Home Activity Your child analyzed character elements in a passage and answered questions about them. Tell your child a few things that have happened to you recently. Have your child explain how you probably felt about these events.

Name______________________________

Sequence

Directions Read the following passage. Then answer the questions below.

First, Jill asked Andy to hold her art project while she ran back to her locker to get an assignment. Andy waited patiently by the door, holding Jill's handmade pottery bowl in both hands. It was really quite pretty, he thought. Next, after about ten minutes, Andy began to wonder where Jill was. He needed to get home—his family was going out for pizza that night. Andy decided to go back into the school and find Jill. Then, just as he reached out to unlatch the door, it came blasting open, knocking right into Jill's bowl and sending it toward the ground. Andy quickly dove to the cement and caught the bowl.

Andy stood up. He could see a small chip in the lip of the bowl. Jill was standing at the door, her mouth wide open.

"Sorry," he said.

Finally, Jill said, "Sorry? That was amazing! Thank you for catching it!"

1. What happened first in the story?

____

____

2. What did Andy think after ten minutes?

____

____

3. What happened when Jill came back?

____

____

4. What did Jill finally say?

____

____

5. What do you think might happen next? Write your answer on a separate sheet of paper.

Home Activity Your child has read a fictional scene and answered questions about the sequence of events. Read a story with your child and discuss the sequence of events in the story.

Name ______________________________

Four Kinds of Sentences

Directions Complete each sentence by adding your own words and the correct end punctuation. The label tells what kind of sentence each should be.

1. People in boats and kayaks ________ (declarative)

____

____

2. Have you ever ________ (interrogative)

____

____

3. Wow! Emergencies ________ (exclamatory)

____

____

4. A class in CPR ________ (declarative)

____

____

5. Please learn ________ (imperative)

____

____

Directions Think about an emergency you saw or were involved in. Write three sentences describing the emergency. Make each sentence a different kind.

____

____

____

____

Home Activity Your child learned how to use four kinds of sentences in writing. Have your child write about his or her homework routine, including at least one declarative, one interrogative, one imperative, and one exclamatory sentence.

Name ____________________

Short Vowel VCCV, VCV

Spelling Words				
distance	method	anger	problem	butter
petals	enjoy	perhaps	figure	channel
admire	comedy	husband	tissue	mustard
shuttle	advance	drummer	regular	denim

Word Search Circle ten hidden list words. Words are down, across, and diagonal. Write the words on the lines.

S	M	D	I	S	T	A	N	C	E	D	H
T	H	E	R	P	E	T	A	L	S	R	U
I	M	U	T	E	C	J	L	I	L	U	S
S	X	L	T	H	G	P	Y	Q	Z	M	B
S	K	R	K	T	O	U	B	C	T	M	A
U	X	O	V	A	L	D	L	Q	T	E	N
E	C	H	A	N	N	E	L	A	G	R	D
A	D	M	I	R	E	Z	G	M	R	K	W

1. ____________
2. ____________
3. ____________
4. ____________
5. ____________
6. ____________
7. ____________
8. ____________
9. ____________
10. ____________

Scramble Unscramble the list words and write them on the lines.

11. cydoem **11.** ____________ **12.** gurife **12.** ____________
13. stamurd **13.** ____________ **14.** mepbolr **14.** ____________
15. medin **15.** ____________ **16.** ynejo **16.** ____________
17. geran **17.** ____________ **18.** teubtr **18.** ____________
19. sahpepr **19.** ____________ **20.** vedanac **20.** ____________

Home Activity Your child has learned to spell longer words with short vowel sounds. Pick two list words and ask your child to use them in a sentence.

Name ______________________________

Character and Plot

- A **character** is a person or animal in a story.
- The **plot** is the pattern of events in a story.

Directions Read the following passage. Then complete the diagram by filling in the elements of the story.

Becky sat in front of me in class, and I knew she was cheating. I wanted her to stop. When we passed our homework to the front, she'd quickly copy mine and turn in her paper like it was her work. I knew I should tell the teacher, but I was afraid of being called a snitch. Finally, I got an idea. One night, I wrote two copies of my homework. One version had the correct answers. The other had answers that sounded good, but were wrong.

The next day, I gave my real homework to my friend, Taka, in the front row. "When the homework passes to you, switch mine with this copy," I said. Taka knew about Becky. "Sure, Audrey!" he agreed. The teacher corrected our homework and returned it at the end of class. "Becky," he asked, handing back "her" homework, "were you asleep when you did this work?" Becky stared at the big "zero" at the top of her page in disbelief. She never copied my homework again.

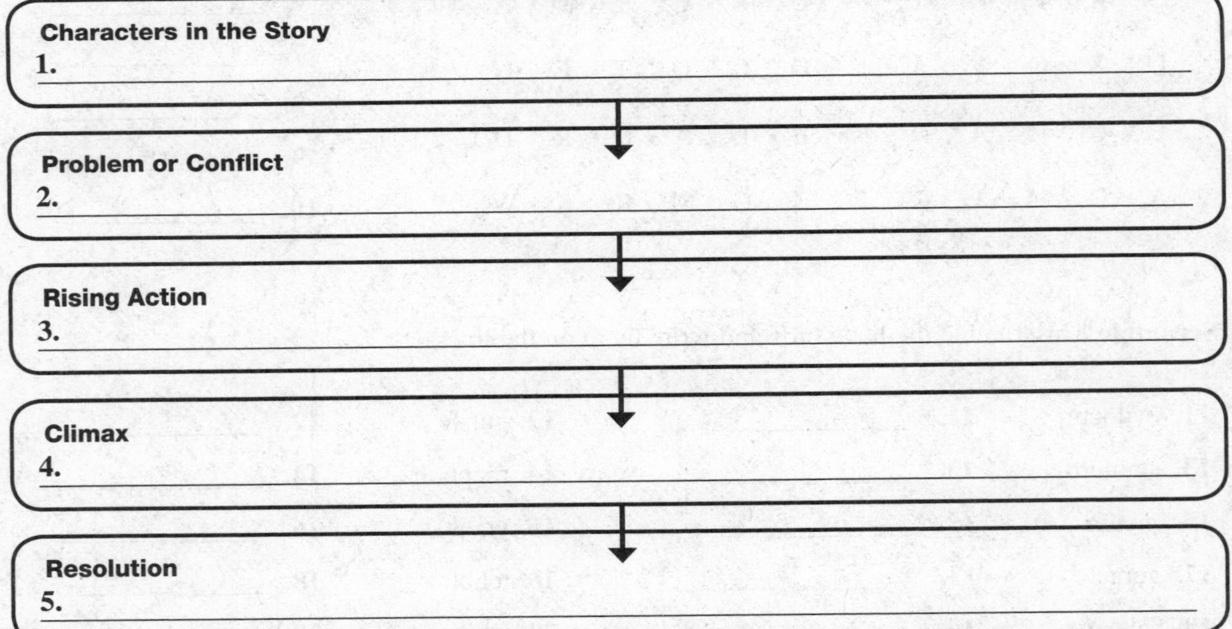

Characters in the Story
1.
Problem or Conflict
2.
Rising Action
3.
Climax
4.
Resolution
5.

Home Activity Your child identified characters and plot details in a short passage. Discuss the plot of a favorite book or movie with your child, analyzing how its events lead toward the resolution of the problem or conflict established in the beginning of the story

Name ______________________________

Four Kinds of Sentences

Directions Add the correct end punctuation to each sentence. Then on the line write whether the sentence is *declarative, interrogative, imperative,* or *exclamatory.*

1. Have you ever ridden in a boat ______________

2. It's important to know about boat safety ______________

3. Be sure to wear a life jacket ______________

4. Wow! The water can be dangerous ______________

5. Please learn how to swim ______________

Directions Underline the mistakes in each sentence. Write the correct letter or punctuation mark above each underline.

6. can you paddle a kayak.

7. kayaks are fun in rivers and lakes!

8. watch out for that waterfall?

9. don't let the boat tip over

10. kayaking takes practice

11. always wear a helmet?

Directions Add your own words to complete each sentence. Write the new sentences. Be sure you use end punctuation correctly.

12. Safety rules for boats ________

____

13. A ride in a kayak ________

____

14. Don't ________

____

15. Would you like ________

____

Home Activity Your child reviewed four kinds of sentences. For five minutes, write down what you say to each other. Have your child identify each kind of sentence.

Name____________________

Long Vowel VCV

- **Generalization** Long vowels can be spelled **a: basic**, **e: fever**, **i: climate**, **o: hotel**.

Word Sort Sort words by the long vowel *a*, *e*, *i*, or *o*.

a

1. ____________
2. ____________
3. ____________
4. ____________
5. ____________
6. ____________

e

7. ____________
8. ____________

i

9. ____________
10. ____________
11. ____________
12. ____________
13. ____________
14. ____________

o

15. ____________
16. ____________
17. ____________
18. ____________
19. ____________
20. ____________

Spelling Words

1. fever
2. broken
3. climate
4. hotel
5. basic
6. vocal
7. native
8. silent
9. labor
10. spider
11. label
12. icon
13. agent
14. motive
15. vital
16. acorn
17. item
18. aroma
19. ego
20. solo

School + Home

Home Activity Your child is learning about the long vowel VCV pattern. Say and spell words aloud with your child, and ask your child to identify the long vowel sounds in each word.

Name

Family Times

Summary

Thunder Rose

Thunder Rose is an amazing girl! As a baby she drank milk straight from the cow. Rose constructed a building of iron and wood at age nine, and she could rustle a wild steer with her own hands by twelve. Once, Rose calmed two churning tornadoes with the song her parents sang for her as a baby. All in a day's work for the girl with thunder in her veins.

Activity

The Taller the Better Tall tales use exaggeration to tell the story of impossible events, often because of some superhuman ability of a character. With a family member, make up your own tall tale about someone in your family. Don't hold back—the taller, the better.

Comprehension Skill

Cause and Effect

A **cause** is what makes something happen. An **effect** is what happens as a result of the cause. An effect may have one or more causes. Sometimes authors will use words such as *because* and *so* to show cause and effect.

Activity

The Why of the What Read a story with a family member. After any major event occurs, pause and identify why the event happened. There may be one thing that caused it, or there may be two or more causes.

Lesson Vocabulary

Words to Know

Knowing the meanings of these words is important to reading *Thunder Rose.* Practice using these words.

Vocabulary Words

branded marked by burning the skin with a hot iron

constructed fitted together; built

daintily with delicate beauty; freshly and prettily

devastation waste; destruction

lullaby song for singing to a child

pitch thick, black, sticky substance made from tar or turpentine

resourceful good at thinking of ways to do things

thieving stealing

veins blood vessels that carry blood to the heart from all parts of the body

Conventions

Subjects and Predicates

A complete sentence must have a **subject** and a **predicate.** The subject is the word or group of words that tells whom or what the sentence is about. The predicate is the word or group of words that tell something about the subject. *For example: Michael is supposed to go to bed.* "Michael" is the *subject* and "is supposed to go to bed" is the *predicate*. If a sentence does not have one of each, it is not a sentence but a **sentence fragment.**

Activity

Sentence Junction With a family member, have one of you write down six numbered subjects on a piece of paper. They could be words like "I," "My dog," etc. Have the other person write down six numbered predicates on a separate sheet of paper. These could be phrases like "stared at my homework," "do silly things," etc. Now take turns rolling two numbers on a number cube. Use each pair of numbers to join subjects and predicates from your lists into new sentences. What kinds of inventive sentences can you come up with together?

Practice Tested Spelling Words

Name________________________________

Cause and Effect

- A **cause** is what makes something happen. An **effect** is what happens as a result of the cause.
- If there are no clue words, ask yourself, "What made this event happen? What happened as a result of this event?"
- An effect may become the cause of another effect.

Directions Read the following passage. Then answer the questions below.

Walking home, Arthur could hardly see where he was going. The fierce wind whipped the snow around. At least a foot of snow covered the sidewalks. His socks, shoes, and pant legs were soaked, and his hands felt like ice. He knew his dad would be home from work when he got there. He just hoped that there would be some warm cocoa and popcorn waiting. Finally, he reached his door. As he hurried inside, he could smell cocoa and popcorn. Arthur changed out of his wet clothes and sat down to enjoy his snack with his dad. But the best part of all was the news on television. Because of the bad storm that Arthur had walked through, there would be no school the next day!

1. Why was Arthur unable to see where he was going?

____

2. What were some of the effects of the snowstorm in the neighborhood?

____

3. What was an effect of the snowstorm that pleased Arthur?

____

____

4. If you had a day off from school because of bad weather, what would you do with it?

____

____

5. What was the cause of the last day you had off from school, other than a weekend?

____

____

Home Activity Your child read a short passage and answered questions about cause and effect. With your child, write a short story about a hero. Include what caused the person to act heroically and the effects of his or her heroism.

Name______________________________

Character and Plot

Directions Read the scene. Then answer the questions below.

Alice was rearranging her collection of glass birds. She'd just added a tiny and fragile glass hummingbird to her collection. Just as she finished, her neighbor Jim stopped by with his dog, a nervous and jumpy cocker spaniel. Jim asked, "Can you feed my dog while I'm away tomorrow?" Before she could answer, the phone rang, and Alice left the room to answer it. As she hung up, a crack of thunder pounded through the air. Alice heard Jim's dog barking frantically and then heard a loud crash! Alice didn't dare imagine what devastation the dog had caused. The veins in her head throbbed as she returned to the living room. She saw Jim looking guilty with his dog hiding behind his legs. Jim looked up at Alice and said, "I hope I didn't startle you. I was going to the recycling center after I left here. I dropped my bag of bottles when I heard the thunder." Alice turned to look at the display case with her glass birds. Every bird was in its place. Alice told Jim, "No problem. It was quite a noise. By the way, I'd be happy to feed your dog."

1. What was Alice doing at the beginning of the story?

____

2. What did Alice think had happened when she heard the crash?

____

3. How did the writer describe the dog? How does the description of the dog fit with what Alice thought happened?

____

____

4. How are Jim and his dog described when Alice returns to the living room? How does their behavior fit with what Alice thought happened?

____

____

5. On a separate sheet of paper, write a version of this story in which Jim's dog breaks Alice's collection of birds. Try to use what you know about Alice, Jim, and the dog from this passage to help you figure out how they will react.

Home Activity Your child has read a short passage and answered questions about the characters and the plot. Tell your child a story about a family member and have them identify the plot and the characters.

Name ____________________

Subjects and Predicates

Directions Use each noun and verb pair as part of the subject and predicate. Add words to make a complete sentence. Underline the complete subject once and the complete predicate twice.

1. tall tales include

____

____

2. hero is

____

____

3. stories make

____

____

4. Pecos Bill lassoed

____

____

5. Paul Bunyan rode

____

____

Directions This paragraph contains fragments and a run-on. Rewrite the paragraph. Add words and punctuation to make sure every sentence has a subject and a predicate.

Davy Crockett was a real person he was also the hero of many tall tales. A good frontiersman and hunter. Killed a bear when he was only three. This "king of the wild frontier."

____

____

____

____

Home Activity Your child learned how to write sentences that have subjects and predicates. Name a familiar person. Have your child write three sentences about the person and underline the complete subject and circle the complete predicate in each sentence.

Name______________________________

Long Vowel VCV

Spelling Words				
fever	broken	climate	hotel	basic
vocal	native	silent	labor	spider
label	icon	agent	motive	vital
acorn	item	aroma	ego	solo

Scrambled Words Unscramble the list words and write them on the line.

1. oslo **1.** ____________
2. calvo **2.** ____________
3. marao **3.** ____________
4. coin **4.** ____________
5. racon **5.** ____________
6. ernkbo **6.** ____________
7. vietom **7.** ____________
8. vainte **8.** ____________
9. tinsel **9.** ____________
10. livat **10.** ____________
11. baell **11.** ____________
12. cabsi **12.** ____________
13. oge **13.** ____________
14. dresip **14.** ____________
15. rabol **15.** ____________
16. mite **16.** ____________

Hidden Words Each of these small words can be found inside one of the list words. Write the list word that contains the small word.

17. mate **17.** ____________ **18.** ever **18.** ____________
19. hot **19.** ____________ **20.** age **20.** ____________

Home Activity Your child has unscrambled words with long vowel sounds. Ask your child to scramble two list words and see if you can unscramble them.

Name ________________________________

Cause and Effect

- A **cause** is what makes something happen. An **effect** is what happens as a result of the cause.
- If there are no clue words, ask yourself, "What made this event happen? What happened as a result of this event?"
- An effect may become the cause of another effect.

Directions Read the following passage.

Anna wished she hadn't done it. She didn't even like snowball fights. She was just leaving the library with a novel she couldn't wait to read. A bunch of kids from her school came running up the street, laughing and throwing snowballs at one another. Anna knew one of the girls, Lucy, so when Lucy tossed a snowball at Anna, Anna tossed one back. But who knew that Lucy was going to slip on some ice at that exact moment? The snowball flew right over Lucy's head and squarely into Mr. Anderson's nose. Anna rushed over to apologize. Mr. Anderson was about to say something angry. But when he saw the book Anna was carrying, he started to smile. "Do you know," he said, "when I was your age that was my favorite book. I hope you enjoy it as much as I did." "I'm sure I will," Anna replied with surprise. "I can't wait to read it!"

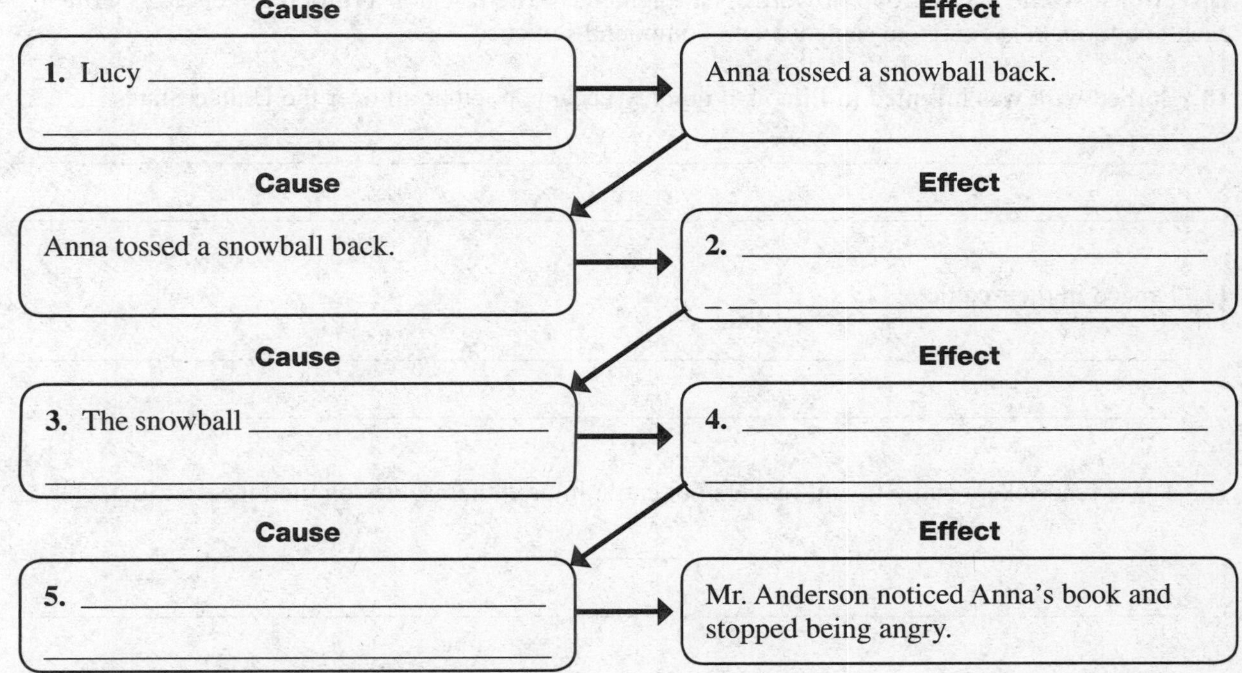

Cause	Effect
1. Lucy ____________	Anna tossed a snowball back.
Anna tossed a snowball back.	2. ____________
3. The snowball ____________	4. ____________
5. ____________	Mr. Anderson noticed Anna's book and stopped being angry.

Home Activity Your child read a short passage and identified the causes and effects. Read a short story with your child. Have your child explain to you the effects of one of the story's causes. Then ask your child to figure out if the effect becomes the cause of another effect.

Name ______________________________________

Subjects and Predicates

Directions Draw a line between the complete subject and the complete predicate in each sentence.

1. A blacksmith was important to the pioneer community.
2. People called this metal worker a smithy.
3. He could mend a plow, and he could mend tools.
4. The powerful man pounded steel on his anvil.
5. Fascinated children watched the smithy at work.

Directions Identify the part of the sentence that is underlined. Write *complete subject,* or *complete predicate.*

6. Patient oxen were once beasts of burden. ______________________________
7. A pair of oxen might pull a wagon. ______________________________
8. These big animals could plow all day. ______________________________
9. The farmer walked along behind. ______________________________

Directions: Write *F* if a group of words is a fragment. Write *R* if it is a run-on sentence. Rewrite each one to make a complete sentence or a compound sentence.

10. Barbed wire was invented in Illinois it quickly became popular all over the United States. ______

____

____

11. Fenced in their cattle. ______

____

____

12. These fences kept cattle in and rustlers out cattle injured themselves on the fences at first. ______

____

____

Home Activity Your child reviewed subjects, predicates, fragments, and run-ons. Ask your child to make a note card for each term with the definition on one side and an example on the other.

Name ______________________________

Long Vowel Digraphs

- **Generalization** Long *a* is sometimes spelled **ai**: **paint**. Long *e* is sometimes spelled **ee** and **ea**: **speech**, **feast**. Long *o* is sometimes spelled **oa** and **ow**: **coast**, **arrow**.

Word Sort Sort words by the spelling of the long vowel sound.

ai

1. ______________
2. ______________
3. ______________
4. ______________
5. ______________
6. ______________
7. ______________

ee

8. ______________
9. ______________
10. ______________
11. ______________

ea

12. ______________
13. ______________
14. ______________
15. ______________

oa

16. ______________
17. ______________

ow

18. ______________
19. ______________
20. ______________

Spelling Words

1. coast
2. feast
3. speech
4. wheat
5. Spain
6. paint
7. arrow
8. needle
9. charcoal
10. praise
11. faint
12. maintain
13. crease
14. grain
15. breeze
16. willow
17. appeal
18. bowling
19. complain
20. sneeze

Home Activity Your child is learning about different spelling patterns for long vowel sounds. Select three list words and ask your child which pattern spells the long vowel in each word.

Name ______________________________

Family Times

Summary

Island of the Blue Dolphins

Karana is an Indian girl stranded alone on an island. While waiting years for a ship to come near and rescue her, she finds inventive ways of living on an island inhabited by wild dogs. She makes a cave house, creates her own tools, finds food, and survives many years on her own.

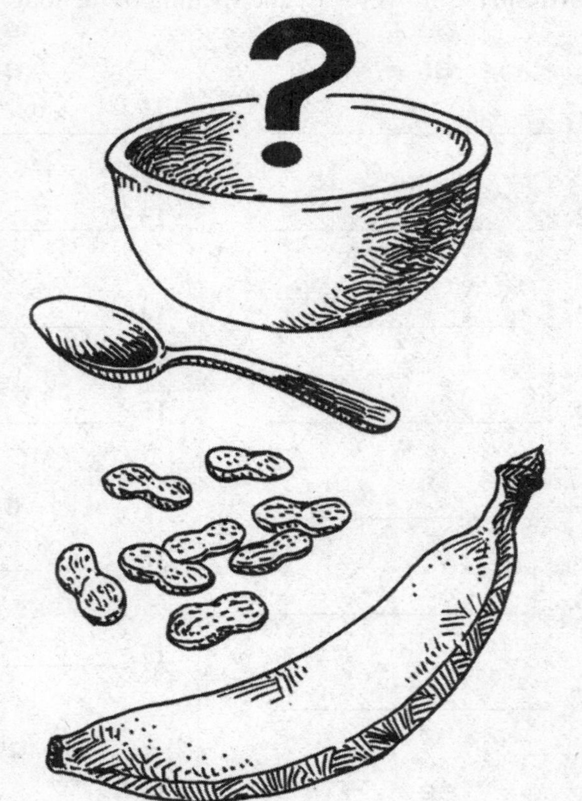

Activity

Kitchen Foraging With a member of your family, look through your kitchen and try to plan a lunch or dinner for the two of you. But here's the catch: you can't look in the refrigerator, you can only use one utensil, and you're allowed to use only a small amount of water from the sink. *Bon appétit!*

Comprehension Skill

Theme and Setting

The **theme** is the underlying meaning of a story. The **setting** is where and when the story takes place. Setting often helps determine how a story's characters think and behave.

Activity

Far Away Pretend you're stranded on a faraway island with a member of your family. Describe what the island looks like, the animals you encounter, and the trees and plants you see. What's the first thing you would do there: Find food? Build a shelter? Why did you make the choices you made?

Lesson Vocabulary

Words to Know

Knowing the meanings of these words is important to reading *Island of the Blue Dolphins*. Practice using these words.

Vocabulary Words

gnawed bitten or worn away

headland narrow ridge of high land jutting out into water; promontory

kelp any of various large, tough, brown seaweeds

lair den or resting place of a wild animal

ravine a long, deep, narrow valley eroded by running water

shellfish a water animal with a shell. Oysters, clams, crabs, and lobsters are shellfish.

sinew tendon

Conventions

Independent and Dependent Clauses

A clause is a group of related words that has a subject and a predicate. If a clause makes sense by itself, it is an **independent clause.** If a clause does not make sense by itself, it is a **dependent clause.** *For example: Tim had a ticket that he bought with his own money.* "Tim had a ticket" is the *independent clause* because it makes sense by itself. However, "that he bought with his own money" is *dependent* because it does not make sense by itself.

Activity

Clause Connection Create a T-chart on a sheet of paper. Cover the right column and have a family member write five independent clauses in it. Now cover the left column and write five dependent clauses. Then uncover the chart and take turns creating new sentences by combining an independent clause from the table with one (or more) dependent clauses.

Practice Tested Spelling Words

______	______	______	______
______	______	______	______
______	______	______	______
______	______	______	______
______	______	______	______

Name ______________________________

Theme and Setting

- The **theme** is the underlying meaning of a story. It is often not stated. You can figure out a theme from events and other evidence in the story.
- The **setting** is where and when the story takes place. Writers use details, such as sights and sounds, to describe it.

Directions Read the following passage. Then answer the questions below.

Jessica had never seen a real Native American village. Standing in the pueblo, she realized that her books hadn't prepared her for what it would be like. Under the pale spring sunshine, the red clay buildings at the center of the pueblo looked so different than the ones she had read about and seen in books back home. But when she entered one of the shops, it looked very familiar. It had the same kind of display cases, the same food, even the same posters she saw in shops at home.

The lady behind the counter gave Jessica a big smile and said hello. The lady was wearing a t-shirt with the name of the same college Jessica's father attended, the same college Jessica hoped to attend one day. Jessica didn't feel so far away from home anymore.

1. What is the setting of the above passage?

____

2. Where had Jessica learned about pueblos before her arrival?

____

3. Why does everything in the store look so familiar to Jessica?

____

____

4. What is the underlying theme of this passage?

____

____

5. On a separate sheet of paper, write down the visual memories you have of a place you visited for the first time. It could be a new town, someone's home, a new school, etc.

Home Activity Your child answered questions about setting and theme in a fictional passage. Find a family photo that shows a place you have been to and have your child describe the setting in his or her own words. Try to make up a story with your child based on the picture.

Name ______________________________

Character and Plot

Directions Read the article. Then answer the questions below.

George was lost. He could see the darkening blue sky when he looked up through the dense tree cover. He'd never make it back to base camp in the dark. Darkness was falling fast and the night time sounds of the mountains were growing louder. He knew he'd have to survive out here alone. He had forgotten his emergency kit, too, which only made him angrier at himself. He searched the rocks for a crevice or opening of some kind where he could sleep safely. He had two granola bars in his pack, and he'd been drinking his water sparingly. Every new rustle he heard put him on edge. Bears ruled these mountains, and he didn't want to meet one at night. He found a small opening at the base of a large rock formation. He eased himself into the space slowly, squinting and listening as hard as he could. When he was completely inside, he stood up. Inside the cave, everything seemed quiet and safe.

1. Why does George have to sleep overnight in the mountains?

____

____

2. Why is George angry with himself?

____

3. Why does George look for a safe place to sleep for the night?

____

4. The night sounds put George on edge. What might he be imagining?

____

____

5. On a separate sheet of paper, describe the resolution to George's problem. What do you think will happen next?

Home Activity Your child has read a fictional passage and answered questions about the plot and the main character. Have your child summarize this passage to you. Then ask your child to explain how he or she would feel if stuck in the same situation.

Name ____

Independent and Dependent Clauses

Directions Add an independent clause to each dependent clause to create a sentence that makes sense. Write the sentence.

1. because the natives depended on the sea for food

2. so that they could make a boat

3. after the tree was cut down

4. when the ashes were scraped out

5. since the boat was made by digging out wood

6. so that they would be watertight

7. because the boats were so well made

Home Activity Your child learned how to write sentences that combine an independent and a dependent clause. With your child, read an article about Native Americans. Have your child look for sentences that have both kinds of clauses.

Name ____________________________________

Long Vowel Digraphs

Spelling Words				
coast	feast	speech	wheat	Spain
paint	arrow	needle	charcoal	praise
faint	maintain	crease	grain	breeze
willow	appeal	bowling	complain	sneeze

Crossword Puzzle Write list words to complete the puzzle.

Across
2. fold
4. compliment
6. land along the sea
7. bow and ___
11. used to sew with
12. kind of tree
13. a talk
14. use color
15. light wind
16. request
17. to keep up

Down
1. banquet
2. used to BBQ
3. a country
5. family sport
8. pass out
9. cough and ___
10. whine
12. a grain

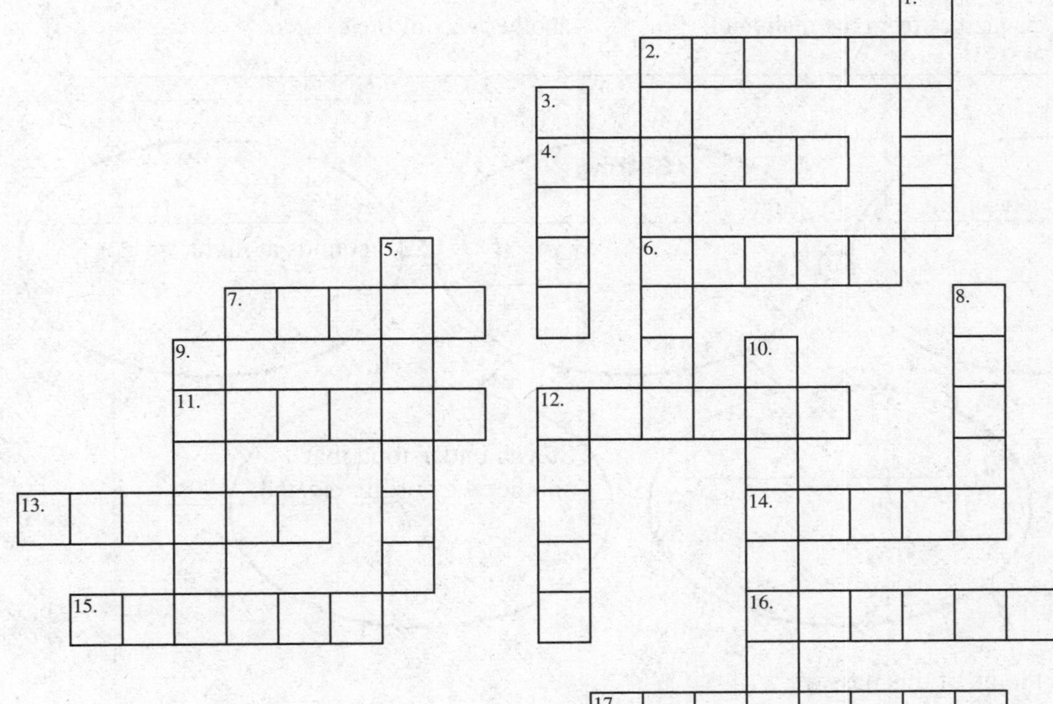

Home Activity Your child has learned to read, write, and spell words with long vowel digraph patterns. Look through books with your child to find three new words with long vowel digraphs.

Name ________________________________

Theme and Setting

- The **theme** is the underlying meaning of a story. It is often not stated. You can figure out a theme from events and other evidence in the story.
- The **setting** is where and when the story takes place. Writers use details, such as sights and sounds, to describe it.

Directions Read the following passage. Then, complete the graphic below, by filling in the *Setting* circle in the middle, and then writing in some of the sights, sounds, and feelings from the passage.

As a child, living on a tropical island was all Steven knew. He climbed rustling palm trees and ate coconuts. He kept colorful lizards as pets. The sounds of the jungle lulled him to sleep at night. As he got older, he understood how much his parents tried to keep in touch with the world they had left behind. Relatives sent books and magazines from the mainland. His parents even rigged up an Internet connection using a satellite dish. Visitors often came to the island to learn about his mother's work. Everyone would sit around the rough wooden table and share stories of life back on the mainland. Although he lived far away from the world of airports and subway trains, he understood that another way of life existed.

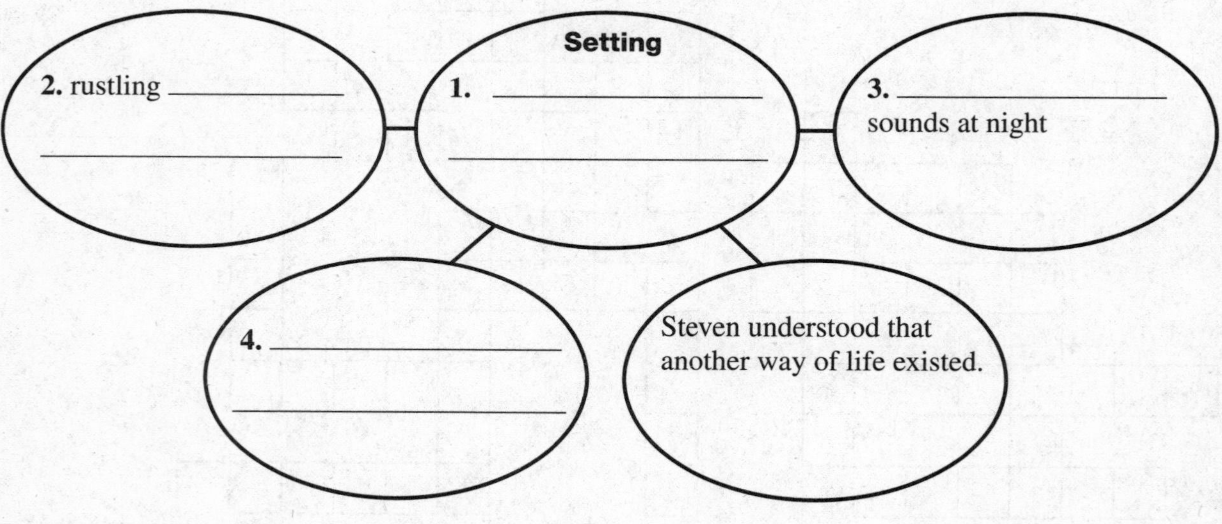

5. What is the theme of this passage?

____

Home Activity Your child identified the setting and theme in a fictional passage. Discuss one of your child's favorite stories with him or her. Have your child describe the story's setting, major characters, and main conflict.

Name ____________________

Independent and Dependent Clauses

Directions Write *I* after each independent clause. Write *D* after each dependent clause.

1. some Native Americans built homes of wood ________
2. where they lived year-round ________
3. others made tipis of skins and poles ________
4. so that they could move their homes ________
5. the cone-shaped tipi was useful ________
6. because it was efficient and portable ________
7. when the herd moved on ________
8. the tipis were quickly taken down ________
9. the natives followed the bison ________
10. until the herd reached new grazing land ________

Directions: Write sentences combining each pair of clauses in the first exercise. Use correct capitalization and punctuation.

11. (Clauses 1 and 2) ____________________

____

12. (Clauses 3 and 4) ____________________

____

13. (Clauses 5 and 6) ____________________

____

14. (Clauses 7 and 8) ____________________

____

15. (Clauses 9 and 10) ____________________

____

Home Activity Your child reviewed independent clauses and dependent clauses. With your child, look through a newspaper article. Have your child find sentences with independent and dependent clauses and mark the clauses *I* and *D*.

Name ______________________________

Adding *-ed, -ing*

- **Generalization** In words that end in **e**, drop the **e**: **decided**, **deciding**. In words that end **CVC**, double the final consonant: **admitted**, **admitting**. In words that end in **y**, change **y** to **i** when adding **-ed** and keep the **y** when adding **-ing**: **supplied**, **supplying**.

Word Sort Sort the list words into groups that have *-ed* and *-ing* endings.

-ed (no change)

1. ____________

-ed (change)

2. ____________

3. ____________

4. ____________

5. ____________

6. ____________

7. ____________

8. ____________

9. ____________

10. ____________

-ing (no change)

11. ____________

12. ____________

13. ____________

14. ____________

15. ____________

16. ____________

-ing (change)

17. ____________

18. ____________

19. ____________

20. ____________

Spelling Words

1. supplied
2. supplying
3. denied
4. denying
5. decided
6. deciding
7. included
8. including
9. admitted
10. admitting
11. occurred
12. occurring
13. qualified
14. qualifying
15. identified
16. identifying
17. delayed
18. delaying
19. satisfied
20. satisfying

Home Activity Your child is learning about adding *-ed* and *-ing* endings. Give your child two list words and ask if the spelling is changed in either word when *-ed* or *-ing* is added.

Name

Family Times

Summary

Satchel Paige

Satchel Paige was one of the greatest baseball pitchers who ever lived. Because baseball was segregated, he played in the Negro Leagues. Paige liked traveling the country almost as much as he liked baseball. He could strike out the best hitters with his crazy pitches and long-legged windup. Even when he settled down and started a family, he could not keep away from his first love—baseball.

Activity

Crazy Cards Work with a family member to create baseball-style "trading cards" for members of your family. On one side, draw a picture of a family member that shows a real or imaginary claim to fame—was Grandpa the first person to swim across the Atlantic? Did Aunt Mae eat the most hot dogs in recorded history? On the back, describe your family member and his or her story.

Comprehension Skill

Fact and Opinion

A **statement of fact** can be proved true or false. A **statement of opinion** is what someone thinks or feels. Statements of opinion often contain words that make judgments, such as *interesting* or *beautiful.* A single sentence might contain both a statement of fact and a statement of opinion.

Activity

Play-by-Play While a member of your family is doing something (cooking, cleaning, playing), try to describe every action they take as you might hear a sports announcer do it. Use both facts and opinions in your description.

Lesson Vocabulary

Words to Know

Knowing the meanings of these words is important to reading *Satchel Paige*. Practice using these words.

Vocabulary Words

confidence firm belief in yourself; self-confidence

fastball a pitch thrown at high speed with very little curve

mocking laughing at; making fun of

outfield the three players in the outfield of a baseball field

unique having no like or equal; being the only one of its kind

weakness a weak point; slight fault

windup a swinging movement of the arms while twisting the body just before pitching the ball

Conventions

Compound and Complex Sentences

A **compound sentence** contains two simple sentences joined with a comma and a word such as *and*, *but*, and *or*. *For example: I went to the game, but Juan stayed home*. The comma and the word *but* joins two simple sentences into one compound sentence. On the other hand, a **complex sentence** is made up of a simple sentence and another part. The other part has a subject and verb, but it is a dependent clause, which means it doesn't make sense by itself. *For example: After he finished his homework, Juan came and joined me*. "After he finished his homework" does not make sense by itself—it is a dependent clause.

Activity

If, And, or But Work with a family member to create a graphic organizer. Put a simple sentence in a bubble in the center. Take turns adding new bubbles to the main simple sentence to create compound sentences. See who can make the silliest sentence.

Practice Tested Spelling Words

______	______	______	______
______	______	______	______
______	______	______	______
______	______	______	______
______	______	______	______

Name ____________________

Fact and Opinion

- A **statement of fact** can be proved true or false.
- A **statement of opinion** is what someone thinks or feels.

Directions Read the following passage.

Born in Puerto Rico the youngest of seven children, Roberto Clemente became a professional baseball player. After he was offered a contract to play with the Montreal Royals, Clemente played with that team until he went to the Pittsburgh Pirates in 1954. Playing in a culture different from his own was probably a great challenge for him. Clemente played eighteen seasons in the majors and was awarded the National League's Most Valuable Player Award in 1966. He won twelve Gold Glove Awards. He was elected to the Hall of Fame in 1973, becoming the first Latin American to be selected.

I think Clemente was a selfless person because he did charity work both in Puerto Rico and Latin American countries. He died in a plane crash in 1972 while traveling to help victims of an earthquake in Nicaragua.

Directions Write *F* or *O* to identify facts and opinions. Rewrite the facts as opinions.

______ **1.** Clemente was the youngest of seven children. ____________________

______ **2.** He won twelve Gold Glove Awards. ____________________

______ **3.** Playing in a culture different from his own was probably a great challenge for him.

______ **4.** He was the first Latin American elected to the Hall of Fame.

______ **5.** I think Clemente was a selfless person. ____________________

Home Activity Your child read a short passage and identified facts and opinions. Read a newspaper sports article with your child. Have your child explain which statements are facts and which are opinions.

Name ______________________________

Cause and Effect

Directions Read the following passage. Then fill in the answers on the lines.

Mia Hamm started playing soccer at a young age. When she was six, her family moved to Italy, where the sport is very popular. She watched the game and began playing it. Mia Hamm continued playing when her family moved back to the United States. Mia was always a good athlete, but as a child, she had a medical problem with her legs and had to wear casts on them. Because she was determined and confident, Mia overcame her challenges and became a great soccer player.

Mia Hamm became known as one of the greatest athletes, male or female, ever to play the game. In 1999, she led the U.S. Women's Soccer team to win the World Cup. Hamm retired from soccer after leading the U.S. Olympic Women's Soccer team to a gold medal in 2004. For women and girls who play soccer today, Mia Hamm remains an inspiration.

Cause	Effect
1. ______________________________	Mia Hamm started playing soccer at age six.
2. ______________________________	As a child, Mia Hamm wore leg casts.
Mia Hamm was determined and confident.	**3.** ______________________________
4. ______________________________	Mia Hamm is an inspiration to women athletes.
5. The 1999 U.S. Women's Soccer team was a great team.	**5.** ______________________________

Home Activity Your child read a short passage and identified causes and effects in it. Read an article about a famous athlete with your child and ask him or her to talk about the reasons that athletes became great.

Name ______________________________

Compound and Complex Sentences

Directions Add a clause from the box to complete each sentence. Write *compound* or *complex* to tell what kind of sentence each one is.

He was the first African American player in the white major leagues
and a hero's skin color does not matter to them
the jeers soon turned to cheers
Since Jackie Robinson was the only African American on the field
and in 1962 he was elected to the Baseball Hall of Fame

1. Baseball fans love the stars of the game, ______________________________
______________________________. ______________

2. ______________________________
______________________________, he endured anger and jeers at first. ______________

3. Because he showed great skill and grace, ______________________________
______________________________. ______________

4. The public admired Robinson, ______________________________
______________________________. ______________

5. ______________________________
______________________________, but he soon was not the only one. ______________

Directions Write several sentences about your favorite sports hero or performer. Use at least one compound sentence and one complex sentence. Use commas and conjunctions correctly.

____
____
____
____
____
____

Home Activity Your child learned how to use compound and complex sentences in writing. Ask your child to read you a story and to point out examples of compound and complex sentences.

Name ______________________________

Adding *-ed*, *-ing*

Spelling Words				
supplied	supplying	denied	denying	decided
deciding	included	including	admitted	admitting
occurred	occurring	qualified	qualifying	identified
identifying	delayed	delaying	satisfied	satisfying

Directions Write list words that tell about an action that happened in the past.

Two *-ed* words in which the final consonant is doubled:

1. ____________ **2.** ____________

Two *-ed* words in which the final *e* is dropped.

3. ____________ **4.** ____________

Five *-ed* words in which *y* is changed to *i*

5. ____________ **6.** ____________ **7.** ____________

8. ____________ **9.** ____________

Word Endings Write list words by adding the ending in parentheses.

10. supply (ing) **10.** ____________

11. deny (ing) **11.** ____________

12. decide (ing) **12.** ____________

13. include (ing) **13.** ____________

14. admit (ing) **14.** ____________

15. occur (ing) **15.** ____________

16. qualify (ing) **16.** ____________

17. identify (ing) **17.** ____________

18. delay (ed) **18.** ____________

19. satisfy (ing) **19.** ____________

20. delay (ing) **20.** ____________

Home Activity Your child has learned to read, write, and spell words with *-ed* and *-ing* endings. Have your child pick the five hardest words on the list. Go over the spellings with your child.

Name____________________

Fact and Opinion

- A **statement of fact** can be proved true or false.
- A **statement of opinion** is what someone thinks or feels. Statements of opinion often contain words that make judgments, such as *interesting* or *beautiful.*
- A sentence might contain both a statement of fact and a statement of opinion.

Directions Read the following passage. Fill in the diagram below.

Choosing the right baseball mitt is the most important thing for any baseball player. I think a baseball mitt should fit your hand, position, and ability exactly. A catcher's mitt has a thumb pocket and mitten, instead of fingers. A mitt is also called a glove. An infielder's glove is shorter and has five fingers. There are gloves designed for women, men, and children. There are closed-back and open-back gloves. I prefer the closed-back gloves. There are some beautiful gloves for sale in the athletic department.

Statement	Can it be proved true or false?	Fact? Opinion? Or both?
Choosing the right baseball mitt is the most important thing for any baseball player.	**1.**	**2.**
A catcher's mitt has a thumb pocket and mitten, instead of fingers.	**3.**	**4.**
There are some beautiful gloves for sale in the athletic department.	The first part can't be proved true, but the second part can.	**5.**

Home Activity Your child read a short passage and identified whether statements were facts or opinions. Listen to a sportscast on the news and decide together whether the speaker uses facts and opinions in his or her report.

Name ________________________

Compound and Complex Sentences

Directions Join each pair of simple sentences to form a compound sentence. Use the conjunction that makes sense (*and, but,* or *or*). Put a comma before the conjunction. Write the compound sentence on the lines.

1. Julia loves sports.
She cannot decide which one to try first.
Julia loves sports, but she cannot decide which one to try first

2. She could play softball.
She could join a soccer team.
She could play softball, or she could join a

3. Her older brother plays on a traveling soccer team.
Her mom is an umpire for the softball league.
Her older brother plays on a traveling soccer team, and Her mom is an umpire for the softball league.

4. Marcus runs like the wind.
He is quite strong.
Marcus runs like the wind, and he's quite strong.

Directions Write *compound* after each compound sentence and underline the conjunction. Write *complex* after each complex sentence and underline the dependent clause.

5. His name was George Herman Ruth, but everyone called him Babe. Compound

6. He was a left-handed pitcher when he began his career in 1914. complex

7. He pitched 163 games, and he won 92 of them. compound

8. If you can believe it, he was greatest of all at hitting home runs. Complex

Home Activity Your child reviewed compound and complex sentences. Ask your child to explain how a game is played, using some compound and complex sentences.

Name ______________________

Contractions

- **Generalization** In contractions, an apostrophe (') takes the place of letters that are left out: **they are** becomes **they're**.

Word Sort Sort the list words into nouns/pronouns and verbs.

nouns/pronouns	verbs
1. ______	9. ______
2. ______	10. ______
3. ______	11. ______
4. ______	12. ______
5. ______	13. ______
6. ______	14. ______
7. ______	15. ______
8. ______	16. ______
	17. ______
	18. ______
	19. ______
	20. ______

Spelling Words

1. they're
2. you've
3. weren't
4. needn't
5. there'd
6. they've
7. mustn't
8. what'll
9. doesn't
10. hadn't
11. could've
12. would've
13. should've
14. might've
15. wouldn't
16. who've
17. shouldn't
18. who'd
19. this'll
20. couldn't

Home Activity Your child is learning about contractions. Ask your child to tell you what role the apostrophe plays in contractions.

Name

Family Times

Summary

Ten Mile Day

On April 28, 1869, 1,400 workers from the Central Pacific Railroad agreed to a challenge. On a bet from Thomas Durant, president of another railroad, the Union Pacific, the workers attempted to lay ten miles of railroad track in one day. Laboring with almost impossible strength, speed, and organization, the workers succeeded.

Activity

Taking Care of Business Very few people alive today know what it's like to carry thousands of pounds of steel by hand over ten miles in one day. Almost everyone, however, has put in a long day's work of one kind or another. With a family member, write a description of hard work that needs to be done in your home. List the skills and traits that can help get the jobs done.

Comprehension Skill

Cause and Effect

The **cause** is what made something happen. The **effect** is what happened as a result of the cause. An effect may have more than one cause, and a cause may have more than one effect. Sometimes authors use clue words such as *because* and *so* to show a cause-and-effect relationship.

Activity

One Thing Leads to Another Pick a favorite story about something funny or dramatic that happened to you or one of your relatives in the past. Talk with a family member about the cause (or causes) that made this event occur.

Lesson Vocabulary

Words to Know

Knowing the meanings of these words is important to reading *Ten Mile Day*. Practice using these words.

Vocabulary Words

barren unable to grow plant life

deafening so loud as to cause a loss of hearing

lurched moved suddenly

previous occurring earlier in time or position

prying moving up, apart, open, or out with force

surveying measuring the size, borders, and shape of (as a plot of land)

Conventions

Common Nouns, Proper Nouns, and Appositives

A **common noun** names any person, place, or thing. *For example: girl, city, building*. A proper noun names a particular person, place, or thing. Proper nouns include titles of books and movies, as well as many abbreviations. Capital letters are used for the first letter and each important word of a proper name. *For example: Nadine, Mexico City, White House, The Wizard of Oz, U.S.A.* When two nouns refer to each other in the same sentence, they are known as **appositives.** In the sentence: My friend Nadine came over my house to watch a movie, the common noun "friend" and the proper noun "Nadine" are appositives of each other.

Activity

The Proper Way With a family member, make two separate lists of ten common nouns. Exchange your lists and try to change each common noun into a proper noun.

Practice Tested Spelling Words

______	______	______	______
______	______	______	______
______	______	______	______
______	______	______	______
______	______	______	______

Name ____________________

Cause and Effect

- A **cause** is what makes something happen. An **effect** is what happens as a result of the cause.
- An effect may have more than one cause, and a cause may have more than one effect.

Directions Read the following passage. Then answer the questions below.

In the early part of the twentieth century, there were a large number of immigrants who came to the United States. Many people came from eastern European countries like Poland, Italy, and Russia. Because large U.S. cities offered an easier transition into American culture, many ethnic neighborhoods developed in major cities. These cities offered jobs and public transportation was widespread. Immigrants were able to be near other relatives who'd moved to the U.S., and a community of familiar languages and customs was welcoming to newcomers. These areas where immigrants settled helped define the neighborhoods that became a part of big cities like Chicago, New York, and Boston.

1. What were the nationalities of many immigrants in the early twentieth century?

2. What features of big cities appealed to immigrants?

3. What do you think happened to the population in big cities during this time? What do you think was the cause of this effect?

4. How were the immigrants' cultural backgrounds preserved in the new country?

5. Write a summary of the passage in one or two sentences.

Home Activity Your child read a short passage and answered questions about cause and effect. Read an article about your city or a neighborhood where you live. See if you can identify some of the reasons why your city or neighborhood is the way that it is.

Name

Graphic Sources

Directions Read the passage. Then use the time line to answer the questions below.

Mike Nee came to America when he was 21 years old. Until then he had spent his entire life on the west coast of Ireland. Once in America, he found work with the local gas company. Within a couple of years, he was able to buy a house. Soon after that, he met Ellen, who was also from Ireland. They married in 1932 and, although they struggled in their first years of marriage, hoped to have a large family. They were determined to share the good life in their new country with children of their own. Mike and Ellen welcomed their first child Mary into the world in 1943.

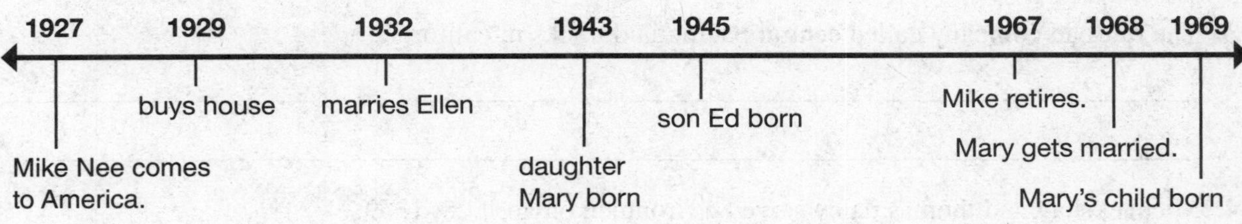

1. When did Mike Nee come to America?

2. How many years after Mike's coming to America did he marry Ellen?

3. What year did Mike buy a house?

4. How many years passed between Mike and Ellen's marriage and the birth of their daughter?

5. How old was Mike's daughter when his grandchild was born?

Home Activity Your child has read a time line and answered questions about when events occurred. Together, read a short section from a history book and have your child plot events on a time line.

Name ___________________________________

Common, Proper, and Collective Nouns

Directions Rewrite each sentence. Capitalize all proper nouns.

1. Many workers came from china and ireland to build the railroad.

____

____

2. Some workers were supervised by charles crocker and james strobridge.

____

____

3. The railroad company called central pacific laid tracks in california.

____

____

4. Michael shay and thomas daley served as ironmen on april 28, 1869.

____

____

Directions Add the date, greeting, signature, and information needed in the body of the letter. Use correct capitalization.

____

Dear ____________________,

Please come to a birthday party for ____________________ (person) on ____________ (day of week), ____________________ (date), at ________ (time of day). The party will be held at

____________________________ (name of place)

____________________________ (address)

____

We really hope you can come and help us celebrate.

Best wishes,

____________________________ (signature)

Home Activity Your child learned how to use common and proper nouns in writing. Ask your child to write a note inviting a friend to a special event. He or she should capitalize all proper nouns.

Name ___________________________________

Contractions

Spelling Words				
they're	you've	weren't	needn't	there'd
they've	mustn't	what'll	doesn't	hadn't
could've	would've	should've	might've	wouldn't
who've	shouldn't	who'd	this'll	couldn't

Contractions Complete the chart.

	Word	Word	Contraction
1.	should	have	
2.	who	would	
3.	this	will	
4.	should	not	
5.	had	not	
6.	what	will	
7.	they	have	
8.	does	not	
9.	could	have	
10.	they	are	

Writing Contractions Put the apostrophe in the correct place in each word. Write each word.

11. w o u l d n t **11.** ____________ **12.** w h o v e **12.** ____________

13. w e r e n t **13.** ____________ **14.** w o u l d v e **14.** ____________

15. m u s t n t **15.** ____________ **16.** c o u l d n t **16.** ____________

17. y o u v e **17.** ____________ **18.** t h e r e d **18.** ____________

19. n e e d n t **19.** ____________ **20.** m i g h t v e **20.** ____________

Home Activity Your child has learned to spell contractions. Have your child pick the five hardest words on the list. Go over the spellings with your child.

Name ___________________________

Cause and Effect

- A **cause** is what makes something happen. An **effect** is what happens as a result of the cause.
- An effect may have more than one cause, and a cause may have more than one effect.

Directions Read the following passage and complete the diagram below.

When Abraham Lincoln was elected President in 1860, most Americans didn't even vote for him. Four men ran for President that year, and no one won more than 50% of the vote. Lincoln won because he got enough electoral votes to win. Without a majority, however, his presidency was difficult from the very start. Many Southern states wanted their own separate country in which slavery would continue to be legal. But Lincoln promised to end slavery.

Some people were so opposed to Lincoln's goals that they threatened his life. He had to be brought to Washington, D.C., secretly in the dark of night. In spite of the threats, Lincoln did not change his mind about his goals. Unfortunately, the Southern states did not want to change either, and the Civil War started.

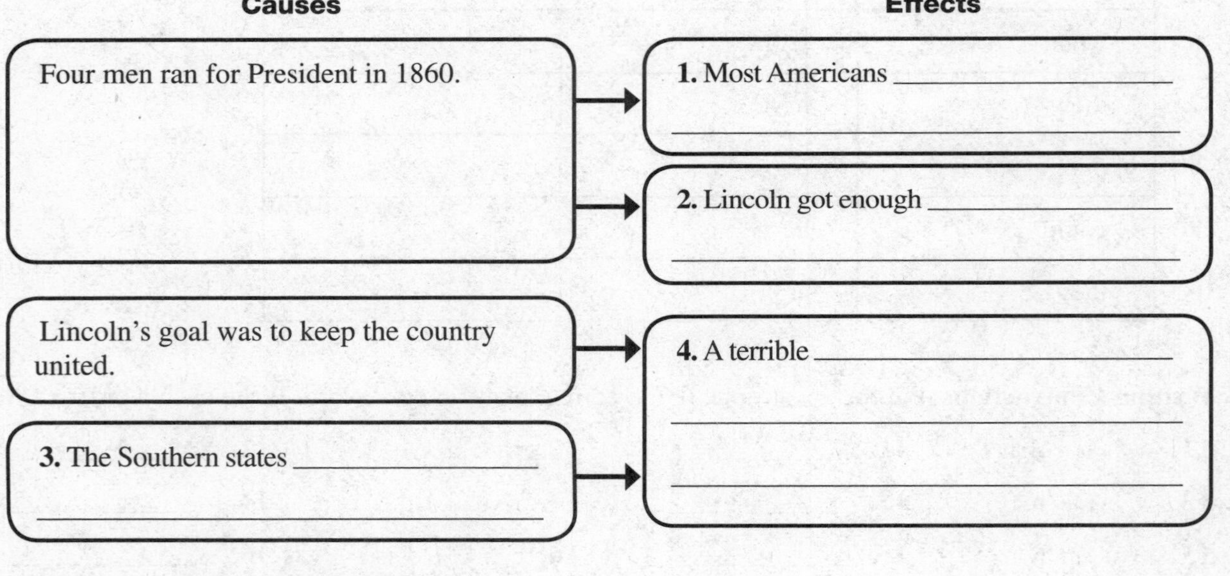

Causes
Effects
Four men ran for President in 1860.
1. Most Americans ___________________________
2. Lincoln got enough ___________________________
Lincoln's goal was to keep the country united.
3. The Southern states ___________________________
4. A terrible ___________________________

5. Write a summary of the passage.

____

____

Home Activity Your child read a short passage and identified causes and effects. Read an article about a government officeholder and talk about how he or she has caused things to happen in your community.

Name ______________________________

Common, Proper, and Collective Nouns

Directions Match the letter of each common noun on the right with a proper noun on the left. Then write another proper noun that fits in that category.

____ **1.** Japan ______________________ **A.** city

____ **2.** *Oliver Twist* ______________________ **B.** country

____ **3.** Ms. Kopeki ______________________ **C.** team

____ **4.** Atlanta Braves ______________________ **D.** book

____ **5.** London ______________________ **E.** teacher

Directions Write *C* if the group of words is capitalized correctly. If the group of words is not capitalized correctly, rewrite it using correct capitalization.

6. Helen and her cousins ______________________

7. mr. Jorge Ruiz, sr. ______________________

8. the greatest City in the Midwest ______________________

9. fourth of july ______________________

10. Mississippi River ______________________

11. holidays in november ______________________

12. south bend, In 46614 ______________________

Directions Rewrite each sentence. Use capital letters where they are needed.

13. On friday we went to a restaurant on east 18th st. called hot tamales.

____

____

14. It is owned by ms. marie dablontez, who is from mexico.

____

____

School + Home **Home Activity** Your child reviewed common and proper nouns. Ask your child to write a note inviting a friend to do something. Have him or her check to be sure proper nouns are capitalized correctly.

Name ______________________

Family Times

Selection Summaries

Week 1 *Red Kayak*
A boating accident forces a teenager to courageously meet challenges.

Week 2 *Thunder Rose*
Rose is an amazing cowgirl with thunder in her veins and a powerful lullaby in her heart.

Week 3 *Island of the Blue Dolphins*
Karana must be resourceful to survive when she is left all alone on an island.

Week 4 *Satchel Paige*
A great pitcher overcomes challenges in the early days of major league baseball.

Week 5 *Ten Mile Day*
Teams of builders of the Transcontinental Railroad try to set a record for laying the most rails in one day.

Activity
Tell a member of your family more about each of the five stories. Be sure to remember characters, plot, theme, and setting. Then choose your favorite and write three reasons why you like it the best.

Comprehension Skills Review

In Unit 1, you learned and used many skills while reading the stories and selections.

- The **plot** is what happens in a story.
- **Characters** are the people who experience the events of a story.
- The **cause** is why an event happens and the **effect** is what happens.
- The **setting** is where and when the story takes place.
- **Theme** is the "big idea" that holds the entire story together.
- **Sequence** refers to the order in which the events happen. In nonfiction, it means the steps in a process.

Activity
Ask a member of your family to tell you a story about something that happened to him or her when he or she was your age. Try to identify the setting, conflict, and resolution together. Discuss why you think it happened. Then discuss what you learned about the people in the story by the things they did and said and how they reacted to each other. Ask the family member what lesson he or she learned from these events. Finally, retell the story to another family member in the exact order in which the real events happened.

Unit Vocabulary Skills

Homographs are words that are spelled the same as other words but have different meanings and sometimes have different pronunciations.

Activity With a family member, take turns brainstorming words that are homographs. Use a dictionary to check your answers.

Homonyms are words spelled and pronounced alike but with different meanings.

Activity With a family member, take turns brainstorming words that are homonyms. Use a dictionary to check your answers.

Multiple-meaning words are words that have more than one meaning.

Activity Read a newspaper, magazine, or book looking for multiple-meaning words. Make a list of ones you find. Use context clues to figure out which meaning of the word is being used.

Unknown Words

When you find words in your reading that you don't know, you can look them up in a dictionary or a glossary.

Activity With a family member, read a newspaper article and identify words you do not know. Use a dictionary to check their meanings.

Antonyms are words that mean the opposite of other words.

Activity Jot down verbs and adjectives you find in the selections. Use a thesaurus to find antonyms of those words.

Unit Spelling Rules

Short Vowel VCCV, VCV

When a syllable ends with a single vowel and a single consonant, the vowel stands for its short sound. VCCV: *butter* VCV: *regular*

Long Vowel VCV When a single vowel appears at the end of a word or syllable, the vowel usually stands for its long sound. VCV: *silent*

Long Vowel Digraphs If a word has two vowels in a row, the first vowel is usually long, and the second vowel is silent. For example: *faint.*

Adding *-ed, -ing* Remember the following three things when adding *-ed* and *-ing*:

- the final consonant is doubled before adding the ending
- in words that end in *y*, the *y* is changed to *i* before adding *-ed*: *horrified*
- in words that end in *y*, keep the *y* when adding *-ing: horrifying*

Contractions Remember that in contractions, an apostrophe takes the place of letters that are left out. For example, *were not* becomes *weren't*.

Activity With a family member, identify as many words in books, magazines, or newspapers that follow this Unit Spelling Rules. Make a list of these words.

Name ___

Homographs

The cornstalks grew in rows.

The girl uses oars whenever she rows her boat.

The children have many rows over the bicycle.

Which word in each sentence is a homograph? Say the word as it is pronounced in each sentence.

- A **homograph** is a word that is spelled the same as another word or words but has a different meaning and may have a different pronunciation. Circle the Word to Know that is a homograph.

Words to Know

compressions
grumbled
insistently
intentionally
minute
neutral
normally

Practice Read the following sentences. Fill in the blanks with one of the Words to Know. Then circle the letter of the correct meaning of the homograph that is underlined in each sentence. Use a dictionary to check your answers.

1. The ___ the sky ___ the way it did, Ernesto could project that a dangerous storm was near.

   a. to make a prediction b. a special assignment

2. Rather than remaining ___ during the rescue, Ernesto ___ took the lead.

   a. a soft metallic element b. command

3. Ernesto ___ moved to the bow of the boat where he ___ kept the first-aid kit.

   a. a weapon for shooting arrows b. the forward part of a vessel

4. Ernesto knew he had to close open cuts and apply ___ to stop bleeding.

   a. block b. near

On Your Own As you read "The Big Game," look for one of the homographs above. Pronounce the word as it is used in the story.

Home Activity Your child reviewed how to use a dictionary to check the meaning of homographs. With your child, look for homographs in newspapers, magazines, or ads.

Name ______________________________

Character and Plot

- A **character** is a person or an animal that takes part in the events of a story.
- The **plot** is the sequence of events in a selection. The plot starts with a *problem* or *conflict*, continues with *rising action* as the conflict builds, and reaches a *climax* when the problem or conflict is faced. The plot ends with a *resolution* or *outcome*.

Practice Look at the chart. Then answer the questions below.

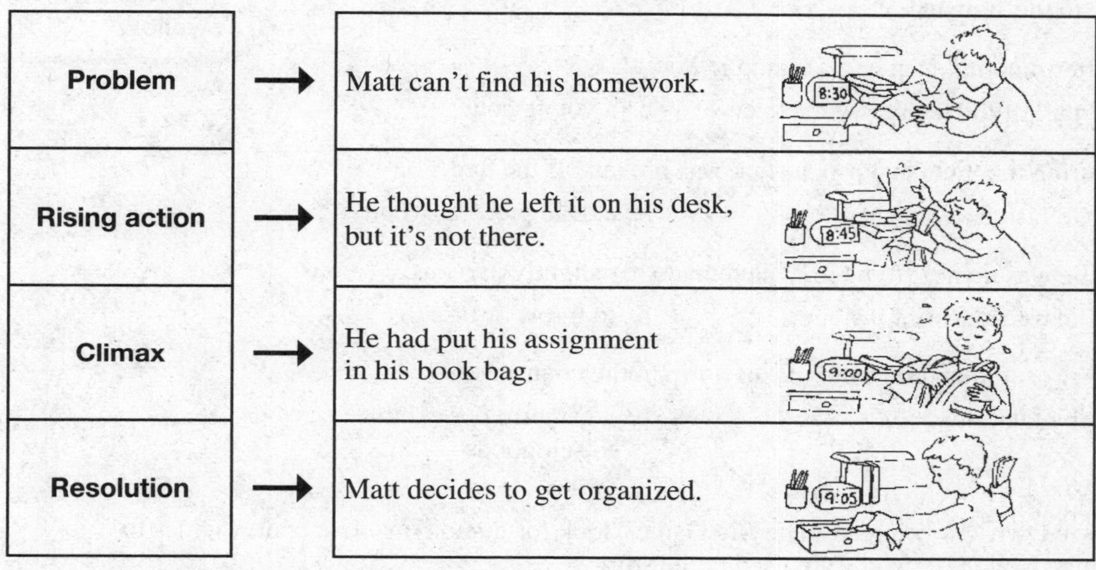

Problem	→	Matt can't find his homework.
Rising action	→	He thought he left it on his desk, but it's not there.
Climax	→	He had put his assignment in his book bag.
Resolution	→	Matt decides to get organized.

1. Who is the main character in the story on the chart above?

____

2. What is Matt's problem?

____

3. What is the climax of the story?

____

4. What is the resolution?

____

On Your Own Use what you know about character and plot as you read "The Big Game."

Home Activity Your child reviewed using the skills character and plot. Retell one of your favorite stories or movies. Discuss who the characters are. Have your child explain the problem, rising action, climax, and resolution of the story or movie.

Name____

Homonyms

- **Homonyms** are words spelled and pronounced alike but with different meanings.

Words to Know

- calf
- fair
- pitch
- stick
- swallow

Practice Read the following sentences. Use context clues to choose the definition that best matches the underlined homonym. Circle the correct definition's letter.

1. The young swallow stayed in its nest during the rain.
   a. to pass through the mouth to the stomach
   b. a small bird
2. After running, Dan had a cramp in his calf.
   a. part of the leg below the knee
   b. a young cow
3. During the thunderstorm, a stick was broken off the tree.
   a. to fasten or attach
   b. a dead piece of wood
4. Julie was up next to pitch, which made her slightly nervous.
   a. the steepness of a slope
   b. to throw or toss
5. Every summer, our family takes a trip to the county fair.
   a. by the rules
   b. a gathering or exhibit to sell goods

On Your Own As you read "The Big Game," look for homonyms. Use context clues to determine how these words are used in the story.

School + Home

Home Activity Your child used context clues in sentences to determine the correct meaning of homonyms. With your child, make a list of as many homonyms as you can. Use each word in a sentence and have your child tell you the correct meaning of the word as it is used in your sentence.

Name ______________________

Cause and Effect

- Clue words such as *because, so,* and *since* may signal causes and effects.
- Ask yourself "What happened?" and "Why did it happen?" to determine causes and effects.

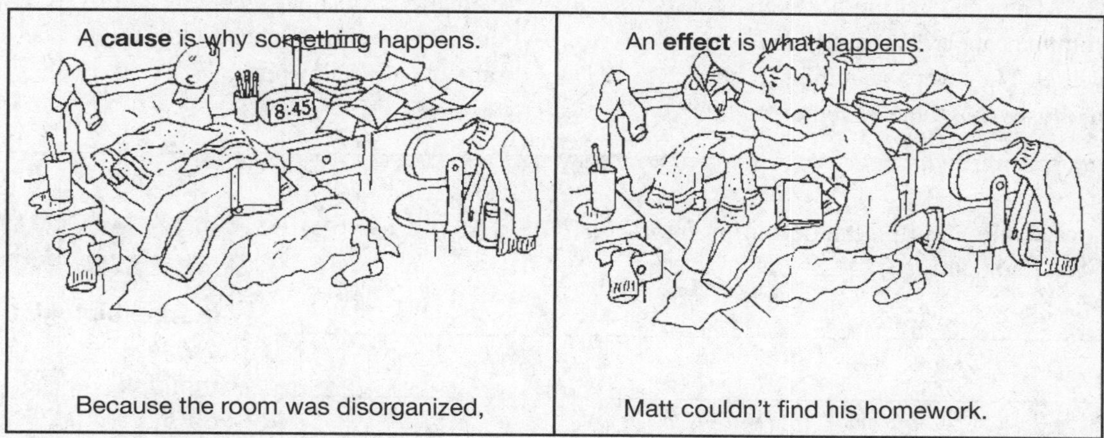

A **cause** is why something happens.
8:45
Because the room was disorganized,
An **effect** is what happens.
Matt couldn't find his homework.

Practice In the boxes below, write the words that identify the cause and effect in each sentence. If there is a clue word, circle it.

1. Matt's homework wasn't on his desk so he searched his book bag.

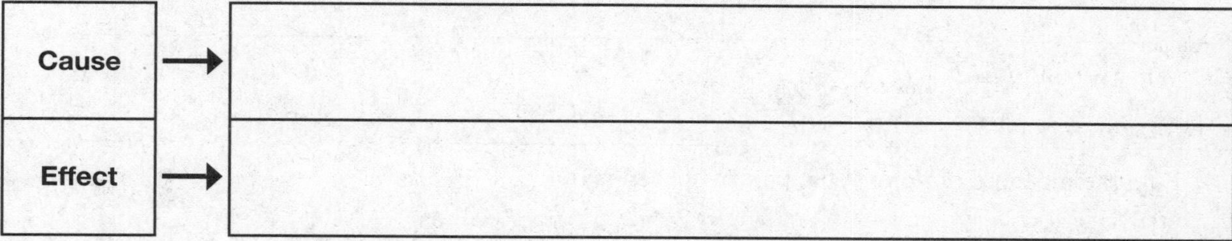

2. He was tired because it was almost bedtime.

On Your Own Use what you know about cause and effect as you read "The Big Game."

Home Activity Your child reviewed how to determine causes and effects. Think of a cause, and have your child supply the effect. For example, say "Because it was raining outside..." and have your child finish the sentence.

Name ______________________________

Unknown Words

Practice Read the passage. Then answer the questions. Use a dictionary for help.

Gina's mother was a marine biologist. Gina and her mother spent most summers aboard a scientific research vessel. They were searching for the mollusks that Gina's mother studied.

Gina helped the scientists chart their data collection. Most days went by calmly. But one day the ship's sonar picked up the remains of a shipwreck!

Words to Know

marine biologist
vessel
mollusk
data
sonar

1. How would you find the definition of *marine biologist*? Write its meaning.

____

____

____

____

2. What is the meaning of *vessel*?

____

3. What is a *mollusk*?

____

4. Find the meaning of *data.* What part of speech is it?

____

____

5. Define *sonar* in a complete sentence.

____

____

On Your Own As you read "The Big Game," look for unknown words. Use a dictionary to find the meanings of these words and write a sentence for each word.

Home Activity Your child reviewed using a dictionary to find the meanings of unknown words. With your child, read a passage from a favorite book. Have your child select an unknown word and find its meaning in the dictionary.

Name ________________________________

Theme and Setting

- The **theme** is the "big idea" of a story. The reader determines theme from the events and characters in a story.
- The **setting** is the time and place in which a story takes place.

Practice Think about Matt's story from this week. Look at the picture. Answer the questions.

1. What is the theme of Matt's story?

____

2. Writers use details such as sights and sounds to describe the setting. List what you would see and hear if you were in Matt's room.

____

____

____

3. Imagine if the setting were Matt's dining room at dinner. What might the sights and sounds be?

____

____

4. If Matt were an organized person, what might his room look like?

____

____

On Your Own Use what you know about theme and setting as you read "The Big Game." Write a statement of what the theme and setting are in the passage.

Home Activity Your child reviewed theme and setting. Name the title of a favorite book or movie. Have your child explain the theme and identify the setting of it.

Name ____

Antonyms

confidence weakness windup fastball unique outfield mocking

- An **antonym** is a word that has the opposite meaning of another word. A thesaurus helps identify antonyms of words. Often context clues such as *unlike, while, on the other hand,* and *even though* also help.

Practice Fill the blanks with the Words to Know that correctly complete each sentence. Circle the two words in each sentence that are antonyms. Use a thesaurus to help you determine the antonyms. Then underline the context clues that show a contrast.

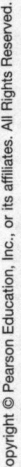

Words to Know

confidence
fastball
mocking
outfield
unique
weakness
windup

1. His greatest ________________, on the other hand, can also be his greatest strength.
2. A ________________ can be ________________ even though it is common to baseball.
3. He displays a lot of ________________ in his ________________ when he pitches, unlike his timidity when at bat.
4. Some spectators took to ________________ the players in the ________________, while others were cheering them on.

On Your Own As you read "A Real Winner," look for the words *win, created, best, rough,* and *easy.* Use a thesaurus to list some antonyms for each. Read the context in which the words are used in the selection for any clue words that can help determine their opposites.

Home Activity Your child reviewed using a thesaurus to determine the meanings of antonyms, words that have the opposite meanings of other words. Take turns saying a word and having the other person name an antonym.

Name____

Fact and Opinion

- A statement of **fact** can be proved true or false.
- A statement of **opinion** is what someone thinks or feels.
- A single sentence might contain both a statement of fact and a statement of opinion.

Practice Read the following passage. Fill in the diagram below.

In the early 1800s, many European immigrants came to America seeking a better life. At the time, some people in Europe experienced hunger and warfare or were treated unfairly because of their religious or political beliefs. Most immigrants probably thought life in America looked much better. But some immigrants were very disappointed. Factory jobs offered long hours and poor wages and working conditions. It must have been hard for immigrants to adjust when they did not speak English.

Arriving from the east, many immigrants settled in cities along the Atlantic coast. From there, some of these settlers moved to the midwestern states. Finally, some settlers forged trails in covered wagons to try their luck out west. I think immigrants who traveled west were happier than those who stayed in the east.

Statement	Can it be proved true or false?	Fact? Opinion? Or both?
Some people in Europe experienced hunger and warfare.	**1.**	**2.**
Most immigrants probably thought life in America looked much better.	**3.**	**4.**
	5. The first part cannot be proved true, but the second part can be.	contains both fact and opinion

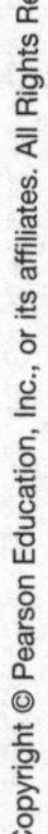

On Your Own Identify facts as you read "A Real Winner."

Home Activity Your child identified facts and opinions in a story. With your child, read an article in a newspaper or magazine and have him or her identify facts and opinions.

Name ________________________________

Multiple-Meaning Words

- A **multiple-meaning word** has more than one meaning. Context clues can help determine the meaning that is intended for a multiple-meaning word.

Words to Know

- barren
- deafening
- lurched
- previous
- prying
- surveying

Practice Read the following sentences. Fill in the blanks using one of the Words to Know. Then use context clues to determine which definition of the underlined multiple-meaning word is being used in each sentence. Circle the letter of the correct definition.

1. Workers grabbed hold of each side of the crate and began ________________ it open to reach their supplies.
   a. a surface that is not the front, back, top, or bottom of an object
   b. position or point of view
2. They began ________________ the ________________ land before laying a single railroad track.
   a. footprint
   b. metal rail
3. The continuous hammering sounds of stakes being struck were the cause of major ear ________________.
   a. greater
   b. military rank
4. A team of iron men that at a ________________ time stood still, now ________________ forward to move the crates.
   a. group
   b. partner

On Your Own As you read "A Real Winner," look for multiple-meaning words. Use context clues to determine how these multiple-meaning words are used in the selection.

Home Activity Your child reviewed using context clues to determine the meanings of multiple-meaning words. Choose a passage from a favorite book and list all of the multiple-meaning words you find.

Name________________________________

Cause and Effect

- A **cause** is why something happens, and an **effect** is what happens. Sometimes an effect may have more than one cause, and a cause may have more than one effect.

Matt had a baseball game late in the afternoon.

Matt and his family usually eat dinner at 6:00 in the evening.

Matt finished his homework late in the evening.

Matt always makes sure he has his homework finished before going to bed.

Matt is usually in bed by 9:00.

Practice Read the following questions and answer them on the lines below.

1. What caused Matt's family to eat dinner later than usual?

____

____

2. What two events caused Matt to finish his homework later in the evening?

____

____

3. What was the effect of Matt finishing his homework later in the evening?

____

____

4. What were two effects of Matt's family eating dinner later than usual?

____

____

On Your Own Use what you know about cause and effect as you read "A Real Winner." What do you think were the effects in the story? What caused such effects?

Home Activity Your child reviewed identifying multiple causes and effects. Discuss how a situation might have many effects or how a situation might have many causes.

Name____________________

Setting Underline the words in the first paragraph that help you visualize how the setting looks, smells, and feels.

Character Circle words and phrases that show Berta's personality.

Homographs What does *close* mean as it's used in paragraph 6?

____

Name a homograph of *close* and define it.

____

____

____

Cause and Effect What causes Marisol to play in the game?

____

____

____

Homonyms What does the word *shot* mean as it is used in this story?

____

____

____

The Big Game

Marisol strolled innocently into the Middlebrook school gym and inhaled the fresh pine scent that sprang from the sparkling clean floors of the basketball court. *The gym is like an icebox this early in the morning*, she thought. *I'll probably spend the entire game freezing on the sidelines.* She zipped up her Middlebrook Stingrays sweatshirt and took her regular place on the bench. She had no idea of the devastation to come.

Today was the Stingrays' big game against the Prairie View Lions. The Stingrays were guaranteed to win since Berta was on the team. Marisol glanced at the court and saw Berta skillfully dribbling the ball. As usual, the group of players who worshipped Berta surrounded her.

"Watch this, I can dribble the ball through my legs," Berta boasted. The obedient group was impressed.

I wish I could play like that, Marisol grumbled.

The referee's whistle brought Marisol back to reality. Both teams took their positions on the court. Marisol stayed on the bench. The scoreboard blasted its horn, and the crowd cheered for the Stingrays. The ball echoed as it slapped against the wood floors, and the athletes' shoes squeaked with every sudden move. The gym buzzed with the intensity of a swarming beehive.

Berta was definitely the star of the show, sinking one ball after another. With two minutes left in the fourth quarter, the score was close: Berta: 29 Lions: 28. Suddenly, Marisol heard a horrified gasp from the crowd. Marisol was stunned to see Berta on the floor clutching her ankle in pain.

"Marisol! Looks like you'll finally have the chance to get acquainted with the court. You're going in for Berta," the coach said. "Do you see Number 6? Cover her like peanut butter on jelly."

Wow, thanks for the great advice, Marisol thought sarcastically. She felt her stomach drop, and she willed herself to walk onto the court. For a moment she thought she might faint. The two guards for the Lions quickly dribbled the ball down the court, and the *thump* pounded in Marisol's ears. *Just follow Number 6. Just follow Number 6,* she repeated to herself.

The ball whizzed back and forth. Number 6 faked left and then right. Marisol jumped right and then left. The point guard threw the ball over Marisol's head. Number 6 caught it, pivoted toward the basket, and shot. The ball bounced off the rim and flew straight toward Marisol.

"Rebound!" the crowd screamed.

Name ______________________________

Without thinking, Marisol stuck her hands out and caught the ball. Her mind raced. *What do I do now?* Behind the sound of her heartbeat, she could hear the crowd cheering her on. Number 6 was moving toward her. Marisol turned toward the basket and set up her shot. The crowd went wild. *What are they saying?* Marisol thought. *Go? Go?* Marisol threw the ball and watched with amazement as it swished through the basket. *I made it! I made my first basket!* Marisol was overjoyed.

The sound of the buzzer ended the game, and the crowd grew strangely silent. Marisol heard the slow *thump* of the ball as it bounded away on its own. Then the Lions formed a circle and chanted, "We're number one!" All at once, it hit Marisol. She had scored two points for the Lions. Her team had lost the game because of her.

Marisol left the gym quickly. Her embarrassment and disappointment gnawed at her and she mumbled, "How could I have done something like that?"

"Hey, Marisol, wait up!" Berta limped over. "What an awesome shot! You know that was an impossible angle to shoot from."

"Really? It would have been better if I'd shot it in the right basket," Marisol said dryly.

"Well, if I hadn't been so busy showing off, I might not have hurt myself and could have stayed in the game. Or if we'd made all of our free throws, we might still have won by a point."

"I hadn't thought of it that way."

"Hey, want to practice with me?" asked Berta. "The angle you shot from is my weakness."

"Sure, that would be great," Marisol answered. *I guess it takes a whole team to win or lose a game,* she thought as she skipped home.

What is another meaning of *shot*?

____

____

____

Cause and Effect What is the effect of Marisol's shot?

____

Plot Draw a box around the climax of the story.

Unknown Words Use a dictionary to find the meaning of *awesome.*

____

____

____

____

Theme What is the theme of the story?

____

____

____

____

____

____

Home Activity Your child read a selection and used comprehension and vocabulary skills from Unit 1. Have your child retell the selection and identify the characters and plot.

Name____

Fact and Opinion Is the last sentence in Paragraph 2 a fact or an opinion?

____

____

____

Cause and Effect Underline the cause of Jackie going to military court.

Multiple-Meaning Words What does *scout* mean as it's used in the selection?

____

____

____

What is another definition of *scout*?

____

____

____

Antonyms What is an antonym for *terrible*?

____

____

____

A Real Winner

Jack Roosevelt Robinson faced challenges all his life. They started soon after he was born in rural Georgia in 1919. The Robinson family moved to Pasadena, California, in 1920, but circumstances didn't make them feel welcome. Many businesses, schools, and even professional sports teams kept white people apart from black people. This was called *segregation*.

Jack, better known as "Jackie," was a natural athlete and team leader. Through high school and junior college Jackie excelled at football, basketball, track, and baseball. In 1939 he won a scholarship to the University of California in Los Angeles, where he was the first student to win a letter in all four sports.

In the spring of 1941 Jackie left college to get a job. In December of that year, Pearl Harbor in Hawaii was attacked, and the United States entered World War II. Jackie enlisted in the army in 1942 and went to Fort Riley, Kansas. He wanted to become an officer, but African American soldiers weren't allowed to be officers at the time. However, he met Sgt. Joe Lewis. Joe Lewis was the world heavyweight boxing champion. Sgt. Lewis spoke up, and Jackie and several other black servicemen were admitted to Officers' Candidate School.

Later Jackie was sent to Fort Hood, Texas. Though military regulations said that any soldier could sit anywhere on a military bus, one day Jackie was told by a higher-level officer to move to the back. Because he refused and stood his ground, he was sent to military court. He was found innocent in 1944 and then asked for, and received, an honorable discharge.

In April 1945 Jackie was hired to play shortstop with the Kansas City Monarchs, a team in the Negro Leagues. Black baseball players who were not allowed to play in white major league ball clubs had created this league. The low pay and terrible conditions he faced in the league discouraged Jackie, but this did not get him down. Soon his reputation as a star player caught the attention of major league baseball scouts.

Branch Rickey, general manager of the Brooklyn Dodgers, had sent scouts to observe Jackie in action. Mr. Rickey wanted to build the best team he could. Rickey was told of the talent and confidence of Jackie Robinson. When the two men met in August of 1945, Rickey told Jackie he was looking for a unique player "with guts enough not to fight back" against the attacks of bullies. Jackie accepted his assignment. Rickey advised him to marry his college sweetheart, Rachel Isum, so that he would have someone by his side during rough times.

Name ____________________

In 1946, Jackie played with the Montreal Royals, the Dodgers' minor league "farm" team. In many U.S. cities, the newcomer to a baseball team was jeered and called terrible names. The sound of the crowd was sometimes deafening. Jackie and his wife got hate mail and threats. But with Jackie on the team, the Royals won the minor league pennant.

In 1947 the Dodgers announced that Jackie would play first base for them as Number 42. He later played second and third base and even the outfield. He was a powerful hitter and set records for stealing bases. He was named National League Rookie of the Year the first year on the team. But it wasn't easy. Some of his own teammates wrote a petition to get rid of him. Branch Rickey stood his ground and kept Jackie on the team.

In 1949 Jackie was named Most Valuable Player. In his ten years with the Dodgers, the team won the National League pennant six times and also the 1955 World Series.

When Jackie retired in 1956, he won the Spingarn Medal for his work with black youth. In 1962 he was the first African American named to the Baseball Hall of Fame. He worked hard for the civil rights of all Americans until his death in 1972.

Jackie Robinson is still honored for opening most professional sports to all athletes. In 1997, Number 42 was retired forever. From that point forward, no one entering the league will wear that number.

Fact and Opinion Tell how you know this statement is a fact: Jackie Robinson was named Most Valuable Player in 1949.

____

____

____

How can you prove this is a fact?

____

____

____

____

Cause and Effect What is the effect of Jackie Robinson's number being retired?

____

____

____

____

____

Home Activity Your child read a selection and used comprehension and vocabulary skills from Unit 1. Have your child summarize the selection and identify facts as well as causes and effects.

Name ______________________________

Digraphs *th, sh, ch, ph*

- **Generalization** Words can have two consonants together that are pronounced as one sound: **southern, shovel, chapter, hyphen**.

Word Sort Sort the list words by digraphs **th**, **sh**, **ch**, and **ph**.

th

1. ______________
2. ______________
3. ______________
4. ______________
5. ______________

sh

6. ______________
7. ______________
8. ______________
9. ______________
10. ______________

ch

11. ______________
12. ______________
13. ______________
14. ______________
15. ______________
16. ______________
17. ______________
18. ______________

ph

19. ______________
20. ______________

Spelling Words

1. shovel
2. southern
3. northern
4. chapter
5. hyphen
6. chosen
7. establish
8. although
9. challenge
10. approach
11. astonish
12. python
13. shatter
14. ethnic
15. shiver
16. pharmacy
17. charity
18. china
19. attach
20. ostrich

Home Activity Your child is learning about four sounds made with two consonants together, called digraphs. Ask your child to tell you what those four sounds are and give one list word for each sound.

Name ______________________________

Family Times

Summary

At the Beach

On a regular day at the beach, Fernando leads three other children on an adventure he knows they shouldn't take. Little Javi unexpectedly gets hurt by a sea urchin. Fernando lies to his parents at first. He eventually confesses, and his mother praises him for telling the truth.

Activity

To Tell or Not to Tell Imagine that you did something you shouldn't have. Would you lie if you thought you could get away with it? Talk over this problem with members of your family. List your reasons for telling the truth.

Comprehension Skill

Compare and Contrast

When writers **compare** and **contrast** things, they tell how things are alike or different. Words such as *same*, *also*, *before*, *although*, and *however* are clues that things are being compared or contrasted.

Activity

Yours and Mine With a family member, find two pairs of shoes from different people in your house and put them side by side. Compare and contrast the size, color, style, and how much wear they show. Try comparing and contrasting other household items by using a Venn Diagram.

Lesson Vocabulary

Words to Know

Knowing the meanings of these words is important to reading *At the Beach.* Practice using these words.

Vocabulary Words

algae a group of related living things, mostly living in water

concealed put out of sight; hidden

driftwood wood carried along by water or washed ashore from the water

hammocks hanging beds or couches made of canvas, cord, etc.

lamented felt or showed grief

sea urchins small, round sea animals with spiny shells

sternly strictly, firmly

tweezers small pincers for picking up small objects

Conventions

Regular and Irregular Plural Nouns

Regular plural nouns name more than one and are formed by adding *-s* or *-es.* **Irregular plural nouns** are formed in unusual ways such as changing a final *f* or *fe* to *v* before adding *-es.* For example, the plural of *leaf* is *leaves.* Other nouns are made into plurals by changing their spellings. An example of this is *man* and *men.* The plural form of *brother-in-law* is *brothers-in-law.* Study and remember irregular plural forms of nouns.

Activity

Irregular Plural Nouns Have a family member help you think of how to spell the irregular plurals of the following nouns. Use a dictionary for help. How many others can you list?

half
staff
mother-in-law
ox
deer
tooth

Practice Tested Spelling Words

______	______	______	______
______	______	______	______
______	______	______	______
______	______	______	______
______	______	______	______

Name ____________________

Compare and Contrast

- When you **compare** and **contrast** two or more things, you show how they are alike and different.
- Clue words, such as *like* or *as* show comparisons. Words such as *but* or *however* show contrast.
- Sometimes, writers do not use clue words when they compare and contrast things.

Directions Read the following passage. Then answer the questions below.

Plagiarism, taking another writer's work and presenting it as one's own, is becoming a big problem in schools. Even though students have a very good chance at getting caught, they still plagiarize. In elementary and secondary schools, students are typically punished by a failing grade, being kicked off teams, or being suspended from school. At the college level, however, the penalties can become more serious. Students are often expelled from the college after only one instance of plagiarism. Teachers and professors usually know, or have a strong suspicion, that a student is plagiarizing.

The student who does his or her own work typically shows improvement slowly over time. A student who copies someone else's work may turn in one assignment that is of poor quality, and then the next week hand in writing that could win prizes. Internet sites that sell or give away finished writing assignments tempt many students who cheat. Like these students, teachers have started using the Internet. Web sites are now available where teachers can upload a student's paper and find out if it has been written by anyone else anywhere in the world.

1. How is plagiarism usually dealt with in elementary and secondary schools?

____

2. How is plagiarism usually dealt with at the college level?

____

3. What is the difference between the work of students who do and don't plagiarize?

____

____

4. How has the Internet made it possible for students to cheat?

____

5. How has the Internet made it possible for teachers to catch plagiarism?

____

Home Activity Your child answered compare and contrast questions about plagiarism. Have your child think about other ways that students are tempted to cheat. Have your child list possible consequences for these offenses.

Name ______________________________

Author's Purpose

Directions Read the following passage. Then answer the questions below.

The sun was high in the sky as it shone down on the men in the pirate ship. Diego tried to untie his wrists before Captain Flemming turned around. "You're a terrible pirate!" Diego shouted at Flemming. "What's that, lad?" Flemming asked. "A pirate? And how exactly would you describe yourself?" Flemming had a good point. Diego was a pirate too. But Diego considered himself an honest one.

"You'd better hope I don't escape this island, Flemming!" Diego warned bitterly. Flemming smiled a wicked grin. "Well, if you ever do, don't forget to bring me my treasure. You buried it! Har, har, har!" Diego had his own reason to be happy. He'd recently spied a small boat hidden in the weeds just beyond the beach. Flemming hadn't noticed the boat. It was just a matter of time before Diego would be free.

1. What is the purpose the author has for writing this passage?

____

2. How can you tell what the author's purpose is?

____

____

3. What type of passage is this?

____

4. Who is Diego?

____

5. Does the author succeed at his or her purpose?

____

____

Home Activity Your child answered questions about the author's purpose for writing a short passage. Read a newspaper article with your child and discuss what the author's purpose might be.

Name I Jackson

Regular and Irregular Plural Nouns

Directions Write a sentence using the plural form of each noun.

1. woman

There are alot of women in my family

2. foot

3. monkey

4. deer

5. leaf

Directions Write the paragraph on the lines. Write the plural form of each noun in ( ). Add a word of your own to describe each plural noun. Write your own ending sentence for the paragraph.

It was a beautiful day, and ___ (family) were enjoying the beach. Near the waves, ___ (boy) made ___ (sand castle). By the dunes, some ___ (man) tossed a football. Several ___ (lady) searched for ___ (seashell). Two ___ (baby) put their ___ (toe) in the water.

School + Home **Home Activity** Your child learned how to use plural nouns in writing. Have your child point out plural nouns on packages and labels and explain the rule for forming each plural.

Name ____________________

Digraphs *th*, *sh*, *ch*, *ph*

Spelling Words				
shovel	southern	northern	chapter	hyphen
chosen	establish	although	challenge	approach
astonish	python	shatter	ethnic	shiver
pharmacy	charity	china	attach	ostrich

Word Search Circle the ten list words below that are hidden in the puzzle. They are across, down, and diagonal. Write the words.

although	chosen	pharmacy	challenge	hyphen
attach	ethnic	approach	establish	southern

E S T A B L I S H C S A
A P H A R M A C Y H O P
T X U Y I Y L G J O U P
T B Q Y P N B N B S T R
A C Q E T H N I C E H O
C D L N A D E Y K N E A
H C H A L L E N G E R C
G G A L T H O U G H N H

1. ____________
2. ____________
3. ____________
4. ____________
5. ____________
6. ____________
7. ____________
8. ____________
9. ____________
10. ____________

Words in Context Finish the story with list words.

The money we raised at the **(11)** ____ auction will **(12)** ____ you. We were able to **(13)** ____ last year's record amount of $585.00. People bid on items such as an **(14)** ____ egg and a book about snakes with a **(15)** ____ on the cover. One **(16)** ____ cup fetched $25.00! An antique **(17)** ____ brought in $20.00. Auctions are exciting. Each time the gavel sounded, a **(18)** ____ of joy went down my spine.

11. ____________
12. ____________
13. ____________
14. ____________
15. ____________
16. ____________
17. ____________
18. ____________

Home Activity Your child has learned to read, write, and spell combined consonants, called digraphs. Have your child underline the digraphs in each list word and then say the word.

Name ______________________________

Compare and Contrast

- When you **compare** and **contrast** two or more things, you show how they are alike and different.
- Clue words such as *but* or *however* show contrasts. The clue words *like* and *as* show comparisons.
- Sometimes, writers do not use clue words when they compare and contrast things.

Directions Read the following passage. Fill in the columns below based on Jorge and Ed's friendship before and after the tornado touched down.

Jorge and Ed grew up on opposite ends of the same street. They went to the same school, and they were sometimes in the same classroom. They were always friendly to each other, but Jorge and Ed didn't really know each other very well.

On the night the tornado touched down, things changed between Jorge and Ed. The roof of Ed's house was blown off. Jorge and his parents were the first people there to help Ed's family. They worked together all night to help clean up Ed's house. That night, Jorge and Ed began to know each other a lot better. They became good friends.

Before	After
1. They lived ______________	**2.** They worked ______________
3. They were sometimes ______________	**4.** They became ______________

5. On a separate sheet of paper, compare and contrast one of your friendships now with what it was like at the beginning. How has it changed? How has it remained the same?

Home Activity Your child compared and contrasted *before* and *after* details from a short passage. Read a favorite story with your child. Identify an important event in the story and compare and contrast what happened before and after that event.

Name ______________________________

Regular and Irregular Plural Nouns

Directions Write the plural forms of the underlined singular nouns.

1. What activity do you enjoy at the beach?

____

2. Some people take blanket and umbrella for sunbathing.

____

3. Child and adult can take class in sailing and surfing.

____

4. Some people ride horse or pony on the sand.

____

Directions Cross out each incorrectly spelled plural noun. Write the correct spelling above the word you crossed out.

5. The sailors' wifes made picnic lunchs for the beach.

6. They served sandwichs, peaches, and tomatos.

7. The antes, flys, and bees did not bother anyone.

8. The women packed colorful glasss and dishs.

Directions Write each sentence. Write the plural forms of the nouns in ( ). Add your own describing word for each plural noun.

9. ____ (country) have ____ (seashore) with ____ (hotel) and ____ (restaurant) nearby.

____

____

10. ____ (beach) with white sand and ____ (wave) are ____ (place) for____ (vacation).

____

____

Home Activity Your child reviewed regular and irregular plural nouns. Ask your child to list things you have in your kitchen and write the plural form for each noun.

Name ______________________________

Irregular Plurals

- **Generalization** Sometimes plurals are formed in irregular ways: **shel<u>ves</u>**, **echo<u>es</u>**.

Word Sort Sort list words by words you know how to spell and words you are learning to spell. Write every word.

words I know how to spell	words I am learning to spell
1. ______	11. ______
2. ______	12. ______
3. ______	13. ______
4. ______	14. ______
5. ______	15. ______
6. ______	16. ______
7. ______	17. ______
8. ______	18. ______
9. ______	19. ______
10. ______	20. ______

Spelling Words

1. staffs
2. ourselves
3. pants
4. scissors
5. loaves
6. volcanoes
7. chiefs
8. buffaloes
9. flamingos
10. beliefs
11. echoes
12. shelves
13. quizzes
14. sheriffs
15. dominoes
16. thieves
17. measles
18. avocados
19. chefs
20. pianos

Home Activity Your child is learning to spell irregular plural nouns. Ask your child to tell you three ways the plural words in the list are formed.

Name

Family Times

Summary

Hold the Flag High

Sergeant William Carney was a soldier in an African American regiment during the Civil War. When Sergeant Carney was hit by a bullet, he bravely caught the flag before it could touch the ground and got it to safety before he collapsed. He was the first African American to win the Congressional Medal of Honor.

Activity

Flag History With a family member, use the library or the Internet to help you find and draw the flags of the Civil War era. How many stars were on the Union flag?

Comprehension Skill

Sequence

A story's **sequence** is the order in which events happen in a story. When you read, think about what happens first, next, and last. Several events may occur at the same time. Words such as *meanwhile* and *during* give clues that two events are happening at the same time.

Activity

Tag-Team Story With a family member, take turns making up a story about your family. You start it, and then the other person continues it for a while, and so on. When the story is finished, try to repeat the sequence of events in order.

Lesson Vocabulary

Words to Know

Knowing the meaning of these words is important to reading *Hold the Flag High*. Practice using these words.

Vocabulary Words

canteen a container that holds drinks
confederacy a group of people, states, or countries that work together
glory praise, honor
quarrel a fight
rebellion a conflict that leads to war
stallion a male horse
union states that are united as one country

Conventions

Possessive Nouns

A **possessive noun** shows ownership. Possessive nouns can be either singular or plural. Singular nouns form singular possessives. *For example: shoe/shoe's, Ron/Ron's.* Plural nouns form plural possessives. *For example: women/women's, girls/girls'.* To form a noun's possessive form, you usually add *-'s* to it. If the noun is a plural noun that ends in *s*, add only an apostrophe. *For example: table/table's, bus/bus's, men/men's, toes/toes'.*

Activity

Whose Favorite? With a family member, try to list the favorite foods of every member of your family you can think of. Identify each family member's favorite food using a complete sentence: "Yin's favorite food is tacos."

Practice Tested Spelling Words

______	______	______	______
______	______	______	______
______	______	______	______
______	______	______	______
______	______	______	______

Name ____________________________

Sequence

- **Sequence** is the order in which events take place, from first to last.
- Clue words such as *first, next,* and *then* may show sequence in a story or article, but not always. Other clues are dates and times of day.
- Sometimes two events happen at the same time. Clue words that show this are *meanwhile* and *in that same year.*

Directions Read the passage. Then answer the questions below.

In November 1860, Abraham Lincoln was elected the 16th President of the United States. This angered many people in the South, as Lincoln promised to end slavery, which was necessary for a large part of the Southern economy. In anticipation of Lincoln's election, South Carolina had already begun preparations to secede from the Union. In December 1860, South Carolina followed through with its threat. Then, in January 1861, Mississippi also seceded from the Union. That same month, Florida, Georgia, Louisiana, and Alabama seceded.

Abraham Lincoln's inauguration was held on March 4, 1861. On April 12, the Confederate army attempted to overtake Fort Sumter. This attack on a federal military post marked the beginning of the Civil War. By June, five more Southern states had seceded from the Union.

1. How many states in all seceded from the Union? ____________________

2. What events took place after South Carolina seceded from the Union?

____

____

3. Which state was the first to secede after South Carolina?

____

4. What event happened about a month before the Confederate army attacked Fort Sumter?

____

5. What clue words help you to understand the order in which events occurred?

____

____

Home Activity Your child has read an informational passage and studied the order in which the events occurred. With your child, read a short story. Have your child explain whether or not the sequence of events in the story affected the story's outcome.

Name_______________________________

Compare and Contrast

Directions Read the passage. Then answer the questions below.

Early in the Civil War, state and local governments provided some of the uniforms for soldiers. Rich citizens donated others. The result was a confusing array of styles and colors on both sides. In time, blue became the official color for the North, while the Confederates wore gray. The colors helped distinguish Union soldiers from Confederate soldiers.

In the North, both officers and enlisted men wore long coats, called sack jackets, and short coats, called shell jackets. Confederate soldiers also wore these. Some Southern men would have worn a waist-length coat called a roundabout. Union soldiers wore blue pants, often with a colored stripe down the side, depending on the soldier's rank. Confederate soldiers wore similar pants, but in a shade of gray. Likewise, both Union and Confederate soldiers wore caps called kepis. These popular caps had a small bill. High-ranking officers on either side might have worn a fully brimmed hat.

1. How were the uniforms of the Union and Confederate soldiers alike?

____

____

2. How were the uniforms of the Union and Confederate soldiers different?

____

____

3. How were the uniforms of high-ranking officers different from the lower-ranking soldiers?

____

____

4. List some of the clue words that show the writer is comparing and contrasting.

____

____

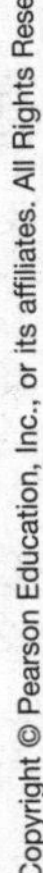

Home Activity Your child compared and contrasted details from a short passage. Discuss with your child two places that your family has visited. Ask your child to make a list of their similarities and differences.

Name ______________________________

Possessive Nouns

Directions Make each sentence less wordy by replacing the underlined words with a possessive noun phrase. Write the sentence on the line.

1. The job of a president is not easy.

   ____

2. The people of a nation do not always agree.

   ____

3. The choices of the president affect everyone.

   ____

4. He makes sure the laws of the country are fair.

   ____

5. The commands of government officials must be obeyed by all.

   ____

   ____

6. The wants of an individual are less important than the well-being of the nation.

   ____

   ____

Directions Write a paragraph describing some of the traits of people in your family. Use possessive nouns to make your writing smooth and less wordy.

____

____

____

____

____

____

____

Home Activity Your child learned how to use possessive nouns in writing. Have your child make labels for the belongings of different family members using possessive nouns.

Name________________________________

Irregular Plurals

Spelling Words				
staffs	ourselves	pants	scissors	loaves
volcanoes	chiefs	buffaloes	flamingos	beliefs
echoes	shelves	quizzes	sheriffs	dominoes
thieves	measles	avocados	chefs	pianos

Alphabetize Write the ten list words in the box below in alphabetical order.

ourselves	scissors
volcanoes	pants
chiefs	measles
buffaloes	chefs
beliefs	loaves

1. ______________
2. ______________
3. ______________
4. ______________
5. ______________
6. ______________
7. ______________
8. ______________
9. ______________
10. ______________

Related Words Write the list word that is the plural of each word below.

11. echo **11.** ______________

12. piano **12.** ______________

13. quiz **13.** ______________

14. shelf **14.** ______________

15. domino **15.** ______________

16. flamingo **16.** ______________

17. thief **17.** ______________

18. avocado **18.** ______________

19. staff **19.** ______________

20. sheriff **20.** ______________

Home Activity Your child has learned to read, write, and spell words with irregular plurals. Have your child underline the irregular ending in each word.

Name ______________________________

Sequence

- **Sequence** is the order in which events take place, from first to last.
- Clue words such as *first, next,* and *then* may show sequence in a story or article, but not always. Other clues are dates and times of day.
- Sometimes two events happen at the same time. Clue words that show this are *meanwhile* and *in that same year.*

Directions Read the passage. Then number the events in order.

In November 1864, Abraham Lincoln was reelected President of the United States. In that same month, General William Sherman conquered Confederate forces in Atlanta, Georgia, and began his infamous March to the Sea. Sherman's army destroyed everything in its path as it marched the 300 miles to Savannah. After taking Savannah in December, Sherman telegraphed President Lincoln and offered him the city as a Christmas present.

By the beginning of 1865, the Confederacy had suffered overwhelming losses, as well as shortages of food and supplies. Starving soldiers began to leave the army. Meanwhile, General Sherman continued his attack through the Carolinas. In April, General Robert E. Lee and his men left Richmond, the Confederate capital. They surrendered to the Union army at Appomattox Courthouse on April 7. Exactly one week later, President Lincoln was assassinated in Washington, D.C.

_____ The Confederate army surrenders.

_____ Sherman takes Savannah.

_____ Abraham Lincoln is assassinated.

_____ Abraham Lincoln is reelected.

_____ Confederate soldiers begin leaving the army.

Home Activity Your child has read an informational passage and studied the order in which the passage's events occurred. With your child, read about a famous historical period. Have your child make a time line of the important events.

Name____

Possessive Nouns

Directions Write each sentence. Change the underlined phrase to show possession.

1. The wishes of the South were not accepted by President Lincoln.

____

____

2. The soldiers of Sergeant Carney paraded through the streets of Boston.

____

____

3. The men of Company C were proud of their uniforms.

____

4. The names of the soldiers were pinned to their backs.

____

Directions Cross out each incorrect possessive noun. Write the correct possessive form above the word you crossed out.

5. The drummers fear was visible to the other men.

6. Sergeant Carney put a blanket around Neds shoulders.

7. The regiments camp was set up near Charleston Bay.

8. Tomorrow, the soldiers's lives would all be changed.

Directions Write a paragraph describing why a young Civil War soldier might be afraid. Use possessive nouns correctly.

____

____

____

____

Home Activity Your child reviewed possessive nouns. Ask your child to write sentences telling what he or she appreciates about home, family, school, and friends. Ask your child to try to use a possessive noun in each sentence.

Name

Vowel Sounds with *r*

- **Generalization** The vowel sound /ôr/ can be spelled **or** and **ore**: **report**, **snore**. The vowel sound /ir/ can be spelled **ear** and **eer**: **appear**, **pioneer**. The vowel sound /âr/ can be spelled **are** and **air**: **spare**, **chair**.

Word Sort Sort words by the way in which the vowel sound with *r* is spelled.

or

1. ____
2. ____
3. ____
4. ____
5. ____

ore

6. ____
7. ____

ear

8. ____
9. ____

eer

10. ____
11. ____
12. ____
13. ____

are

14. ____
15. ____
16. ____
17. ____
18. ____

air

19. ____
20. ____

Spelling Words

1. snore
2. tornado
3. spare
4. appear
5. career
6. square
7. report
8. prepare
9. pioneer
10. chair
11. beware
12. smear
13. repair
14. sword
15. ignore
16. order
17. engineer
18. resort
19. volunteer
20. declare

Home Activity Your child is learning some patterns for spelling vowel sounds with *r*. Have your child read the words aloud and circle the patterns.

Name ______________________

Family Times

Summary

The Ch'i-lin Purse

Hsiang-ling was a spoiled young girl, but on her wedding day, she gave a purse full of riches from her mother to a less fortunate bride getting married on the same day. Later, Hsiang-ling was separated from her husband and son after a horrible storm. She found work taking care of a spoiled young boy in a wealthy home. The boy's mother turned out to be the poor bride Hsiang-ling had helped so long ago. The mother was so grateful that she split her family's fortune with Hsiang-ling and helped her find her husband and son.

Activity

A Gift of Kindness Do something nice for a family member today. Help them finish a chore or task they don't like doing, or offer to take care of something for them to free up a little of their time. You'll be surprised how much small deeds like this are appreciated.

Comprehension Skill

Compare and Contrast

When writers **compare** and **contrast** things, they tell how those things are alike or different. Words such as *same*, *also*, *before*, *although*, and *however* are clues that things are being compared or contrasted.

Activity

On Your Street With a family member, go outside and look at the houses and buildings on your street. Can you guess which ones might have been built by the same company? Do you see similarities? What are some of the differences? Compare and contrast the buildings and houses as you walk down the street.

Lesson Vocabulary

Words to Know

Knowing the meanings of these words is important to reading *The Ch'i-lin Purse*. Practice using these words.

Vocabulary Words

astonished surprised greatly; amazed

behavior manner of behaving; way of acting

benefactor person who has given money or kindly help

distribution the act of giving some to each, of dividing and giving out in shares

gratitude kindly feeling because of a favor received; desire to do a favor in return; thankfulness

procession something that moves forward; persons marching or riding

recommend to speak in favor of; suggest favorably

sacred worthy of reverence; not to be violated or disregarded

traditions customs or beliefs handed down from generation to generation

Conventions

Action and Linking Verbs

Action verbs tell what the subject of a sentence does. *For example: I smiled at the old woman.* "Smiled" is an *action verb*. **Linking verbs** link, or join, the subject to a word or words in the predicate. They tell what the subject of a sentence is like. *For example: Wai's painting looked amazing. Looked* is a *linking verb*. Common linking verbs include *am, is, are, was, were, will be, seem, feel,* and *look*.

Activity

Can You Do It? With a family member, play this fill-in-the-blank word game. Write down a handful of sentences that include an action verb—but leave a blank space where the action verb would normally be. Next, both of you should write ten action verbs on strips of paper. Write the present and past-tense forms of each verb on the strip. Finally, take turns picking a verb strip out of a hat or bowl and using it to fill in a blank in one of your sentences. Make the sentences as silly as you can.

Practice Tested Spelling Words

______	______	______	______
______	______	______	______
______	______	______	______
______	______	______	______
______	______	______	______

Name ____________________

Compare and Contrast

- When you **compare and contrast** things you tell how they are similar and different.
- Sometimes clue words point out comparisons and contrasts, but not always.
- You can compare and contrast different things you read about with one another and also with what you already know.

Directions Read the following passage. Then answer the questions below.

Bill was the head ranger for the town's parks. He had a difficult choice. Two local organizations wanted permits to use River Park at the same time on the very same day. The local middle school wanted to use it for its annual family picnic, and the soccer league wanted to use if for its playoff games.

Bill supported both groups. The picnic brought the school community together. The soccer playoffs had more participants than the middle school picnic, and Bill knew that the teams were a source of pride for the whole town. He didn't know what to do.

1. Which two groups want to schedule an event at River Park?

____

____

2. What do the events have in common?

____

____

3. Name a benefit each event offers the community.

____

____

4. What major differences does Bill see between the events?

____

5. Predict how you think Bill will solve this issue.

____

____

Home Activity Your child read a short passage and answered compare-and-contrast questions. With your child, discuss a current issue. Compare and contrast two opinions about the issue. Make a prediction about how the issue will be resolved.

Name ______________________________

Sequence

Directions Read the following article. Then answer the questions below.

Mary had volunteered for a community organization that built homes for those in need. Mary learned that there are many steps to putting up a wall. First, she put up the wall frame. To do this, she measured and remeasured boards, cut them using a table saw, and screwed and nailed them into place. When the wall frame was up, she learned how to staple the insulation onto it, cutting around the electrical sockets and switches so that she did not cover them. She helped with the drywalling too. She nailed the drywall boards to the wall frame and learned how to tape the seams. By the end of the day, she was exhausted, but she had completed her wall.

1. Which does Mary do first, staple the insulation or "tape" the seams?

____

2. What would happen if Mary nailed the drywall before she stapled the insulation?

____

____

3. Summarize the steps Mary followed to build her wall.

____

____

4. Explain why the sequence of steps is important to building a wall.

____

____

5. Explain the sequence of steps in something you did for the first time.

____

____

____

____

Home Activity Your child read a short passage and answered questions about sequence. With your child, write down the sequence of events that occur at home before school begins.

Name ____________________

Action and Linking Verbs

celebrate	drink	ring
write	sways	dress

Directions Use an action verb from the box to complete each sentence. Write the sentence.

1. People from around the world ________ the new year.

____

2. In China, some people ________ as dragons.

____

3. The dragon's tail ________ as it parades down the street.

____

4. Children in Belgium ________ letters to parents on decorated paper.

____

5. In the United States, people ________ a toast to the new year.

____

6. Bells ________ out at midnight.

____

Directions Write a paragraph describing a celebration. Use vivid action verbs and appropriate linking verbs. Underline the verbs you use.

____

____

____

____

____

____

____

Home Activity Your child learned how to use action and linking verbs in writing. Ask your child to write a description of dinnertime at your home using action verbs and linking verbs.

Name______________________________

Vowel Sounds with *r*

Spelling Words				
snore	tornado	spare	appear	career
square	report	prepare	pioneer	chair
beware	smear	repair	sword	ignore
order	engineer	resort	volunteer	declare

Categorize Write the list word that completes each group.

1. weather, wind, prairie, ___ 1. ____________
2. interest, study, job, ___ 2. ____________
3. sleep, nose, exhale, ___ 3. ____________
4. vacation, travel, hotel, ___ 4. ____________
5. octagon, hexagon, pentagon, ___ 5. ____________
6. explorer, frontier, first, ___ 6. ____________
7. be careful, look out, ___ 7. ____________
8. spread, blur, smudge, ___ 8. ____________
9. announce, say, claim, ___ 9. ____________
10. handle, blade, sheath, ___ 10. ____________

Word Scramble Unscramble the list words and write them on the lines.

11. e s p r a 11. ____________
12. h r c i a 12. ____________
13. p e r r i a 13. ____________
14. r r d o e 14. ____________
15. t v l u n o e r e 15. ____________
16. r i e n g e n e 16. ____________
17. g r n i o e 17. ____________
18. p e a a p r 18. ____________

Home Activity Your child has learned to use patterns to spell vowel sounds followed by *r*. Look in a book or magazine with your child and find two other words that use one of these patterns.

Name ______________________________

Compare and Contrast

- When you **compare** and **contrast** things you tell how they are similar or different.
- Sometimes clue words point out comparisons and contrasts, but not always.
- You can compare and contrast different things you read about with one another and also with what you already know.

Directions Read the following passage.

Serena thought the holidays were the best of both worlds. She loved giving people presents, and she loved receiving them as well. She and her brother usually gave each other gifts of the same value. They both enjoyed making gifts for each other. Serena always asked her brother what he wanted, although he seldom asked her. Serena carefully wrapped her gifts so that the wrapping gave her brother a clue as to what was inside. Her brother would often present his gift to her in a paper bag or wrapped in newspaper. His unusually wrapped gifts always made her smile.

Directions Complete the following graphic organizer. List similarities and differences between Serena and her brother. Then compare them with your experience of gift giving.

Similarities in Text	Differences in Text	Compared with What I Know
1. Serena and her brother gave gifts of ______	**3.** Serena always asked her brother what he wanted, but he ______	**4.** ______
2. They both enjoyed ______	Serena carefully wrapped her gifts, and her brother did not.	**5.** ______

Home Activity Your child read a short passage and made comparisons and contrasts. With your child, compare and contrast details of two activities that your child likes to do.

Name ______________________________

Action and Linking Verbs

Directions Underline the verb in each sentence. Write *A* on the line if the verb is an action verb. Write *L* if it is a linking verb.

1. A governess raises a child in a private home. ________
2. She is important to the family. ________
3. She teaches the child his or her lessons. ________
4. However, a governess is much more than a teacher. ________
5. She shares playtime and mealtime with children. ________
6. She soon seems like one of the family. ________

Directions Match the verb with the phrase that correctly identifies the verb. Write the letter of the phrase on the line.

________	**7.** marries	**A.** linking verb
________	**8.** becomes	**B.** action verb (physical)
________	**9.** wonders	**C.** not a verb
________	**10.** happy	**D.** action verb (mental)

Directions Rewrite each sentence. Add your own verb to make the sentence clear and interesting.

11. People ________ candles and incense for different reasons.

____

12. Candlelight ________ a soft, mysterious mood.

____

13. Fragrant incense ________ pleasant.

____

14. The pleasing light and scent ________ into the air.

____

15. In this way, people ________ holy beings.

____

Home Activity Your child reviewed action and linking verbs. Ask your child to write a letter to a friend or family member using some vivid action verbs and some linking verbs.

Name ________________________________

Final Syllables *-en, -an, -el, -le, -il*

- **Generalization** Vowels in final syllables often sound alike even when they are spelled differently: **veteran, wooden, cancel, chuckle, fossil.**

Word Sort Sort words by the way in which the final syllable is spelled.

-en

1. ____________
2. ____________
3. ____________

-an

4. ____________
5. ____________
6. ____________
7. ____________

-el

8. ____________
9. ____________
10. ____________
11. ____________
12. ____________

-le

13. ____________
14. ____________
15. ____________
16. ____________
17. ____________
18. ____________

-il

19. ____________
20. ____________

Spelling Words

1. example
2. level
3. slogan
4. quarrel
5. scramble
6. evil
7. oxygen
8. wooden
9. double
10. travel
11. cancel
12. chuckle
13. fossil
14. toboggan
15. veteran
16. chisel
17. suburban
18. single
19. sudden
20. beagle

School + Home

Home Activity Your child is learning to spell words with final syllables *-en, -an, -el, -le,* and *-il*. Ask your child to tell you an ending sound and two ways it can be spelled.

Name

Family Times

Summary

A Summer's Trade

Tony is a young Navajo boy who works at the Trading Post to earn money for a saddle. However, when his grandmother has to sell her prized bracelet, Tony knows he must buy it back with what he has earned. Later, Tony is shocked to receive the saddle as a gift from his grandmother.

Activity

Prized Possessions In the story, Tony wants a saddle more than anything. His grandmother's bracelet means everything to her. Have each member of your family name a prized possession. Have everyone explain why their item is so valuable.

Comprehension Skill

Author's Purpose

An **author's purpose** is the reason that the author writes the story. Authors may write to persuade, inform, entertain, or express ideas or feelings.

Activity

What's the Motive? With your family, take turns recounting a story of something that has recently happened. When each person has finished, have the rest of the family try to figure out the storyteller's purpose. Is there more than one? How do you know?

Lesson Vocabulary

Words to Know

Knowing the meaning of these words is important when reading *A Summer's Trade.* Practice using these words.

Vocabulary Words

bandana a square piece of fabric worn on the head or neck
bracelet a piece of jewelry worn around the wrist
hogan a kind of house used by the Navajo people
jostled bumped or jiggled
mesa a rock formation or mountain with a flat top
Navajo a member of the Navajo Indian tribe
turquoise a precious blue-green stone

Conventions

Main and Helping Verbs

Main verbs show the action in a sentence. Main verbs are always the last word in a verb phrase. **Helping verbs** clarify the meaning of the main verb. For instance, they may indicate when the action takes place. They come before the main verb in a sentence. *Have, has, had, will, is, am, are, was,* and *were* can be helping verbs. *For example: Bob is building an airplane. Is* is the *linking verb* and *building* is the *main verb.*

Activity

Say It, Do It With a family member, take turns making statements and have the other person act out the action verb. For example, if someone says "I'm flying over the trees," the other person would act out "flying."

Practice Tested Spelling Words

______	______	______	______
______	______	______	______
______	______	______	______
______	______	______	______
______	______	______	______

Name ____

Author's Purpose

- The **author's purpose** is the reason or reasons the author has for writing.
- An author may write to persuade, to inform, to entertain, or to express ideas and feelings.

Directions Read the following passage. Then answer the questions below.

Traditional Navajo foods that are still enjoyed today include mutton, corn, and fry bread made from flour. This bread is similar to a Mexican tortilla. Fry bread is mostly flat, but puffy in places. This delicious bread can be eaten plain, stuffed with a filling, or dipped into stews.

Fry bread is easy to make. If you want to try Navajo fry bread, you will need flour, salt, baking powder, powdered milk, and water. Follow a recipe and form the dough into little floured patties. These are to be fried in a pan in about one inch of oil. When the dough puffs up, the fry bread is ready to enjoy.

1. What is the author's purpose for writing this passage?

____

____

2. Give an example of an informational statement in the passage.

____

____

3. Which words tell you that the author is being persuasive?

____

____

4. Do you think the author's purpose was achieved?

____

____

5. On a separate sheet of paper, write a passage persuading people to try a new food.

Home Activity Your child learned about author's purpose. Read a newspaper or magazine article with your child and discuss the author's purpose.

Name________________________________

Compare and Contrast

Directions Read the article. Then answer the questions below.

Navajo weavers have produced artistic textiles such as rugs for more than 150 years. Handwoven blankets and rugs were first made for practical purposes. Now they are important to the economy of the Navajo community, since tourists and collectors buy them.

These beautiful rugs are similar to the Middle Eastern *kilims,* which are sometimes called Persian rugs. However, while kilims often included curved and floral lines, typical Navajo rugs used strong geometric patterns with straight lines.

After trade and travel exploded in the late nineteenth century, some kilim designs started to be used in Navajo rugs.

1. What art form do Navajo and the kilim weavers have in common?

____

____

2. Why is textile making important to the Navajo economy now?

____

____

3. How were traditional Navajo rug designs different from kilim designs at first?

____

____

4. How did nineteenth-century trading affect the designs of Navajo rugs?

____

____

5. On a separate sheet of paper, explain how Navajos might have first seen the kilim designs.

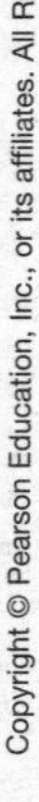

Home Activity Your child compared and contrasted information about Navajo rugs and kilims, which are Persian rugs. Walk around your home and have your child compare and contrast pieces of furniture, rooms, or wall adornments.

Name ______________________________

Main and Helping Verbs

Directions Underline the verb and verb phrases in each paragraph. Circle the verb phrase that expresses the wrong time. Write the correct verb phrase on the line.

1. We are selling more saddles these days. For example, today I am holding a new saddle for a rancher. He was driving over to get it now.

____

2. Last week we visited a Navajo trading post. My parents collect Navajo jewelry. They had brought along a book about traditional necklaces. Soon we all are looking for collectables. Bobbie called. He had found a beautiful piece.

____

3. This winter our family will visit a reservation. Shelly may see her friend Elsie. I will ride a horse to the ocean. We did enjoy the food and dancing at the reservation.

____

4. Tony was saving for a new saddle. He had been working in the store. Tony stacked boxes. He swept the floor. Soon he is helping his father with the flock.

____

Directions Write a paragraph about an animal you might see on a ranch. Use some verb phrases.

____

____

____

____

____

____

____

School + Home

Home Activity Your child learned how to express time correctly using verb phrases. Ask your child to use *be* verbs with action verbs to make up sentences about something he or she did in the past, is doing now, and will do in the future.

Name______________________________

Final Syllables *-en, -an, -el, -le, -il*

Spelling Words				
example	level	slogan	quarrel	scramble
evil	oxygen	wooden	double	travel
cancel	chuckle	fossil	toboggan	veteran
chisel	suburban	single	sudden	beagle

Analogies Write the list word that completes each comparison.

1. Hot is to warm as rapid is to ____. 1. ____________
2. Cart is to wagon as sled is to ____. 2. ____________
3. Plate is to dish as argument is to ____. 3. ____________
4. Grin is to smile as laugh is to ____. 4. ____________
5. Silver is to metallic as oak is to ____. 5. ____________
6. Silly is to funny as wicked is to ____. 6. ____________
7. Chair is to seat as mix-up is to ____. 7. ____________
8. Rush is to hurry as ____ is to one. 8. ____________
9. Fun is to enjoyment as ____ is to experienced. 9. ____________
10. Light is to bright as ____ is to even. 10. ____________

Word Endings Each word has the final syllable spelled incorrectly. Rewrite the list word with the correctly spelled ending.

11. exampel 11. ____________
12. slogen 12. ____________
13. doubel 13. ____________
14. travle 14. ____________
15. cancle 15. ____________
16. fossle 16. ____________
17. chisil 17. ____________
18. suburben 18. ____________
19. beagil 19. ____________
20. oxygan 20. ____________

Home Activity Your child has learned to read, write, and spell words with final syllables *-en, -an, -el, -le, -il.* Take turns saying and spelling each word aloud.

Name ______________________________

Author's Purpose

- The **author's purpose** is the reason or reasons the author has for writing.
- An author may write to persuade, to inform, to entertain, or to express feelings and ideas.
- In persuasive writing, the author tries to convince the reader to agree with an opinion.

Directions Read the passage. Then answer the questions below.

For an unforgettable trip, visit the Navajo Nation, located on about 26,000 square miles of reservation land in parts of Arizona, Utah, and New Mexico. Although it lies within the physical United States, the Navajo Nation is largely independent. Here, the Navajos control their land, economy, government, and culture.

The Navajo economy depends on many components. Traditional practices, such as pottery making, textile weaving, and goat herding are important. However, tourism is another way for the Navajo to support themselves. The beauty of the reservation's landscape, as well as the many national monuments, parks, and historical sites attract many visitors every year. One incredible attraction is the ancient ruins of the ancient Pueblo people. A visit there is a visit to another world.

1. What is the author's purpose in this passage?

____

2. What words give you clues about the author's purpose?

____

____

____

____

3. Underline examples of each purpose. Label it with the author's purpose for that part of the passage.

4. In your opinion, is the author's purpose achieved? Why or why not?

____

____

Home Activity Your child analyzed the author's purpose in a passage about the Navajo Nation. Challenge him or her to make a persuasive argument to you or another family member about making a visit to this area.

Name ____________________

Main and Helping Verbs

Directions Choose a helping verb from the box to complete each sentence. Write the sentence on the line. Underline the verb phrase.

could	should	has	was	had	did

1. My grandfather ______ studied Native American culture for decades.

2. He ______ raised in New Mexico.

3. Even as a little boy, he ______ always read about native cultures.

4. In the desert, he ______ live among the Navajo on a reservation.

5. He ______ not notice the months passing.

6. We ______ admire such devotion to these cultures.

Directions Find the verb phrases. Underline each helping verb. Circle each main verb.

7. Tony has lived on a Navajo reservation all his life.
8. His mother had worked in a restaurant.
9. Tony was helping in the Trading Post.
10. Different items are traded and sold there.
11. He had been saving for his own saddle.
12. He will ride with his father on the ranch.

Home Activity Your child reviewed main and helping verbs. Ask your child to make up sentences using verb phrases to describe an animal's past, present, and future actions.

Name ______________________________

Final Syllables *er, ar, or*

- **Generalization** Words with final syllables **er**, **ar**, and **or** often sound alike even when they are spelled differently: **danger**, **dollar**, **tractor**.

Word Sort Sort the list words by the spelling of the final syllable.

-er

1. ____________
2. ____________
3. ____________
4. ____________
5. ____________
6. ____________
7. ____________
8. ____________
9. ____________
10. ____________

-ar

11. ____________
12. ____________
13. ____________
14. ____________

-or

15. ____________
16. ____________
17. ____________
18. ____________
19. ____________
20. ____________

Spelling Words

1. danger
2. wander
3. tractor
4. dollar
5. harbor
6. eager
7. eraser
8. surrender
9. solar
10. sticker
11. locker
12. helicopter
13. pillar
14. refrigerator
15. caterpillar
16. rumor
17. glimmer
18. linger
19. sensor
20. alligator

Home Activity Your child is learning about final syllables that sound the same but are spelled differently. Ask your child to spell three list words with endings that sound alike but are spelled differently.

Name

Family Times

Summary

The Midnight Ride of Paul Revere

Revolutionary war hero Paul Revere warned the colonists of an advancing attack by the British army. Revere rode his horse through the night warning every village and town. The colonists, prepared by Revere's warning, defeated the British forces.

Activity

Household Poetics With a family member, write a short poem describing something you do every day, like eating lunch or walking to school. Try to make the poem as exciting as possible.

Comprehension Skill

Author's Purpose

The **author's purpose** is the reason or reasons the author has for writing. One purpose is to persuade. When authors write to persuade, they try to convince readers to agree with their opinion.

Activity

Travel Plans Think of some places you really want to visit. Then pick a place you want to go more than all the others. Write a paragraph explaining why the place you want to visit is the perfect choice. Explain what you would want to do there and why other people would have a great time too.

Lesson Vocabulary

Words to Know

Knowing the meanings of these words is important to reading *The Midnight Ride of Paul Revere*. Practice using these words.

Vocabulary Words

fate what becomes of someone or something

fearless without fear; afraid of nothing; brave; daring

glimmer a faint, unsteady light

lingers stays on; goes slowly, as if unwilling to leave

magnified caused something to look larger than it actually is

somber having deep shadows; dark; gloomy

steed a horse, especially a riding horse

Conventions

Subject-Verb Agreement

Subject-verb agreement occurs when the correct singular or plural verb is used to match the singular or plural noun or pronoun in the subject. Singular nouns and pronouns take singular verbs. Plural nouns and pronouns take plural verbs. *For example: Jenny wants to go to Philadelphia. Her parents want to go to Boston instead.* "Jenny" is *singular*, so it takes the singular "wants," but "her parents" is *plural*, so it takes the plural "want."

Activity

Mix 'n' Match With a family member, take a piece of paper and divide it into twelve squares. On six of the squares, write six different subjects (nouns). Make some plural, like *cats*, and some singular, like *dog*. On the other six squares, write six different verbs that agree with the nouns. Then mix up the squares, and match the subjects and verbs in different combinations so they all agree.

Practice Tested Spelling Words

______	______	______	______
______	______	______	______
______	______	______	______
______	______	______	______
______	______	______	______

Name____

Author's Purpose

- The **author's purpose** is the reason or reasons the author has for writing.
- An author may write to persuade, to inform, to entertain, or to express feelings and ideas.

Directions Read the passage. Then answer the questions below.

In 1773, American colonists held the Boston Tea Party, raiding three British ships in Boston Harbor. They dumped more than three hundred crates of British tea into the water. They were protesting England's taxes on the American colonies. Eight months earlier, the British government had created a tax on all tea shipped from England to America. The colonists were furious. On the night of December 16, 1773, approximately one hundred colonists led by Samuel Adams stormed the British ships waiting to unload their tea. By dumping all the tea into the harbor, the colonists let the king know that they would not stand for his high taxation.

1. What is the author's purpose in this passage?

____

2. What happened as a result of the English tax on tea in the American colonies?

____

____

3. List some facts you learned about the Boston Tea Party in this passage.

____

____

____

4. What words or phrases does the author use to show how upset the colonists were with the English taxes?

____

5. In your opinion, is the author's purpose achieved? Why or why not?

____

____

Home Activity Your child analyzed the author's purpose in a passage about the Boston Tea Party. Ask your child to describe an event that happened at school. After he or she has finished, ask your child to explain the purpose in describing the event. Was it to inform, persuade, entertain, express himself or herself, or a combination?

Name______________________________

Literary Elements • Setting and Theme

Directions Read the article. Then answer the questions below.

Patrick Henry was one of the many interesting characters in the American Revolution. He provided us with one of the great sayings in American history As a young man, he tried and failed at being a farmer and shopkeeper. He eventually educated himself and became a lawyer. Patrick Henry became a famous activist in the fight against British control of the colonies. He spoke out against English rule early and often. He urged fellow colonists to revolt. He challenged the British over their restrictions upon American liberty. In 1775, at a meeting of colonial leaders, he spoke his most famous line: "I know not what course others may take, but as for me, give me liberty or give me death." This was the theme of his adult life.

1. When and where did Patrick Henry live?

____

____

2. How do you know Patrick Henry was outspoken?

____

____

3. How did Patrick Henry feel about British rule of the colonies?

____

____

4. Why do you think Patrick Henry said, "Give me liberty or give me death"?

____

____

5. On a separate sheet of paper, describe something you feel so strongly about that you would say something like what Patrick Henry said.

Home Activity Your child read a short passage and answered questions about setting and theme. Discuss the setting of one of your child's favorite places. Ask your child: What does it look like? What do you see there?

Name ______________________________

Subject-Verb Agreement

Directions Add a verb to complete each sentence. Be sure to use the correct verb form.

1. The Liberty Bell ________________ a well-known American symbol.

2. It ________________ in the Liberty Bell Center in Philadelphia.

3. Many tourists ________________ this site.

4. ________________ the bell ever ring?

5. No. A crack ________________ up the side of the bell.

6. The main metals in the bell ________________ copper and tin.

7. The bell ________________ 2,080 pounds.

8. Philadelphia ________________ in southeastern Pennsylvania.

9. More than a million and a half people ________________ there.

10. Tourists ________________ the many historic sites in Philadelphia.

Directions Circle the verb that agrees with each subject. Then write sentences using at least three of the subject-verb pairs.

11. class	is studying	are studying
12. historic site	inspire	inspires
13. teacher	tell	tells
14. some students	sing	sings
15. they	is	are
16. I	feel	feels

Home Activity Your child learned how to write subjects and verbs that agree. Ask your child to make up sentences in the present tense describing favorite animals, first using a singular subject, then a plural subject (dog/dogs, lion/lions, and so on).

Name ____________________

Final Syllables *er*, *ar*, *or*

Spelling Words				
danger	wander	tractor	dollar	harbor
eager	eraser	surrender	solar	sticker
locker	helicopter	pillar	refrigerator	caterpillar
rumor	glimmer	linger	sensor	alligator

Word Scramble Riddle Unscramble each list word and then write the numbered letters on the lines below to answer the riddle.

Riddle: What's the answer to "See you later, alligator!"?

1. RRNDSEURE ___ ___ ___ ___ ___ ___ ___ ___(18) ___ ___
2. ARERSE ___ ___ ___ ___ ___ ___(6)
3. EOERRIRRFAGT ___ ___ ___(4) ___ ___ ___ ___ ___ ___ ___ ___(2) ___
4. RAERPCTALIL ___ ___ ___(3) ___ ___ ___ ___ ___ ___ ___ ___
5. LEMMGRI ___ ___(11) ___ ___ ___ ___ ___
6. LOLDAR ___ ___(5) ___ ___ ___ ___
7. PALIRL ___ ___ ___ ___ ___ ___(14)
8. EINGLR ___ ___(19) ___ ___ ___ ___
9. RLAITALGO ___ ___(20) ___ ___(10) ___ ___ ___ ___ ___
10. CISKTRE ___ ___ ___ ___(13) ___ ___ ___
11. OSRAL ___ ___ ___ ___(7) ___
12. LCERKO ___ ___(15) ___ ___ ___ ___
13. NGDREA ___ ___ ___(1) ___ ___(21) ___
14. UMRRO ___ ___ ___ ___(17) ___
15. RNEWAD ___(8) ___ ___ ___ ___ ___
16. ATOCRTR ___ ___ ___ ___(16) ___ ___ ___
17. HRRABO ___(9) ___ ___ ___ ___ ___
18. AGREE ___(12) ___ ___ ___ ___

___ ___ ___   ___ ___ ___   ___   ___ ___ ___ ___ ___   ___ ___ ___ ___ ___ ___ ___ ___ ___
1 2 3   4 5 6   7   8 9 10 11 12   13 14 15 16 17 18 19 20 21

Home Activity Your child has learned to spell words with final syllables *er*, *ar*, and *or*. Look through a book or magazine with your child and find four other words with the same endings.

Name___________________________

Author's Purpose

- The **author's purpose** is the reason or reasons the author has for writing.
- An author may write to persuade, to inform, to entertain, or to express feelings and ideas.

Directions Read the passage. Then fill in the chart below and answer the questions.

No one is exactly sure who fired the first shot of the American Revolution. When the British army arrived in Lexington, about seventy militiamen met them. The British were there to disarm the colonists, but the colonists were ready. The two sides stood face-to-face. After some yelling back and forth, a shot was fired. A battle followed. When it was over, eight colonists were dead. Later, both sides blamed the other for firing first, but many claimed they had no idea who started shooting first. Still others said the first shot came from behind a hedge or from inside a tavern. The truth is, with all the confusion, we may never know who fired "the shot heard 'round the world."

Author's Purpose	How You Know
1.	**2.**

3. If the author wished to use this same story to entertain, what could be done differently?

____

____

4. Was the author successful in achieving his or her purpose in this passage?

____

____

5. On a separate sheet of paper, rewrite the paragraph with a different purpose, such as persuading, entertaining, or expressing an idea.

Home Activity Your child analyzed the author's purpose in a historical account. Show your child an example of historical nonfiction and an example of historical fiction. Ask your child to explain the different purposes the authors had in the two examples.

Name ______________________________

Subject-Verb Agreement

Directions Underline the subject of each sentence. Circle the verb in ( ) that agrees with the subject.

1. Paul Revere (is, are) a legendary figure of the Revolutionary War.
2. Americans (love, loves) hearing about his midnight ride.
3. I (imagine, imagines) that night.
4. Three men (ride, rides) from Boston to Concord.
5. Danger (lurk, lurks) around every bend.
6. An English scout (yell, yells) "Stop! Who goes there?"
7. His companions (stop, stops) one of the three riders.
8. One man (go, goes) no farther that night.
9. It (is, are) Paul Revere.
10. Few people (know, knows) that fact.

Directions Add a present tense verb to complete each sentence. Be sure the verb agrees with the subject in number.

11. This portrait ____________________ a serious man.
12. It ____________________ a portrait of Paul Revere.
13. Several objects ____________________ on the table next to him.
14. They ____________________ a silversmith's tools.
15. The man's right hand ____________________ his chin thoughtfully.
16. His left hand ____________________ a silver teapot.
17. Americans still ____________________ the silver work of Revere.
18. A silver piece by Paul Revere ____________________ great value today.

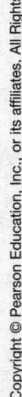

Home Activity Your child reviewed subject-verb agreement. Ask your child to read a newspaper or magazine article and point out singular and plural subjects. Have him or her explain why the verbs agree with those subjects.

Name ______________________________

Family Times

Selection Summaries

Week 1 *At the Beach*
When a boy gets hurt while following Fernando on a forbidden adventure, Fernando lies about what happened.

Week 2 *Hold the Flag High*
In an African American regiment during the Civil War, one soldier displays extraordinary bravery.

Week 3 *The Ch'i-lin Purse*
A bride's kindness is repaid years later.

Week 4 *A Summer's Trade*
Tony is saving money from his summer job. Then he hears that his grandmother has had to pawn her favorite bracelet.

Week 5 *The Midnight Ride of Paul Revere*
After spreading word of a British invasion, Paul Revere becomes a hero.

Activity
Tell a member of your family more about each of the five stories. Be sure to remember characters, plot, theme, and setting. Write three reasons why you like one story the most.

Comprehension Skills Review

In Unit 2, you learned and used many skills while reading the stories and selections.

- When you **compare** and **contrast,** you tell how things are alike and different.
- The **author's purpose** is the reason the author wrote a story.
- **Sequence** refers to the order in which the events happen.

Activity
Doing the right thing isn't always easy. Sometimes we're afraid to do the right thing because we might get into trouble. Talk with a family member about a time when he or she did the right thing, even though it was difficult. Then tell about a time when you did the right thing. How were your experiences alike? How were they different?

Unit Vocabulary Skills

Unfamiliar Words

When you find an **unfamiliar word** while reading, you can try to find its meaning from the words and sentences around it.

Activity As you read, write each unfamiliar word on an index card. Write the meaning you infer on the other side.

Greek and Latin Roots

Many English words have **Greek and Latin roots.** You can use a dictionary to find out a word's root.

Activity As you read, look for words that seem similar and check their roots in a dictionary. Do they come from the same root word?

Unknown Words

When you find an **unknown word** while reading, you can look in a dictionary or glossary to find its meaning.

Activity Make a list of unknown words that you encounter while reading. Then put them in alphabetical order and check their definitions.

Endings, *-s, -ed, -ing*

Endings *-s, -ed,* and ***-ing*** are added to the end of a word to create a new word with a new meaning. If you are unsure about the meaning of a word with an ending of *-s*, *-ed*, or *-ing*, check the dictionary.

Activity Make a list of six words and then add *-s*, *-ed*, or *-ing* to the words to change their meanings. Write the new words in a second list.

Unit Spelling Rules

Digraphs *th, sh, ch, ph*

Consonant digraphs are two consonants together that stand for one new sound.

Irregular Plurals

Regular plurals follow the rules. Irregular plurals often have base word changes. Some irregular plurals are the same as the singular form.

Vowel sounds with *r*

Vowels and vowel sounds have a slightly different sound when they are followed by *r*. Vowels followed by *r* are called *r*-controlled vowels.

Final syllables *en, an, el, le, il*

Vowels in unaccented syllables often stand for the same sound, /ə/.

Final syllables *er, ar, or*

Final syllables *er*, *ar*, and *or* often sound alike even when they are spelled differently. Some sounds can be spelled in different ways.

Activity With a family member, identify as many words as possible in books, magazines, or newspapers that follow the Unit Spelling Rules. Make a list of these words.

Name ______________________

Unfamiliar Words

- **Unfamiliar Words** As you read, you may come across some words that you are not sure about. You can use context clues or check the meanings of words that you are unsure of in a dictionary.

Words to Know

algae
concealed
driftwood
hammocks
lamented
sea urchins
sternly
tweezers

Practice Guide words appear on the top of each dictionary page to show the first and the last word on each page. For each Word to Know, circle the correct set of guide words.

1. driftwood
   a. document – donkey b. dried – drink
2. algae
   a. aluminum – amalgam b. aleph – alphabet
3. sternly
   a. stepson – sticker b. steam – steed
4. hammocks
   a. hardly – harrowing b. hamburger – Hamptons
5. concealed
   a. conjure – contrite b. collect – concentrate
6. sea urchins
   a. seatmate – secret b. secret agent – sedative
7. tweezers
   a. turnabout – turtle b. turtledove – twilled
8. lamented
   a. landmass – lap b. lame – landmark

On Your Own As you read "Augie's Present," look for words that are unfamiliar to you. Find their definitions in a dictionary.

Home Activity Your child reviewed how to use a dictionary to check the meanings of unfamiliar words. With your child, look for unfamiliar words in a newspaper or magazine. Look up the words together, using guidewords when necessary, and discuss their meanings.

Name______________________________

Compare and Contrast

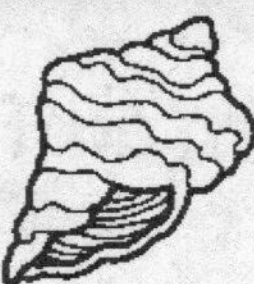

- When you **compare and contrast,** you tell how things are similar to and different from each other.

Practice Read the following passage. Then answer the questions below.

Mariska had always loved swimming in the calm waters of the lake near her house. Today, however, she was at the ocean for the first time! She shivered as the brisk wind came off the water. The great stretch of sandy beach astonished her. The lake near her house was much smaller. It didn't have waves like these, either.

Mariska laughed at the little sea birds as they ran away from the oncoming water. Her lake had birds, too, but they were bigger ones like ducks and loons. Mariska gasped as she felt the sand being washed away from under her feet. "This place is amazing!" she said. "Especially at high tide!"

1. What is going on in the passage?

____

2. What does Mariska notice about the ocean that is different from the lake she is used to?

____

____

3. What does Mariska notice that is the same?

____

4. Did Mariska prefer the beach or the lake?

____

____

On Your Own Use what you know about drawing conclusions as you read "Augie's Present."

Home Activity Your child reviewed the skill of drawing conclusions. Share a magazine article and work together to draw conclusions from what you read.

Name ______________________________

Unknown Words

- Remember that **unknown words** are words you have not seen before or do not know. When you come to an unknown word in your reading, you can look up its meaning in a dictionary or glossary.

Practice Read the following passage. Fill in the blanks with the correct Words to Know from the list.

Sitting on top of his ________________, the cavalry soldier took a drink of water from the ________________ and looked around. He was a Yankee from the North. He was in this war to stop the ________________ of Southern states. He knew the Union army needed to smash the ________________. His father did not agree with the war. They had a loud ________________ when he left. But his father was wrong. He was not seeking personal ________________. He was battling to preserve the ________________ of the United States of America.

Words to Know

- canteen
- confederacy
- glory
- quarrel
- rebellion
- stallion
- union

On Your Own As you read "Franklin Delano Roosevelt," look up unfamiliar words in the dictionary. Make a list of the words you find.

School + Home **Home Activity** With your child, read a newspaper or magazine feature article. As you read, pause to look up unfamiliar words in a dictionary.

Name ___

Sequence

- **Sequence** is the order in which events happen.

Jesse gets up every day at 7 A.M.

After getting dressed and brushing his teeth, he eats breakfast.

Jesse walks six blocks to school, through the town square.

School starts at 9 in the morning.

Practice Read the following questions and answer them on the lines below.

1. What time does Jesse get up on school days?

2. What does Jesse do before having breakfast?

3. What does Jesse do after breakfast?

4. What time does Jesse have to be at school?

5. On a separate sheet of paper, write a paragraph describing your own morning routine.

On Your Own Use what you know about sequence as you read "Franklin Delano Roosevelt."

Home Activity Your child reviewed sequences of events. Discuss the sequence of events that your family follows when doing a regular activity, such as making dinner.

Name ______________________________

Greek and Latin Roots

- **Greek and Latin roots** are used in many English words. When you find a word you don't know, being familiar with its Greek or Latin root may help you understand what the word means.

Practice Read the following sentences and fill in the blanks with the Words to Know. Then circle the correct meaning of each underlined word.

Words to Know

astonished
behavior
benefactor
distribution
gratitude
procession
recommend
sacred
traditions

1. My family is Chinese-American, and we benefit from having many interesting Chinese ________________. For example, we burn paper money to show ________________ to our ancestors.
   a. get something good from   b. get nothing good from

2. I left a big gratuity, or tip, for the waiter in the restaurant. My family was ________________ until I explained that he had done a great job and that I wanted to thank him for his considerate ________________.
   a. money that someone gives to show they are pleased   b. money that someone has to pay even if they don't want to

3. The villagers made a long ________________ through their town to check on the ________________ of food to everyone. All the families who were hungry felt grateful for this kindness.
   a. helpful   b. thankful

4. In some parts of the world, cows are considered beneficial and ________________, so people will not kill or eat them.
   a. something that needs help   b. something that is good for all

5. You have been such a generous ________________ to my family and me. Can you ________________ a way for us to pay you back and show our gratefulness?
   a. a feeling of being pleased or thankful   b. a feeling of needing help from someone

On Your Own As you read "Augie's Present," look for words that have Greek or Latin roots. Make a list of the words you find.

Home Activity Your child reviewed Greek and Latin roots, which are often parts of English words. Discuss with your child the roots he or she learned about and look for words with similar roots in magazines and newspapers.

Name ___________________________

Compare and Contrast

- When you **compare** two things, you tell the ways in which they are similar.
- When you **contrast** two things, you tell the ways they are different.

This is Amy and her dog. When she takes her dog for a walk, her dog holds his head up as Amy holds the leash tight.

This is Ann and her dog. When Ann takes her dog for a walk, her dog walks with his head down.

Practice Read the following questions and answer them on the lines below.

1. Amy and Ann are sisters. Compare their pictures. How are Amy and Ann alike?

____

____

____

2. Now, contrast Amy and Ann. How are they different?

____

____

____

On Your Own Use what you know about comparing and contrasting as you read "Augie's Present."

Home Activity Your child reviewed comparing (telling how things are alike) and contrasting (telling how things are different). Discuss two favorite games or books with your child, and ask him or her to compare and contrast them.

Name ______________________

Unfamiliar Words

- Use context clues to help you figure out **unfamiliar words**. Context clues are the words and sentences around the unfamiliar words.

Words to Know

bandana
bracelet
hogan
jostled
mesa
Navajo
turquoise

Practice Read the following sentences. Fill in the blanks with the correct words from the Words to Know list. Then choose the definition that best matches the word and circle its letter.

1. Cyrus tied a ______________ around his face to keep the dust out of his nose and mouth.

a. large handkerchief b. ski mask

2. Grandmother wore her favorite silver ______________ on special occasions only.

a. wristwatch b. band or chain worn on the wrist

3. Many ______________ people live on the reservation.

a. members of a Native American group b. visiting

4. Waiting in line at the theater, we were ______________ by the crowd.

a. cut in front of b. shoved against someone roughly

5. A ______________ stone is blue, while a ruby is red.

a. reddish gemstone b. blue-green mineral

On Your Own On a separate sheet of paper, write sentences using the words *mesa* and *hogan.*

School + Home

Home Activity Your child reviewed unfamiliar words. As you read a book or newspaper together, challenge your child to find the meanings of some new words using context clues.

Name____________________

Author's Purpose

- The **author's purpose** is the reason the author wrote the text. Authors write to entertain, to inform, to persuade, and to express their feelings and ideas.

Authors write for many different reasons.

Practice Draw a line from the kind of writing to the author's purpose for writing it.

Newspaper editorial	to inform
Poem	to express himself or herself
User's Guide	to entertain
Novel	to persuade

Practice Read the sentence or sentences after each number below. On the lines below, write what the author's purpose is, and tell how you know.

1. The dog growled at Stacy. She shuddered. Then, to her amazement, the dog said, "Hey, why are you so scared?"

____

2. If you use this brand of shampoo, you will have the most beautiful hair.

____

3. The firefighters responded to the report of a fire at 822 North Street at 6:30 P.M.

____

____

4. I just want to thank you for the gift—it was such a nice surprise!

____

____

5. Looking to the trees/The happy breeze/Sets my mind at ease.

____

On Your Own After reading "Franklin Delano Roosevelt," write a sentence describing what you think the author's purpose was for writing it.

Home Activity Your child reviewed the purposes authors have for writing. Flip through a newspaper and discuss the purposes of the people who wrote letters to the editor, the articles, and the columns.

Name________________________________

Inflected Endings *-s, -ed, -ing*

- **Inflected endings *-s, -ed,*** and ***-ing*** are added to the end of a word to create a new word with a new meaning. If you are unsure about the meaning of a word with an inflected ending, check the dictionary.

Words to Know	
fate	magnified
fearless	somber
glimmer	steed
lingers	

Practice Read the passage. Write the base of each underlined word on the lines below.

"I am very somber today," <u>sighed</u> the king, "as I must give all of my kingdom to the evil knight, Sir Specter, who has laid siege to my castle."

"But King Horace, as long as the Silver Knight still <u>lives</u>, there is a bright light of hope," offered the king's servant.

"But even the Silver Knight will be <u>frightened</u> of Sir Specter," said the king. "I fear it is our fate that Sir Specter shall rule the kingdom forever."

Just then, hoof beats rang out, magnified by the loud <u>echoing</u> on the stone castle walls. A voice called, "It is I, the Silver Knight! I come with good news. I have driven the evil Sir Specter from the kingdom! The crown can again rest atop the head of our rightful king!"

The Silver Knight's steed <u>reared</u> up. Knight and horse made a dazzling sight. The Silver Knight took off her helmet and her long hair shone in the sunlight. "Thank you, Lady Gwen!" said the king. "I hope you will join us for a feast to celebrate your victory. After all, a hero must be hungry after <u>saving</u> the day!"

1. ______________________ 4. ______________________

2. ______________________ 5. ______________________

3. ______________________ 6. ______________________

On Your Own As you read "Franklin Delano Roosevelt," look for words with inflected endings.

School + Home **Home Activity** Your child reviewed the inflected word endings *-s, -ed,* and *-ing.* Have a contest with your child to see who can find the most inflected words in a newspaper article.

Name ____________________

Author's Purpose

- The **author's purpose** is the reason the author wrote the text. Authors write to entertain, to inform, to persuade, and to express their feelings and ideas.

Practice Read the following passage. Then complete the diagram and answer the question below.

You can help take care of Earth by making little changes in your life. One way is to reduce what you use. Your family can reduce the gas you use by riding bicycles instead of driving a car. You can save water by turning off the faucet while brushing your teeth. The next step is to reuse old products. Making things from recycled materials is cheaper and causes less pollution. Use your old jeans to make a schoolbag. Lastly, everybody can recycle. When you finish a bottle or can, don't throw it away—put it in your bag and recycle it later.

1. **Detail:** You can save water by ____________________ →
2. **Detail:** Making things from recycled material is ____________________ →
3. **Detail:** After you finish a bottle or can, ____________________ →

4. **Author's Purpose:** ____________________

5. Does the author succeed at his or her purpose? Why or why not?

____

____

On Your Own Use what you know about the author's purpose as you read "Franklin Delano Roosevelt."

Home Activity Your child reviewed the purposes authors have for writing. Look at some other articles about environmental issues and have your child state the author's purpose.

Name ___________________________

Franklin Delano Roosevelt

"The only thing we have to fear is fear itself." So said one of our country's most brilliant and well-spoken Presidents, Franklin Delano Roosevelt. This brave leader was President of the United States from 1933 to 1945. He was elected to serve an extraordinary four terms in office when no other President had served more than two. Millions of Americans listened to Roosevelt's radio broadcasts, known as "fireside chats." His voice carried across the darkness, traveling through the radio to people who were hungry, afraid, and poor. Americans listened to their President and heard a voice that would lead them to a brighter future.

From the moment he was born, Franklin Delano Roosevelt was given wealth and privileges. His rich parents educated him at home until the age of 14. He then went to Groton, a private school in Massachusetts, and then went to college at Harvard University. Franklin was accustomed to having money, but he was also taught to be generous to others. While at Harvard, he became inspired by his fifth cousin, President Theodore Roosevelt. It was Theodore who first turned Franklin's attention to politics and economics.

Franklin later met Theodore's niece, Eleanor. Eleanor and Franklin were soon engaged, and the young couple married in 1905. Eleanor, who worked with the poor in New York City, opened Franklin's eyes to the problems of hunger and poverty in America.

Franklin Delano Roosevelt went into politics and was elected to the New York Senate in 1910. He was reelected in 1912, and later became Assistant Secretary of the Navy in 1913. During World War I, Roosevelt proved he was a capable leader who strengthened and organized the navy.

Then disaster hit. While vacationing at Campobello Island in Canada, the healthy young Roosevelt was struck down with polio, a dangerous disease that causes paralysis. At the time, no cure or vaccine for polio existed. Roosevelt would have to spend the rest of his life in a wheelchair or leg braces.

Despite these intense difficulties, Franklin was able to continue his political career, thanks in part to the help of Eleanor and others. In 1928, he was elected as New York governor, and he went on to serve several years in that position. As governor, Franklin worked to provide tax relief, cheaper utilities, employment, and help to those in need. His achievements as governor paved the way for his election to the presidency in 1932.

Sequence Were Franklin and Eleanor Roosevelt married before or after Roosevelt went into politics?

____

Unknown Words Find the word *accustomed* in the second paragraph and circle it. Can you tell what it means? Check a dictionary for its definition.

____

Author's Purpose What do you think is the author's purpose in this passage?

____

____

____

Unfamiliar Words Circle the words in the fifth paragraph that help you understand the meaning of the word *paralysis*.

Author's Purpose What does the author try to persuade you of in the first paragraph?

____

____

____

Name ______________________________

Unfamiliar Words What words help you to understand the meaning of *neutrality* in the fourth paragraph?

____

____

____

Sequence What event happened after Pearl Harbor was bombed?

____

____

____

Endings Find examples of words from the story with the inflected endings, *-s, -ed,* and *-ing.* Write them on the lines.

____

____

____

Author's Purpose Do you think the author's purpose was achieved?

____

____

____

____

When Franklin was elected President in 1932, the United States was in deep trouble. A time of poverty and hardship called the Great Depression was ravaging the country. People were out of work, farmers couldn't earn a living, and banks were closing. For many, food was scarce and money was tight. Americans were in desperate need of a good leader.

As his first order of business, President Roosevelt started the New Deal, a series of programs and policies that helped farmers and the unemployed. Roosevelt stabilized the banks, created more jobs, and provided aid to those in need. When it was time for reelection in 1936, Roosevelt won by a landslide.

The Great Depression left many Americans focused only on their problems at home. But in Europe and Asia, more troubles were brewing. Roosevelt became increasingly worried about the political environment in Germany, Italy, and Japan. Then in 1939, World War II erupted in Europe. Americans hoped to distance themselves from the violence overseas, but Roosevelt knew this would be difficult. He offered as much assistance to the Allied Forces as he could, short of officially entering the war.

With the world in turmoil, Roosevelt was elected in 1940 to a third term in office. Then on December 7, 1941, Japan bombed Pearl Harbor, a naval base on Honolulu, Hawaii. More than 2,500 people died in the bombing. That was the end of the United States's neutrality. The very next day, President Roosevelt declared war.

During the war, Roosevelt worked hard to strengthen his relationships with the representatives of Britain and the Soviet Union. He was elected to his final term as President in 1944. Roosevelt worked constantly to bring an end to the war, but his health was beginning to fail. He died on April 12, 1945, leaving behind a country that would mourn the loss of its beloved and fearless leader.

Home Activity Your child read a selection and used comprehension and vocabulary skills from Unit 2. Have your child summarize the selection using sequence words and identifying facts and opinions.

Name ______________________________

Augie's Present

The year was 1942. I looked through my dirty window at the even dirtier gray sky beyond it. Nothing felt right anymore, not since my brother Augie had joined the army and left for Europe nearly three months ago. His birthday was coming up soon. I hoped he'd have a chance to celebrate somehow.

On the street down below, cars and people were beginning to stir. *Stay safe today, Augie,* I thought to myself.

The smell of porridge curled through the air, and Ma was soon knocking on my bedroom door. "Get up, Susan," she told me. "Breakfast will be ready soon, and you need to get to school."

I sighed and pulled myself out of bed. That was Ma—practical to a fault. Nothing worried or scared her.

By the time I was ready to leave, Ma was halfway through cleaning our small apartment. She was always bustling through life, working hard to make ends meet. We didn't have much, but we had enough to get by.

"Out you go," Ma told me, kissing me on the cheek. "And don't you forget—learning is a privilege and a luxury. I won't have you missing school and moping about just because you're thinking of your brave brother overseas. He did the right thing by leaving."

I nodded quietly. "His birthday's coming up soon, Ma," I said. "We have to find a way to make it special."

"I know, honey," she told me. "We will." Then she shooed me out the door.

The school day went by quickly. Mrs. Heaton passed out some arithmetic homework and gave us a reading assignment. Then at recess, my friends and I gossiped about the war. It was all anyone ever talked about. After a few more hours of writing and geography, it was time to head back home.

I wandered slowly toward our apartment, thinking all the while about Augie. Ma and I had received a brief letter from him last week. *All's well,* he had written. *Surely sister Susie's staying sweet.* It was something Augie often wrote—a tongue twister with extra meaning. Both my brother and I had a terrible sweet tooth.

I was walking past a bakery when an idea began to form inside my head. I peered into the window at a large case full of pastries and cookies. I was sure they cost more than we could afford, but perhaps I could find a way to earn them.

Compare and Contrast How does Augie's being in Europe affect the way Susan behaves? How does this compare to the way Ma behaves?

____

____

____

____

____

Unfamiliar Words Circle the word that helps you to understand the meaning of *luxury*.

Compare and Contrast What do Augie and Susan have in common?

____

____

____

Name ______________________________

Greek and Latin Roots The Latin root *gratus* means "pleasing." What word in this story has this root?

____

Compare and Contrast Compare and contrast how Susan feels at the beginning of the story to how she feels at the end.

____

____

____

____

____

____

____

____

____

A large man inside was sweeping up the dust and flour off the floor. He coughed and grumbled to himself, obviously annoyed by his work. When he saw me standing at the window of his shop, he frowned and continued sweeping. I'm sure he could tell just by looking at me that I hadn't a spare cent to buy anything. But I wasn't going to let that stop me. I took a deep breath and entered the store. The doorbell rang softly above my head.

I cleared my throat and watched the man keep sweeping. "Excuse me, sir," I said to him.

Finally, he looked up. "What is it?" His broom continued to kick clouds of flour dust into the air.

"Could you use some help?" I paused, seeing his unsmiling face, then kept talking. "I could sweep for you, if you like."

"I'm quite capable of doing it myself, young lady," he said sternly, emptying a dustpan.

"Oh, I'm sure you are," I told him. "But you'd probably like to be doing other things…like baking, or…" My voice trailed off. This wasn't working. The baker stopped sweeping for a moment to look at me. He narrowed his eyes and waited. "I'd work for cookies," I said.

The man looked me up and down. Then he tossed me the broom. "I guess you could use a few cookies, kid," he said. "You're awfully skinny. Tell you what. You sweep for me every day this week, and by Friday, you'll have yourself a big box of cookies to take home."

With gratitude, I began sweeping what was left of the mess.

Later when I got home, Ma eyed me suspiciously. "You're late," she told me. "What happened?"

My eyes twinkled. "I found a present for Augie. Something absolutely delicious."

Ma looked at me, astonished. "Well, young lady, just how do you think we'll afford that?"

I told her about my brand-new job. She smiled and patted me on the shoulder. "Your brother will love his present," she told me. I nodded happily. Soon Augie would have his cookies and a birthday message to keep him company all the way across the ocean.

Home Activity Your child read a selection and used comprehension and vocabulary skills from Unit 2. Have your child retell the selection, comparing and contrasting the characters.

Name ______________________

Words with Schwa

- **Generalization** In many words, the schwa in an unaccented syllable gives no clue to its spelling: **jewel**, **factory**, **garage**, **tropical**.

Word Sort Sort the list words by words you know how to spell and words you are learning to spell.

words I know how to spell	words I am learning to spell
1. ______	11. ______
2. ______	12. ______
3. ______	13. ______
4. ______	14. ______
5. ______	15. ______
6. ______	16. ______
7. ______	17. ______
8. ______	18. ______
9. ______	19. ______
10. ______	20. ______

Spelling Words

1. jewel
2. kingdom
3. gasoline
4. factory
5. garage
6. tropical
7. pajamas
8. estimate
9. tomorrow
10. humidity
11. Chicago
12. bulletin
13. carnival
14. illustrate
15. elegant
16. census
17. terrific
18. celebrate
19. operate
20. celery

School + Home

Home Activity Your child is learning about the sound of schwa. Name three words from the list and ask your child to tell you which sound in each word is the schwa.

Name

Family Times

Summary

The Fabulous Perpetual Motion Machine

The Pérez Twins, Carla and Carlos, are determined to win this year's science fair. Because they are fabulous, they definitely don't want to do anything boring. What could be less boring than a machine that needs no power and *never stops?* Gathered together with parents, a reporter, and their friends Larry and Effie, they give their perpetual motion machine a test run to make sure it works. The machine does seem to run forever, but with one small problem—everything in the house that runs on electricity stops working! The fabulous twins lose no time looking for another fabulous project to enter in the science fair.

Activity

People throughout history have come up with ideas for inventions that aren't possible. Think of a crazy invention that would help you and your family if only you could make it work. The more fantastic it is, the better! Either draw a diagram of your machine with labels for the different parts, or write a description about what it does and how it works.

Comprehension Skill

Sequence

Sequence is the order in which the events of a story or article take place, from first to last. Clue words such as *first*, *next*, and *then* may show sequence, but not always. Other clues are dates and times of day. Sometimes two events happen at the same time. Clue words that show this are *meanwhile* and *in that same year.*

Activity

Look up a recipe in a cookbook. Then write what the directions told you to do *first*, *next*, and *last*. Why is the order of the directions important when following a recipe?

Lesson Vocabulary

Words to Know

Knowing the meanings of these words is important to reading *The Fabulous Perpetual Motion Machine*. Practice using these words.

Vocabulary Words

applauds shows approval by clapping hands, shouting, etc.

browsing looking here and there

fabulous wonderful; exciting

inspecting looking over carefully; examining

project a special assignment planned and carried out by a student or group of students

Conventions

Past, Present, and Future Tenses

Present tense verbs show action that is happening now. *For example: walk, bounce, talk.* **Past tense** verbs show action that happened in the past. Most past tense verbs are formed by adding *-ed* to the present tense. *For example: walked, bounced, talked.* **Future tense** verbs show action that will happen in the future. Future tense verbs are formed by adding the word *will* or a form of *is going to* to the present tense. *For example: will walk, will bounce, is going to talk.* Some verbs, however, do not follow the usual past tense rules. These verbs are called **irregular verbs,** and their past tense forms must be memorized. *For example: fly/flew; eat/ate; write/wrote.*

Activity

Verb Verse Work with a family member to write a poem using the past tense, present tense, and future tense of the same verbs. Be as creative and clever as possible. Perform the poem for other family members.

Practice Tested Spelling Words

________	________	________	________
________	________	________	________
________	________	________	________
________	________	________	________
________	________	________	________

Name ______________________________________

Sequence

- **Sequence** is the order in which events take place, from first to last.
- Clue words such as *first, next,* and *then* may show sequence in a story or article, but not always. Other clues are dates and times of day.
- Sometimes two events happen at the same time. Clue words that show this are *meanwhile* and *in that same year.*

Directions Read the passage. Then answer the questions below.

I watched Judge Roberts walk up and down the rows of projects at the school science fair. First, he looked at all the fourth grade projects, inspecting them for about five minutes each. Then, he studied all the fifth grade projects, including mine. When he finished, he went over and whispered in our science teacher's ear. As Judge Roberts walked back toward the projects, my hands started to sweat. Then he pulled two blue ribbons from his coat. He hung the fourth grade ribbon on Jeanne Peacock's project. Then he hung the fifth grade ribbon on my project. I was so excited I almost hugged him.

1. What was the first thing that Judge Roberts did?

____

2. If there were six fourth grade projects, about how long did Judge Roberts spend inspecting those projects?

____

3. Whose project got the first blue ribbon?

____

4. In the story, what two events happen at the same time? What word tells you this?

____

____

____

5. What clue words do you recognize in the story that helped explain the sequence of events?

____

Home Activity Your child has read a fictional passage and studied the sequence in which the events occurred. Ask your child to explain his or her morning routine in sequence using clue words to help put things in the proper order.

Name ___________________________________

Cause and Effect

Directions Read the following passage. Then answer the questions below.

Do you know anyone who has had polio? There's a reason why you probably don't. Jonas Salk, M.D., led a team of scientists that developed a vaccine against the crippling disease. Every summer during the 1940s and 1950s, thousands of children became infected with polio. Every summer parents were anxious and afraid. Polio also affected adults. For example, President Roosevelt came down with polio as an adult.

In 1955, Americans received the news of Dr. Salk's success. It made him famous overnight. Dr. Salk said the vaccine he discovered belonged to everyone. Therefore, the vaccine was made available to people around the world. The disease began to disappear.

1. Why do you think you do not know anyone who has had polio?

____

____

2. Every summer in the 1940s and 1950s, thousands of children became infected. What effect did this have on parents?

____

____

3. What made Dr. Salk famous overnight?

____

4. Dr. Salk said the vaccine he discovered belonged to everyone. What effect did that have? Which word helped you identify the effect?

____

____

5. Explain the effects of a new vaccine.

____

____

Home Activity Your child read a short passage and identified causes and effects. Work with your child to identify the cause and effect of three important events in his or her own life.

Name ______________________________

Past, Present, and Future Tenses

Directions Underline the verb or verbs that use the wrong tense. Write the correct tense.

1. Last year, Teresa made a fascinating science project. It shows the ice in Antarctica. Teresa demonstrates the ice shrinking. When the projects were judged, Teresa won first place.

____

2. We will work on our project next week. I discuss my ideas with my group. It will be interesting to hear everyone's ideas. ______________________

3. The play is about an amazing invention. It describes a very useful machine. Today's inventors were creative. ______________________

Directions Replace each underlined verb with the verb in the correct tense. Use the correct tense to make the order of events clear. Write the paragraph.

4. People <u>begin</u> using electrical power in the 1800s. **5.** Edison <u>invent</u> the electric light. **6.** Today, everyone <u>depend</u> on electricity. **7.** People <u>used</u> electricity for work and play. **8.** In the future, the demand for electrical power <u>increase</u>.

____

____

____

____

____

Directions Pretend that you have created an invention that will change the world. Write a paragraph about how you came up with the invention, what it does, and how it will change the future.

____

____

____

____

____

____

Home Activity Your child learned how to use present, past, and future tenses in writing. With your child, talk about an activity he or she completed, an ongoing activity, and a future activity.

Name ______________________________

Words with Schwa

Spelling Words				
jewel	kingdom	gasoline	factory	garage
tropical	pajamas	estimate	tomorrow	humidity
Chicago	bulletin	carnival	illustrate	elegant
census	terrific	celebrate	operate	celery

Categorize Write the list word that completes each group.

1. New York, Los Angeles, Boston, ____ 1. ____________

2. car, mechanic, car lift, ____ 2. ____________

3. assembly line, plant, workshop, ____ 3. ____________

4. diamond, sapphire, ruby, ____ 4. ____________

5. chic, classic, smart, ____ 5. ____________

6. counting, poll, survey, ____ 6. ____________

7. stalk, vegetable, green, ____ 7. ____________

8. draw, explain, show, ____ 8. ____________

9. guess, approximate, ____ 9. ____________

10. run, control, drive, ____ 10. ____________

Words in Context Write the list word that completes each sentence.

11. The ____ has rides, games, and performers. 11. ____________

12. It's not the heat, it's the ____. 12. ____________

13. Do not put off for ____ what you can do today. 13. ____________

14. A ____ is ruled by a king or queen. 14. ____________

15. Before I go to bed, I change into my ____. 15. ____________

16. We ____ Flag Day on June 14. 16. ____________

17. Florida has a ____ climate. 17. ____________

18. That was a ____ skateboard move! 18. ____________

19. A news ____ cut in on our television show. 19. ____________

20. Most cars are still powered by ____ fuel. 20. ____________

Home Activity Your child has learned to read, write, and spell words with schwa sounds. Take turns saying and spelling each word aloud.

Name ____________________

Sequence

- **Sequence** is the order in which events take place, from first to last.
- Clue words such as *first, next,* and *then* may show sequence in a story or article, but not always. Other clues are dates and times of day.
- Sometimes two events happen at the same time. Clue words that show this are *meanwhile* and *in that same year.*

Directions Read the following passage. Then write the order of events in the chart and answer the question.

The Space Elevator will be a revolution in space travel! Once it is built, space travel will be clean, safe, and affordable to everyone. No fuel will be used, so there will be no pollution from emissions. The space elevator will also be safe because, instead of launching and landing, it will work like a ski lift. Preparations will begin soon. First, scientists will build one huge pulley on the ground and another one up in space. Next, cables that run between the pulleys will be attached to cars as big as buses. Then, Earth's gravity and rotation will turn the pulleys around and around sending the cars into space. Finally, the Space Elevator will be ready to take people into space. While the Space Elevator is being built, Motion, Inc. will be making reservations for future space tourists.

1. First	
2. Next	
3. Then	
4. Finally	

5. What will be happening at the same time that the Space Elevator is being built? What clue word shows you this?

____

____

Home Activity Your child used a graphic organizer to identify sequence in a short passage. Have your child use the sequence words *first, next, then,* and *last* to write a short paragraph describing how to do an activity that he or she enjoys. Discuss the sequence of events he or she wrote about.

Name ______________________________

Past, Present, and Future Tenses

Directions Identify the tense of each underlined verb. Write *past, present,* or *future.*

1. You will enjoy this book about inventions. ______________
2. Inventors create new machines. ______________
3. Each machine does a different task. ______________
4. In the past, people invented steam engines. ______________
5. Later, other people made computers. ______________
6. Today, inventors work on new energy sources. ______________
7. They think of saving the environment. ______________
8. Perhaps they will succeed someday. ______________
9. I will invent a bed-making machine. ______________
10. It will save me much work. ______________

Directions Rewrite each sentence twice. First, change the underlined verb to past tense. Then change it to future tense.

11. The computer is a useful invention.

    Past: ______________________________

    Future: ______________________________

12. We get information on computers.

    Past: ______________________________

    Future: ______________________________

13. Computers make our lives more productive.

    Past: ______________________________

    Future: ______________________________

Home Activity Your child reviewed past, present, and future tenses. With your child, list verbs that describe what your family does each day. Challenge your child to write the present, past, and future tenses of the verbs and use them in sentences.

Name ______________________________

Compound Words

- **Generalization** A compound word is smaller words joined together. Keep all the letters when spelling compounds: **water + proof = waterproof**.

Word Sort Sort the list words by words you know how to spell and words you are learning to spell. Write every word.

words I know how to spell	words I am learning to spell
1. ________	11. ________
2. ________	12. ________
3. ________	13. ________
4. ________	14. ________
5. ________	15. ________
6. ________	16. ________
7. ________	17. ________
8. ________	18. ________
9. ________	19. ________
10. ________	20. ________

Spelling Words

1. waterproof
2. teaspoon
3. grasshopper
4. homesick
5. barefoot
6. courthouse
7. earthquake
8. rowboat
9. scrapbook
10. countryside
11. lightweight
12. fishhook
13. spotlight
14. blindfold
15. whirlpool
16. tablespoon
17. greenhouse
18. postcard
19. hummingbird
20. thumbtack

Home Activity Your child is learning about compound words. Help your child draw a line to separate the two words that make up each compound word.

Name

Family Times

Summary

Leonardo's Horse

The year is 1452. The Duke of Milan wants a statue of a horse to give to his father. The great artist, Leonardo da Vinci, believes he alone can make it. He begins work on it at the age of 30, but is never able to complete it.

Activity

Art Action Think about a work of art you would like to make. Talk with a family member about the materials you would need, how you would make it, and what it would look like.

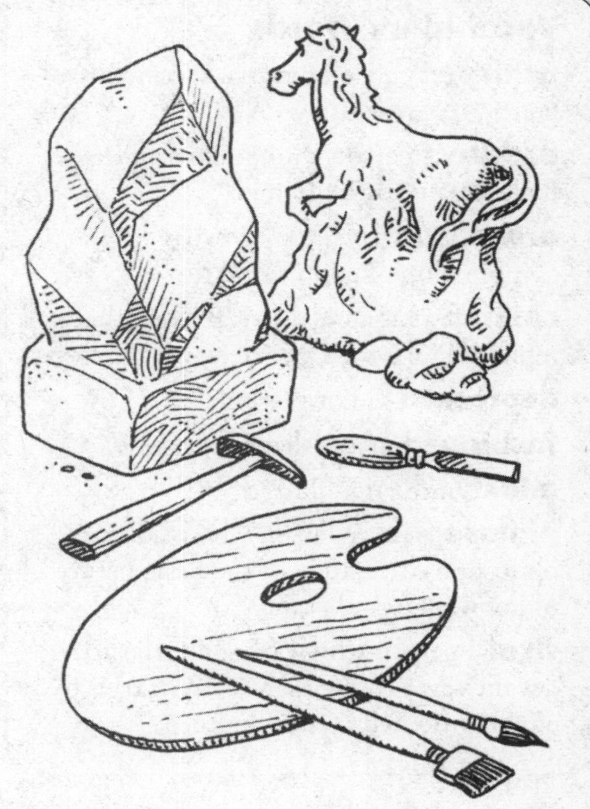

Comprehension Skill

Main Idea and Details

The **main idea** is the most important idea about a paragraph, passage, or article. Supporting **details** are small pieces of information that tell more about the main idea.

Activity

Cats or Dogs? Express a general idea about a pet or animal you are familiar with. *For example: Cats make better pets than dogs.* Have a family member suggest specific details that support your main idea. *For example: You don't have to walk a cat.*

Lesson Vocabulary

Words to Know

Knowing the meanings of these words is important to reading *Leonardo's Horse*. Practice using these words.

Vocabulary Words

achieved carried out to a successful end

architect person who designs and makes plans for buildings

bronze a dark yellow-brown combination of copper and tin

cannon a big gun, especially one that is mounted on a base or wheels

depressed sad or gloomy

fashioned made, shaped, or done

midst in the middle

philosopher a person who studies philosophy, the study of the basic nature of knowledge and reality

rival a person who wants and tries to get the same thing as another, or tries to equal or do better than another

Conventions

Principle Parts of Regular Verbs

A verb's tenses are formed from its **principle parts:** the present, the past, and the past participle. **Regular verbs** add *–d* or *–ed* to form the past tense. *For example: walk/walked, use/used.* To form the past participle, use *has* or *have* with the past-tense form. *For example: have walked, has used.*

Activity

Pass it on In groups of two, play "Pass it on." The first person selects a verb and says its present participle and past tense. The second person repeats the first person's statement, then adds the verb's past participle, and then chooses a new verb and says the new verb's present participle and past tense. Play continues back and forth, each person adding three words to the growing list, until one player cannot recite the entire list.

Practice Tested Spelling Words

______	______	______	______
______	______	______	______
______	______	______	______
______	______	______	______
______	______	______	______

Name ______________________________

Main Idea and Details

- The **topic** is what a paragraph or article is all about.
- The **main idea** is the most important idea about a paragraph, passage, or article.
- **Details** are small pieces of information that tell more about the main idea.

Directions Read the following passage. Then answer the questions below.

When most people think of the Renaissance in England, they think of William Shakespeare (1564–1616). He is considered by many to be the greatest writer of the English language. He wrote 154 poems called sonnets, but he is most remembered for his 38 plays.

Shakespeare is probably the best-known writer of plays in the world. His writing still influences writers today. Today, 400 years after his death, audiences fill theaters to see his plays. High school and college students read, study, and perform them. Since 1899, many of his plays have been made into popular movies. We can be certain that the great works of Shakespeare will have a positive influence on readers of future generations.

1. What is the topic of the passage?

____

2. Write the sentence that gives the main idea of the passage.

____

____

3. What is one detail that tells more about the main idea?

____

____

4. What is another detail about the main idea?

____

____

5. Write a one-sentence summary of this passage.

____

____

Home Activity Your child identified the main idea and supporting details in a short passage. Read a magazine article or story about an artist or writer with your child. Work together to identify the main idea and details. Ask your child to write a short summary.

Name ______________________________

Fact and Opinion

Directions Read the article. Then answer the questions below.

I think the Renaissance artist Raphael (1483–1520) was the greatest painter of all time. According to biographers and historians at the time, he was handsome and charming. For this reason, he was given the nickname "the prince of painters."

One of his paintings is the popular *St. George and the Dragon.* It shows St. George as a young knight in armor riding on a white horse. With his right arm he drives a long spear into the body of a fierce dragon. His horse is rearing back away from the dragon. In the background, a young woman is kneeling. I believe she is praying for the knight's success.

1. In the first sentence, which words help you decide whether or not it's a statement of fact or of opinion? What kind of statement is it?

____

____

2. Is the second sentence a statement of fact or of opinion? How do you know?

____

____

3. Is the first sentence of the second paragraph a statement of fact or of opinion? How do you know?

____

____

4. In the second paragraph, sentences 2 through 4 are all statements of fact. Explain how you could check to see if they are true or false.

____

____

5. The eighth sentence states a fact that can be verified by looking at the painting. Is there any way to tell what the woman is thinking? Explain your answer.

____

____

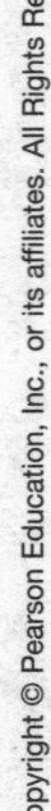

Home Activity Your child has identified facts and opinions in a short passage. Read a movie or book review with your child. Ask your child to identify which statements are fact and which are opinion.

Name________________________________

Principal Parts of Regular Verbs

Directions Write a complete sentence using the past participle form of the verb in ( ) with *have* or *has.*

1. Ms. Wissing (instruct) this art class for two years.

____

2. The students (enjoy) her hands-on teaching style.

____

3. For several weeks our art class (study) how to draw life-forms.

____

4. Tonya (sketch) the head of a woman.

____

5. I (complete) my drawing of a horse.

____

6. The teacher (encourage) my efforts in the past.

____

Directions Write a paragraph about something you have planned to invent or create. Include past participle forms of verbs where needed.

____

____

____

____

____

____

____

____

____

Home Activity Your child learned how to write principal parts of regular verbs correctly. Ask your child to write about a project he or she has completed recently at school or at home. Remind him or her to use correct verb tenses.

Name ______________________________

Compound Words

Spelling Words				
waterproof	teaspoon	grasshopper	homesick	barefoot
courthouse	earthquake	rowboat	scrapbook	countryside
lightweight	fishhook	spotlight	blindfold	whirlpool
tablespoon	greenhouse	postcard	hummingbird	thumbtack

Mixed-Up Words Draw a line to connect the words to make a list word. Then write the list word on the line.

1. earth	weight	**1.** ____________
2. bare	proof	**2.** ____________
3. table	hook	**3.** ____________
4. country	spoon	**4.** ____________
5. fish	fold	**5.** ____________
6. light	tack	**6.** ____________
7. grass	side	**7.** ____________
8. water	foot	**8.** ____________
9. blind	hopper	**9.** ____________
10. thumb	quake	**10.** ____________

Word Scramble Unscramble the words and write them on the lines.

11. thsoueourc	**11.** ____________
12. looplirhw	**12.** ____________
13. stapoone	**13.** ____________
14. regensehou	**14.** ____________
15. mirdmibungh	**15.** ____________
16. watboor	**16.** ____________
17. mecksiho	**17.** ____________
18. dracstop	**18.** ____________

Home Activity Your child has learned to read, write, and spell compound words. Look in other books to find three other compound words.

Name ____

Main Idea and Details

- The **main idea** is the most important idea about a paragraph, passage, or article.
- **Details** are small pieces of information that tell more about the main idea.

Directions Read the passage and complete the diagram. State the main idea of the passage and then list supporting details.

Leonardo da Vinci was not only a great artist. He was also a scientific thinker who drew up plans for many inventions. Flight interested Leonardo, so he drew plans for flying machines and parachutes. Construction was another of his interests, so he drew plans for bridges and cranes. Human anatomy interested him, so he drew detailed diagrams on how human body parts look and function. These drawings may have been the first accurate diagrams of human body parts.

Main Idea

1. Leonardo da Vinci was not just an artist but also a ______________

____

Detail

2. His interest in flight led to ______________

____

____

____

Detail

3. His interest in construction led to

____

____

____

Detail

4. His interest in anatomy led to

____

____

____

5. Write a one-sentence summary of this passage.

____

____

Home Activity Your child identified the main idea and details of a short passage. Read an article about a famous person. Work with your child to identify the main idea and details of the article. Ask your child to summarize the article.

Name ____________________

Principal Parts of Regular Verbs

Directions Write *present, present participle, past,* or *past participle* to identify the form of the underlined verb.

1. Machines existed in Leonardo's day. ____________
2. For example, waterwheels turned millstones. ____________
3. As a boy, Leonardo had watched machines closely. ____________
4. By adulthood, he had analyzed how each part worked. ____________
5. Unlike others, Leonardo combined parts in new ways. ____________
6. He thought, "Aha! This change improves the machine!" ____________
7. He reasoned, "This invention is working better with different parts." ____________
8. He explained his analyses in journals. ____________
9. Grateful engineers still study his sketches. ____________
10. These illustrations are serving as blueprints for us. ____________

Directions Write the sentence using the principal part of the underlined verb indicated in ( ).

11. Leonardo refuse all meat. (past)

____

12. He always love animals. (past participle)

____

13. Vegetarians still follow his habit. (present).

____

14. I stop eating meat too. (past participle)

____

15. Fruits and vegetables provide plenty of nutrition. (present)

____

Home Activity Your child reviewed principal parts of regular verbs. Have your child identify examples of the use of present, past, and past participle forms in an article or a familiar book.

Name____________________________________

Consonant Sounds /j/, /ks/, /sk/, and /s/

- **Generalization** The sound /j/ can be spelled **g**, **j**, and **dge**: **ginger**, **journal**, **dodge**. The sound /ks/ can be spelled **x**: **excuse**. The sound /sk/ can be spelled **sch**: **schedule**. The sound /s/ can be spelled **sc**: **scene**.

Word Sort Sort words by the spelling of the consonant sounds.

g

1. ____________
2. ____________

dge

3. ____________
4. ____________
5. ____________

x

6. ____________
7. ____________
8. ____________
9. ____________

j

10. ____________
11. ____________

sch

12. ____________
13. ____________
14. ____________
15. ____________

sc

16. ____________
17. ____________
18. ____________
19. ____________
20. ____________

Spelling Words

1. excuse
2. scene
3. muscle
4. explore
5. pledge
6. journal
7. science
8. schedule
9. gigantic
10. scheme
11. Japan
12. excellent
13. exclaim
14. fascinate
15. ginger
16. scholar
17. scent
18. dodge
19. smudge
20. schooner

Home Activity Your child is learning to spell words with consonant sounds /j/, /ks/, /sk/, and /s/. Have your child name one list word with each of these sounds.

Name

Family Times

Summary

The Dinosaurs of Waterhouse Hawkins

The year is 1853. The place is London. Waterhouse Hawkins has created the first-ever dinosaur models in his workshop. Afterward, he holds a great party to celebrate with guests such as Queen Victoria and Prince Albert. No one has ever seen a model of a dinosaur, and they are all astonished.

Activity

Artist's Workshop Find books about dinosaurs and look through them. Compare illustrations of the various dinosaurs. Select one that you and a family member like and draw your own versions of it.

Comprehension Skill

Fact and Opinion

You can prove a **statement of fact** true or false. A **statement of opinion** cannot be proved true or false. Statements of opinion express somebody's thoughts or feelings.

Activity

Can you prove it? State a fact about something you know. *For example: Our dog is a golden retriever.* Have others suggest how that fact could be stated as an opinion. *For example: Our retriever is the best dog ever!* Then turn it around and start with an opinion.

Lesson Vocabulary

Words to Know

Knowing the meanings of these words is important to reading *The Dinosaurs of Waterhouse Hawkins*. Practice using these words.

Vocabulary Words

erected put up; built

foundations parts on which the other parts rest for support; bases

mold a hollow shape in which anything is formed, cast, or solidified

occasion a special event

proportion a proper relation among parts

tidied put in order

workshop space or building where work is done

Conventions

Principle Parts of Irregular Verbs

An **irregular verb** is one that does not add *–ed* to form the past tense. Most irregular verbs have different spellings for the past and the past participle. For example, for the verb *buy*, *bought* is the past tense, and *has*, *have*, or *had bought* is the past participle.

Activity

Irregular Verb Charts Work with a family member to make a graphic organizer of irregular verbs. Write an irregular verb in a central square, the past tense and the past participles in the circles around the square, and then write a sentence using each form of the verb in a rectangle next to each circle. Create more charts using new irregular verbs such as *write* and *know*.

Practice Tested Spelling Words

______	______	______	______
______	______	______	______
______	______	______	______
______	______	______	______
______	______	______	______

Name ____________________

Fact and Opinion

- You can prove a **statement of fact** true or false. You can do this by using your own knowledge, asking an expert, or checking a reference source such as an encyclopedia or a nonfiction text.
- A **statement of opinion** gives ideas or feelings, not facts. It cannot be proved true or false.
- A sentence may contain both a statement of fact and a statement of opinion.

Directions Read the following passage and answer the questions below.

Dinosaurs are really interesting. I wanted to find out what happened to them so I went to the library to read some articles and books. This is what I found out: About 65 million years ago, dinosaurs became extinct. They had lived on Earth for about 165 million years. That's much longer than humans have been around! Suddenly, they all began to die off. No one knows for sure why this happened.

According to many scientists, an asteroid believed to be about 4.9 miles wide crashed to Earth and caused the extinction. When it crashed it might have scattered dust into the atmosphere, created tidal waves, and caused huge fires. This could have caused sunlight to be blocked for months and for the temperature to drop. Living things on Earth would have had difficulty surviving.

1. Give an example of an opinion from the passage.

____

2. How can you tell this is an opinion?

____

3. Give an example of a fact from the passage.

____

4. How would you prove that this is a fact?

____

____

5. Select one statement of fact from the passage. On a separate piece of paper, list as many ways as you can think of to verify it.

Home Activity Your child read a short passage and identified facts and opinions. Together, read an editorial from a newspaper or magazine. Identify facts and opinions in the editorial. Ask your child how he or she can tell the difference between the facts and opinions.

Name ____________________

Main Idea and Details

Directions Read the following passage. Then answer the questions below.

As a young girl, Mary Nicol was interested in prehistory and fossils. When she was a child, she had a difficult time in school. But as soon as she was old enough, she began attending classes about prehistory at the University of London. She was a talented illustrator and soon had a chance to illustrate a book by a famous researcher, Louis Leakey. They married, and she changed her name to Mary Leakey. The Leakeys went to Africa to find fossils in 1935.

While in Africa, Mary made several important discoveries that changed how scientists thought about early humans. In 1948, she found the first skull of a fossil ape. It was twenty million years old. In 1959, she found a two-million-year-old fossilized skull of an early human. In 1978 she uncovered a footprint trail. It was left in volcanic ash nearly 2.3 million years ago. This proved that there were humanlike beings in those days that walked upright on two feet.

1. What is the topic of the passage?

____

2. What is the passage's main idea?

____

____

3. Give an example of a detail.

____

____

4. Give another example of a detail.

____

____

5. Summarize the passage in a few sentences.

____

____

____

Home Activity Your child has read a short passage and answered questions about its main ideas and details. Read a nonfiction story with your child. Ask him or her to identify the main idea of a paragraph and the details.

Name ______________________________

Principal Parts of Irregular Verbs

Directions Write a complete sentence using the past participle form of the verb in ( ) with *has* or *have*.

1. Mr. Hancock (run) the museum for five years.

____

2. He (choose) May as membership drive month.

____

3. He (speak) to many organizations.

____

4. The membership list (grow) quite large.

____

5. I (do) it!

____

6. The new dinosaur education wing (draw) new members.

____

Directions Write a paragraph about dinosaurs. Include some past and past participle forms of such irregular verbs as *be, find, come, know,* and *think.*

____

____

____

____

____

____

____

____

____

Home Activity Your child learned how to write principal parts of irregular verbs correctly. Ask your child to write about a favorite prehistoric animal. Encourage him or her to use forms of *become, is, see, think, go,* and *eat* when writing.

Name____

Consonant Sounds /j/, /ks/, /sk/, and /s/

Spelling Words				
excuse	scene	muscle	explore	pledge
journal	science	schedule	gigantic	scheme
Japan	excellent	exclaim	fascinate	ginger
scholar	scent	dodge	smudge	schooner

Crossword Puzzle Use the clues to find the list words. Write each letter in a box.

Across
1. promise
4. timetable
5. smear
6. spice
7. log
8. avoid
9. boat

Down
2. huge
3. a strong ___
4. student
5. plan

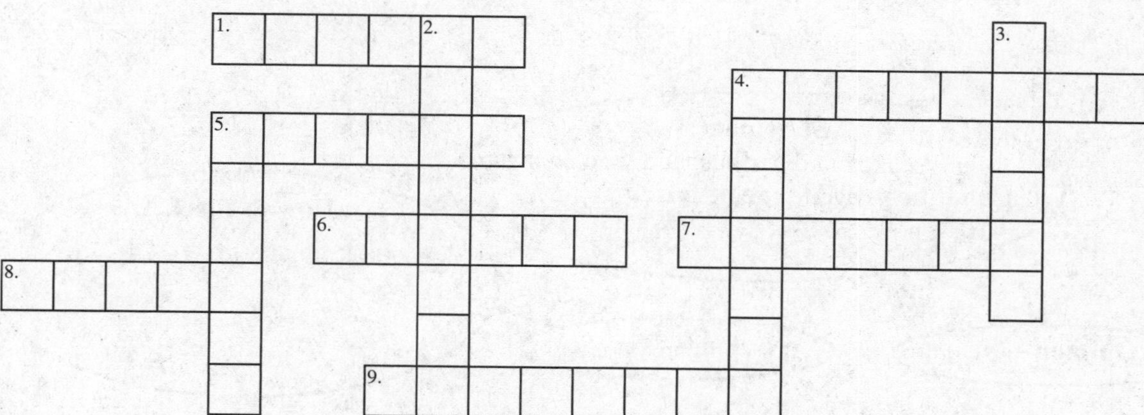

Words in Context Finish the story using list words.

Some foods from **(10)**____ are flavored with **(11)**____. The **(12)**____ of the cooking is delicious. The tasty foods will surely **(13)**____ your taste buds. It is a great experience to **(14)**____ the foods of different countries.

10. ______________

11. ______________

12. ______________

13. ______________

14. ______________

Home Activity Your child has learned to read, write, and spell words with consonant sounds spelled in special ways. Take turns spelling aloud the list words with your child.

Name ____________________________

Fact and Opinion

- You can prove a **statement of fact** true or false. You can do this by using your own knowledge, asking an expert, or checking a reference source such as an encyclopedia or a nonfiction text.
- A **statement of opinion** gives ideas or feelings, not facts. It cannot be proved true or false.
- A sentence may contain both a statement of fact and a statement of opinion.

Directions Read the following passage. Then complete the diagram and answer the questions below.

When I grow up, I want to hunt for fossils like Mary Leakey. We seem to be a lot alike. She wanted to find fossils. So do I. She wanted to learn about early humans. So do I. I read all about her discoveries in Africa. I think her most exciting discovery was the skull from the Stone Age, which was almost two million years old. Her work in Africa gave us new information about stone tools and Stone Age cultures. In 1962, she and her husband, Louis Leakey, won the National Geographic Society's highest honor.

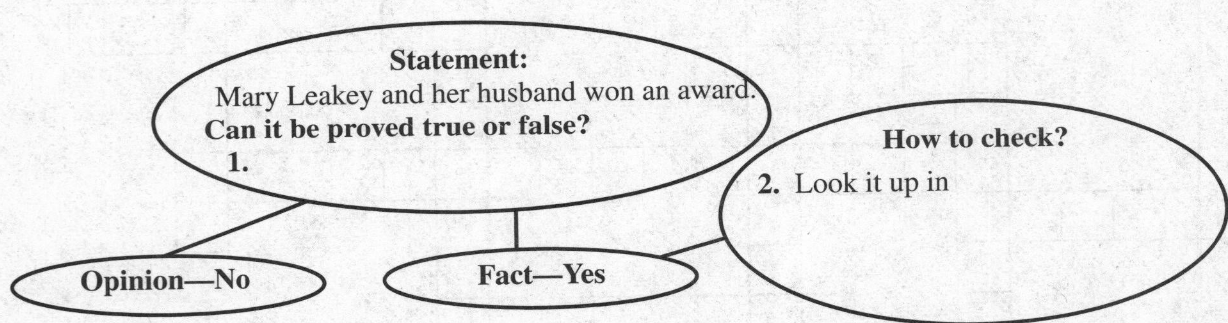

3. How do you know "We seem to be a lot alike" is a statement of opinion?

   Because there is no way to ____________________________

4. Which sentence contains both a fact and an opinion?

   ____

   ____

5. In the eighth sentence, the author expresses an opinion that the discovery of the Stone Age skull was the most exciting. What kind of details would support this opinion?

   Details about how other people ____________________________

Home Activity Your child read a short passage and identified facts and opinions. Read a news article and have your child make a list of facts and opinions in the passage.

Name ____________________

Principal Parts of Irregular Verbs

Directions Write *present, present participle, past,* or *past participle* to identify the underlined verb form.

1. The diners eat for eight hours. ____________
2. Each diner has told at least one story. ____________
3. Hawkins chose the iguanodon model. ____________
4. He had set a dining table inside it. ____________
5. His guests become excited. ____________
6. Hawkins thought they would be. ____________
7. The guests told about this event for years. ____________
8. The dinosaur fad had begun. ____________
9. Today we find Hawkins's models odd. ____________
10. We are making more discoveries about dinosaurs. ____________

Directions Write the sentence using the principal part of the underlined verb indicated in ( ).

11. We know a great deal about the past. (present)

____

12. In 1850, scientists know much less. (past)

____

13. They find some fossils of dinosaur bones. (past participle)

____

14. Sometimes animals freeze in glaciers. (present)

____

15. Explorers find the remains of these animals. (present participle)

____

16. A little of Earth's history freeze with them. (past participle)

____

Home Activity Your child reviewed principal parts of irregular verbs. Have your child identify examples of the use of present, present participle, past, and past participle forms in a cookbook or history book.

Name ______________________________

One Consonant or Two

- **Generalization** Many words have two consonants that stand for the same sound: **address**, **committee**.

Word Sort Sort the list words by words you know how to spell and words you are learning to spell. Write every word.

words I know how to spell	words I am learning to spell
1. ________	11. ________
2. ________	12. ________
3. ________	13. ________
4. ________	14. ________
5. ________	15. ________
6. ________	16. ________
7. ________	17. ________
8. ________	18. ________
9. ________	19. ________
10. ________	20. ________

Spelling Words

1. address
2. collar
3. mirror
4. recess
5. committee
6. collect
7. Mississippi
8. immediate
9. command
10. appreciate
11. announce
12. possess
13. Tennessee
14. gallop
15. opponent
16. barricade
17. broccoli
18. accomplish
19. allowance
20. zucchini

School + Home

Home Activity Your child is learning about words with double consonants. Have your child circle the double consonants in each list word.

Name

Family Times

Summary

Mahalia Jackson

In this story, a grandfather tells his granddaughter about the music he loves, the blues. He explains that the blues is not just a feeling. It's a kind of music. The he tells her about the great blues singer, Mahalia Jackson.

Activity

Making Music Pretend you are starting a family band together. What kind of music will you play? Who will play what instruments? Together, write the lyrics of your first song. Set it to a melody you already know or make up your own.

Comprehension Skill

Main Idea and Details

The **main idea** makes a point about a topic and has at least one supporting detail. **Details** are smaller pieces of information that tell more about the main idea.

Activity

Lyrical Reading Read through the lyrics of a favorite song, or listen to the lyrics very closely when you hear it played. What is the main idea expressed in the song? Sum it up in your own words. What details in the song support the main idea?

Lesson Vocabulary

Words to Know

Knowing the meanings of these words is important to reading *Mahalia Jackson*. Practice using these words.

Vocabulary Words

appreciate to think highly of; value; enjoy

barber person whose business is cutting hair and shaving or trimming beards

choir group of singers who sing together, often in a church service

released to permit to be published, shown, sold, etc.

religious devoted to religion

slavery the condition of being owned by another person and being made to work without wages

teenager a person in his or her teens

Conventions

Troublesome Verbs

Troublesome verbs are pairs of verbs that are confusing because they have similar meanings or because they look alike. *For example: lay/laid; lie/lay.*

Activity

Troublesome Verb Rhymes

Together with a family member, discuss the meanings of the following words and when to use them (you can use a dictionary for help): *lay/lie*, *set/sit*, *let/leave*, *teach/learn*, and *may/can*. Then, create a rhyme that will help you remember the correct way to use at least one of the verb pairs.

Practice Tested Spelling Words

______	______	______	______
______	______	______	______
______	______	______	______
______	______	______	______
______	______	______	______

Name ______________________________

Main Idea and Details

- The **main idea** is the most important idea about the topic.
- **Details** are small pieces of information that tell more about the main idea.

Directions Read the following passage. Then answer the questions below.

Louis Armstrong is remembered as the greatest trumpeter in jazz history. He grew up in New Orleans and got to know many leading jazz musicians there. As a young man, he played the trumpet in marching bands. In 1922, he had the opportunity to play and record with King Oliver's band in Chicago. Before Armstrong, the trumpet was not a solo instrument. It supported the band as a whole. Armstrong changed this. He was able to create solo pieces for the trumpet that the band supported. Later in his career, he starred in films and performed as a comedian. He also sang. He made many jazz recordings. Some of the songs he's most famous for are "Hello, Dolly!," "Goldfinger," and "What a Wonderful World."

1. What is the topic of this passage?

____

2. What is the main idea of the passage?

____

____

3. What is one important detail that supports the main idea?

____

____

4. What is another detail that supports the main idea?

____

____

5. On a separate piece of paper, create a graphic organizer to show the main idea and details in this passage.

Home Activity Your child read a short passage and identified the main idea and details. Read a magazine article about a musician with your child. Together, create a graphic organizer to show the main idea and supporting details in the article.

Name ____

Fact and Opinion

Directions Read the following passage. Then answer the questions below.

I was lucky to have once heard Ray Charles perform in person. It was an experience I will always remember. Ray Charles lost his sight when he was seven years old. I believe his lack of sight must have enhanced his ability with music.

Both his parents died by the time he was fifteen, and he had to earn a living. He began as a blues and jazz pianist in the style of Nat King Cole. He went on to combine blues and gospel, creating his own musical style. When he sang, he swayed on the piano bench as if he were living the songs.

He was still in his twenties when his hit song, "What'd I Say," hit the charts. It sold over a million copies. I can't imagine life without Ray Charles's best sellers "Georgia on My Mind" and "I Can't Stop Loving You."

1. Explain why "Ray Charles lost his sight when he was seven years old" is a statement of fact or a statement of opinion.

____

____

2. Is "I believe his lack of sight must have enhanced his ability with music" a statement of fact or a statement of opinion? How do you know?

____

____

3. Explain why "He was still in his twenties when his hit song, 'What'd I Say,' hit the charts" is a statement of fact or a statement of opinion.

____

____

4. Is "I can't imagine life without Ray Charles's best sellers 'Georgia on My Mind' and 'I Can't Stop Loving You'" a statement of fact or a statement of opinion? How do you know?

____

____

5. Find a sentence that contains both a statement of fact and statement of opinion.

____

Home Activity Your child read a short passage and identified statements of fact and statements of opinion. Read a review of a musical performance in the newspaper. Ask your child to identify facts and opinions and ask how the facts could be checked.

Name______________________________

Troublesome Verbs

Directions Choose the form of the underlined verb indicated in ( ). Use the chart to help you. Write the sentence on the line.

Present	Past	Past Participle
lie ("to rest," "to recline")	lay	(has, have, had) lain
lay ("to put," "to place")	laid	(has, have, had) laid

1. Wes lay the sheet music on the shelf. (past)

____

2. The twins lie beside the pool relaxing. (past)

____

3. Their towels lie on the concrete all day. (past participle)

____

4. We lay the groundwork for next year's concert. (past participle)

____

5. In this song, lay the heaviest emphasis on long vowels. (present)

____

6. The secret lie in hours of practice. (present)

____

Directions Write a paragraph describing a photograph of your family or friends. Use as many principal parts of *sit, set, lie, lay, leave,* and *let* as you can.

____

____

____

____

____

____

____

Home Activity Your child learned how to write principal parts of troublesome verbs correctly. Ask your child to write sentences about cleaning a room. Encourage him or her to use forms of *lie, lay, sit, set, leave,* and *let.*

Name ___________________________

One Consonant or Two

Spelling Words				
address	collar	mirror	recess	committee
collect	Mississippi	immediate	command	appreciate
announce	possess	Tennessee	gallop	opponent
barricade	broccoli	accomplish	allowance	zucchini

Double Puzzle Unscramble the words. Write the numbered letters in the boxes below to find the answer to the riddle.

Riddle: What is the name of a dark, rich chocolate dessert?

1. CINUCZIH ___ ___ ___ ___ ___ ___ ___ ___ (16)
2. GPLALO ___ ___ ___ ___ ___ ___ (9)
3. MIRORR ___ ___ ___ ___ ___ ___ (1)
4. SADDRSE ___ ___ ___ ___ ___ ___ ___ (14, 4)
5. DETIAMIME ___ ___ ___ ___ ___ ___ ___ ___ ___ (2)
6. UNOCEANN ___ ___ ___ ___ ___ ___ ___ ___ (13, 17)
7. SSNEEEENT ___ ___ ___ ___ ___ ___ ___ ___ ___ (6)
8. POICSHCALM ___ ___ ___ ___ ___ ___ ___ ___ ___ ___ (15, 5, 7)
9. BDCIERARA ___ ___ ___ ___ ___ ___ ___ ___ ___ (8)
10. TAIARPECEP ___ ___ ___ ___ ___ ___ ___ ___ ___ ___ (10)
11. PSESSSO ___ ___ ___ ___ ___ ___ ___ (3)
12. EIOETTCMM ___ ___ ___ ___ ___ ___ ___ ___ ___ (12, 11)

___ ___ ___ ___ ___ ___ ___ ___ ___ ___ ___   ___ ___ ___   ___ ___ ___
1 2 3 4 5 6 7 8 9 10 11   12 13 14   15 16 17

Synonyms Write the list word that has the same or nearly the same meaning.

13. foe ________________
14. part of a shirt ________________
15. green vegetable ________________
16. order ________________
17. payment ________________
18. gather ________________
19. speak to ________________
20. time off ________________

Home Activity Your child has learned to read, write, and spell words with double consonants. Look at magazines and newspapers with your child and find three other words that have double consonants.

Name________________________________

Main Idea and Details

- The **main idea** is the most important idea about the topic.
- **Details** are small pieces of information that tell more about the main idea.

Directions Read the following passage. Then complete the diagram below.

Motown started as an African American-owned independent record company in Detroit. It became home to many of the greatest singers of popular music. Its name came from Detroit's nickname, "Motor City." In 1961, owner Berry Gordy discovered The Temptations, who became one of the most popular singing groups during the 1960s and 1970s. The discovery of singer and songwriter Smokey Robinson and his group The Miracles made Motown famous. The company recorded many popular stars, like Marvin Gaye and Stevie Wonder. However, nothing could beat the popularity of Diana Ross and The Supremes. Berry Gordy sold Motown in 1988.

Main Idea

1. Motown is ________________________________

Supporting Details

2. Berry Gordy ____________

3. ____________

4. Marvin Gaye ____________

5. ____________

Home Activity Your child read a short passage and identified its main idea and details. Read a magazine article about a musical group with your child. Work together to identify the main idea and details in the article by using a graphic organizer.

Name ____

Troublesome Verbs

Directions Write the letter of the definition of the underlined verb.

_____ **1.** You left without your music. **A** am seated

_____ **2.** She had set it on the piano. **B** has allowed

_____ **3.** Lay the tickets on the counter. **C** has rested or reclined

_____ **4.** I sit and listen to the players. **D** went away

_____ **5.** Joan has lain in the sun too long. **E** place or put

_____ **6.** Tim has not let that bother him. **F** had put (a thing) somewhere

Directions Choose a verb from the box to complete each sentence. Write the sentence on the line.

lay	leave	let	lain	sit	set

7. __________ the oven at 350° before you leave.

____

8. Everyone, please __________ at the table.

____

9. Mom and Dad __________ for their voice lesson at 7:15.

____

10. They __________ us fix our own dinner.

____

Directions Underline the verb that correctly completes the sentence.

11. I have (laid, lain) in a hammock.

12. Yesterday you (sat, set) up front.

13. The music teacher (left, let) the room.

14. First she (laid, lain) the chalk on the desk.

Home Activity Your child reviewed principal parts of troublesome verbs. Have your child write a joke using different forms of *sit, set, lie, lay, leave,* and *let* correctly.

Name ____

Prefixes *un-, de-, dis-*

- **Generalization** When prefixes **un-**, **de-**, or **dis-** are added to words, the base word does not change: **uncover**, **defrost**, **discourage**.

Word Sort Sort the list words by their prefixes.

un-

1. ____________
2. ____________
3. ____________
4. ____________
5. ____________
6. ____________
7. ____________
8. ____________

de-

9. ____________
10. ____________
11. ____________
12. ____________

dis-

13. ____________
14. ____________
15. ____________
16. ____________
17. ____________
18. ____________
19. ____________
20. ____________

Spelling Words

1. uncover
2. defrost
3. uncomfortable
4. discourage
5. disadvantage
6. unfortunate
7. unfamiliar
8. disability
9. discomfort
10. deodorant
11. unemployed
12. deflate
13. disbelief
14. unpredictable
15. disapprove
16. disappoint
17. unpleasant
18. dehydrated
19. disqualify
20. undecided

Home Activity Your child is learning to spell words with prefixes *un-*, *de-*, and *dis-*. Have your child circle the prefix in each list word.

Name ______________________________

Family Times

Summary

Special Effects in Film and Television

Have you ever wondered how movie monsters and dinosaurs can seem so real? In this article, we follow the process of a group of special effects artists as they create a miniature model of a prehistoric landscape, complete with dinosaurs that move!

Activity

Your Own Miniature Model Using materials you find around the house and outside, such as scrap wood, cardboard, construction paper, rocks, and sand, create a miniature model of a scene from a favorite story that you would like to see made into a movie.

Comprehension Skill

Graphic Sources

Graphic sources are visual materials such as pictures, time lines, maps, charts, and diagrams that make information easy to understand. Previewing graphic sources before reading a story or article can help you predict what it will be about.

Activity

Get the Picture? Take turns describing stories or articles that this picture might accompany. Create as many captions as you can for the picture.

Lesson Vocabulary

Words to Know

Knowing the meanings of these words is important to reading *Special Effects in Film and Television.* Practice using these words.

Vocabulary Words

background the part of a picture or scene toward the back

landscape a view of scenery on land

miniature smaller in size or scale than others of its type

prehistoric of or belonging to periods before recorded history

reassembled came or brought together again

Conventions

Prepositions and Prepositional Phrases

A **preposition** is a word that shows a relationship between a noun and another noun. *For example: Maria stood between her parents*. The *preposition* "between" shows where Maria (a noun) stood in relation to her parents (also a noun).

A **prepositional phrase** begins with a preposition and ends with a noun called the **object of the preposition**. *For example: Samuel crawled under the porch.* "Under" is the *preposition*, "porch" is the *object of the preposition*, and "under the porch" is the *prepositional phrase.*

Activity

Where Are You Going? Many prepositions describe location. Write five prepositional phrases that answer the question, "Where are you going?" Have a family member write the object of the preposition for each of your phrases, and then check their work. When you are done, switch roles.

Practice Tested Spelling Words

____________	____________	____________	____________
____________	____________	____________	____________
____________	____________	____________	____________
____________	____________	____________	____________
____________	____________	____________	____________

Name ______________________

Graphic Sources

- Some **graphic sources** are maps, time lines, charts, diagrams, and pictures with captions.
- A **graphic source** makes information easy to see and understand.

Directions Study the diagram for a miniature neighborhood below. Then answer the questions that follow.

Miniature Neighborhood Layout Diagram

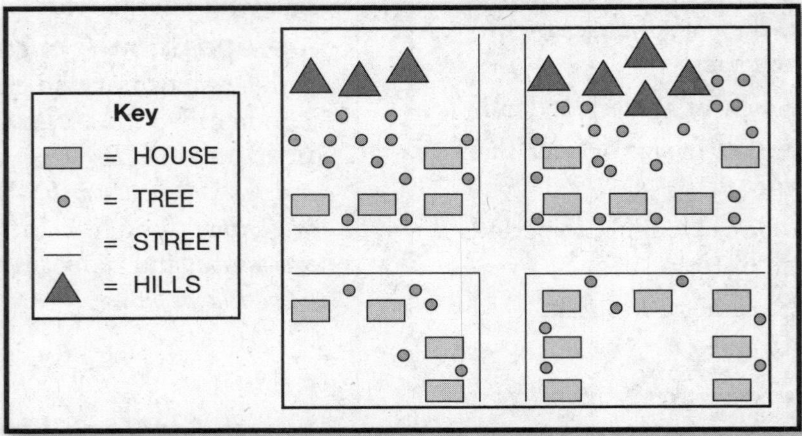

1. What does this diagram show?

____

____

2. What shape represents a tree?

____

3. How many more houses than hills are there?

____

4. Why would this diagram be helpful to special-effects artists?

____

____

5. What prior knowledge did you have about this topic that helped you understand it?

____

____

Home Activity Your child used a graphic source to answer questions. Together, make a diagram of your home. Create a title and a key for your diagram. Challenge your child to use prior knowledge of diagrams to construct it.

Name ______________________________

Author's Purpose

Directions Read the passage. Then answer the questions below.

Jack had studied dinosaurs for twenty years, and he'd lived in Dinosaur Park for all twenty of them. Nothing about dinosaurs could surprise him. This thought calmed his nerves as he walked toward the lodge at the other end of the park.

After an hour, he pulled out his GPS-DL (dinosaur locator) to check the position of the dinosaurs. The path was still clear for miles. So why did he feel so uneasy? Sweat was running down his cheeks. He felt dizzy.

Then a thundering blast filled the air. The earth shook. A foul smell hit him like a punch. A roar split the sky. It was like nothing he'd heard before. And it was coming straight toward him.

1. What is the author's purpose?

____

2. How do you know?

____

3. Do you think the author met his or her purpose for writing? Why or why not?

____

____

4. Notice the sentences get shorter in the second half of the passage. Why do you think the author did this?

____

____

5. How did the author's purpose affect your reading pace?

____

____

Home Activity Your child has read a fictional passage and identified the author's purpose for writing it. Choose a story to read. Have your child preview the story first, looking at the cover, title, and pictures, to predict the author's purpose. Read the story to find out if the prediction was correct.

Name ______________________________

Prepositions and Prepositional Phrases

Directions Add a preposition to complete each sentence. Write the sentence on the line.

1. I usually lie ______________ the floor when I watch TV.

____

2. When I get hungry, I get a snack ______________ the refrigerator.

____

3. We have several movies stored ______________ the television.

____

4. I would rather see a movie ______________ the theater.

____

5. The big screen and the smell ______________ popcorn create a memorable experience.

____

Directions Add a prepositional phrase of your own to complete each sentence. Write the sentence.

6. Let's make Dad a cartoon ______________.

____

7. I'll get the paper and markers ______________.

____

8. You draw the scenes in pencil, and I'll color them ______________.

____

9. What colors shall we use ______________?

____

10. Dad will hang this cartoon ______________.

____

Home Activity Your child learned how to use prepositions and prepositional phrases in writing. Ask your child to write about his or her favorite animated film using at least one prepositional phrase in each sentence.

Name ____________________

Prefixes *un-*, *de-*, *dis-*

Spelling Words				
uncover	defrost	uncomfortable	discourage	disadvantage
unfortunate	unfamiliar	disability	discomfort	deodorant
unemployed	deflate	disbelief	unpredictable	disapprove
disappoint	unpleasant	dehydrated	disqualify	undecided

Adding Word Parts Write the list words that contain the words below.

approve **1.** ____________

pleasant **2.** ____________

qualify **3.** ____________

cover **4.** ____________

courage **5.** ____________

odor **6.** ____________

fortunate **7.** ____________

predictable **8.** ____________

advantage **9.** ____________

frost **10.** ____________

Word Search Find ten list words hidden in the puzzle. Words are found down and across. Then write the words.

D	I	S	C	O	U	R	A	G	E	D	N
K	D	E	O	D	O	R	A	N	T	E	D
U	N	D	E	C	I	D	E	D	W	F	E
U	N	P	L	E	A	S	A	N	T	R	F
D	I	S	B	E	L	I	E	F	P	O	L
U	N	F	A	M	I	L	I	A	R	S	A
D	I	S	C	O	M	F	O	R	T	T	T
D	E	H	Y	D	R	A	T	E	D	Y	E

11. ____________

12. ____________

13. ____________

14. ____________

15. ____________

16. ____________

17. ____________

18. ____________

19. ____________

20. ____________

Home Activity Your child has learned to read, write, and spell words with prefixes. Take turns spelling aloud the list words with your child.

Name____________________

Graphic Sources

- Some **graphic sources** are maps, time lines, charts, diagrams, and pictures with captions.
- A **graphic source** makes information easy to see and understand.

Directions Study the bar graph. Then answer the questions.

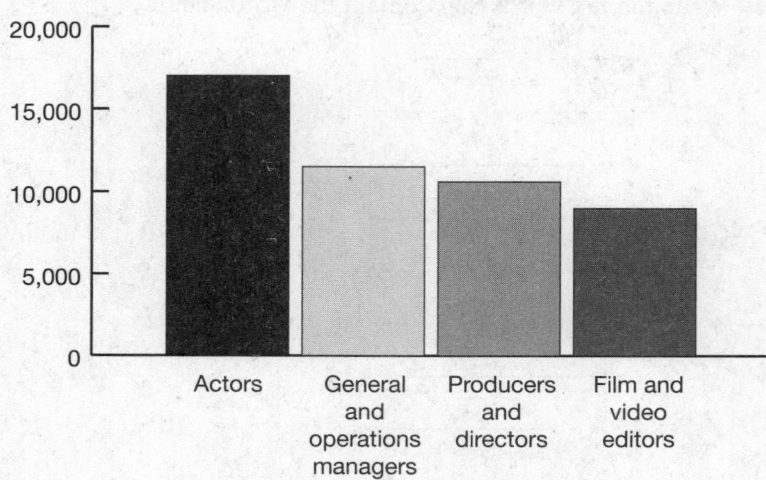

1. What does this bar graph show?

____

2. What kind of article might include this graphic source?

____

____

3. How many editor jobs were there in 2002?

____

4. Which group had the most jobs?

____

5. What prior knowledge helped you understand this subject and graph?

____

Home Activity Your child used a graphic source to answer questions. Look at the graphic sources in a newspaper. Challenge your child to study them on his or her own and then explain them to you.

Name ____

Prepositions and Prepositional Phrases

Directions Underline each prepositional phrase. The number in ( ) tells how many prepositional phrases are in that sentence.

1. *Bambi* is an animated movie about a deer. (1)
2. It begins with Bambi's birth in the forest. (2)
3. All the forest creatures are filled with joy at the birth. (2)
4. They welcome the new prince of the forest. (1)
5. Bambi makes two friends of the closest kind. (1)
6. Thumper is a bunny with attitude, who has a sense of fun. (2)
7. Bambi discovers a shy skunk in the flowers and names him Flower. (1)

Directions Write *P* if the underlined word is a preposition. Write *O* if it is the object of the preposition.

8. Today we learned <u>about</u> computer animation. ______
9. We enjoy cartoons thanks <u>to</u> this technique. ______
10. Artists create drawings on the <u>computer</u>. ______
11. With <u>software</u>, they manipulate these drawings. ______
12. <u>Before</u> computers, animation artists drew every frame. ______
13. Now computers move the cartoon <u>for</u> the artist. ______
14. Software also applies colors in the <u>shapes</u>. ______

Directions Underline the prepositional phrase in each sentence. Write *P* above the preposition. Write *O* above the object of the preposition.

15. *Toy Story* is an animated film about a boy's toys.
16. The toys remain loyal to their owner.
17. There is jealousy and competition among the toys.
18. They finally become friends and work together for their own good.

Home Activity Your child reviewed prepositions and prepositional phrases. Have your child see how many prepositional phrases he or she can find on the label of a box or can of food. Have your child identify the prepositions.

Name ____________________

Family Times

Selection Summaries

Week 1 *The Fabulous Perpetual Motion Machine*

The science fair will never be the same, thanks to the Pérez twins' amazing project.

Week 2 *Leonardo's Horse*

What is it about this horse statue that makes it impossible for the great Leonardo da Vinci to complete it?

Week 3 *The Dinosaurs of Waterhouse Hawkins*

Finding dinosaurs took the skill of scientists, but bringing them to life took the unique vision of a remarkable artist.

Week 4 *Mahalia Jackson*

In this story, a grandfather tells his granddaughter about the music he loves, and about one of the greatest blues singers of them all.

Week 5 *Special Effects in Film and Television*

Movies and TV have created a whole new kind of artist—one who can make us think we see things that don't exist.

Activity

Tell a member of your family more about each of the five stories. Tell which one is your favorite, and why you liked it best.

Comprehension Skills Review

In Unit 3, you learned and used many skills while reading the stories and selections.

- Every piece of writing contains the **author's viewpoint,** or how the author feels about the topic. Some authors show a strong **bias** for or against their topic.
- The **main idea** of a piece of writing is what the text is mostly about.
- A **fact** can be proved true. An **opinion** is what someone thinks or believes and cannot be proved true.
- A **graphic source** shows or explains information in the text. Pictures, tables, charts, diagrams, time lines, and maps are all graphic sources.

Activity

What do you imagine? Do you dream of castles and knights, or of fantastic flying machines? Imagination is essential for artists, singers, writers, scientists, and inventors. Talk with a trusted family member about imagination and what you would like to do with your life.

Unit Vocabulary Skills

Multiple-Meaning Words

Multiple-meaning words are words that have more than one meaning.

Activity Read a newspaper and look for words with multiple meanings. List the words and their different meanings.

Greek and Latin Roots

Many English words have **Greek and Latin roots.** You can use a dictionary to find out a word's roots.

Activity As you read, check word roots in a dictionary; make a list of words that come from Latin or Greek.

Homonyms

Homonyms are words spelled and pronounced alike but with different meanings and roots.

Activity Make a list of five words that are spelled and pronounced alike. Are they homonyms? Check a dictionary to see if they come from the same root.

Antonyms

Antonyms are words that mean the opposite of other words.

Activity Use a thesaurus to find the antonyms of words you have learned recently.

Prefixes

A **prefix** is a word part added to the beginning of a word to change its meaning.

Activity Make a list of words in your reading that have the prefix *pre-*, and add their meanings from the dictionary.

Unit Spelling Rules

Schwa

In many words, the schwa in an unaccented syllable gives no clue to its spelling. Any vowel can stand for the schwa sound.

Compound Words

A compound word is smaller words joined together. To decode a compound word, divide it and sound out each smaller word.

Consonant Sounds /j/, /ks/, /sk/, /s/

These consonant sounds can be spelled in different ways:

- /j/ can be spelled *g*, *j*, and *dge*, as in *ginger*, *journal*, and *dodge*.
- /ks/ can be spelled *x*, as in *excuse*.
- /sk/ can be spelled *sch*, as in *schedule*.
- /s/ can be spelled *sc*, as in *scene*.

One Consonant or Two

When the same consonant appears twice in a row in a word, it stands for a single sound.

Prefixes *un-, de-, dis-*

When the prefixes *un-*, *de-*, and *dis-* are added to a base word, the base word does not change. These three prefixes all mean "not" or "the opposite of."

Name ______________________________

Multiple-Meaning Words

Running six miles can *tire* you out.

He fixed the flat *tire* on his bicycle.

Words to Know

applauds
browsing
fabulous
inspecting
project

- A **multiple-meaning word** is a word that has more than one meaning. In the pictures above identify the multiple-meaning word and its two different meanings.

Practice Read the following sentences. Fill in the blanks using the Words to Know. Then choose the definition that best matches the underlined word.

1. Kyle's <u>homework</u> for his science fair ________________ includes observing magnets.

a. an assignment   b. stick out from   c. forecast

2. Even the <u>judge</u> who is ________________ it can't quite understand the machine.

a. one at a trial   b. one at a contest   c. one with an opinion

3. Kyle explains his ________________ machine prevents deer from ________________ in people's <u>gardens</u>.

a. land for plants   b. public place   c. raises vegetables

4. "When the deer <u>approach</u>, the machine ________________," Kyle says, "scaring the deer away without hurting them."

a. to deal with something   b. to land   c. draw near to

On Your Own As you read "The Baseball Mitt," look for multiple-meaning words.

School + Home **Home Activity** Your child used context clues to determine the correct meanings of multiple-meaning words. With your child, make a list of as many multiple-meaning words as you can.

Name ____________________

Sequence

- **Sequence** refers to the order of events, or the steps in a process. Clue words, such as *first, next,* and *then* can help you follow the sequence of events. Dates are also clues as to when events happened.

First, immigrants would settle in one of the cities along the Atlantic Ocean.

In 1825, the Erie Canal was completed. Settlers moving west sailed up the Hudson River from New York City to reach the canal.

Next, settlers would use flatboats to navigate the Ohio and Mississippi Rivers to St. Louis, Missouri.

Finally, settlers would travel in overland wagons on trails leading to California.

Practice Look at the pictures and read the captions. Then answer the questions.

1. Where did the immigrants first settle?

2. Circle the sequence clue words in each caption. List them.

3. In what year was the Erie Canal completed?

4. Would settlers moving west travel on the Ohio and Mississippi Rivers before or after using the Erie Canal?

5. What was the final destination for settlers heading west?

On Your Own Use what you know about sequence as you read "The Baseball Mitt." Make a flowchart showing the order of events.

Home Activity Your child reviewed using clue words to determine a sequence of events. With your child, list the sequence of events for getting ready and going to a family event.

Name ____________________

Greek and Latin Roots

- Many English words come from ancient Greek and Latin words. Sometimes you can use **Greek and Latin roots** to figure out the meaning of an unfamiliar word.
- The Greek root *sophia* means "knowledge." The Latin root *spect* means "look at." The Greek root *bio* means "life."

Practice Read the following sentences. Fill in the blanks using the Words to Know. Then choose the definition that best matches the underlined word.

Words To Know

achieved
architect
bronze
cannon
depressed
fashioned
midst
philosopher
rival

1. The ____________ designed the skyscraper, and she ____________ such fame that the building is mentioned in her biography.

a. a book about someone's life b. a book about building

2. The building inspector came to see the finished structure, which was a statue of the famous ____________ Plato, ____________ totally of ____________.

a. one who creates b. one who examines

3. A ____________ from another firm was ____________ to see his philosophy of design being used by a competitor.

a. knowledge about a topic b. desire to study a new topic

4. On the day of the grand opening, spectators stood in the ____________ of a large crowd, while a memorial ____________ gave a grand salute.

a. people who watch an event b. people who compete in an event

On Your Own As you read "The Wizard of Menlo Park," look for words with Greek or Latin roots.

Home Activity With your child, list as many words as you can with the same root words as *philosopher* and *architect.*

Name ____

Main Idea and Details

- The **main idea** of a piece of writing is what the piece of writing is mostly about.
- **Details** help support and expand on the main idea.

Bree is a tall girl.

Her parents, brother, and sister are all tall too.

Bree does not feel self-conscious about her height.

She says being tall can come in handy.

Practice Fill in the graphic organizer below with the main idea and details.

Main Idea	Supporting Detail	Supporting Detail	Supporting Detail

On Your Own Use what you know about main idea as you read "The Wizard of Menlo Park." List the details that support the main idea.

School + Home **Home Activity** Your child reviewed main idea. Work with your child to make a graphic organizer that shows the main idea and details of an article about an artist.

Name ______________________________ **Unit 3 Week 3 Interactive Review**

Homonyms

- **Homonyms** are words spelled and pronounced alike but with different meanings. Context clues can help you determine what meaning of a homonym an author is using.

Practice Read the following sentences. Fill in the blanks using the Words to Know. Then choose the definition that best matches the underlined homonym. Use context clues to help you.

Words to Know

- erected
- foundations
- mold
- occasion
- proportion
- tidied
- workshop

1. I was sad that I had to miss Jenna's welcome home party because it was going to be an ______________ of immense ______________ for her family.

   a. to fail to attend b. an unmarried woman

2. Now that there is an artists' ______________ at the college, I hope that an experienced painter there will train me to use watercolors. This will set down the ______________ for the paintings I hope to create for my friends.

   a. a set of railroad cars pulled by an engine b. teach

3. The new building was ______________ on the banks of the Ohio River, and it has a beautiful view of the water.

   a. places where money is kept b. high ground next to a body of water

4. While I ______________ the room before the guests arrived, the caterer handed me the bill for the food.

   a. a statement of money owed b. the beak of a bird

5. After the basement flooded, there was ______________ on the boxes we used to store down there.

   a. a place where goods are sold b. to put away for future use

On Your Own As you read "The Wizard of Menlo Park," look for homonyms. Make a list of the words you find, and write down their meanings.

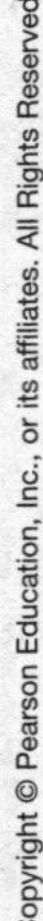

School + Home **Home Activity** Your child reviewed homonyms. Invite your child to list three homonyms and tell you more than one meaning for each one.

Name____

Fact and Opinion

- A **fact** is something that can be proved true or false.
- An **opinion** is a belief or judgment that cannot be proved true or false.

Directions Read each statement. If it is a fact, write *F* on the line. If it is an opinion, write *O*.

______ The playwright's name is Starr Smith.

______ Her house was flooded by a storm.

______ The play is really great.

______ The actor playing the lead could have been better.

______ I would like to see the play again.

Practice Read the following passage. Underline the statements of fact.

Starr Smith's new play, *Chasing Roger,* opened last night before a full house at the Hippodrome Theater. The playwright is only 25 years old, but I was pleasantly surprised by the play's quality. The play is a comedy about a man trying to track down an ex-roommate who took some of his property. Lead actor William Dunst took several scenes to become comfortable in the role, which was unfortunate. With a better actor in the lead role, *Chasing Roger* may have been the best play of the year. The play ran for two hours, with a fifteen-minute intermission. I think we can expect great things from Ms. Smith in the future.

On Your Own Use what you know about fact and opinion as you read "The Wizard of Menlo Park." Decide which are facts and which are opinions in the selection.

Home Activity Your child reviewed fact and opinion. Discuss the ways in which you can tell facts from opinions and how they differ.

Name ____________________

Antonyms

- An **antonym** is a word that means the opposite of another word. A thesaurus is a useful tool for finding antonyms.

Practice Answer each question with one of the Words to Know. Use a thesaurus to look up any words you do not know.

Words to Know
- appreciate
- barber
- choir
- released
- religious
- slavery
- teenager

1. Which word means the opposite of *soloist?*

   ____

2. Which word means the opposite of *freedom?*

   ____

3. Which word means the opposite of *captured?*

   ____

4. Which word means the opposite of *disparage?*

   ____

5. Which word means the opposite of *secular?*

   ____

6. Which word means the opposite of *adult?*

   ____

On Your Own As you read "The Wizard of Menlo Park," notice how the author uses antonyms. Make a list of the antonyms you find.

Home Activity Your child reviewed antonyms. Play a game with one of you saying a word and the other answering with the word's antonym. Use a thesaurus for help if you get stumped.

Name_______________________________________

Main Idea and Details

- The **main idea** of a piece of writing is what the piece of writing is mostly about.
- **Details** help support and expand on the main idea.

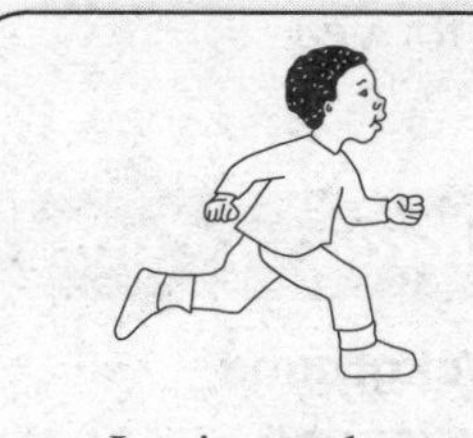			
Louis was born in 1900.	He liked to play with other kids.	Then he discovered the trumpet.	Louis Armstrong grew up to be a famous musician.

Practice Fill in the graphic organizer below with the main idea and details.

Main Idea	Supporting Detail	Supporting Detail	Supporting Detail

On Your Own Use what you know about main idea as you read "The Wizard of Menlo Park." Decide what the main idea is and what details support the main idea in the selection.

School + Home **Home Activity** Your child reviewed main idea. Together, read a magazine article and determine the main idea of the article.

Name ______________________________

Prefixes

- A **prefix** is a word part added to the beginning of a word to change its meaning. The prefix *pre-* means "before" or "the opposite of." The prefix *re-* means "again" or "back."

Practice Add the prefix *pre-* or *re-* to the words below and write the new words formed. Then write a definition for each new word.

re + cycle = ______________________________

pre + record = ______________________________

pre + teen = ______________________________

re + new = ______________________________

Words to Know

background
landscape
miniature
prehistoric
reassembled

Practice Read the following sentences. Fill in the blanks with one of the Words to Know. Then answer the question about the underlined word in each sentence.

1. For their science diorama of a ______________ era, Lashawn and Queen went online to review depictions of early mammals.

   Review probably means: a. look at again b. repeat

2. They were fascinated by a Web site that re-created a ______________ where ______________ horses lived.

   Re-created probably means: a. made previously b. made again

3. Because the clay trees they made drooped, they ______________ the background, using precut broccoli crowns from the grocery store.

   Precut probably means: a. cut again b. cut before

On Your Own As you read "The Wizard of Menlo Park," look for antonyms and how they are used in the story. Make a list of the antonyms you find.

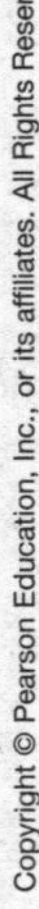

Home Activity Your child reviewed prefixes. Choose a common prefix and see who can list the most words with the prefix in a minute.

Name____

Graphic Sources

- **Graphic sources,** such as maps, charts, tables, illustrations, and diagrams, make information easy to understand and use. Graphic sources depict information that would take a great deal to describe in words visually in a small amount of space.

Practice Read the questions and then answer them on the lines below.

Science Project Timetable: Ms. Carter's Class

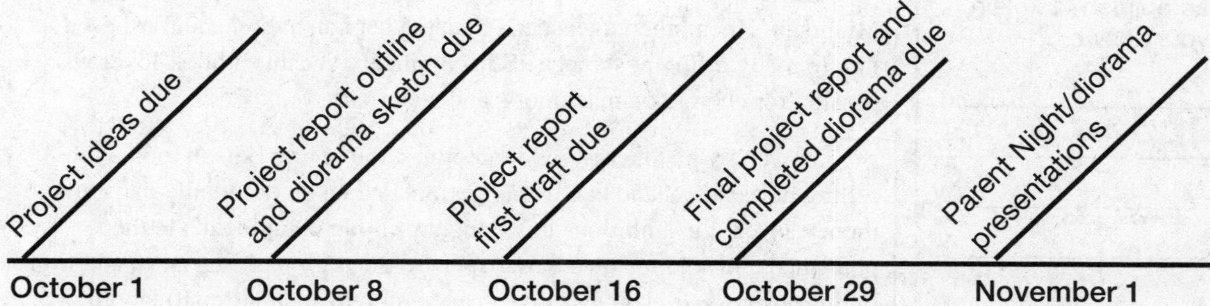

1. On what date do Ms. Carter's students have to give her their project ideas?

2. What is due to Ms. Carter on October 8?

3. By what date must the students hand in their completed dioramas?

4. At what event will the class present their projects?

On Your Own Use what you know about graphic sources as you read "The Wizard of Menlo Park."

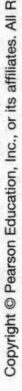

Home Activity Your child reviewed graphic sources. Flip through a magazine or newspaper and count how many different graphic sources you can find.

Name ______________________________

Main Idea What is the topic of this passage?

____

Fact and Opinion Is the first sentence of the passage a fact or an opinion? Explain your answer.

____

Homonyms What is the meaning of the word *light* in paragraph one?

____

What is another meaning for *light*?

____

The Wizard of Menlo Park

Every time we turn on a light, we should feel grateful to Thomas Alva Edison. Edison officially created and patented more inventions than anyone in history. Some of these inventions, such as the phonograph, the motion picture camera, and the incandescent light bulb, had a huge impact on American society.

Early Years

Edison was born in 1847 and spent his childhood in Port Huron, Michigan. His mother, a teacher, educated her son at home and exposed him to many different subjects. Edison quickly became a book-lover with a passion for chemistry, machinery, and electricity.

Driven by his interest in locomotives, the young Edison took a job selling newspapers and candy on the train. When he eventually had enough money saved, the ambitious boy bought printing equipment. He then published and sold his own newspapers to the train passengers. In addition to this business, Edison was given permission to set up a small laboratory in the train's baggage car. The eager boy-scientist conducted experiments there, until an accidental fire brought the locomotive lab to an abrupt end.

Telegraphy and Edison's First Invention

In 1862, when Edison was still a teenager, he risked his life to save a three-year-old boy from an oncoming train. The boy's father thanked Edison by teaching him about the telegraph, a way of sending messages over wires using electricity. At the time, the telegraph was the chief method for communicating across long distances. Edison soon became a skilled telegraph operator, working around the country.

In 1869, Edison patented his very first invention: the electric vote-recording machine. Patents are handed out by the United States government. When someone gets a patent for a new invention, it means that he or she will get money if people use their idea. But Edison's vote machine didn't sell. No politicians were interested in using it! Despite this failure, Edison's first official invention taught him a valuable lesson. From that moment on, he would be sure to invent devices that people would use.

Name ___________________________________

Edison's Career Takes Flight

Edison eventually landed a well-paying job and achieved several successful patents and good business deals. After he had enough money saved, he built what he called "an invention factory" in Newark, New Jersey. He hired dozens of engineers and produced numerous products. His work was so successful that he eventually moved his creative workshop to a larger facility in Menlo Park, New Jersey, and later again to West Orange, New Jersey. As his fame grew, he became known as the "Wizard of Menlo Park."

His Most Famous Inventions

Of the more than 1,000 patents that Edison received during his lifetime, a few of his inventions stand out above the rest. First, he decided to rework Alexander Graham Bell's telephone, improving its sound quality and clarity. Then in 1877, Edison invented the phonograph, or record player, a device that would play back sound.

Edison, though, was most famous for his work on the incandescent light bulb. Other inventors had already discovered that when an electric current was sent through a wire, the wire became hot and glowed. This glowing was known as incandescence—the giving off of light. The wire that people used, however, only lasted for a short time before burning out. It was Edison who discovered that a thin piece of scorched cotton thread would provide light for many hours without burning out too quickly.

After the invention of the incandescent light bulb, Edison also collaborated with his assistant, William Dickson, to create a motion picture camera and viewer, known respectively as the Kinetograph and the Kinetoscope. These early devices helped to lay the groundwork for modern movies.

Over his lifetime, Edison was granted more than 1,000 patents, at times receiving an average of one patent for an invention every five days. He achieved great success and his hard-working philosophy made him famous throughout the world. Today, our cultural landscape would not be the same if weren't for the Wizard of Menlo Park.

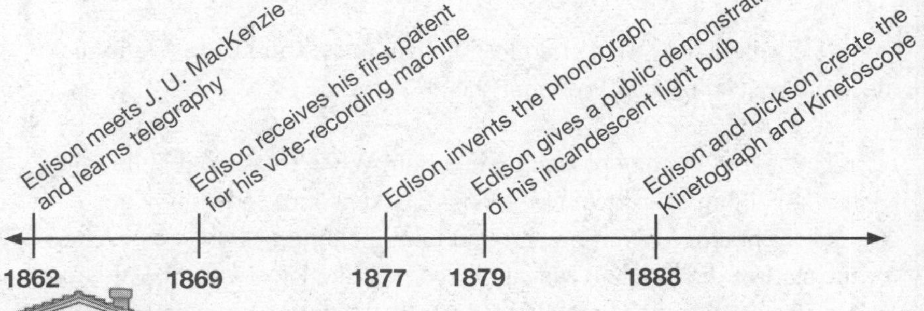
Edison meets J. U. MacKenzie and learns telegraphy
Edison receives his first patent for his vote-recording machine
Edison invents the phonograph
Edison gives a public demonstration of his incandescent light bulb
Edison and Dickson create the Kinetograph and Kinetoscope
1862
1869
1877
1879
1888

Antonyms What is an antonym for *numerous?*

____

____

Main Idea What is the main idea of the first paragraph?

____

____

____

____

____

____

Prefixes What is the prefix in *rework?*

____

Greek and Latin Roots What word on this page contains the Greek root *philo-?*

____

Graphic Sources Circle the date on the time line that tells you when Edison presented his light bulb to the public.

School + Home **Home Activity** Your child read a selection and used comprehension and vocabulary skills from Unit 3. Have your child summarize the main ideas of the selection, using the time line to help with the summary.

Name ____________________

Sequence Did Rico's dad remind him of baseball practice before or after breakfast?

____

____

____

____

____

The Baseball Mitt

Rico woke up on Monday morning when his bed tossed him onto the floor. *I guess I'll need to do some work on my mattress alarm,* he thought while rubbing his head. Then he looked at his watch and yelped. He was running fifteen minutes behind schedule! Quickly, he activated his A.M. Machine and watched his room slip into action. His bedroom light flipped on, his bureau drawer flew open, and his bedspread rolled neatly into place. Within minutes, Rico was dressed, his room was tidy, and he was ready to head down for breakfast.

"Morning, Rico," his mother said, handing him a piece of toast. Rico ate it hungrily and gathered his things for school. In the corner of the kitchen, his little brother sat in a high chair busily coating himself in oatmeal. Rico made a mental note to invent some stain-resistant fabric for later.

Right before Rico left for school, his father called him over. "Don't forget, kiddo," his dad said. "Baseball practice starts today. I'll see you on the field."

Rico gave a weak smile and stared uncomfortably at his feet. Rico's father was the baseball coach, and this year, he'd signed up his son for the team. Rico hadn't had the heart to tell his father he would rather be home working on whatever new project he'd invented. That was more fun for him than running bases or fielding balls.

At least Rico had one new invention that might help him out on the baseball field. He ducked into the garage and carefully slipped his secret baseball glove into his backpack. Already he was dreading the afternoon practice, but there was nothing he could do to stop it.

At lunch, Rico sat with his friend, Jamil, discussing his practice game plan. "All I need to do is flip the glove's switch," Rico said, "and the vacuum will suck up the ball. I'll never have to worry about catching a thing. The glove will do it all for me."

"Let's hope it works," Jamil said. "If it does, I'm hiring you to make me some special baseball running shoes."

The rest of the day passed by in a blur. When the school bell rang, Rico dragged himself down to the boys' locker room and slowly got dressed for practice. Everyone around him, including Jamil, was excited for the start of the baseball season. It seemed like Rico was the only one wishing he were somewhere else. Carefully, he pulled his secret glove out of his backpack and headed for the baseball diamond.

Name ___________________________________

When the team had assembled on the field, Rico's dad began to speak. "Okay, guys. Let's try some fielding. Everyone get out there and show your stuff!" Rico swallowed hard. He felt like a prisoner awaiting his sentence.

When no one was looking, he flipped the switch on his glove. It made a noise like a small vacuum cleaner, but none of his teammates seemed to notice. For several minutes, Rico waited for a ball. He was just beginning to wonder if one would come his way when suddenly a pop fly began plummeting in his direction. *Please work*, he thought to himself as he squeezed his eyes shut and held up his glove.

A moment later, Rico felt a hard and solid thud in his hand. He opened his eyes to see the ball resting firmly in his glove. "Nice job, Rico," his father called from home plate. Rico stared in astonishment. His invention had worked!

"Here comes one more," his father yelled. In a flash, Rico's glove grabbed the second ball, too. Now Rico began to panic. He hadn't expected so many baseballs to fly at him all at once. In desperation, he held out his mitt, accidentally sucking up two more pop flies meant for other teammates.

By now, a curious crowd had gathered in a circle. "What's going on, Rico?" his father shouted over the noise of the vacuum.

Finally, Rico flipped the glove's switch and four baseballs promptly fell to the ground. "I invented this glove," Rico said. "It makes the catch for you."

His father's eyes were thoughtful as he started inspecting the mitt. "Rico, this is a fabulous invention—I'm proud that you made it! But it wouldn't be fair to use it when we're playing. We all need to use our own skills—not a glove that does the work for us."

"I know," Rico admitted. "But maybe I can use the mitt to collect the baseballs after fielding practice is over."

Rico's father laughed. "Sounds like a deal," he said. "Now everyone," he continued, turning to his team, "let's play ball!"

Multiple-Meaning Words What is the meaning of *sentence* as it is used in the passage?

____

____

What is another meaning for *sentence* not used in the passage?

____

____

____

____

Sequence When did Rico's special glove start to work?

____

____

____

____

Home Activity Your child read a selection and used comprehension and vocabulary skills from Unit 3. Have your child retell the selection, focusing on the author's viewpoint and bias regarding the characters.

Name ______________________________

Words from Many Cultures

- **Generalization** Many words in English come from other languages and may have unexpected spellings: **k<u>h</u>aki**, **bal<u>let</u>**.

Word Sort Sort the list words by words you know how to spell and words that you are learning to spell. Write every word.

words I know how to spell	words I am learning to spell
1. ______	11. ______
2. ______	12. ______
3. ______	13. ______
4. ______	14. ______
5. ______	15. ______
6. ______	16. ______
7. ______	17. ______
8. ______	18. ______
9. ______	19. ______
10. ______	20. ______

Spelling Words

1. khaki
2. hula
3. banana
4. ballet
5. waltz
6. tomato
7. vanilla
8. canyon
9. yogurt
10. banquet
11. macaroni
12. polka
13. cobra
14. koala
15. barbecue
16. safari
17. buffet
18. stampede
19. karate
20. kiosk

Home Activity Your child is learning to spell words that come from other cultures. Look up each word in the dictionary with your child.

Name ______

Family Times

Summary

Weslandia

Wesley doesn't have friends at school. To make himself happy during the summer, he uses his imagination and some of the things he learned at school to start a garden. This garden becomes his own world. In time, the world he creates interests the kids who once tormented him.

Activity

Your Own World Discuss the following with a family member: What if you had the chance to create your own little world? What would it look like? Who would live there? What would you do there? Draw your own little worlds and discuss them with each other.

Comprehension Skill

Draw Conclusions

To **draw a conclusion** is to form an opinion after thinking about what you have read. When you draw a conclusion, be sure it makes sense and is supported by details.

Activity

"Drawing" Conclusions On a piece of paper, draw pictures about the things or people that are important to you. Have another person look at your picture, and draw a conclusion from it about your personality.

Lesson Vocabulary

Words to Know

Knowing the meanings of these words is important to reading *Weslandia*. Practice using these words.

Vocabulary Words

blunders stupid mistakes

civilization the ways of living of a people or nation

complex made up of a number of parts; hard to understand

envy feeling of discontent, dislike, or desire because another person has what you want

fleeing running away

inspired filled with a thought or feeling; influence

rustling causing a light, soft sound of things gently rubbing together

strategy the skillful planning and management of anything

Conventions

Subject and Object Pronouns

Pronouns used in the subjects of sentences are called **subject pronouns.** *For example: I, you, he, she, it, we, you, they*. Pronouns used as direct objects or objects of prepositions are **object pronouns.** *For example: me, you, him, her, it, us, you, them.*

Activity

Pronoun Paragraph Ask someone in your family to write a sentence or two that doesn't have any pronouns. Then, rewrite each sentence by substituting in subject and object pronouns. Take turns writing original sentences and rewriting them.

Practice Tested Spelling Words

Name ____________________

Draw Conclusions

- A **conclusion** is a decision you make after thinking about the details in what you read.
- Often your prior knowledge can help you draw, or make, a conclusion.
- When you draw a conclusion, be sure it makes sense and is supported by what you have read.

Directions Read the following passage. Then answer the questions below.

When Kyoung first arrived in the United States, he saw tall buildings, cars, and people. It looked just like he'd seen in the movies. Everyone and everything moved very quickly. There also was so much more of everything than in his village in his old country. It wasn't until he got to his new home in Maryville that time seemed to slow down.

At school, students didn't talk to him much because he didn't speak English. His teacher suggested that he have a different student buddy each week. The students talked to him more. They asked about his life before he came to the United States. He tried to explain, but it was difficult. The cultures were very different and he was still learning English. Nevertheless, he told them a little each time they asked.

1. How do you think Kyoung felt when he first reached the U.S.?

___

2. What parts of the text helped you reach the conclusion you described above?

___

___

3. What things that you already knew helped you reach the conclusion you described above?

___

4. Do you think pairing Kyoung with other students was a good idea?

___

5. How do you think Kyoung felt when other students asked him about his past? Is your conclusion based on the passage, on your own experience, or both?

___

___

Home Activity Your child drew conclusions from the details of a brief story. Read an article or story with your child about a faraway place. Ask him or her questions about how someone from there of your child's age might adapt to life in the United States.

Name______________________________________

Theme and Setting

Directions Read the passage. Then answer the questions below.

Rebecca was out picking blueberries when she glanced up, startled. The sun was getting lower in the sky. "Better check the sundial in the garden," she thought. Mother would want Rebecca and her sisters home with full baskets before sundown. Mother would contribute their blueberries for the village meal. Rebecca picked up the hem of her frock so she could run faster. It wouldn't do to be late today, when Mistress Goody was in charge of the cooking. Rebecca was glad to do her part to keep their village going. The villagers were never sure they'd have enough food for the winter. Some people were even afraid of a drought coming.

1. Where and when do you think this story takes place?

____

____

2. What clues helped you to know the setting?

____

____

3. How would you state the theme of the passage?

____

____

4. What helped you identify the theme?

____

____

5. On a separate sheet of paper, write a plan for how you could grow or find your own food.

Home Activity Your child identified theme and setting in a short passage. Using a book of familiar tales, ask your child to identify the theme and setting of a few.

Name ______________________________

Subject and Object Pronouns

Directions Use a pronoun from the box to complete each sentence. Write the sentence.

they	he	I	us
them	she	me	you

1. My mom and ____________ plant a garden every summer.
2. ____________ lets me pick out the seeds we will plant.
3. Some new flowers surprised ____________ both this season.
4. ____________ looked very strange among the roses and daisies.
5. As we watched ____________ grow, we became more and more amazed.
6. Their enormous leaves and huge white flowers puzzled Mom and ____________.
7. Finally, Dad confessed. ____________ had planted moonflower seeds to surprise us!
8. Would ____________ have fallen for his joke?

Directions Write a paragraph about a unique person you know. Use subject and object pronouns correctly.

____

____

____

____

____

____

____

____

____

____

____

Home Activity Your child learned how to use subject and object pronouns in writing. Ask your child to write a description of something he or she did with a friend or a group. Remind your child to use subject and object pronouns correctly.

Name ______________________________

Words from Many Cultures

Spelling Words				
khaki	hula	banana	ballet	waltz
tomato	vanilla	canyon	yogurt	banquet
macaroni	polka	cobra	koala	barbecue
safari	buffet	stampede	karate	kiosk

Words in Context Write list words to complete the menu.

1. Welcome to the 5th Grade ____.
2. Eat all you want at the ____!

1st Course Appetizer

3. green salad with ____
4. cucumber with ____ dressing

2nd Course Entrée

5. chicken served fresh from the ____
6. ____ and cheese

3rd Course Dessert

7. ____ split sundae

Your choice of

8. ____, chocolate, or strawberry ice cream

1. ____________
2. ____________
3. ____________
4. ____________
5. ____________
6. ____________
7. ____________
8. ____________

Word Search Find ten list words hidden in the puzzle. Words are down, across, and diagonal. Write the words on the lines.

S	S	C	S	S	F	S	J	K	D	A	L
T	T	J	O	K	L	S	Y	O	M	T	K
B	K	A	I	B	Q	S	Y	A	N	J	H
A	X	A	M	E	R	W	R	L	H	H	A
L	H	S	R	P	S	A	F	A	R	I	K
L	N	U	U	A	E	W	A	L	T	Z	I
E	B	D	L	P	T	D	K	I	O	S	K
T	V	H	L	A	T	E	E	L	J	U	H

9. ____________
10. ____________
11. ____________
12. ____________
13. ____________
14. ____________
15. ____________
16. ____________
17. ____________
18. ____________

Home Activity Your child has learned to read, write, and spell words from other cultures. Take turns spelling the list words.

Name ______________________________

Draw Conclusions

- A **conclusion** is a decision you make after thinking about the details of what you read.
- Often your prior knowledge can help you draw, or make, a conclusion.
- When you draw a conclusion, be sure it makes sense and is supported by what you have read.

Directions Read the following passage. Then complete the diagram.

People have played games throughout history. There are all kinds of games—card games, board games, sports games, children's games, and problem-solving games. People have invented games that can be played by one person, a few people, or by whole teams. Games give people a chance to challenge their minds and bodies. They also give people the thrill of winning. Best of all, games are fun.

Detail:	**Detail:**	**Detail:**	**What you know:**
1. People have played games ______	2. There are many different ______	3. Games challenge people's ______	4. ______

Conclusion

5. People everywhere ______________________

Home Activity Your child drew conclusions from facts or details found in a reading passage about games. Read a story or an article with your child. Work with him or her to draw conclusions from the details in it.

Name ____

Subject and Object Pronouns

Directions Write the letter of each pronoun next to the correct category.

______	**1.** Singular subject pronoun	**A**	we
______	**2.** Plural object pronoun	**B**	she
______	**3.** Singular object pronoun	**C**	me
______	**4.** Plural subject pronoun	**D**	you
______	**5.** Singular and plural, subject and object pronoun	**E**	them

Directions Write *S* if the underlined word is a subject pronoun. Write *O* if the word is an object pronoun.

6. We learned about the Anasazi people. ______

7. They built a civilization in the Southwest. ______

8. Like many civilizations, it depended on crops. ______

9. Maize and pumpkins provided the staple foods for them. ______

10. Little rain fell, but the Anasazi hoarded it to water crops. ______

11. The teacher asked Lia and me to report on cliff dwellings. ______

Directions Underline the correct pronoun in ( ) to complete each sentence.

12. My family and (I, me) visited Chaco Canyon.

13. (Us, We) learned about the pueblos the Anasazi built there.

14. Their skill in building with adobe amazed Sara and (I, me).

15. The people who lived here disappeared 800 years ago and took little with (them, they).

16. Why they left is a mystery to (us, we).

17. Scientists and (they, them) agree that drought may have forced them to migrate.

Home Activity Your child reviewed subject and object pronouns. Challenge your child to write sentences using *you, he, she, it, him, her,* and *them* correctly.

Name ______________________

Prefixes *over-*, *under-*, *sub-*, *super-*, *out-*

- **Generalization** When the prefixes **over-**, **under-**, **sub-**, **super-**, and **out-** are added to words, the base word stays the same: **overlook**, **underline**, **subway**, **supermarket**, **outlet**.

Word Sort Sort words by their prefixes.

over-

1. ______
2. ______
3. ______
4. ______

under-

5. ______
6. ______
7. ______
8. ______

sub-

9. ______
10. ______
11. ______
12. ______
13. ______

super-

14. ______
15. ______
16. ______
17. ______

out-

18. ______
19. ______
20. ______

Spelling Words

1. overlook
2. underline
3. subway
4. subset
5. supermarket
6. outlet
7. underground
8. overboard
9. undercurrent
10. superstar
11. overtime
12. supersonic
13. submarine
14. undercover
15. overcast
16. outfield
17. output
18. supernatural
19. subdivision
20. subhead

Home Activity Your child is learning about prefixes. Have your child tell you the five prefixes used in the list words.

Name

Family Times

Summary

Tripping Over the Lunch Lady

Jinx is a little bit clumsy, but she wants to learn to square dance. When the teacher decides to have square dancing in gym class, Jinx knows her dream has come true. Unfortunately, there is still the problem of Jinx's clumsiness.

Activity

Funny Memories Have you ever done something silly that was embarrassing at the time but later seemed funny? Talk with your family about something that happened to you or another family member that seems funny now. Write about the event as a comic story.

Comprehension Skill

Generalize

To **generalize** is to make a broad statement or rule that applies to several examples. Authors sometimes use clue words such as *most, all, usually,* and *never* to help readers generalize. Some generalizations are valid, or supported by facts and details. Others are faulty, or not supported. Active readers pay close attention to what authors tell them about story characters and make generalizations about those characters as they read.

Activity

Guess Who Play this game with your family or friends. Make a general statement about one person without naming the person. For example, it could be something the person always does or always likes. Have others try to guess whom the generalization is about and supply details supporting the generalization. Have everyone take a turn. When you are finished, decide who made the best generalization.

Lesson Vocabulary

Words to Know

Knowing the meaning of these words is important to reading *Tripping Over the Lunch Lady*. Practice using these words.

Vocabulary Words

Dalmatian a dog that has a white coat with black or brown spots

frilly clothing that has ruffles

promenading to be walking for show

sprained to be injured by a sudden twist

substitute a person or thing taking the place of another

Conventions

Pronouns and Antecedents

A **pronoun** is a word that replaces a noun or noun phrase. *For example: I, you, he, she, it, me, him, her, we, you, they, us*. The word or words that a pronoun stands for—such as *Julie, my father,* or *our cat Mouffette*—is called the pronoun's **antecedent.** *For example: Laurene saw George, so she waved to him.* In the example, the nouns "Laurene" and "George" are the *antecedents* of the *pronouns* "she" and "him."

Activity

Creative Captions With a family member, look through a picture book with which you both are familiar. Write captions on a separate piece of paper for the pictures that you see. Circle each pronoun that appears in your captions.

Practice Tested Spelling Words

______	______	______	______
______	______	______	______
______	______	______	______
______	______	______	______
______	______	______	______

Name ____

Generalize

- An author may write similar details about different things or people. You can use these similar details to make a general statement that covers all the things or people. This statement is called a **generalization.**
- A **valid** generalization can be supported by facts or details. A **faulty** generalization cannot.

Directions Read the first paragraph of the passage and make a prediction about what the rest of the passage will be about. Finish reading the passage. Then answer the questions below.

In July, 1968, Eunice Kennedy Shriver opened the first Special Olympics Games. She knew many athletes would win, but she also knew many would not. She wanted to encourage all of the athletes to do their best. So she told them what the gladiators in Rome said, "Let me win, but if I cannot win, let me be brave in the attempt." This became the Special Olympics Athlete Oath.

Through Special Olympics, many people with intellectual disabilities realize their full potential and become productive members of society. They train all year and compete in a variety of sports. In the process, they develop physical fitness, demonstrate courage, and experience joy. Special Olympics also creates an environment of acceptance for people with intellectual disabilities.

1. Write a generalization from this passage about how the Special Olympics affects its participants.

____

____

2. How did you know this was a generalization?

____

3. What detail supports the generalization?

____

4. What other detail supports the generalization?

____

5. After you read the first paragraph, what did you predict the rest of the article would be about? Was your prediction accurate?

____

____

Home Activity Your child read a short passage and recognized a generalization using clue words. Read an article together and challenge your child to find generalizations.

Name ____________________

Draw Conclusions

Directions Read the passage. Then answer the questions below.

At our school, about half of the students bring their lunches in brown bags. The others buy the school lunch. Bringing your lunch in a brown bag is okay, if you like mushy sandwiches and warm milk. The best way to bring lunch is to have each item packed in a separate container that keeps it fresh. Of course, then you have to carry all those containers home again, which is harder than throwing out a brown bag. Buying your lunch can be tricky too, because there might be a day when you don't like what the school is offering. The lunch lady gives you a big heap of goo on a plate. Sometimes you can't even tell what it is without checking the menu. Most days, I wish I could go home for lunch!

1. What conclusion can you draw about this writer regarding school lunch?

2. Which words and phrases tell you this?

3. What conclusion can you draw about the school lunches offered?

4. Which words and phrases tell you this?

5. What do you think the student should do about school lunch?

School + Home

Home Activity Your child reviewed drawing conclusions. Read several letters to the editor in a newspaper and draw conclusions about the viewpoint of the writers.

Name ______________________________

Pronouns and Antecedents

Directions Write a sentence or a pair of sentences using the noun or noun phrase and pronoun. Use each noun as an antecedent of each pronoun.

1. Mr. Deimeister and Jinx/they

____

____

2. Jinx/her

____

3. the other students/them

____

____

4. Victoria/she

____

____

5. square dancing/it

____

Directions Write a paragraph about someone who works hard to overcome an obstacle. Use at least four pronouns with their antecedents. Underline the antecedent for each pronoun.

____

____

____

____

____

____

School + Home **Home Activity** Your child learned how to use pronouns and antecedents in writing. With your child, write a paragraph about a hard worker you admire. Have your child point out pronouns and underline their antecedents.

Name ____________________

Prefixes *over-, under-, sub-, super-, out-*

Spelling Words				
overlook	underline	subway	subset	supermarket
outlet	underground	overboard	undercurrent	superstar
overtime	supersonic	submarine	undercover	overcast
outfield	output	supernatural	subdivision	subhead

Complete the Word Add a prefix to each word to make a list word. Write the complete word on the line.

1. ___way　　1. ____________
2. ___put　　2. ____________
3. ___natural　　3. ____________
4. ___market　　4. ____________
5. ___line　　5. ____________
6. ___head　　6. ____________
7. ___division　　7. ____________
8. ___current　　8. ____________

Word Search Find and circle ten list words hidden in the puzzle. Words are down, across, and diagonal. Write the words on the lines.

U	S	D	L	T	J	J	I	G	O	S	S
R	N	J	D	Z	D	F	F	H	V	U	U
T	O	D	S	X	O	W	Y	O	E	B	B
G	O	V	E	R	L	O	O	K	R	M	H
S	U	P	E	R	S	T	A	R	B	A	E
B	T	Q	A	R	C	P	C	T	O	R	A
B	P	K	D	N	C	O	L	K	A	I	D
S	U	B	S	E	T	A	V	W	R	N	H
L	T	X	E	A	J	Y	S	E	D	E	V
S	U	B	W	A	Y	B	P	T	R	O	L

9. ____________
10. ____________
11. ____________
12. ____________
13. ____________
14. ____________
15. ____________
16. ____________
17. ____________
18. ____________

Home Activity Your child has learned to read, write, and spell words with prefixes. See if you can recombine prefixes and list words to make other words such as *outline*.

Name______________________________

Generalize

- An author may write similar details about different things or people. You can use these similar details to make a general statement that covers all the things or people. This statement is called a **generalization.**
- A **valid** generalization can be supported by facts or details. A **faulty** generalization cannot.
- Sometimes an author makes a generalization and uses a clue word such as *all, many,* or *generally* to signal it.

Directions Read the following passage. Then complete the diagram below.

Deafness is the inability to hear. In general, there are two types of deafness. The first kind can be caused by earwax. Earwax blocks the pathway of sound from outside the ear into the inner ear in the head. This kind of deafness can usually be cured when a doctor softens the wax and flushes it out of the ear pathway.

A second kind of deafness is not curable. This is caused by a damaged nerve in the inner ear. Some babies are born without hearing. In other people, the nerve dies over a period of years. Extremely loud noises can damage the ear nerve. After injury the nerve cannot be healed.

General Statement

1. In general,

2. Clue word(s):

Supporting Details

3. The first kind

4. The second kind

5. Some babies

Home Activity Your child read a short passage and recognized a generalization using clue words. Read a newspaper or magazine article together and circle all the clue words that point to a generalization.

Name ____

Pronouns and Antecedents

Directions Match the pronoun with the noun or noun phrase that could be its antecedent. Write the letter of the correct antecedent next to the pronoun.

_____	**1.** Jinx	**A** he
_____	**2.** Mr. Deimeister	**B** it
_____	**3.** Victoria and I	**C** they
_____	**4.** trampoline	**D** we
_____	**5.** square dancers	**E** she

Directions Circle the antecedent of the underlined pronoun in each sentence.

6. Jinx got that name because <u>she</u> was clumsy.

7. Victoria broke her foot after Jinx asked <u>her</u> to learn square dancing.

8. Mr. Deimeister's fishing rod broke after the girl dropped a weight on <u>it</u>.

9. Jinx scared Tony as she bounced right over <u>him</u>.

10. Uncle Jeff thought of the name, but <u>he</u> was clumsy too.

Directions Write a pronoun to replace each underlined noun or noun phrase.

11. Cody had forgotten Chelsea was visiting until <u>Chelsea</u> knocked on his door.

____

12 Cody had a baseball game in 15 minutes, so <u>Cody</u> took Chelsea along.

____

13. The team needed another player, so <u>the team</u> convinced Chelsea to play.

____

14. Baseball was fun for Cody, and <u>baseball</u> was his favorite sport.

____

15. Chelsea scored four runs, and the team thanked <u>Chelsea</u>.

____

Home Activity Home Activity Your child reviewed pronouns and antecedents. Have your child dictate sentences about what he or she learned about overcoming obstacles today. Ask your child to underline pronouns and circle any antecedents in the sentences.

Name ______________________________

Homophones

- **Generalization** A homophone is a word that sounds exactly like another word but has a different spelling and meaning: **cent**, **sent**.

Word Sort Sort the list words by words you know how to spell and words that you are learning to spell. Write every word.

words I know how to spell	words I am learning to spell
1. ____________	11. ____________
2. ____________	12. ____________
3. ____________	13. ____________
4. ____________	14. ____________
5. ____________	15. ____________
6. ____________	16. ____________
7. ____________	17. ____________
8. ____________	18. ____________
9. ____________	19. ____________
10. ____________	20. ____________

Spelling Words

1. cent
2. sent
3. scent
4. threw
5. through
6. weather
7. whether
8. their
9. there
10. they're
11. chili
12. chilly
13. tide
14. tied
15. pale
16. pail
17. aloud
18. allowed
19. course
20. coarse

Home Activity Your child is learning about homophones. Ask your child to look at the word, say it, and then spell it.

Name

Family Times

Summary

Exploding Ants: Amazing Facts About How Animals Adapt

Animals adapt in many ways. They adapt to escape, trick, or overpower enemies. Some animals use their bodies to help out their species. Some adapt in order to survive. The soldier ants of the *Camponotus saundersi* burst in order to defend their colony. An owl eats its dinner whole and then spits up the bones and excess material the next day. More adaptations and interesting facts can be found in this selection.

Butterflies taste with their feet.

Activity

Animal Magic What is the strangest fact you know about an animal? Talk with members of your family about interesting animal facts.

Comprehension Skill

Graphic Sources

Graphic sources are visual ways of showing information. They include charts, graphs, maps, and time lines. You'll understand what you read better if you preview graphic sources. During reading, you should compare any graphic sources with the text. To help you remember what you read, create your own graphic source, such as a diagram or time line.

Activity

What's Coming Up? Look at the graphs, charts, and photographs that go with a magazine article. Discuss with a family member what you think the article is about, based on the information you have learned from the graphic sources.

Lesson Vocabulary

Words to Know

Knowing the meanings of these words is important to reading *Exploding Ants: Amazing Facts About How Animals Adapt*. Practice using these words.

Vocabulary Words

critical being important to the outcome of a situation

enables gives ability, power, or means to; makes able

mucus a slimy substance produced in the nose and throat to moisten and protect them

scarce hard to get; rare

specialize to develop in a special way

sterile free from germs

Conventions

Possessive Pronouns

A **possessive pronoun** is used in place of a possessive noun. Like the possessive noun, it shows who or what owns something. Like a pronoun, it takes the place of a noun, such as a person, animal, or thing. *For example: my/mine, your/yours, his, her/hers, its, our/ours, their/theirs.* Remember that possessive pronouns do not take apostrophes. *For example: its head, its handle.*

Activity

Pronoun Exchange With a family member, look for sentences in a book or newspaper that use possessive nouns. Then substitute a possessive pronoun for each possessive noun. Be sure you check each other's ideas!

Practice Tested Spelling Words

______	______	______	______
______	______	______	______
______	______	______	______
______	______	______	______
______	______	______	______

Name ______________________________

Graphic Sources

- A **graphic source,** such as a picture, diagram, or chart, organizes information visually.
- Preview the graphic sources to help you predict what you will be reading about.

Directions Study the following map. Then answer the questions below.

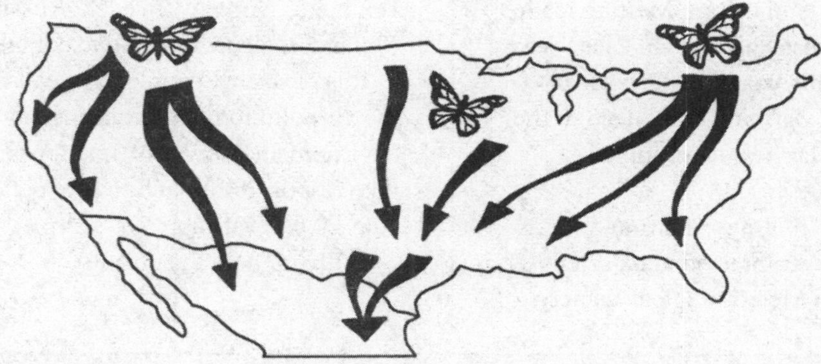

The Fall Migration of Monarch Butterflies (September – November)

1. What does the map show you?

____

2. In what kind of article might you see this graphic source?

____

____

3. In what main direction do the butterflies migrate?

____

4. How many months does the process of migration take? How do you know?

____

____

5. Good readers make sure they understand what they read, including graphic sources. If you were confused by something in this graphic source, what could you do?

____

____

Home Activity Your child used a graphic source to find information, and he or she also suggested how to respond to confusion about some part of the graphic source. Read a nonfiction article about animals with your child. Discuss what steps he or she could take to clear up confusion about some aspect of the article.

Name ____

Author's Purpose

Directions Read the following passage. Then answer the questions below.

Temperatures in the Arctic are rising ten times faster than elsewhere. The change is caused by the increasing amount of carbon dioxide in the air. Melting ice in Greenland and elsewhere could cause sea levels to rise. This would disturb ocean currents. Arctic warming could lead to the extinction of polar bears and some seals by the year 2100.

These are the findings of a four-year study made by over three hundred scientists of the American Meteorological Society. They examined the issue at the request of the Arctic Society. This group includes members from the United States, Canada, Denmark, Norway, Sweden, Russia, Finland, Iceland, and native communities.

It is clear that people have caused the air pollution that threatens our environment. Now it is time for people to take responsibility and to take action to stop global warming.

Will you help the effort?

1. What do you think is the author's purpose in this passage?

____

____

2. What could be affected by rising temperatures in the Arctic?

____

____

3. How does the information about the American Meteorological Society and the Arctic Society support the author's purpose?

____

____

4. Why do you think the author mentions Canada, Russia, and other countries?

____

____

5. In your opinion, does the author achieve his or her purpose? Why or why not?

____

____

Home Activity Your child analyzed the author's purpose in a nonfiction passage about global warming. Challenge him or her to make a persuasive argument to you or another family member about helping your community in some way.

Name____

Possessive Pronouns

Directions Underline the error in each sentence. Write the correct possessive pronoun in the space above the error.

(1) Each animal is adapted to it's environment. **(2)** For example, snakes have temperature-sensing organs on they're heads. **(3)** They can use these organs to locate there prey in the dark. **(4)** My corn snake Lolamae can take a whole mouse or egg in hers mouth. **(5)** She can unhinge her's bottom jaw to fit in a big meal. **(6)** The aquarium in the corner is her. **(7)** Lolamae will be happy to slither up yours arm. **(8)** It took mine mom a long time to get used to Lolamae too.

Directions Write a paragraph about pets you and your friends have owned. Describe some unique features of the pets. Use at least five possessive pronouns. Underline the possessive pronouns in your paragraph.

Home Activity Your child learned how to use possessive pronouns in writing. Have your child write interview questions to ask you about a prized possession and then write your answers below the questions.

Name ____________________

Homophones

Spelling Words				
cent	sent	scent	threw	through
weather	whether	their	there	they're
chili	chilly	tide	tied	pale
pail	aloud	allowed	course	coarse

Word Search Circle ten list words that are hidden in the puzzle. Words are down, across, and diagonal. Write each word you find.

B	T	J	A	H	Z	T	Z	C	Q	I	D
L	W	H	E	T	H	E	R	O	E	M	Y
T	X	F	R	U	Y	P	O	U	G	N	C
H	M	C	Q	O	Z	F	S	R	N	J	T
E	I	T	L	A	U	R	M	S	V	B	E
R	Z	A	H	B	T	G	A	E	G	E	M
E	W	I	V	E	L	S	H	B	R	H	A
U	P	Y	K	A	I	T	D	P	A	I	L
T	I	E	D	H	Y	R	O	M	K	E	O
D	L	R	L	A	I	L	N	E	D	X	U
H	Q	Y	J	S	O	E	R	Y	A	G	D
W	K	G	D	C	H	I	L	L	Y	N	T

1. ____________
2. ____________
3. ____________
4. ____________
5. ____________
6. ____________
7. ____________
8. ____________
9. ____________
10. ____________

Words in Context Write a list word to complete each sentence.

11. I'm worried because ____ late getting here. 11. ____________
12. The pitcher ____ the ball over the plate. 12. ____________
13. We had ____ with our hot dog. 13. ____________
14. The ____ was perfect for the beach. 14. ____________
15. The boy needs sunscreen on his ____ skin. 15. ____________
16. Swimming is not ____ when the lifeguard is off duty. 16. ____________
17. She ____ her classmate a party invitation. 17. ____________
18. The rose had a wonderful ____. 18. ____________
19. We looked for seashells when the ____ was out. 19. ____________
20. The ____ fabric was itchy. 20. ____________

Home Activity Your child has learned to read, write, and spell homophones. Say a homophone and spell it. Ask your child to say and spell the other homophone or homophones.

Name______________________________

Graphic Sources

- A **graphic source,** such as a picture, diagram, or chart, organizes information visually.
- Preview the graphic sources to help you predict what you will be reading about.

Directions Study the following diagram. Then answer the questions below.

The Butterfly's Life Cycle

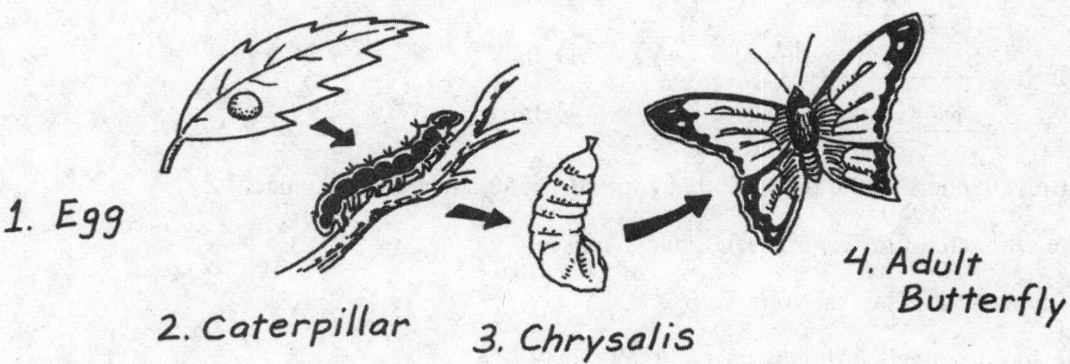

1. What tells you the topic of this graphic source?

____

2. What is the second stage of a butterfly's life?

The second stage is ______________________________

3. How does the diagram tell you the different stages in the life of a butterfly?

To show the different stages, the diagram uses ______________________________

____

4. How does the diagram help you to understand the life cycle of the butterfly?

The diagram helps you picture ______________________________

____

5. Where might you see a graphic source like this?

____

____

Home Activity Your child answered questions using a graphic source. Find a nonfiction article that includes a diagram or illustrations. Together, examine the graphic source and make predictions about what the article will be about. Then read the article to check your predictions.

Name ______________________________

Possessive Pronouns

Directions Write the letter of the possessive pronoun that can replace the underlined word or words in each phrase.

_____ **1.** Aaron's and Mike's question	**A**	her
_____ **2.** Mr. Shaefer's lesson	**B**	their
_____ **3.** the book's index	**C**	our
_____ **4.** Sam's and my interest	**D**	its
_____ **5.** Mom's degree	**E**	his

Directions Underline the pronoun that correctly completes each sentence.

6. We will catch fireflies in (theirs, our) hands.

7. Which of these jars is (your, yours)?

8. Be sure to punch air holes in (it's, its) top.

9. Dusk is (their, theirs) time to glow and flash.

10. I have ten fireflies in (my, mine) jar.

11. The light flashes from (their, it's) abdomen.

12. We let the fireflies go. Our friends released (their, theirs) later.

Directions Write the possessive pronoun that can replace the underlined word or words.

13. A snake sheds a snake's skin when it outgrows it.

____

14. This bleached-out turtle shell is the one belonging to me.

____

15. Zara and Ted explained that the rat was Zara's and the hamster was Ted's.

____

Home Activity Your child reviewed possessive pronouns. Ask your child to list the possessive pronouns on this page, use each one in an example sentence, and tell you what possessive noun the possessive pronoun replaces.

Name ____________________

Suffixes *-ible, -able*

- **Generalization** When adding the suffix **-ible** or **-able**, there is no sound clue to help you decide which form to use: **flex<u>ible</u>, agree<u>able</u>**.

Word Sort Sort the list words by their suffixes.

-ible	-able
1. ________	7. ________
2. ________	8. ________
3. ________	9. ________
4. ________	10. ________
5. ________	11. ________
6. ________	12. ________
	13. ________
	14. ________
	15. ________
	16. ________
	17. ________
	18. ________
	19. ________
	20. ________

Spelling Words

1. sensible
2. washable
3. available
4. agreeable
5. fashionable
6. valuable
7. flexible
8. reasonable
9. favorable
10. breakable
11. convertible
12. forgettable
13. laughable
14. sociable
15. allowable
16. divisible
17. hospitable
18. reversible
19. responsible
20. tolerable

School + Home

Home Activity Your child is learning about the suffixes *-ible* and *-able*. Say and spell the list words with your child.

Name

Family Times

Summary

The Stormi Giovanni Club

After Stormi Giovanni Green moves for the thousandth time, she decides she is not going to make new friends at her new school, because she would just have to say good-bye to them anyway. At first, Stormi really dislikes her new surroundings. But by the second day, she decides that making new friends isn't such a bad idea after all.

Activity

Script It Imagine the play someone might write about an event in your own life. What event would it focus on? Would the play be funny, sad, or both? Would the characters talk to the audience, as in *The Stormi Giovanni Club?* Discuss your thoughts with a family member. You may wish to write a scene from the play.

Comprehension Skill

Generalize

To **generalize** is to make a broad statement or rule that applies to several examples. Active readers pay close attention to what authors tell them about story characters and make generalizations about those characters as they read.

Activity

Character Generalizations Think about your favorite character from a story or book. In general, what is the character like? Along with a family member, discuss how the character's actions and personality support this generalization.

Lesson Vocabulary

Words to Know

Knowing the meanings of these words is important to reading *The Stormi Giovanni Club*. Practice using these words.

Vocabulary Words

cavities hollow places in teeth caused by decay
combination a series of numbers or letters dialed in opening a certain kind of lock
demonstrates shows how a thing is done
episode one part of a story that is published or broadcast in several parts, one at a time
profile *low profile:* moderate attitude or position, deliberately chosen in order to avoid notice
strict very careful in following a rule or in making others follow it

Conventions

Indefinite and Reflexive Pronouns

Indefinite pronouns do not refer to a particular person or thing. They can be used in the subject or predicate of a sentence. *For example: anybody, both, either, everyone.* **Reflexive pronouns** reflect the action of the verb back on the subject. They cannot be used as the subject of a sentence. *For example: himself, themselves, herself, myself, ourselves.*

Activity

Pronoun Hunt Choose an article from a magazine or newspaper. With a family member, pick sentences from the article and exchange their pronouns with examples of indefinite and reflexive pronouns. Discuss how the sentences' meanings change when the pronouns are changed.

Practice Tested Spelling Words

____________	____________	____________	____________
____________	____________	____________	____________
____________	____________	____________	____________
____________	____________	____________	____________
____________	____________	____________	____________

Name ______________________________

Generalize

- To **generalize** is to make a broad statement or rule that applies to several examples.
- Active readers pay close attention to what authors tell them about story characters and make generalizations about those characters as they read.

Directions Read the following scene from a play. Then answer the questions below.

PRINCIPAL: We're welcoming a student who's new to Harper School. Everyone, meet Dylan. Dylan, do you have any questions for the other students?

DYLAN: What do I need to know?

KAMALI: Most kids wear jeans.

KIM: And T-shirts. But if you have bad words on your T-shirt, you'll be in the principal's office.

DAVID: Also, there's lunch.

DYLAN (sounding stressed): I guess every school is different…

KAMALI: You have to get your tray a certain way.

KIM: And only teachers sit by the door.

DAVID: And there are Harper terms. The "field" is the blacktop, and "breakfast club" is detention.

DYLAN: Wait, wait! I'm getting the feeling it's hard to fit in here.

DAVID: Don't worry, we'll take you through it.

KIM: Yes, we'll show you the ropes. You'll like it here.

DYLAN: Thanks a lot!

1. What is the purpose of the meeting with the new student?

____

2. What generalization can you make about the attitude of Harper students at the meeting?

____

3. How can you generalize about the kind of advice the students give?

____

4. How does the advice make Dylan feel at first? How do you think Dylan's feelings change?

____

5. Explain the structure of this scene. How does a problem grow during the rising action and come to a climax? What is the outcome?

____

____

____

Home Activity Your child read a short passage and made generalization about the characters. Read a story about school with your child. Work together to make generalizations about the main character.

Name ______________________________

Draw Conclusions

Directions Read the following scene from a play. Then answer the questions below.

KARA: Mom, I don't want to go back to this new school. Everyone's so mean!

MOM: Kara, give it a chance.

KARA: No one talks to me.

MOM: Believe me, you'll be happy once you get to know people.

(TWO WEEKS LATER)

MOM: How's school?

KARA: It's funny—the kids in class told me that they had thought I was mean.

MOM: Why?

KARA: Because I didn't talk to anyone.

MOM: Then what happened?

KARA: The other day a new girl named Kate came into our class. She was even more miserable than I was, so I sat with her at lunch and tried to cheer her up.

MOM: So the other kids saw how nice you are?

KARA: Yeah, and they're pretty nice too. So is Kate.

1. What conclusion can you draw about how Kara felt at first at her new school?

____

____

2. Why did Kara think the kids at school were mean?

____

____

3. Why did Kara start making an effort at school?

____

____

4. Why did the kids at school change their attitude about Kara?

____

____

5. What conclusion can you draw about Kara's mother's advice? Explain your conclusion.

____

____

School + Home

Home Activity Your child has read a short passage and drew conclusions. Read a short story to your child. Ask him or her to draw conclusions about the characters.

Name ______________________________

Indefinite and Reflexive Pronouns

ourselves	everyone	yourself	few
myself	anyone	herself	both

Directions Choose a pronoun from the box to complete each sentence correctly. Be sure indefinite pronouns used as subjects agree in number with their verbs.

1. "Tell us about ____________, Tonya," says the teacher.
2. I think to ____________, "This is going to be good!"
3. ____________ leans forward to listen.
4. Tonya is a cowgirl who taught ____________ to ride.
5. ____________ of us know anything at all about horses.
6. Tonya says that ____________ can ride her gentle horse Bluebonnet.
7. All of us think to ____________, "I might not be able to!"
8. My friend Tonya has two horses, and ____________ are beautiful.

Directions Write several sentences about a time you made a new friend. Use some indefinite and reflexive pronouns. Underline the indefinite and reflexive pronouns you use.

____

____

____

____

____

____

____

____

____

____

____

Home Activity Your child learned how to write indefinite and reflexive pronouns. Have your child write these pronouns on cards. Choose several cards at a time and ask him or her to write sentences using the pronouns.

Name Stormi Giovanni

Suffixes *-ible*, *-able*

Spelling Words				
sensible	washable	available	agreeable	fashionable
valuable	flexible	reasonable	favorable	breakable
convertible	forgettable	laughable	sociable	allowable
divisible	hospitable	reversible	responsible	tolerable

Crossword Puzzle Use clues to find the list words. Write each letter in a box.

Across

6. friendly
7. levelheaded
8. silly
9. welcoming
10. positive

Down

1. stylish
2. bearable
3. unmemorable
4. precious
5. bendable

1. 2. 3. 4. 5. 6. 7. 8. 9. 10.

Definitions Write the list word that fits the definition.

11. anything that can be cleaned with soap and water 11. ________
12. separable into equal parts 12. ________
13. able to obtain 13. ________
14. fragile and delicate 14. ________

Home Activity Your child has learned to read, write, and spell words with suffixes. Have your child pick out the five hardest words to review with you.

Name ______________________

Generalize

- To **generalize** is to make a broad statement or rule that applies to several examples.
- Active readers pay close attention to what authors tell them about story characters and make generalizations about those characters as they read.

Directions Read the following passage.

Dan was amazed that he had made such great new friends at his new school. One was Jeff, who liked the same sports teams he did. Jeff also played on three sports teams himself. He even carried around a radio to make sure he didn't miss any sports scores. Other friends included Sam, who played in a band. He wrote song lyrics and liked the same music Dan did. Dan met Carlos when they were both in the school play. Carlos wrote plays too. Annie, another new friend, made up the funniest jokes he'd ever heard. She would go up to kids she didn't even know and tell them jokes. That's how Dan had met her. He was glad he'd met all four of his new friends.

Directions Complete the diagram by making a generalization about Dan's new friends and including supporting details.

Generalization

1. Dan's new friends ______________________

____

Support from Text

2. Jeff ______________________

Support from Text

3. Sam ______________________

Support from Text

4. Carlos ______________________

Support from Text

5. Annie ______________________

Home Activity Your child read a short passage and made a generalization about the characters. Work with your child to make generalizations about characters in a story you read together.

Name ____________________

Indefinite and Reflexive Pronouns

Directions Underline the pronoun in each sentence. Write *indefinite* or *reflexive* to identify the kind of pronoun it is. Then write *singular* or *plural* to show its number.

1. Everyone wants friends. __________ __________
2. Anna told herself to smile. __________ __________
3. A smile multiplies itself. __________ __________
4. Many begin to smile at Anna. __________ __________
5. Anybody can give a smile. __________ __________

Directions Underline the correct pronoun in ( ) to complete each sentence.

6. (Someone, Both) are friendly.
7. (Everyone, Many) agrees they are good friends
8. (No one, Others) are welcome in our club.
9. (Several, Anybody) have inquired about joining.
10. The boys signed (himself, themselves) up for bowling class.
11. (Anybody, Yourself) can try out for the class play.
12. Marcus and I practiced our parts by (himself, ourselves).

Directions Choose a pronoun from the box to complete each sentence correctly. Be sure indefinite pronouns used as subjects agree in number with their verbs.

ourselves	everybody	themselves	few

13. __________ in class was to choose an after-school activity.
14. A __________ of us are signing up for poetry.
15. Ms. Lonway will let us choose a poet for __________.
16. Humorous poets don't take __________ too seriously.

Home Activity Your child reviewed indefinite and reflexive pronouns. Have your child reread a favorite story and identify the indefinite and reflexive pronouns in it as singular or plural.

Name ____________________

Negative Prefixes

- **Generalization** When adding prefixes **il-**, **in-**, **im-**, and **ir-**, make no change in the base word: **illegal**, **invisible**, **impossible**, **irregular**. All of the prefixes mean "not."

Word Sort Sort the list words by their prefixes.

il-

1. ____________________
2. ____________________
3. ____________________

in-

4. ____________________
5. ____________________
6. ____________________
7. ____________________
8. ____________________
9. ____________________
10. ____________________
11. ____________________

im-

12. ____________________
13. ____________________
14. ____________________
15. ____________________
16. ____________________
17. ____________________

ir-

18. ____________________
19. ____________________
20. ____________________

Spelling Words

1. invisible
2. illiterate
3. irregular
4. irresistible
5. impossible
6. informal
7. illegal
8. impatient
9. independent
10. incorrect
11. inactive
12. imperfect
13. impolite
14. immature
15. illogical
16. indefinite
17. inappropriate
18. immobile
19. irresponsible
20. inexpensive

Home Activity Your child is learning about prefixes that mean "not." Have your child tell you four prefixes that mean "not."

Name

Family Times

Summary

The Gymnast

What is it like to try gymnastics? As a young boy, Gary envies his cousin who takes gymnastics. Gary tries to learn too. He vividly describes his feelings as he rolls, flips, and cartwheels for the first time.

Activity

Sports Center With your family, recall outstanding sports moments you each have seen or experienced. Then talk with family members about what sport they would like to succeed at.

Comprehension Skill

Draw Conclusions

A **conclusion** is a decision you reach when you think about facts and details. Draw conclusions as you read. Your conclusions should be logical and well supported.

Activity

How Was Your Day? Ask a family member to tell you about the things that happened during his or her day. When you have heard your family member's story, decide whether he or she probably felt it was a good day or a bad day. Explain the thinking you used as you drew your conclusion.

Lesson Vocabulary

Words to Know

Knowing the meanings of these words is important to reading *The Gymnast.* Practice using these words.

Vocabulary Words

bluish somewhat blue; somewhat like the color of the clear sky in daylight

cartwheels sideways handsprings with the legs and arms kept straight

gymnastics a sport in which very difficult exercises are performed

hesitation act of failing to act promptly; doubt; indecision

limelight center of public attention and interest

skidded slipped or slid sideways while moving

somersault to run or jump, turning the heels over the head

throbbing beating rapidly or strongly

wincing drawing back suddenly; flinching slightly

Conventions

Who and Whom

Use **who** as the subject of a sentence. *For example: Who is calling?* Use **whom** as the object of a preposition such as *to*, *for*, or *from*, or as a direct object. *For example: Whom is that from? Whom are you calling?* To check whether you should write *who* or *whom* in a question, think of a sentence with *he* or *him* in place of *who* or *whom*. If *he* is correct, then write *who*. If it is not correct, write *whom*.

Activity

Boo-Who Play this game with your family. In teams, make up questions that use *who/whom*, such as *Who/Whom does the quarterback pass to?* The other team's job is to decide whether *who* or *whom* is correct in that sentence. Call out "boo-who" if the team answers incorrectly.

Practice Tested Spelling Words

______	______	______	______
______	______	______	______
______	______	______	______
______	______	______	______
______	______	______	______

Name ______________________________

Draw Conclusions

- A **conclusion** is a sensible decision you make after you think about facts or details that you read.
- Drawing conclusions may also be called making inferences.
- Use your prior knowledge to help you draw conclusions.

Directions Read the following passage. Then answer the questions below.

When Lance Armstrong was 20, he made the U.S. Olympic cycling team. Three years later, he won an important cycling race, the Tour Du Pont, a premier U.S. cycling event. In 1996, he made the U.S. Olympic team again. That same year, he was diagnosed with cancer. He suffered terrible pain during his treatments and fought hard to get back to cycling. Five months after his diagnosis, he was training again determined to return to the sport he loved. Even though he was weakened from the disease, he wouldn't give up. In 1998, he finally returned to professional cycling. In 1999 he won the Tour de France. In 2005, he became the first seven-time winner of the Tour de France. Lance Armstrong inspires many people with his courage and abilities.

1. What conclusion can you draw about Lance Armstrong's character?

2. What is one detail from the passage that supports your conclusion?

3. What is another detail from the passage to support your conclusion?

4. What conclusion can you draw about how Lance Armstrong inspired other people?

5. How does visualizing help you understand what you read about Lance Armstrong?

Home Activity Your child read a short passage and drew conclusions based on details in the passage. Read a newspaper or magazine article about a famous athlete with your child. Ask your child to visualize the details. Afterward, ask your child to draw a conclusion about this sports star.

Name ______________________________

Generalize

Directions Read the passage. Then answer the questions below.

Many schools require every student to play at least one sport. By playing sports, many young people say that they meet new friends. By being on a team, a young person can learn cooperation and fair play. Playing a sport can build strength, flexibility, and endurance, and improve fitness. Many experts say young people get a boost in self-confidence as they succeed with new skills they learn through playing sports. Finally, for most young athletes, playing sports is simply a lot of fun.

1. Based on the passage, what is a generalization you can make about playing sports?

____

____

2. Which detail from the passage supports this generalization?

____

____

3. What other detail supports this generalization?

____

____

4. What is a generalization that is stated in the passage?

____

____

5. Write a generalization of your own about sports. Write at least one detail to back it up.

____

____

____

____

____

Home Activity Your child read a short passage and made a generalization based on the passage. Tell your child some specific details about a subject you think is important. Ask him or her to make a generalization about the subject.

Name ______________________________

Using *Who* and *Whom*

Directions Choose *who* or *whom* to correctly complete each sentence. Then write this sentence and answer or explain it with another sentence or two.

1. A person who/whom I admire is ____________________.

2. To who/whom do I go for advice?

3. Who/Whom is my good friend?

4. Who/Whom is a person from history I'd like to meet?

Directions Write two sentences about a sport you would like to learn and the person whom you would like as a coach. Use *who* or *whom* correctly in each sentence.

5. ______________________________

6. ______________________________

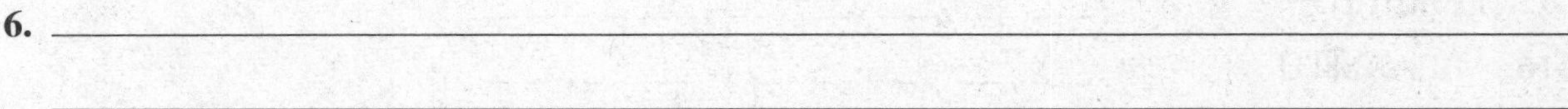

Home Activity Your child learned how to use *who* and *whom* correctly in writing. Ask him or her to write a fictional news story about sports and use the pronouns *who* and *whom* in it.

Name ______________________

Negative Prefixes

Spelling Words				
invisible	illiterate	irregular	irresistible	impossible
informal	illegal	impatient	independent	incorrect
inactive	imperfect	impolite	immature	illogical
indefinite	inappropriate	immobile	irresponsible	inexpensive

Complete the Word Add a prefix to each word to make a list word. Write the word.

1. ___appropriate 1. ______________
2. ___correct 2. ______________
3. ___definite 3. ______________
4. ___formal 4. ______________
5. ___legal 5. ______________
6. ___logical 6. ______________
7. ___mature 7. ______________
8. ___patient 8. ______________
9. ___perfect 9. ______________
10. ___regular 10. ______________

Double Puzzle Unscramble each word. Write one letter on each line. Write the numbered letters to find the answer to the question.

What is the date when the United States celebrates its independence?

11. ALRGIERUR ___ ___ ___ ___ ___ ___ ___ ___ ___ (3)
12. MALFIRON ___ ___ ___ ___ ___ ___ ___ ___ (1, 9)
13. TOCNRRIEC ___ ___ ___ ___ ___ ___ ___ ___ ___ (4)
14. CRMEPIFET ___ ___ ___ ___ ___ ___ ___ ___ ___ (7, 5)
15. PEIMILTO ___ ___ ___ ___ ___ ___ ___ ___ (2)
16. MIEARMTU ___ ___ ___ ___ ___ ___ ___ ___ (8)
17. OCLILGLAI ___ ___ ___ ___ ___ ___ ___ ___ ___ (6)

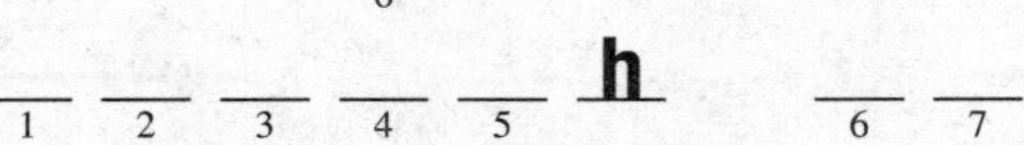

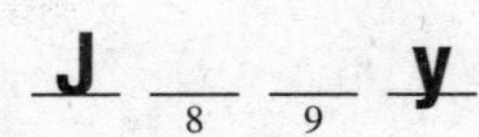

Home Activity Your child has learned to read, write, and spell words with prefixes. Take turns using list words in sentences that you say aloud. Ask your child to spell aloud the list word that is used in each sentence.

Name____________________

Draw Conclusions

- A **conclusion** is a sensible decision you make after you think about facts or details that you read.
- Drawing conclusions may also be called making inferences.
- Use your prior knowledge to help you draw conclusions.

Directions Read the following passage. Then complete the diagram below.

Gymnastics has existed for more than five thousand years. It dates back to ancient Egyptian times. In modern times, gymnastics developed first in Germany and then came to the United States in the 1800s. For many years it was based in local clubs and organizations. U.S. schools then began teaching gymnastics at the end of the nineteenth century. Still, gymnastics was not popular in schools and grew mainly through clubs outside of school. The first world competitions for gymnastics began about a hundred years ago, in 1903. Women did not compete in Olympics gymnastics until 1928. Finally, in 1970 the U.S. Gymnastics Federation was formed to oversee the sport in this country. By then gymnastics had earned its place as a competitive sport in the United States.

What does the text say?

1. Gymnastics began ____________

What does the text say?

2. In the 19th century, ____________

What does the text say?

3. ____________

What do I already know?

4. ____________

What can I conclude?

5. It took many years for ____________

Home Activity Your child read a short passage and drew a conclusion based on the facts in the passage. Together with your child, read an article about an unfamiliar sport. Have your child draw a conclusion about why people participate in that sport.

Name ______________________________________

Using *Who* and *Whom*

Directions Write *subject, object of preposition,* or *direct object* to identify how the underlined word is used.

1. To whom did Rosa speak? ______________________
2. Who likes tumbling? ______________________
3. A gymnast is someone who is agile and strong. ______________________
4. The girl with whom Jordan practices has real talent. ______________________
5. People who are flexible are better at somersaults. ______________________
6. Whom did you choose as a partner? ______________________

Directions Underline *who* or *whom* to complete each sentence correctly.

7. (Who, Whom) said that gymnastics is easy?
8. No one (who, whom) has studied gymnastics would say that.
9. Harry, (who, whom) I have coached for three years, shows promise.
10. To (who, whom) shall we give the "Most Improved" award?
11. Marla is the gymnast with (who, whom) most teammates want to work.
12. Our grandfather, (who, whom) is now 65, competed on his college gymnastics team.
13. (Who, Whom) will win Olympic gold this year?
14. (Who, Whom) made the banner congratulating the team?

Directions Cross out mistakes in the use of *who* and *whom* in the paragraph. Write the correct pronoun above the line.

(15) Kids whom live in the same family often compete with each other. **(16)** They want to see who the parents like best. **(17)** Parents, whom love all their children equally, try not to play favorites. **(18)** Although brothers and sisters like to see whom is faster or stronger, they love each other too.

Home Activity Your child reviewed using *who* and *whom*. Read a story with your child, and then ask him or her to tell about favorite characters, using *who* and *whom* correctly.

Name ______________________

Family Times

Selection Summaries

Week 1 ***Weslandia***
Wesley uses his imagination and some of the things he learned at school to start a very special garden.

Week 2 ***Tripping Over the Lunch Lady***
A clumsy, accident-prone girl decides to take up square-dancing.

Week 3 ***Exploding Ants***
From soldier ants that self-destruct to save their colony to owls that literally gulp down their dinner, animals have developed amazing adaptations.

Week 4 ***The Stormi Giovanni Club***
Stormi decides making friends isn't worth the pain of saying goodbye to them. But on the second day of school, she changes her mind.

Week 5 ***The Gymnast***
Gary tells his experiences as he learns to roll, flip, and cartwheel in gymnastics.

Activity
Retell in your own words one of the selections from the unit to a family member. Explain why you chose that selection.

Comprehension Skills Review

In Unit 4, you learned and used many skills while reading the stories and selections.

- When you **draw a conclusion**, you form an opinion based on what you know or on the facts and details in a text.
- An **author's viewpoint** is how the author feels about the topic. Some authors show a strong **bias** for or against their topic.
- A **graphic source** shows or explains information in the text. Pictures, tables, charts, and maps are all graphic sources.
- An author may write similar details about different things or people, and these details can be used to **generalize** about the things or the people.

Activity
Sometimes we have to learn to do things differently, such as when we start a new grade with a different teacher or move to a new home. Write about a time when you've had to adapt to something new. Tell what was good about it, and what was not so good.

Unit Vocabulary Skills

Suffixes

A **suffix** is attached to the end of a word to change its meaning. You can check the meanings of suffixes in the dictionary.

Activity Look for words that contain suffixes as you read the selections, and make a list of what you find.

Unfamiliar Words

When you come across an **unfamiliar word,** use context clues—the words and sentences near the word—to help you figure out the word's meaning.

Activity As you read, look for words you are not familiar with and make a list of them. Use context clues to figure out their meanings, and check the dictionary.

Synonyms

A **synonym** is a word that has a similar meaning to another word. You can find synonyms in a thesaurus.

Activity As you read, keep a list of any adjectives you find. Use a thesaurus to find synonyms for those words.

Unfamiliar Words

When you come across an **unfamiliar word,** use context clues—the words and sentences near the word—to help you figure out the word's meaning.

Activity As you read, look for words you are not familiar with and make a list of them. Use context clues to figure out their meanings, and check the dictionary.

Unit Spelling Rules

Words from Many Cultures

Many words in English come from other languages. These may have unexpected spellings that do not follow the usual English spelling rules.

Prefixes *over-, under-, sub-, super-, out-*

When these prefixes are added to words, the base word stays the same. The base word is also pronounced the same way as it was before the prefix was added.

Homophones

A homophone is a word that sounds exactly like another word but has a different spelling and meaning (for example, *sent*, *cent*, and *scent*).

Suffixes *-ible, -able*

When adding these suffixes, there are no sound clues to help you decide which form to use. The vowel sound spelled by the letters *ib* and *ab* in these suffixes is the schwa sound and can be spelled many different ways.

Negative Prefixes

The prefixes *il-*, *in-*, *im-*, and *ir-* all mean "not." When adding these prefixes, make no change in the base word. Remember that vowels before double consonants usually have a short sound. These prefixes have a short vowel sound in words like *impossible* and *illegal*.

Name ___________________________

Inflected Endings *-s, -es, -ed, -ing*

- **Inflected endings *-s, -es, -ed,*** or ***-ing*** are added to the end of a word to create a new word with a new meaning. If you are unsure about the meaning of a word with an inflected ending, check the dictionary.

Words to Know

blunders
civilization
complex
envy
fleeing
inspired
rustling
strategy

Practice Write the base of the word listed. Then add the ending shown to make a new word, and write it on the line. Check your spelling in a dictionary.

1. **blundered** ____________ **+ -s =** ____________
2. **inspired** ____________ **+ -ing =** ____________
3. **civilizes** ____________ **+ -ed =** ____________
4. **envying** ____________ **+ -es =** ____________
5. **rustles** ____________ **+ -ing =** ____________

On Your Own On a separate sheet of paper, write sentences using the words *complex, fleeing,* and *strategy.*

School + Home

Home Activity Your child reviewed the inflected endings *-s, -es, -ed,* and *-ing.* List four words for your child and ask him or her to write a new word using an inflected ending.

Name ____________________

Draw Conclusions

- When you **draw a conclusion**, you use what you already know and the facts you get from the text to form an opinion.
- When you read something, check your conclusion by asking: Does it make sense? Are the facts correct?

Fact: Jack's plan for becoming famous involved building a toothpick tower.
Fact: He wanted to break the world's record.
Conclusion: Jack would become famous if he broke the world's record.

Fact: The team made mistakes while building the tower.
Fact: The tower collapsed.
Conclusion: Jack did not succeed in breaking the world's record.

Practice Read the facts. Draw a conclusion and write it in the box.

1. Fact: Jack designed the toothpick tower. Fact: The tower fell over.

2. Fact: Jack really wants to become famous. Fact: His first plan to become famous failed.

On Your Own Use what you know about drawing conclusions while you read "City Blues." Make a conclusion about life in the city.

Home Activity Your child reviewed drawing conclusions. Together, read a newspaper article and see what conclusions you can draw.

Name ______________________________

Unfamiliar Words

- When you come across an **unfamiliar word**, look at the words and sentences around it. These context clues can help you figure out its meaning.

Practice Fill the blanks with the Words to Know. Then use context clues to choose the definition that best matches the underlined word.

Words to Know

accurate
dwindled
edible
extraordinary
unexplainable
uprooted

1. When I looked out the window one morning, I saw the branches of a most ________________ and unusual <u>conifer</u> towering over the house.

   a. bush b. shrub c. tree

2. Its <u>instantaneous</u> growth and ________________ cones were simply ________________.

   a. absurd b. quick c. tall

3. Even though the <u>cynical</u> newspaper reporter, at first, refused to believe that the tree had grown overnight, a professor from the local college confirmed that our assertions were ________________.

   a. someone who doubts what other people tell her b. someone who studies hard to understand things c. someone who tries to show kindness to all

4. Our cranky neighbor wanted to have the tree ________________, but her hopes ________________ as the crowds <u>swelled</u>, from a few people to many hundreds, to see our marvelous tree!

   a. divided b. grew c. visited

On Your Own As you read "Urban Wildlife," use context clues to determine the meanings of unfamiliar words.

Home Activity Your child has reviewed using context clues to determine the meanings of unfamiliar words. Together, read a story and look for unfamiliar words. Use context clues to determine their meanings, and check your ideas with a dictionary.

Name ____________________________________

Generalize

- To **generalize** is to use a broad statement or rule that applies to many examples. Clue words such as *all, most, every, always, usually,* and *generally* signal generalizations.

Practice Read the following passage. Think about the generalizations based on facts in the text. Fill in the diagram bewlow

Extreme Trucks just came out with three new models. The *Sport* is built for almost any outdoor adventure. It's made for off-road trails. Also, the bed of the truck converts to a tent.

The *Mountain* is built for the snow. This truck has traction control, so there is no slipping or sliding. There are also mounts built in for skis and snowboards. This truck makes every passenger feel safe and warm in a winter storm.

The *Hauler* is built for work. It has a big cargo load, so the truck's bed holds almost anything you would ever need. It has an extended cabin, so more people can ride inside. It also has a built-in toolbox.

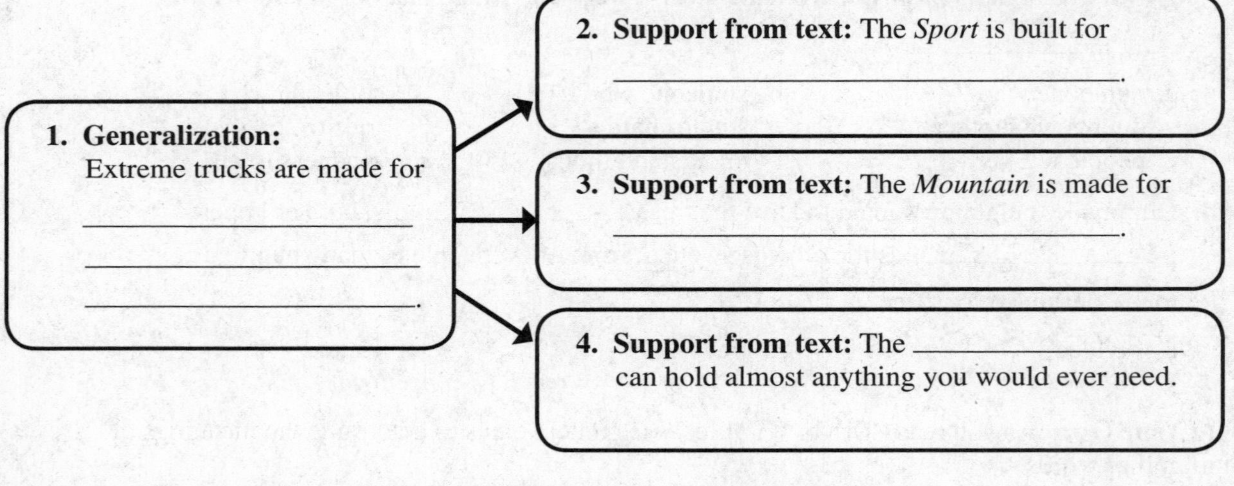

1. Generalization: Extreme trucks are made for ______________________.
2. Support from text: The *Sport* is built for ______________________.
3. Support from text: The *Mountain* is made for ______________________.
4. Support from text: The ____________ can hold almost anything you would ever need.

5. Identify three words in the text that tell you sentences are generalizations.

____

On Your Own Use what you know about generalizations as you read "Urban Wildlife." Identify the statements that are generalizations.

Home Activity Your child reviewed making generalizations. Read several letters to the editor in your newspaper and discuss any generalizations you find.

Name ______________________________

Synonyms

- A **synonym** is a word that means the same or almost the same as another word. A thesaurus lists the synonyms of words.

Words to Know
critical
enables
mucus
scarce
specialize
sterile

Practice Fill in the blanks with Words to Know. Then use a thesaurus to help you find the answers to the questions that follow.

Dr. Muldoon is an epidemiologist. Epidemiologists ______________ in studying disease. For her work, it is ______________ that she obtains samples, such as ______________. She examines the samples under ______________ conditions, which ______________ her to determine what bacteria and viruses are present. People who do her job are pretty ______________.

1. Which Word to Know means the same or almost the same as *rare?*

   ____

2. Which Word to Know means the same or almost the same as *vital?*

   ____

3. Which Word to Know means the same or almost the same as *helps?*

   ____

4. Which Word to Know means the same or almost the same as *clean?*

   ____

5. Which Word to Know means the same or almost the same as *concentrate?*

   ____

6. Which Word to Know means the same or almost the same as *slime?*

   ____

On Your Own As you read "Urban Wildlife," look for synonyms of words that you already know. Write them in a list in alphabetical order. Then look up the words in a thesaurus.

Home Activity Your child reviewed synonyms. Read a magazine together and make a list of words you want to find synonyms for.

Name____

Graphic Sources

- A **graphic source** shows or explains information in the text. Pictures, tables, charts, diagrams, time lines, and maps are all graphic sources.

Illnesses Studied by Dr. Muldoon		
Name	**Caused by**	**Studied since**
Chicken Pox	Virus	1984
Flu	Virus	1996
Lyme Disease	Bacteria	2005
Mumps	Virus	1977
Salmonella	Bacteria	2001
Strep	Bacteria	1989

Practice Use the table above to answer the following questions. Circle the letter in front of your answer.

1. In what year did Dr. Muldoon start studying strep?

a. 1977 b. 1989 c. 1996

2. Dr. Muldoon has been studying salmonella about _____ years longer than she has been studying Lyme Disease.

a. 2 b. 4 c. 6

3. Which three illnesses shown on the chart are caused by a virus?

a. chicken pox, flu, and mumps b. chicken pox, mumps, and salmonella c. flu, Lyme Disease, and strep

4. According to the table, which illness has Dr. Muldoon been studying for the longest time?

a. flu b. Lyme Disease c. mumps

On Your Own Use what you know about graphic sources as you read "Urban Wildlife." Make a chart that shows the reasons for the changes in urban wildlife population.

School + Home

Home Activity Your child reviewed using graphic sources to obtain information. Together, look through a how-to book and talk about how the graphic sources make the information easier to understand.

Name___________________________________

Unfamiliar Words

- When you come across an **unfamiliar word,** look at the words and sentences around it. These context clues can help you figure out its meaning.

Practice Read the following sentences. Fill in the blanks using the Words to Know. Then use context clues to figure out the meaning of the underlined word.

Words to Know

cavities
combination
demonstrates
episode
profile
strict

1. Kelsey once again forgot her locker ________________, and to Mr. Hall that ________________ that she is in <u>dire</u> need of getting organized.

a. bland b. professional c. serious

2. After that <u>mortifying</u> ________________, Kelsey tried to keep a low ________________ in school.

a. attractive b. embarrassing c. rowdy

3. However, Mr. Hall is ________________ when he wants a student to do something. He followed up with Kelsey by providing her with a school <u>agenda</u>, to help her organize her time and activities each day.

a. list of topics b. motive c. planner

4. "This will help fill any ________________ in your memory," Mr. Hall <u>asserted</u>.

a. laughed b. said slowly c. said with certainty

On Your Own As you read "City Blues," look for words unfamiliar to you and use context clues to figure out their meanings. Check your ideas in the dictionary.

Home Activity Your child reviewed unfamiliar words. With your child, read a magazine article and use context clues to figure out their meanings.

Name ______________________________

Generalize

- To **generalize** is to use a broad statement or rule that applies to many examples.
- Clue words such as *all, most, every, always, usually,* and *generally* signal generalizations.

Ted usually has a hard time with the livestock.

Roslyn has always had a way with animals.

Their cousin Lyra is afraid of all animals.

Practice Look at the pictures above. Based on the generalizations you have read, choose the letter in front of the person's name that the statement is most likely about.

1. handles the animals well

a. Lyra b. Roslyn c. Ted

2. is uncomfortable on a farm

a. Lyra b. Roslyn c. Ted

3. might decide to become a veterinarian

a. Lyra b. Roslyn c. Ted

4. should ask for help handling the animals

a. Lyra b. Roslyn c. Ted

5. has probably not spent lots of time with animals

a. Lyra b. Roslyn c. Ted

On Your Own Use what you know about generalization as you read "City Blues." Make a list of generalizations as you read the passage.

Home Activity Your child reviewed making generalizations. Talk about how generalizations can be useful, but how they have their limits too.

Name____________________

Suffixes

- A **suffix** is attached to the end of a word to change its meaning. The suffix *-ish* means "similar to something, or like something." The suffix *-ion* means "the act or state of being."

Practice Read the following sentences. Fill in the blanks with one of the Words to Know. Then choose the meaning of each underlined word. You can use a dictionary to help you.

Words to Know

bluish
cartwheels
gymnastics
hesitation
limelight
skidded
somersault
throbbing
wincing

1. Chris asked Sara to teach her ____________, and Sara found herself ____________ at the request because Chris lacks coordination.
   a. a person who is coordinated
   b. the state of being coordinated

2. Yet Sara agreed without ____________ because Chris is her dearest friend, even though Sara knew the gymnastics lesson might be nightmarish.
   a. the opposite of a nightmare
   b. similar to a nightmare

3. After tumbles and ____________, Chris tried a disastrous ____________ and stood up holding her arm. Her fascination with gymnastics had turned a bit painful!
   a. the state of being fascinated by something
   b. a good reason to be fascinated by something

4. Chris admitted that her arm was ____________, but she didn't want to be childish, so she didn't cry.
   a. similar to or like a child
   b. much older than a child

5. A few weeks later, to show her appreciation for the gymnastics lesson, Chris taught Sara to skate. Now Chris was in the ____________, while Sara was clumsy as she ____________ across the ____________ ice and fell.
   a. the act of appreciating something
   b. not ever appreciating anything

On Your Own As you read "City Blues," look for words that have suffixes. List them and remove the suffix, then look up the base word in the dictionary.

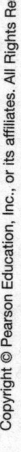

Home Activity Your child reviewed suffixes. Work together to list as many words as you can that end with suffixes you know. Discuss the suffixes' meanings.

Name ____________________

Draw Conclusions

- **Drawing conclusions** is forming an opinion based on what you know or on the facts and details in a text.

Chris is showing Sara how to skate. | At first, Sara feels wobbly on the ice. | But after a while, Sara can skate by herself.

Practice Look at the pictures above and read the captions. Then answer the questions.

1. Which girl is a better skater? Tell how you know.

____

2. List the details in the pictures and the captions that help you know that Sara is just learning to skate.

____

____

3. Do you think Sara is learning to be a better skater? Why or why not?

____

____

4. Based on the pictures and captions, what kind of a friend is Chris?

____

____

On Your Own Use what you know about drawing conclusions as you read "City Blues." Make a conclusion about the main character's feelings about living in the city.

School + Home **Home Activity** Your child reviewed drawing conclusions. With your child, talk about any conclusions you can reach after reading a newspaper article together.

Name ____________________

Urban Wildlife

If you've ever noticed a pigeon flying past city buildings or a cockroach scuttling along the kitchen floor, then you've witnessed urban wildlife. Sure, pigeons and cockroaches aren't the most glamorous of animals, but when you think about how these creatures have made their homes in our cities, it's easy to see how remarkably talented they are.

Plenty of species are visible right outside our doors. Birds, squirrels, deer, raccoons, bats, insects, and mice are just a few of the animals that suburban- and urban-dwellers are likely to see on any given day. But there are countless other species too. Some are living in, under, or on top of our homes! Scientists believe, in fact, that the number of urban species is increasing due to cities' expansion and improved urban environmental actions.

Where exactly do these wild animals make their homes? Our streets, buildings, gardens, streams, and railroads are just some of the places they choose to live. What's more, plentiful food supplies—including our steady stream of garbage—provide creatures with a choice of tasty snacks and meals.

Amazingly, some animals whose numbers have dwindled in their natural habitats have made a comeback in urban areas. One such animal is the redstart bird, which has recently been found throughout abandoned factories and city rooftops in London. Peregrine falcons have also made a comeback, particularly in New York City. These swift birds can hurtle down toward their prey, traveling at over one hundred fifty miles per hour! Many people have helped these extraordinary creatures by placing special peregrine nesting boxes on ledges high off the ground.

Birds will find places to roost in just about every urban nook and cranny. Look at highway overpasses, train tunnels, hidden corners in churches and skyscrapers—even streetlights and stoplights—for signs of these animals. Beneath the skies and in the waters, the number of fish and waterfowl has also increased thanks to cleaner rivers and other waterways.

But the news isn't always good. One of the reasons that animals have moved into our neighborhoods is because we have encroached on their territory. As our cities grow past their limits, natural habitats can become scarce.

Generalize After you read the first page of "Urban Wildlife," write a sentence that makes a generalization about the information.

____

____

____

____

____

____

Draw Conclusions Why does garbage attract animals?

____

____

Synonyms What is a synonym for *swift*?

____

____

Suffixes What is the suffix in *expansion*?

____

Unfamiliar Words Underline the words in the passage that help you understand the meaning of *encroached.*

Name ______________________________

Generalize Write a sentence that makes a generalization about why wild animals move away from their old habitats.

____

____

____

____

____

____

Draw Conclusions How might foreign species affect native species?

____

____

____

____

____

Graphic Sources According to the chart, what types of animals might you see in the air?

____

____

Another reason that animals have moved away from their natural habitats is because of the chemicals and pesticides being used on farmland. Due to these poisons, open meadows and forests are no longer as friendly to living creatures as they once were. Plants are disappearing, along with the species that relied on them. Fortunately for us, some types of animals, such as butterflies and beetles, are finding their needed food sources in the woodsy parts of suburbs, where pesticides and other chemicals are not widely used.

Some urban wildlife may also be affected by non-native species that have shifted to the area. For example, two birds—the house sparrow and the starling—were originally brought to the United States in the 1800s and have since multiplied in cities and suburbs across North America. Some people believe they have brought down the numbers of other native birds, such as bluebirds and woodpeckers.

Yet regardless of whether species are native or foreign, nature conservationists agree that it is important to care for all wildlife. Several organizations throughout the United States provide resources and information for people interested in getting to know their wild neighbors. Are you curious about what lives in your region? Then hit the streets and see what urban animals you can find.

City Slickers in the Limelight Wild animals live among us in our cities and towns. Which animals can you find near you?

On Land	In the Sky	In the Water
Skunks	Bats	Fish
Mice	Birds	Frogs
Lizards	Butterflies	Turtles

Home Activity Your child read a selection and used comprehension and vocabulary skills from Unit 4. Have your child summarize the selection, drawing conclusions about the author's viewpoint and bias.

Name____

City Blues

At five in the morning, Jada woke up to the sound of a motorcycle revving its loud engine down her busy street. She moaned and pulled the pillows over her head. Sleeping would be so much easier if she could simply turn off the noises of the city.

Moments later, when the deafening sound of a garbage truck rumbled beneath her window, Jada threw her pillows onto her bed and decided it was time to get up. She grabbed her journal and got herself some cereal. Then she sat on her parents' new couch that still smelled like the furniture store.

Day 5, Jada wrote in her journal. *Note to self: buy earplugs. Still miss Gran and her garden. Living here is the pits.*

Jada stared out of her tenth-story apartment window at the highway just a few blocks away. Leaving Gran behind had been the worst part of Jada's move. Back at home, it was Gran who had taken Jada for fish tacos and root beer at the Cactus Café. It was Gran who had explained the ins and outs of every soap opera episode and the strategies behind game shows. And it was Gran who had taught Jada about the desert plants that grew across her dusty backyard.

Now Jada was living three hours away in a new civilization, one that was full of concrete and cars. There wasn't so much as a single cactus in sight. The only thing cities were good for were sirens and office buildings.

Just as Jada was finishing her last bite of breakfast cereal, her mother padded into the living room. "Morning, honey," she yawned. "You're up early, again."

"Couldn't sleep," Jada said. She turned on her dad's computer and began checking her e-mail, where she found a new message from Gran. *Dear Jays,* she read. *My cactus, George, is missing you. It's hotter than blue blazes here. Hope you're keeping cool. Love, G.*

Jada sighed. A twinge of envy rippled through her body. How she wished she were with Gran on her back porch, staring at the brown and jagged mountain skyline.

A few hours later, when the sun had risen high overhead, Jada's father asked her if she wanted to go for a swim. "There's a new pool at the recreation center down the street," he explained. "Might as well take advantage of it, now that we're here!"

Suffixes What is the suffix in *moaned?*

____

Draw Conclusions Why does Jada want to buy earplugs?

____

____

____

Generalize Look at the fifth paragraph. Underline the generalization that Jada makes about the city.

Unfamiliar Words What do you think *jagged* means?

____

____

What nearby words help you to determine the meaning of *jagged?*

____

Name_______________________________________

Draw Conclusions Why do you think Jada is so upset when her book gets wet?

____

____

____

____

____

Generalize Before Jada meets George, how do you think she feels? Make a generalization about her attitude.

____

____

____

____

"I guess so," Jada said, though she wasn't too convinced.

A combination of adults and kids were swimming in the pool by the time Jada and her parents got there. Jada had to admit that the cool water looked inviting, but she knew she had better things to do with her time. Finding a chair in a shady spot, she sat down to browse through her new book on desert plants. The book had been a good-bye present from Gran. *By the time you come back to visit me,* she'd said, *you'll be telling me what to do with my garden.*

Jada was in the midst of admiring the pictures when a piercing voice rang through the air. "Cannonball!" the voice cried. Instantly, Jada was splashed from head to toe by a boy who had jumped into the pool. She looked down at her new book to find it sopping wet.

"Sorry about that!" she heard someone say. Jada looked up to see the boy standing in front of her with water dripping down his hair and nose. She felt like fleeing back to her apartment and bit her lip to hold back the tears.

"You ruined my book," she said quietly.

The boy's face fell. "Hey, I'm sorry. I didn't mean to." He stared at the wet pages apologetically, then noticed the book's photographs and took a closer look. "Actually," he said in surprise, "my dad has lots of books like this one. He gets them from working at the botanical gardens. He'd let you borrow one if you want."

"There are botanical gardens here?" Jada asked in astonishment. "I thought nothing grew in the city."

"Of course things grow," the boy said. "This isn't the planet Mars, you know. Are you new here or something?"

Jada flushed. "Kind of," she said.

"Well, come over any time," the boy told her, "and I'll show you some of my dad's books. My name's George, by the way."

Just like Gran's cactus, Jada thought to herself, with a small smile. Then she introduced herself and looked toward the pool. "Maybe I'll go in," she said. "I've already gotten wet anyway."

"How about a water race?" George asked with a gleam in his eye.

"You're on," Jada said, leaping into the pool.

Home Activity Your child read a selection and used comprehension and vocabulary skills from Unit 4. Have your child retell the selection, making generalizations and drawing conclusions about the characters.

Name ____________________

Multisyllabic Words

- **Generalization** When spelling words with many syllables, look carefully at each word part.

Word Sort Sort the list words by words you know how to spell and words that you are learning to spell. Write every word.

words I know how to spell	words I am learning to spell
1. ______	11. ______
2. ______	12. ______
3. ______	13. ______
4. ______	14. ______
5. ______	15. ______
6. ______	16. ______
7. ______	17. ______
8. ______	18. ______
9. ______	19. ______
10. ______	20. ______

Spelling Words

1. elementary
2. vehicle
3. miniature
4. probability
5. opportunity
6. substitute
7. variety
8. literature
9. elevator
10. Pennsylvania
11. ravioli
12. cafeteria
13. mosaic
14. tuxedo
15. meteorite
16. fascination
17. cylinder
18. intermediate
19. centennial
20. curiosity

School + Home

Home Activity Your child is learning about words with many syllables. Have your child say each word very slowly, pausing in between each syllable.

Name

Family Times

Summary

The Skunk Ladder

Creativity turns to chaos when two friends decide to dig a hole as a way to pass the time. Unfortunately, some ideas are destined to cause trouble no matter what. All it takes is a curious skunk and a suspicious father to fall into the trap of youthful imagination.

Activity

I Remember When... Children are often forbidden to do some things because their families know from experience that the results will be disastrous. With your family, discuss some of the brilliant yet misfired ideas they had when they were young. Discuss how those experiences compare with some of your "brilliant" ideas.

Comprehension Skill

Character and Plot

Traits are the qualities shown by a story's **characters,** such as bravery or shyness. We see their traits in their words, actions, and how other characters treat them. The **plot** is the pattern of events in a story.

Activity

What's She Like? Think about a character you know from a book, movie, or television show. How would you describe him or her to someone? Sit down with a family member and describe him or her. Think about the character's personality traits as well as how he or she looks.

Lesson Vocabulary

Words to Know

Knowing the meanings of these words is important to reading *The Skunk Ladder*. Practice using these words.

Vocabulary Words

abandoned gave up on, dismissed
attempt try or make an effort
bellow shout or roar like a bull
cavern a large cave
feat a difficult or skillful act
immensely very greatly
savage wild, ferocious, angry

Conventions

Contractions and Negative Contractions

A **contraction** is a shortened form of two words. An apostophe takes the place of one or more letters. Contractions can be formed from a pronoun and a verb. *For example: I + am = I'm; she + will = she'll; you + are = you're.*
A **negative contraction** is when you combine a verb with *not*. An apostrophe takes the place of the letter *o* in *not*. *For example: do + not = don't; are + not = aren't; will + not = won't.*

Activity

Cut It Down Newspapers usually avoid using contactons in their articles. Choose a newspaper article and read a few sentences to a family member. Then read the sentences again, this time using contractions wherever you can. Discuss with your family member how this changes the way the article sounds.

Practice Tested Spelling Words

Name ________________________________

Character and Plot

- **Traits** are the qualities, such as bravery or shyness, of **characters,** or the people and animals in a story. We see characters' traits in their words and how other characters treat them.
- The **plot** is the pattern of events in a story. Usually, the events are told in sequence, from start to finish.

Directions Read the following passage. Then answer the questions below.

Every day, Nipper, Jack's favorite sheepdog, and Bowser, the German Shepherd, ran through the pastures on Jack's farm, protecting and corralling Jack's large sheep herd. The main job for the dogs was to keep the sheep from wandering too close to the woods, where a pack of wolves was known to live. A wolf could be very dangerous to a sheep.

One day a large grey wolf wandered onto the farm. It snuck around the farmhouse, crept slowly up behind the herd, and was getting ready to pounce on one of the sheep. From across the field, Nipper and Bowser sprang into action. They raced like rockets across the field, barking like crazy. They ran straight toward the wolf. The wolf ran as fast as it could back into the woods. Jack drove up in his pickup truck shortly after the wolf ran away. He walked over, petted the dogs and asked, "Why do you guys seem so excited?"

1. Who are Nipper and Bowser?

____

2. What traits might describe the dogs?

____

3. What do Nipper and Bowser do when they see the wolf get ready to pounce on the sheep?

____

4. Are they successful? How do you know?

____

5. If Nipper and Bowser could have answered Jack's question, what might they have said?

____

Home Activity Your child answered questions about plot and character based on a short passage. With your child, describe a character from a favorite book or movie.

Name___________________________________

Author's Purpose

Directions Read the article. Then answer the questions below.

The restless look on Winnie's face made me nervous. "There's nothing to do around here," she complained. She was right. Our town was boring. "We should protest something," Winnie declared. Winnie loved to protest. She became energized when she made signs and handed out flyers.

Suddenly, Winnie's face brightened. "What about the senior center?" she asked.

"Winnie, our town doesn't have a senior center," I said.

"Exactly!" she exclaimed. "We'll demand that the town turn the abandoned factory downtown into a senior center. It'll be our best protest ever!" she said. "After we succeed, the senior citizens will be so grateful that they will give us a hand in our next protest!"

1. What is the author's purpose in the passage above?

____

____

2. Does the narrator or Winnie make the big decision in the story?

____

____

3. What do the narrator and Winnie plan to do?

____

____

4. What is the motivation, or purpose, behind Winnie's plans?

____

____

5. Does the author succeed at his or her purpose? Why or why not?

____

____

Home Activity Your child has answered questions about an author's purpose in a fictional passage. Read a short story with your child and identify how the author succeeds or fails to write a humorous or dramatic tale.

Name ______________________________

Contractions and Negatives

Directions Use contractions to replace the underlined words. Rewrite the sentence.

1. There is plenty to do on a farm in the summer.

____

____

2. Those boys will not just swim or fish.

____

3. They have thought of some new projects to try.

____

4. I do not think the pond is big enough for a submarine.

____

____

5. Their plane is not ready to take off.

____

6. What is that hole for?

____

Directions Rewrite the sentences, correcting any double negatives.

7. No one never dug a hole that deep before.

____

8. There isn't no better place to dig a hole.

____

9. The boys didn't think nothing could get into the hole.

____

10. There weren't no animals around when they were digging.

____

Home Activity Your child learned how to write negatives and contractions correctly. Ask your child to write a paragraph about what he or she likes to do during the summer, using several contractions and negatives. Have him or her underline these words.

Name ____

Multisyllabic Words

Spelling Words				
elementary	vehicle	miniature	probability	opportunity
substitute	variety	literature	elevator	Pennsylvania
ravioli	cafeteria	mosaic	tuxedo	meteorite
fascination	cylinder	intermediate	centennial	curiosity

Classifying Write the word that completes the group.

1. Philadelphia, Liberty Bell, ____ **1.** ____________
2. interest, attraction, appeal, ____ **2.** ____________
3. car, bus, truck, ____ **3.** ____________
4. text, poetry, novels, ____ **4.** ____________
5. dining room, mess hall, ____ **5.** ____________
6. assortment, selection, ____ **6.** ____________
7. shooting star, moon rock, ____ **7.** ____________
8. tiles, grout, pattern, ____ **8.** ____________
9. hundred, anniversary ____ **9.** ____________
10. tube, can, ____ **10.** ____________

Word Search Find ten list words that are hidden in the puzzle. Words are across, down, up, backward, and diagonal. Write the words on the lines.

```
I L C C E X E I P R M S Z
E N X V D T L C R O I T O
T E T K H O A F O T N G P
U C V E I E D F B A I E P
T D M V R X K V A V A N O
I O A J M M G Q B E T U R
T R T E T U E B I L U T T
S T U X E D O D L E R C U
B T N O I T I N I F E D N
U Z E L E M E N T A R Y I
S N F L G C P E Y N T Z T
C P Y T I S O I R U C E Y
```

11. ____________
12. ____________
13. ____________
14. ____________
15. ____________
16. ____________
17. ____________
18. ____________
19. ____________
20. ____________

Home Activity Your child has learned to read, write, and spell multisyllabic words. Take turns using the words in a sentence.

Name________________________________

Character and Plot

- **Traits** are the qualities, such as bravery or shyness, of **characters,** or the people and animals in a story. We see characters' traits in their words and how other characters treat them.
- The **plot** is the pattern of events in a story. Usually, the events are told in sequence, from start to finish.

Directions Read the following passage. Fill in the diagram below.

Finding that old bottle did something to Maribel. As it turned out, the bottle was just her first discovery of many from a two-hundred-year-old dump. After finding the bottle, Maribel became immensely interested in history. She wanted to know everything about the lives of the people who had lived on her street in the 1800s.

Maribel cautiously dug up more bottles, pottery, and other artifacts from the past. She delicately cleaned them and took them to the local historical museum, where a museum employee helped her identify what the bottles were used for. Soon Maribel's history grades improved. She also started to enjoy writing and faithfully kept a journal of all her historical finds. When her teacher asked where Maribel's new enthusiasm for learning came from, her father answered, "She found it in a junk pile."

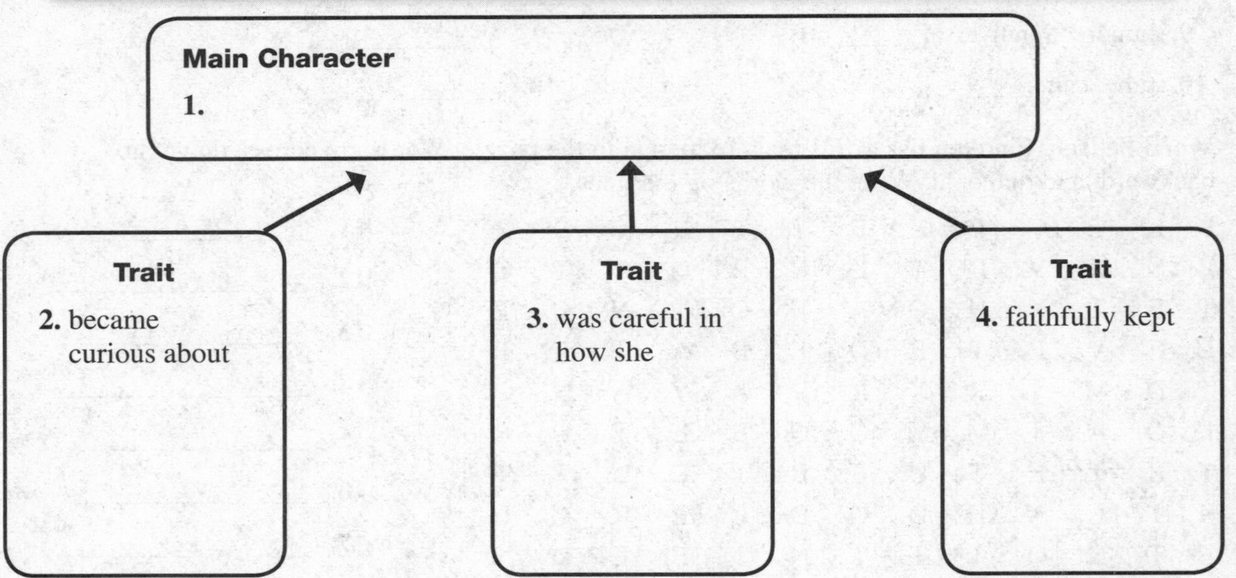

Home Activity Your child answered questions about character and plot in a fictional passage. Have your child come up with words that describe some of the traits he or she admires in a best friend or relative.

Name____

Contractions and Negatives

Directions Underline the contraction in each sentence. Write the words that make up the contraction.

1. What's our next project going to be? ____________________
2. I've got a great idea. ____________________
3. We'll build a bridge across the creek. ____________________
4. It'll be made out of firewood. ____________________
5. I am the best engineer you've ever seen. ____________________

Directions Draw a line to connect each contraction with the words used to form it.

6. could've	you are
7. they'll	it is
8. who'd	could have
9. you're	who would
10. it's	they will

Directions Circle the word in ( ) that correctly completes each sentence.

11. Crazy Eddie didn't (ever, never) run out of ideas.
12. There hasn't ever been (anybody, nobody) as creative as he was.
13. His dad found out there was (anything, nothing) Eddie wouldn't try.
14. Of course, his projects didn't (ever, never) turn out perfect.
15. I bet Eddie's chemistry experiments aren't (ever, never) boring.

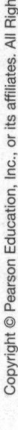

Home Activity Your child reviewed contractions and negatives. Ask him or her to write a story that uses at least five contractions and five negatives correctly. Have your child highlight these words and read you the story.

Name ______________________________

Related Words

- **Generalization** Related words often have consonants that are spelled the same but pronounced differently: **music**, **musician**.

Word Sort Sort word pairs by the consonant that is pronounced differently.

c

1. ______________ ______________

2. ______________ ______________

3. ______________ ______________

t

4. ______________ ______________

5. ______________ ______________

6. ______________ ______________

7. ______________ ______________

g

8. ______________ ______________

9. ______________ ______________

n

10. ______________ ______________

Spelling Words

1. music
2. musician
3. select
4. selection
5. sign
6. signal
7. part
8. partial
9. haste
10. hasten
11. protect
12. protection
13. magic
14. magician
15. resign
16. resignation
17. electric
18. electrician
19. condemn
20. condemnation

Home Activity Your child is learning about related words that have consonants that are pronounced differently. Say and spell words aloud with your child, and ask your child to identify which consonant is pronounced differently.

Name

Family Times

Summary

The Unsinkable Wreck of the R.M.S. Titanic

Seventy-four years after the *Titanic's* tragic collision with an iceberg, two explorers took the mini-submarine *Alvin* two-and-a-half miles down to the ocean's bottom to view the wreck of the *Titanic.* They were the first people to ever see the wreckage. They found that the ocean floor was littered with personal items that serve to this day as a reminder of the accident.

Activity

Uncover Your History With a family member, dig through some boxes your family has stored in an attic or garage. If possible, ask a grandparent or older relative if you can explore his or her house. Try to determine the age of the items you find.

Comprehension Skill

Graphic Sources

Graphic sources include charts, tables, graphs, maps, illustrations, and photographs. Before you read an article, look closely at any graphic sources that accompany it.

Activity

Worth a Thousand Words Pick up a newspaper or magazine and flip through it until you come across a chart. With a family member, study the chart and the information it provides. Then, both of you make a guess as to what the article will be about. Read the article and see how close you came to being right.

Lesson Vocabulary

Words to Know

Knowing the meanings of these words is important to reading *The Unsinkable Wreck of the R.M.S.* Titanic. Practice using these words.

Vocabulary Words

cramped shut into a small space
debris scattered fragments; ruins
interior inner surface or part; inside
ooze a soft mud or slime, especially at the bottom of a pond or river or on the ocean bottom
robotic of or for a machine with moving parts and sensing devices controlled by a computer
sediment material that settles to the bottom of a liquid
sonar device for finding the depth of water or for detecting and locating underwater objects. Sonar sends sound waves into water, and they are reflected back when they strike the bottom or any object.

Conventions

Adjectives and Articles

An **adjective** is a word that modifies a noun or pronoun. It usually, but not always, comes before the noun it describes. When an adjective is used to modify a pronoun, it usually comes after the pronoun and follows a linking verb such as *is*, *was*, *look*, or *seem*. Most adjectives answer the questions *What kind?*, *How many?*, *How much?*, or *Which one?* The words *a*, *an*, and *the* are special adjectives called **articles**.

Activity

Whose News? Select a few sentences from a newspaper article. Circle all the adjectives in the text and number them. Next, create a numbered list with the same number of blank entries as the number of adjectives in the news article. Have a family member write one adjective on each blank. Now read the news article aloud, inserting the new adjectives where the old adjectives were. What kind of story does the article tell now?

Practice Tested Spelling Words

______	______	______	______
______	______	______	______
______	______	______	______
______	______	______	______
______	______	______	______

Name ______________________

Graphic Sources

- **Graphic sources** include charts, tables, graphs, maps, illustrations, and photographs.
- Before you read, look closely at graphic sources that accompany a selection. They will give you an idea of what you will read.

Directions Study the illustration of the Hubble Telescope. Then answer the questions below.

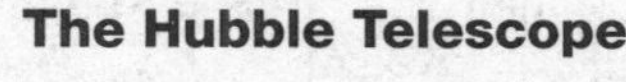

The Hubble Telescope

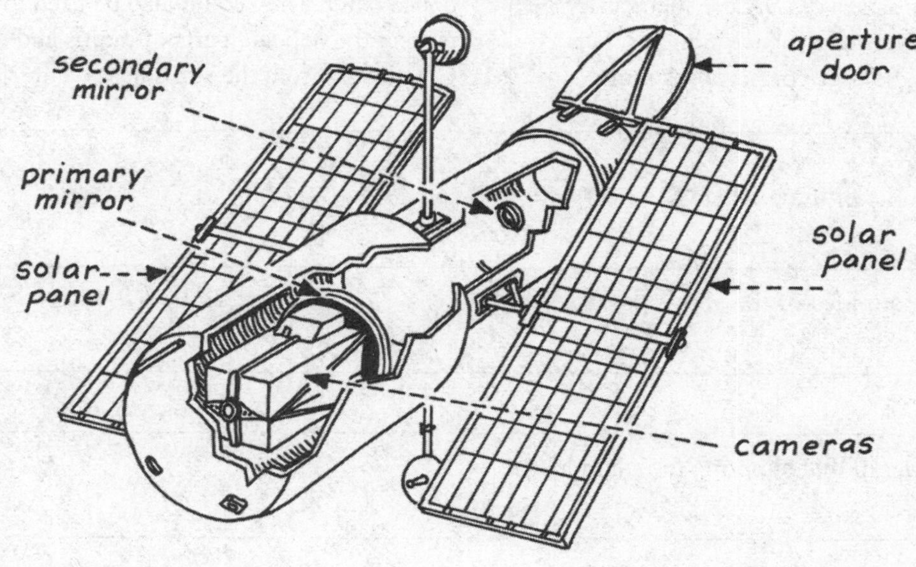

1. How many solar panels are there on the Hubble Telescope?

____

2. Why do you think the Hubble Telescope might need an extra solar panel?

____

____

3. Where are the two cameras located on the Hubble Telescope?

____

4. Can you tell how big the Hubble Telescope is? Why or why not?

____

5. An *aperture* is an opening or hole that lets light into the lens of a camera. Why do you think the Hubble has a door to cover the aperture?

____

____

Name ______________________________

Main Idea and Details

Directions Read the passage. Then answer the questions below.

NASA has developed many materials for astronauts that are later used in everyday products. A recent invention, thermoplastic polymers, are materials that become hard when cooled and soft when heated. Scientists at NASA use them as a protective covering on space vehicles, but they can also be used for purposes more common than space flight. Thermoplastics are designed to protect against the sun's ultraviolet rays, so they could have many uses. They could be used as a coating for outdoor statues, other art pieces, and house paint. They could also be used to protect the delicate parts of radios and CD players from the sun's heat.

1. What is the topic of the passage?

____

2. What is the main idea of the above passage?

____

____

3. What is one detail that supports the main idea?

____

____

4. What is another detail that supports the main idea?

____

____

5. Write a summary of the passage in one or two sentences.

____

____

____

Home Activity Your child read a short passage and identified its main idea and details. Read a newspaper or magazine article with your child and have him or her identify the main idea and details in the article.

Name ____

Adjectives and Articles

Directions Choose an adjective from the box to complete each sentence.

hollow	Greek	strange	deep-sea
several	five	4,500	

1. *Bathys* is a ______________ word meaning "deep," and a *sphere* is a globe or ball.
2. The bathysphere was the first ______________ machine that took people far beneath the waves.
3. This ______________ steel ball, which weighed ______________ pounds, was raised and lowered by a cable.
4. It was about ______________ feet in diameter and was fitted inside with oxygen tanks.
5. Divers reported news of the ______________ animals they saw via a telephone cable to a ship on the surface.
6. ______________ creatures had never been seen by humans before!

Directions Think about what you would like to see on a visit to the ocean floor. Write a sentence to answer each question below. Use adjectives and articles and underline them.

7. How far down would you travel?

____

____

8. What equipment would you take?

____

____

9. What would you look for?

____

____

10. What do you think it would look like?

____

____

Home Activity Your child learned how to write adjectives and articles correctly. Ask your child to write a paragraph describing what it is like to move under water. Have him or her circle adjectives and articles used.

Name ______________________________

Related Words

Spelling Words			
music	musician	select	selection
sign	signal	part	partial
haste	hasten	protect	protection
magic	magician	resign	resignation
electric	electrician	condemn	condemnation

Scrambled Words Unscramble the list words and write them on the line.

1. giciaanm **1.** ______________________

2. ngsial **2.** ______________________

3. orttepncio **3.** ______________________

4. ciisamnu **4.** ______________________

5. astnhe **5.** ______________________

6. gciam **6.** ______________________

7. treelicc **7.** ______________________

8. steah **8.** ______________________

9. repoctt **9.** ______________________

10. ings **10.** ______________________

11. triilaccnee **11.** ______________________

12. mondcen **12.** ______________________

Hidden Words Each of the smaller words can be found inside two of the list words. Write the list words that contain the smaller words.

elect **13.** ______________________ **14.** ______________________

sign **15.** ______________________ **16.** ______________________

art **17.** ______________________ **18.** ______________________

nation **19.** ______________________ **20.** ______________________

Home Activity Your child has unscrambled related words. Ask your child to scramble two list words and see if you can unscramble them.

Name ____

Graphic Sources

Directions Study the map. Then answer the questions below.

Columbus's First Voyage to the Americas

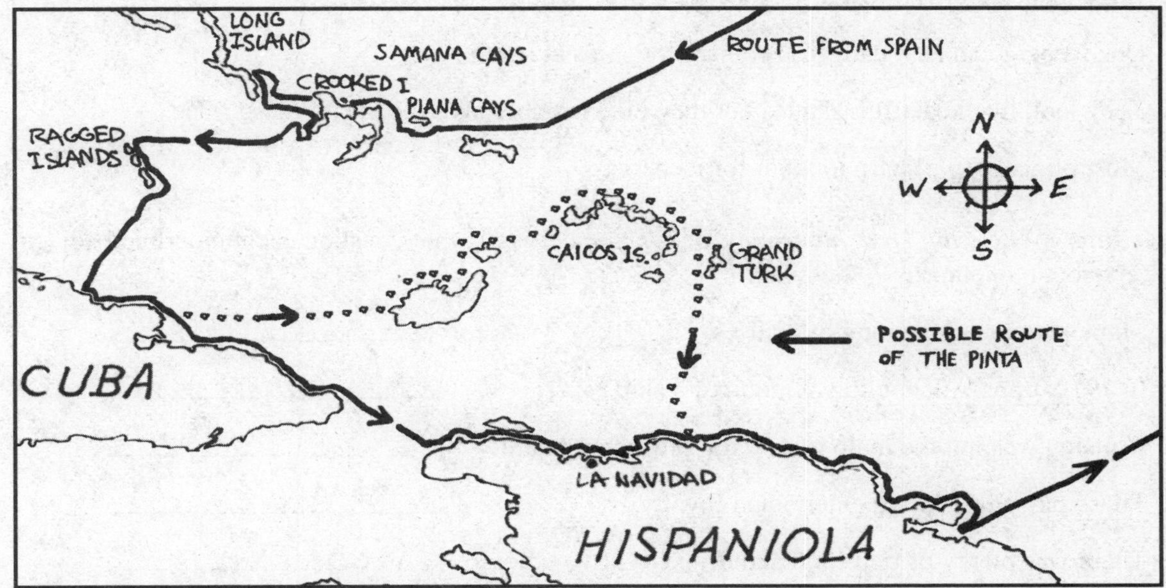

1. Where did Columbus land first, Ragged Islands or La Navidad?

____

2. What direction did Columbus travel after he reached the first island?

____

3. What was the name of the island Columbus departed from to return to Spain?

____

4. What do you think the arrow pointing off the right side of the map means?

____

5. What does the dotted line in the map represent?

____

____

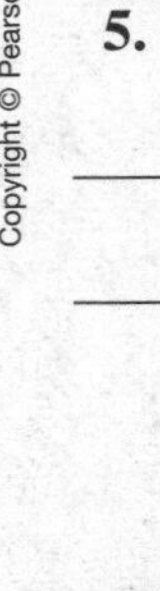

Home Activity Your child examined graphic sources and answered questions about them. Help your child draw a map of how your family gets from your house to a friend's house.

Name ____

Adjectives and Articles

Directions Underline the articles and circle the adjectives in each sentence.

1. Huge icebergs break off the vast ice near Greenland.
2. One iceberg can be a dangerous object for ships at sea.
3. They look like beautiful islands, but they hide treacherous ice beneath the surface.
4. Most pilots keep a sharp lookout for icebergs.

Directions Write *what kind, how many,* or *which one* to tell what question each underlined adjective answers about a noun.

5. Many people enjoy going on cruises. ____________________
6. In 1912, trans-Atlantic travel required a ship. ____________________
7. Cruising was not the main reason for getting on board. ____________________
8. Those passengers were entertained royally. ____________________
9. There was plenty of rich food and drink. ____________________

Directions Write *a, an,* or *the* in the blank to complete each sentence. Choose the article that makes sense and follows the rules for articles.

10. They dressed for dinner almost ________ hour before it was served.
11. Mrs. Astor was escorted to her table by ________ captain.
12. ________ elegant glass dome rose over the grand staircase.
13. Fine linen, china, and silver gleamed upon ________ tables.
14. This glamour would all be gone in ________ few short hours.
15. But for now, the room was ________ magical place.
16. It was ________ most special spot in the world.

School + Home **Home Activity** Your child reviewed adjectives and articles. With your child, read an encyclopedia article about the *Titanic*. Ask your child to point out adjectives and articles in at least one paragraph.

Name ______________________________

Greek Word Parts

- **Generalization** Many words are formed from the Greek word parts **-ology,** meaning "study of"; **phobia** meaning "fear of," **-ism** meaning "condition of being," and **-ist** meaning "person who."

Word Sort Sort the list words by their Greek word part.

-ology

1. ______________
2. ______________
3. ______________
4. ______________
5. ______________
6. ______________

phobia

7. ______________
8. ______________
9. ______________
10. ______________

-ism

11. ______________
12. ______________
13. ______________
14. ______________
15. ______________

-ist

16. ______________
17. ______________
18. ______________
19. ______________
20. ______________

Spelling Words

1. artist
2. tourism
3. biology
4. phobia
5. heroism
6. geology
7. cartoonist
8. technology
9. journalism
10. hydrophobia
11. violinist
12. ecology
13. patriotism
14. vocalist
15. meteorology
16. zoology
17. claustrophobia
18. capitalism
19. novelist
20. technophobia

Home Activity Your child is learning about four Greek word parts. Have your child explain what each Greek word part means.

Name

Family Times

Summary

Talk with an Astronaut

Answering questions submitted by students across the country, NASA astronaut Ellen Ochoa talks about her experiences, how she decided to be an astronaut, and what it's like to be weightless in space. Ochoa also gives her thoughts about being a mom and an astronaut, as well as the chances of making contact with other beings in space.

Activity

Press Box Pretend you're a reporter for your local paper and interview a family member. First, write down five questions you want to ask. Then ask the person the questions and write down their answers. Give your interview a title when you are finished.

Comprehension Skill

Author's Purpose

An **author's purpose** is the main reason an author writes a selection. An author may write to persuade, to inform, to entertain, or to express ideas and feelings. An author may write with more than one purpose. What the author says and details given help you figure out the author's purpose.

Activity

Why in the World? With members of your family, take turns making up three stories about space exploration and travel. The purpose for each story should be different. Discuss the words that are the same in each kind of story and the words that are different. Are the differences related to the different purposes?

Lesson Vocabulary

Words to Know

Knowing the meanings of these words is important to reading *Talk with an Astronaut.* Practice using these words.

Vocabulary Words

accomplishments things that have been done with knowledge, skill, or ability; achievements

focus the central point of attraction, attention, or activity

gravity the natural force that causes objects to move or tend to move toward the center of the Earth

monitors screens connected to a computer that show information and instructions

role a part played by a person in real life; *role model:* person whose patterns of behavior influence someone else's actions and beliefs

specific definite; precise; particular

Conventions

Demonstrative Pronouns: *This, That, These, and Those*

This, *that*, *these*, and *those* are **demonstrative pronouns.** They demonstrate the position of an object. *This* and *these* refer to things that are nearby. *That* and *those* refer to things that are at a distance. These pronouns have singular and plural forms. *This* and *that* are used to indicate single objects, and *these* and *those* indicate multiple objects.

Activity

Near and Far Take turns with a family member using demonstrative pronouns. One person names something around your home. Use both singular and plural nouns: *door, shoes, bananas, dog.* The other person then flips a coin. If the coin shows heads, the coin-flipper should describe the object as if it were nearby: *this door, these shoes.* If the coin shows tails, describe the object as if it were far away: *those bananas, that dog.*

Practice Tested Spelling Words

______	______	______	______
______	______	______	______
______	______	______	______
______	______	______	______
______	______	______	______

Name____

Author's Purpose

- An **author's purpose** is the reason or reasons an author has for writing.
- An author may write to persuade, to inform, to entertain, or to express ideas or feelings.
- Authors often have more than one reason for writing.

Directions Read the following passage. Then answer the questions below.

Sally Ride was the first American woman in space. But as a teenager, Ride was more interested in sports than space. She trained to be a tennis player from a very early age. She even dropped out of college to pursue a pro tennis career, but she soon left the pros and decided to return to college. She was studying astrophysics when she read that NASA was looking for new astronauts.

Ride was one of 8,000 people who applied. She began the training program in 1977. In 1983, she was aboard the space shuttle *Challenger,* becoming the first American woman in space. Over the next four years, she would log 343 hours of space travel. As a child Sally Ride might have had her eye on the ball, but as an adult, her head was in the clouds.

1. What is the author's main purpose for writing the above passage?

2. When she was a little girl, what did Sally Ride want to be when she grew up?

3. Based on the number of years it took for Ride to reach outer space from the time she began her astronaut training, do you think it is easy to become an astronaut? Why or why not?

4. Based on her hours of space flight, approximately how many days was Sally Ride in space?

5. If you needed to answer questions about Sally Ride, what fix-up strategies could you use to do so?

Home Activity Your child answered questions about an author's purpose and fix-up strategies. Have your child practice taking notes while reading an article about space.

Name____

Graphic Sources

Directions Study the diagram of the Space Shuttle and answer the questions below.

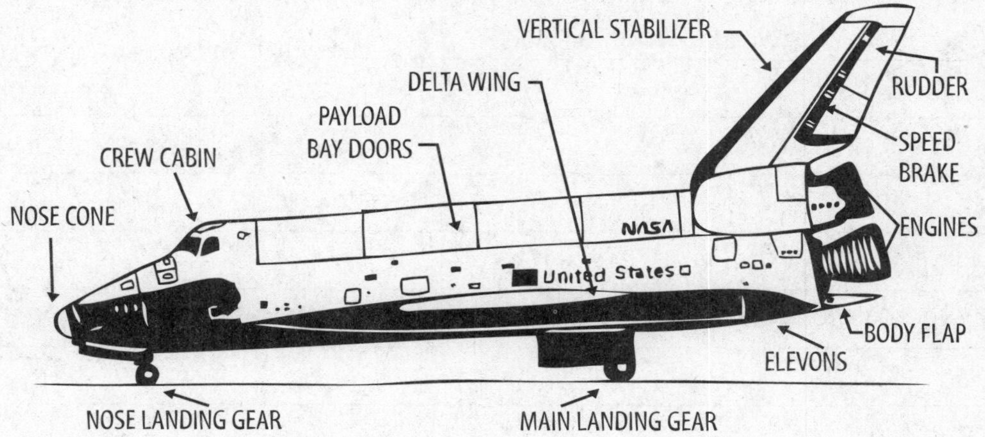

1. What does the Space Shuttle use to land when returning to Earth?

____

2. According to this diagram, what part of the Shuttle do you think is the *most* different from a non-military airplane?

____

____

3. Where is the large equipment stored for each mission?

____

4. How do you think the Shuttle is designed like an airplane?

____

____

5. Pretend you are an airplane pilot flying the Space Shuttle for the first time. On a separate sheet of paper, describe what you think would be different when landing the Shuttle compared to an airplane.

School + Home **Home Activity** Your child has answered questions about a graphic source. Find an owner's guide to a piece of equipment in the house (oven, microwave, car, radio) and look at the detailed diagram with your child.

Name ______________________________

This, That, These, and *Those*

Directions Think of an exciting new product that might come from the space program. Complete the following ad for this product. Use the adjectives *this, that, these,* or *those* and underline them.

These ______________________________ are what America has been waiting for!

____

____

____

____

____

____

______________________________ This ad has been brought to you by

____

Directions Think about an object that you treasure. Tell what makes it special. Use the adjectives *this*, *that*, *these*, and *those* correctly.

____

____

____

____

____

____

____

____

____

____

____

____

Home Activity Your child learned how to use *this, that, these,* and *those* in writing. Ask your child to write sentences about things near and far, using each of the four adjectives correctly.

Name ____

Greek Word Parts

Spelling Words				
artist	tourism	biology	phobia	heroism
geology	cartoonist	technology	journalism	hydrophobia
violinist	ecology	patriotism	vocalist	meteorology
zoology	claustrophobia	capitalism	novelist	technophobia

Double Puzzle Unscramble the list words. Write each letter on a line. Write the numbered letters below to solve the riddle.

What can everyone do to help the environment?

1. OOLEGGY ___ ___(11) ___ ___(17) ___ ___ ___
2. GLRTMEEOOOY ___ ___ ___ ___(13) ___ ___(7) ___ ___ ___ ___ ___
3. TOTOARNCIS ___(16) ___ ___(12) ___ ___ ___ ___ ___ ___ ___
4. COOLGEY ___(8) ___ ___ ___ ___ ___ ___(15)
5. SPROTHOABILCUA ___(14) ___ ___ ___(9) ___ ___ ___ ___ ___ ___ ___ ___ ___ ___
6. CEGHLNOOTY ___ ___(18) ___ ___ ___ ___ ___ ___ ___ ___
7. LISTEVON ___ ___ ___ ___(6) ___ ___ ___ ___
8. LISTAVOC ___ ___ ___(5) ___ ___ ___ ___ ___
9. OURNAILSMJ ___ ___ ___(4) ___ ___ ___ ___ ___ ___ ___
10. ROMESHI ___ ___(2) ___ ___ ___ ___(10) ___
11. HOBODRYHIAP ___ ___ ___(3) ___(1) ___ ___ ___ ___ ___ ___ ___

___(1) ___(2) ___(3) ___(4) ___(5) ___(6)   ___(7) ___(8) ___(9) ___(10) ___(11)   ___(12) ___(13) ___(14) ___(15) ___(16) ___(17) ___(18)

Connect the Words Draw a line from the word part to its Greek word part. Then write the word.

12. techno	ism	**12.** ____________________
13. zo	phobia	**13.** ____________________
14. violin	ology	**14.** ____________________
15. patriot	ist	**15.** ____________________

Home Activity Your child has learned to read, write, and spell words with Greek word parts. Have your child pick out the ten hardest words to review with you.

Name________________________________

Author's Purpose

- An **author's purpose** is the reason or reasons an author has for writing.
- An author may write to persuade, to inform, to entertain, or to express ideas or feelings.
- Authors often have more than one reason for writing.

Directions Read the following passage and fill in the diagram below.

Carl Allen was sure of one thing: if he was too young to fly to the Moon with the real astronauts, he would start training for it on his own. Carl set out a training schedule for himself. He ran around his yard a lot, he monitored the temperature everywhere in his house, and he practiced floating in the bathtub on his back, pretending to be weightless. Then Carl discovered a refrigerator box by a neighbor's trash. He started making it into his own space capsule. He had his mom help cut out a window and a small door, and he spent weeks drawing and pasting a control board inside the capsule. Even though he was still in his house, when Carl sat in his box with his football helmet on, it was like he was on the Moon!

AUTHOR'S PURPOSE	**1.** The author is writing to
DETAIL What did Carl make his space capsule from?	**2.**
DETAIL Name two things Carl did as part of his astronaut training.	**3.** Carl ran **4.** Carl monitored

5. Did the author meet his or her purpose successfully? Why do you feel this way?

____

____

Home Activity Your child answered questions about author's purpose in a fictional passage. Discuss the author's purpose in one of your child's favorite stories.

Name____

This, That, These, and *Those*

Directions Match each adjective with the phrase that describes it.

______ **1.** this	**A**	modifies plural nouns that are close by
______ **2.** that	**B**	modifies singular nouns that are close by
______ **3.** these	**C**	modifies singular nouns that are far away
______ **4.** those	**D**	modifies plural nouns that are far away

Directions Underline the word in ( ) that completes each sentence correctly.

5. (This, Those) summer I am going to space camp.

6. At (that, these) camp we will train like astronauts.

7. Astronauts must take many tests, and one of (them, those) tests involves gravity.

8. Gravity pulls us to Earth. (This, These) force becomes very great when we try to leave Earth's atmosphere.

9. Takeoff pushes the spacecraft into space. During (this, those) minutes, the body has to withstand strong G-forces.

10. In space the body floats because it is weightless. I want to imitate (this, these) experience at camp.

Directions Write the sentences correctly.

11. Ellen Ochoa invented an optical system. That there system "sees" flaws in a repeating pattern.

____

____

____

12. Ochoa holds three patents for inventions. Them inventions all involve optical systems or robotics.

____

____

____

Home Activity Your child reviewed *this, that, these,* and *those*. Have your child read an encyclopedia or Internet biography about Ellen Ochoa and then summarize it using *this, that, these,* and *those*.

Name ______________________________

Latin Roots

- **Generalization** Many words are formed with the Latin roots **spec** meaning "look," **scrib** or **scrip** meaning "write," **rupt** meaning "break," and **ject** meaning "throw."

Word Sort Sort the list words by their Latin root.

ject

1. ______________
2. ______________
3. ______________
4. ______________

spec

5. ______________
6. ______________
7. ______________
8. ______________
9. ______________

scrib or scrip

10. ______________
11. ______________
12. ______________
13. ______________
14. ______________
15. ______________

rupt

16. ______________
17. ______________
18. ______________
19. ______________
20. ______________

Spelling Words

1. describe
2. interruption
3. inspection
4. scribble
5. respectful
6. bankrupt
7. project
8. injection
9. manuscript
10. suspect
11. subscription
12. spectacular
13. eruption
14. eject
15. abruptly
16. prescribe
17. reject
18. aspect
19. rupture
20. inscribe

Home Activity Your child is learning about Latin roots. Have your child explain what each Latin root in this lesson means.

Name

Family Times

Summary

Journey to the Center of the Earth

In Jules Verne's classic tale of underground adventure, young Harry, his professor uncle, and their guide Hans encounter a raging battle between two multi-headed monsters. The monsters look like combinations of dinosaurs and mammals. The explorers watch in fear and amazement as they realize they are the first to see these incredible creatures.

Activity

What Could It Be? Imagine you are exploring the Earth's core. What kind of animals (or monsters) might you see there? With a family member, draw an imaginary monster and write a few sentences about the beast.

Comprehension Skill

Cause and Effect

A **cause** is what makes something happen. An **effect** is what happens. An effect may have one or more causes. Sometimes authors will use words like *because* and *so* to show cause and effect.

Activity

Why Oh Why? With a family member, recall an event that happened at home recently. Maybe something spilled, or you did a great job cleaning your room. The event itself is the effect. Now make a list of the causes that brought the event about.

Lesson Vocabulary

Words to Know

Knowing the meanings of these words is important to reading *Journey to the Center of the Earth.* Practice using these words.

Vocabulary Words

armor any kind of protective covering
encases covers completely; encloses
extinct no longer existing
hideous very ugly; frightful; horrible
plunged fell or moved suddenly downward or forward
serpent snake, especially a big snake

Conventions

Comparative and Superlative Adjectives

A **comparative adjective** is used to compare two people, places, things, or groups. Add *–er* to most adjectives to make them comparative. *For example: Ben is faster than Ellen.* A **superlative adjective** is used to compare three or more people, places, things, or groups. Add *–est* to most adjectives to make them superlative. *For example: Alice is the fastest sprinter on the team.* Remember that there is no need to combine the word *more* with comparative or superlative adjectives in your writing.

Activity

Better-Best With a family member, write out five statements about people you know—family, friends, teachers, etc. —that use adjectives. *For example: My sister is loud. Uncle Steve is funny.* Then go back and make all of the adjectives comparative. After that, change them all to superlative adjectives.

Practice Tested Spelling Words

____	____	____	____
____	____	____	____
____	____	____	____
____	____	____	____
____	____	____	____

Name ___________________________

Cause and Effect

- A **cause** (what makes something happen) may have several effects. An **effect** (what happens as a result of a cause) may have several causes.
- Sometimes clue words such as *since, as a result, caused, thus, therefore,* and *consequently* are used to show cause-and-effect relationships.

Directions Read the following passage. Then answer the questions below.

Why are people so fascinated with dinosaurs? Young and old alike, people are interested in the great beasts that once roamed this planet. Museums have been built to showcase what dinosaurs might have looked like, thousands of books have been written on the subject, and many television shows and movies have been made about them.

Are we fascinated by dinosaurs because they are so strange and unlike any animal we know? Is it because many of them were so huge? Maybe it's because some dinosaurs seem scary, and some people find it thrilling to be scared. Some scientists have made their life's work studying dinosaurs, and maybe that same curiosity is at the heart of all dinosaur fans.

1. What are two causes for people to be fascinated with dinosaurs?

____

2. What are two effects of people's fascination with dinosaurs?

____

3. Using your own experience, what might be the most important reason we like dinosaurs?

____

4. Why do you think older people and young people are interested in dinosaurs?

____

____

5. Write a summary of this passage in one or two sentences.

____

____

____

Home Activity Your child read a short passage and answered questions about causes and effects. With your child, discuss the reasons you think dinosaurs are fascinating. Ask your child to summarize your thoughts on dinosaurs.

Name ____________________

Author's Purpose

Directions Read the following passage. Then answer the questions below.

In 1912, a German scientist named Alfred Wegener suggested a theory to explain why the Earth's continents came to be in the places they are today. According to Wegener's theory, a large landmass he called Pangaea covered more than half the planet. It drifted apart slowly over many millions of years. One example he uses as evidence is that the west coast of Africa appears to fit exactly into the east coast of South America. Another example he uses is that the coasts of both countries share many similar fossils of plants and animals, suggesting they were once joined together.

1. What is the author's purpose for writing this passage?

2. How do you know that this is the author's purpose?

3. How did the author's purpose affect your reading rate?

4. Why might Africa and South America have been joined together at one point in time?

5. Write a sentence or two to persuade people to take a vacation on Pangaea.

Home Activity Your child read a short passage and has answered questions about the author's purpose. Together read an article from the travel section of the newspaper or from a travel book. Ask your child to identify the author's purpose for the article.

Name ______________________________

Comparative and Superlative Adjectives

Directions Write a comparative or superlative form of the adjective in ( ) to make each sentence precise.

1. I think Jules Verne was a ______________________ writer than Philip K. Dick. (inventive)
2. From childhood, he had been ______________________ of all when observing how things worked. (happy)
3. He always researched the very ______________________ scientific ideas. (new)
4. I like his books ______________________ than those of Charles Dickens. (good)
5. Verne included the ______________________ details possible in his novels. (realistic)
6. The submarine, motorcar, and navigable airship are just three inventions he anticipated from a ______________________ age. (late)

Directions Write a paragraph to persuade a classmate to read one of your favorite books. Include comparative and superlative adjectives.

____

____

____

____

____

____

____

____

____

____

____

____

Home Activity Your child learned how to use comparative and superlative adjectives in writing. Ask your child to compare two of his or her favorite book characters using comparative and superlative adjectives.

Name ______________________________________

Latin Roots

Spelling Words				
describe	interruption	inspection	scribble	respectful
bankrupt	project	injection	manuscript	suspect
subscription	spectacular	eruption	eject	abruptly
prescribe	reject	aspect	rupture	inscribe

Alphabetize Put the list words in the box below in alphabetical order.

describe	interruption	respectful	bankrupt	project
injection	suspect	subscription	eject	prescribe

1. ____________ 2. ____________ 3. ____________

4. ____________ 5. ____________ 6. ____________

7. ____________ 8. ____________

9. ____________ 10. ____________

Crossword Puzzle Use the clues to find the list words. Write each letter in a box.

Across

1. distinct feature or element
3. burst, split, or break
8. organized or official examination
9. refuse to accept
10. dramatic, sensational in appearance

Down

2. sudden violent outbreak
4. quickly and without warning
5. scratch or cut into a material
6. write carelessly
7. handwritten book or document

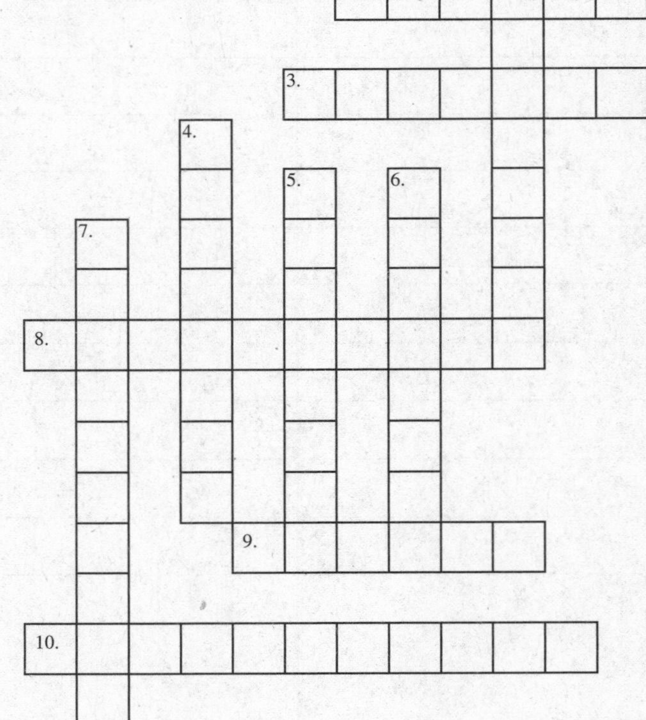

Home Activity Your child has learned to read, write, and spell words with Latin roots. Challenge your child to think of other words that use these Latin roots.

Name ______________________________

Cause and Effect

- A **cause** (what makes something happen) may have several effects. An **effect** (what happens as a result of a cause) may have several causes.
- Sometimes clue words such as *since, as a result, caused, thus, therefore,* and *consequently* are used to show cause-and-effect relationships.

Directions Read the following passage. Then complete the diagram below.

A good way to understand how a volcano erupts is by shaking a bottle of soda. The shaking causes pressure to build up inside the bottle. When you open the bottle—splat! The soda bursts out of the top.

Volcanoes work in a similar way. The Earth's magma, which is a thick liquid between the crust and the fiery core of the Earth, is like the soda pop. When the tectonic plates that sit below the continents shift and move, it's like shaking up the soda bottle. After enough pressure builds up, the magma rises to the Earth's surface, eventually causing volcanoes to erupt.

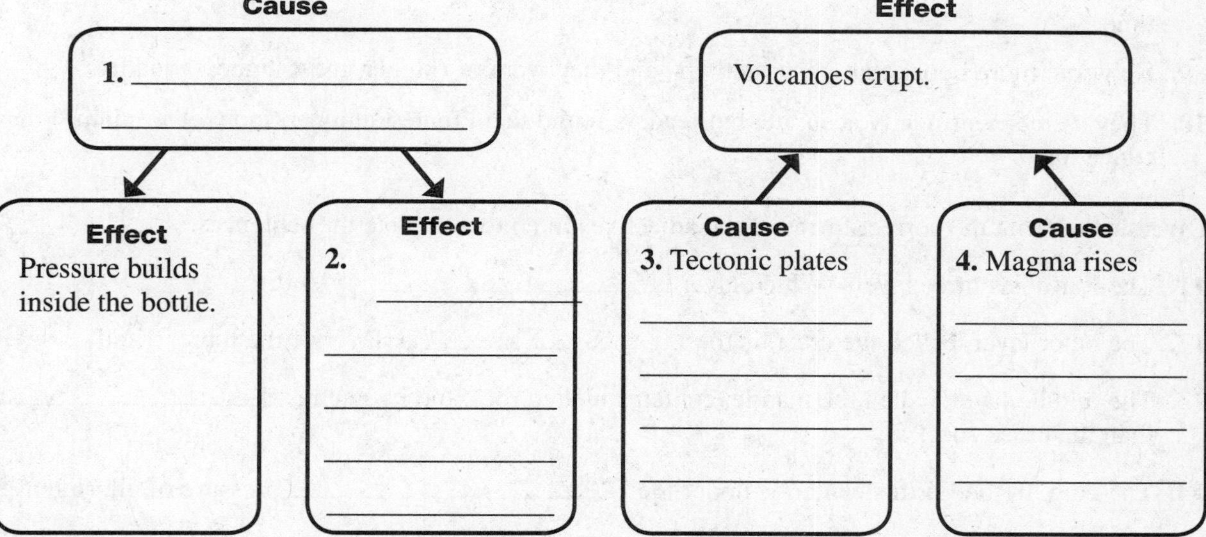

5. Write a summary of this passage in one or two sentences.

____

____

Home Activity Your child read a short passage and identified causes and effects. Based on one of your child's favorite movies, discuss the causes and effects.

Name ______________________________

Comparative and Superlative Adjectives

Directions If the adjective forms are correct, write *Correct* on the line. If they are not correct, write the comparative and superlative forms correctly on the line.

	Adjective	Comparative	Superlative	
1.	happy	more happier	most happiest	____________
2.	hungry	hungrier	hungriest	____________
3.	beloved	beloveder	belovedest	____________
4.	sad	more sadder	most saddest	____________

Directions Underline the adjective form in ( ) to complete each sentence correctly.

5. Jules Verne was (most unhappy, most unhappiest) as a stockbroker.

6. He was (happier, more happier) writing plays.

7. However, he was a much (more better, better) novelist than a playwright.

8. He left business and went on to become the (more successful, most successful) writer of his time.

9. He wrote more books than other authors, and they were of (higher, most highest) quality.

10. They were scientifically accurate, but readers found them (entertaininger, more entertaining) than educational.

Directions Write the correct forms of the adjectives in ( ) to complete the sentences.

11. The Earth has three layers. Which layer is ______________? (thin)

12. The outer layer, called the crust, is the ______________ layer of the three. (rigid)

13. The middle layer, called the mantle, contains melted rock and is much ______________ than the crust. (hot)

14. The core, in the Earth's center, is under the ______________ pressure of all. (intense)

15. Jules Verne's idea for a journey to the core is ______________ than realistic. (fantastic)

Home Activity Your child reviewed comparative and superlative adjectives. Reread the selection with your child. Have him or her describe the fighting monsters using comparative and superlative adjectives.

Name ______________________________

Greek Word Parts

- **Generalization** Many words are formed from the Greek word parts **tele** meaning "over a long distance," **photo** meaning "light," **meter** meaning "measure," and **graph** meaning "write."

Word Sort Sort the list words by their Greek word part.

tele

1. ______________
2. ______________
3. ______________
4. ______________

photo

5. ______________
6. ______________

meter

7. ______________
8. ______________
9. ______________
10. ______________
11. ______________
12. ______________
13. ______________
14. ______________

graph

15. ______________
16. ______________
17. ______________
18. ______________

tele and **photo**

19. ______________

tele and **graph**

20. ______________

Spelling Words

1. telephone
2. graphic
3. thermometer
4. photographer
5. centimeter
6. paragraph
7. telescope
8. diameter
9. photocopy
10. speedometer
11. telegraph
12. millimeter
13. autograph
14. television
15. barometer
16. telecommute
17. pedometer
18. phonograph
19. kilometer
20. telephoto

Home Activity Your child is learning about Greek word parts. Have your child explain what each Greek word part in this lesson means.

Name ______________________________

Family Times

Summary

Ghost Towns of the American West

In the mid-1800s, large numbers of Americans headed west in search of land and riches. The result was many small towns being built seemingly overnight. These same towns were deserted when the promised wealth didn't materialize. To this day, you can see ghost-like remnants of these small, temporary towns.

Activity

Uncover Your History Take a look through the closets or storage areas at your house for "ghost toys" you once played with all the time but now don't think about. Pull one out and with a family member write a short description about the "olden days" when you used to play with the toy.

Comprehension Skill

Generalize

To **generalize** means to make a broad statement or rule that applies to several examples. Clue words such as *all*, *many*, and *most* can signal that an author is making a generalization. If these generalizations are supported by the text, they are *valid*. If not, they are *faulty generalizations*.

Activity

Nose for News With a family member, read an article from a newspaper or current events magazine. As you read, look for instances where the author uses generaliza-tions. When you find a generalization, examine the text to see if it is valid or faulty.

Lesson Vocabulary

Words to Know

Knowing the meanings of these words is important to reading *Ghost Towns of the American West.* Practice using these words.

Vocabulary Words

economic of or about the management of the income, supplies, and expenses of a household, government, etc.

independence freedom from the control, influence, support, or help of others

overrun to spread over

scrawled written or drawn poorly or carelessly

vacant not occupied

Conventions

Adverbs

An **adverb** tells how, when, or where something happens. It can describe a verb, an adjective, or another adverb. Many adverbs that tell how end in *-ly*. You can change adjectives to adverbs by adding *–ly*. A **comparative adverb** compares two people, places, things, or groups. Add *–er* to most adverbs to make them comparative. *For example: longer, faster*. A **superlative adverb** is used to compare three or more people, places, things, or groups. Add *–est* to most adverbs to make them superlative. *For example: longest, fastest*.

Activity

Mix 'n' Match With a family member, cut up some squares of paper and write down a variety of adjectives (e.g., *quiet, cool, dark, slow*). Put the squares in a hat or cup, and then take turns picking out squares one at a time. With each square, create an adverb and write it on a sheet of paper. It can be a simple adverb (adding *–ly*) or a comparative or superlative adverb.

Practice Tested Spelling Words

______	______	______	______
______	______	______	______
______	______	______	______
______	______	______	______
______	______	______	______

Name ____________________

Generalize

- To **generalize** means to make a broad statement or rule that applies to several examples. Clue words such as *all, many,* and *most* can signal generalizations.
- If generalizations are supported by the text, they are *valid generalizations.* If they are not supported by the text or by logic, they are *faulty generalizations.*

Directions Read the following passage. Then answer the questions that follow.

Railroads first appeared in the United States in the 1820s. During the next few decades, more and more track was laid, connecting towns and cities in different regions of the country. Railroads began to change the way Americans traveled, worked, did business, and settled.

During the mid-1800s, many people chose to settle in areas west of the Mississippi River served by railroads. In the 1850s and 1860s, railroad lines appeared in Missouri, Arkansas, Texas, and California. Towns that stood near railroad lines prospered. On the other hand, communities that were distant from railroads lost business and population. All in all, railroads were one of the most important factors in the growth and settlement of the American West.

1. What would be a generalization about railroads you could make based upon the text above?

____

____

2. What is one thing in the text that supports your generalization?

____

____

3. What is another thing in the text that supports your generalization?

____

4. What is the word *most* used to describe in the passage?

____

5. Imagine you are a shopkeeper in a western town in the 1850s. On a separate sheet of paper, write a letter to a new railroad company, encouraging them to extend the railroad to your town.

____

____

Home Activity Your child identified a generalization in a nonfiction text and found evidence to support it. Make a generalization about something in your family, such as "Dad is always spilling something on his tie," and work with your child to determine whether the generalization is valid or not.

Name____

Graphic Sources

Directions Study the map of America in 1810. Then answer the questions below.

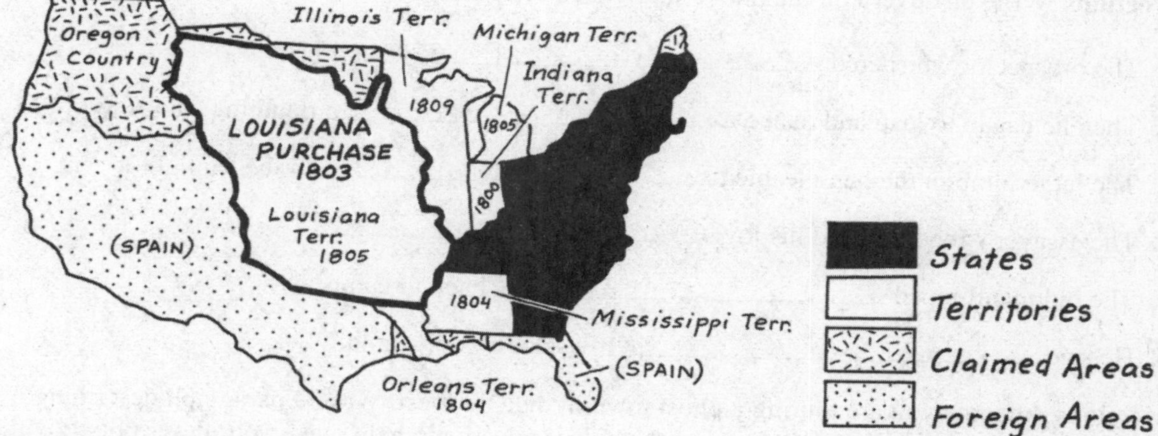

1. What is the purpose of this map?

____

____

2. How many territories belonged to the United States in 1810? What are they?

____

____

3. According to the map, what are the two largest areas that are not states?

____

4. What shading pattern represents the area controlled by foreign countries?

____

5. Imagine that it is 1810 and that you are President Monroe. On a separate sheet of paper, identify which region shown on this map concerns you the most, and tell why it worries you.

____

____

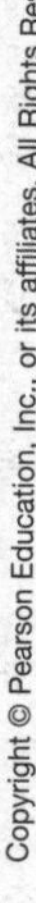

Home Activity Your child has answered questions about a graphic source. Look at a book or newspaper that has a map or chart accompanying some text. Discuss the information in the graphic with your child. Then read the article or passage and discuss with him or her how the graphic aids understanding.

Name ____________________

Adverbs

Directions Write an adverb on the line to make each sentence more lively and colorful.

1. The prospector whispered ____________________, "Can it be?"
2. Then he began to leap and dance ____________________ around the campsite.
3. The large lump in the pan gleamed ____________________ in the sunlight.
4. The assayer's report erased his joy ____________________.
5. The old man limped ____________________ back to camp.
6. He said ____________________, "It was only fool's gold."

Directions Imagine you are touring a ghost town in the Old West. Write a paragraph describing how the town looks and what is happening there. Use adverbs to help make your description vivid and colorful.

Home Activity Your child learned how to use adverbs in writing. With your child, make up a story about a cowboy's trip to town. Encourage your child to include adverbs to make actions vivid and precise.

Name ____________________

Greek Word Parts

Spelling Words				
telephone	graphic	thermometer	photographer	centimeter
paragraph	telescope	diameter	photocopy	speedometer
telegraph	millimeter	autograph	television	barometer
telecommute	pedometer	phonograph	kilometer	telephoto

Double Puzzle Unscramble the list words. Write each letter on a line. Write the numbered letters below to answer the question.

Who were two great Greek teachers?

1. GREEPLATH ___ ___ ___ ___ ___ ___ ___ ___ ___
2. SCEEPTOLE ___ ___ ___ ___ ___(8) ___(3) ___ ___ ___
3. RAIDMEET ___ ___ ___(11) ___ ___ ___ ___ ___
4. METMETECOUL ___(6) ___ ___(10) ___ ___ ___ ___ ___ ___ ___ ___
5. TIELIESNOV ___ ___ ___ ___ ___ ___ ___(8) ___ ___ ___
6. CHOOTPOPY ___ ___ ___(13) ___ ___(2) ___ ___ ___ ___
7. TOAPRAUGH ___(5) ___ ___ ___ ___ ___ ___ ___(9) ___
8. CPHRGAI ___ ___(4) ___ ___ ___ ___ ___
9. MEETSDEEPOR ___(1) ___ ___ ___ ___ ___ ___ ___ ___ ___ ___
10. HOPHOPGRATER ___ ___ ___ ___(12) ___ ___ ___ ___ ___ ___ ___(7) ___

___(1) ___(2) ___(3) ___(4) ___(5) ___(6) ___(7) ___(8), ___(9) ___(10) ___(11) ___(12) ___(13)

Connect the Words Draw a line from the word part to the Greek ending. Then write the word.

11. kilo
12. tele
13. baro
14. phono
15. para
16. centi

graph

meter

11. ____________________
12. ____________________
13. ____________________
14. ____________________
15. ____________________
16. ____________________

Home Activity Your child has learned to read, write, and spell words with Greek word parts. Have your child select the ten hardest words to review with you.

Name ____________________

Generalize

- To **generalize** means to make a broad statement or rule that applies to several examples. Clue words such as *all, many,* and *most* can signal generalizations.
- If generalizations are supported by the text, they are *valid generalizations.* If they are not supported by the text or by logic, they are *faulty generalizations.*

Directions Read the following passage. Complete the diagram by writing a generalization and two ideas that support the generalization. Then answer the questions below.

In the past, many people who left their homes and moved to a new land were following some kind of dream. Often settlers' dreams involved getting rich. For example, in the 1800s thousands of people traveled to the American West to find gold. Other people wanted to find a better life for themselves. For some settlers, this meant owning more land. For others, a better life meant finding a job that made their lives easier or more secure. Still other people moved to a different part of the world to simply seek a change and start a new kind of life.

Generalization

1. In the past, many people moved to a new land to ____________________

Support from Text

2. Often settlers' dreams involved ____________________

Support from Text

3. Other people wished to ____________________

Support from Text

Some people moved to follow their dream of a fresh start in their lives.

4. What word in the answer to question 1 suggests that the statement is a generalization?

____

5. Based on the evidence in the text, is the author's generalization *valid* or *faulty*? Why?

____

____

Home Activity Your child identified a generalization in a nonfiction text and found information in the text to support the generalization. Find a magazine article that includes generalizations, and work with your child to find examples and details in the text that support those generalizations.

Name________________________________

Adverbs

Directions Write the comparative and superlative forms of each adverb.

Adverb	Comparative Adverb	Superlative Adverb
fast	1. ________	2. ________
hard	3. ________	4. ________
eagerly	5. ________	6. ________
badly	7. ________	8. ________

Directions Underline the adverb in each sentence. Circle the word or words that each adverb tells more about.

9. The man looked extremely nervous.
10. He waited impatiently for the stage.
11. It seemed as though it would never arrive.
12. Finally, he heard a storm of hooves.
13. The dusty stage rolled westward toward town.
14. The man greeted his bride warmly.

Directions Underline the correct adverb in ( ) to complete each sentence.

15. California was settled (sooner, more sooner) than many Western states.
16. The promise of gold (first, firstly) drew miners and settlers.
17. Good climate and fertile land held them there (more successfully, most successfully) though.
18. Nevada treated its settlers (harshlier, more harshly) than California.
19. When the silver ran out, miners (quickly, most quickly) left Nevada's hot, dry territory.

School + Home **Home Activity** Your child reviewed adverbs. Have your child clip adjectives from magazine advertisements, change them into adverbs, write the comparative and superlative form of each adverb, and use both forms in sentences.

Name

Family Times

Selection Summaries

Week 1 *The Skunk Ladder*

Two friends dig a marvelous hole, and then discover they have an unwelcome visitor.

Week 2 *The Unsinkable Wreck of the R.M.S.* Titanic

Seventy-four years after the *Titanic*'s tragic collision with an iceberg, two explorers viewed the wreck from a mini-submarine.

Week 3 *Talk with an Astronaut*

NASA astronaut Ellen Ochoa answers questions from students around the country.

Week 4 *Journey to the Center of the Earth*

In an excerpt from a classic novel, Harry and his uncle witness a titanic battle underground between two fearsome creatures.

Week 5 *Ghost Towns of the American West*

Searching for land and riches, people headed west and built towns. When the expected windfall didn't come, they abandoned the towns, which became ghost towns.

Activity

Think about the different ways the selections told their stories. Share your thoughts with a family member. Tell which selection was your favorite, and why.

Comprehension Skills Review

In Unit 5 you learned and used many skills while reading the stories and selections.

- **Plot** is what happens in a story. **Characters** are the people who experience the events.
- A **graphic source** is a picture, table, chart, diagram, time line, or map that shows or explains something in the text.
- The **author's purpose** is the reason the author writes the story.
- A **cause** is why something happens, and an **effect** is what happens.
- To **generalize** is to make a broad statement that applies to several examples.

Activity

Adventures can be found in faraway places or right down the street. Write about a time you had an adventure.

Unit Vocabulary Skills

Greek and Latin Roots

Many English words come from Latin and Greek. Use a dictionary to find out more about **Greek and Latin roots.**

Activity As you read, make a list of Greek and Latin roots you find.

Unfamiliar Words

With an **unfamiliar word**, use context clues and then use the dictionary.

Activity Look for unfamiliar words. Check their meanings in the dictionary. Then create a list of new words and write several sentences using them.

Multiple-Meaning Words

When you come across a **multiple-meaning word**, look the word up in the dictionary or a glossary.

Activity Write two sentences using a multiple-meaning word. The word should have a different meaning in each sentence.

Unknown Words

When you encounter an **unknown word,** use your dictionary or glossary to find the definition.

Activity Look for unknown words. Find their definitions in the dictionary or glossary. Keep a list of your new words as you learn them.

Prefixes

A **prefix** is attached to the beginning of a word to create a new word. Check the meanings of prefixes in the dictionary.

Activity Look up the prefix *over-*. List ten words that begin with it.

Unit Spelling Rules

Multisyllabic Words

When spelling words with many syllables, look carefully at each word part. Often, whether a syllable is stressed or not determines how it is spelled.

Related Words

Related words often have parts that are spelled the same but are pronounced differently: *major*, *majority*. When you say these words, pay close attention to where the stress is placed.

Greek Word Parts

Many English words are formed from Greek word parts. Sometimes the Greek word parts are spelled differently when forming an English word.

Latin Roots

Latin roots show up in many English words—for example, *ject*, meaning "throw," and *aud*, meaning "hear." Not all words that have these letters in them, however, are using the Latin roots. For example, you can see the root *aud* in words like *inaudible*, *audience*, and *auditorium*. However, *gaudy*, meaning "bright or showy," contains *aud* but has nothing to do with hearing.

Name ______________________________

Greek and Latin Roots

- Many words in English have their roots in the older languages Greek and Latin. Look at the roots below to review their meanings.

ex ("out of")	+	cave ("hollow")	+	ation ("act or process of")	=	excavation ("the act of digging up something")

Practice Read the following sentences. Fill in the blanks using the Words to Know. Then circle the letter of the correct definition for each underlined word. Use what you know about word roots to help you. A dictionary can also help if you get stuck.

Words to Know

- abandoned
- attempt
- bellow
- cavern
- feat
- immensely
- savage

1. The crowd pounded their feet with anticipation as the proud explorer, Carl Weisner, began his ______________ to reach the depths of the ______________.

a. to stop anticipating or looking forward to
b. the act or process of anticipating

2. Weisner felt ______________ confident about heading down into the cavernous space, although the ______________ was not easy and other experts had failed.

a. small and full
b. large and hollow

3. Just as the explorer found his first foothold, a ______________ yell erupted from deep within the fissure. It was a terrifying ______________, like the painful roar of someone getting a cavity painfully filled at the dentist!

a. the hard outside part of a tooth
b. a hole or hollow space in a tooth

4. Automatically, everyone thought the attempt would be ______________, but Weisner insisted on continuing down—so the exploration went on.

a. the act or process of exploring
b. being in danger while exploring

On Your Own As you read "On the Hunt," watch out for words that have Greek or Latin roots. Check your ideas against the dictionary.

Home Activity Your child studied Greek and Latin roots. Ask your child to show you how to look for clues to roots in the words.

Name ______________________

Character and Plot

- A **character** is a person or an animal that takes part in the events of a story. The **plot** is what happens in a story.
- The **plot** is the sequence of events in a selection. The plot starts with a *problem* or *conflict*, continues with *rising action* as the conflict builds, and reaches a *climax* when the problem or conflict is faced. The plot ends with a *resolution* or *outcome*.

Practice Read the story. Answer the questions below.

Problem		Rising action		Climax		Resolution
Carl Weisner was beginning to explore a cave live on TV when a huge roar came out of the cavern.	→	The terrible roar frightened everyone except the explorer. They begged him not to go down into the dark cave.	→	He continued his descent into the cavern.	→	The explorer discovered a rival explorer in the cave who pretended to be a monster.

1. Who is Carl Weisner?

____

2. What is Weisner's problem?

____

____

3. What is the climax of the story?

____

____

4. What is the resolution?

____

____

On Your Own Use what you know about character and plot as you read "On the Hunt."

Home Activity Your child reviewed character and plot. Retell one of your favorite books or movies. Discuss who the characters are. Have your child explain the problem, rising action, climax, and resolution of the book or movie.

Name ______________________________

Unknown Words

- When you come across an **unknown word,** use a dictionary or glossary to find its meaning. Dictionaries and glossaries list the words in alphabetical order.

Practice Fill the blanks with the Words to Know. Then choose the definition that best matches the underlined word and circle its letter. Use a dictionary to check your work.

Words to Know

- **cramped**
- **debris**
- **interior**
- **ooze**
- **robotic**
- **sediment**
- **sonar**

1. Dr. Taylor decided to get a <u>specimen</u> of ocean-floor ______________ to complete her research.

a. example　　b. mark

2. Unfortunately, she found the ______________ of the submarine ______________ and began to feel <u>claustrophobic</u>.

a. comfortable to be in a small space　　b. afraid of confined spaces

3. The situation <u>necessitated</u> the use of the sub's ______________ arm to gather the slimy ______________.

a. required　　b. tried

4. Although <u>gratified</u> by the success, she was saddened by the large, under-water ______________ field that the ship's ______________ was tracking.

a. surprised　　b. pleased

On Your Own As you read "Diamond Discoveries," look up the meanings of unknown words in the dictionary. Make a list of new words as you learn them.

School + Home **Home Activity** Your child has reviewed using the dictionary to determine the meanings of unknown words. Together, practice using a print or online dictionary to find new and unusual words.

Name ______________________________

Graphic Sources

- A **graphic source** shows or explains information in the text. Pictures, tables, charts, diagrams, time lines, and maps are all graphic sources.

New Public Buildings Since 1990		
City (Town)	**Total**	**Last Built**
Apogee	7	2005 (library) 2005 (school)
Bonaventure	3	2001 (courthouse)
Hampton	3	2008 (municipal building)
Fishbeim	4	2007 (library)
Karzwell	8	2006 (school) 2006 (park district)

Practice Use the chart to answer the following questions. Circle the letter of the answer you choose.

1. Which city built a new courthouse in 2001?
a. Apogee b. Bonaventure c. Fishbeim

2. The newest school was built in which year?
a. 2004 b. 2005 c. 2006

3. How many public buildings have been built in Fishbeim since 1990?
a. 3 b. 4 c. 7

4. What type of building did Hampton build in 2008?
a. library b. municipal building c. courthouse

5. Which city has the newest library?
a. Fishbeim b. Apogee c. Karzwell

On Your Own Use what you know about graphic sources as you read "Diamond Discoveries." Make a diagram showing the route Fipke takes on his search.

Home Activity Your child reviewed using graphic sources to obtain information. Together, look through a news magazine and talk about what the graphic sources tell you.

Name ______________________________

Multiple-Meaning Words

- A **multiple-meaning word** is a word that has several different meanings. To determine which meaning an author is using in a text use **context clues**. You can also check the word in the dictionary.

Practice Fill in the blanks with Words to Know. Then choose the correct meaning of the underlined multiple-meaning word. Use a dictionary to help you.

Words to Know

accomplishments
focus
gravity
monitors
role
specific

1. Jamal managed some real ______________________ this year.
   a. controlled the use of   b. succeeded in reaching

2. His ______________________ was to improve his scores in math and science.
   a. grades in school   b. musical compositions

3. Even the television ______________________ at home and in the community center did not distract him from his goal.
   a. the finish line in a race   b. something that is desired

4. Now a ______________________ model for younger students, Jamal said that he is working toward his dream of experiencing zero ______________________ as an astronaut in space.
   a. an area of ground of a certain size   b. the area beyond Earth's atmosphere

On Your Own As you read "Diamond Discoveries," look for multiple-meaning words and use the dictionary to find their meanings. Use the new words in sentences.

School + Home **Home Activity** Your child reviewed multiple-meaning words. Together, read a newspaper article and look up any multiple-meaning words in a print or online dictionary.

Name ____________________

Author's Purpose

- The **author's purpose** is the reason the author writes a story. Authors can write to inform, persuade, entertain, and express themselves.

Local student is a fine example to others

Jamal Williams, a student at Centerville Middle School, is an outstanding example of how hard work leads to success. Once a D student, Jamal recently earned all As in his classes. Was this remarkable accomplishment due to some educational video? No, says the young man, it was just deciding he wanted to do better and figuring out how to reach that goal….

Practice Read the article and answer the questions below.

1. Why was the article about Jamal written?

____

____

2. What does the article's author think of Jamal?

____

____

3. Which words helped you identify how the author felt?

____

4. What was Jamal's 'remarkable accomplishment'?

____

On Your Own Use what you know about author's purpose as you read "Diamond Discoveries." Write about the author's purpose in this passage. Did the author succeed?

School + Home

Home Activity Your child reviewed author's purpose. Read several articles in a magazine and discuss the different purposes of the writers.

Name ______________________________

Unfamiliar Words

- As you read, you will come across **unfamiliar words**. Use context clues to help you determine the meanings of these words.

Practice Read the following passage. Fill in the blanks with the correct words from the Words to Know list.

Words to Know

armor
encases
extinct
hideous
plunged
serpent

Kerry and Ricki will spend a day in the museum. They love to look at the glass display that ________________ ancient weapons and shining ________________ once worn by knights. Some of the battle weapons are________________, such as a mace, a spiky iron ball on a club. Others, such as their favorite golden sword, is decorated with a ruby-eyed ________________ crawling up the shaft. These weapons were ________________ into wild beasts that are now ________________, or never existed in the first place!

On Your Own On a separate sheet of paper, write your own sentences using the words from the Words to Know list.

School + Home **Home Activity** Your child reviewed unfamiliar words. As you read a story with your child, ask him or her to figure out the meaning of unfamiliar words using context clues. Then have your child check the definition in a dictionary.

Name ______________________

Cause and Effect

- A **cause** is why something happens, and an **effect** is what happens. Sometimes an effect may have more than one cause, and a cause may have more than one effect.

Practice Read the story and then answer the questions below.

Last Thursday, Hector woke up late. He was supposed to get up at 6:45 but didn't get out of bed until 7:15. Because he left his house late, Hector missed the school bus. As a result, Hector's father had to drive him to school. When he arrived at school, class had already started. Hector's teacher looked up from writing on the board and asked, "Did you oversleep again, Hector?"

1. What caused Hector to miss the bus?

____

2. Why did Hector get a ride from his father to school?

____

____

3. What is a possible cause of why Hector woke up late?

____

____

4. In this example, were there multiple causes, multiple effects or both?

____

____

5. What is another possible effect of Hector waking up late?

____

____

On Your Own Use what you know about cause and effect as you read "On the Hunt." Make a list showing examples of causes and effects in the story.

Home Activity Your child reviewed how to determine cause and effect. Make a list of things your child does every day. Ask him or her to list the effect of each of these activities.

Name ______________________________

Prefixes

- A **prefix** is attached to the beginning of a word to make a new word. You can check the meanings of prefixes in the dictionary. The dictionary will list the prefix by itself and also as part of many words.
- Remember that *in-* can mean "not," and that *over-* means "too much."

Words to Know

economic
independence
overrun
scrawled
vacant

Practice Read the following sentences. Fill in the blanks with one of the Words to Know. Then circle the letter of the correct meaning of each underlined word.

1. My friend Amanda started her own business selling her old puzzles and inactive board games. She hoped that the extra money would give her more ____________.

   a. being used very often b. not being used right now

2. Though the idea sounded like a huge project to her overcautious brother Joe, she ____________ a few signs and hung them around the neighborhood.

   a. being too careful b. not being careful

3. To Joe's surprise, Amanda was ____________ by eager customers, all of whom were incomprehensibly excited to purchase her puzzles!

   a. not easy to understand b. very easy to understand

4. Now her old puzzle closet is ____________, and she is no longer working overtime to get ____________ freedom. Soon, though, she will need to find another creative way to earn some money.

   a. less time than usual b. more time than usual

On Your Own As you read "Diamond Discoveries," look for words that have prefixes. List them and look up the meanings of the prefixes in the dictionary.

School + Home **Home Activity** Your child reviewed prefixes. Work together to list as many words as you can that begin with prefixes.

Name ______________________________

Generalize

- A **generalization** is a broad statement or rule that applies to many examples. Clue words such as *all, most, always, usually,* and *often* can signal generalizations.
- Generalizations that are supported by text evidence and by logic are called *valid generalizations*. Generalizations that are not well supported are called *faulty generalizations*

Amanda is in fifth grade. She often paints after school.

Joe is also in fifth grade. He often plays guitar after school.

Practice Look at the pictures, and read each generalization below. Circle the correct answer to show if you think it is a valid generalization or a faulty generalization. Then explain your answer.

1. Amanda usually enjoys painting.
   a. valid generalization b. faulty generalization

____

____

2. Joe always has his guitar with him.
   a. valid generalization b. faulty generalization

____

____

3. Amanda and Joe never play sports.
   a. valid generalization b. faulty generalization

____

____

On Your Own Use what you know about making generalizations as you read "Diamond Discoveries." List several generalizations you find in the passage.

Home Activity Your child reviewed making generalizations. Together, read a magazine article. Identify any generalizations the writer has made.

Name ______________________

Unknown Words
Circle the word *plummet* in Paragraph 1. Check its meaning in a dictionary and write its definition as it is used in the passage.

____

____

Graphic Sources
After reading the first paragraph of the passage, what graphic source do you think would help you understand the selection?

____

____

Author's Purpose
After reading the first two paragraphs, what do you think is the author's purpose?

____

____

____

____

____

____

Multiple-Meaning Words What is the meaning of *company* as it is used in the passage?

____

____

Diamond Discoveries

If you look at a map of Canada, you will spot the chilly area of the Northwest Territories. These territories cover over 500,000 square miles and consist mainly of forests and frozen lands. During the winters, temperatures can plummet down to –25 degrees Fahrenheit. Only lichen and moss will grow there. The human population is so sparse that, on average, you find one person every twelve and a half miles.

Although this area may seem very remote, one geologist named Charles Fipke braved the cold, harsh climate for a hoard of treasure. His journey first began in 1978 when he was hired by a company to complete a specific task: to locate priceless diamonds in the Canadian wilderness.

Diamonds were expensive, and there was just no telling how much profit could be made. Billions of dollars might be up for grabs. Because the stakes were so high, Fipke wasn't even allowed to tell his team of explorers why they were exploring!

Fipke first set out to search the Colorado Rockies, making his way up past the Canadian border. He knew that finding diamonds would take both talent and a whole lot of luck. Diamonds are located in kimberlite pipes—long channels in the ground created ages ago during volcanic eruptions. Since these pipes are very difficult to find, diamond-hunters may also look for "indicator minerals." These special minerals, such as garnets and chromites, are often found near the kimberlite pipes. Not all pipes, however, have diamonds in them. Many pipes are empty, while others are just too small to mine.

By 1981, Fipke and his team had moved farther east, into the Northwest Territories. When Fipke heard that competitors were looking for diamonds just a hundred miles away, he decided to spy on their operation. The information that he gathered from the soil and sediment samples there helped to further his own mission.

Soon after the espionage incident, Fipke's employer abruptly ended the diamond search. But that wasn't about to stop Fipke from looking on his own! Without any help from an outside company, Fipke and a fellow geologist, Stewart Blusson, pooled their economic resources together and started on their own diamond quest.

Name ____________________

The pair made their way farther east to an area now known as the Barren Lands. Concerned that rivals would hear about their explorations, they kept extra quiet and took many precautions. They hiked through areas they knew didn't have diamonds, just to throw competitors off the scent. Blusson would also fly a helicopter without telling anyone where he was going. He was afraid that others would track his flight patterns and then head in the same direction in search of diamonds. Once when Blusson was alone in the icy wasteland, his freezing helicopter would not restart. Since no one knew of his location, he had to save himself. Blusson eventually built a fire, heating the plane's engine until it was warm enough to turn on again.

For years, the men searched for diamond traces while suffering through insanely cold winter temperatures and vicious summer mosquitoes. Their expeditions were enormously expensive, and still no kimberlite pipes were in sight.

Work continued at a constant pace with the help of other funds. Then in the late 1980s, newly published geological research helped Fipke to pinpoint a potential diamond source located in an area among thousands of tiny lakes.

While Blusson was on other expeditions, Fipke and a new team set up a camp near this new lake area. Fipke was feverish with anticipation, and his team began racing against the clock. Everyone was afraid that rivals would hear about their location and soon swoop down to look for diamonds themselves.

Tensions mounted. Where was the kimberlite? It had to be around there somewhere.

Finally, Fipke found a kimberlite pipe beneath one of the many lakes—and yes, there were diamonds inside! With the help of a large company, he quickly staked his claim of land. After years and years of searching, Fipke's fortune was finally made, and his accomplishments were announced to the world!

Graphic Sources How could a time line help you better understand this passage?

____

____

____

____

____

Prefixes What is the prefix in *insanely*?

____

Generalize Underline a generalization in the fourth paragraph.

Author's Purpose Do you think the author achieved her purpose? Why or why not?

____

____

____

____

____

Generalize What generalization could you make about Fipke?

____

____

____

Home Activity Your child read a selection and used comprehension and vocabulary skills from Unit 5. Have your child summarize the selection, drawing conclusions about the facts and making generalizations about the text.

Name____

Character/Plot What is the problem in the story?

____

____

____

____

____

Unfamiliar Words Find the word *eagerly* in the first paragraph and circle it. Define this word. What context clues can help you?

____

____

____

____

____

Cause and Effect What caused the shouts and cheering in paragraph 2?

____

____

____

____

____

____

On the Hunt

The gym was full of excitement as the fifth-grade school scavenger hunt was about to start. Deval, Sofia, and Evan chattered together eagerly as the sky grew dark outside. They were determined to win the scavenger hunt and the prize of the free movie passes.

When all of the kids had settled down, Principal Taylor began to speak. "Good evening, everyone," she said. "I know you're all eager to begin, so I'll make this introduction quick. Your teachers and I will soon be passing out the list of scavenger hunt questions. First team to answer all of the questions correctly wins the prize! When the game is over, we'll finish the evening with a pizza party here in the gym." At the end of this announcement, the entire fifth grade erupted in shouts and cheering.

Papers were quickly handed out, and the teams plunged into action. Deval, Sofia, and Evan high-fived and ran to their starting location: Ms. Kyle's first-grade classroom. Evan looked at the paper and read clue number one aloud. "My name is Ted. I like to rhyme. I wrote *Green Eggs* in little time."

"Green eggs?" asked Deval. "Sounds pretty gross, if you ask me."

Sofia thought for a moment and ran over to the bookshelf. "Maybe the clue means *Green Eggs and Ham.* You know—the book by Dr. Seuss." She found a copy of the story and opened the front cover. Lying inside was a little note. *Congratulations, super sleuth!* it read. *You've answered the first question. Ted Geisel, otherwise known as Dr. Seuss, was the writer of* Green Eggs and Ham. *Now head to the library where you'll find the answer to question two.*

"Nice!" Deval said to Sofia. Then the group bolted to the library, and Evan read the next clue.

"According to this book, yesterday always follows today."

"What could that possibly mean?" Sofia pondered. All of the kids scratched their heads and waited for a burst of inspiration. Deval began pacing through the aisles, skimming the library titles as he went. The scavenger clue didn't seem to make any sense.

Name ______________________________

Evan peered into a heavy reference book that was sitting on a podium. "Hey, check it out—Dr. Seuss's name is listed in the dictionary!"

"Wait a second!" Deval shouted. "That's it! When you look up something in a dictionary, *yesterday* comes after *today*. Alphabetical order!" He raced over to where Evan was standing and lifted the front cover of the dictionary. Sure enough, another slip of paper was waiting for them there. *You know your ABCs, detective! Now head to the main office where the answer to your last clue awaits.*

"I can almost feel those movie tickets in my hand right now," Sofia said. Quickly, the team abandoned the library and took off for the main office.

They slowed their steps as they got near Principal Taylor's doorway. "This place gives me the creeps," Evan said.

"That's because the only time you're ever here is when you've gotten in trouble."

"Teachers shouldn't blame me for talking in class all of the time!" Evan said. "I can't help it. Everyone in my family talks—just look at my parents, and my sisters, and my auntie, and my dog—"

"Later," Sofia said. "We don't have the time. Deval, what's the last clue?"

Deval looked at the paper and read, "You'd think my name would mean 'I sew,' but actually I run the show."

"Oh, that's an easy one!" Evan said.

Sofia and Deval stared in disbelief. "Easy?" they asked. "So what's the answer?"

"Principal Taylor, of course," Evan said. "Get it? Taylor? Tailor?"

Sofia and Evan laughed hysterically. "Who knew your spectacular feat of genius would be inspired by all your visits to the office!" Sofia said. Then all three of them ran to find their principal.

Principal Taylor smiled at the kids when they arrived. "Looks like you've solved my little puzzle," she said.

"And just in time for dinner," Sofia replied. "I'm starving for some pizza!"

Cause and Effect What effect does going to the principal's office have on Evan?

____

____

Character/Plot Underline two sentences on this page that help you to understand Evan's personality.

Greek and Latin Roots The Latin root *spec-* means "look or see." How does this root help you to understand the meaning of *spectacular*?

____

____

____

____

Home Activity Your child read a selection and used comprehension and vocabulary skills from Unit 5. Have your child retell the selection, focusing on the sequence of events in the plot.

Name ______________________________

Suffixes *-ous*, *-sion*, *-ion*, *-ation*

- **Generalization** When adding **-ous, -sion, -ion,** and **-ation,** some base words change. A final **e** or **y** may be dropped: **famous, furious.** Some words have other changes: **decision.**

Word Sort Sort the list words by their suffix.

-ous

1. ______________
2. ______________
3. ______________
4. ______________
5. ______________

-sion

6. ______________
7. ______________
8. ______________

-ion

9. ______________
10. ______________
11. ______________
12. ______________

-ation

13. ______________
14. ______________
15. ______________
16. ______________
17. ______________
18. ______________
19. ______________
20. ______________

Spelling Words

1. famous
2. invention
3. election
4. furious
5. imagination
6. education
7. nervous
8. explanation
9. various
10. decision
11. relaxation
12. conversation
13. tension
14. humorous
15. exhibition
16. attraction
17. invasion
18. creation
19. occupation
20. destination

Home Activity Your child is learning about suffixes. Have your child tell you the four suffixes studied and spell each for you.

Name ______________________

Family Times

Summary

The Truth About Austin's Amazing Bats

In Austin, Texas, you can see over a million bats in the night sky. The reconstruction of the Congress Avenue Bridge unintentionally created a perfect habitat for bats. The massive number of bats that pours out from under the bridge attracts many tourists. People come to watch them from high spots and low spots; some watch even from boats. Today Austin loves its bats—although that was not always true!

Activity

Going Batty Are you afraid of bats? Use the library or Internet resources to list the kind of bats common to your area. Find out their habits and what they eat. Try to see real bats in a zoo or wildlife refuge. Find out how and where to see them in the night sky. Then tell your family what you learned about bats.

Comprehension Skill

Draw Conclusions

When you **draw a conclusion,** you form an idea based on what you know or on the facts and details in a text. You can check your conclusions by asking yourself: Is this the only logical choice? Are the facts accurate?

Activity

Make a bat scrapbook, using photos or drawings of bats that are local as well as from other areas. Label the pictures, listing the areas the bats are found and a few details about each one. Then try to draw a conclusion about what makes bats scary to some people. Are they really scary or mainly harmless creatures? Explain your findings to your family.

Lesson Vocabulary

Words to Know

Knowing the meaning of these words is important to reading *Austin's Amazing Bats*. Practice using these words.

Vocabulary Words

bizarre strange; weird; very unusual
breathtaking so surprising, impressive, or beautiful that it could make people gasp
headline the title of an article in the newspaper
high-pitched describes a sound that is higher than most other sounds
roost a place to rest and sleep
vital necessary; crucial

Conventions

Modifiers

Remember to use **modifiers** correctly. A modifier is a word that limits the meaning of another word. Keep modifiers close to the words they modify. Sometimes using modifiers incorrectly changes the meaning of a sentence. For example, *Only Ken visits* has a different meaning from *Ken only visits*. Prepositional phrases should be kept close to the words they modify too. For example: *The gift from France is on the table* has a different meaning than *The gift is on the table from France*.

Activity

Mixed-Up Modifiers With a family member, make a list of seven words or phrases you can use as modifiers. *Tight*, *rich*, and *very rich* are a few examples of modifiers. Then pick a sentence out of a newspaper, magazine, or book. Make a new sentences by inserting as many modifiers as you can from your list into the sentences you choose. How are the meanings of the new sentences similar to the meanings of the original sentences? How are they different?

Practice Tested Spelling Words

______	______	______	______
______	______	______	______
______	______	______	______
______	______	______	______
______	______	______	______

Name ___________________________

Draw Conclusions

- Active readers **draw conclusions,** or make decisions, based on information in the text and their own knowledge.
- Examine your own conclusions as you read. Ask yourself, "Can I support them with information from the text or with facts I already know?"

Directions Read the following passage. Then answer the questions below.

Coral reefs are formed from the hard skeletons of sea animals. They are found in oceans around the world, but mainly in clear, warm tropical seas. Coral reefs provide food and shelter for many different kinds of fish and sea creatures. For example, they protect animals such as sponges from their enemies. In addition, coral reefs protect shorelines from erosion. They act as a barrier to the pounding waves. Coral reefs may even contribute to the well-being of human beings. Substances gathered from tiny animals growing on coral reefs may one day be made into medicines. Finally, coral reefs are known for their beauty. They attract tourists to vacation areas, allowing local people to earn a living.

1. What conclusion can you draw about the functions of coral reefs?

____

____

2. What is an important fact that supports this conclusion?

____

3. What is another important fact that supports the conclusion?

____

4. What are two more facts that support the conclusion?

____

____

5. What details in the passage help you to visualize a coral reef? How did visualizing details help you to understand the passage?

____

____

Home Activity Your child drew and supported a conclusion in a nonfiction text. With your child, read a magazine article about the ocean. Work together to draw a conclusion based on the text and your prior knowledge. Find and talk about details in the text that support your conclusion.

Name

Generalize

Directions Read the following passage. Then answer the questions below.

Paul was planning to bake his mother's birthday cake. His father claimed to hate to cook and never missed a baseball game, but Paul asked him if he wanted to help bake the cake anyway. "Sorry, I'd rather watch the game," his father said. Paul always had a good attitude, so he found a good recipe in a cookbook, made a list of ingredients, and then rode his bike to the supermarket. When he got home, Paul lined up the ingredients on the table in the order he would need them. Then he turned on his favorite music and put on an apron, singing all the while.

In the living room, his father was watching the game and heard Paul making noise out in the kitchen. He looked in to see Paul, flour all over his face, singing and mixing ingredients. His father had to smile. "It looks like you're having fun. Do you have another apron for me?" Paul's father asked.

1. What did Paul want to do?

2. Why didn't Paul's father want to help?

3. What generalization about Paul's father do you see with the word *never*?

4. What generalization about Paul do you see with the word *always*?

5. Write a statement to generalize what happens in this story.

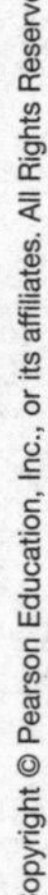

Home Activity Your child read a story and determined and made generalizations. With your child, find and read a story and help your child generalize about the outcome.

Name____________________________________

Modifiers

Directions Add adjectives, adverbs, and prepositional phrases to these sentences. Use modifiers to create a more specific, interesting picture.

1. The bridge held bats.

____

____

2. A bat appeared.

____

____

3. The creatures scattered.

____

____

4. The bats searched.

____

____

Directions Imagine you find something interesting in a tree. Write a description of what you find and how you find it. Use modifiers to create a vivid word picture.

____

____

____

____

____

____

____

____

School + Home **Home Activity** Your child learned how to use modifiers in writing. Give your child simple sentences such as those in items 1–4 on this page and have him or her add modifiers to make interesting story starters.

Name ______________________________

Suffixes *-ous, -sion, -ion, -ation*

Spelling Words				
famous	invention	election	furious	imagination
education	nervous	explanation	various	decision
relaxation	conversation	tension	humorous	exhibition
attraction	invasion	creation	occupation	destination

Match Suffixes Draw a line from the word or word part to its suffix. Write the word on the line.

attract	ion	1. ________	humor	ous	6. ________
creat	sion	2. ________	imagin	ation	7. ________
deci	ous	3. ________	occup	ous	8. ________
exhibit	ion	4. ________	relax	ation	9. ________
furi	ion	5. ________	vari	ation	10. ________

Double Puzzle Unscramble the list words. Use the numbered letters to find the answer to the question.

What is a destination for fun, attractions, and relaxation?

11. ASFUMO ___ ___ ___(4) ___ ___ ___
12. ESNVOUR ___(9) ___ ___ ___ ___ ___ ___
13. ONTNEIS ___ ___ ___ ___(6) ___ ___ ___
14. CNPAIUCTOO ___ ___ ___ ___ ___(11) ___(1) ___ ___ ___ ___
15. ESOOTRACNIVN ___ ___ ___ ___ ___ ___(13) ___ ___(3) ___ ___ ___ ___
16. XOHNIEBITI ___(7) ___ ___ ___ ___ ___ ___ ___ ___ ___
17. VINANOIS ___ ___ ___ ___(12) ___ ___ ___ ___(2)
18. ARECNTOI ___ ___ ___(8) ___ ___ ___ ___ ___
19. NINVETNIO ___ ___ ___ ___ ___ ___(10) ___ ___ ___
20. DEUNCAIOT ___ ___ ___(5) ___ ___ ___ ___ ___ ___

___(1) ___(2) ___(3) ___(4) ___(5) ___(6) ___(7) ___(4) ___(8) ___(9) ___(10)

___(11) ___(12) ___(13) k

Home Activity Your child has learned to read, write, and spell words with suffixes. Look through books or magazines with your child and try to find four other words with the same endings.

Name ______________________________

Draw Conclusions

- Active readers **draw conclusions,** or make decisions, based on information in the text and their own knowledge.
- Examine your own conclusions as you read. Ask yourself, "Can I support them with information from the text or with facts I already know?"

Directions Read the following passage. Then complete the diagram and answer the question.

David and his friends were at the beach one day. They noticed a lifeguard's chair and laughed. "We know how to swim. We don't need a lifeguard!" they chuckled.

While they were out in the water swimming, David suddenly shouted in pain. After the boys helped him to shore, they saw his leg had long, bright red marks across it. No one knew how to stop the pain until a lifeguard found them.

"You've been stung by a jellyfish," he told David. "Jellyfish float out in the water. Their stingers cause pain." He rinsed David's leg with seawater and removed the jellyfish stingers with tweezers. He applied a cream from his first-aid kit and bandaged the leg. "Keep your leg still, and check with your doctor," he told David.

Before long, David's leg and spirits both began to feel better.

What Can I Conclude?

1. Lifeguards have the ability

What Does the Text Say?

2. The lifeguard knew

3. The lifeguard also knew

4. David's leg

5. What is another conclusion you might draw from the text about swimming at a beach?

____

____

Home Activity Your child drew conclusions based on the details of a story. As you read a story together, work with your child to draw conclusions about the characters and events.

Name______________________________

Modifiers

Directions Underline the prepositional phrase in each sentence. Write *adverb* or *adjective* to identify how the prepositional phrase is used.

1. We observed some insects with red eyes. ____________________

2. Up the glass crept a graceful brown spider. ____________________

3. A firefly flashed its light across the dim room. ____________________

4. The ladybug had four black spots on its back. ____________________

5. We saw a bee with a long stinger. ____________________

6. Black bats fluttered around the cage. ____________________

Directions Underline the adjectives, adverbs, and prepositional phrases in each sentence. The number in ( ) tells how many modifiers a sentence contains. (Do not underline the articles *a* and *the*.)

7. The scientist has several unusual specimens in her collection. (3)

8. There is a tiny black Free-tail from Mexico. (3)

9. In the spring, she found a bright blue butterfly on a flower. (4)

10. She carefully preserves the rare creatures. (2)

11. Winged creatures add beauty and color to the world. (2)

Directions Underline the misplaced modifier in each sentence. Rewrite the sentence, and put the modifier where it belongs.

12. He only studies Mexican bats—nothing else.

____

____

13. She saw a rare small-footed bat resting with her binoculars.

____

____

14. The bats amazed the students with their sharply curved wings.

____

____

Home Activity Your child reviewed modifiers. Have your child use a magazine article or story to show you good examples of adjectives, adverbs, and prepositional phrases that make the writing specific and interesting.

Name______________________________

Final Syllable *-ant, -ent, -ance, -ence*

- **Generalization** There is no sound clue to help you decide whether to use an **a** or **e**: **important**, **intelligent**, **instance**, **experience**.

Word Sort Sort the list words by their ending.

-ant

1. ____________
2. ____________
3. ____________
4. ____________

-ent

5. ____________
6. ____________
7. ____________

-ence

8. ____________
9. ____________
10. ____________
11. ____________
12. ____________
13. ____________
14. ____________

-ance

15. ____________
16. ____________
17. ____________
18. ____________
19. ____________
20. ____________

Spelling Words

1. important
2. experience
3. ignorant
4. entrance
5. difference
6. instance
7. absence
8. appearance
9. intelligent
10. evidence
11. pollutant
12. clearance
13. confidence
14. conference
15. insurance
16. ambulance
17. hesitant
18. consistent
19. excellence
20. persistent

Home Activity Your child is learning about final syllables. Have your child choose and spell a list word for each of the four final syllables being studied.

Name

Family Times

Summary

The Mystery of Saint Matthew Island

The reindeer herd on Saint Matthew Island had grown to six thousand animals. Suddenly, almost all of the reindeer died. A scientist tries to figure out why. His research rules out the usual causes: predators, disease, and old age. He discovers that the reindeer had starved, and a brutal winter sealed their fate.

Activity

Survival Strategies Imagine you and members of your family are scientists studying animals in the wild. Talk with your family about how animals survive. Discuss the different things that can threaten a wild animal's survival, both natural and man-made.

Comprehension Skill

Main Idea and Details

The **main idea** is an important point that has at least one supporting detail. **Details** are smaller pieces of information that tell more about the main idea.

Activity

Zero In Ask members of your family for their opinions about certain animals. For each opinion, or main idea, discuss ideas for supporting details. Make a list of the main ideas and the details that support them.

Lesson Vocabulary

Words to Know

Knowing the meanings of these words is important to reading *The Mystery of Saint Matthew Island.* Practice using these words.

Vocabulary Words

bleached whitened by exposure to sunlight or by use of chemicals

carcasses bodies of dead animals

decay process of rotting

parasites living things that live on or in others, from which they get their food, often harming the others in the process

scrawny having little flesh; lean; thin; skinny

starvation suffering from extreme hunger

suspicions beliefs, feelings, thoughts

tundra a vast, treeless plain in the arctic regions

Conventions

Conjunctions

A **conjunction** is a word that joins words, phrases, or entire sentences. *And*, *or*, and *but* are conjunctions. You can use conjunctions to join subjects, predicates, and objects. *For example: John and Kathleen; rice or noodles.* Sometimes two sentences about related topics can be combined, using a comma and a conjunction or a subordinating conjunction such as *because*, *if*, *then*, or *when*. *For example: We went to the zoo because we love tigers.*

Activity

Be a Joiner Make a three-column chart. In the first and third columns, write three simple sentences. In the middle column, write *and*, *or*, and *but*. Cut the paper so there is one sentence on each cut piece of paper. Take turns combining sentences using different conjunctions. Do this by moving the sentences in front of and after each conjunction.

Practice Tested Spelling Words

Name ______________________________

Main Idea and Details

- The **topic** is the overall subject of a piece of writing. The **main idea** of a selection is the most important idea about the topic of that selection. **Details** are small pieces of information that tell more about the main idea.

Directions Read the following passage. Then answer the questions below.

Sometimes a certain species of animal dies off naturally or through another cause, such as hunting by humans. In these cases, there will be an increase in the number of the animals that the dying species feeds on.

An example of this process can be seen in the relationship among wolves and panthers and deer. Wolves and panthers have largely disappeared from the United States. Consequently, their natural prey, deer, have multiplied. There are more deer in the country now than there were before colonists settled the land centuries ago. Because the deer population has become very large, herds of deer quickly eat up all the food in some areas. Of course, when food is lacking, the animals starve. Human beings can help an area recover its natural balance. In some cases, people introduce natural enemies into an area to control the numbers of the prey animal.

1. In one or two words, what is the topic of this passage?

____

2. What is the main idea of the passage?

____

3. What is one important detail that tells more about the main idea?

____

____

4. What is another detail that supports the main idea?

____

____

5. Identify the text structure used in each paragraph of this article.

____

Home Activity Your child identified the main idea and details of a nonfiction passage. Together, read a magazine article about another wild animal. Work together to identify the main idea and details of the article.

Name ____

Sequence

Directions Read the following article. Then answer the questions below.

Before the school was built in 1950, the land on which it stands was a swamp. Back then, the earth was soft, wet, and marshy. Beavers, otters, and turtles slid through the watery land. Cranes, herons, hawks, and egrets swooped overhead or waded in the water.

Then, after the town decided to build the school, the land was filled in. First, truckloads of dirt were added to provide a firm base. Afterward, earth movers were used to shape the land, creating a flat surface with a few low hills. Finally, the school was constructed on top of the newly sculpted land. When the building was finished, no swamp animals or water birds remained. Now students and teachers have taken the place of toads and turtles.

1. According to the article, what was the land like originally? What clues tell you this condition was present before the building of the school?

____

____

2. What first lived on the land? Who is there now?

____

____

3. What was the first change that was made to the land?

____

____

4. What was the next step before the school was constructed?

____

____

5. On a separate sheet of paper, explain how clues clarify the sequence of changes described in the second paragraph. How do these clues help you to understand the article?

Home Activity Your child has identified the sequence of changes that a piece of land has undergone. Together, read a newspaper article. Work with your child to make a time line to clarify the sequence of events.

Name ______________________________

Conjunctions

Directions Write a conjunction on each line to complete the paragraph.

(1) The island features spectacular cliffs ____________ volcanic mountains. **(2)** That odd seabird you observed might be a petrel ____________ a fulmar. **(3)** The climate is extremely cold, ____________ many birds are able to live here. **(4)** They build their nests in the cliffs ____________ raise their young. **(5)** Birds can breed on the island, ____________ they need not stay all year. **(6)** Some birds migrate to warmer winter headquarters, ____________ others build up an insulating layer of fat. **(7)** One bird you are sure to see is McKay's bunting, which breeds here ____________ nowhere else.

Directions Combine the short sentences to make one longer, smoother sentence. Use conjunctions. Write the new sentence.

8. In 1944, voles lived on St. Matthew Island. So did arctic foxes.

____

____

____

____

9. The Coast Guard introduced 24 female reindeer to the island. They also introduced 5 males.

____

____

____

____

10. Years before there were reindeer everywhere. Now only a few remained.

____

____

____

____

Home Activity Your child learned how to use conjunctions in writing. Have your child read about reindeer and write simple sentences about them. Ask your child to find ways to combine some of the related sentences.

Name______________________________

Final Syllable *-ant*, *-ent*, *-ance*, *-ence*

Spelling Words				
important	experience	ignorant	entrance	difference
instance	absence	appearance	intelligent	evidence
pollutant	clearance	confidence	conference	insurance
ambulance	hesitant	consistent	excellence	persistent

Alphabetical Order Write the list word that fits in alphabetical order between the two words.

1. amazement/ambush — 1. ______________
2. clay/clef — 2. ______________
3. igloo/illness — 3. ______________
4. herb/hickory — 4. ______________
5. above/absorb — 5. ______________
6. permit/person — 6. ______________
7. cone/confess — 7. ______________
8. poll/pomp — 8. ______________
9. ewe/exit — 9. ______________
10. ill/impress — 10. ______________

Word Search Circle ten list words that are hidden in the puzzle. Write each word.

K	L	K	A	D	O	Q	V	L	H	E	C	E	E	11. ______________
G	D	S	V	P	I	T	K	S	O	S	O	X	N	12. ______________
F	K	N	B	W	P	F	M	E	O	D	N	P	T	13. ______________
S	X	O	A	Q	M	E	F	U	J	R	F	E	R	14. ______________
I	P	H	J	K	G	Y	A	E	U	X	I	R	A	15. ______________
E	V	I	D	E	N	C	E	R	R	P	D	I	N	16. ______________
I	N	S	U	R	A	N	C	E	A	E	E	E	C	17. ______________
C	O	N	S	I	S	T	E	N	T	N	N	N	E	18. ______________
I	N	T	E	L	L	I	G	E	N	T	C	C	V	19. ______________
I	N	S	T	A	N	C	E	O	S	A	E	E	E	20. ______________

Home Activity Your child has learned to read, write, and spell words with final syllable spellings *-ant*, *-ent*, *-ance*, and *-ence*. Take turns saying and spelling the words aloud.

Name ______________________________

Main Idea and Details

- The **topic** is the overall subject of a piece of writing.
- The **main idea** of a selection is the most important idea about the topic of that selection.
- **Details** are small pieces of information that tell more about the main idea.
- Sometimes the author states the main idea in a single sentence. When the author does not state the main idea, the reader must figure it out.

Directions Read the following passage. Then complete the diagram below.

Mari wondered why the numbers of some species swing up or down. Her science teacher explained that environment controls an animal's population size.

"Food, shelter, water, and space all have an effect," Mr. Gonzalez explained. "The animals' numbers are limited by whichever one of these is least available."

"But what about other animals?" Mari asked. "Don't they have an effect too?"

"Yes, that's the other part of the puzzle," said Mr. Gonzalez. "Enemies can cut down an animal's numbers. Some species are reduced because other animals are competing for the same food. Also, if there is a lack of prey for an animal, that animal's numbers will drop."

Main Idea

1. Animal numbers are determined by ______________________________

Details

2. One thing that limits an animal's numbers is availability of ______________

3. Also limiting an animal's numbers is lack of ______________________

4. An animal's numbers will decline if others are ______________________

5. What is the main idea? ______________________________

____

Home Activity Your child identified the main idea and details of a nonfiction passage. Work with your child to identify the main idea and details of individual paragraphs in a magazine article about wild animals.

Name______________________________

Conjunctions

Directions Underline the conjunction in each sentence.

1. Birds and small mammals live on the island.

2. Did a fox or a rabbit make that nest?

3. Count the animals on the island, and we will make a chart.

4. You can count them but cannot determine their sex.

5. We will find out what happened or guess the cause of the die-off.

Directions Underline the conjunction in ( ) that completes each sentence.

6. Nature holds many mysteries, (and, or) scientists want to solve them.

7. Scientists use logic and scientific method, (or, but) imagination is also important.

8. Dr. David Klein had to count (and, or) also weigh reindeer on St. Matthew Island.

9. He knew the reindeer were not killed by diseases (but, or) parasites.

10. Low weight (or, and) missing bone marrow suggested the deer had starved.

Directions Use the conjunction *and, but,* or *or* to join each pair of sentences. Write the new sentences. Remember to add a comma.

11. Polar mammals have fur and fat to keep them warm. People have to dress warmly.

____

____

____

____

12. Layers of clothing trap warm air next to the skin. This keeps people warm in cold weather.

____

____

____

____

Home Activity Your child reviewed conjunctions. With your child, make a favorite food. Ask your child to talk about the process, using the conjunctions *and, but,* and *or* to describe actions and choices in the process.

Name ______________________________

Latin Roots

- **Generalization** Many words are formed with the Latin roots **aud** meaning "hear," **dict** meaning "say," **port** meaning "carry," **dec** meaning "ten," and **terr** meaning "land."

Word Sort Sort the list words by their Latin root.

aud

1. ______________
2. ______________
3. ______________
4. ______________

dict

5. ______________
6. ______________
7. ______________
8. ______________

port

9. ______________
10. ______________
11. ______________
12. ______________
13. ______________

dec

14. ______________
15. ______________
16. ______________
17. ______________

terr

18. ______________
19. ______________
20. ______________

Spelling Words

1. portable
2. audience
3. decade
4. territory
5. auditorium
6. dictionary
7. terrace
8. reporter
9. December
10. contradict
11. export
12. decimal
13. audit
14. transport
15. audition
16. prediction
17. import
18. jurisdiction
19. decathlon
20. terrain

Home Activity Your child is learning about Latin roots. Have your child explain what each Latin root in this lesson means.

Name

Family Times

Summary

King Midas and the Golden Touch

King Midas loves only one thing more than his gold: his daughter. When he is granted a magic wish, he wishes that all he touches turns to gold. He realizes the tragedy of this wish when he turns his daughter to gold. He is overjoyed when he can give up the golden touch and have his daughter back.

Activity

The Wish Game Imagine that you could have one wish granted. What would you wish for? See what your family members would wish for, and make a list. Talk about the consequences of each wish.

Comprehension Skill

Compare and Contrast

Compare and **Contrast** means to tell how two or more things are alike or different. Clue words such as *but*, *like*, *similarly*, and *as* show comparisons. Words such as *but*, *however*, and *instead* show differences.

Activity

Before and After With your family, choose some significant events in your life, such as entering school, starting lessons, making friends, or playing sports. Compare and contrast how things were alike and different for you before and after these milestones.

Lesson Vocabulary

Words to Know

Knowing the meanings of these words is important to reading *King Midas and the Golden Touch*. Practice using these words.

Vocabulary Words

adorn to add beauty to; put ornaments on; decorate

cleanse to make clean

lifeless without life

precious having great value; worth much

realm kingdom

spoonful as much as a spoon can hold

Conventions

Commas

A **comma** is a punctuation mark that indicates a short pause. A comma is used to set off or separate words or groups of words. Use a comma after a person's name when you directly address that person. *For example: Meg, come here.* Use commas to separate three or more words in a series. *For example: The blouse is blue, green, and pink.* Use commas to set off an appositive, which is an explanation placed next to a word. *For example: Our dog, a boxer, is named Pug.* In the example, *a boxer* is an appositive.

Activity

Comma Keeper Look in a newspaper to find sentences that use commas. Make a chart that shows examples of commas used for direct address, series, and appositives.

Practice Tested Spelling Words

______	______	______	______
______	______	______	______
______	______	______	______
______	______	______	______
______	______	______	______

Name ______________________________

Compare and Contrast

- Writers sometimes use **comparison** and **contrast** to organize their writing. Clue words such as *same, also, before, although,* and *however* signal comparisons and contrasts.
- Good readers notice the author's comparisons and contrasts and make their own as they read.

Directions Read the following passage. Then answer the questions below.

In every culture, certain qualities are considered precious. But these qualities might not be the same in every culture. Beauty, for example, is valued in many cultures. But what is considered beautiful in one culture may not be beautiful in others. Wealth is also valued in many cultures. But some cultures place a higher value on it than others. In the United States today, youth is greatly valued. Japan, China, and India treat their elders with honor and respect. The oldest members of a family have the highest status.

1. What qualities are being compared and contrasted in the passage?

2. How do attitudes about old age compare in Japan, China, and India?

3. How do attitudes about old age in Japan, China, and India contrast with U.S. attitudes?

4. What is another quality that you might compare and contrast across cultures?

5. How does your prior knowledge about different cultures help you compare and contrast the qualities that those cultures find precious?

Home Activity Your child read a short passage and identified comparisons and contrasts. Read a magazine article about a different culture. Work together with your child to identify some of the culture's values and compare them with your own.

Name

Draw Conclusions

Directions Read the following article. Then answer the questions below.

For months, Meg had been trying to talk her dad into getting a dog. She thought of so many good reasons that finally he gave in. Meg named her new puppy Hap, and she had a lot of fun playing with him all summer.

When her friends would call, she'd say she was too busy. From the time she got up in the morning until the time she went to bed, she was training and chasing Hap. When her friend Callie had a birthday party, Meg said she had to take care of her puppy. She ran home right after swim practice, even though her friends pleaded with her to hang out with them at the pool.

Once school started, though, it was a lot of trouble to run home right after school every day to walk Hap. Meg wanted to be with her friends instead. However, she felt lonely because she wasn't close to her friends anymore. They seemed to have moved on.

1. What conclusion can you draw about Meg based on how she gets her dog? Explain.

2. What conclusion can you draw about Meg during the summer?

3. What is a detail from the story that supports your conclusion?

4. What is another detail from the story that supports your conclusion?

5. What conclusion can you draw about Meg's friends? What details support your conclusion?

Home Activity Your child read a short passage and drew conclusions about its characters. Read a short story to your child. Ask him or her to draw conclusions about the main character.

Name ______________________________

Commas

Directions Add commas in the sentences to make the meaning clear. Rewrite the paragraph.

(1) Some things are necessities items we could not live without. **(2)** Food water and shelter fit in this category. **(3)** What more do we need dear reader to live and be happy? **(4)** Many people believe they would be happy if only they had lots of money possessions and free time. **(5)** In fact people's real needs are quite different. **(6)** The happiest people are those who have good health loving relationships and useful work.

____

____

____

____

____

____

____

____

____

____

Directions Write sentences to answer each question. Use commas to set off words in a series, appositives, words of direct address, and introductory words.

7. What are three possessions that are precious to you?

____

____

____

8. Explain why one of these objects is important to you. Address your sentences to a friend.

____

____

____

Home Activity Your child learned how to use commas in writing. With your child, read a story or article. Have your child point out commas that are used to set off series, appositives, introductory words, and nouns of direct address.

Name ______________________________

Latin Roots

Spelling Words				
portable	audience	decade	territory	auditorium
dictionary	terrace	reporter	December	contradict
export	decimal	audit	transport	audition
prediction	import	jurisdiction	decathlon	terrain

Alphabetize Put the list words in the box below in alphabetical order.

portable	audience	auditorium	terrace	December
contradict	decimal	transport	jurisdiction	decathlon

1. ______________ 2. ______________

3. ______________ 4. ______________

5. ______________ 6. ______________

7. ______________ 8. ______________

9. ______________ 10. ______________

Crossword Puzzle Use the clues to find the list words. Write each letter in a box.

Across

3. opposite of import
6. book of words
10. one who tells the news

Down

1. shape of the land
2. forecast
4. ten years
5. land area, region
7. try out
8. review of money
9. opposite of export

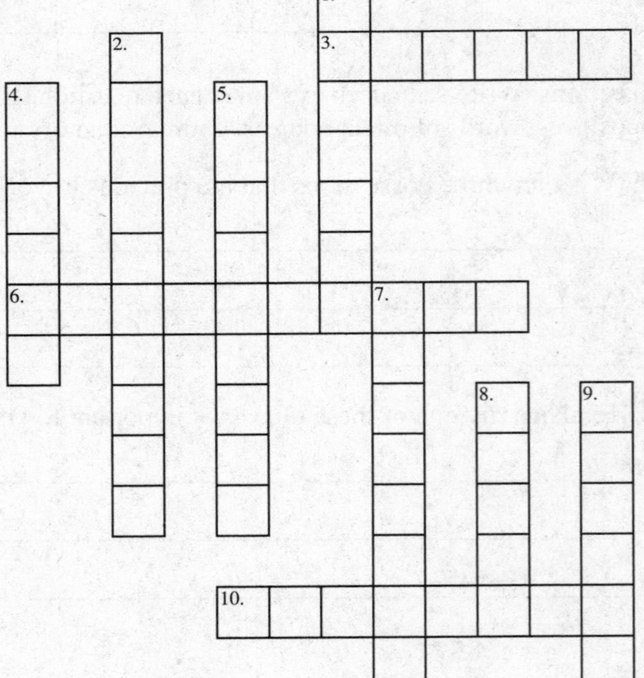

Home Activity Your child has learned to read, write, and spell words with Latin roots. Challenge your child to think of other words that use these Latin roots.

Name ___________________________________

Compare and Contrast

- Writers sometimes use **comparison** and **contrast** to organize their writing. Clue words such as *same, also, before, although,* and *however* signal comparisons and contrasts.
- Good readers notice the author's comparisons and contrasts and make their own as they read.

Directions Read the following passage. Then complete the diagram below.

White gold and platinum are both metals used to make jewelry. They are both silver or white in color and therefore don't interfere with the color of gemstones. Even though they look similar to most people, they are different metals. White gold is made by mixing gold with other metals. It is very dense and is easily molded into jewelry. To appear truly white rather than gray, white gold is coated with rhodium, another white metal. White gold needs to be recoated after several years for it to continue looking white. Platinum is used for jewelry in almost pure form so it is heavier than white gold. It does not need to be coated to appear white. Platinum is more rare than gold and is two times more expensive than white gold.

Advantages and Disadvantages of Using White Gold for Jewelry Instead of Platinum	
Advantages	**Disadvantages**
White gold is less expensive than platinum.	**3.** White gold is not ____________ ____________
1. The color of white gold does not interfere ____________	**4.** White gold needs to be ____________ ____________
2. White gold is easily ____________ ____________	**5.** White gold is less ____________ ____________

Home Activity Your child read a short passage and made comparisons and contrasts. Read an article about two different time periods or places. Work with your child to compare and contrast the two.

Name ____________________

Commas

Directions Add commas to each sentence where they are needed.

1. Many tales involve kingdoms magic creatures and wishes.
2. Have you noticed Danny that humans always seem to use these wishes foolishly?
3. Yes tales also often have a young person as the hero.
4. Tales usually have a talking animal stone or tree.
5. One tale featured Excalibur a sword with a mind of its own.
6. Mr. Wickness our reading teacher said we could write a tale a mystery or a poem.

Directions Rewrite each sentence. Add commas where they are needed.

7. Gold has been used for centuries to make coins jewelry and accessories.

____

____

8. Can you tell me Mr. Liakos if the king's crown is made of gold?

____

____

9. Yes it is made of gold and inset with precious gems.

____

____

10. Both crown and scepter a staff symbolizing the king's power were made of valuable materials.

____

____

11. In fact the scepter has more diamonds on it than the crown does.

____

____

Home Activity Your child reviewed commas. Ask your child to write an imaginary conversation between two friends about their favorite things. Have your child highlight the commas in another color.

Name ______________________

Related Words

- **Generalization** Related words often have vowels that are spelled the same but pronounced differently: **clean, cleanse**.

Word Sort Sort word pairs by the vowel that is pronounced differently.

a

1. ______ 2. ______

3. ______ 4. ______

5. ______ 6. ______

e

7. ______ 8. ______

9. ______ 10. ______

i

11. ______ 12. ______

13. ______ 14. ______

15. ______ 16. ______

17. ______ 18. ______

19. ______ 20. ______

Spelling Words

1. clean
2. cleanse
3. inspire
4. inspiration
5. legal
6. legality
7. define
8. definition
9. please
10. pleasant
11. combine
12. combination
13. human
14. humanity
15. organ
16. organist
17. crime
18. criminal
19. recognize
20. recognition

Home Activity Your child is learning about related words that are spelled similarly but pronounced differently. Review the pairs of words with your child and ask him or her to point out the ways in which the pronunciation of the two words in each pair is different.

Name

Family Times

Summary

The *Hindenburg*

Hugo Eckener was intent on developing dirigibles, and his *Hindenburg* was the largest one ever. In fact, it was the largest object ever to fly. In 1937, the *Hindenburg* exploded over New Jersey during its tenth transatlantic flight, and thirty-one people died. Instantly, the era of the dirigible ended.

Activity

Surprises Compare notes with your family about unexpected events in the news. Discuss how to plan for the unexpected.

Comprehension Skill

Fact and Opinion

A **fact** is something that can be proved. An **opinion** is something that is a belief, thought, or feeling, and cannot be proved. Opinions often include words that make judgments, such as *best*, *beautiful*, or *interesting*.

Activity

Facts You Can Use In a local newspaper, find a list of events that will take place in the near future. With a family member make a list of opinions about the events. For example, tell why children might like the event or why it will be fun. Use words such as *best* and *interesting*.

Lesson Vocabulary

Words to Know

Knowing the meanings of these words is important to reading The *Hindenburg*. Practice using these words.

Vocabulary Words

criticizing finding fault with; disapproving of; blaming

cruised traveled at the speed at which the vehicle operates best

drenching wetting thoroughly; soaking

era a period of time or history

explosion act of bursting with a loud noise; a blowing up

hydrogen a colorless, odorless gas that burns easily

Conventions

Quotations and Quotation Marks

A **quotation** is the exact words a speaker says. In your writing, put a quotation in **quotation marks.** Use commas to set off the words that introduce a quotation. Also, place the end punctuation or the comma that ends the quotation inside the quotation marks. *For example: Sandy said, "If it rains tomorrow, we can't go to the beach." "I'll keep my fingers crossed then," said Kate.*

Activity

Quote Me Make a chart with two columns. In the left column, write down questions you will ask your family members, such as *Whom do you most admire?* or *What is your biggest strength?* In the right column, record their answers. Be sure to put quotation marks around the words they say.

Practice Tested Spelling Words

___	___	___	___
___	___	___	___
___	___	___	___
___	___	___	___
___	___	___	___

Name ______________________________

Fact and Opinion

- **Statements of fact** are objective, not personal. They can be proved true or false. **Statements of opinion** are personal judgments or beliefs. They cannot be proved true or false.
- Statements of opinion can be valid or faulty. **Valid** statements can be supported by facts and common sense. **Faulty** statements cannot.
- Examine statements of opinion by using your prior knowledge. Based on what you have seen or read or what you know, ask, *Is the statement valid or faulty?*

Directions Read the following passage. Then answer the questions below.

As far as I'm concerned, air travel is king. Over the past twenty years, traveling by plane has become safer and more affordable than it used to be. I also believe that air travel is more comfortable and convenient than traveling by train or by car. In the modern world, everybody enjoys traveling by plane. Safer and faster airplanes are being developed all the time. The aircraft of the future will probably make air travel seem like a vacation in the sky. Whenever possible, we should travel by air to support the development of more planes.

1. Is the first sentence a statement of fact or opinion? How can you tell?

____

____

2. Is the second sentence a statement of fact or opinion? How can you tell?

____

3. Is the statement of opinion in the fourth sentence valid or faulty? Why?

____

____

4. In the final sentence, how does the word *should* help you know whether the sentence is a statement of fact or of opinion?

____

____

5. What question could you ask to check your understanding of this passage?

____

Home Activity Your child recognized statements of fact and opinion in a nonfiction passage and generated questions based on the passage. Together, read an editorial about transportation. Work together to identify statements of fact and opinion. Encourage your child to ask questions during and after reading.

Name ______________________________

Main Idea and Details

Directions Read the following passage. Then answer the questions below.

Rail travel was very popular during the 1920s and 1930s, but later it was replaced by automobiles and airplanes as the leading form of transportation. At the peak of rail travel in 1920, 1.2 billion passengers rode trains. During the 1930s, sleek, streamlined trains were developed, and these grew very popular. During World War II, trains were used extensively to carry soldiers and military equipment. At the end of the war, two-thirds of paying passengers were traveling by train.

However, during the next twenty years, the use of trains fell off. Cars, which had been around since the beginning of the century, became the top choice for going from one place to another. At the same time, the use of airplanes grew for long-distance travel. By the 1950s, more people were traveling by air than by train. Trains were viewed as old-fashioned.

1. In one or two words, what is the topic of this passage?

____

2. What is the main idea of this passage?

____

____

3. What is one detail that supports the main idea?

____

____

4. What is another detail that supports the main idea?

____

____

5. On a separate sheet of paper, write a summary of this article.

Home Activity Your child identified the main idea and details in a nonfiction passage. Together, read a short nonfiction article about a topic that interests both of you. Work with your child to state the main idea and to identify details.

Name ______________________________

Quotations and Quotation Marks

Directions Choose a sentence from the box that supports the ideas in each paragraph. Write the sentence, adding quotation marks and correct punctuation.

A radio announcer moaned over the airwaves Oh, the humanity!

Modern airships are generally known only as flying billboards one expert says.

As airship historian R. D. Layman explains A balloon cannot be piloted in any sense of the word.

1. The hot air balloon and airship differ in important ways. An airship is powered by a motor and propellers, but a balloon is not. An airship's horizontal path can be controlled, but a balloon's cannot. A balloon can be raised or lowered by adjusting the propane burner that heats the air inside it. However, it goes wherever the wind takes it.

____

____

2. The burning of the *Hindenburg* on May 6, 1937, is the most famous airship disaster. The spectacular accident was witnessed by many and actually covered on the air. It turned the public away from airships. They watched as the enormous fireball plummeted from the sky and people lost their lives. One cry in particular spoke for the American public.

____

____

Directions Do you think airship travel should have been abandoned or continued? On another sheet of paper, write a paragraph to persuade readers that your opinion is correct. Use quotations from *The Hindenburg* to support your argument. Use quotation marks and punctuation to set off your quotations correctly.

____

____

____

____

____

____

____

Home Activity Your child learned how to use quotations and quotation marks in writing. With your child, write dialogue for characters in a story about flying. Have your child punctuate the dialogue correctly.

Name ____________________

Related Words

Spelling Words				
clean	cleanse	inspire	inspiration	legal
legality	define	definition	please	pleasant
combine	combination	human	humanity	organ
organist	crime	criminal	recognize	recognition

Directions Unscramble the list words and write them on the line.

1. miinlrac 1. ____________
2. abciimnnoto 2. ____________
3. pasalent 3. ____________
4. ganro 4. ____________
5. iiinnsprato 5. ____________
6. eseapl 6. ____________
7. eseancl 7. ____________
8. mirec 8. ____________
9. stganroi 9. ____________
10. eancl 10. ____________
11. niecomb 11. ____________
12. spineri 12. ____________

Hidden Words Each of the smaller words can be found inside two of the list words. Write the list words that contain the smaller words.

13. gal ____________ 14. ____________
15. fin ____________ 16. ____________
17. man ____________ 18. ____________
19. cog ____________ 20. ____________

Home Activity Your child has learned to read, write, and spell related words that have differences in the way their vowels are pronounced. Ask your child to use two pairs of related words in sentences.

Name________________________________

Fact and Opinion

- **Statements of fact** are objective, not personal. They can be proved true or false. **Statements of opinion** are personal judgments or beliefs. They cannot be proved true or false.
- Statements of opinion can be valid or faulty. **Valid** statements can be supported by facts and common sense. **Faulty** statements cannot.
- Examine statements of opinion by using your prior knowledge. Based on what you have seen or read or what you know, ask, *Is the statement valid or faulty?*

Directions Read the following passage. Then complete the chart using statements of fact and statements of opinion from the passage.

I believe that airships should be built and used again, because they have many advantages over airplanes. First of all, they are cheaper to fly, because they need less fuel than planes. Secondly, they are larger and can carry more cargo. They are quiet, graceful machines, too. In addition, they can take off without a runway, since they rise straight up into the air. When airships were flown in the 1920s and 1930s, they made thousands of safe flights. Then came the *Hindenburg* explosion in 1937. Today's new technology would surely make airships safer. There is no reason to be frightened of airship travel. Because airships are fantastic in many ways, they should be in the skies again.

Statement of Opinion	Support	Valid or Faulty?
I believe that airships should be built and used again, because they have many advantages over airplanes.	**1.** They are cheaper to fly, larger, and they can	**2.**
3. There is no	**4.**	**5.**

Home Activity Your child identified facts and opinions in a nonfiction passage. Together, look through print advertisements for automobiles, air travel, and other forms of transportation. Identify as many statements of fact and statements of opinion as you can.

Name

Quotations and Quotation Marks

Directions Rewrite each sentence. Add quotation marks where they are needed.

1. Tell us about blimps, requested Sean.

2. What do you want to know? asked the museum guide.

3. Sean asked Do they have a framework inside to give them shape?

4. They do not, replied the guide. They get their shape from the gas inside them.

Directions Write each sentence correctly. Add capital letters, quotation marks, and other punctuation as needed.

5. Blimps are filled with helium he continued

6. how are they used asked Sean

7. the military has used blimps he replied to learn where land mines are located

8. some companies use them for advertising he continued and for aerial views of sports events

Home Activity Your child reviewed quotations and quotation marks. Ask your child to write sentences about the *Hindenburg* and include dialogue. Remind your child to use quotation marks and other punctuation correctly.

Name ______________________________

Easily Confused Words

- **Generalization** Some words are easily confused because they have similar pronunciations and spellings: **quiet**, **quite**.

Word Sort Sort the list words by words you know how to spell and words you are learning to spell. Write each word.

words I know how to spell	words I am learning to spell
1. ____________	11. ____________
2. ____________	12. ____________
3. ____________	13. ____________
4. ____________	14. ____________
5. ____________	15. ____________
6. ____________	16. ____________
7. ____________	17. ____________
8. ____________	18. ____________
9. ____________	19. ____________
10. ____________	20. ____________

Spelling Words

1. quiet
2. quite
3. finely
4. finally
5. except
6. accept
7. than
8. then
9. since
10. sense
11. affect
12. effect
13. from
14. form
15. later
16. latter
17. adapt
18. adopt
19. medal
20. metal

Home Activity Your child is learning about easily confused words. Ask your child to say each list word and spell it aloud.

Name

Family Times

Summary

Sweet Music in Harlem

C.J. wants to play jazz like Uncle Click, who's being photographed for a magazine. As C.J. tries to find Uncle Click's hat, he gathers lots of people to be in the photo with Click. To cap off the day, Uncle Click gives C.J. a new clarinet, and they even find Click's hat. Click is C.J.'s biggest fan.

Activity

Meeting the Music What kind of music do you like? Talk with your family members about the music each of them likes and why. See if there is any type of music that you all like.

Comprehension Skill

Sequence

The **sequence** of events is the order in which they take place, from first to last. Clue words such as *first*, *next*, and *then* may show sequence in a story or an article, but not always. Other clues are dates and times of day. Sometimes two events happen at the same time. Clue words that show this are *meanwhile* and *in that same year*.

Activity

What Happened Next? With members of your family, tell a familiar story out of order. Then challenge each other to tell the events of the story in the correct order.

Lesson Vocabulary

Words to Know

Knowing the meanings of these words is important to reading *Sweet Music in Harlem*. Practice using these words.

Vocabulary Words

bass the largest, lowest sounding stringed instrument in an orchestra or band

clarinet a woodwind instrument, having a mouthpiece with a single reed and played by means of holes and keys

fidgety restless; uneasy

forgetful apt to forget; having a poor memory

jammed made music with other musicians without having practiced

nighttime time between evening and morning

secondhand not new; used already by someone else

Conventions

Punctuation

Use a **semicolon** to join the parts of a compound sentence when no conjunction is used. *For example: Rob pitched; Denise caught.* Use a **colon** to introduce a list. *For example: He played the following sports: baseball, soccer, and tennis.* Use a **hyphen** in compound nouns, such as *great-uncle*, and compound adjectives before a noun, such as *out-of-town guests.* Use **parentheses** for words inserted as a comment. *For example: Ken (a musician) played at the wedding.*

Activity

Wait, Punctuate! Make a chart on a large sheet of paper. Make four boxes in the chart and label them "Semicolons," "Colons," "Hyphens," and "Parentheses." Find a magazine that is OK to cut up. Find sentences that use the four punctuation marks. Cut out the sentences and glue them on the chart.

Practice Tested Spelling Words

______	______	______	______
______	______	______	______
______	______	______	______
______	______	______	______
______	______	______	______

Name ______________________________

Sequence

- **Sequence** is the order of events in a selection. Dates and times of day or clue words such as *first, next,* and *then* can help you follow the sequence of events.
- Clue words such as *meanwhile* and *during* signal events happening at the same time.

Directions Read the following passage. Then answer the questions below.

Tamara loved to play the trumpet, and she wanted to play like the jazz greats she heard on the radio, including Wynton Marsalis, Miles Davis, and Freddie Hubbard. Then one day her family was invited to a reception in Harlem where Miles Davis was playing. Overjoyed, she and her family went to the party, bringing her beloved trumpet in case she could get it autographed. She waited for what seemed like hours, but finally Miles Davis played. She felt like she was in heaven. Then, at the end of the performance, he asked for someone from the audience to come onstage and help him play. When Tamara was picked, she got to stand next to Miles Davis and wail out some tunes!

1. What happens first in this story?

____

2. What happens next? Then what happens before the performance?

____

3. What happens at the end of the performance? How does it compare with what Tamara wanted?

____

____

4. What clue words help to show sequence in the story? Why is it important that the events occur in this sequence?

____

____

5. What do you know about jazz, trumpet, or jazz trumpeters? How does this knowledge help you to understand the story?

____

____

Home Activity Your child identified the sequence of events in a story and applied his or her prior knowledge to help understand the story. Tell your child a story about music, but first talk about your child's prior knowledge on the subject. Then work together to identify the sequence of events.

Name ______________________________

Draw Conclusions

Directions Read the story. Then answer the questions below.

Throughout Harlem, Danielle was known as the little girl with the big horn. Saxophone was her instrument, and she tried to imitate Charlie Parker, John Coltrane, and Kenny Garrett. When she practiced jazz on an old secondhand sax, the neighbors hung out of their windows to listen.

"You have talent," her music teacher told her as she gave her an extra lesson at no charge.

No one had to encourage Danielle. She practiced any time she had a chance. Then disaster hit. Her saxophone broke. She took it to her uncle, who fixed instruments, but he told her that he could not repair it. The price of a new instrument was way beyond her reach. She was disappointed. The neighbors were also disappointed when the music stopped. A few weeks later, on Danielle's birthday, the neighbors pitched in and presented her with a gift—a secondhand sax! She wrote a song to thank them.

1. How skilled do you think Danielle is at the saxophone? Explain why.

____

____

2. What can you tell about the community Danielle lives in? Explain.

____

____

3. What do you think Danielle's attitude is toward playing the saxophone?

____

____

4. Why do you think the music teacher gives Danielle a free lesson and tells her she has talent?

____

____

5. On a separate sheet of paper, explain how you think Danielle feels when she receives the saxophone. What effect do you think the gift will have on her and why?

Home Activity Your child has read a story about playing the saxophone and drawn conclusions about the characters. Read a short story to your child. Challenge him or her to identify the characters' traits and motives.

Name____________________

Punctuation

Directions Add the punctuation named in ( ) to make the meaning of the sentence clear. Write the sentence.

1. These woodwind instruments are reed instruments clarinet, saxophone, bassoon, English horn, and oboe. (colon)

____

____

2. Woodwinds were once made of wood now they are also made of other materials. (semicolon)

____

____

3. The after school program will show the movie The Music Man at 300 P.M. (hyphen, underlining, colon)

____

____

Directions Add punctuation to the following paragraph to make it clear. Rewrite the paragraph.

The clarinet is a single reed woodwind instrument. Its thin, flat reed is attached to the mouthpiece. The clarinet player takes the mouthpiece in her mouth and blows then the reed vibrates against the mouthpiece. Vibrating air is pushed through the straight, tube shaped instrument. Fingers press keys to open and close holes. A good clarinet player that's not me yet can make a wide range of smooth sounds.

____

____

____

____

____

____

____

____

Home Activity Your child learned how to use punctuation in writing. With your child, write a letter to a music store asking about a special CD. Be sure your child includes appropriate punctuation marks.

Name ____________________

Easily Confused Words

Spelling Words				
quiet	quite	finely	finally	except
accept	than	then	since	sense
affect	effect	from	form	later
latter	adapt	adopt	medal	metal

Word Scramble Unscramble each word to write a list word.

1. taapd — 1. ____________
2. telam — 2. ____________
3. ofrm — 3. ____________
4. ratel — 4. ____________
5. fftcee — 5. ____________
6. neess — 6. ____________
7. petcac — 7. ____________
8. etqui — 8. ____________
9. liynef — 9. ____________
10. neth — 10. ____________

Sound-alike Words Write a list word that sounds like each word listed below.

11. quiet — 11. ____________
12. finely — 12. ____________
13. accept — 13. ____________
14. then — 14. ____________
15. sense — 15. ____________
16. effect — 16. ____________
17. later — 17. ____________
18. form — 18. ____________
19. metal — 19. ____________
20. adapt — 20. ____________

Home Activity Your child unscrambled words and matched sound-alike words. Ask your child to pick a list word and spell it.

Name ______________________________

Sequence

- **Sequence** is the order of events in a selection. Dates and times of day or clue words such as *first, next,* and *then* can help you follow the sequence of events.
- Clue words such as *meanwhile* and *during* signal events happening at the same time.

Directions Read the following passage. Then complete the diagram by finishing the sentences that tell the sequence of events.

Three friends got together and wanted to play music, but they didn't have any instruments. "We have a garbage can," said Ken. Then he started trying to fashion it into a kettle drum. That inspired Jason to make his bicycle into an instrument, using strings, bowls, cans, and bells. Next, Ken's dad came along and told them about a cigar box guitar, made from a box, a stick, and wire. When Carin heard about that, she tried to make one. A few days later, they had three instruments to play. Next, they gave two friends sticks to clack and a hollow reed for a kind of flute. Then all five friends started practicing. Before long, they were making music together.

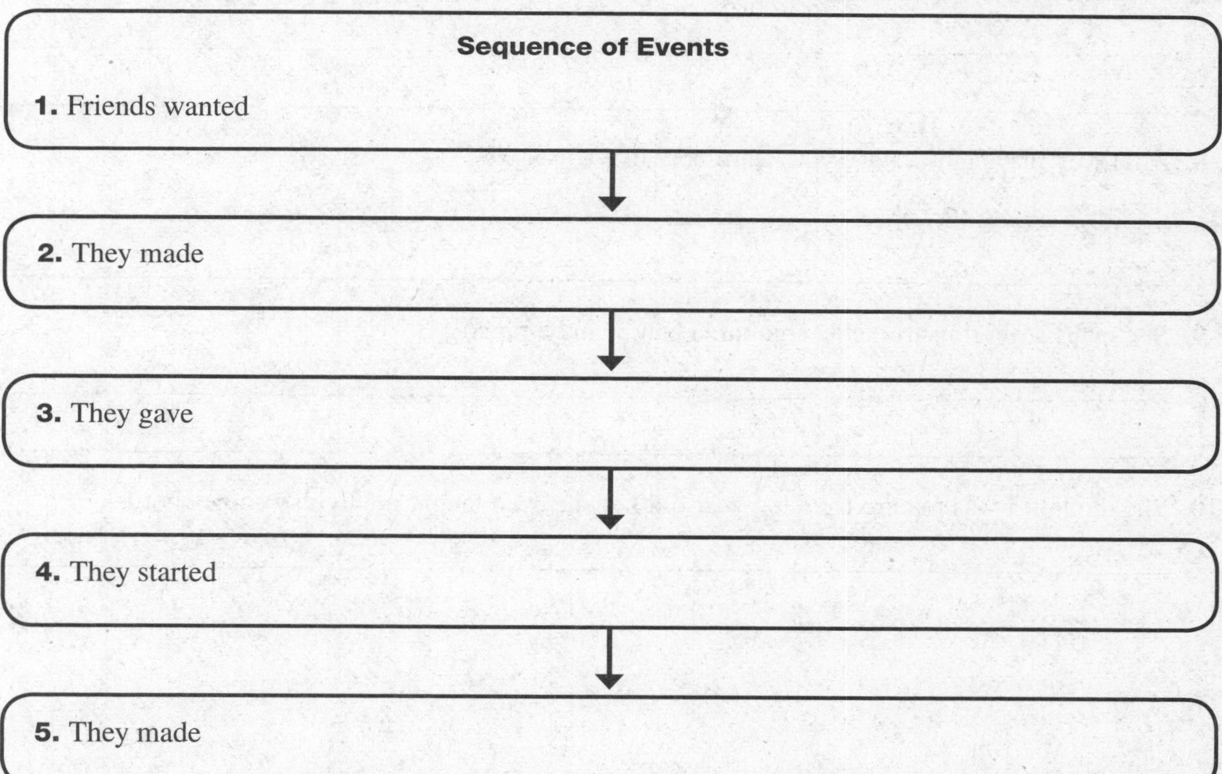

Sequence of Events
1. Friends wanted
2. They made
3. They gave
4. They started
5. They made

Home Activity Your child identified the sequence of events in a story using clue words. Read a newspaper story with your child and ask him or her to put the events of the story in sequence. Work with your child to identify clue words.

Name ______________________________

Punctuation

Directions Match the punctuation mark with the correct description.

_____ **1.** colon (:)

_____ **2.** semicolon (;)

_____ **3.** dash (—)

_____ **4.** italics (*Big*)

_____ **5.** hyphen (-)

A used to set off material that interrupts

B used in some compound words

C used after the salutation of a business letter

D used to join two independent clauses

E used to indicate titles

Directions Rewrite each sentence. Add the missing punctuation marks.

6. Troy doesn't like the old fashioned music that WDQB plays from 1030 to midnight.

____

____

7. I began my letter, "Dear Sir Please cancel my subscription to Music Classics."

____

____

8. Aunt Kay plays guitar have you heard her? like a pro.

____

____

9. She owns several instruments a guitar, a banjo, and a piano.

____

____

10. She thought I was mature for a ten year old kid she even taught me to play some chords.

____

____

Home Activity Your child reviewed punctuation. Have your child make a list of favorite books and magazines with correct underlining.

Name ______________________

Family Times

Selection Summaries

Week 1 *The Truth About Austin's Amazing Bats*

When the people of Austin, Texas, build a new bridge, they accidentally get a bat colony too.

Week 2 *The Mystery of Saint Matthew Island*

After a 1,000-member herd of reindeer disappears, a scientist sets out to find out why.

Week 3 *King Midas and the Golden Touch*

When the king gets to wish for anything he wants, his choice leads to despair.

Week 4 *The Hindenburg*

Hugo Eckener built the largest flying object ever, but when the dirigible exploded, an era ended.

Week 5 *Sweet Music in Harlem*

C.J. wants to play jazz like his Uncle Click, who is being photographed for a magazine. The photo shoot leads to unexpected results.

Activity

Where do stories come from? Discuss with a family member how you think the authors of these selections got their ideas.

Comprehension Skills Review

In Unit 6, you learned and used many skills while reading the stories and selections.

- The **sequence** of events is the order in which they take place, from first to last. Clue words such as *first*, *next*, and *then* may show sequence.
- The **main idea** of a text is what it is mostly about. **Details** support and expand on the main idea.
- When you **compare** two things, you tell how they are alike. When you **contrast** them, you tell how they are different.
- A **fact** is something that can be proved. An **opinion** is something that is a belief, thought, or feeling, and cannot be proved.

Activity

Unexpected developments can be unpleasant, like a sudden storm, or delightful, like a surprise party. Try writing your own story about an expected event, pleasant or not.

Unit Vocabulary Skills

Unknown Words

Use a dictionary or glossary to find the meaning of an **unknown word.**

Activity As you read, list unknown words and the meanings you looked up.

Endings

Endings, such as *-s* and *-es* are added to a word to create a new word with a new meaning. If you are unsure about the meaning of a word with an ending, check the dictionary.

Activity Make a list of six words and then add *-s* or *-es* to the words to change their meanings.

Suffixes

A **suffix** is attached to the end of word to create a new word.

Activity Find a word with a suffix and cover the suffix. How does the suffix change the base word's meaning?

Unfamiliar Words

Use context clues to help you figure out the meaning of an **unfamiliar word.**

Activity As you read, list unfamiliar words and the meanings you devised based on context clues.

Homographs

Homographs are words that are spelled the same but have different meanings or pronunciations.

Activity Brainstorm homographs and try using them in sentences. Use a dictionary to find other homographs.

Unit Spelling Rules

Suffixes *-ous, -sion, -ion, -ation*

When adding these suffixes, some base words change. A final *e* or *y* may be dropped: *famous*, *furious*. Some words have other changes: *decision*.

Final Syllable *-ant, -ent, -ance, -ence*

There is no sound clue to help you decide whether to use an *a* or an *e* in these word endings. The schwa sound in the endings can be spelled in different ways.

Latin Roots

Many English words come from Latin. For example, the Latin root *port*, which means "to carry," is used in the English words *portable*, *export*, and *transportation*. If you see *port* in a word and it has something to do with carrying, it probably comes from the Latin root *port*.

Related Words

Related words often have parts that are spelled the same but are pronounced differently: *please*, *pleasant*. When you say these words, pay close attention to where the stress is placed.

Easily Confused Words

Some words can be tricky to spell because they sound very much like another word, but they have different meanings and spellings: *except*, *accept*. Memorize the spellings and meanings of these words.

Name ______________________

Unknown Words

- As you read, you will come across **unknown words,** or words that are new to you. You can check the meanings of words that you don't know in a dictionary or glossary.

Practice Read the following sentences. Fill in the blanks with one of the Words to Know. Then choose the definition that best matches the underlined word.

Words to Know

- bizarre
- breathtaking
- headline
- high-pitched
- roost
- vital

1. Kiley's parents studied bats that inhabited a nearby ______________.

a. attacked b. lived in

2. The scientific studies were ______________ to the welfare of the bat colony.

a. group of animals b. cave

3. Kiley brought a recorded sample of the bats' ______________ squeals to school.

a. not difficult b. example

4. Kiley thought the sounds were ______________ and beautiful, but the other kids thought they were ______________ and unusual.

a. not usual b. normal

5. Kiley and the other kids thought of an inventive ______________ for their school newspaper: Bats in Our Belfry.

a. creative b. boring

On Your Own On a separate sheet of paper, write a story about what you would see if you were watching a bat. Use some of the words from the Words to Know list in your sentences.

Home Activity Your child reviewed unknown words. As you read a book or the newspaper together, challenge your child to find the meanings of some new words in a dictionary.

Name ______________________________

Draw Conclusions

- Active readers **draw conclusions,** or make decisions, based on information in the text and their own knowledge.
- Examine your own conclusions as you read. Ask yourself, "Can I support them with information from the text or with facts I already know?"

Directions Read the following story. Then complete the diagram by writing a conclusion and listing details from the story that support your conclusion.

On most summer weekends, Tina went to the beach with her aunt and younger cousins. She built sand castles with her cousins and watched the kids carefully as they toddled near the shore. If they waded into the water, Tina held their hands. She taught them to watch out for big waves, and she showed the older cousins how to swim. She also brought snacks for all the children to share. When it was time to go home, Tina carried the youngest cousins to keep their feet from burning on the sand. On the way home, she was already looking forward to the next day at the beach.

What Can I Conclude?

1.

What Does the Text Say?

2.

3.

4.

What Do I Already Know?

5.

Home Activity Your child drew a conclusion based on the details of a passage. Together, read a story about children. Work with your child to draw one or more conclusions about a character or event, using the text and prior knowledge.

Name ____________________

Endings

- An **ending** is attached to the end of a word to create a new word with a new meaning. If you are unsure about the meaning of a word with an ending, check the dictionary.

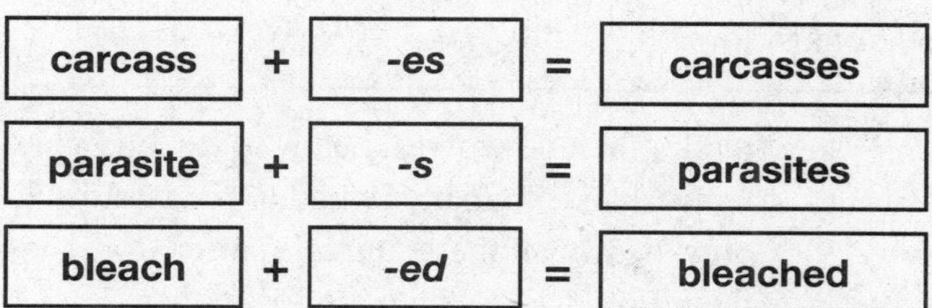

carcass	+	*-es*	=	carcasses
parasite	+	*-s*	=	parasites
bleach	+	*-ed*	=	bleached

Practice Read the following sentences. Fill in the blanks using the Words to Know. Circle the letter of the meaning of the underlined word. Use a dictionary to help you.

Words to Know
- bleached
- carcasses
- decay
- parasites
- scrawny
- starvation
- suspicions
- tundra

1. After finding the ____________ of two sheep, the farmer has his ____________ about what caused their deaths.

a. one sudden death b. more than one death

2. Because one sheep was noticeably ____________, the farmer decided that ____________ had caused the sheep's ____________.

a. is making a decision about something b. made a decision about something

3. The farmer expressed his concerns about raising sheep to his wife, who had always thought that they lived too close to the ____________ for the sheep to thrive.

a. more than one concern b. one very important concern

4. Because their barn had been ____________ by the sun and the cabin was beginning to ____________, they finally took the sheep and moved south.

a. will be going somewhere b. went somewhere

On Your Own As you read "Dirty Snowballs," look for words that include endings, and check their meanings in the dictionary. Make a list of these new words.

Home Activity Your child reviewed endings. Together, make a list of words from a book or a magazine article that contain the endings *-s, -es, -ed,* and *-ing*. Then write new sentences using those words.

Name ___________________________________

Main Idea and Details

- The **main idea** of a text is what it is mostly about.
- **Details** support and expand on the main idea.

Practice Read the passage and answer the questions below.

Despite the cold of the tundra, it is home to a variety of wildlife. Large herbivores, or plant-eaters, such as caribou and musk-ox, live in herds. Smaller plant-eaters, such as mice, shrews, and hares, live here too. The predators of the tundra include wolves, bears, foxes, and wolverines. No matter whether predator or prey, nearly all these animals suffer from the biting insects, such as mosquitoes, black flies, and deer flies.

1. What is the main idea of the passage?

____

____

2. What details support the main idea?

____

____

____

3. Which of the following sentences would also support the main idea?

a. Birds such as snowy owls, ducks, and geese also find a home in the tundra.

b. The tundra becomes very cold during the winter.

On Your Own Use what you know about main idea as you read "Dirty Snowballs." List details in the passage that support the main idea.

School + Home **Home Activity** Your child reviewed main idea and details. Together, read a newspaper article and ask your child to point out the main idea and details.

Name ______________________

Suffixes

- A **suffix** is attached to the end of a word to create a new word with a new meaning. If you are unsure about the meaning of a word with a suffix, check the dictionary.

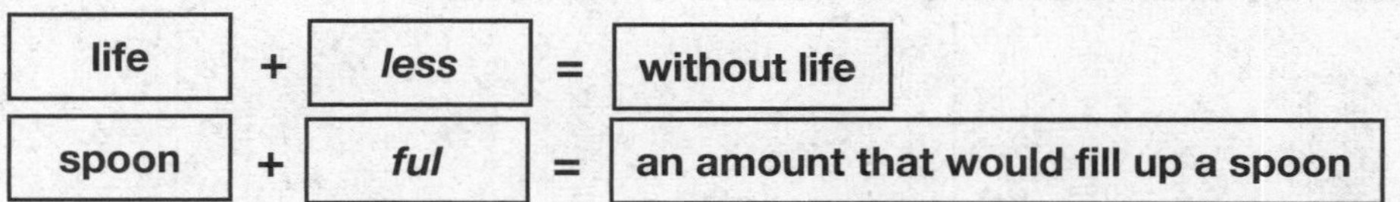

life + *less* = without life
spoon + *ful* = an amount that would fill up a spoon

Practice Fill in the blanks with Words to Know. Then circle the letter of the meaning of the underlined word that contains a suffix. Use what you know about the suffixes *-ful* and *-less* to help you.

Words to Know

- adorn
- cleanse
- lifeless
- precious
- realm
- spoonful

1. My mother declared that we were going to spend a peaceful afternoon at home, during which we would ______________ every inch of it.
   a. filled with peace b. without peace
2. After I realized it was hopeless to try to change her mind, she declared that the living room was my ______________.
   a. having strong hope of success b. having no hope of success
3. I grabbed a mop and poured a large ______________ of detergent in a bucket. I was ceaseless in my scrubbing and sweeping, and soon the room was so clean and empty that it looked almost ______________.
   a. without stopping or ceasing b. getting ready to stop or cease
4. "Looks like you got a bit carried away," Mom said, as she successfully used a few ______________ objects to ______________ the bare room.
   a. with great success b. without much success

On Your Own As you read "The Comet Racer," make a list of words with suffixes. Write sentences for these new words.

Home Activity Your child reviewed suffixes. Together, play a game of adding suffixes to different words to see how their meanings change.

Name ______________________________

Compare and Contrast

- When you **compare** two things, you tell how they are alike.
- When you **contrast** them, you tell how they are different.

Practice Look at the pictures above. Then answer the questions.

1. Describe the room in the first picture. What do you see?

____

____

____

2. Describe the room in the second picture. What do you see?

____

____

3. How is the room the same in the both pictures?

____

____

4. How is the room different?

____

____

On Your Own Use what you know about compare and contrast as you read "The Comet Racer." Write one thing that compares and one that contrasts in the passage.

Home Activity Your child reviewed comparing and contrasting. Together, compare and contrast two of your family's favorite places.

Name ____________________

Unfamiliar Words

- If you encounter an **unfamiliar word** while you are reading, you can use the words and sentences around it, or context clues, to help you figure out the meaning.

Practice Read the following sentences. Fill in the blanks using the Words to Know. Then circle the letter of the correct definition for each underlined word. Use context clues to help you.

Words to Know

- **criticizing**
- **cruised**
- **drenching**
- **era**
- **explosion**
- **hydrogen**

1. After taking off in a downpour, our airplane gained altitude until it ____________ high above the ____________ rain.

a. depth b. height c. speed

2. The gas turbine engines propelled our craft through the air, burning jet fuel in a controlled ____________.

a. stored b. burned c. moved

3. Although I was secure in the plane, I missed riding in the ____________-powered car that my father devised.

a. invented b. crashed c. suspended

4. While my aunt was ____________ his daydreams, my father maintained that his invention was the start of a new ____________ in transportation.

a. insisted b. worried c. trained

On Your Own As you read "Dirty Snowballs," list unfamiliar words and their meanings based on context clues. Write sentences using the new words from the passage.

School + Home **Home Activity** Your child reviewed unfamiliar words. Together, check the list of word meanings your child derived from context clues against a print or online dictionary.

Name ______________________________

Fact and Opinion

- A **fact** is something that can be proved.
- An **opinion** is something that is a belief, thought, or feeling, and cannot be proved. Opinions often include words that make judgments, such as *best, beautiful,* or *interesting.*

Practice Read the passage and then answer the questions below.

My family and I went to the zoo on Saturday. It was the best time. I saw all kinds of animals. My favorite animals were the cougars. The zoo built the cougars a natural habitat, so it was like watching them in the wild. Cougars stalk their prey. That means they hide and then surprise them. We saw one cougar practice by stalking another cougar. Watching it leap out was one of the most exciting things I've ever seen.

My least favorite animals were the elephants. They smelled really bad, and they kept throwing dirt everywhere. You could ride them if you wanted, but I chose not to. I didn't want to smell like that for the rest of the day.

1. What is one fact about the cougars?

____

2. What is one opinion about the elephants?

____

3. Write another fact from the story.

____

4. Write another opinion from the story.

____

5. How could opinions in this passage influence readers?

____

____

On Your Own Use what you know about facts as you read "Dirty Snowballs." Then write a few opinions about what it would be like to see a comet.

Home Activity Your child reviewed facts and opinions. Ask your child to share some facts and one opinion about where he or she goes to school.

Name ______________________________

Homographs

- **Homographs** are two words that are spelled the same but have different meanings and may have different pronunciations.

present (adjective):
in attendance
present (verb): to give
something to someone

Practice Read the following sentences. Fill in the blanks with one of the Words to Know. Then circle the letter of the correct meaning of the homograph that is underlined in each sentence. Use a dictionary to check your answers.

Words to Know

bass
clarinet
fidgety
forgetful
jammed
nighttime
secondhand

1. Hugh was <u>content</u> with the ____________ trumpet and ____________ that he owned.

   a. happy   b. information

2. He said that he is so ____________, he would <u>refuse</u> better instruments out of the worry he would accidentally leave them somewhere.

   a. trash, garbage   b. say no to something

3. At ____________, he went to the corner coffeeshop and ____________ with other musicians. He wanted to <u>exploit</u> every chance he had to practice.

   a. to take advantage of an opportunity   b. a bold, unusual, daring action

4. The ____________ player did not <u>object</u> to Hugh's ____________ manner.

   a. a thing   b. speak out against

On Your Own As you read "The Comet Racer," watch out for words that are homographs, and check their meanings in the dictionary. Write a sentence using the word.

Home Activity Your child reviewed homographs. With your child, look up a list of homographs online and challenge each other to use each word in a sentence.

Name ____________________

Sequence

- **Sequence** refers to the order of events, or the steps in a process. Clue words such as *first, next,* and *then* can help you follow the sequence of events.

Practice Read the recipe for making a salad. Then answer the questions below.

First, wash a head of lettuce. My favorite is green leaf, but you can use any kind you like. Then tear the lettuce apart and add it to a large bowl. Next, prepare the fresh vegetables. Have an adult slice or chop tomatoes, cucumbers, onions, and olives, or any other vegetables that you like. Then add them to the bowl. Next, add salad dressing and croutons, if you like them.

Finally, toss the salad so it mixes evenly. The whole process should take about fifteen minutes.

1. What is the last step in making a salad?

____

2. When should you add fresh vegetables to the salad?

____

____

3. What is the first thing you should do when you are making a salad?

____

4. What should you do before adding the vegetables to the salad?

____

____

5. How long should it take to make a salad?

____

____

On Your Own Use what you know about sequence as you read "The Comet Racer." Write what comes first, next, and last in the story.

Home Activity Your child reviewed sequence. Have your child list the sequence of events from this past day. Remind him or her to use clue words.

Name______________________________________

Dirty Snowballs

Comets have fascinated people for centuries. From Earth, these outer-space bodies look like fuzzy smudges of light in the night sky. But what are comets, and what do we know about them?

A comet is a frozen object in outer space, made of ice and dust. For this reason, some astronomers call them "dirty snowballs." There are three main parts to a comet: the nucleus, the coma, and the tail.

The nucleus is the solid inner part of the comet. It is made up of ice, dust, and gases. It is covered with a black crust that absorbs heat as the comet travels. As the nucleus absorbs the heat of the sun, the ice inside it starts to melt, pressure builds, and the weakest parts of its crust start to rupture, or break up.

Jets of gas shoot out of the weakening nucleus. Each explosion of gas adds to a growing halo of dust and gas that surrounds the nucleus. This halo is called the coma. Together, the coma and the nucleus form the head of the comet. An invisible layer of hydrogen gas surrounds the coma. This is called the hydrogen envelope, and it becomes larger when the comet approaches the sun.

Usually, a comet's nucleus and coma will only be about six miles across. But some are much larger. One famous comet, the Great Comet of 1811, had a coma about as big across as the diameter of the sun!

The comet's tail is also made up of the dust particles and gas molecules that evaporate from the nucleus. The tail is easily visible because the dust particles reflect the sunlight, and it can be millions of miles long. The Great Comet of 1843 had a tail that was more than 150 million miles long.

Comets come into being far outside our solar system, billions or even trillions of miles away from the sun. Scientists think that there are ancient clouds of dust and gas out there that are left over from billions of years ago, when our solar system began.

Most comets never get close enough to Earth for us to see them, even with our most powerful telescopes. But a few do travel close enough for humans to glimpse. Usually comets that can be seen with the naked eye only show up once every five to ten years.

Comets are unpredictable in how they appear to us. Some may linger in the sky for weeks, while others may fade in and out of view in just a few hours. Sometimes one comet will split up into several and continue to move together in the same direction.

Suffixes What is the suffix of the word *snowballs*?

____

What is the suffix of the word *gases*?

____

Unfamiliar Words Underline the words in the third paragraph that help you understand the meaning of *rupture.*

Main Idea and Supporting Details Underline the main idea in the fourth paragraph.

Fact and Opinion Write a fact you learned about comets from Paragraph 2. How do you know it's a fact?

____

____

____

____

____

Name ___________________________________

Main Idea and Supporting Details
Underline the details in the second paragraph that support the idea that we can't see from Earth how fast comets are moving.

Fact and Opinion
Write an opinion that the author could have included in this passage.

____

____

____

____

____

____

____

Remember that comets start out billions of miles away from the sun. When a comet has cruised into our solar system and moves closer to the sun, the dust and ice in the comet heat up and evaporate. This evaporation is what produces the long tails of gas and dust that can be seen from Earth. Comets with extremely long tails can be seen with the naked eye. Those only show up about once every ten years.

Even the comets we can see from Earth are millions of miles away. Because of this, we can't easily see their movement across the sky. This is one way in which comets are very different from meteors, or "shooting stars," which seem to streak across the sky and then disappear. Usually, the only way to tell that a comet is moving is to watch it for several nights. Then you can see that it is moving in relationship to the stars around it.

Sometimes, the sun's gravity will pull comets into an elliptical orbit. An elliptical orbit is more oval-shaped than circle-shaped. These comets can orbit the sun for thousands of years. However, other comets orbit too close to the sun. These comets will melt like an ice cube near a flame. Over thousands of years, the comet will shrink and melt away.

Long ago, people thought comets were bad omens. They thought a comet was a sign that something terrible was about to happen, such as a plague or a war. In our own era, most people don't see comets as messengers of disaster. However, people today continue to be interested in these interstellar snowballs.

One of the most famous comets is Halley's comet. Halley's comet is famous because it returns about every 76 years. Its most recent sighting was in 1985, and it is predicted to return again in 2061. Astronomers have noted every single appearance of Halley's comet since ancient times.

If you ever do see a comet through a telescope or with your naked eye, remember that it was made from the most ancient building blocks of our nebula. The dust and gas that formed that comet is the same dust and gas that formed our own solar system billions of years ago!

Home Activity Your child read a selection and used comprehension and vocabulary skills from Unit 6. Have your child point out the main idea and supporting details of each paragraph in the selection. In addition, have your child point out words with suffixes and explain how the suffix changes the meaning of the base word.

Name______________________________________

The Comet Racer

Jaz put on his Black Violet Visor and felt a trickle of sweat run down his back. All around him was the emptiness of space. The electric engine pulse of his ship, the Sorcerer, seemed to match his own frantic heartbeat.

The race master's voice came over Jaz's headset. "Contestants, do you copy?" said the voice. "Comet Kettleboom is approaching at the stargate. Start your engines and line up at the raceway."

Jaz flipped off the idle switch on his dashboard and flew the Sorcerer into its proper lane. Fidgety with excitement, he wondered if he should have had that third glass of Rocketwave Juice an hour earlier.

Back on Earth, Jaz knew the immense crowds were cheering for the fourteen different spaceships getting ready to begin. All across the globe, hovering air-screens were projecting images of each ship's location and pilot. Jaz glanced at his own contestant's badge hung around his neck: *Comet Quest Competitor 00904: Jaz Morse. June 1, 2189*

Jaz had worked hard to get to this point. For three years, his precious time had been filled with flight exams, astrophysics lab work, and anti-gravity engineering. When the Comet Quest committee had announced that he would be the fourteenth competitor in the upcoming race, Jaz just knew this was his chance to make history. No single ship had been able to surpass a flying comet—at least, not yet.

The race master's voice jolted Jaz back to reality. "Contestants, do you copy?" There was a brief pause as everyone responded. "All ships on course and ready for velocity activation. Comet Kettleboom 5,000 miles away and counting." Jaz quickly did the calculations in his head. The comet would be here in just over two minutes. He counted to himself as he braced the steering wheel.

"In 10," said the race master, "9… 8… 7… 6… 5… 4… 3… 2… GO!" In the lifeless vacuum of space, fourteen ships bolted forward with a furious burst of blazing heat. Jaz saw Comet Kettleboom flying several hundred miles to his right, as he launched the Sorcerer into action.

The speed gauge on the dashboard registered 15 miles per second, but Jaz knew he was going to have to travel a whole lot faster if he was going to beat that comet. He ramped up the engine core and increased his speed to 20 miles per second. In a few more moments, he was up to 30. *C'mon Sorcerer,* Jaz thought to himself, *I know you're one whizzing wizard of a ship!*

Sequence Circle the words that tell you whether Jaz had Rocketwave Juice before or after starting his engine.

Draw Conclusions After reading Paragraph 5, draw a conclusion about what Jaz intends to do.

____

____

____

Sequence What happened after the race master's countdown?

____

____

Draw Conclusions After reading this page, what conclusions can you draw about Jaz?

____

____

____

____

____

Name ______________________________

Homographs What is the meaning of *lead* in Paragraph 1?

____

What is another meaning of *lead*?

____

Compare and Contrast Compare the Comet Quest race with a running race. Name one similarity and one difference.

____

____

____

____

____

____

____

Unknown Words Circle the word *disoriented* in Paragraph 7. Check its meaning in a dictionary and write its definition as it is used in the passage.

____

____

____

His on-screen monitors showed his rivals nearby as the comet propelled ahead. Now was the time for Jaz to hit the flash grid core accelerator. With a cool, steady hand and a madly beating heart, Jaz shifted on the accelerator and felt his body push back into his seat. Now he was flying at 40 miles per second—just as fast as Comet Kettleboom. The Sorcerer began to emerge into the lead as the other ships fell behind. "Aces!" Jaz shouted as he sped into the blackness.

Soon he was traveling just under 45 miles per second. He could see the distance shrinking between himself and the racing comet. There it was—that dirty ball of ice just daring him to pass by. "You're mine," Jaz said as he rushed straight ahead.

In the two seconds that followed, Jaz gave one final blast to the thrusters and felt his ship bolt to the front. His heart flip-flopped inside his chest as he called into his headset, "Race master, this is Jaz Morse. I've passed the comet's coma." But no sooner had Jaz made the announcement when he felt his ship give a lurch. A red light suddenly began flashing on his dashboard. Something dreadful was wrong.

Jaz checked his control panel and realized quickly that the dust from the comet had chipped at his ship's outer hull. A mechanism had failed and he was beginning to spin out of control. "Morse to base," Jaz called out. "Requiring immediate assistance." Without a moment to spare, Jaz switched off the flash grid core accelerator. His speed dropped down, but the Sorcerer was still spinning. He cut power to the thrusters and felt his stomach whirling. "C'mon, Sorce!" Jaz yelled. "Please don't fail me now." Madly, he held on to his seat as he tried to pull on the stuck emergency brake.

Just when Jaz thought he'd lose his lunch and his life, he gave one last dramatic pull and felt his ship begin to slow down.

"Race master to Jaz, do you copy? Do you copy?"

Jaz felt a little ill and disoriented as he clutched his contestant's badge. "Did I win?" he groaned into his headset.

"You've won, my boy!" the race master said. "You're the first to fly faster than a speeding comet. Can you make it back to base?"

"Can I move?" would be a better question, Jaz thought to himself. But he straightened in his chair and patted his control panel. "Fine work, Sorcerer. Really fine work."

Home Activity Your child read a selection and used comprehension and vocabulary skills from Unit 6. Have your child retell the selection, comparing and contrasting the plot details and noting the importance of the setting.

Reveal MATH®

Student Edition

Grade K • Volume 2

Back cover: Velvetfish/iStock/Getty Images

mheducation.com/prek-12

Send all inquiries to:
McGraw Hill
8787 Orion Place
Columbus, OH 43240

ISBN: 978-0-07-683903-2
MHID: 0-07-683903-6

Printed in the United States of America.

6 7 8 9 QSX 24 23 22

Contents in Brief

Volume 1

Volume 2

Welcome to *Reveal Math*!

We are excited that you have made us part of your math journey.

Throughout this school year, you will explore new concepts and develop new skills. You will expand your math thinking and problem-solving skills. You will be encouraged to persevere as you solve problems, working both on your own and with your classmates.

With *Reveal Math*, you will experience activities to spark your curiosity and challenge your thinking. In each lesson, you will engage in sense-making activities that will make you a better problem solver. You will have different learning experiences to help you build understanding.

We look forward to revealing to you the wonder and excitement of math.

The *Reveal Math* authors

The *Reveal Math* Authorship Team

McGraw Hill teamed up with expert mathematicians to create a program centered around you, the student, to make sure each and every one of you can find joy and understanding in the math classroom.

Ralph Connelly, Ph.D.
Authority on the development of early mathematical understanding.

Annie Fetter
Advocate for students' ideas and student thinking that fosters strong problem solvers.

Linda Gojak, M.Ed.
Expert in both theory and practice of strong mathematics instruction.

Sharon Griffin, Ph.D.
Champion for number sense and the achievement of all students.

Ruth Harbin Miles, Ed.S.
Leader in developing teachers' math content and strategy knowledge.

Susie Katt, M.Ed.
Advocate for the unique needs of our youngest mathematicians.

Nicki Newton, Ed.D.
Expert in bringing student-focused strategies and workshops into the classroom.

John SanGiovanni, M.Ed.
Leader in understanding the mathematics needs of students and teachers.

Raj Shah, Ph.D.
Expert in both theory and practice of strong mathematics instruction.

Jeff Shih, Ph.D.
Advocate for the importance of student knowledge.

Cheryl Tobey, M.Ed.
Facilitator of strategies that drive informed instructional decisions.

Dinah Zike, M.Ed.
Creator of learning tools that make connections through visual-kinesthetic techniques.

Unit 8

Addition and Subtraction Strategies

Unit 9

Numbers 11 to 15

Numbers 16 to 19

Unit
11

3-Dimensional Shapes

Count to 100

Unit 13

Analyze, Compare, and Compose Shapes

Compare Measurable Attributes

Let's Talk About Math!

This year, you will explore the language of mathematics together as you talk about math with your classmates. You are going to learn many new words. Use these resources as you expand your vocabulary.

Glossary

In the back of this book, you will find a glossary with definitions.

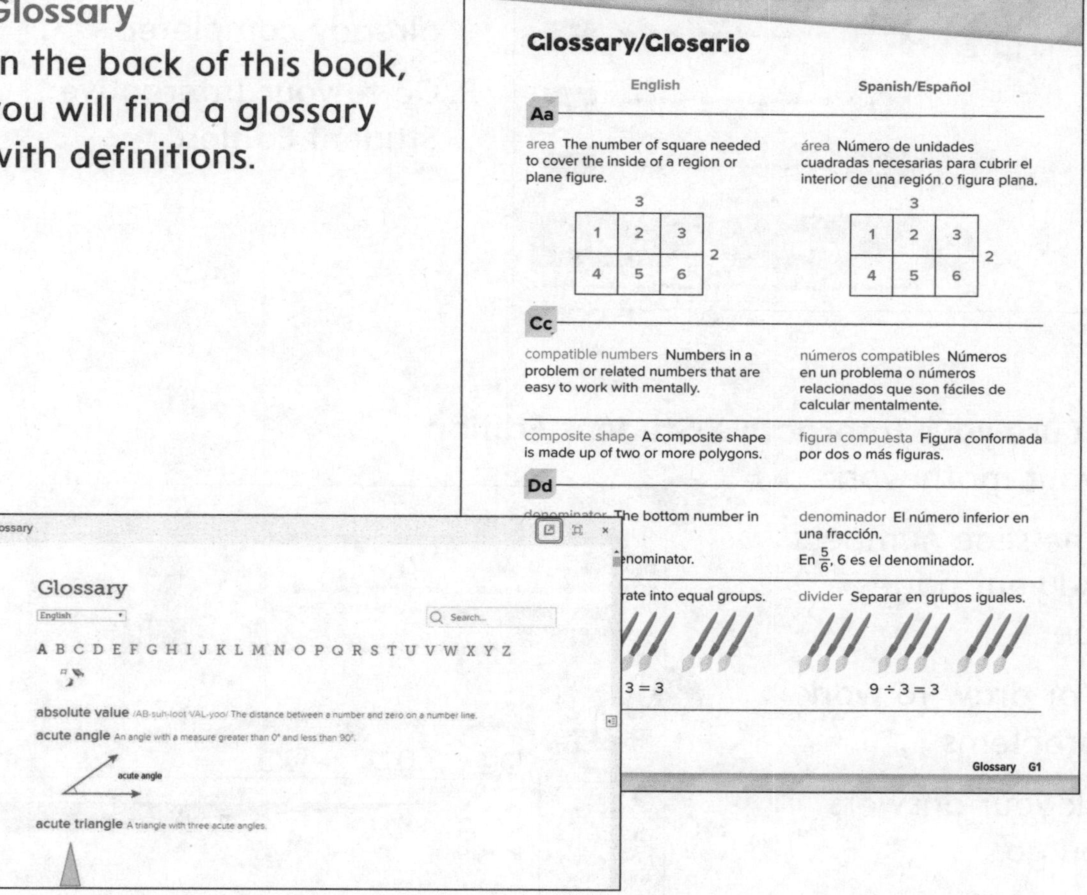

Interactive Glossary

The Interactive Glossary will support you as you work in your Interactive Student Edition.

Jump into Learning!

You can find all the resources you need from your **Student Dashboard**.

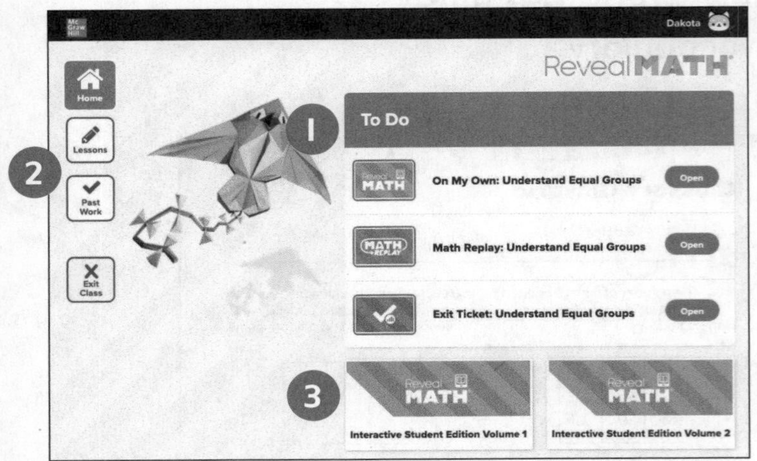

1. See your work in the To-Do List.
2. See the work you already completed.
3. Go to your Interactive Student Edition.

You can use your **Interactive Student Edition** for all your math work.

1. Use the slide numbers to find your page number.
2. Type or draw to work out problems.
3. Check your answers as you go.

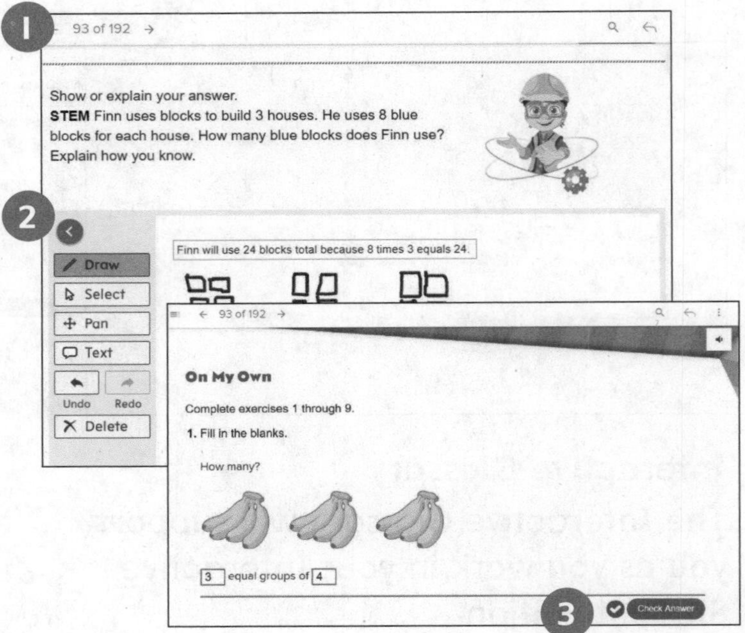

Access Lesson Supports Online!

You can also use these to support while you practice.

Need an Instant Replay of the Lesson Content?

Each lesson has a **Math Replay** video that provides a 1–2 minute overview of the lesson concept.

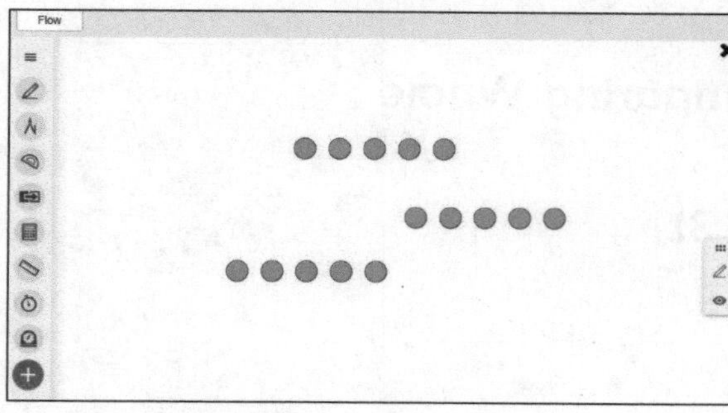

Virtual Tools to Help You Problem Solve

You can access the eToolkit at any time from your Student Dashboard. You can access these tools:

- Counters
- Base-Ten Blocks
- Array Builder
- Fraction Model
- Bucket Balance
- Geometry Sketch
- Money
- Fact Triangles
- Number Line
- and more!

Key Concepts and Learning Objectives

Key Concept Habits of Mind and Classroom Norms

- I can describe ways we use math in our lives and our world. (Unit 1)
- I can describe my strengths as a doer of math. (Unit 1)
- I can explain what a problem is. (Unit 1)
- I can see mathematics in the real-world. (Unit 1)
- I can explain my thinking. (Unit 1)
- I can work well on my own and in a group. (Unit 1)
- I know the steps I can take to solve a problem. (Unit 1)
- I can describe patterns. (Unit 1)

Key Concept Representing and Comparing Whole Numbers

- I can count objects to 10. (Units 2, 3)
- I can show numbers 1–10. (Units 2, 3)
- I can identify 0. (Unit 2)
- I can explain how to identify the number that is one more. (Units 2, 3)
- I can tell whether groups are equal. (Units 2, 3)
- I can compare two groups of objects or numbers. (Units 2, 3)
- I can write numbers to show how many. (Unit 3)
- I can represent numbers 11–19. (Units 9, 10)
- I can make groups of 11–19 objects. (Units 9, 10)

- I can decompose groups of 11–19 objects. (Units 9, 10)
- I can count by 1s and 10s to 100. (Unit 12)
- I can describe patterns when counting by 1s and 10s to 100. (Unit 12)
- I can count by 1s to 100, starting at any number. (Unit 12)
- I can count to answer "how many?" about as many as 20 things. (Unit 12)

Key Concept **Addition and Subtraction**

- I can represent and solve addition and subtraction problems. (Units 6, 7)
- I can solve addition and subtraction equations within 5 fluently. (Unit 8)
- I can compose and decompose numbers to 10 in different ways. (Unit 8)

Key Concept **Measurement and Data**

- I can sort and describe objects by attribute. (Unit 4)
- I can describe and compare objects using length, height, weight, and capacity. (Unit 14)

Key Concept **Describing Shapes and Space**

- I can name and describe 2-dimensional shapes. (Unit 5)
- I can describe the relative position of 2-dimensional and 3-dimensional shapes. (Units 5, 11)
- I can name and describe 3-dimensional shapes. (Unit 11)
- I can compare and contrast 2-dimensional and 3-dimensional shapes. (Unit 13)
- I can draw and build 2-dimensional and 3-dimensional shapes. (Unit 13)

Math is...

How would you complete this sentence?

Math is.....

Math is not just adding and subtracting.

Math is...

- working together
- finding patterns
- sharing ideas
- listening thoughtfully to our classmates
- sticking with a task even when it is a little challenging

In *Reveal Math,* you will develop the habits of mind that strong doers of math have. You will see that math is all around us.

Let's be Doers of Mathematics

Remember, math is more than getting the right answer. It is a tool for understanding the world around you. It is a language to communicate and collaborate. Be mindful of these prompts throughout the year to access the power of math.

1. **Math is... Mine**
   - Mindset
2. **Math is... Exploring and Thinking**
   - Planning
   - Connections
   - Thinking
3. **Math is... My World**
   - In My World
   - Modeling
   - Choosing Tools
4. **Math is... Explaining and Sharing**
   - Explaining
   - Sharing
   - Precision
5. **Math is... Finding Patterns**
   - Patterns
   - Generalizations
6. **Math is... Ours**
   - Mindset

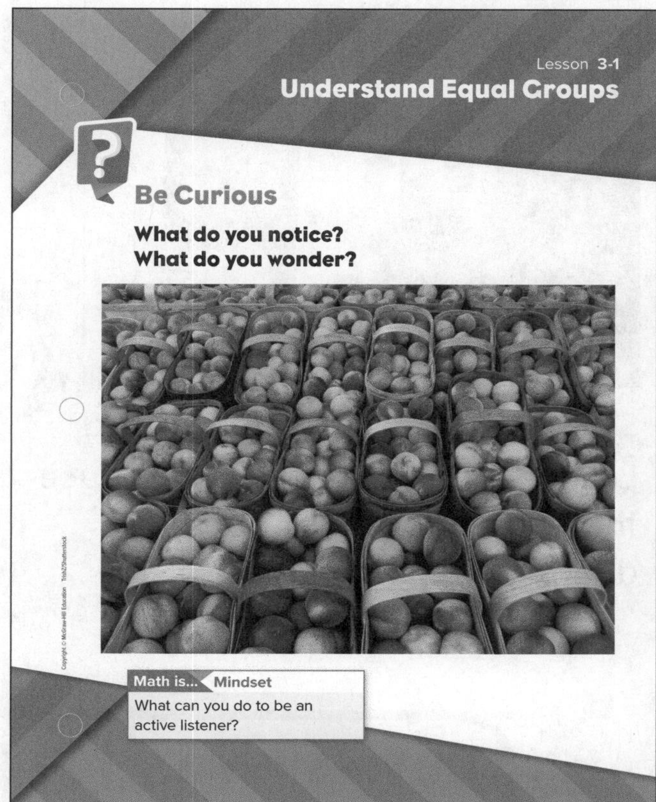

Lesson 3-1
Understand Equal Groups
Be Curious
What do you notice?
What do you wonder?
Math is... Mindset
What can you do to be an active listener?

Math is... Mindset

What can you do to be an active listener?

Explore the Exciting World of STEM!

Ever wonder how math applies in the real world? In every unit, you will learn about a STEM career, from protecting our parks to exploring outer space. You will learn about the STEM career through digital simulations and projects.

STEM Career Kid: Meet Sienna

Let the STEM Career Kid introduce their career and talk about the different responsibilities.

Math In Action: Nutritionist

Watch the Math in Action to see how the math you are learning applies to the real world.

Hi, I'm Sienna.

I want to be a nutritionist to help people eat to feel great!

Unit 8

Addition and Subtraction Strategies

Focus Question

How can I make and decompose numbers in more than one way?

Hi, I'm Deven.

I want to be a sound engineer. I will be using 6 microphones! I can use 3 to record the drums and 3 to record the guitars. How else can I arrange the microphones?

Name

How Many Are Covered?

Work Mat

Directions: Listen to your teacher. Use counters to make amounts.

Lesson **8-1**

Add within 5

Be Curious

Math is... Mindset

Directions:
What do you notice? What do you wonder?

Learn

$3 + 2 = 5$

Work Together

$3 + 1 =$ ___

Work Together: How can you count on to find 3 + 1? Color the starting number. Count on 1. Circle the stopping number. What is the sum?

On My Own

MATH REPLAY | GO ONLINE

Name ______________________

1
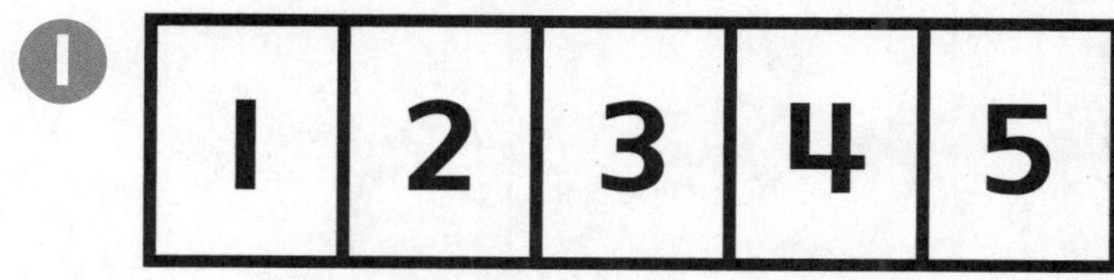

2 + 1 = ____

2
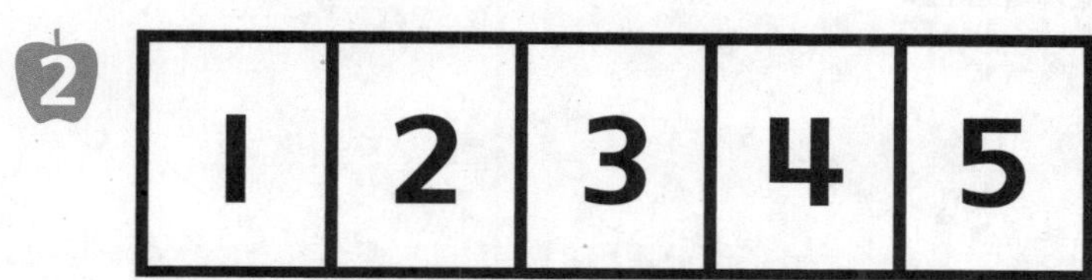

4 + 1 = ____

3
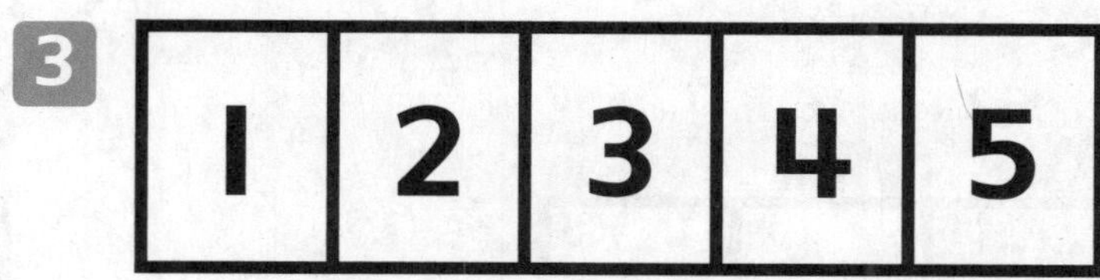

2 + 2 = ____

Directions: **1.** How can you count on to find 2 + 1? Color the starting number. Count on 1. Circle the stopping number. What is the sum? **2.** How can you count on to find 4 + 1? Color the starting number. Count on 1. Circle the stopping number. What is the sum? **3.** How can you count on to find 2 + 2? Color the starting number. Count on 2. Circle the stopping number. What is the sum?

1	2	3	4	5

I + I = ___

1	2	3	4	5

2 + 3 = ___

Reflect

1	2	3	4	5

Directions: 4. How can you count on to find I + I? Color the starting number. Count on I. Circle the stopping number. What is the sum? **5. Extend Your Thinking** Two students are on the playground. Three more join. Color the starting number. Count on 3. Circle the stopping number. What is the sum?

Reflect: How can a number path help you find 3 + I?

Lesson 8-2

Subtract within 5

Be Curious

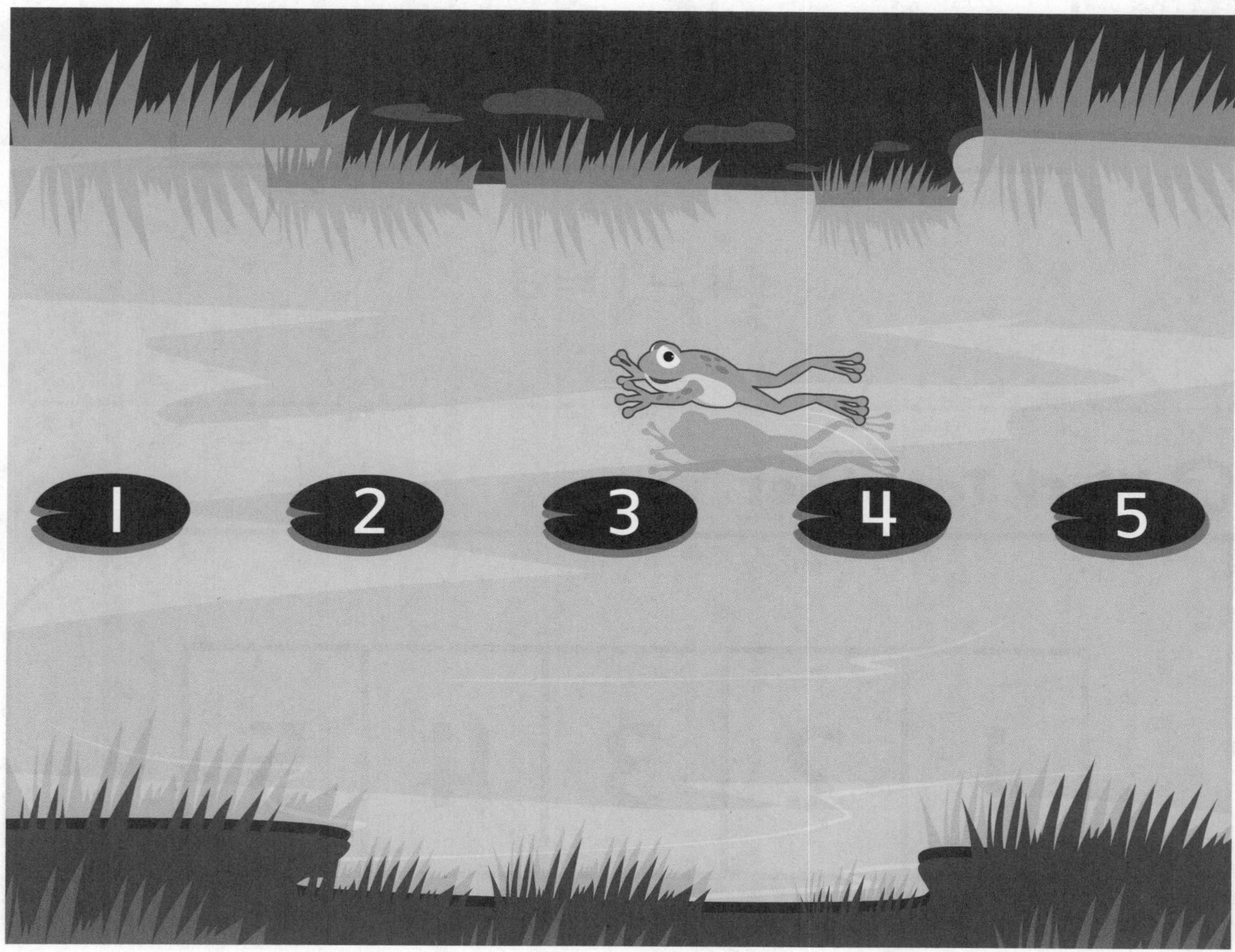

Math is... Mindset

Directions:
What do you notice? What do you wonder?

Learn

$4 - 1 = 3$

Work Together

1	2	3	4	5

$4 - 2 =$ ______

Work Together: How can you count back to find 4 − 2? Color the starting number. Count back 2. Circle the stopping number. What is the difference?

On My Own

MATH REPLAY | GO ONLINE

Name ______________________

1

$3 - 2 =$ ____

2

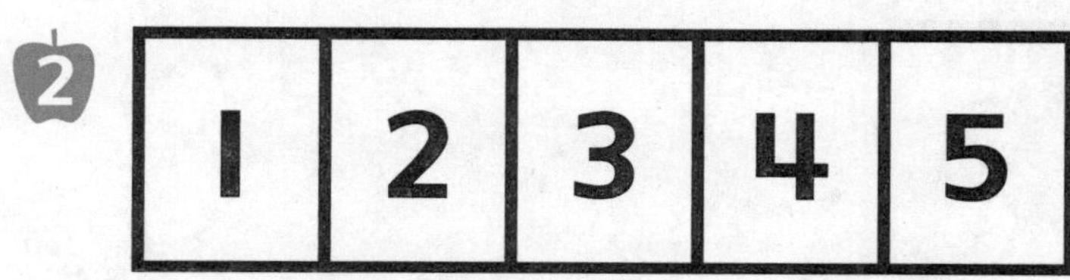

$5 - 2 =$ ____

3

$2 - 1 =$ ____

Directions: 1. How can you count back to find 3 − 2? Color the starting number. Count back 2. Circle the stopping number. What is the difference? **2.** How can you count back to find 5 − 2? Color the starting number. Count back 2. Circle the stopping number. What is the difference? **3.** How can you count back to find 2 − 1? Color the starting number. Count back 1. Circle the stopping number. What is the difference?

1	2	3	4	5

3 – 1 = ___

1	2	3	4	5

5 – 3 = ___

Reflect

1	2	3	4	5

Directions: 4. Error Analysis Trevor says 3 – 1 = 1. Use the number path to help Trevor find 3 – 1 and complete the equation. **5. Extend Your Thinking** Five frogs were on the grass. Three jumped in the water. Color the starting number. Count back 3. Circle the stopping number. What is the difference?

Reflect: How can a number path help you find 5 – 1?

Ways to Make 6 and 7

Be Curious

Math is... Mindset

Directions:
How are they the same? How are they different?

Learn

6

$1 + 5 = 6$

$4 + 2 = 6$

7

$2 + 5 = 7$

$4 + 3 = 7$

Work Together

6

___ + ___ = ___

Work Together: How can you make 6? Use two colors to show a way to make 6. Write the equation to match.

MATH REPLAY | GO ONLINE

On My Own

Name ________________

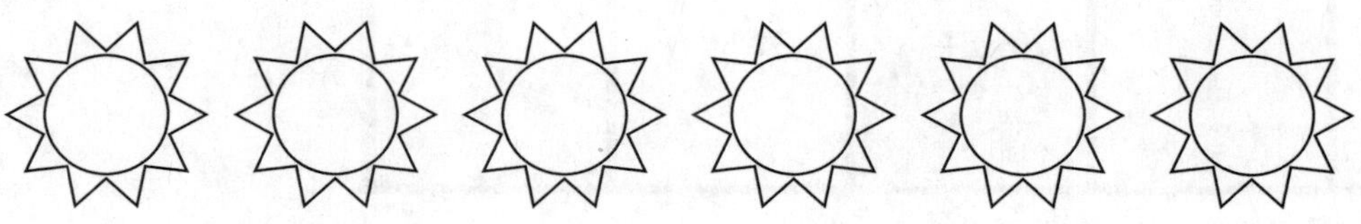

___ + ___ = ___

2

___ + ___ = ___

3

___ + ___ = ___

Directions: **1.** How can you make 6? Use two colors to show a way to make 6. Write the equation to match. **2.** How can you make 7? Use two colors to show a way to make 7. Write the equation to match. **3.** How can you make 6? Use two colors to show a different way to make 6. Write the equation to match.

4

___ + ___ = ___

5

___ + ___ = ___

___ + ___ = ___

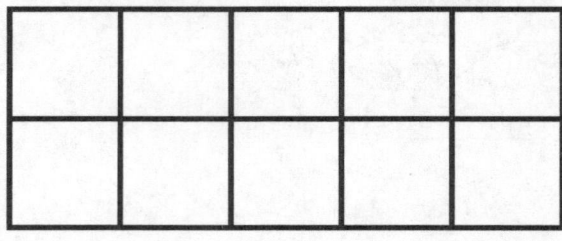

Reflect

6

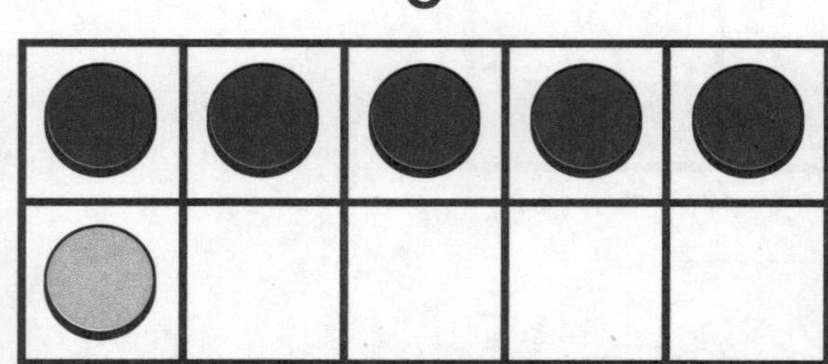

7

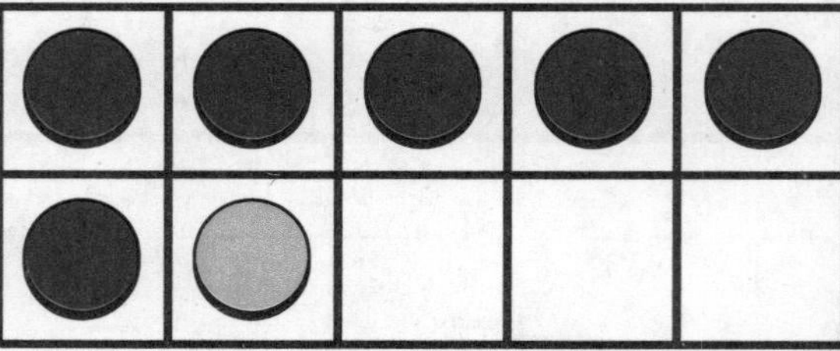

Directions: 4. STEM Connection How can you make 7? Use two colors to show a different way to make 7. Write the equation to match. **5. Extend Your Thinking** Draw counters to show two ways to make 7. Write the equations to match.

Reflect: What other ways can you make 6 and 7?

Ways to Decompose 6 and 7

Be Curious

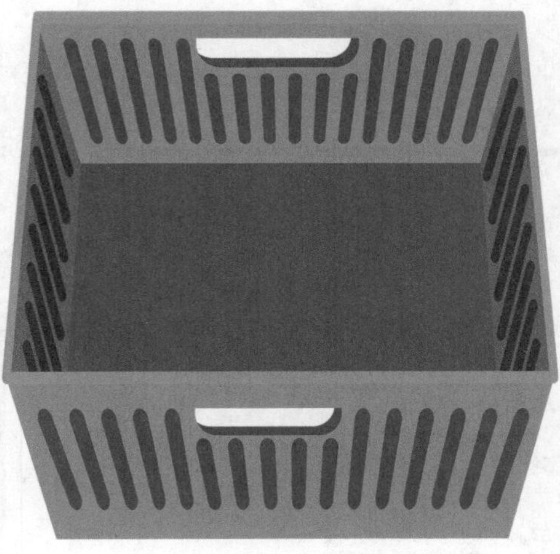

Math is... Mindset

Directions:
What question could you ask?

Learn

6

6 = 1 + 5　　　6 = 3 + 3

7

7 = 3 + 4　　　7 = 5 + 2

Work Together

7

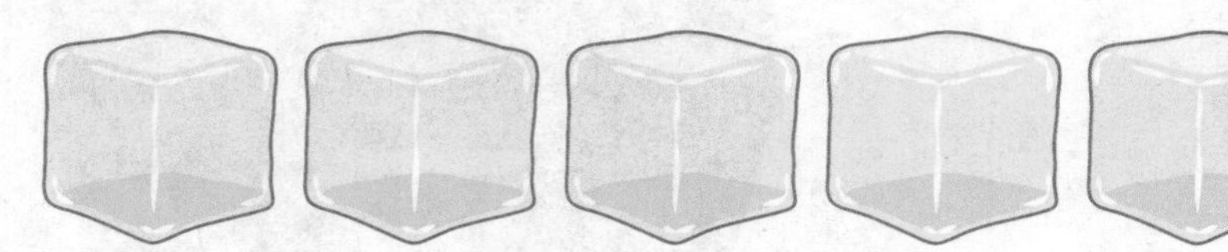

___ = ___ + ___

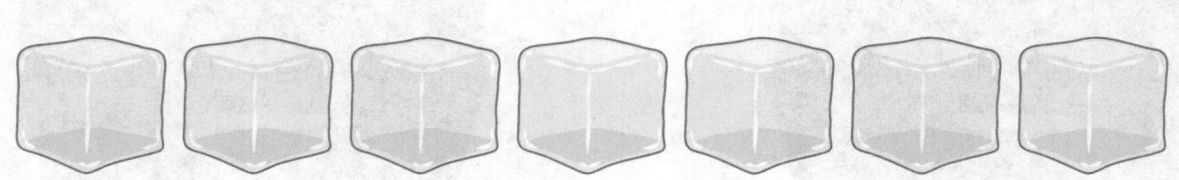

Work Together: How can you decompose 7? Circle groups to show a way to decompose 7. Write the equation to match.

On My Own

MATH REPLAY | GO ONLINE

Name ______________________________

___ = ___ + ___

2

___ = ___ + ___

3

___ = ___ + ___

Directions: 1. How can you decompose 6? Circle groups to show a way to decompose 6. Write the equation to match. **2.** How can you decompose 7? Circle groups to show a way to decompose 7. Write the equation to match. **3.** How can you decompose 6? Circle groups to show a different way to decompose 6. Write the equation to match.

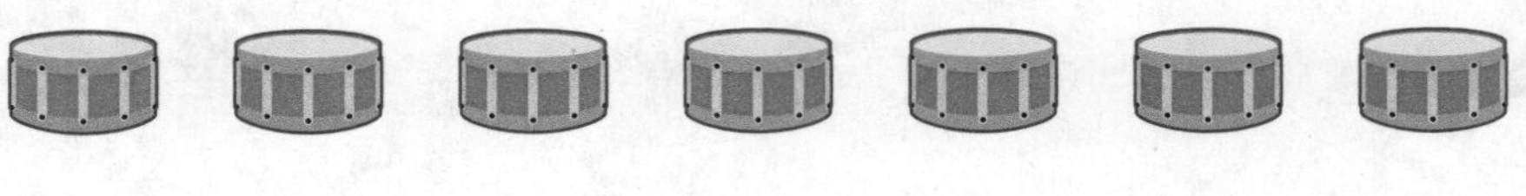

___ = ___ + ___

5

6

6

___ = ___ + ___

___ = ___ + ___

Reflect

6 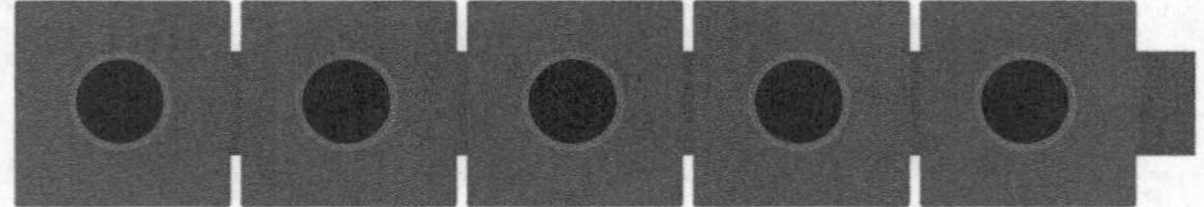 

7 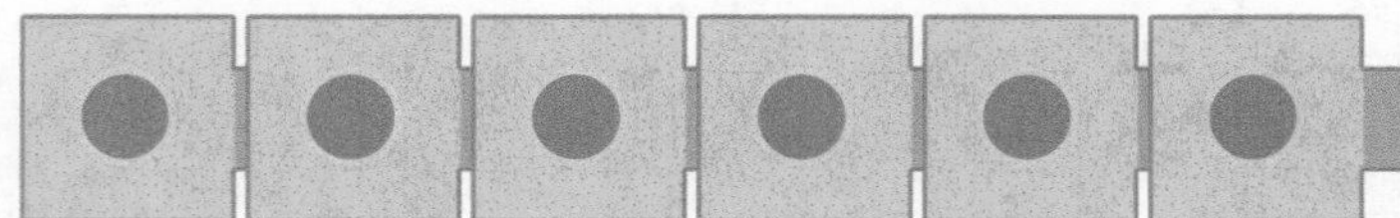 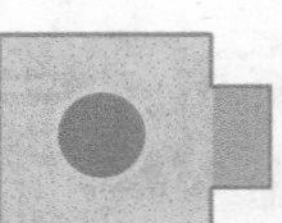

Directions: 4. STEM Connection How can you decompose 7? Circle groups to show a different way to decompose 7. Write the equation to match. **5. Extend Your Thinking** How can you decompose 6? Draw connecting cubes to show two different ways to decompose 6. Write the equations to match.

Reflect: What is a different way to decompose 6 and 7 than what is shown?

Unit 8

Ways to Make and Decompose 5, 6, and 7

Name ______________________________

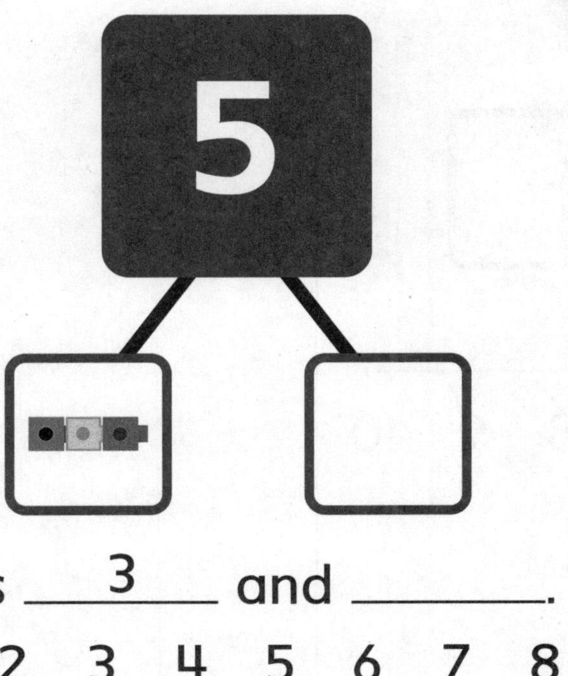

5 is ___3___ and ______.

1 2 3 4 5 6 7 8

Tell or show why.

2

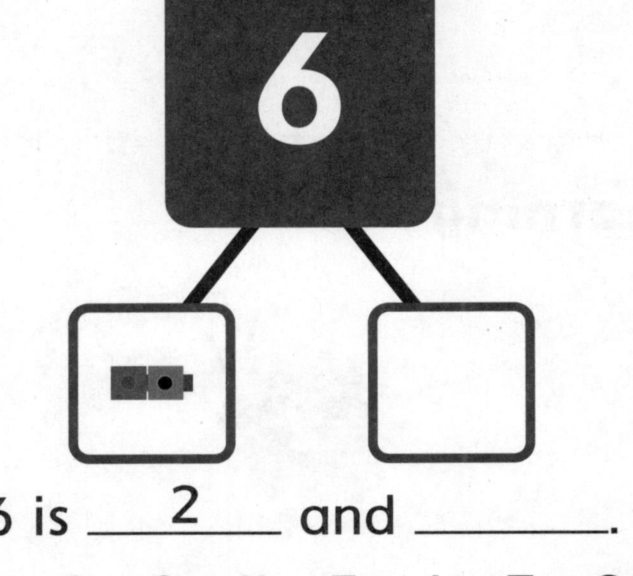

6 is ___2___ and ______.

1 2 3 4 5 6 7 8

Tell or show why.

Directions: Circle the correct number. Tell or show why you circled that number.

3

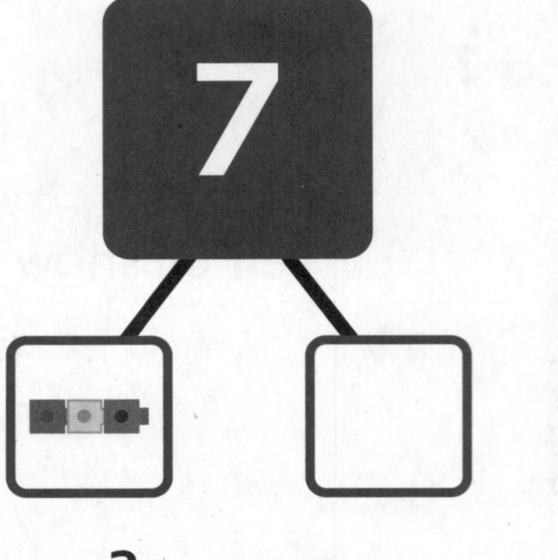

7 is 3 and ________.

3 4 5 6 7 8 9 10

Tell or show why.

Reflect On Your Learning

Directions: Circle the correct number. Tell or show why you circled that number.
Reflect On Your Learning: Do you understand? Circle to show your understanding.

Lesson 8-5

Ways to Make 8 and 9

Be Curious

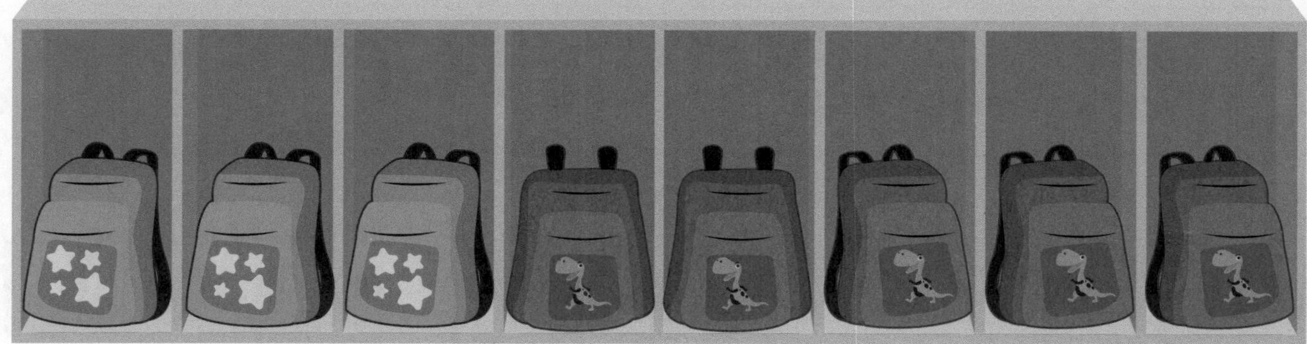

Math is... Mindset

Directions:
How are they the same? How are they different?

Learn

8

6 + 2 = 8

3 + 5 = 8

9

7 + 2 = 9

3 + 6 = 9

Work Together

9

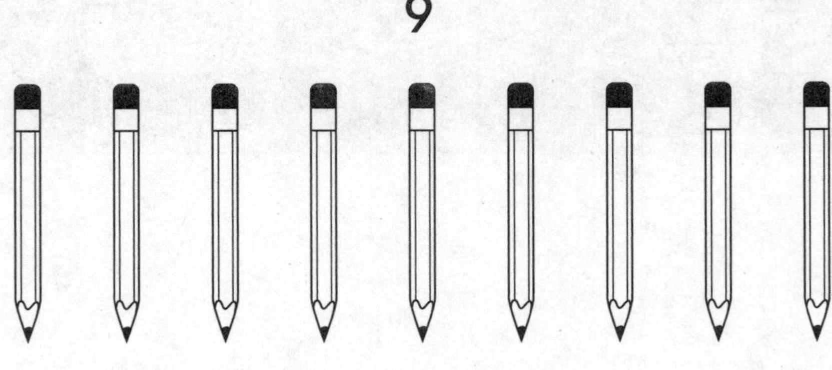

___ + ___ = ___

Work Together: How can you make 9? Use two colors to show a way to make 9. Write the equation to match.

On My Own

Name

1

____ + ____ = ____

2

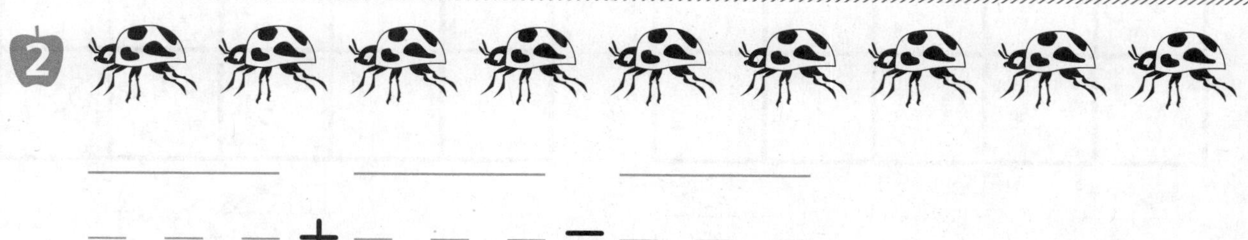

____ + ____ = ____

3

____ + ____ = ____

Directions: 1. How can you make 8? Use two colors to show one way to make 8. Write the equation to match. **2.** How can you make 9? Use two colors to show one way to make 9. Write the equation to match. **3.** How can you make 9? Use two colors to show a different way to make 9. Write the equation to match.

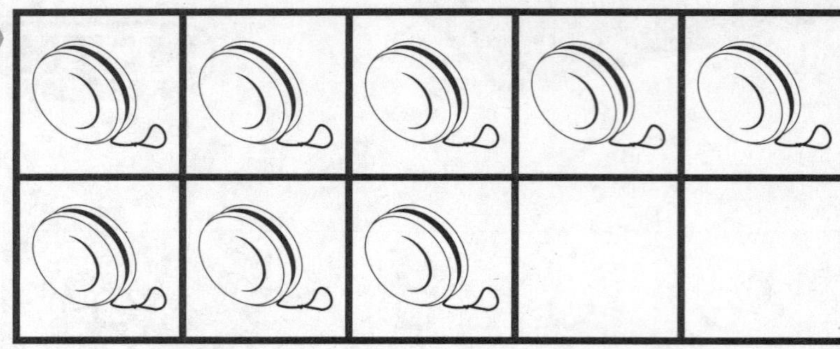

___ + ___ = ___

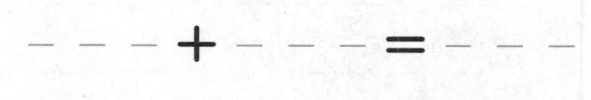

___ + ___ = ___ ___ + ___ = ___

Reflect

8 9

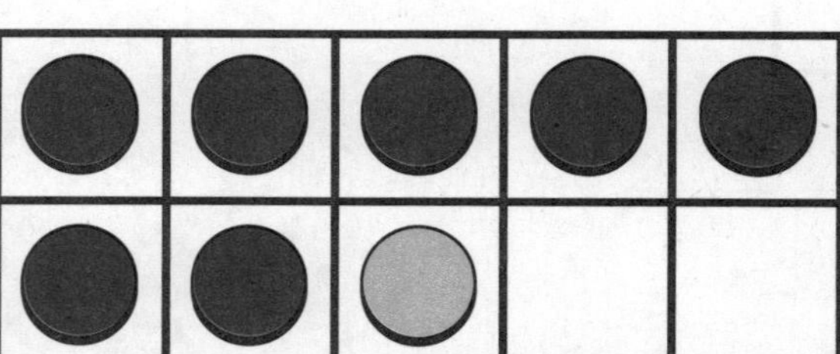

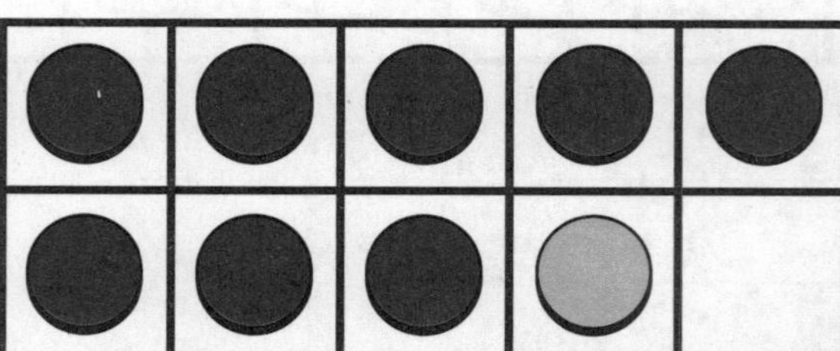

Directions: 4. STEM Connection How can you make 8? Use two colors to show a different way to make 8. Write the equation to match. **5. Extend Your Thinking** Draw counters to show two ways to make 9. Write the equations to match.

Reflect: What other ways can you make 8 and 9?

Ways to Decompose 8 and 9

Be Curious

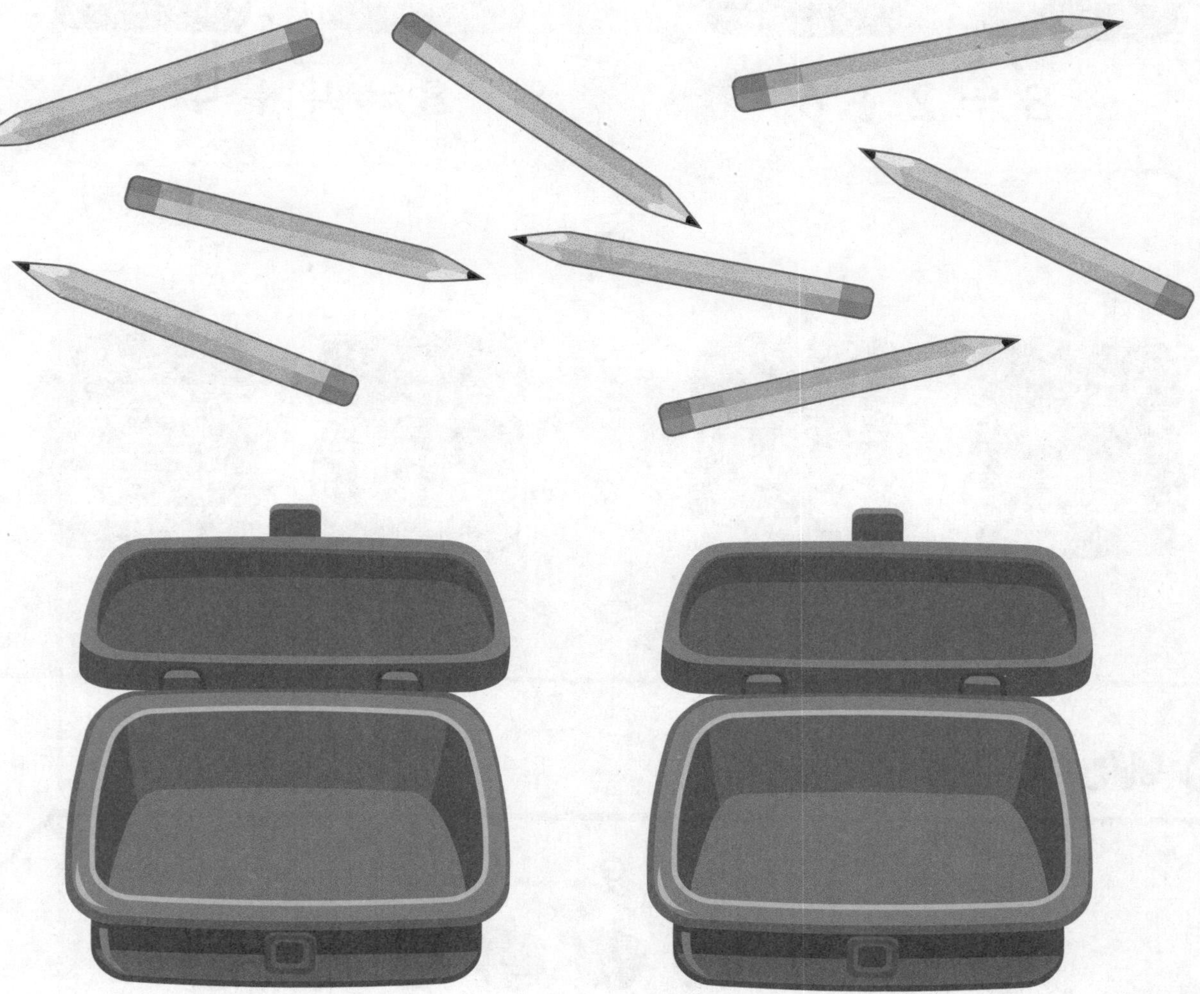

Math is... Mindset

Directions:
What question could you ask?

Learn

8

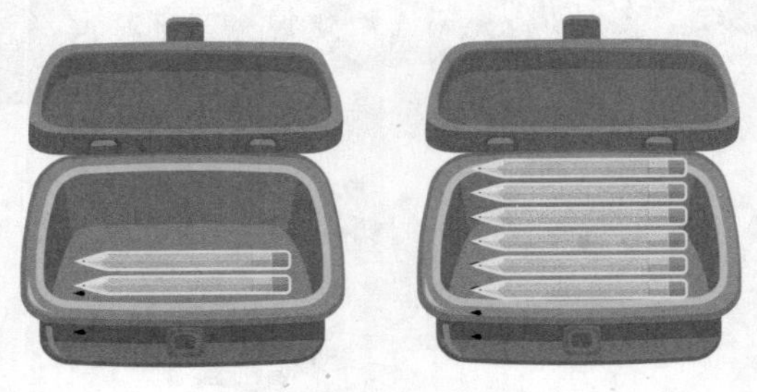

8 = 2 + 6

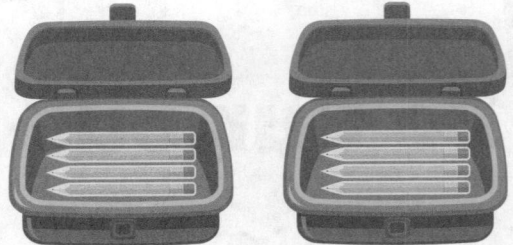

8 = 4 + 4

9

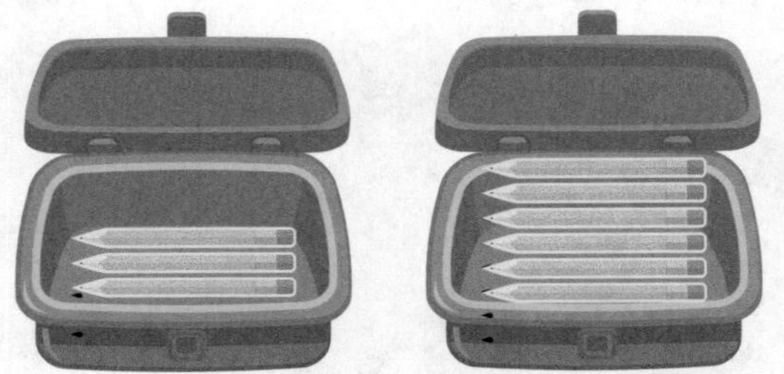

9 = 3 + 6

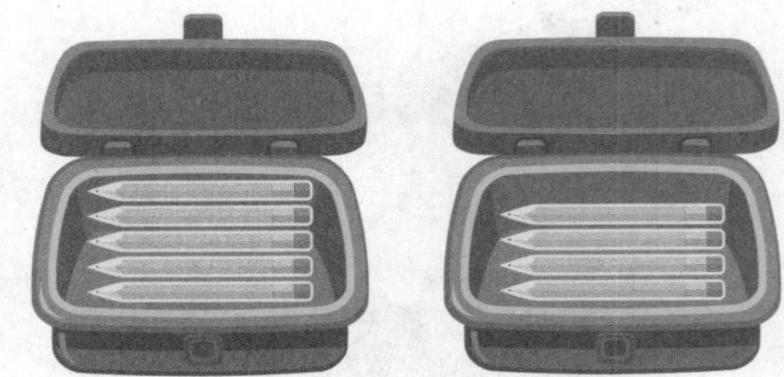

9 = 5 + 4

Work Together

9

___ = ___ + ___

Work Together: How can you decompose 9? Circle groups to show a way to decompose 9. Write the equation to match.

On My Own

Name ______________________________

1

___ = ___ + ___

2

___ = ___ + ___

3

___ = ___ + ___

Directions: **1.** How can you decompose 8? Circle groups to show a way to decompose 8. Write the equation to match. **2.** How can you decompose 8? Circle groups to show a different way to decompose 8. Write the equation to match. **3.** How can you decompose 9? Circle groups to show a way to decompose 9. Write the equation to match.

4

___ = ___ + ___

5

9

9

___ = ___ + ___

___ = ___ + ___

Reflect

8

9

Directions: 4. How can you decompose 9? Circle groups to show a different way to decompose 9. Write the equation to match. **5. Extend Your Thinking** How can you decompose 9? Draw connecting cubes to show two different ways to decompose 9. Write the equations to match.

Reflect: What is a different way to break apart 8 and 9 than what is shown?

Lesson 8-7

Ways to Make 10

Be Curious

5 + 5	6 + 4 = 10
	4 + 1

Math is... Mindset

Directions:
Which doesn't belong?

Learn

10

3 + 7 = 10

5 + 5 = 10

Work Together

10

___ + ___ = ___

Work Together: How can you make 10? Use two colors to show a way to make 10. Write the equation to match.

On My Own

MATH REPLAY | GO ONLINE

Name ______________________________

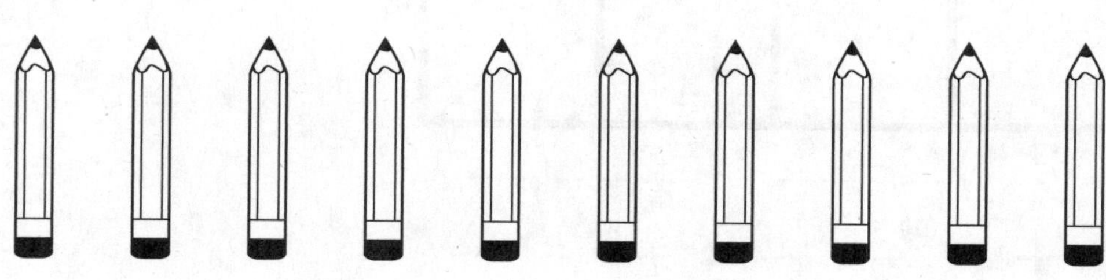

___ ___ ___ + ___ ___ ___ = ___ ___ ___

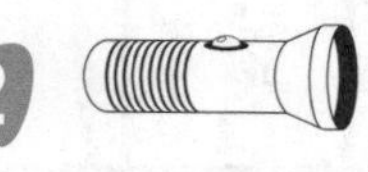

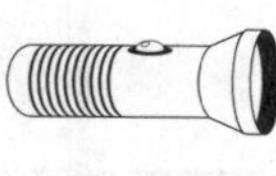

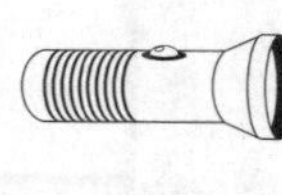

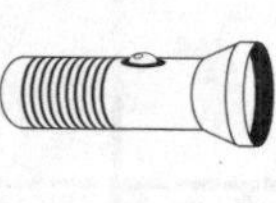

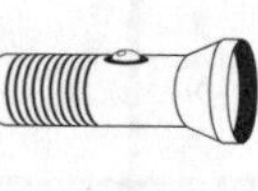

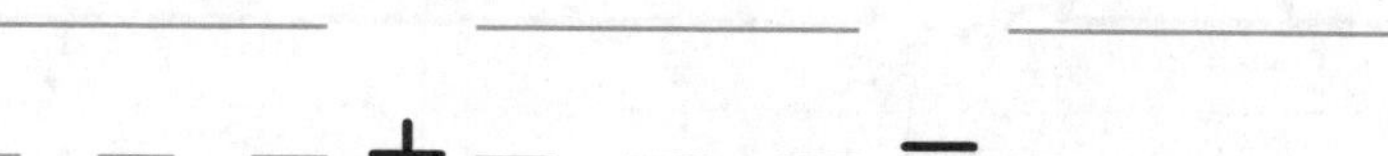

___ ___ ___ + ___ ___ ___ = ___ ___ ___

3

___ ___ ___ + ___ ___ ___ = ___ ___ ___

Directions: 1. How can you make 10? Use two colors to show one way to make 10. Write the equation to match. **2.** How can you make 10? Use two colors to show a different way to make 10. Write the equation to match. **3.** How can you make 10? Use two colors to show a different way to make 10.

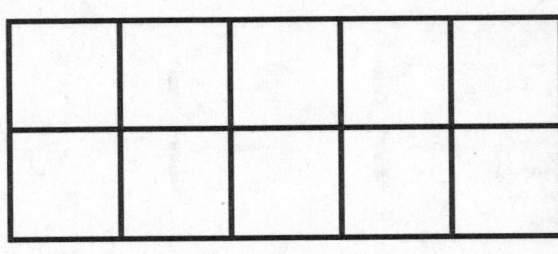

4

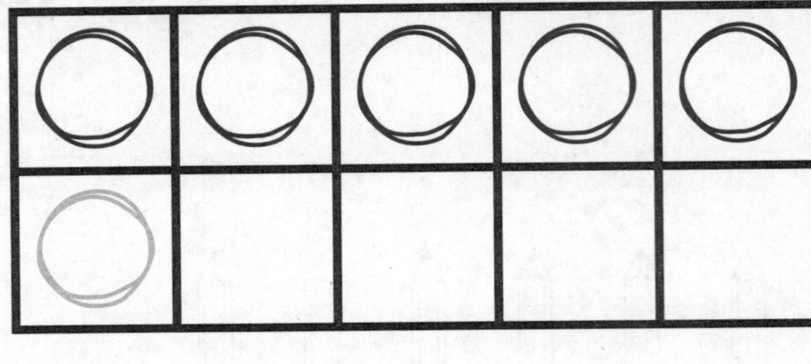

___ + ___ = ___

5

___ + ___ = ___

___ + ___ = ___

Reflect

10

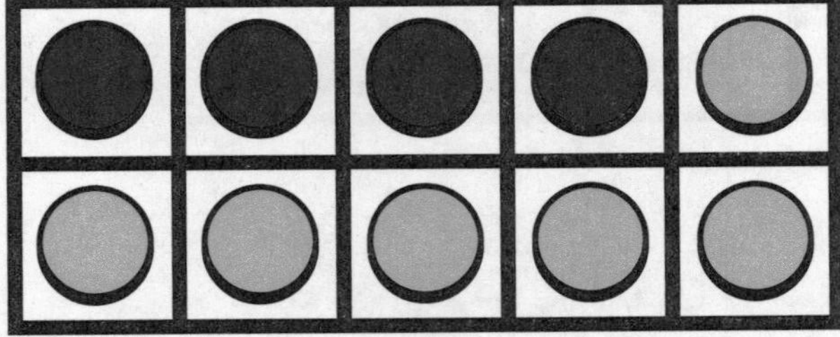

Directions: 4. Error Analysis Jenna wants to show a way to make 10. Draw counters to help finish Jenna's picture. Write an equation to match. **5. Extend Your Thinking** Draw counters to show two ways to make 10. Write the equations to match.

Reflect: What is a different way to make 10 than what is shown?

Ways to Decompose 10

Be Curious

Math is... Mindset

Directions:
What question could you ask?

Learn

10

10 = 4 + 6

10 = 5 + 5

Work Together

10

___ = ___ + ___

Work Together: How can you decompose 10? Circle groups to show a way to decompose 10. Write the equation to match.

On My Own

MATH REPLAY | GO ONLINE

Name

1

___ = ___ + ___

2

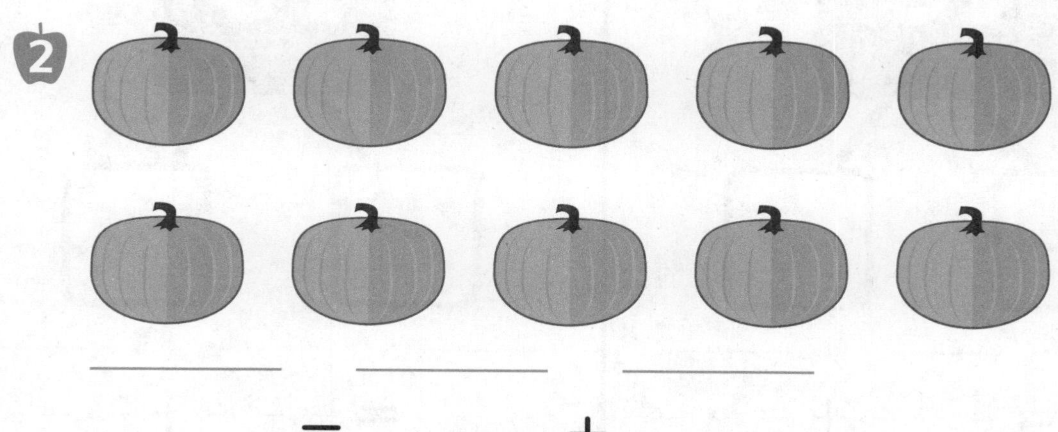

___ = ___ + ___

3

___ = ___ + ___

Directions: **1.** How can you decompose 10? Circle groups to show a way to decompose 10. Write the equation to match. **2.** How can you decompose 10? Circle groups to show a different way to decompose 10. Write the equation to match. **3.** How can you decompose 10? Circle groups to show a different way to decompose 10. Write the equation to match.

$9 = 6 + 3$

___ = ___ + ___

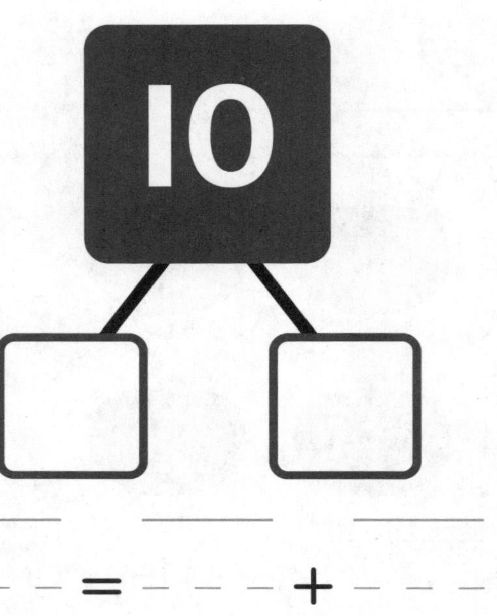

10

___ = ___ + ___

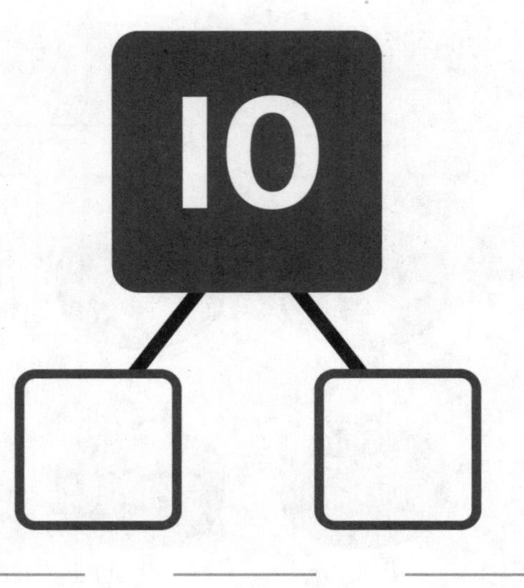

10

___ = ___ + ___

Reflect

10

Directions: 4. Error Analysis Angie circled groups to show a way to decompose 10 and wrote an equation. Is her equation correct? How can you help Angie write an equation that matches her picture? **5. Extend Your Thinking** How can you decompose 10? Draw connecting cubes to show two different ways to decompose 10. Write the equations to match.

Reflect: What is a different way to decompose 10 than what is shown?

Unit Review

Name

Vocabulary Review

1

− +

2

− +

3

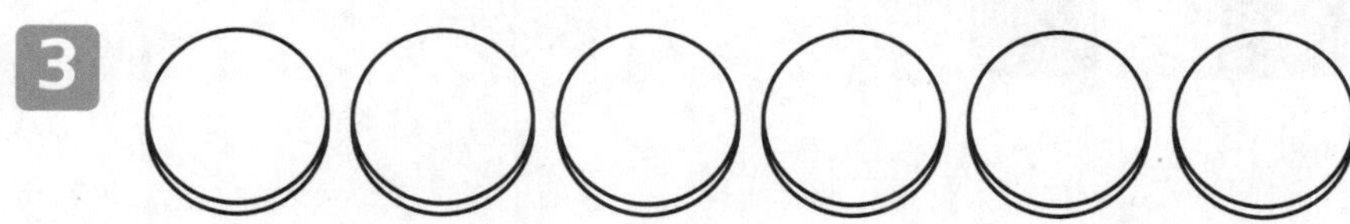

4

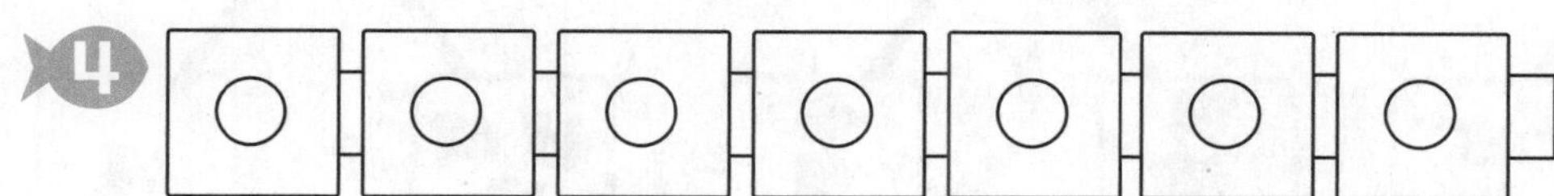

Directions: **1.** Which symbol tells you to add? Circle the symbol that tells you to add. **2.** Which symbol tells you to subtract? Circle the symbol that tells you to subtract. **3.** How can you show one way to make 6? Color the counters red or yellow to show 2 and 4 is 6. **4.** How can you show one way to decompose 7? Color the cubes red or yellow to show 7 is 1 and 6.

Review

5

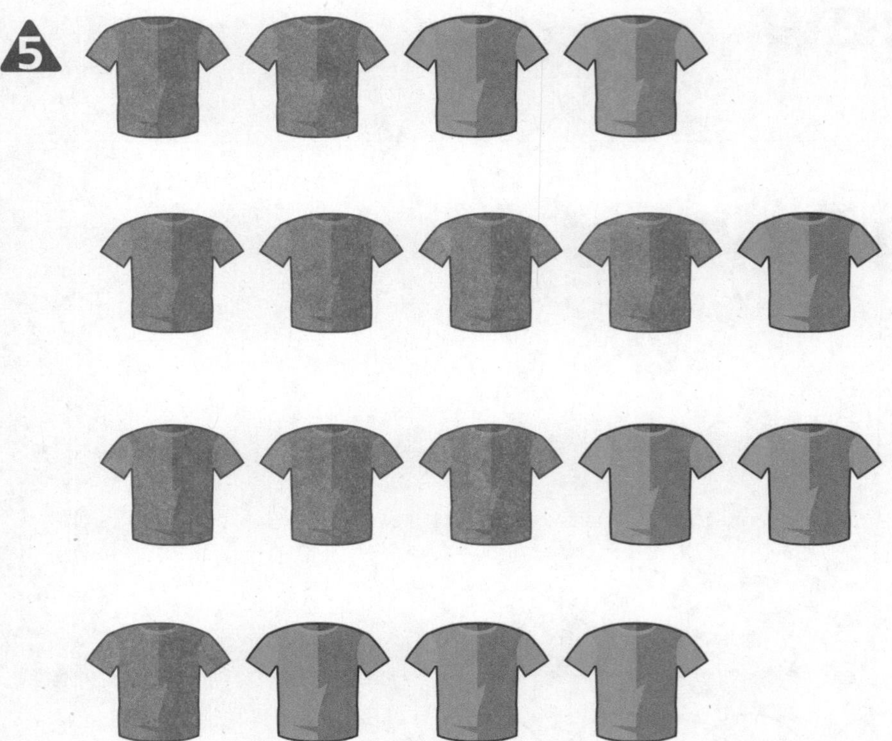

6

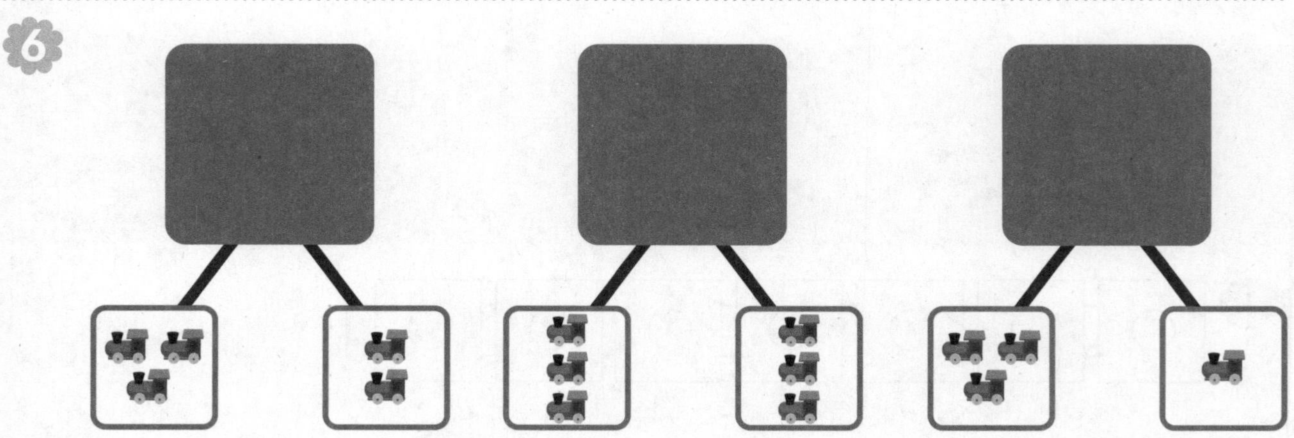

Directions: 5. Which show a sum of 5? Circle the groups that show a sum of 5. **6.** Which shows a way to decompose 6? Circle the number bond that shows one way to decompose 6.

7

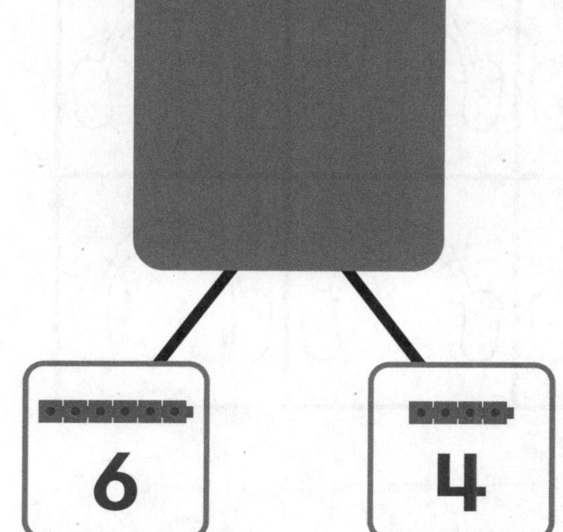

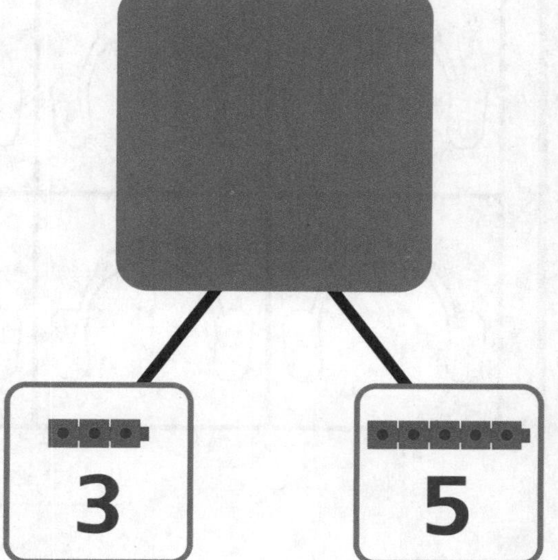

8

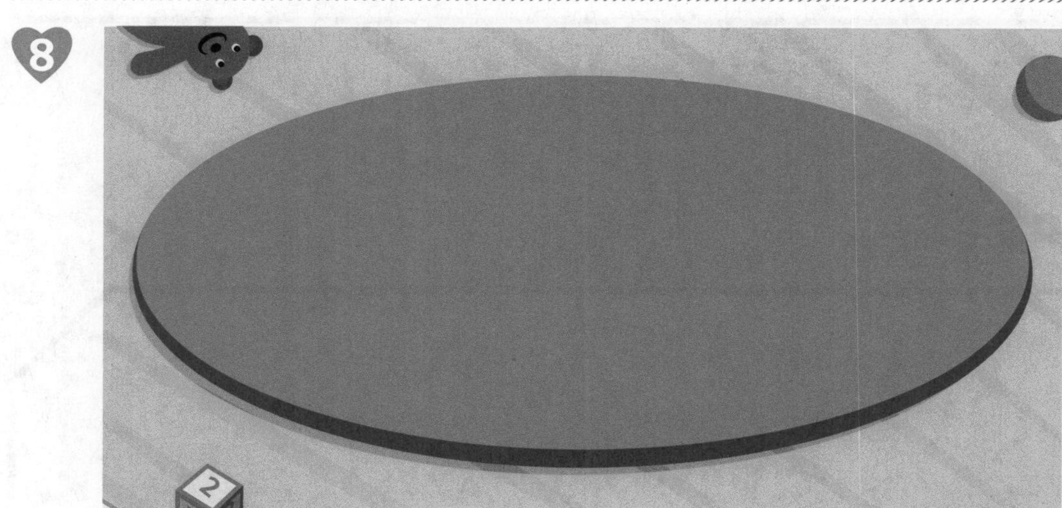

Directions: 7. Which shows a way to decompose 10? Circle the number bond that shows one way to decompose 10. **8.** How can you make 6? Draw red cars and blue cars to show one way to make 6.

Performance Task

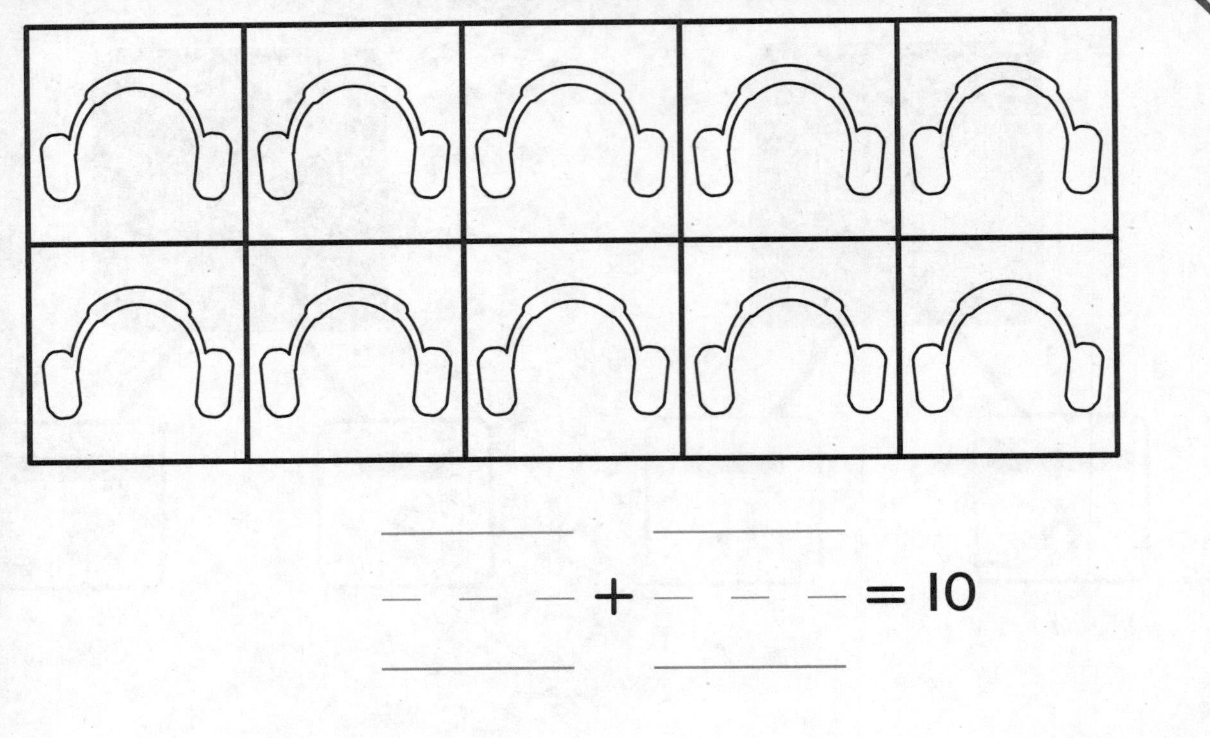

___ + ___ = 10

Reflect

Performance Task: A sound engineer has 10 headphones. Some are black. Some are blue. How many of each color headphones could the sound engineer have? Color the headphones to show one way to make 10. Write the numbers to complete the equation.

Reflect: How can you decompose a number?

Unit 8

Fluency Practice

Name ______________________________

Fluency Strategy

Fluency Flash

1

2

Directions: Fluency Strategy: You can count the number of objects in each group to compare the groups. The group of 9 crayons has more than the group of 8 pens.
Fluency Flash: 1. Which group has less? Count. Write the numbers. Circle the group that has less objects. **2.** Which group has more objects? Count. Write the numbers. Circle the group that has more objects.

Fluency Check

3

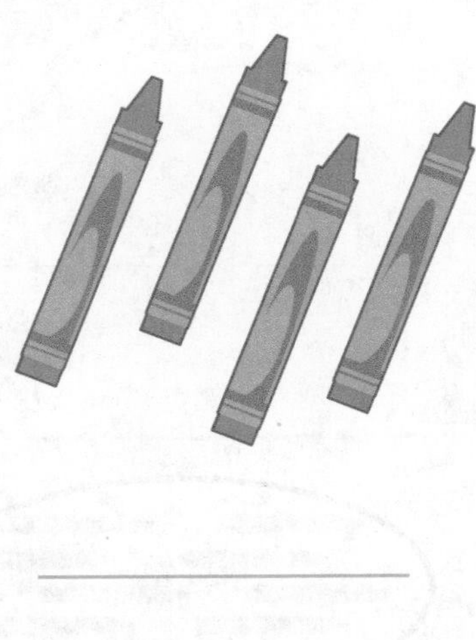

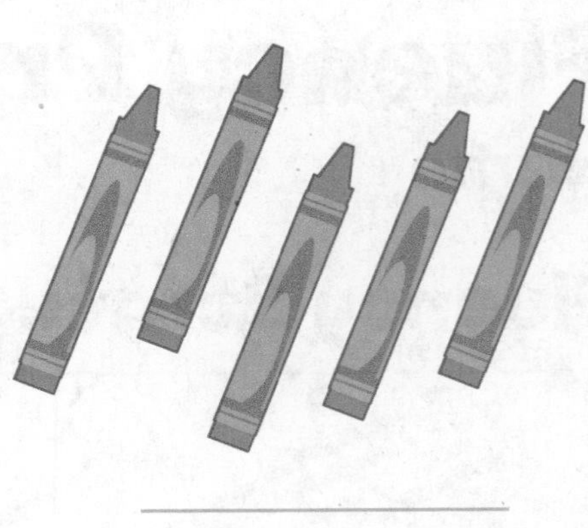

4

Fluency Talk

Directions: Fluency Check: 3. Which group has less? Count. Write the numbers. Circle the group that has less crayons. **4.** Which group has more? Count. Write the numbers. Circle the group that has more objects. **Fluency Talk:** Look at the crystals and diamonds in Exercise 4. How did you decide which group has the greater number of objects?

Numbers 11 to 15

Focus Question

How can I represent, make, and decompose numbers 11 to 15?

Hi, I'm Hugo.

I want to be a meteorologist. I love weather. The first ten days and the last three days of August were hot! Ten days and three more days is 13 days. What a hot month!

Name ______________________________

Secret Hops

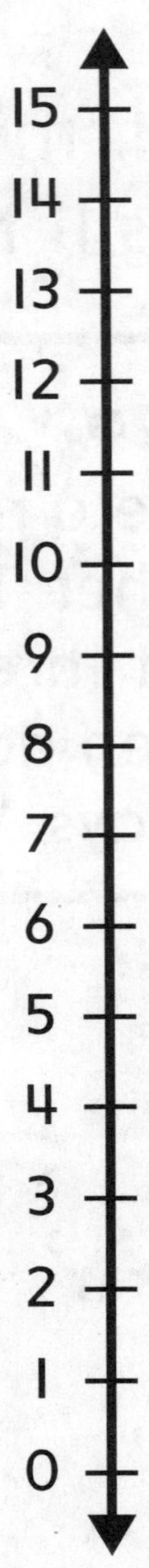

Directions: Use counters to make "secret hops." Find the sums.

Lesson 9-1

Represent 11, 12, and 13

Be Curious

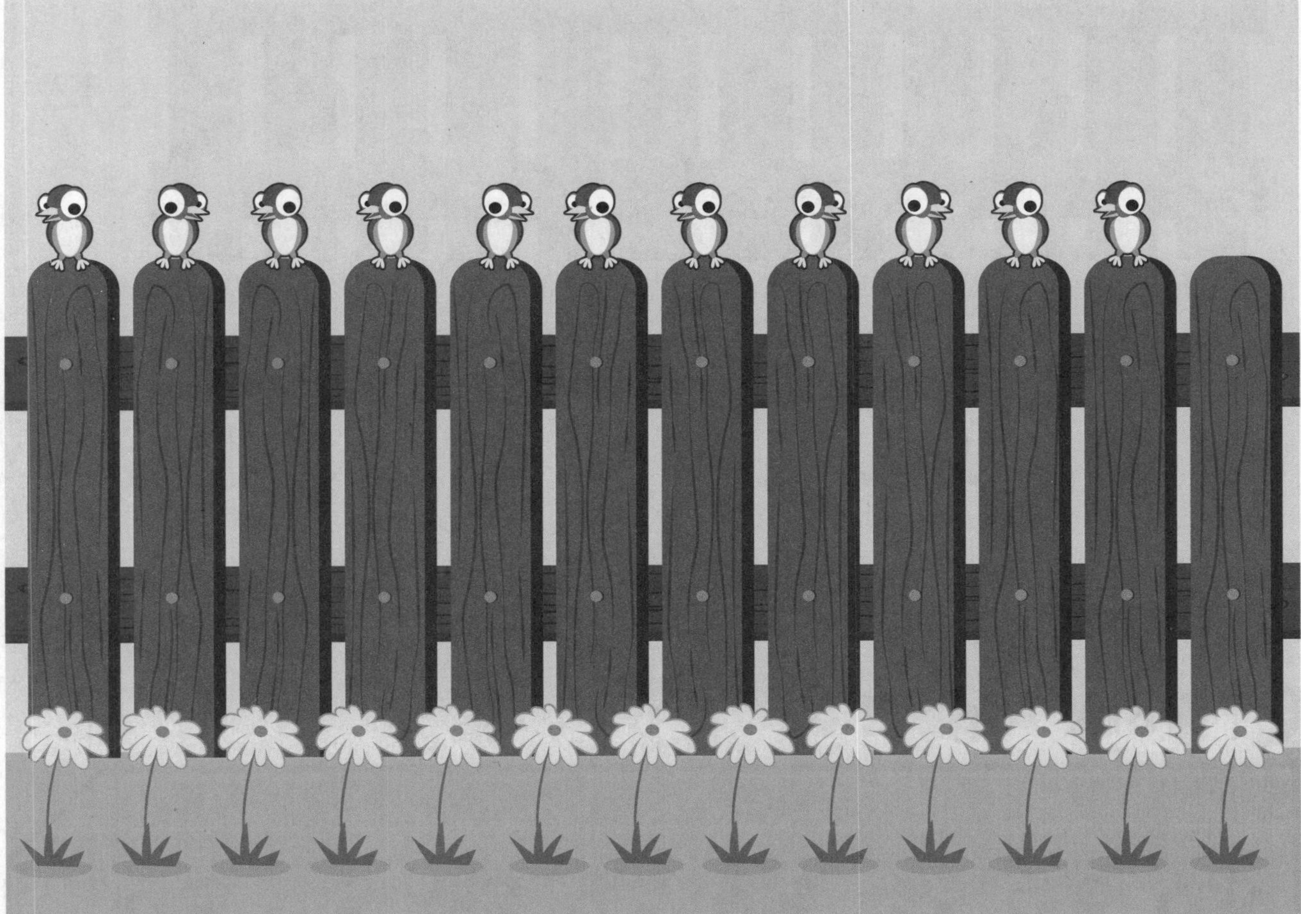

Math is... Mindset

Directions:
What do you notice? What do you wonder?

Learn

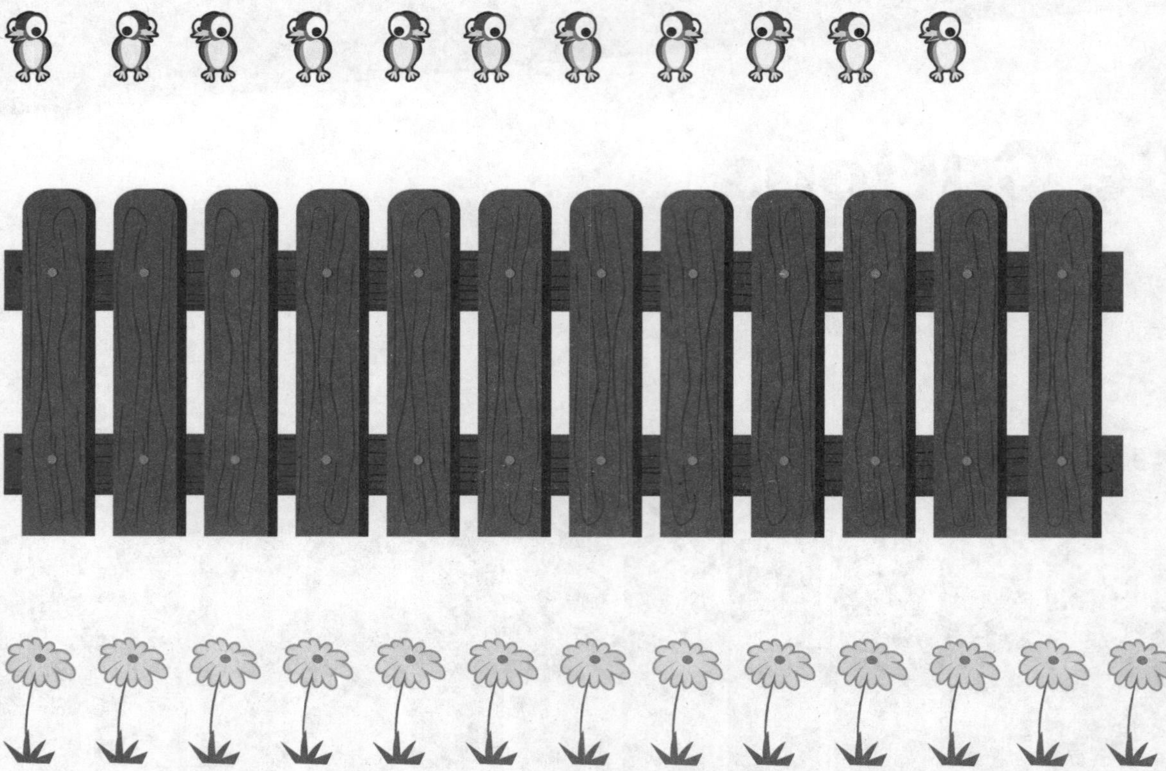

11

12

13

Work Together

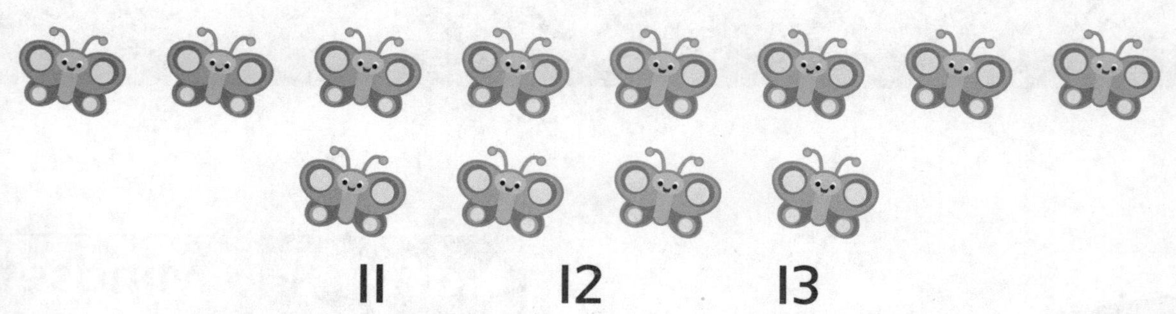

11 12 13

Work Together: How many butterflies? Count. Circle the number to show how many.

On My Own

MATH REPLAY | GO ONLINE

Name ____________________

1

11 12 13

2

11 12 13

3

11 12 13

Directions: 1. How many ladybugs? Count. Circle the number to show how many. **2.** How many acorns? Count. Circle the number to show how many. **3.** How many bunnies? Count. Circle the number to show how many.

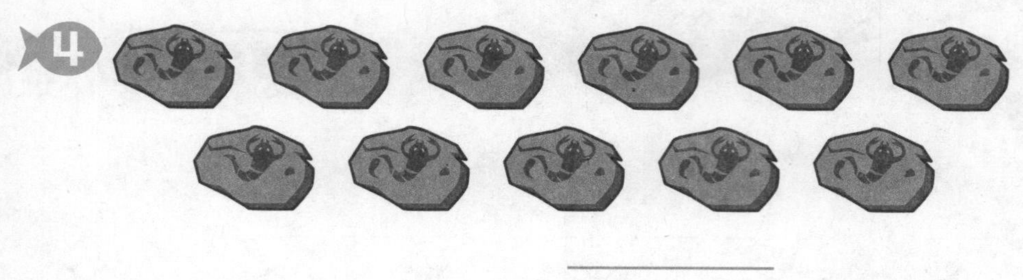

Reflect

Directions: 4. STEM Connection How many rocks? Count. Write the number to show how many. **5. Extend Your Thinking** How many chipmunks are there? Circle 10 chipmunks. Then circle 2 more. Write the number to show how many.

Reflect: How can you show the number of bees?

Make 11, 12, and 13

Be Curious

Math is... Mindset

Directions:
How are they the same? How are they different?

Learn

10 + 1 = 11

10 + 2 = 12

10 + 3 = 13

Work Together

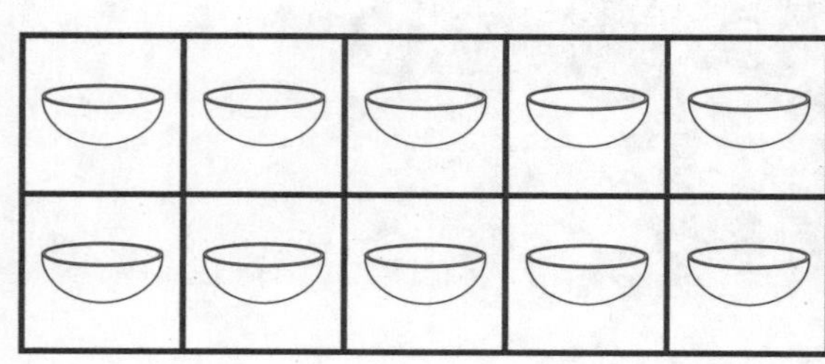
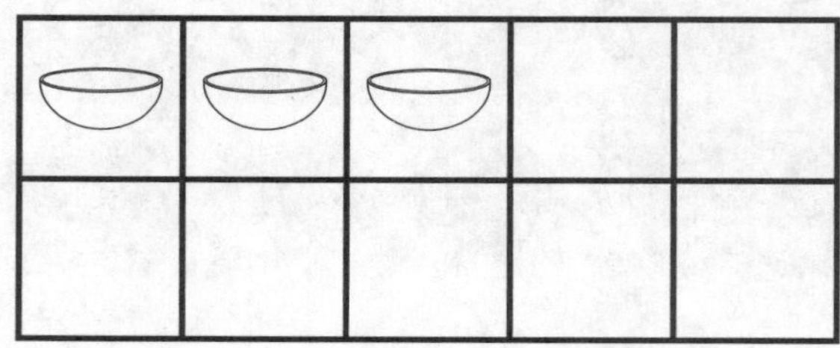

____ + ____ = 13

Work Together: How can you make 13? Use one color to show 10 ones. Then use another color to show 3 more ones. Complete the equation to match.

On My Own

MATH REPLAY | GO ONLINE

Name ______________________________

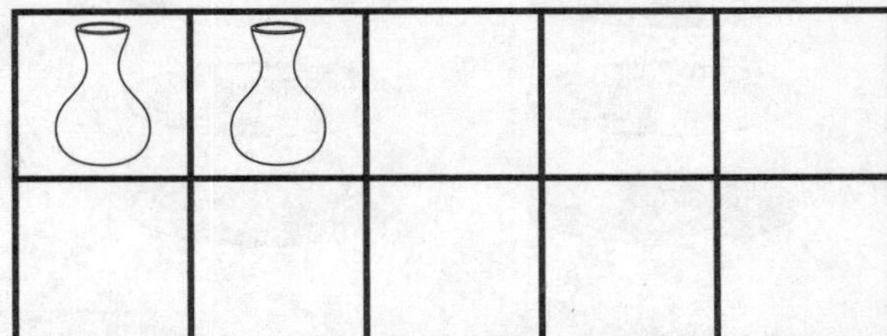

______ + ______ = 12

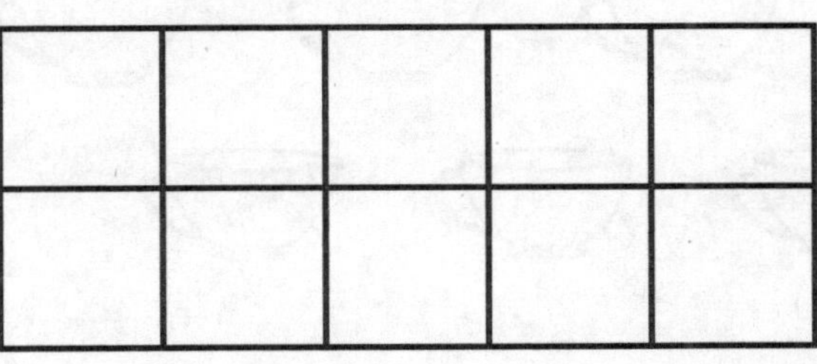
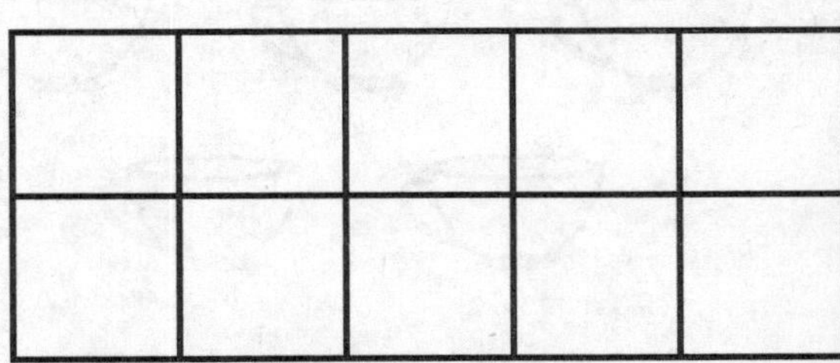

______ + ______ = 13

3
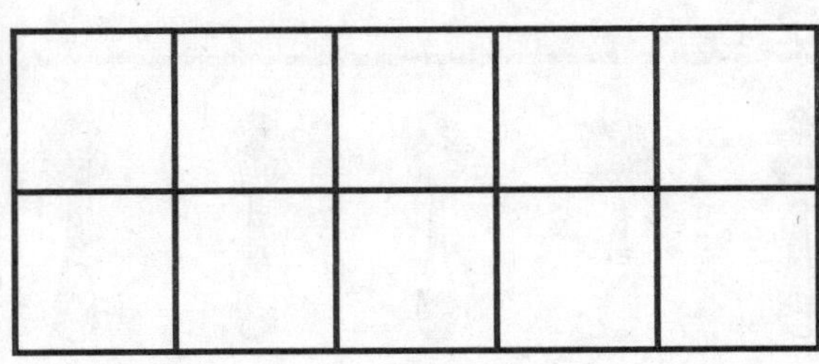
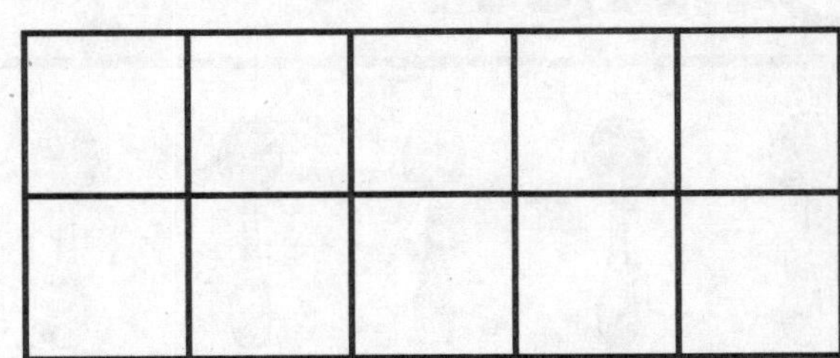

______ + ______ = 11

Directions: 1. How can you make 12? Use one color to show 10 ones. Then use another color to show 2 more ones. Complete the equation to match. **2.** How can you make 13? Draw counters to show a group of ten ones and some more ones. Complete the equation to match. **3.** How can you make 11? Draw counters to show a group of ten ones and some more ones. Complete the equation to match.

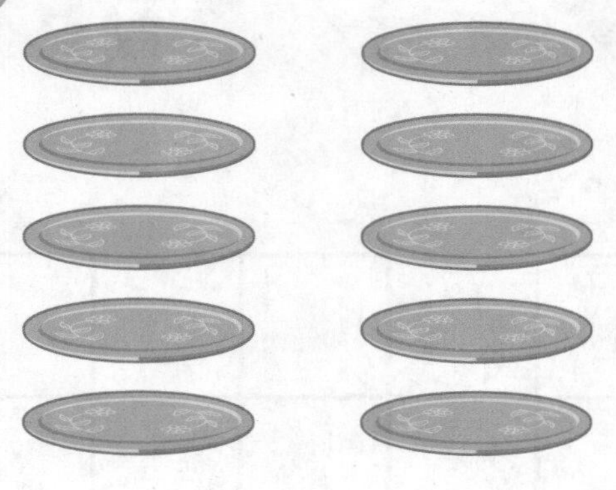

10 + ___ = 13

___ + ___ = 11

Reflect

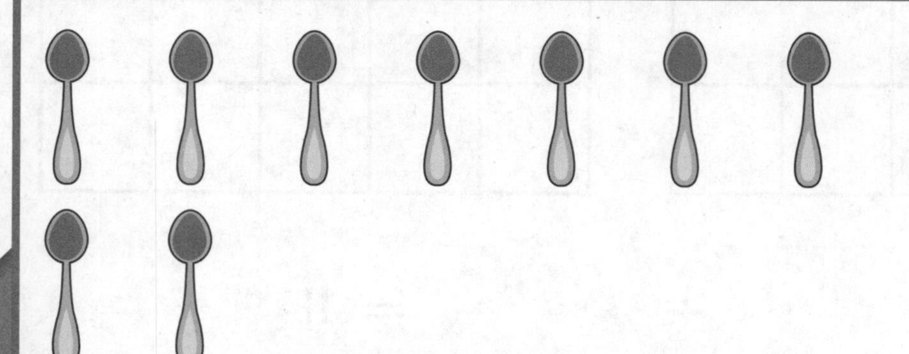

Directions: 4. Error Analysis Josh says there are 10 plates and 2 more plates. Carl says there are 10 plates and 3 more plates. Complete the equation to show how many more plates there are. **5. Extend Your Thinking** Use one color to show 10 ones. Then use another color to show 1 more one. Complete the equation to match.

Reflect: How can you make a group of 10 and some more?

Lesson 9-3

Decompose 11, 12, and 13

Be Curious

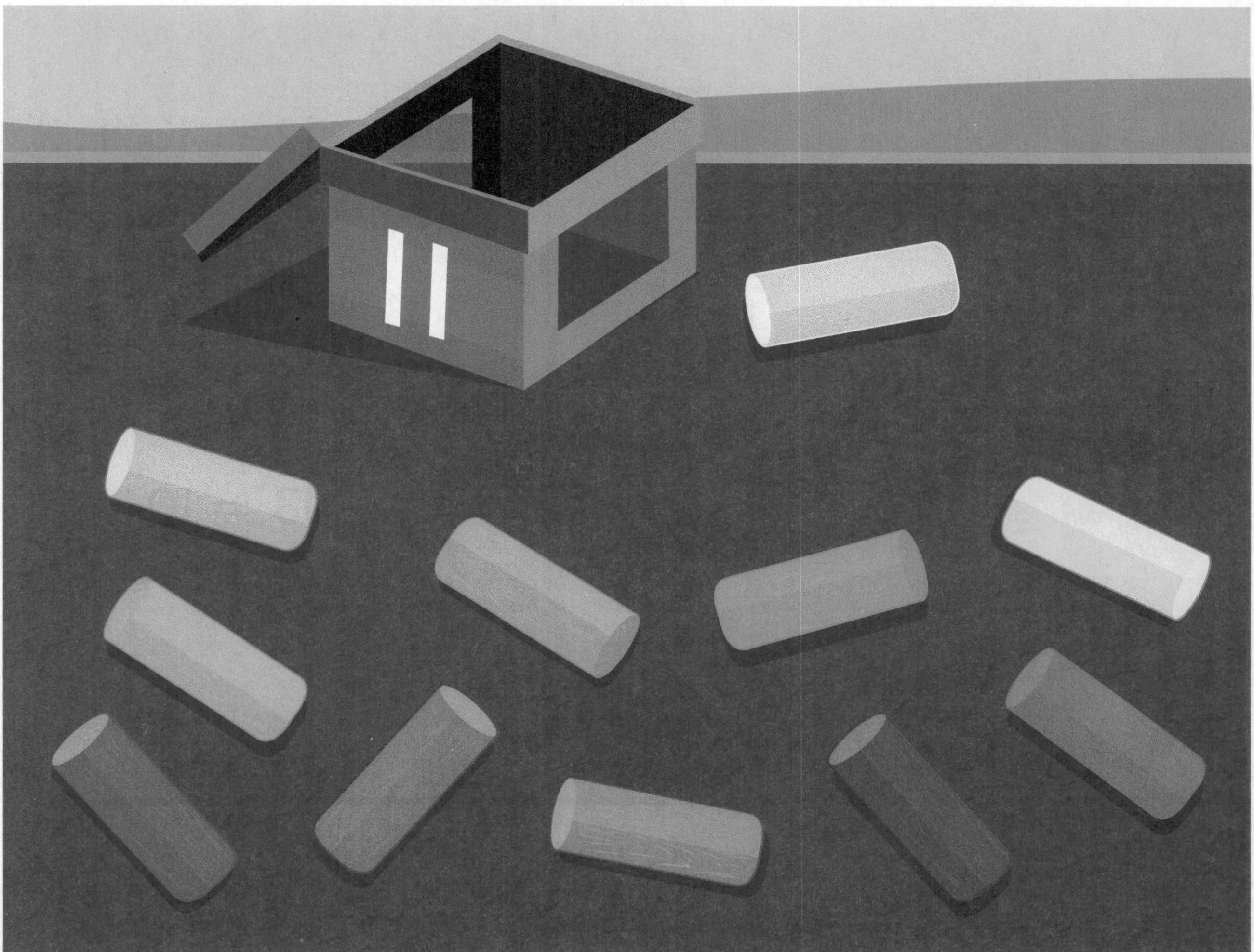

Math is... Mindset

Directions:
What question could you ask?

Learn

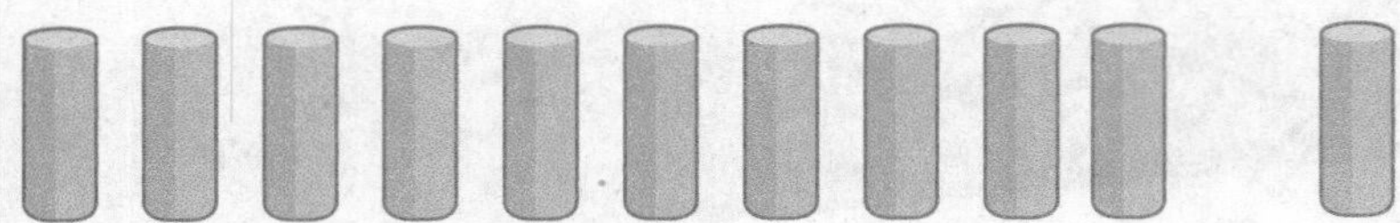

$11 = 10 + 1$

$12 = 10 + 2$

$13 = 10 + 3$

Work Together

$11 = 10 +$ ___

Work Together: How can you decompose 11? Circle groups to decompose 11 into ten ones and some more ones. Complete the equation to match.

On My Own

MATH REPLAY | GO ONLINE

Name ____________________

1

12 = ____ + ____

2

11 = ____ + ____

3

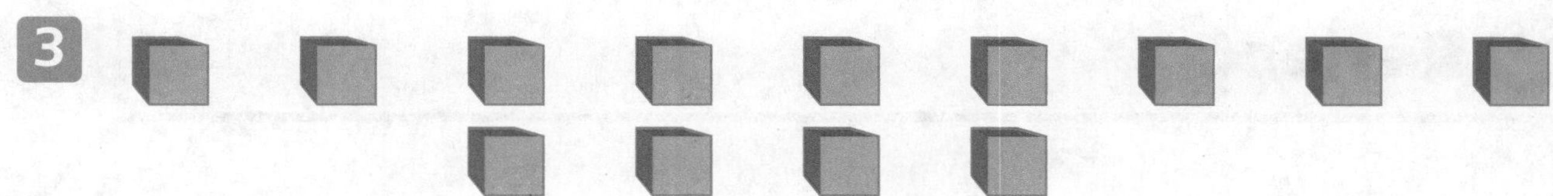

13 = ____ + ____

Directions: **1.** How can you decompose 12? Circle groups to decompose 12 into ten ones and some more ones. Complete the equation to match. **2.** How can you decompose 11? Circle groups to decompose 11 into ten ones and some more ones. Complete the equation to match. **3.** How can you decompose 13? Circle groups to decompose 13 into ten ones and some more ones. Complete the equation to match.

4

12 = ___ + ___

5

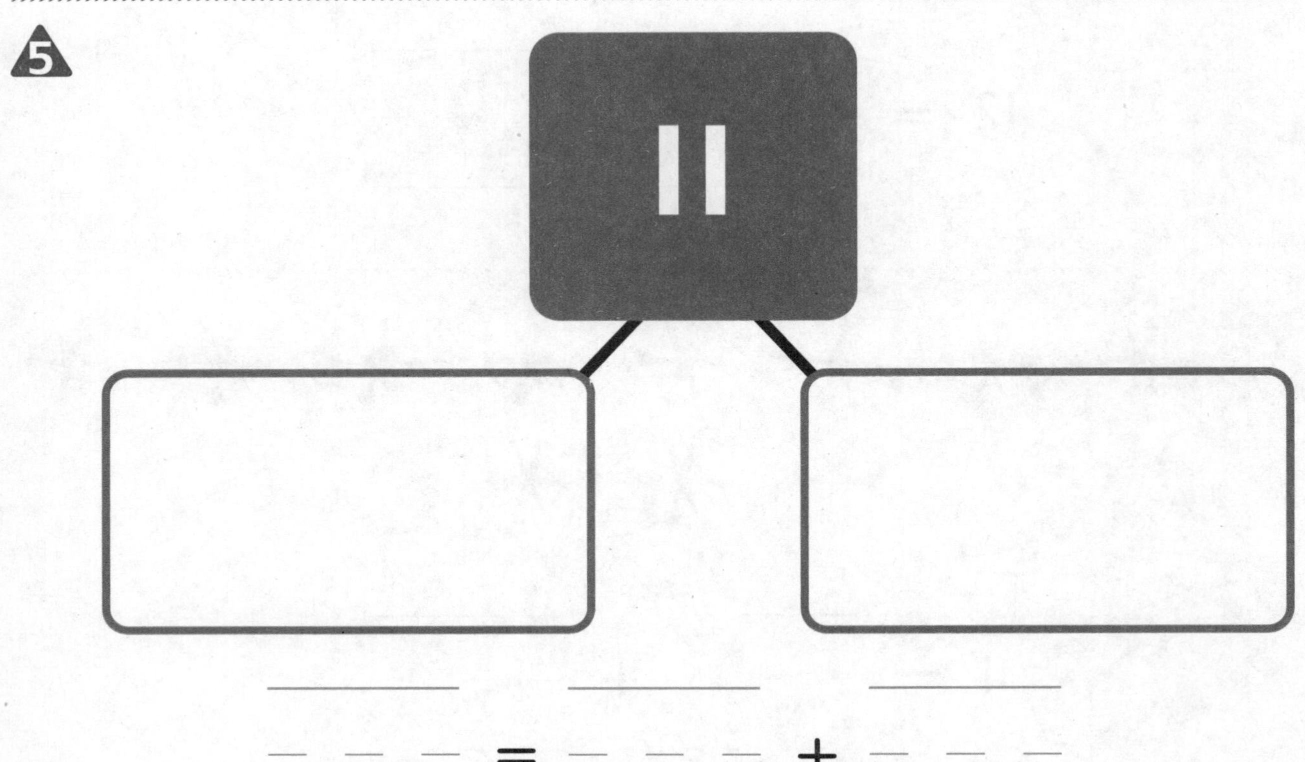

___ = ___ + ___

Reflect

Directions: 4. How can you decompose 12? Circle groups to decompose 12 into ten ones and some more ones. Complete the equation to match. **5. Extend Your Thinking** How can you decompose 11? Draw connecting cubes to decompose 11 into ten ones and some more ones. Write the equation to match.

Reflect: How can you decompose 13 into 10 ones and some more ones?

Represent 14 and 15

Be Curious

Math is... Mindset

Directions:
What do you notice? What do you wonder?

Learn

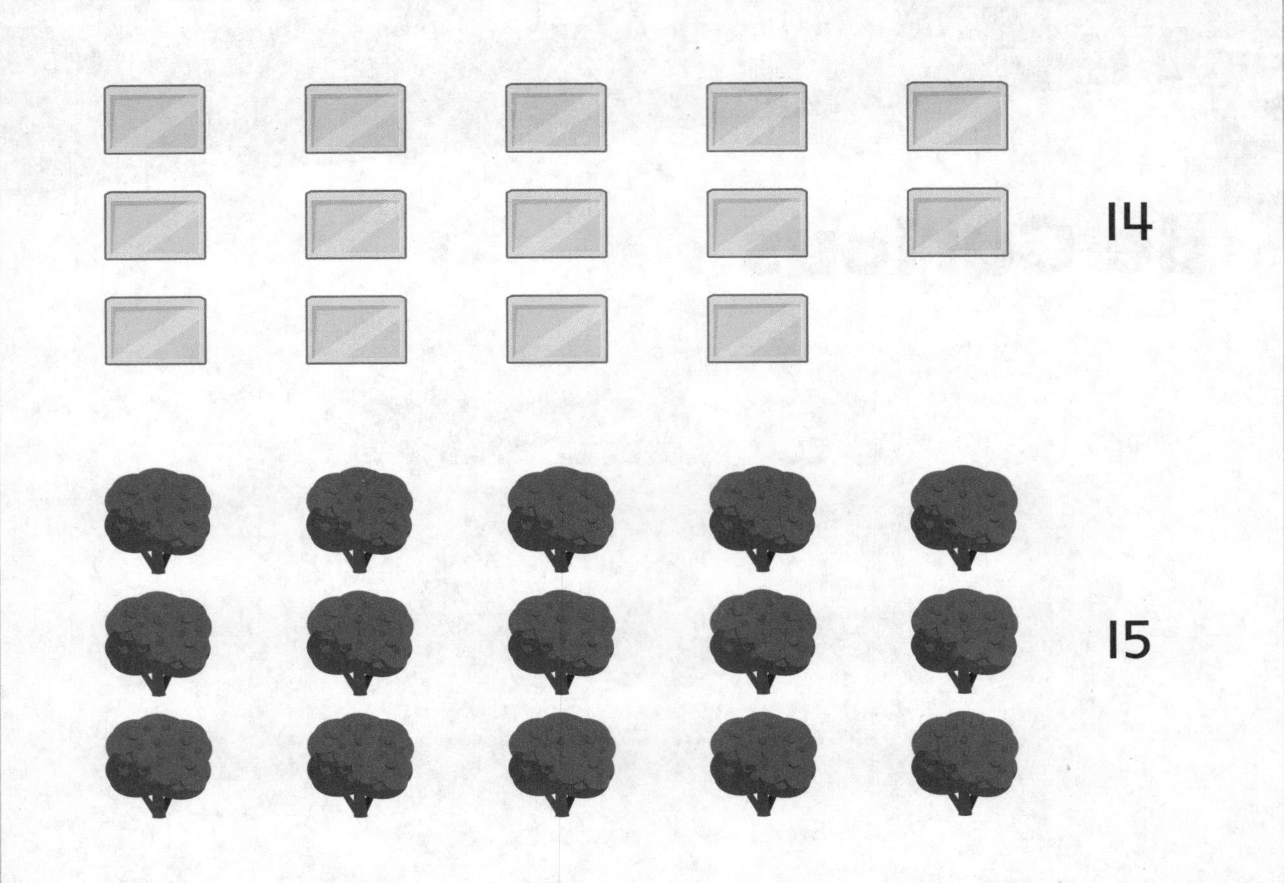

Work Together

14 15

Work Together: How many keys? Count. Circle the number to show how many.

On My Own

MATH REPLAY | GO ONLINE

Name ____________________

1

14 15

2

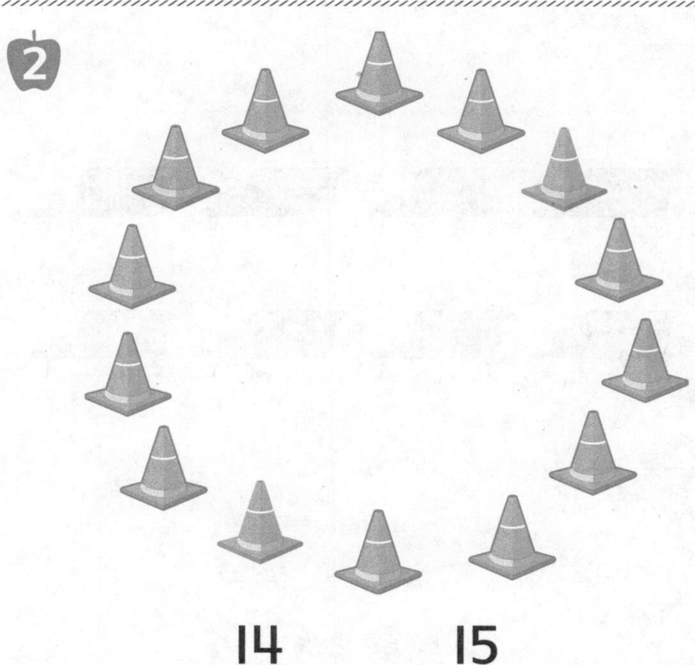

14 15

3

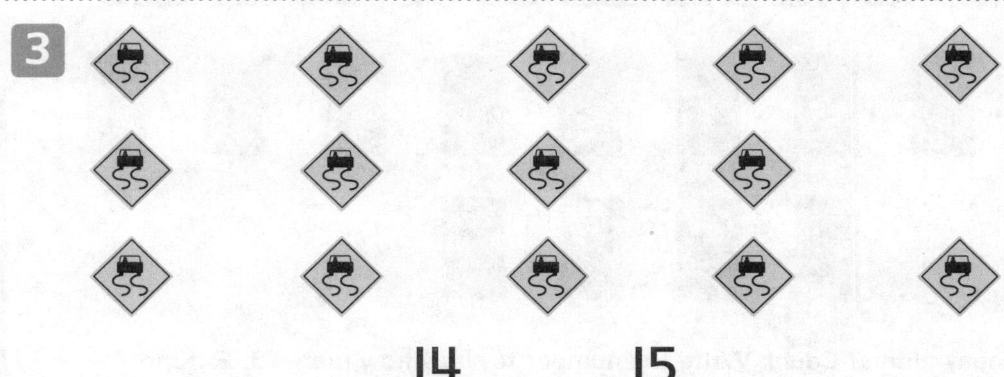

14 15

Directions: 1. How many trees? Count. Circle the number to show how many. **2.** How many cones? Count. Circle the number to show how many. **3.** How many signs? Count. Circle the number to show how many.

4

5

Reflect

Directions: 4. How many plants? Count. Write the number to show how many. **5. Extend Your Thinking** How many benches are there? Circle 10 benches. Then circle 4 more. Write the number to show how many.

Reflect: How can you show the number of doors?

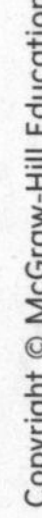

Unit 9

Counting Counters

Name ______________________________

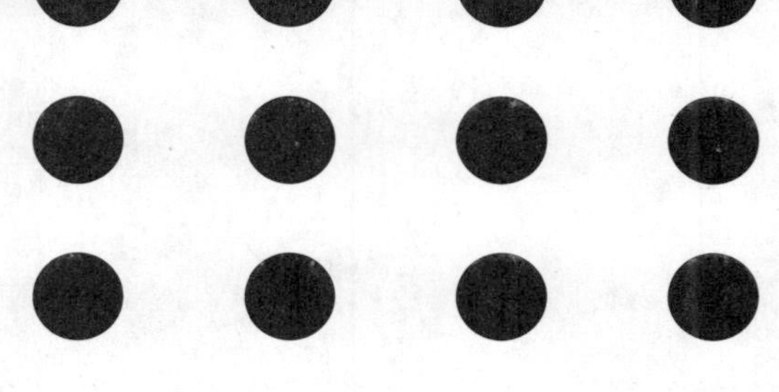

1

10 11 12 13 14 15

Tell or show why.

2

10 11 12 13 14 15

Tell or show why.

Directions: How many counters do you see? Circle the number. Tell or show why you circled that number.

3

10 11 12 13 14 15

Tell or show why.

4

10 11 12 13 14 15

Tell or show why.

Reflect On Your Learning

Directions: How many counters do you see? Circle the number. Tell or show why you circled that number.

Reflect On Your Learning: Do you understand? Circle to show your understanding.

Make 14 and 15

Be Curious

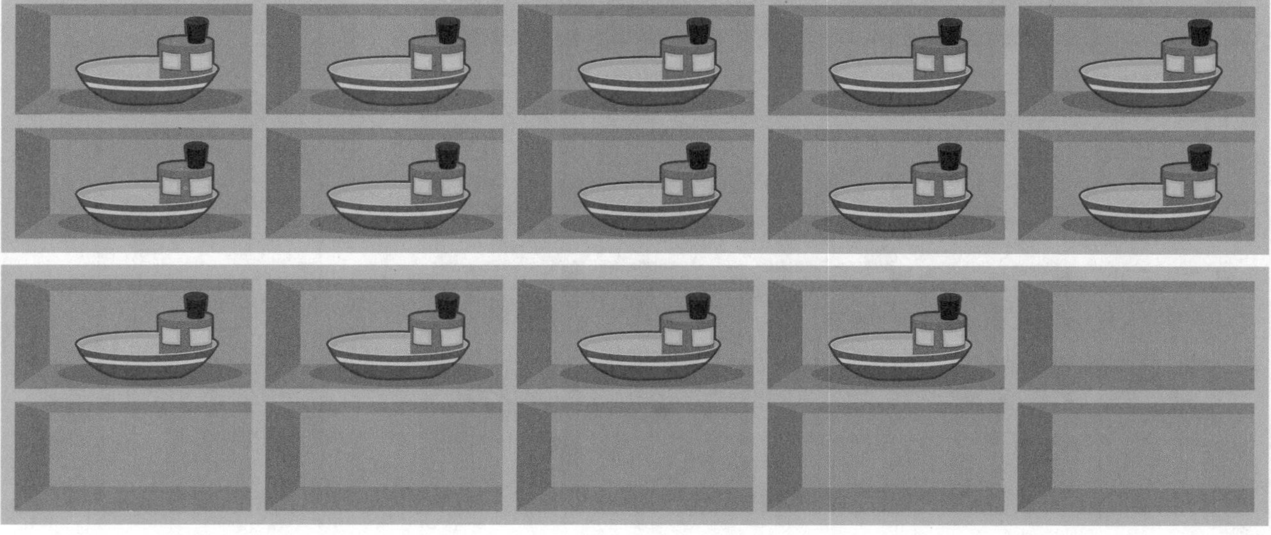

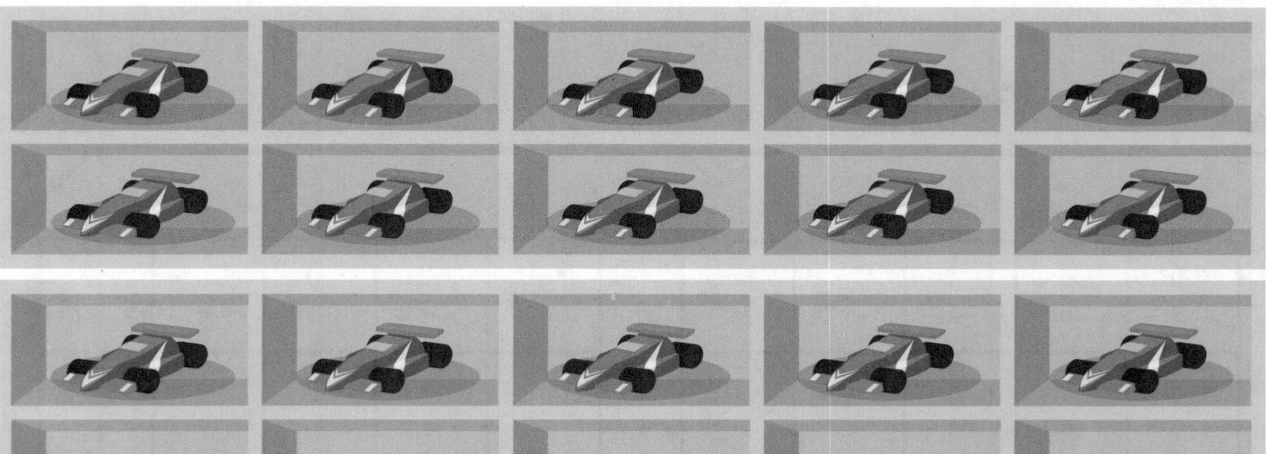

Math is... Mindset

Directions:
How are they the same? How are they different?

Learn

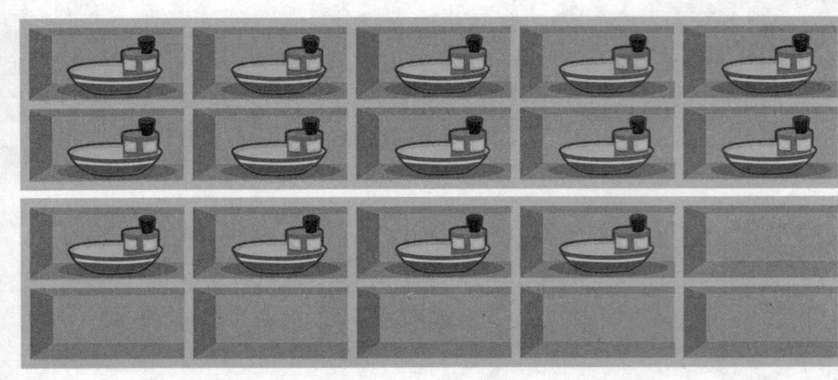

10 + 4 = 14

10 + 5 = 15

Work Together

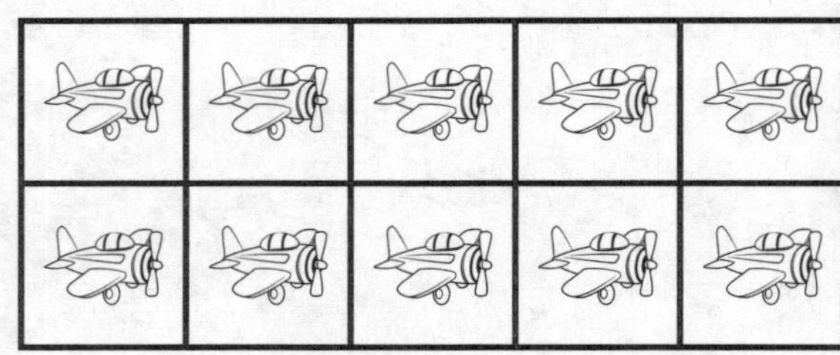

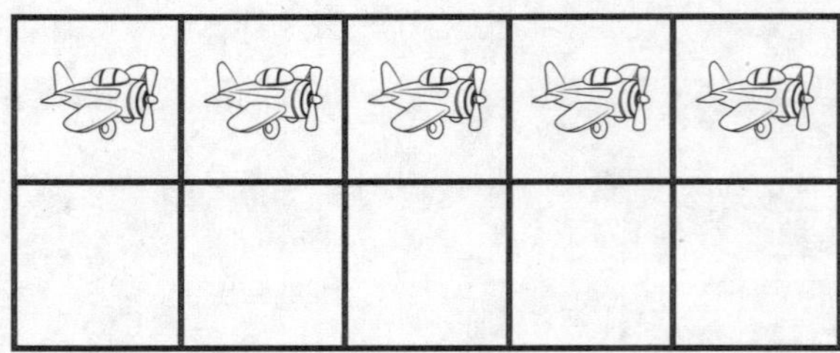

___ + ___ = 15

Work Together: How can you make 15? Use one color to show 10 ones. Then use another color to show 5 more ones. Complete the equation to match.

On My Own

MATH REPLAY | GO ONLINE

Name ____________________

1

___ + ___ = 14

2

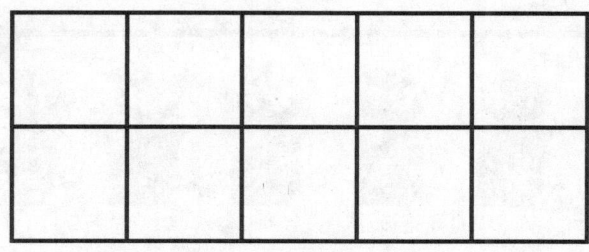

___ + ___ = 15

3

___ + ___ = 14

Directions: **1.** How can you make 14? Use one color to show 10 ones. Then use another color to show 4 more ones. Complete the equation to match. **2.** How can you make 15? Draw counters to show a group of ten ones and some more ones. Complete the equation to match. **3.** How can you make 14? Draw counters to show a group of ten ones and some more ones. Complete the equation to match.

4

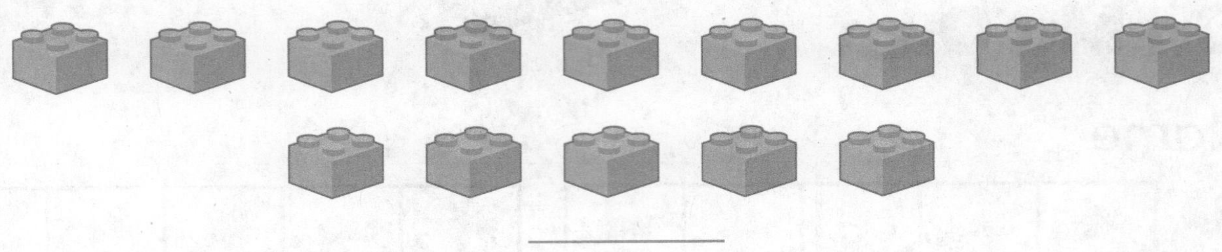

$10 + \_\_\_ = 14$

5

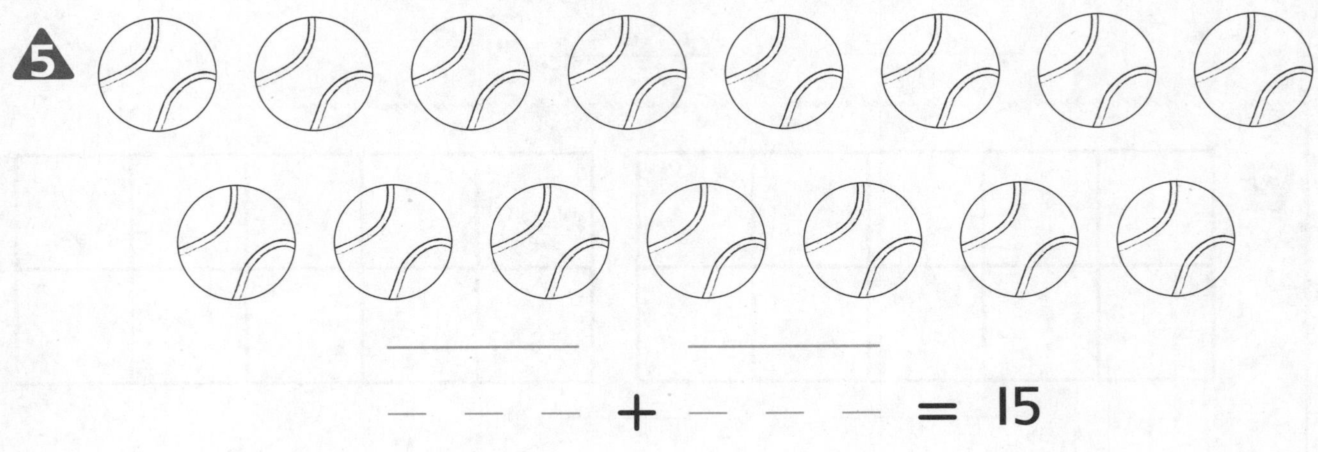

$\_\_\_ + \_\_\_ = 15$

Reflect

Directions: 4. Error Analysis There are 14 blocks. Janet says the missing number in the equation is 4. Marcy says the missing number is 5. Complete the equation to show who is correct. **5. Extend Your Thinking** Use one color to show 10 ones. Then use another color to show 5 more ones. Complete the equation to match.

Reflect: How can you make a group of 10 and some more?

Decompose 14 and 15

Be Curious

Math is... Mindset

Directions:
What question could you ask?

Learn

$14 = 10 + 4$

$15 = 10 + 5$

Work Together

$15 = 10 +$ ____

Work Together: How can you decompose 15? Circle groups to decompose 15 into ten ones and some more ones. Complete the equation to match.

On My Own

MATH REPLAY | GO ONLINE

Name ______________________

1

14 = ___ + ___

2

15 = ___ + ___

3

14 = ___ + ___

Directions: **1.** How can you decompose 14? Circle groups to decompose 14 into ten ones and some more ones. Complete the equation to match. **2.** How can you decompose 15? Circle groups to decompose 15 into ten ones and some more ones. Complete the equation to match. **3.** How can you decompose 14? Circle groups to decompose 14 into ten ones and some more ones. Complete the equation to match.

14 = ___ + ___

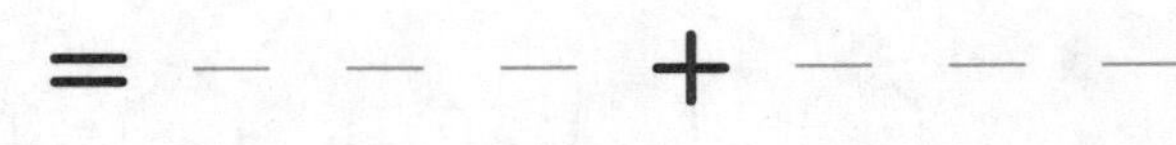

___ = ___ + ___

Reflect

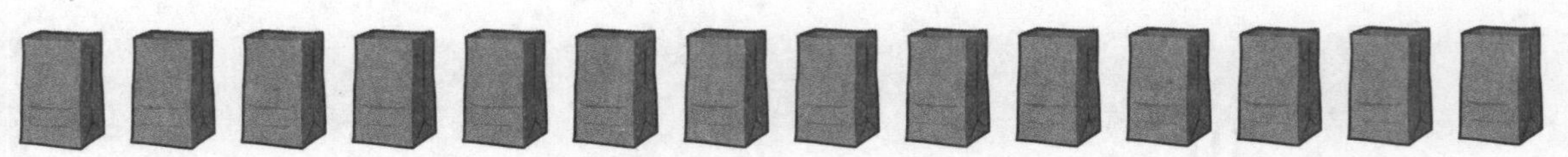

Directions: 4. STEM Connection How can you decompose 14? Circle groups to decompose 14 into ten ones and some more ones. Complete the equation to match. **5. Extend Your Thinking** How can you decompose 15? Draw connecting cubes to decompose 15. Write the equation to match.

Reflect: How can you decompose 14 into ten ones and some more ones?

Unit Review

Name ______________________

Vocabulary Review

1

11

12

13

2

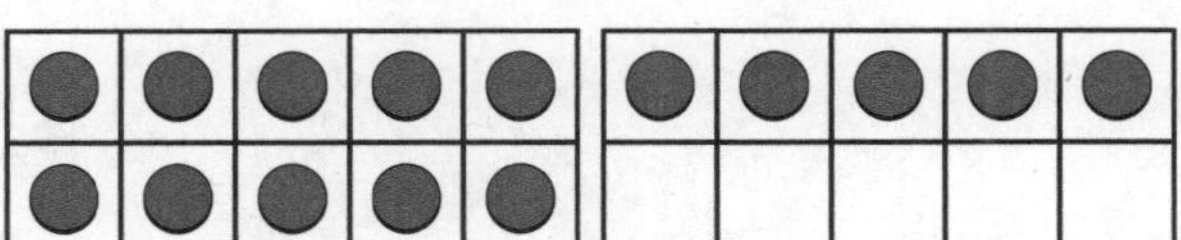

3

14 15

Directions: 1. How many toys? Match the numbers to the pictures to show how many. **2.** How many cubes? Write the number that shows how many. **3.** How many counters? Circle the number that shows how many.

Review

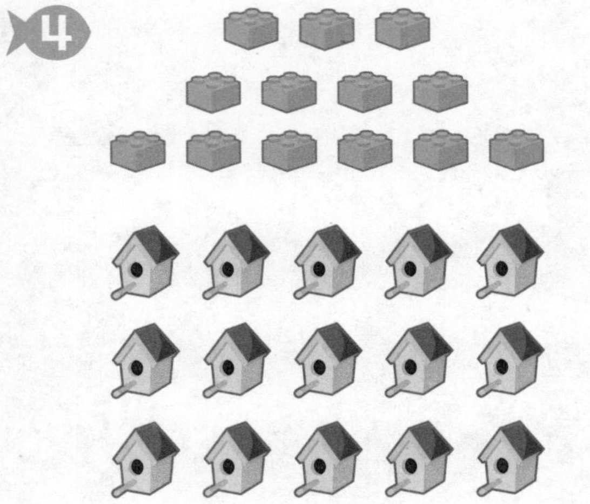

12

15

13

___ + ___ = 14

Directions: 4. How many objects? Match the pictures to the numbers to show how many. Not all numbers will be used. **5.** How can you make 14? Draw counters to show 14 as ten ones and some more ones. Complete the equation to match the counters.

6

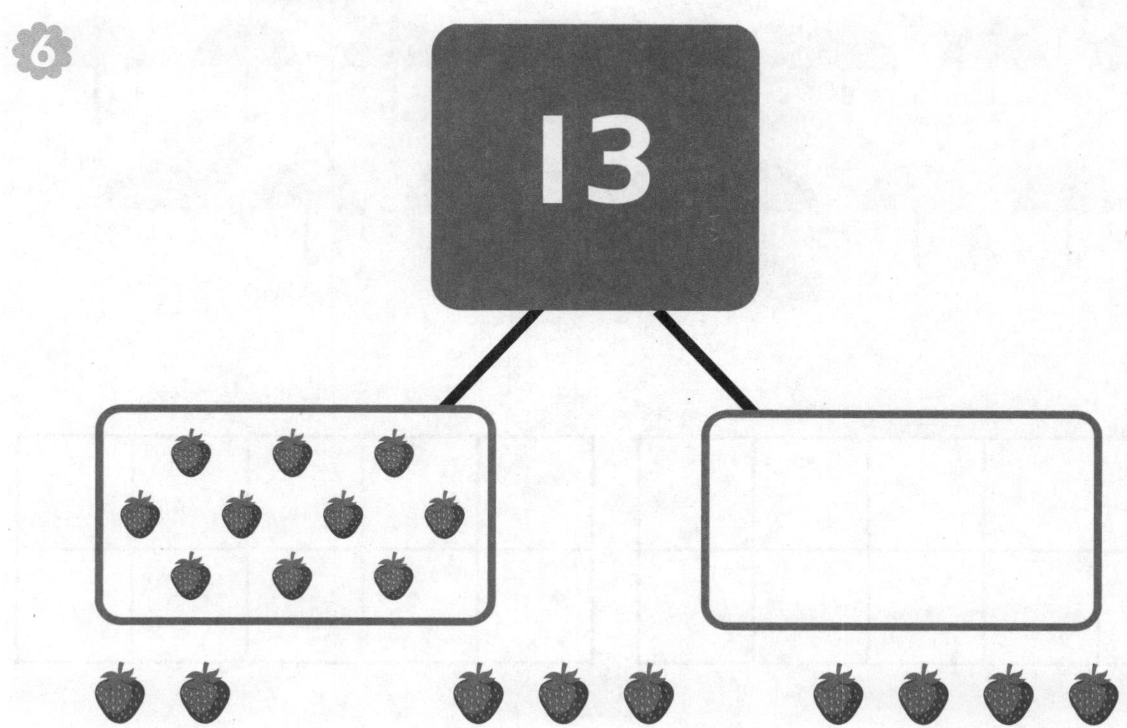

7

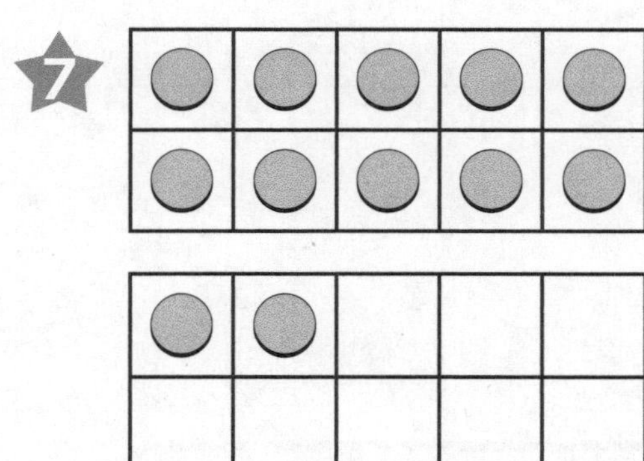

11 12 13

8

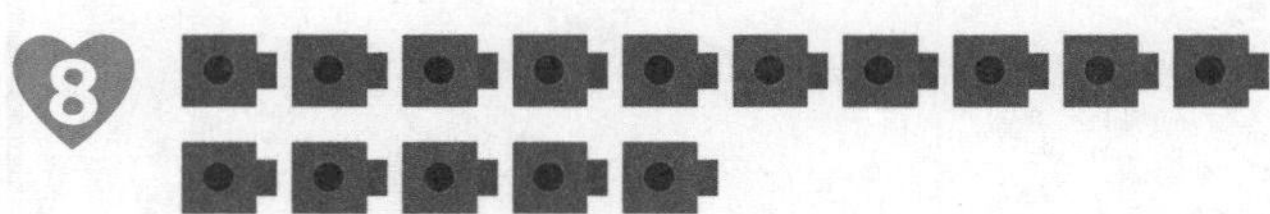

15 = 10 + 3 15 = 10 + 4 15 = 10 + 5

Directions: 6. How can you decompose 13 into ten strawberries and some more strawberries? Circle the group of strawberries that completes the number bond. **7.** How many counters? Circle the number that shows how many. **8.** How many connecting cubes? Circle the equation that matches the picture.

Performance Task

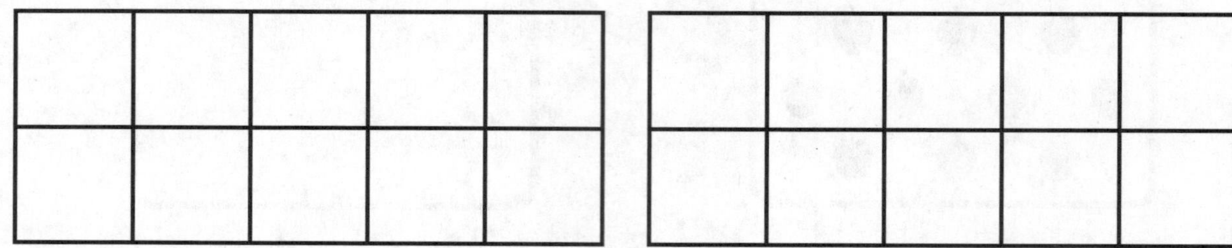

10 + ___ = 14

Reflect

Performance Task: A meteorologist is predicting rain. The school has 14 umbrellas for teachers to use. How can you make 14? **Part A** Circle 14 umbrellas. **Part B** Draw counters to show 14 as ten ones and some more ones. **Part C** Complete the equation to show how to make 14 as ten ones and some more ones.

Reflect: What are different ways you can count, read, and show numbers 11 to 15?

Unit 9

Fluency Practice

Name ______________________

Fluency Strategy

7

(9)

1

7

6

Fluency Flash

2

8

9

3

10

8

Directions: **Fluency Strategy:** You can compare two numbers. 9 is greater than 7. **1.** How can you compare numbers? Circle the number that is greater than the other number. **Fluency Flash:** **2.** How can you compare numbers? Circle the number that is greater than the other number. **3.** How can you compare numbers? Circle the number that is less than the other number.

Fluency Check

9

6

Fluency Talk

Directions: Fluency Check: 4. How can you compare numbers? Circle the number that is greater than the other number. **5.** Which group has more? Circle the group that has the greater number of objects. Write numbers to show how many. **6.** Which group has less? Circle the group that has less objects. Write numbers to show how many.
Fluency Talk: Look at the numbers 9 and 6 in Exercise 4. How did you decide which number was greater?

Numbers 16 to 19

Focus Question

How can I represent, make, and decompose numbers 16 to 19?

Hi, I'm Emily.

I want to be an aerospace engineer. I will need to know how many passengers an airplane will hold. I can count seats to find how many. I will use numbers to do my job.

Name

Cross Out the Numbers

Round 1

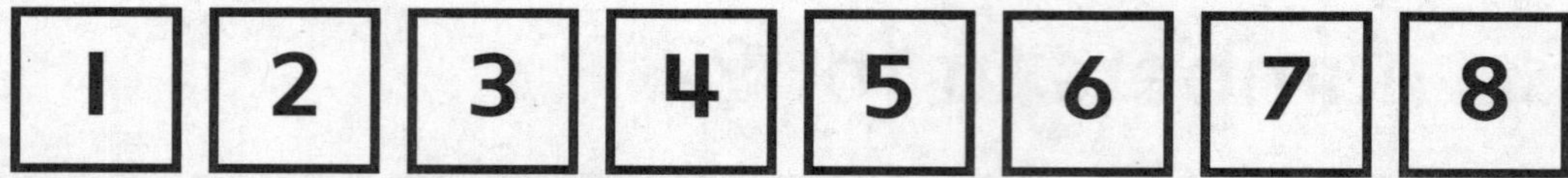

Round 2

Round 3

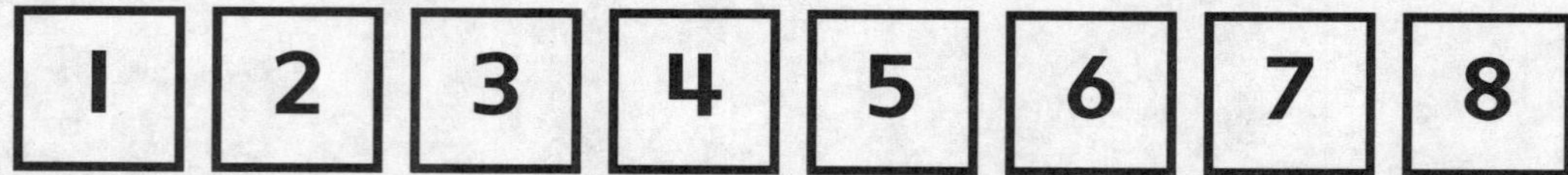

Bonus Round

Directions: Cross out each number that you use.

Represent 16 and 17

Be Curious

Math is... Mindset

Directions:
What do you notice? What do you wonder?

Learn

16

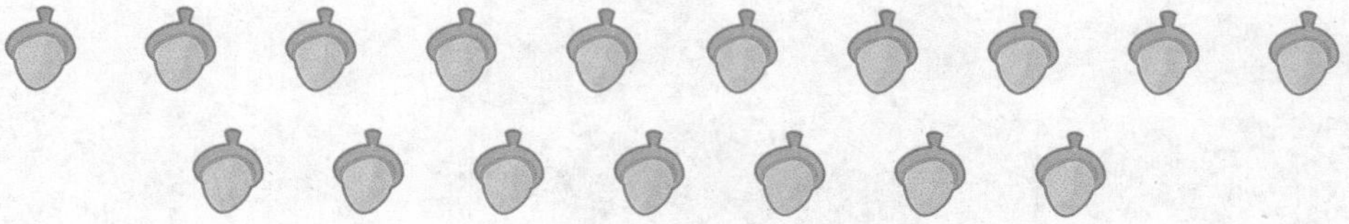

17

Work Together

16 17

Work Together: How many flowers? Count. Circle the number to show how many.

On My Own

Name ____________________

1

2

3

Directions: 1. How many squirrels? Count. Write the number to show how many. **2.** How many birds? Count. Write the number to show how many. **3.** How many flowers? Count. Write the number to show how many.

Reflect

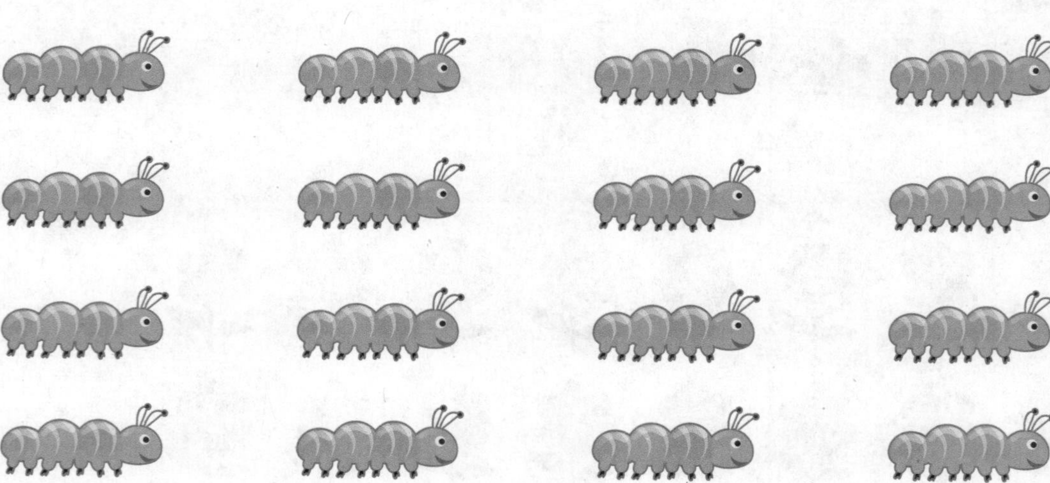

Directions: **4.** How many trees? Count. Write the number to show how many. **5. Extend Your Thinking** How can you show 17? Draw counters to show 17.

Reflect: How can you count the number of animals?

Unit 10

How Many Counters?

Name ________________

1

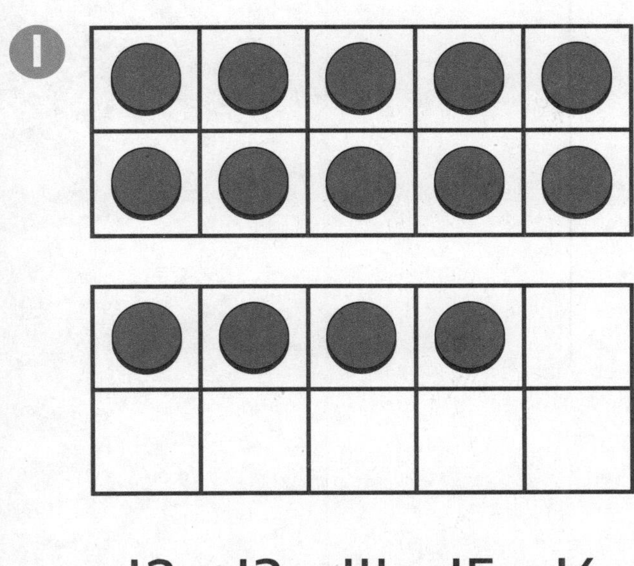

12 13 14 15 16

Tell or show why.

2

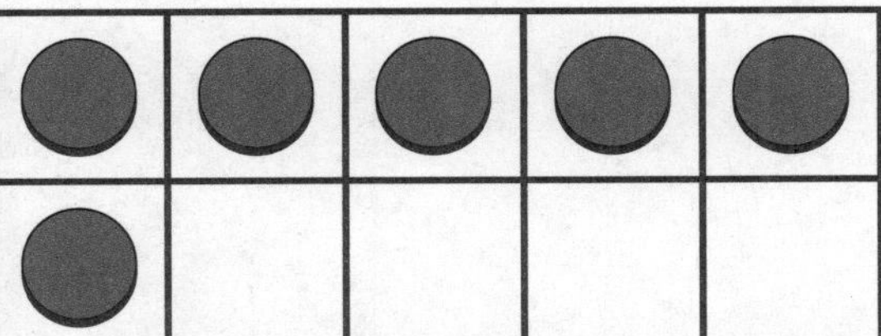

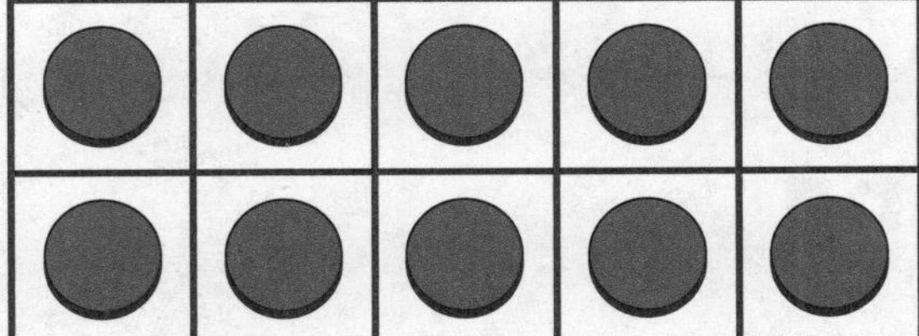

14 15 16 17 18

Tell or show why.

Directions: How many counters do you see? Circle how many there are in all. Tell or show why.

3

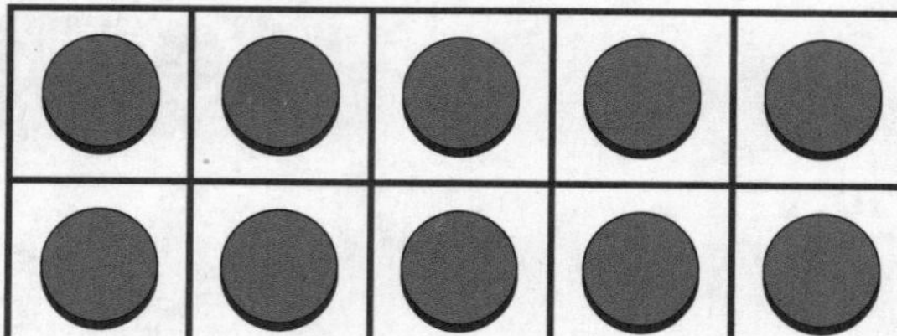

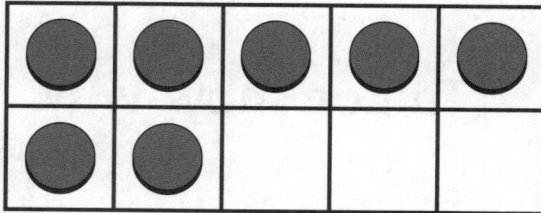

13 14 16 17 18

Tell or show why.

Reflect On Your Learning

Directions: How many counters do you see? Circle how many there are in all. Tell or show why.
Reflect On Your Learning: Do you understand? Circle to show your understanding.

Lesson 10-2

Make 16 and 17

Be Curious

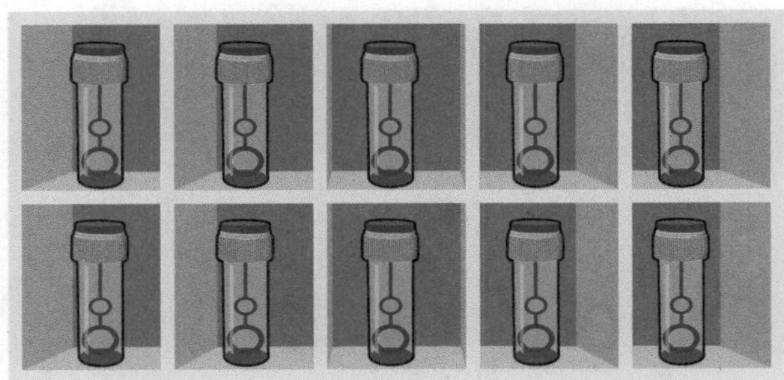
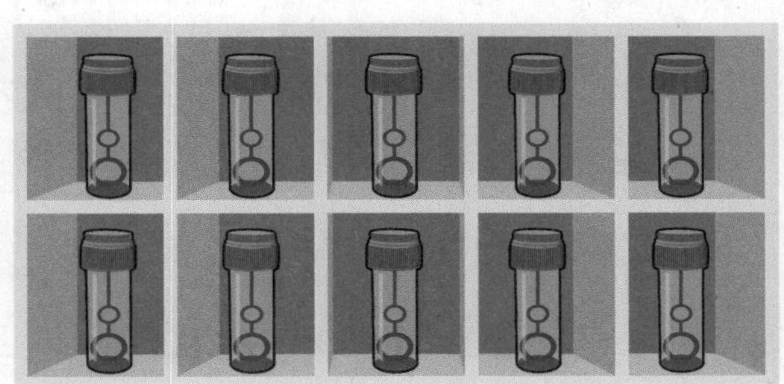
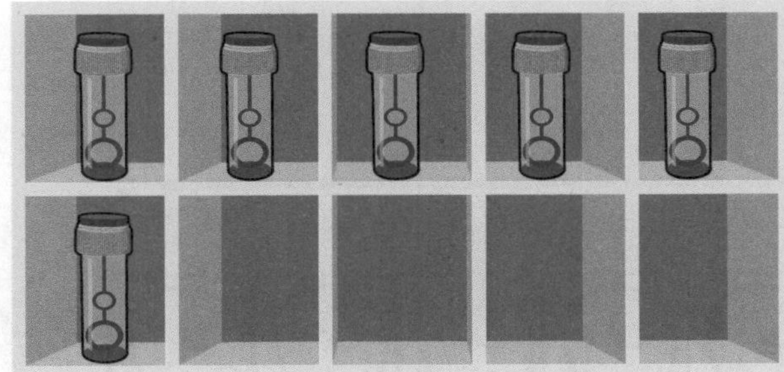
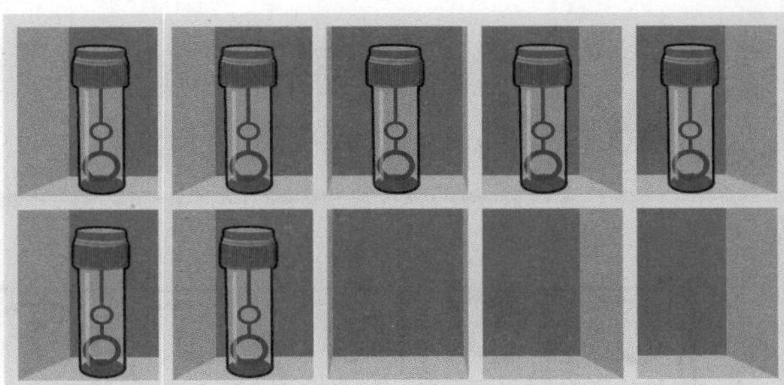

Math is... Mindset

Directions:
How are they the same? How are they different?

Learn

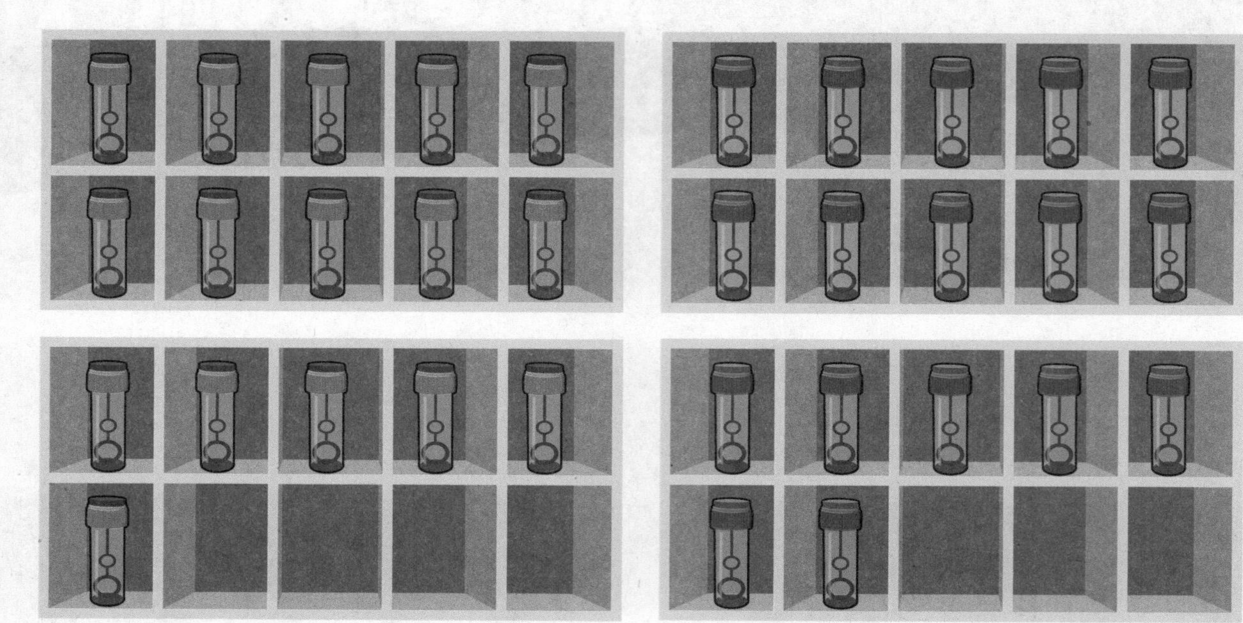

$10 + 6 = 16$ $10 + 7 = 17$

Work Together

___ + ___ = 16

Work Together: How can you make 16? Use one color to show 10 ones. Then use another color to show 6 more ones. Complete the equation to match.

On My Own

MATH REPLAY | GO ONLINE

Name ______________________

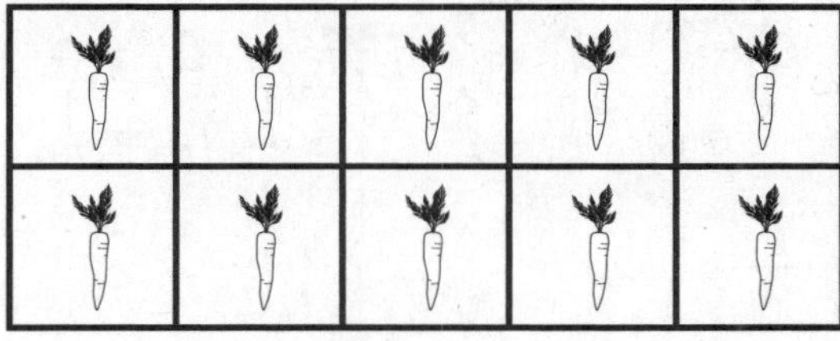

___ + ___ = 17

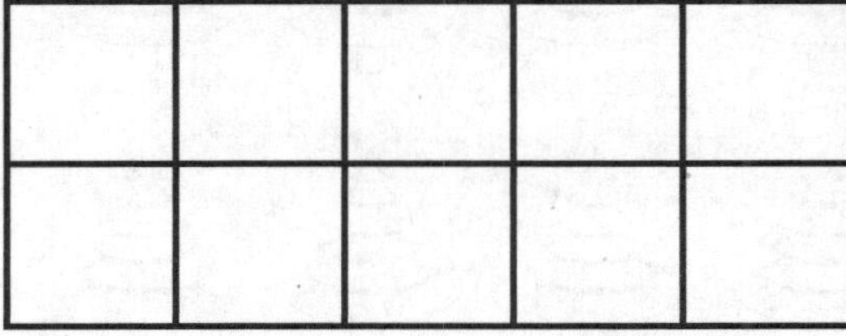

___ + ___ = 16

3

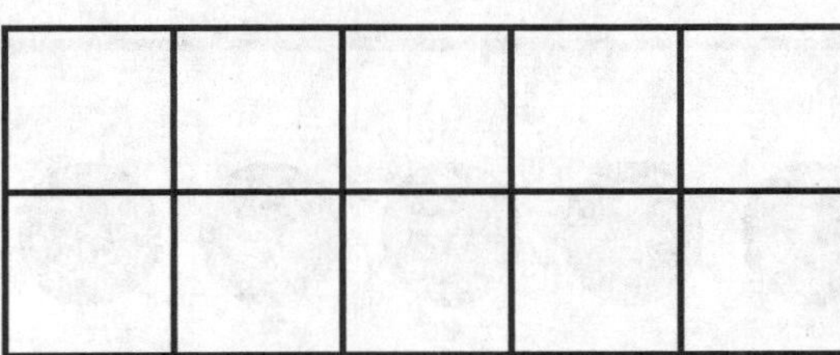

___ + ___ = 17

Directions: 1. How can you make 17? Use one color to show 10 ones. Then use another color to show 7 more ones. Complete the equation to match. **2.** How can you make 16? Draw counters to show a group of ten ones and some more ones. Complete the equation to match. **3.** How can you make 17? Draw counters to show a group of ten ones and some more ones. Complete the equation to match.

4

$10 + \_\_\_ = 17$

5

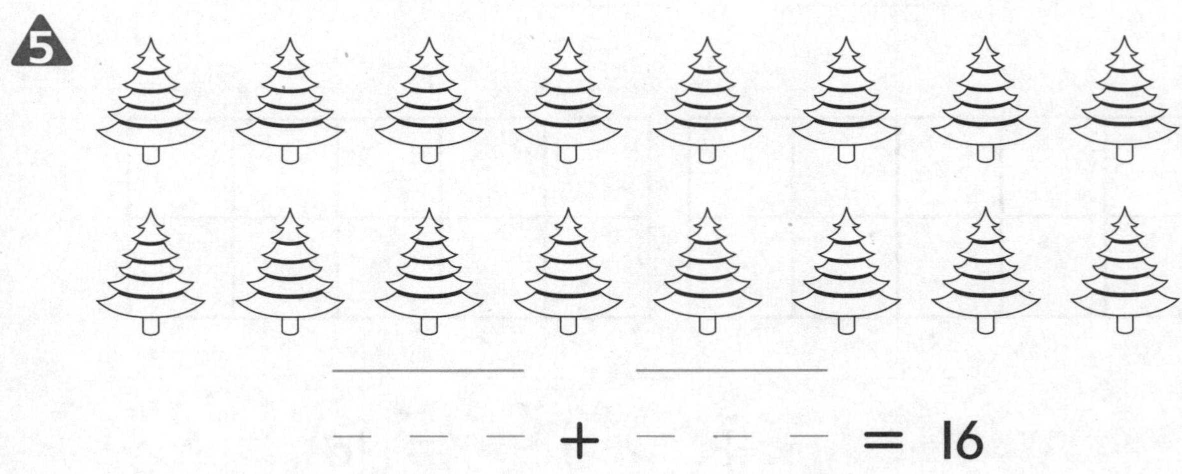

$\_\_\_ + \_\_\_ = 16$

Reflect

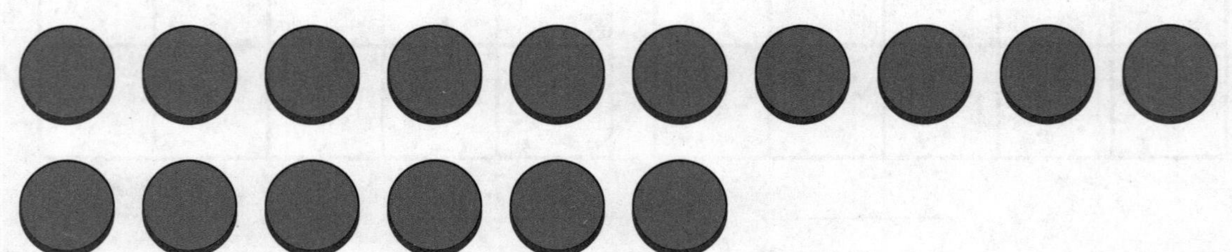

Directions: 4. Error Analysis Carrie says there are 10 cats and 6 more cats. Shelly says there are 10 cats and 7 more cats. Complete the equation to show who is correct. **5. Extend Your Thinking** Use one color to show 10 ones. Then use another color to show 6 more ones. Complete the equation to match.

Reflect: How can you make a group of 10 and some more?

Decompose 16 and 17

Be Curious

Math is... Mindset

Directions:
What question could you ask?

Learn

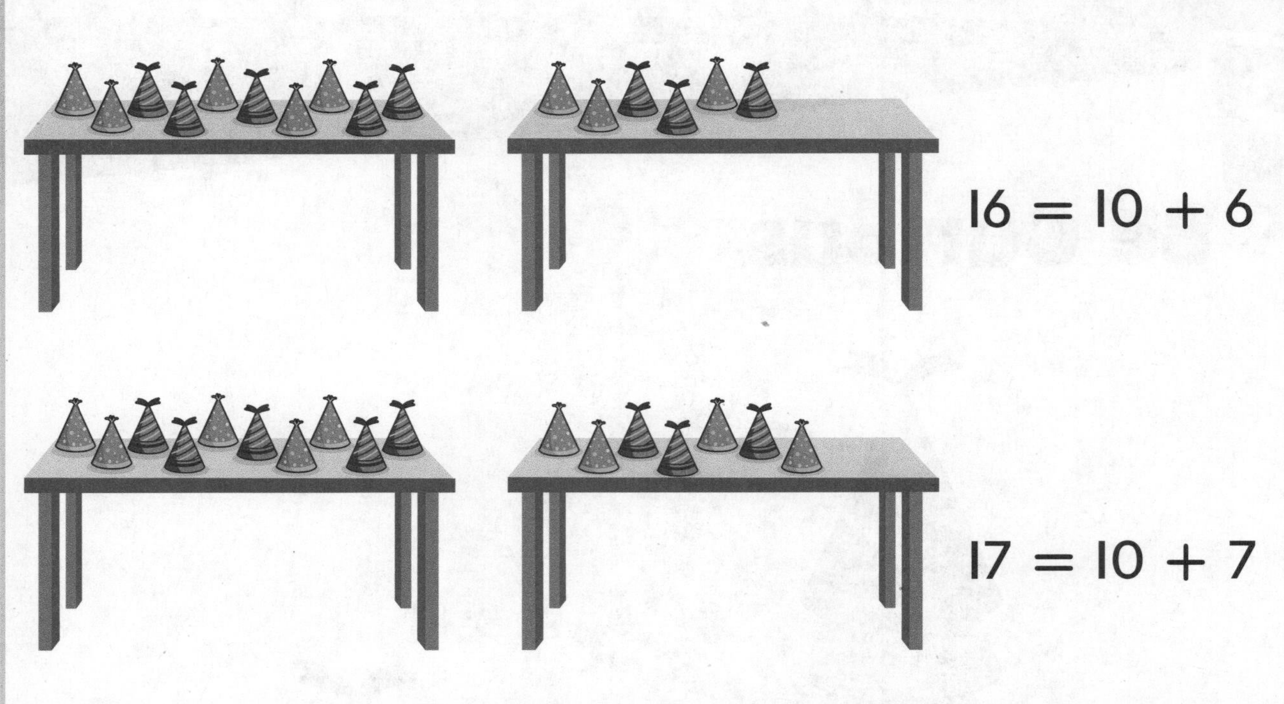

Work Together

17 = 10 + ___

Work Together: How can you decompose 17? Circle groups to decompose 17 into ten ones and some more ones. Complete the equation to match.

On My Own

MATH REPLAY | GO ONLINE

Name ______________________________

1

17 = ______ + ______

2

16 = ______ + ______

3

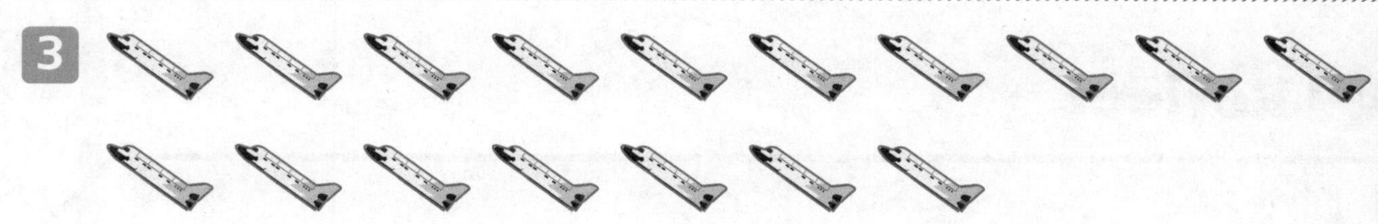

17 = ______ + ______

Directions: **1.** How can you decompose 17? Circle groups to decompose 17 into ten ones and some more ones. Complete the equation to match. **2.** How can you decompose 16? Circle groups to decompose 16 into ten ones and some more ones. Complete the equation to match. **3. STEM Connection** How can you decompose 17? Circle groups to decompose 17 into ten ones and some more ones. Complete the equation to match.

4

16 = ___ + ___

5

___ = ___ + ___

Reflect

Directions: 4. How can you decompose 16? Circle groups to decompose 16 into ten ones and some more ones. Complete the equation to match. **5. Extend Your Thinking** How can you decompose 17? Draw connecting cubes to decompose 17 into ten ones and some more ones. Write the equation to match.

Reflect: How can you decompose a number?

Represent 18 and 19

Be Curious

Math is... Mindset

Directions:
What do you notice? What do you wonder?

Learn

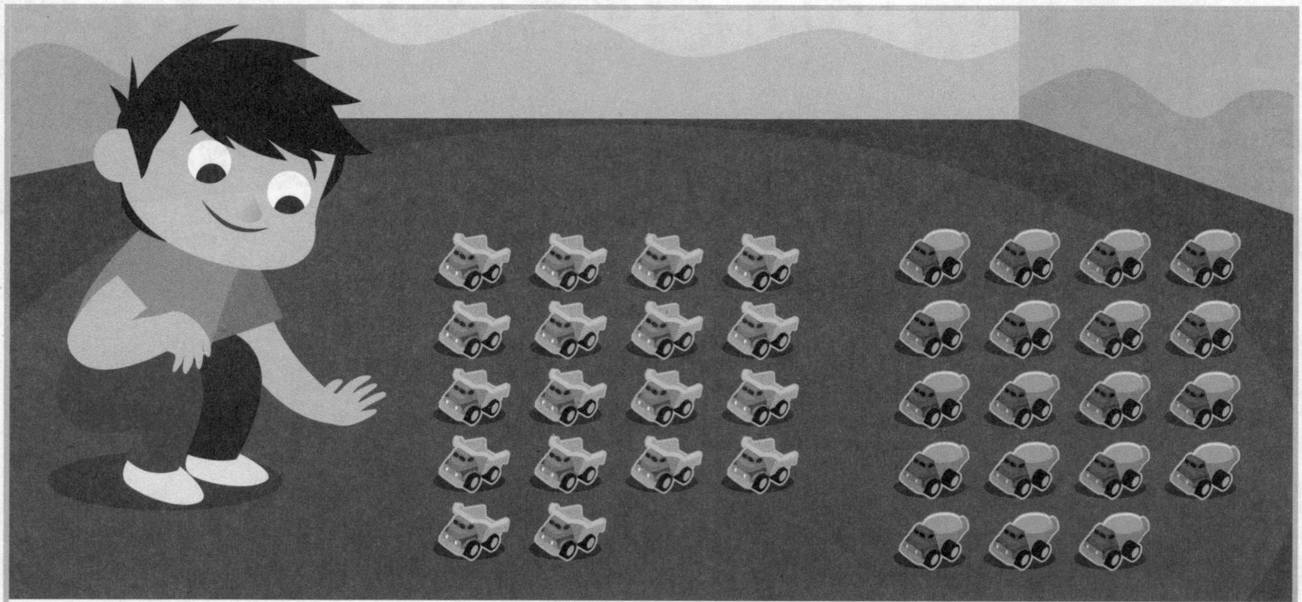

18

19

Work Together

18 19

Work Together: How many blocks? Count. Circle the number to show how many.

On My Own

Name

1

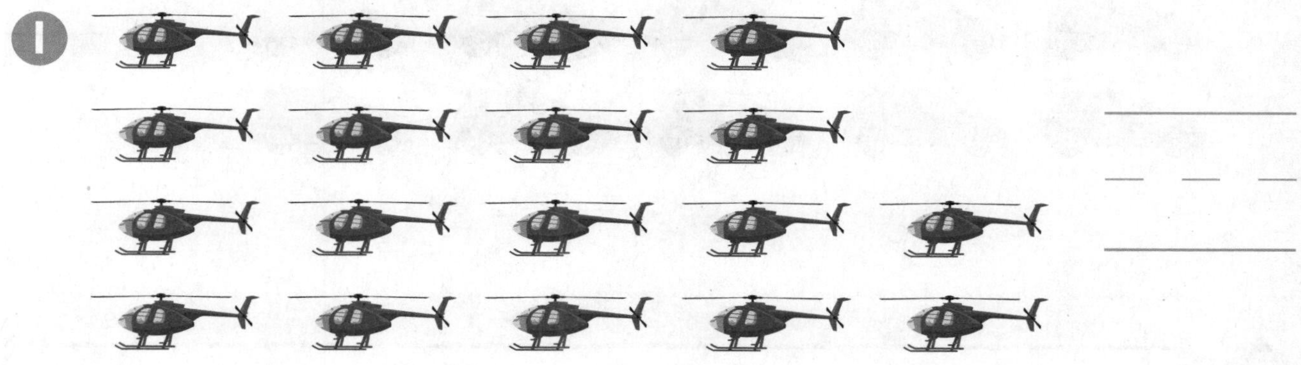

2

3

Directions: 1. STEM Connection How many helicopters? Count. Write the number to show how many. **2.** How many bicycles? Count. Write the number to show how many. **3.** How many trucks? Count. Write the number to show how many.

Reflect

Directions: **4.** How many cars? Count. Write the number to show how many. **5. Extend Your Thinking** How can you show 18? Draw counters to show 18.
Reflect: How can you count the number of scooters?

Lesson 10-5

Make 18 and 19

Be Curious

Math is... Mindset

Directions:
How are they the same? How are they different?

Learn

10 + 8 = 18

10 + 9 = 19

Work Together

_____ + _____ = 19

Work Together: How can you make 19? Use one color to show 10 ones. Then use another color to show 9 more ones. Complete the equation to match.

On My Own

MATH REPLAY | GO ONLINE

Name ________________

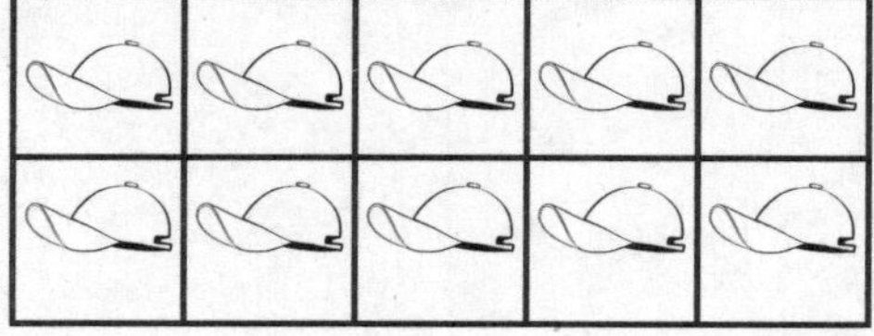 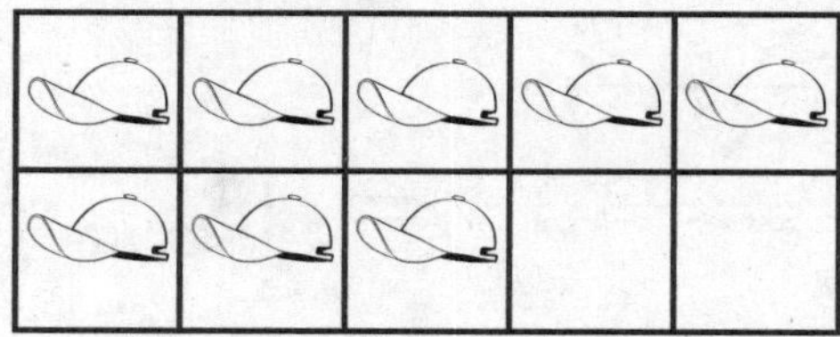

___ + ___ = 18

2

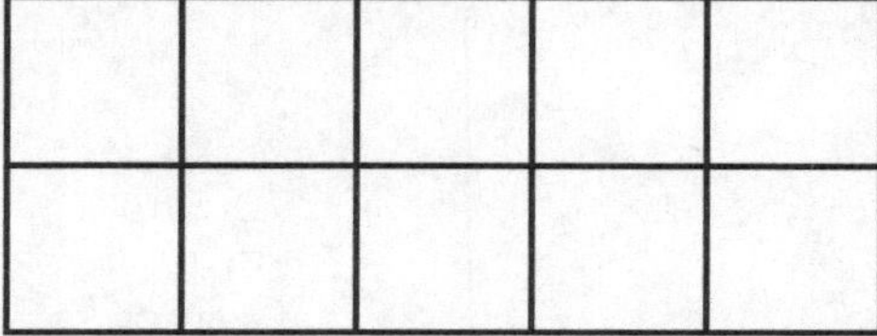 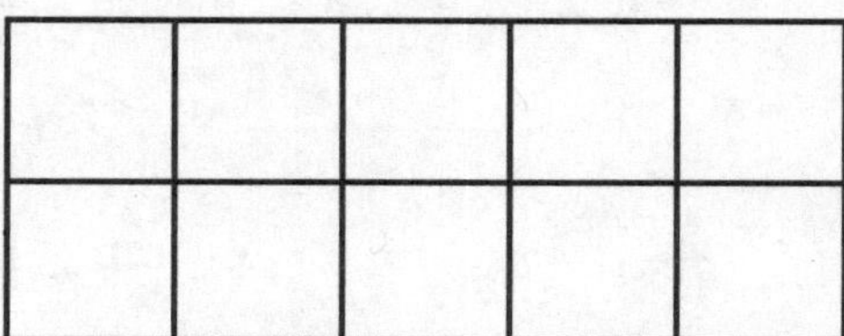

___ + ___ = 19

3

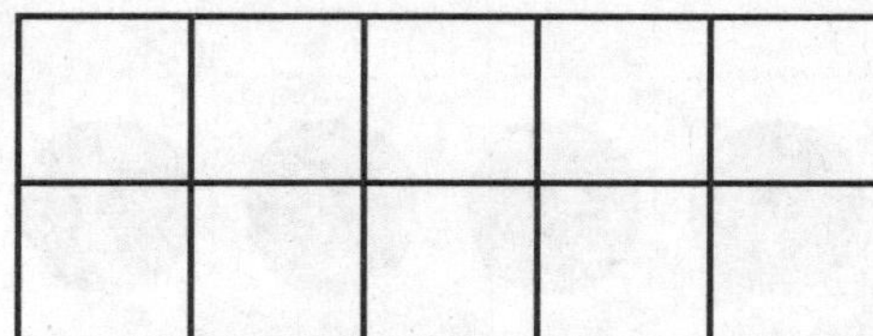 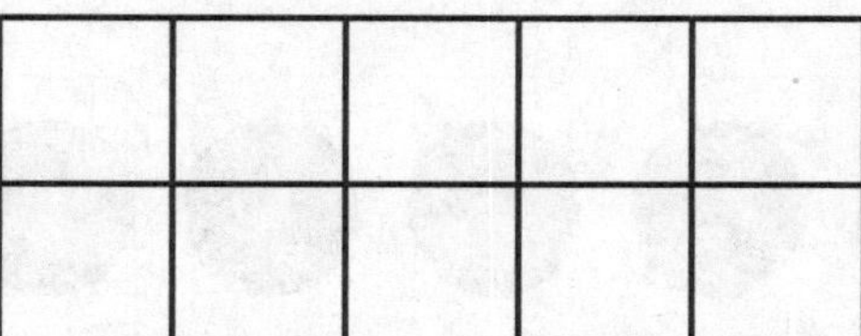

___ + ___ = 18

Directions: **1.** How can you make 18? Use one color to show 10 ones. Then use another color to show 8 more ones. Complete the equation to match. **2.** How can you make 19? Draw counters to show a group of ten ones and some more ones. Complete the equation to match. **3.** How can you make 18? Draw counters to show a group of ten ones and some more ones. Complete the equation to match.

4

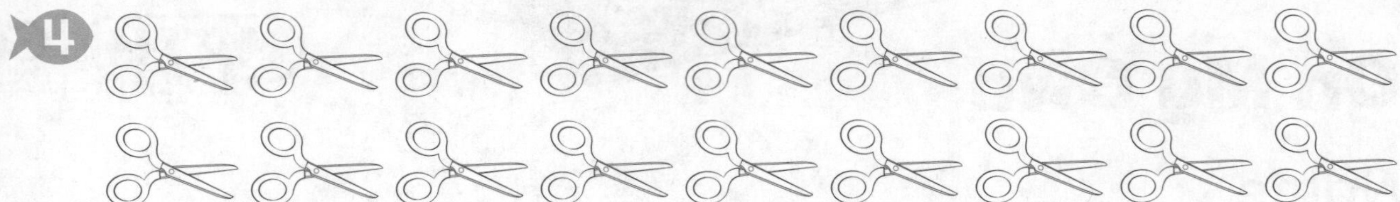

10 + ___ = 18

5

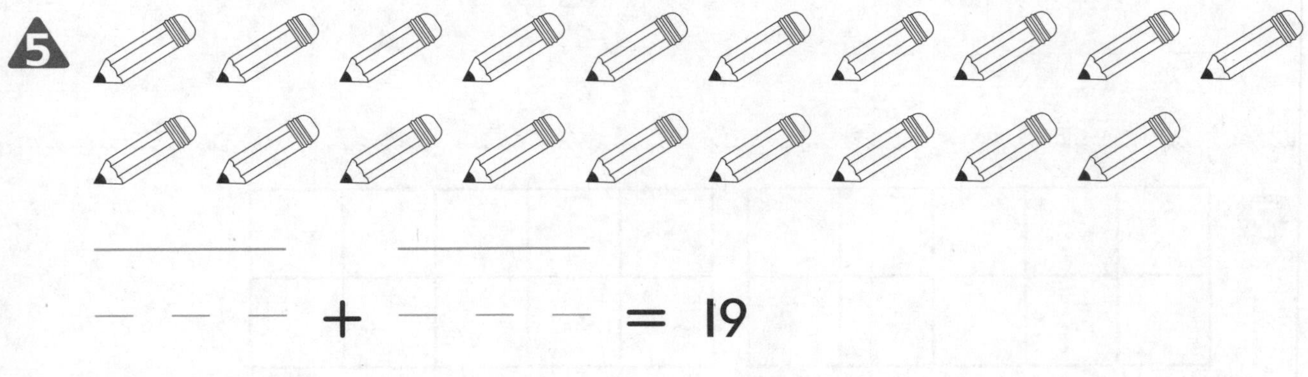

___ + ___ = 19

Reflect

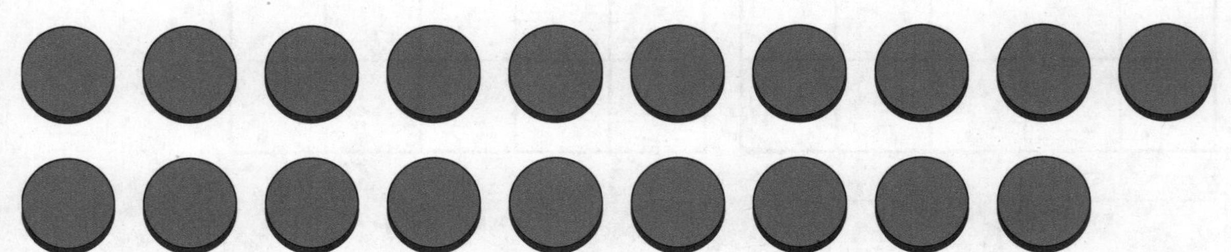

Directions: 4. Error Analysis There are 18 scissors. Jill says the missing number in the equation is 8. Mandy says the missing number is 9. Complete the equation to show who is correct. **5. Extend Your Thinking** Use one color to show 10 ones. Then use another color to show 9 more ones. Complete the equation to match.
Reflect: How can you make a group of 10 and some more?

Decompose 18 and 19

Be Curious

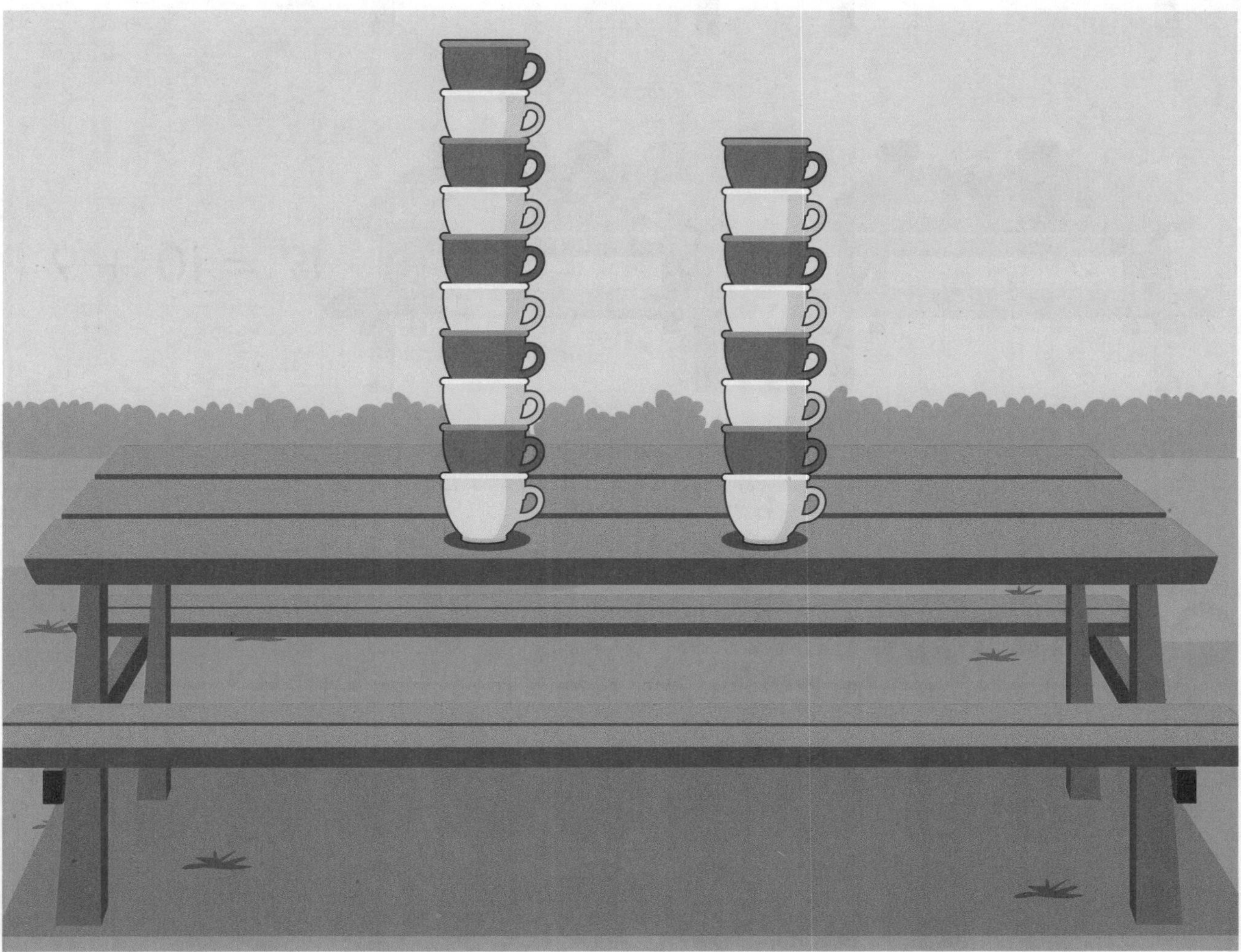

Math is... Mindset

Directions:
What question could you ask?

Learn

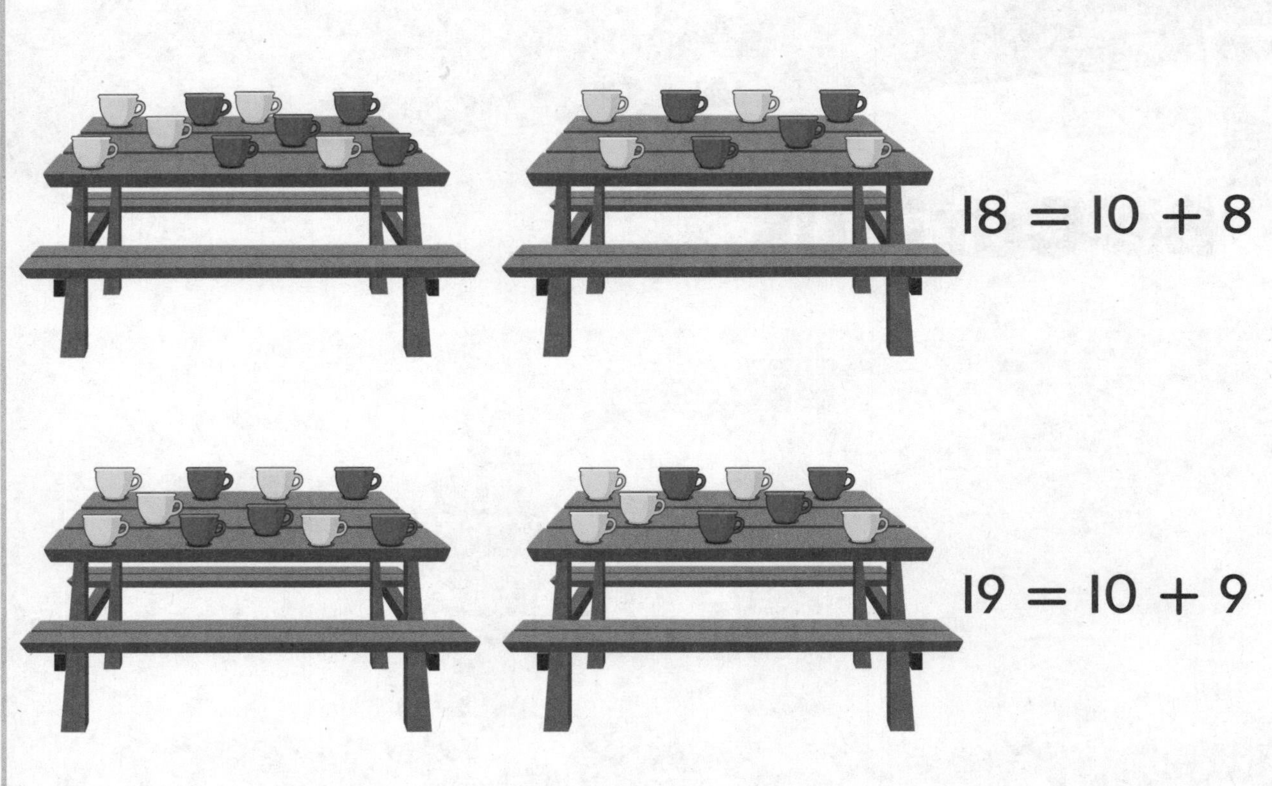

$18 = 10 + 8$

$19 = 10 + 9$

Work Together

$18 = 10 +$ ___

Work Together: How can you decompose 18? Circle groups to decompose 18 into ten ones and some more ones. Complete the equation to match.

MATH REPLAY | GO ONLINE

On My Own

Name ______________________

1

18 = ___ + ___

2

19 = ___ + ___

3

18 = ___ + ___

Directions: **1.** How can you decompose 18? Circle groups to decompose 18 into ten ones and some more ones. Complete the equation to match. **2.** How can you decompose 19? Circle groups to decompose 19 into ten ones and some more ones. Complete the equation to match. **3.** How can you decompose 18? Circle groups to decompose 18 into ten ones and some more ones. Complete the equation to match.

4

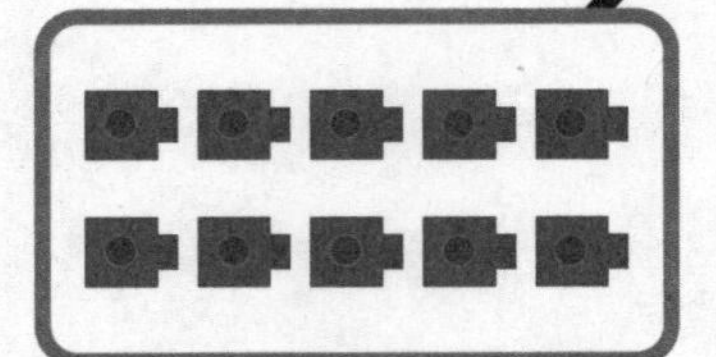

18 = ___ + ___

5

Reflect

Directions: 4. Error Analysis Nate is decomposing 18. He says the equation is 18 = 10 + 9. Do you agree? Complete the equation to correct his thinking. **5. Extend Your Thinking** How can you decompose 18? Draw connecting cubes to decompose 18 into ten ones and some more ones.

Reflect: How can you decompose a number?

Unit Review

Name ________________

Vocabulary Review

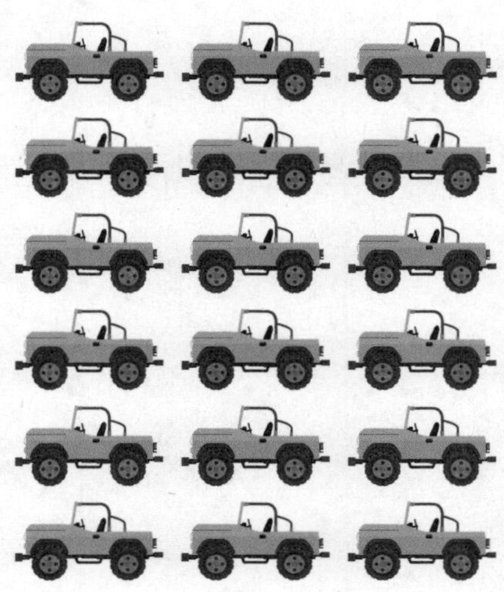

Directions: **1.** Circle the group of 16 toys. **2.** Draw an X on the group of 19 toys. **3.** Underline the group of 18 toys. **4.** Draw a box around the group of 17 toys.

Review

5

16 17 18

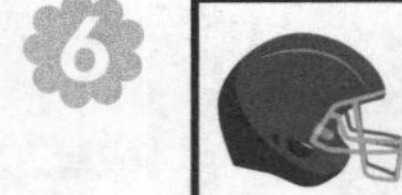

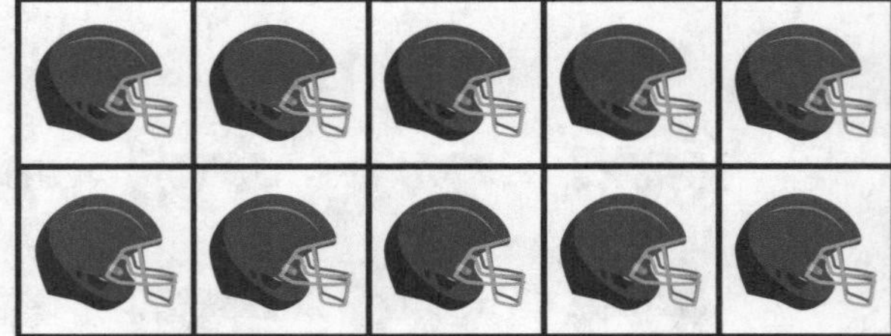

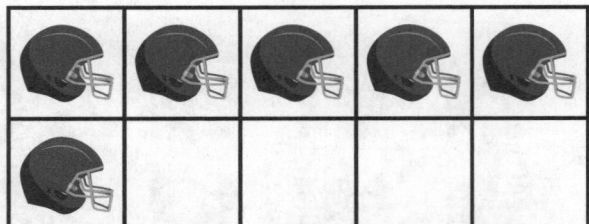

$10 + 6 = 16$ $10 + 7 = 17$ $10 + 8 = 18$

Directions: 5. How many skateboards? Count. Circle the number to show how many.
6. How can you make 16? Circle the equation that shows how to make 16.

7

18

17

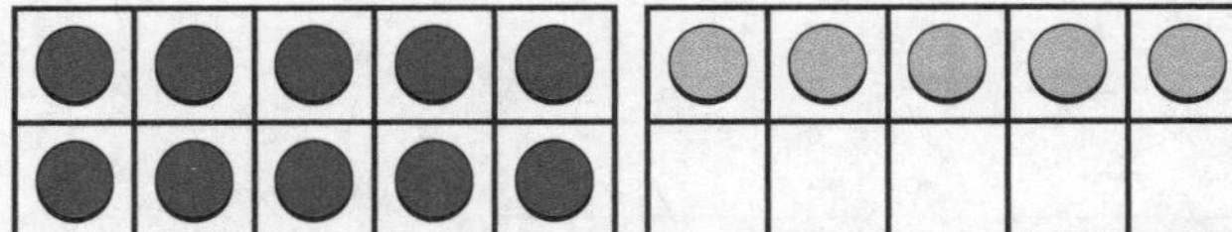

$10 + 8 = 18$

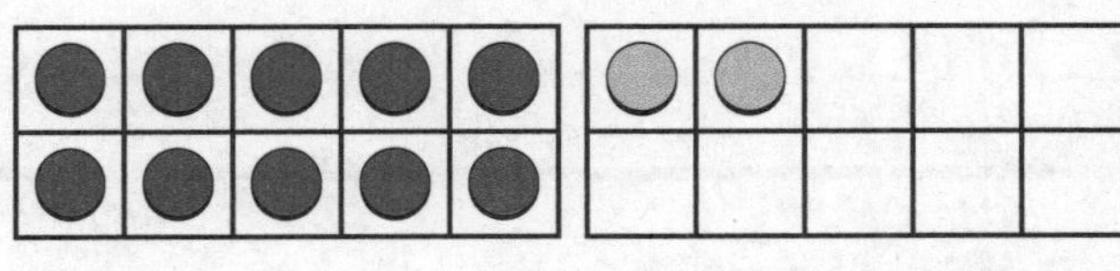

$10 + 2 = 12$

$10 + 5 = 15$

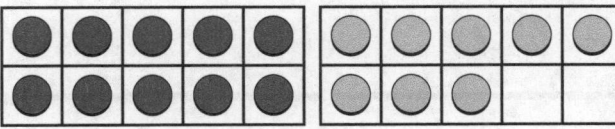

Directions: 7. How many? Match the numbers to the pictures to show how many in each group.
8. How can you make a number? Match the equations to the counters.

Performance Task

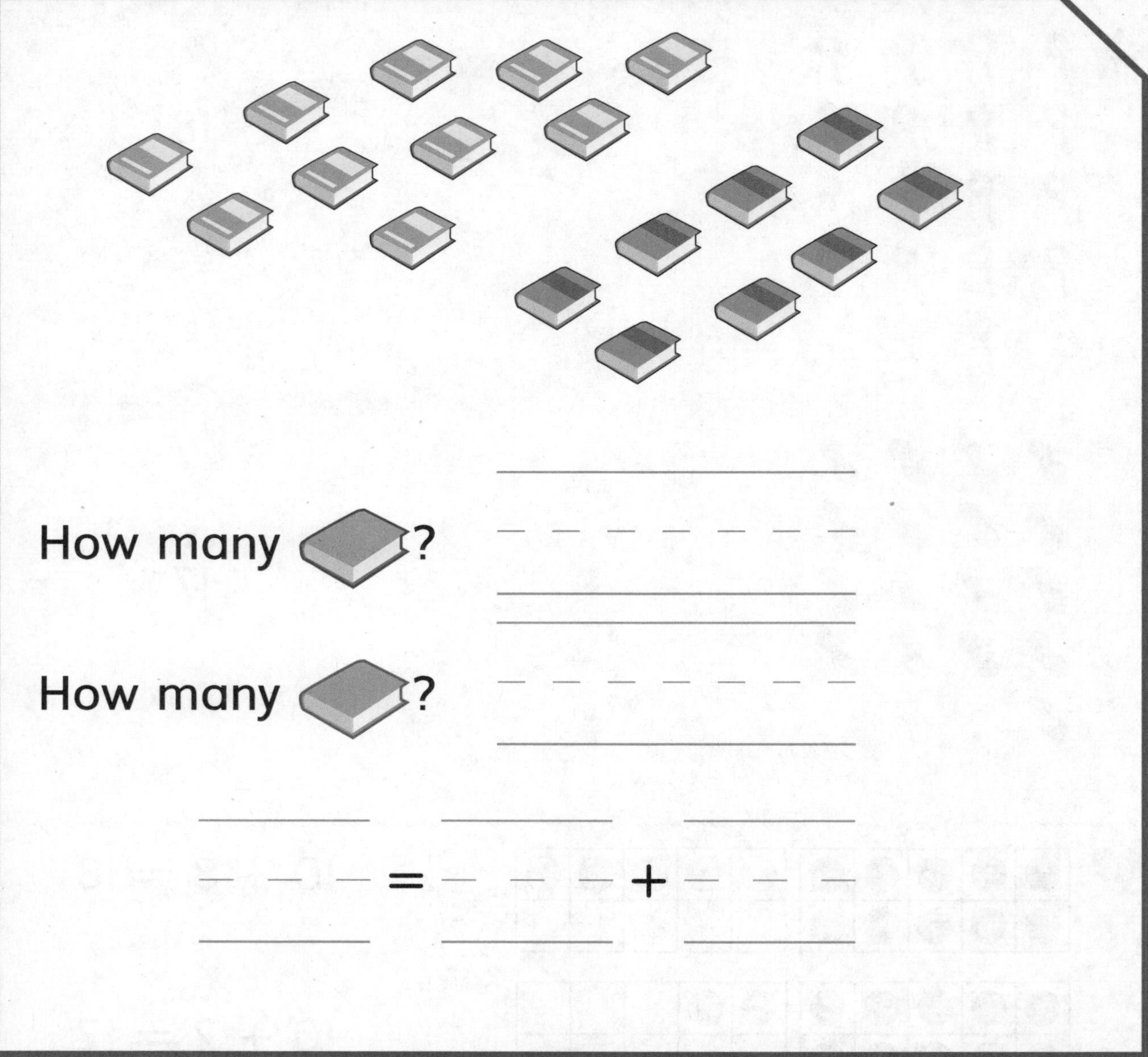

Reflect

Performance Task: An aerospace engineer has books about space to put away. **Part A** How many blue books? Count and write the number. How many green books? Count and write the number. **Part B** Write an equation to show how the aerospace engineer can put the books away into a group of ten books and some more books.

Reflect: What are different ways you can count, read, and show numbers 16 to 19?

Unit 10

Fluency Practice

Name ____________________

Fluency Strategy

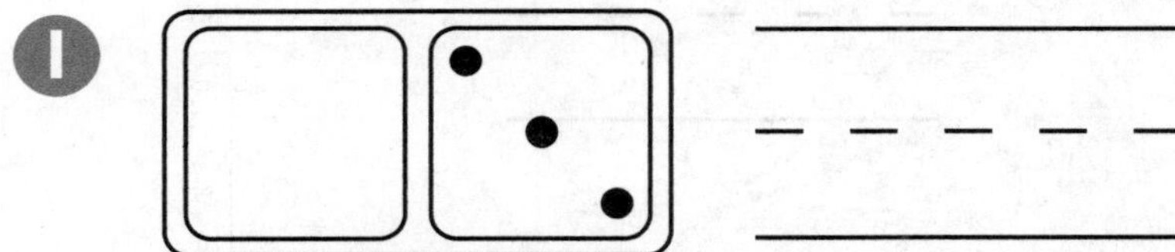

Fluency Flash

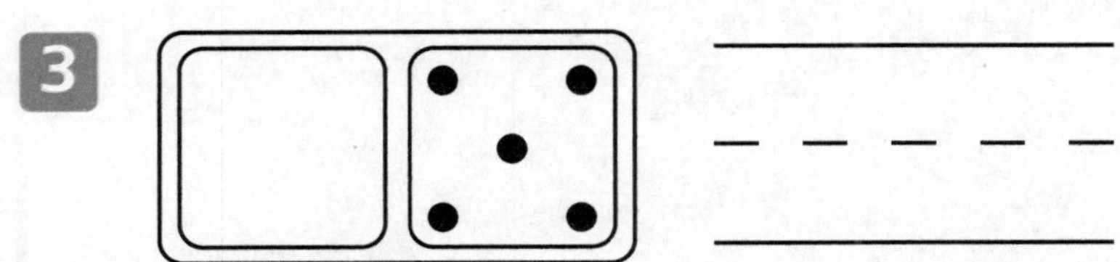

Directions: Fluency Strategy: You can visually determine the number of dots. There are 4 dots. **1.** How many dots does the domino have? Write the total number of dots you see. **Fluency Flash: 2.** How many dots does the number cube have? Write the total number of dots you see. **3.** How many dots does the domino have? Write the total number of dots you see.

Fluency Check

4 8

10

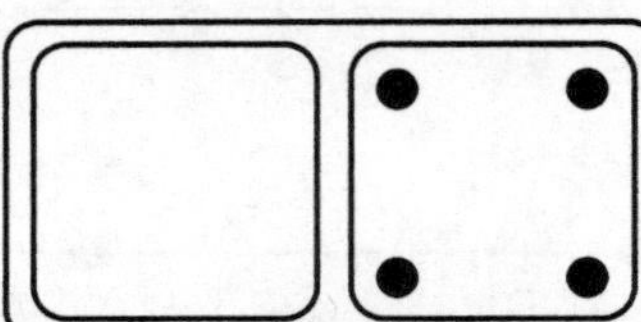

5

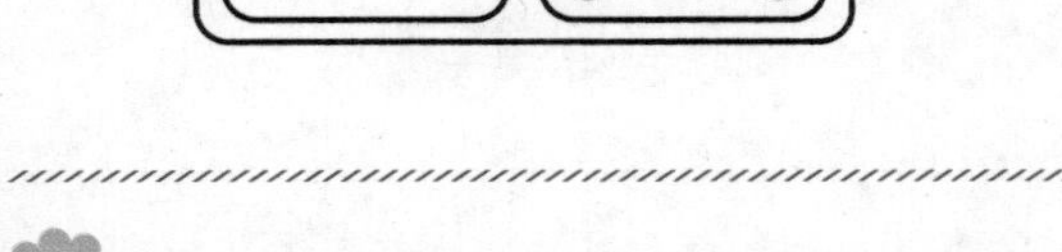

6

Fluency Talk

Directions: Fluency Check: 4. Which number is greater? Circle the number that is greater. **5.** How many dots does the domino have? Write the total number of dots you see. **6.** Which group has more? Circle the group that has a greater number of objects. Write numbers to show how many.
Fluency Talk: Look at the domino in Exercise 5. How did you determine the total number of dots?

3-Dimensional Shapes

Focus Question

How can I identify 3-dimensional shapes?

Hi, I'm Kayla.

I want to be a landscape architect. I like to take care of plants and watch them grow. Plants can be shaped like cubes, cones, and spheres!

Name

Which Shape Is Different?

Group 1

Group 2

Group 3

Directions: Tell how one shape is different than the other two.

Lesson 11-1

2-Dimensional and 3-Dimensional Shapes

Be Curious

Math is... Mindset

Directions:
How are they the same? How are they different?

Learn

Work Together

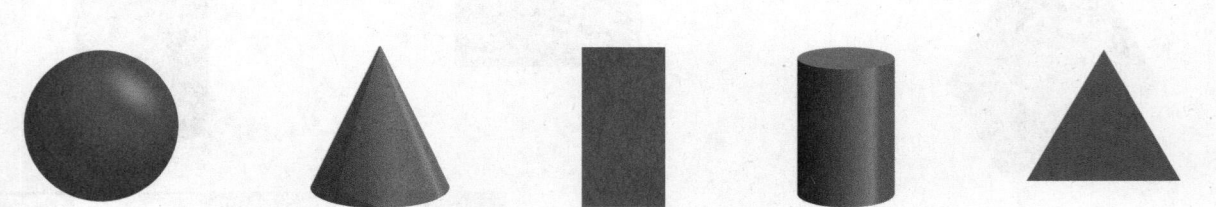

Work Together: Which shapes are 3-dimensional? Circle all the 3-dimensional shapes.

On My Own

Name ______________________________

1

2

3

Directions: I. Which shape is 2-dimensional? Circle the 2-dimensional shape. **2.** Which shapes are 3-dimensional? Circle all the 3-dimensional shapes. **3.** Which shapes are 2-dimensional? Circle all the 2-dimensional shapes.

4

5

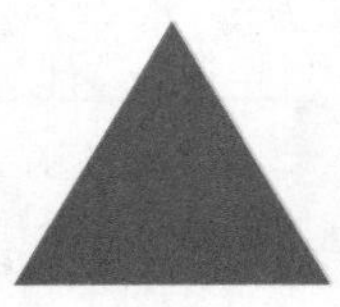

Reflect

Directions: 4. Error Analysis Mary says the larger shape is 3-dimensional. Janine says the smaller shape is 3-dimensional. Who is correct? Circle the 3-dimensional shape. **5. Extend Your Thinking** Which shape is not like the others? Circle the shape that is not like the others.
Reflect: How can you tell if a shape is 2-dimensional or 3-dimensional?

Unit 11

Flat Shape or Solid Shape?

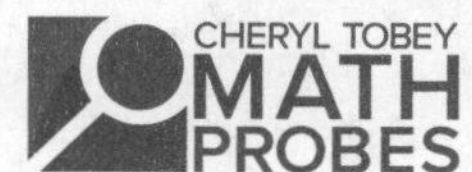

Name ____________________

Flat Shapes

Solid Shapes

A.

B.

C.

D.

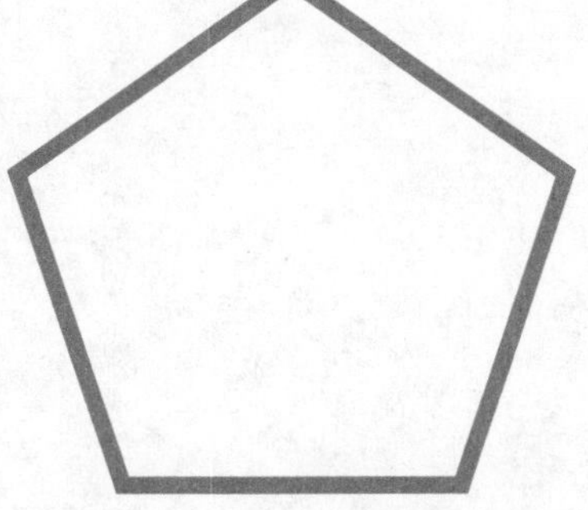

Directions: Is the shape flat or solid? Sort the shapes by flat shapes and solid shapes.

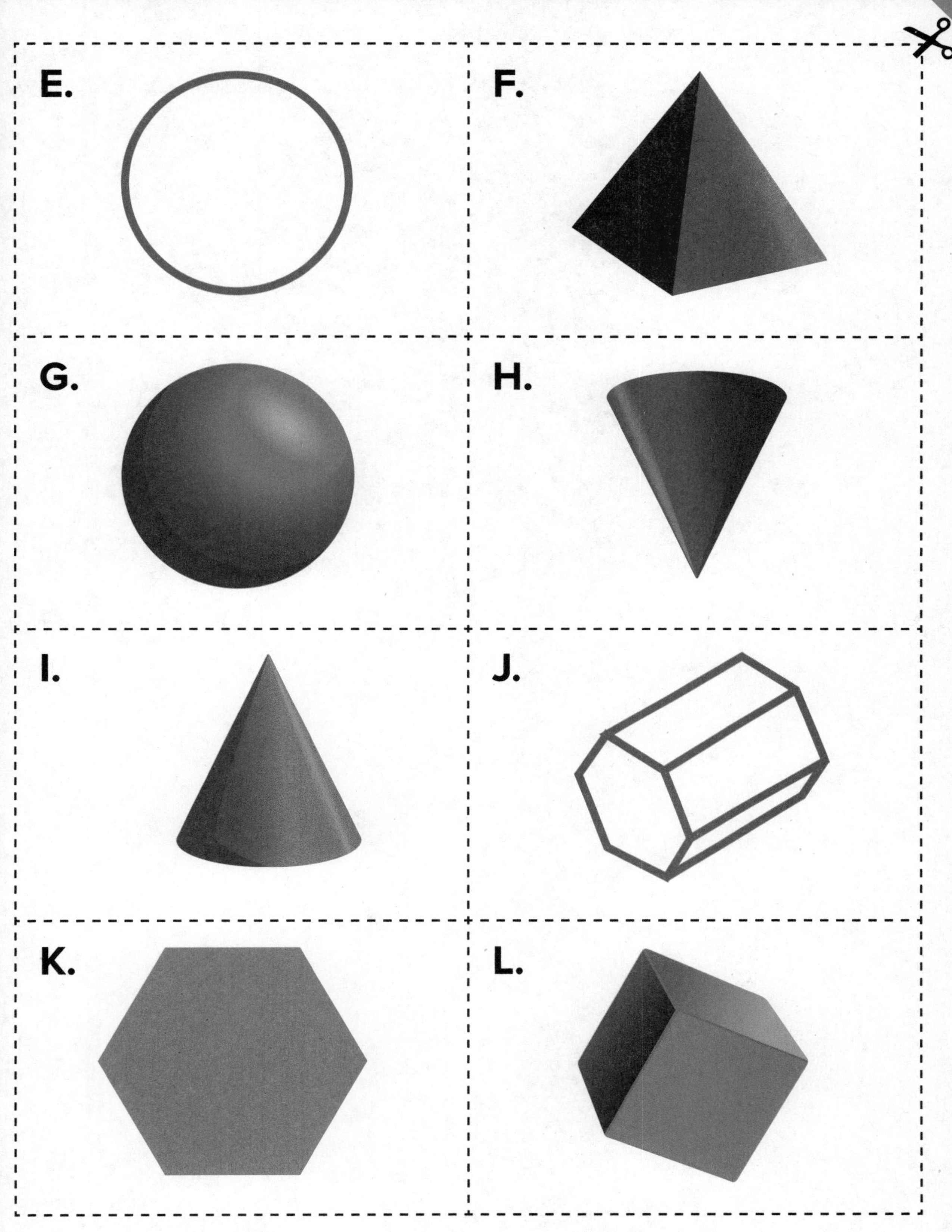

Directions: Is the shape flat or solid? Sort the shapes by flat shapes and solid shapes.

Cubes

Be Curious

Math is... Mindset

Directions:
Which doesn't belong?

Learn

Work Together

Work Together: Which shapes are cubes? Circle all the cubes.

On My Own

MATH REPLAY | GO ONLINE

Name ______________________________

2

3

Directions: 1-2. Which shape is a cube? Circle the cube. **3.** Which shapes are cubes? Circle all the cubes.

4

5

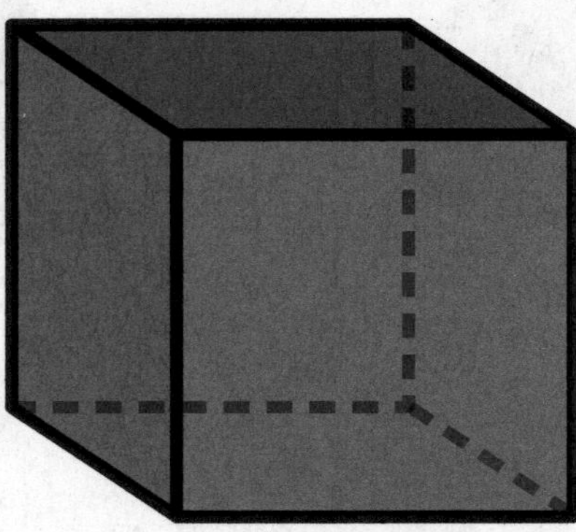

2 4 6

Reflect

Directions: 4. Which shape is not a cube? Circle the shape that is not a cube. **5. Extend Your Thinking** How many faces does a cube have? Circle the number of faces.

Reflect: How can you describe this shape?

Lesson 11-3

Spheres

Be Curious

Math is... Mindset

Directions:
Which doesn't belong?

Learn

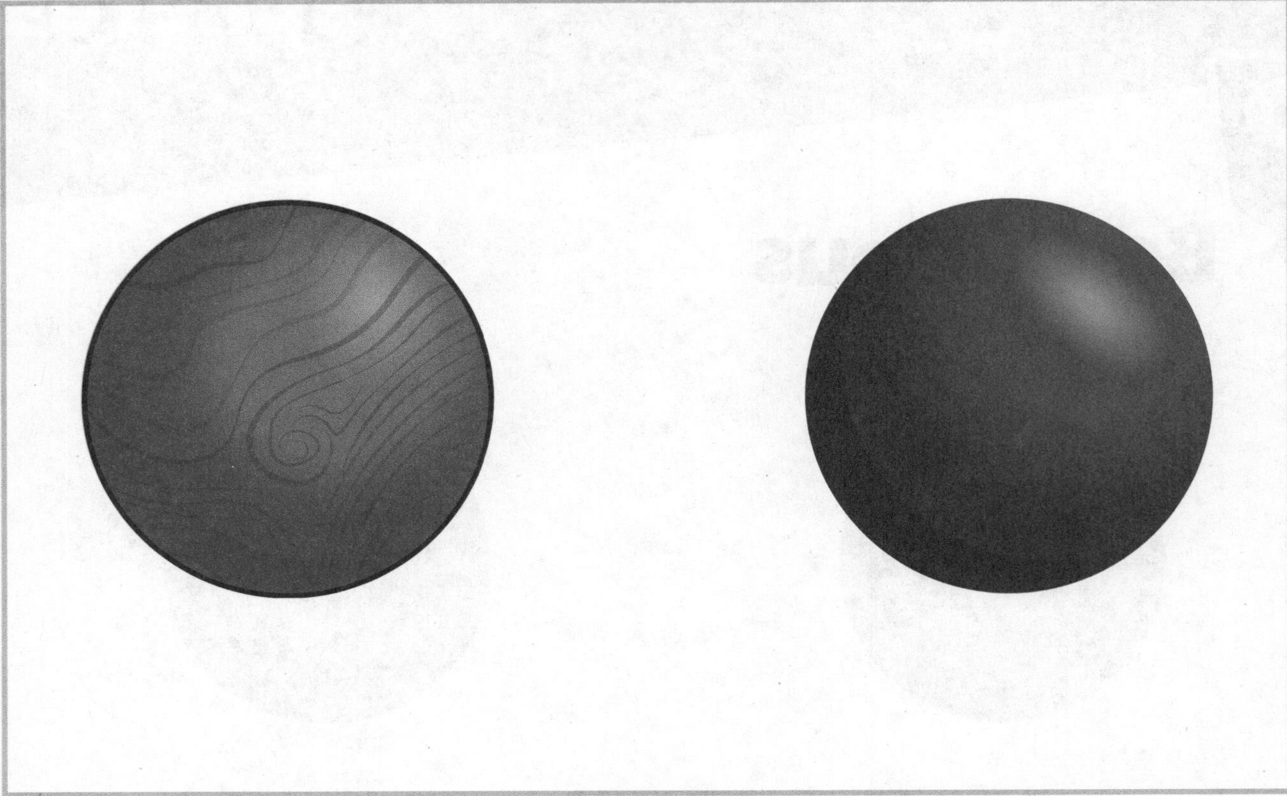

Work Together

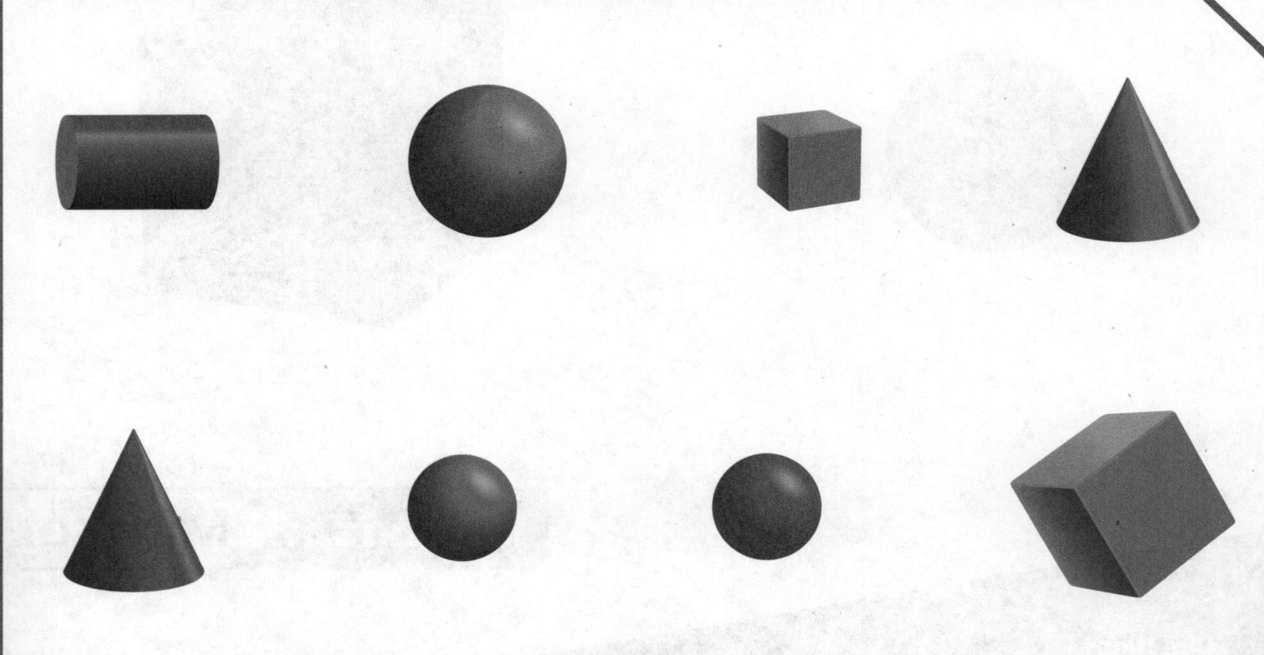

Work Together: Which shapes are spheres? Circle all the spheres.

On My Own

Name

2

3

Directions: 1. Which shape is a sphere? Circle the sphere. **2.** Which shape can roll? Circle the shape that can roll. **3.** Which shapes are spheres? Circle all the spheres.

1 2 3

Reflect

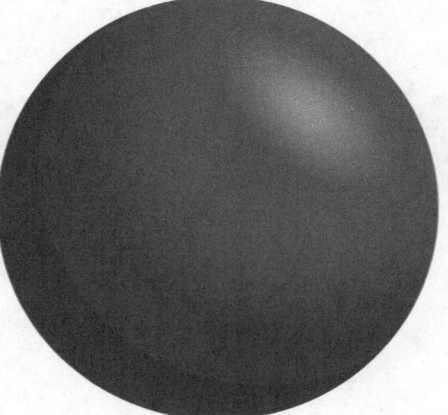

Directions: 4. STEM Connection An aerospace engineer designs aircraft for space travel. How many spheres are in the picture? Circle the number of spheres. **5. Extend Your Thinking** Jeff has a collection of spheres. Which shape does not belong in his collection?

Reflect: How can you describe this shape?

Cylinders

Be Curious

Math is... Mindset

Directions:
Which doesn't belong?

Learn

Work Together

Work Together: Which shapes are cylinders? Circle all the cylinders.

On My Own

Name ______________________________

1

2

3

Directions: 1. Which shape is a cylinder? Circle the cylinder. **2.** Which shape can be stacked? Circle the shape that can be stacked. **3.** Which shapes are cylinders? Circle all the cylinders.

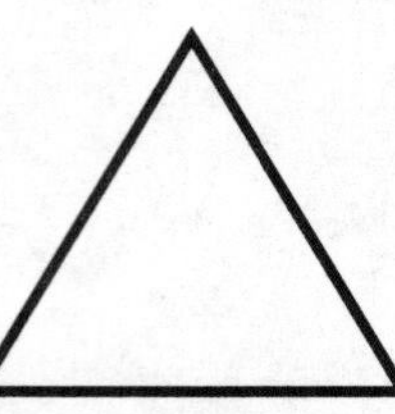

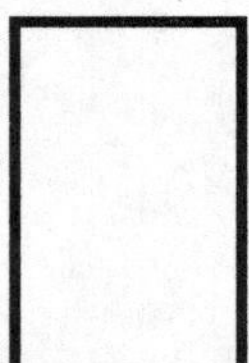

Reflect

Directions: 4. Error Analysis Tom says all of the shapes can roll and stack. Is he correct? Circle the shape or shapes that can both roll and stack. **5. Extend Your Thinking** Circle the 2-dimensional shape that shows what one of the bases of a cylinder looks like.

Reflect: How can you describe this shape?

Cones

Be Curious

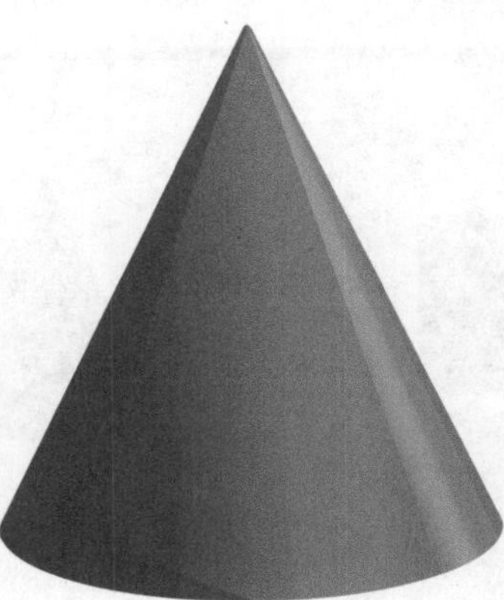

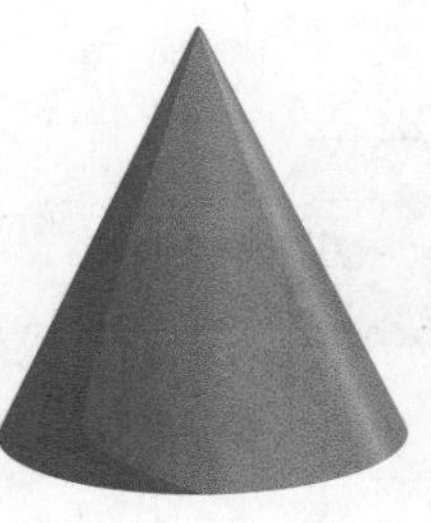

Math is... Mindset

Directions:
Which doesn't belong?

Learn

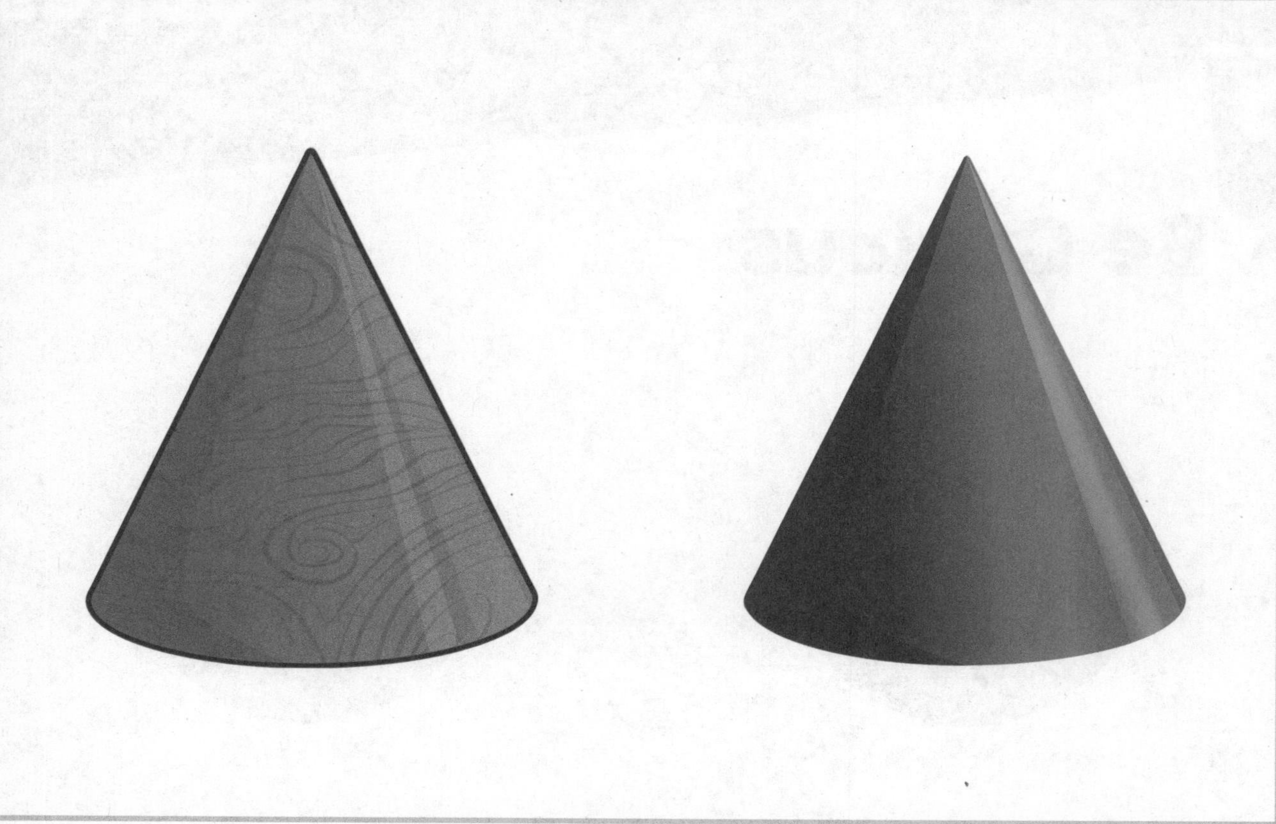

Work Together

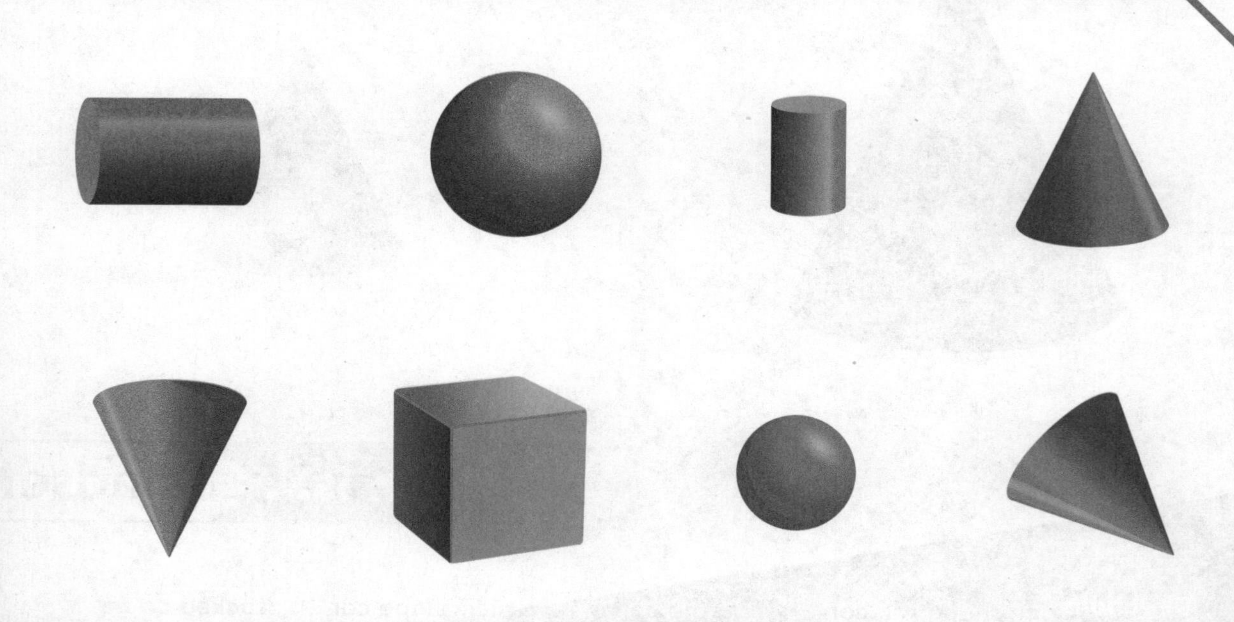

Work Together: Which shapes are cones? Circle all the cones.

On My Own

Name ______________________________

3

Directions: 1. Which shape is a cone? Circle the cone. **2.** Which shape can be stacked on top of another shape? Circle the shape that can be stacked. **3.** Which shapes are cones? Circle all the cones.

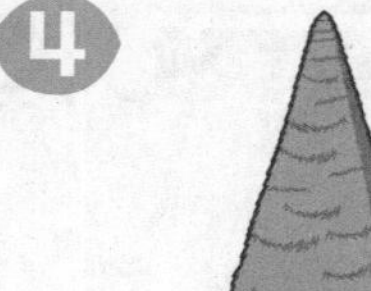
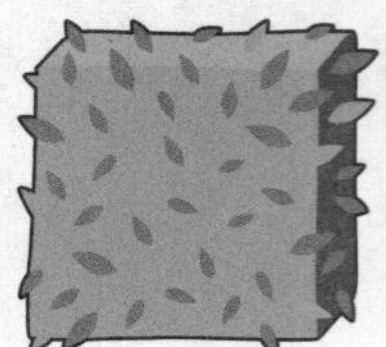

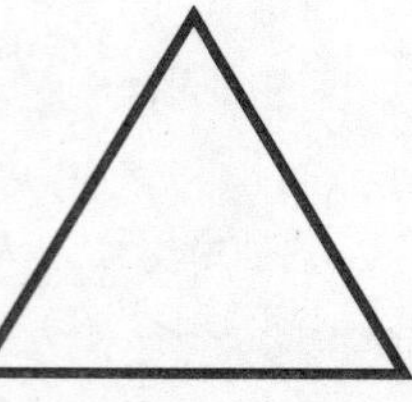

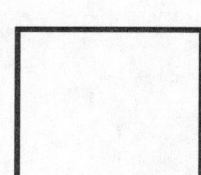

Reflect

Directions: 4. STEM Connection A landscape architect cut some bushes into 3-dimensional shapes. Circle the bush that looks most like a cone. **5. Extend Your Thinking** Circle the 2-dimensional shape that shows what the base of a cone looks like.

Reflect: How can you describe this shape?

Lesson 11-6

Describe 3-Dimensional Shapes

Be Curious

Math is... Mindset

Directions:
What do you see?

Learn

Work Together

Work Together: How can you find an object that is *next to*? Draw an X on the toy that looks like a sphere that is next to the party hat. How can you find an object that is *above*? Circle the toy that looks like a cone that is above the robot.

On My Own

Name ______________________________

3

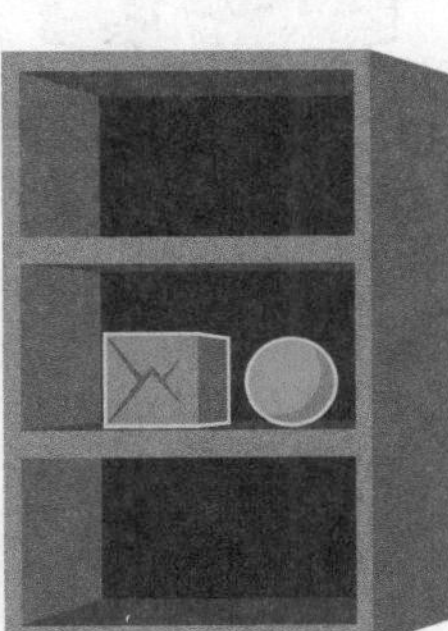
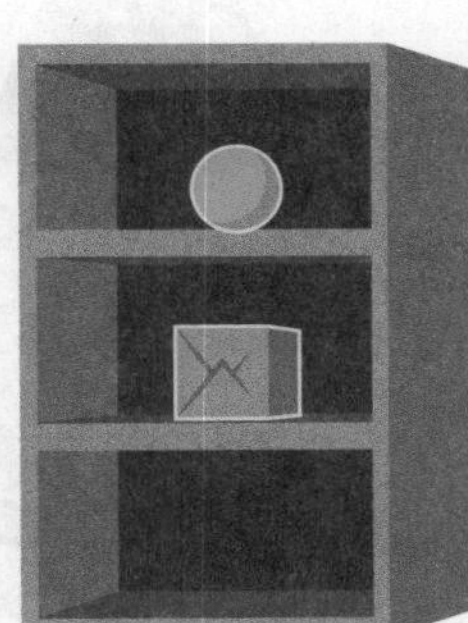
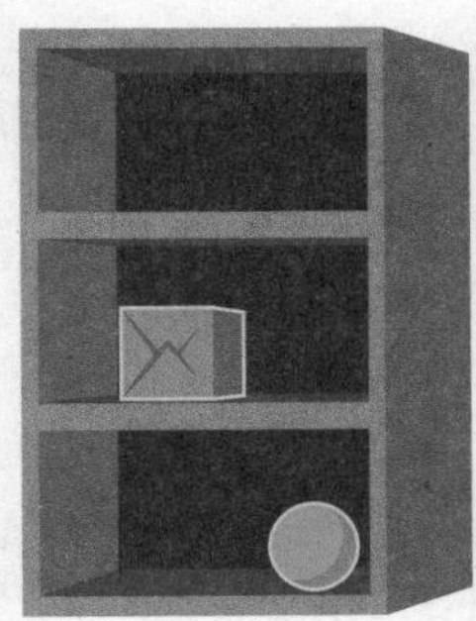

Directions: 1. How can you find an object that is *behind*? Circle the picture that shows the box behind the party hat. **2.** How can you find an object that is *above*? Circle the picture that shows the beach ball above the pool. **3.** How can you find an object that is *below*? Circle the picture that shows the package below the ball.

4

5

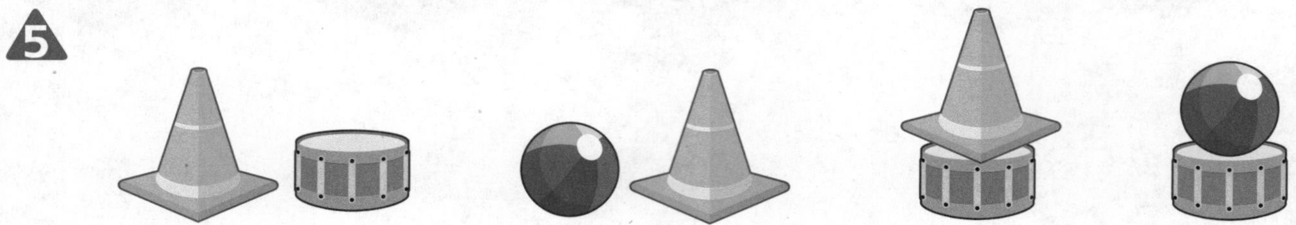

Reflect

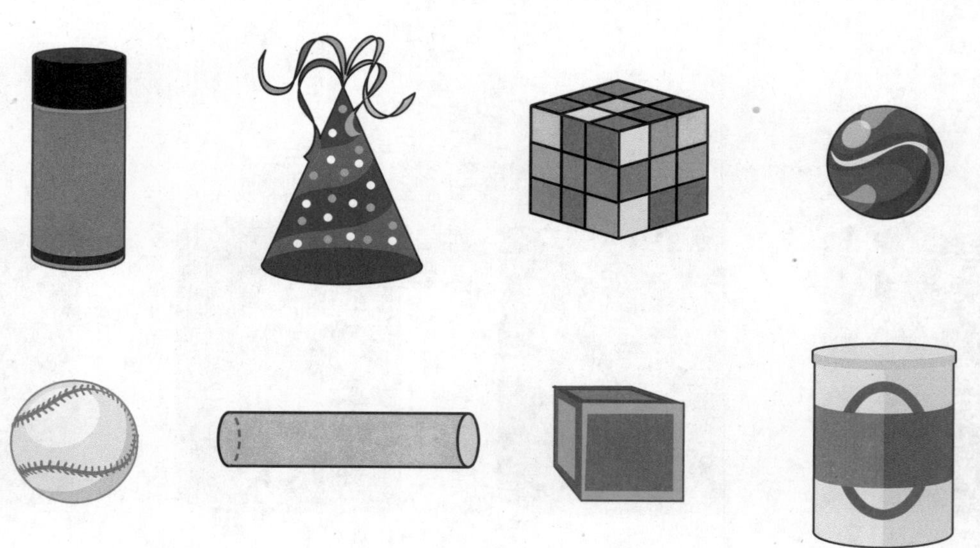

Directions: 4. How can you find an object that *is in front of*? Circle the picture that shows the drum in front of the stool. **5. Extend Your Thinking** How can you find an object that is *beside*? Circle the picture with the cone beside the toy that looks like a cylinder.
Reflect: How can you describe the position of 3-dimensional shapes?

Unit Review

Name

Vocabulary Review

2

3

4

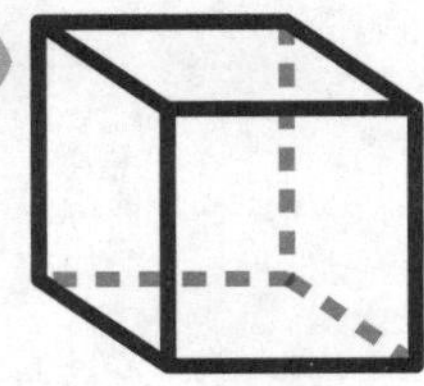

Directions: 1. Which shape is 2-dimensional? Circle the 2-dimensional shape. Which shape is 3-dimensional? Draw an X on the 3-dimensional shape. **2.** Which object looks like a cone? Circle the object that looks like a cone. Which object looks like a cylinder? Draw an X on the object that looks like a cylinder. **3.** Which object looks like a cube? Circle the object that looks like a cube. Which object looks like a sphere? Draw an X on the object that looks like a sphere. **4.** Color one face of the cube blue. Draw a circle around one vertex of the cube.

Review

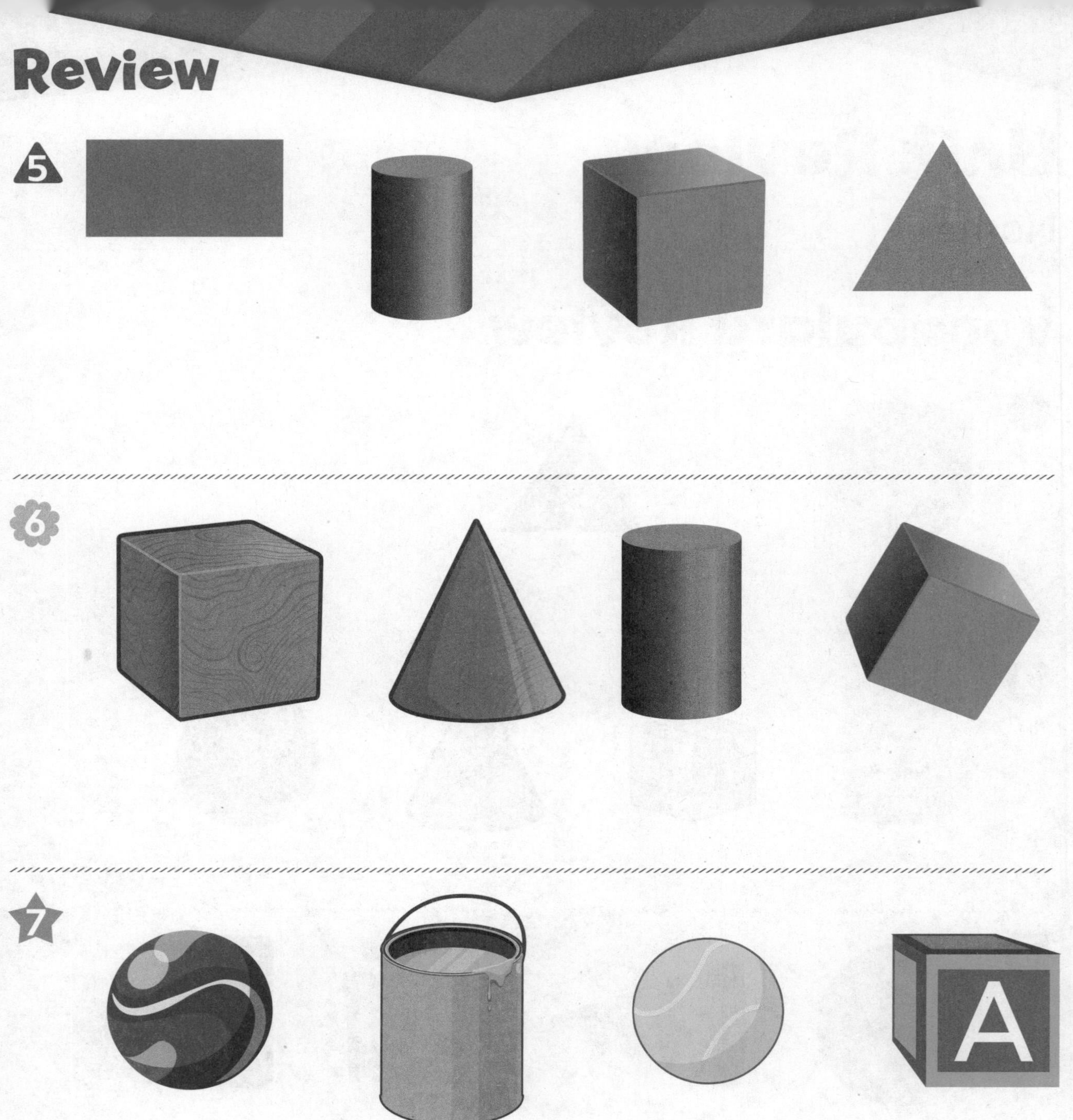

Teacher: 5. Which shapes are 3-dimensional? Circle all the 3-dimensional shapes. **6.** Which shapes are cubes? Circle all the cubes. **7.** Which objects look like spheres? Circle all the objects that look like spheres.

8

9

10

Directions: 8. Which shapes are cylinders? Circle all the cylinders. **9.** Which objects look like cones? Circle all the objects that look like cones. **10.** How can you position the shapes? Draw a line to put the cylinder *above* the table. Draw a line to put the sphere *below* the table. Draw a line to put the cube *next to* the table.

Performance Task

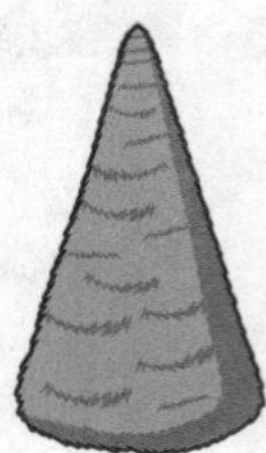
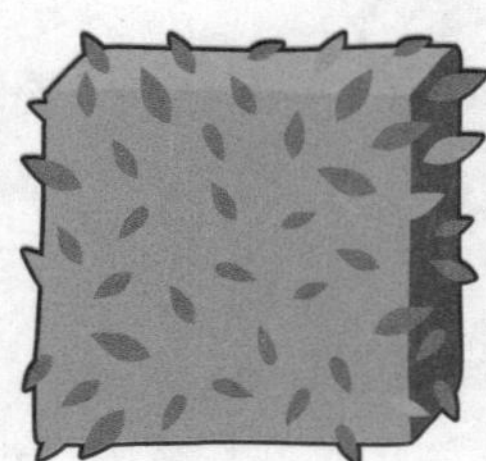

Reflect

Performance Task: Simon works at the botanical garden. He uses special tools to give trees and bushes 3-dimensional shapes. What shapes do you see in the garden? **Part A** Draw an X on the sphere. **Part B** Circle the cube. **Part C** Underline the cone.

Reflect: How can you identify and describe 3-dimensional shapes?

Unit II

Fluency Practice

Name ______________________________

Fluency Strategy

3 + 1 = 4

1. 3 + 2 = ____

Fluency Flash

2. 2 + 2 = ____

3. 4 + 1 = ____

Directions: Fluency Strategy: Count on to add within 5. Count from the first number to add on the second number. **1.** How can you count on to find 3 + 2? Write the sum.

Fluency Flash: 2. How can you count on to find 2 + 2? Write the sum. **3.** How can you count on to find 4 + 1? Write the sum.

Fluency Check

7 9

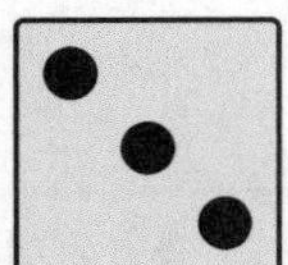

2 + 1 =

Fluency Talk

Directions: Fluency Check: 4. Which number is greater? Circle the number that is greater. **5.** How many dots? Write how many. **6.** How can you count on to find 2 + 1? Write the sum. **Fluency Talk:** Look at 2 + 1. How did you find the sum?

Count to 100

Focus Question

How can I count to 100 by 1s and by 10s?

Hi, I'm Sienna.

I want to be a nutritionist. I love looking for healthy meals and snacks! I will need to be able to count by 1s and 10s to do my job!

STEM video | GO ONLINE

Name

Patterns in a Number Chart

Number Chart

1	2	3	4	5	6	7	8	9	10
11	12	13	14	15	16	17	18	19	20
21	22	23	24	25	26	27	28	29	30
31	32	33	34	35	36	37	38	39	40
41	42	43	44	45	46	47	48	49	50
51	52	53	54	55	56	57	58	59	60
61	62	63	64	65	66	67	68	69	70
71	72	73	74	75	76	77	78	79	80
81	82	83	84	85	86	87	88	89	90
91	92	93	94	95	96	97	98	99	100

Directions: Listen to your teacher. Color squares to find patterns on the number chart.

Count by 1s to 50

? Be Curious

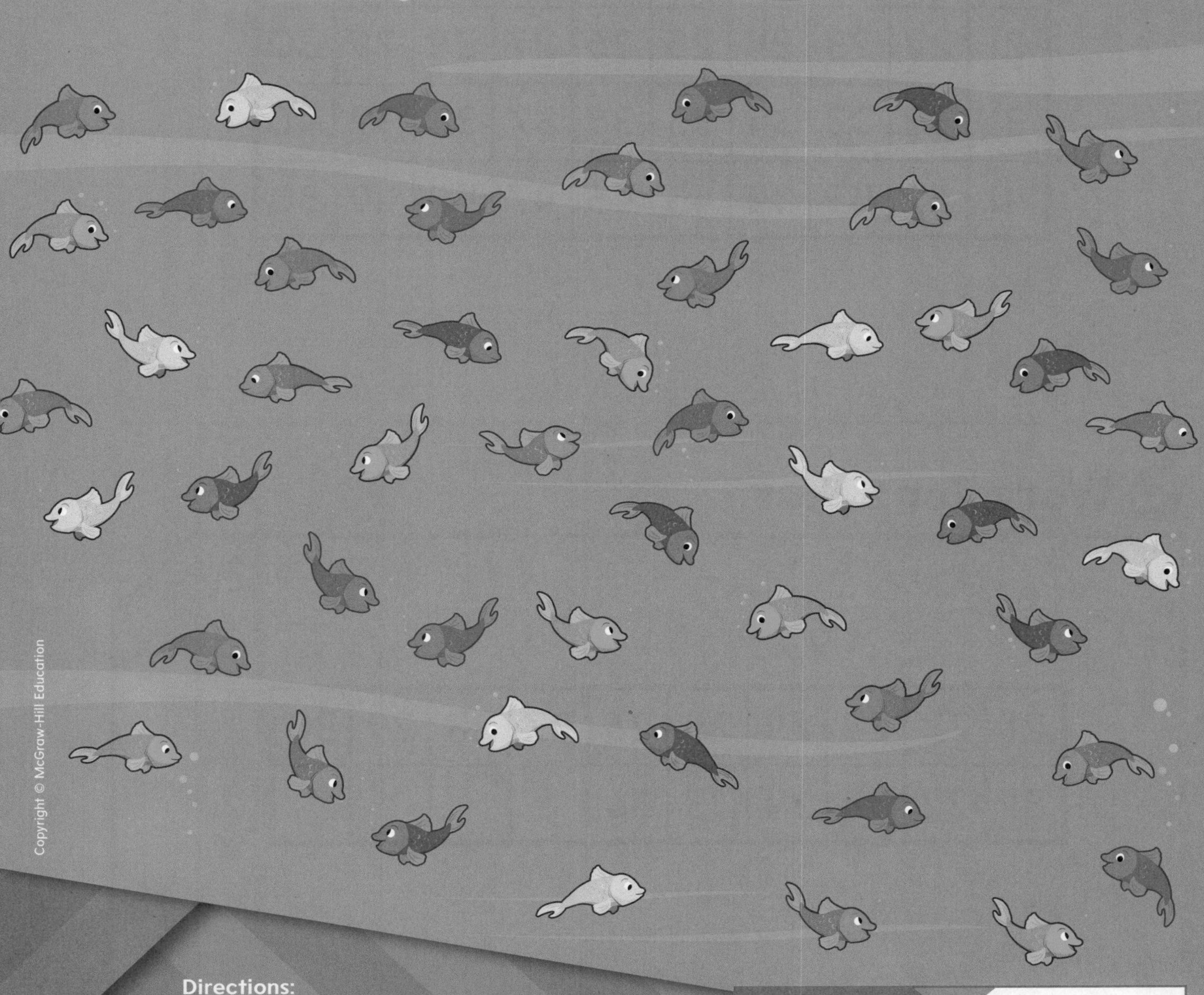

Directions:
What do you see?

Math is... Mindset

Learn

1	2	3	4	5	6	7	8	9	10
11	12	13	14	15	16	17	18	19	20
21	22	23	24	25	26	27	28	29	30
31	32	33	34	35	36	37	38	39	40
41	42	43	44	45	46	47	48	49	50

Work Together

21	22	23	24	25	26	27	28	29	30
31	32	33	34	35	36				

Work Together: Which numbers are missing? Count. Write the missing numbers.

On My Own

MATH REPLAY | GO ONLINE

Name ____________________

11	12	13	14	15	16	17	18	19	20
21	22	_3	_4	_5	26	27	28	29	30

2

21	22	23	24	25	26	27	28	29	30
31	32	33	34	3_	3_	3_	38	39	40

3

31	32	33	34	35	36	37			

Directions: 1–3. Which numbers are missing? Count. Write the missing numbers.

4

41				45	46	47	48	49	50

5

1	2	3	4	5	6	7	8	9	10
11	12	13	14	15	16	17	18	19	20
21	22	23	24	25	26	27	28	29	30
31	32	33	34	35	36	37	38	39	40
41	42	43	44	45	46	47	48	49	50

Reflect

21	22	23	24	25	26	27	28	29	30
31	32	33	34	35	36	37	38	39	40
41	42	43	44	45	46	47	48	49	50

Directions: 4. Which numbers are missing? Count. Write the missing numbers. **5. Extend Your Thinking** How can you count to 50? Touch, count, and color numbers 1 through 10 red, numbers 11 through 25 green, numbers 26 through 40 yellow, and numbers 41 through 50 blue.

Reflect: What patterns do you notice when counting from 21 to 50?

Count by 1s to 100

Be Curious

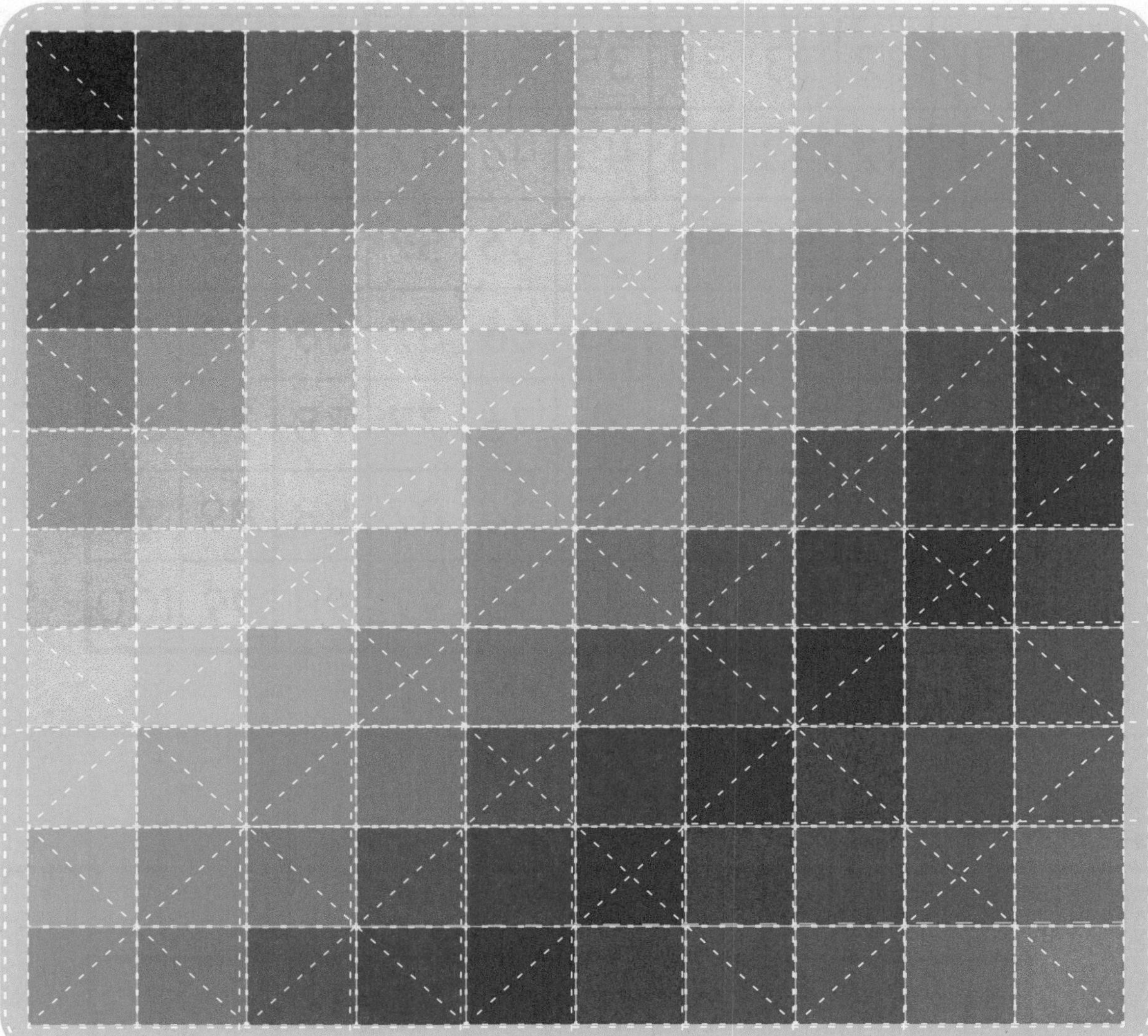

Math is... Mindset

Directions:
What do you see?

Learn

1	2	3	4	5	6	7	8	9	10
11	12	13	14	15	16	17	18	19	20
21	22	23	24	25	26	27	28	29	30
31	32	33	34	35	36	37	38	39	40
41	42	43	44	45	46	47	48	49	50
51	52	53	54	55	56	57	58	59	60
61	62	63	64	65	66	67	68	69	70
71	72	73	74	75	76	77	78	79	80
81	82	83	84	85	86	87	88	89	90
91	92	93	94	95	96	97	98	99	100

Work Together

61	62	63	64	65	66	67	68	69	70
71	72						78	79	80

Work Together: Which numbers are missing? Count. Write the missing numbers.

On My Own

MATH REPLAY | GO ONLINE

Name ______________________

51	52	53	54	55	56	57	58	59	60
61	_2	_3	_4	65	66	67	68	69	70

2

71	72	73	74	75	76	77	78	79	80
81	82	83	84	85	86	87	8_	8_	9_

3

61	62	63	64				68	69	70

Directions: 1–3. Which numbers are missing? Count. Write the missing numbers.

91	92	93	94	95				99	100

51	52	53	54	55	56	57	58	59	60
61	62	63	64	65	66	67	68	69	70
71	72	73	74	75	76	77	78	79	80
81	82	83	84	85	86	87	88	89	90
91	92	93	94	95	96	97	98	99	100

Reflect

51	52	53	54	55	56	57	58	59	60
61	62	63	64	65	66	67	68	69	70
71	72	73	74	75	76	77	78	79	80
81	82	83	84	85	86	87	88	89	90
91	92	93	94	95	96	97	98	99	100

Directions: 4. Error Analysis Aaron says the missing numbers are 86, 87, and 88. Is Aaron correct? Which numbers are missing? Count. Write the missing numbers. **5. Extend Your Thinking** How can you count from 51 to 100? Touch, count, and color numbers 51 through 65 red, numbers 66 through 76 green, numbers 77 through 90 yellow, and numbers 91 through 100 blue.

Reflect: What patterns do you notice when counting from 51 to 100?

Unit 12

What Number Comes After?

Name ______________________________

13
22
24
33

Tell or show why.

2

29
40
49
38

Tell or show why.

Directions: Use a number chart if needed. **1.** When counting, what number comes right after 23? **2.** When counting, what number comes right after 39?

3

66

86

75

77

Tell or show why.

Reflect On Your Learning

Directions: Use a number chart if needed. **3.** When counting, what number comes right after 76?

Reflect On Your Learning: Do you understand? Circle to show your understanding.

Lesson 12-3

Count by 10s to 100

Be Curious

Math is... Mindset

Directions:
What do you notice? What do you wonder?

Learn

1	2	3	4	5	6	7	8	9	10
11	12	13	14	15	16	17	18	19	20
21	22	23	24	25	26	27	28	29	30
31	32	33	34	35	36	37	38	39	40
41	42	43	44	45	46	47	48	49	50
51	52	53	54	55	56	57	58	59	60
61	62	63	64	65	66	67	68	69	70
71	72	73	74	75	76	77	78	79	80
81	82	83	84	85	86	87	88	89	90
91	92	93	94	95	96	97	98	99	100

Work Together

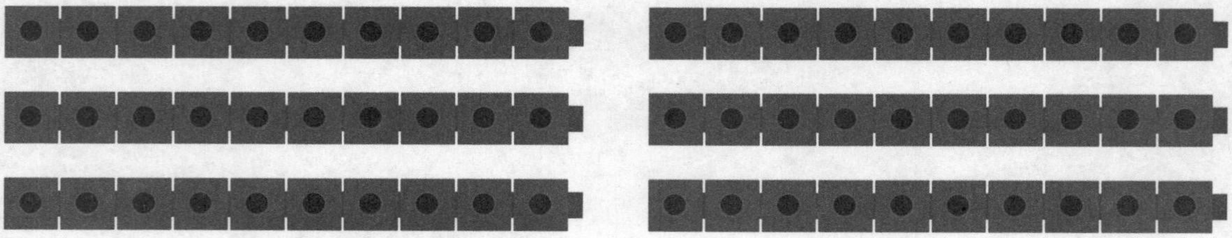

40 50 60

Work Together: How many? Count by 10s. Circle the number that shows how many.

On My Own

Name ____________________

1

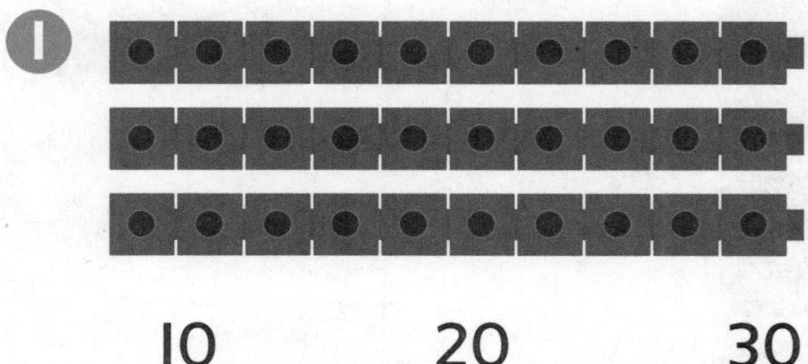

10 20 30

2

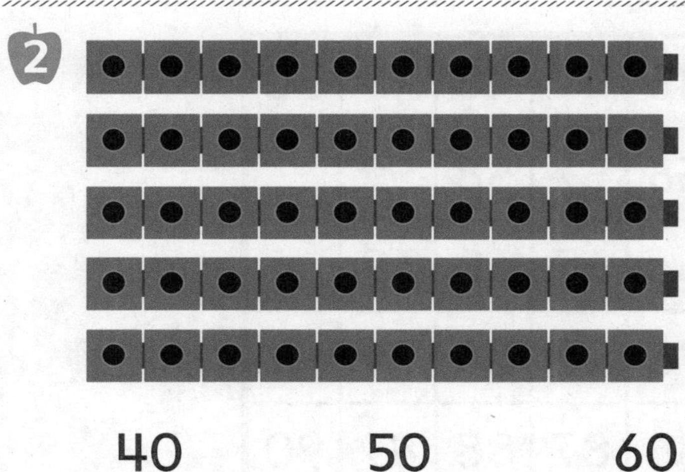

40 50 60

3

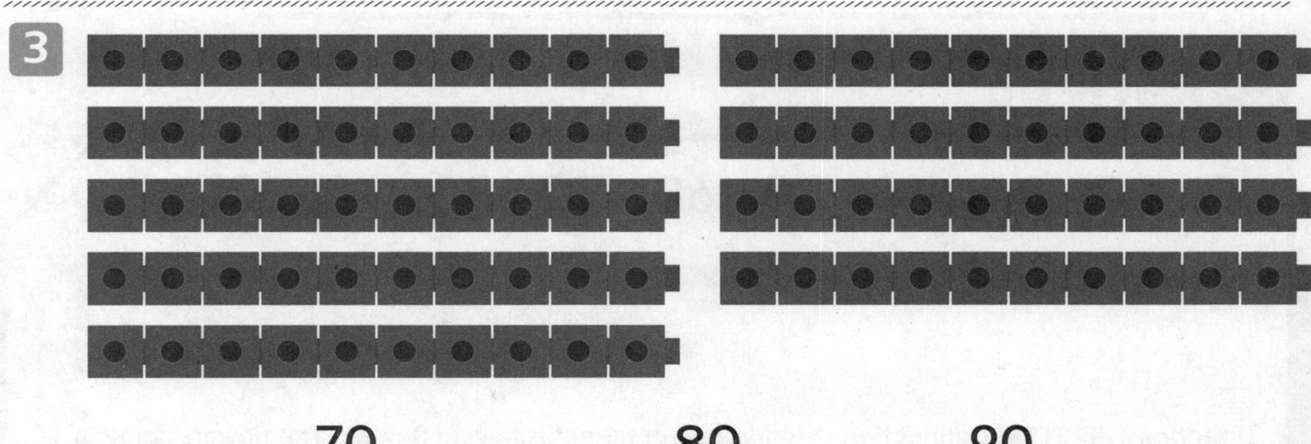

70 80 90

Directions: 1–3. How many? Count by 10s. Circle the number that shows how many.

41	42	43	44	45	46	47	48	49	50
51	52	53	54	55	56	57	58	59	
61	62	63	64	65	66	67	68	69	
71	72	73	74	75	76	77	78	79	
81	82	83	84	85	86	87	88	89	90
91	92	93	94	95	96	97	98	99	

Reflect

10, 20, 30, 40, 50, 60, 70, 80, 90, 100

Directions: 4. STEM Connection A landscape architect is buying flowers. The flowers come in groups of 10. Each row of cubes represents 10 flowers. How many flowers does the landscape architect have? Count by 10s. Write how many. **5. Extend Your Thinking** Which numbers are missing? Count. Write the missing numbers.

Reflect: What patterns do you notice when counting by 10s to 100?

Count From Any Number to 100

Be Curious

Math is... Mindset

Directions:
What do you notice? What do you wonder?

Learn

1	2	3	4	5	6	7	8	9	10
11	12	13	14	15	16	17	18	19	20
21	22	23	24	25	26	27	28	29	30
31	32	33	34	35	36	37	38	39	40
41	42	43	44	45	46	47	48	49	50
51	52	53	54	55	56	57	58	59	60
61	62	63	64	65	66	67	68	69	70
71	72	73	74	75	76	77	78	79	80
81	82	83	84	85	86	87	88	89	90
91	92	93	94	95	96	97	98	99	100

Work Together

45, ________, ________, ________

Work Together: How can you count forward? Start at 45. Write the numbers that come next.

On My Own

MATH REPLAY | GO ONLINE

Name

1

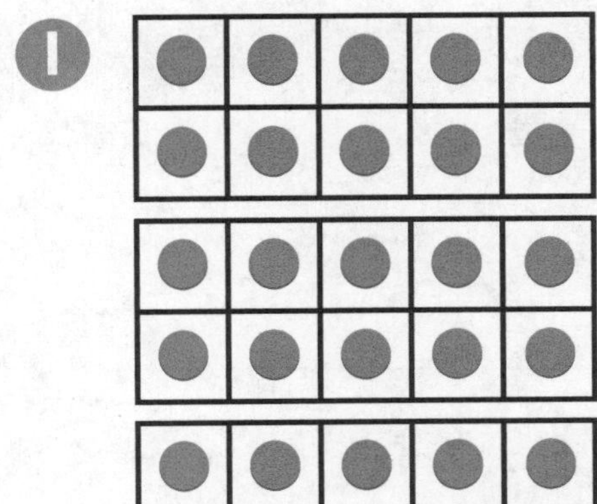

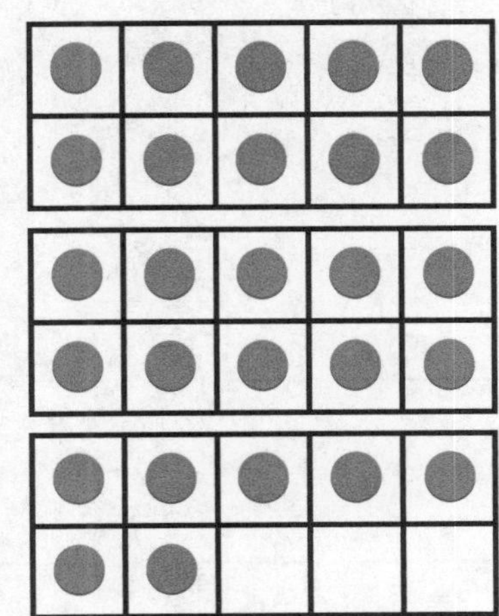

2

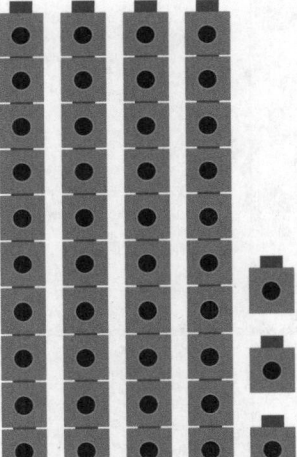

3 58, 59, 60,

Directions: 1-2. How many? Count each group. Then write the number that comes next. **3.** What number comes next? Count. Then write the missing number.

4

_____, 45, 46, _____

5

_____, _____, _____, _____

71	72	73	74	75	76	77		79	80

Directions: 4. Error Analysis Talaysha says the missing numbers are 43 and 48. Is she correct? Count. Then write the missing numbers. **5. Extend Your Thinking** Write any number to start. Then write the numbers that come next when you count forward by 1s.

Reflect: How can you use 77 and 79 to find the missing number?

Lesson 12-5

Count to Find Out How Many

Be Curious

Math is... Mindset

Directions:
What do you notice? What do you wonder?

Learn

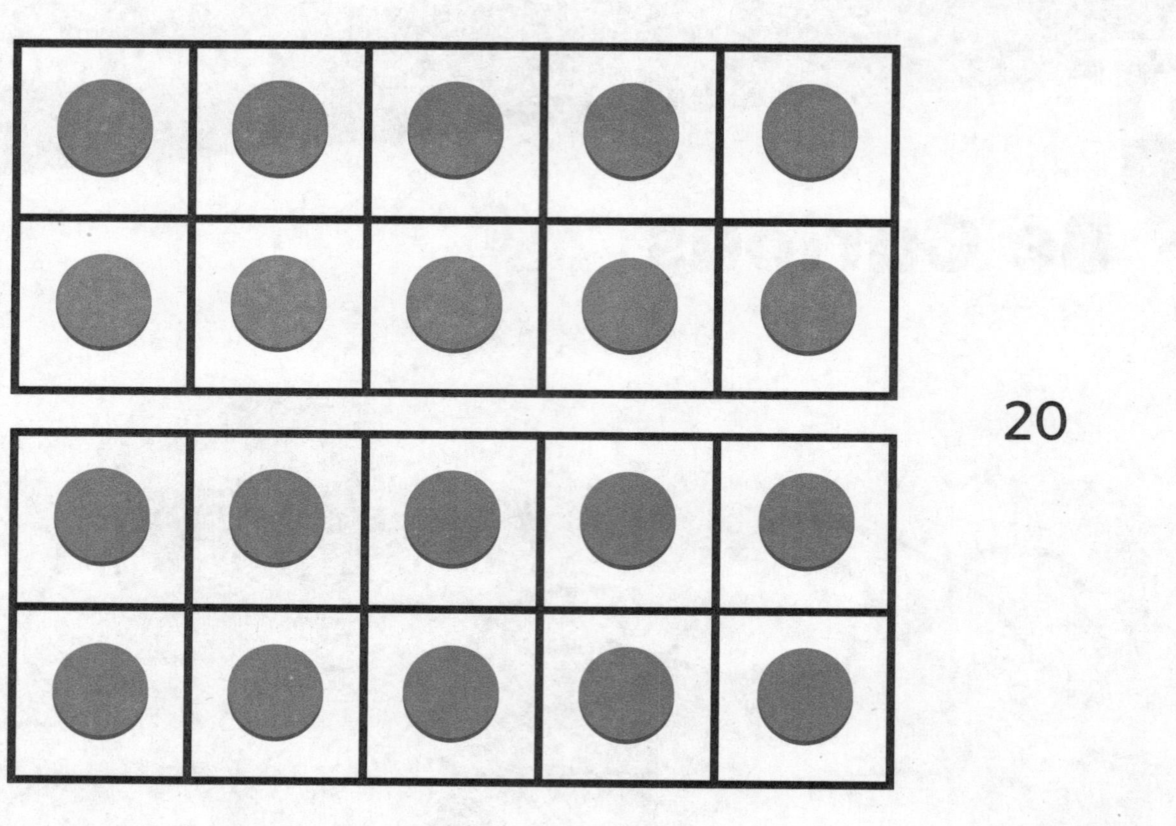

20

Work Together

Work Together: How many? Write the number to show how many puzzle pieces.

On My Own

Name

1

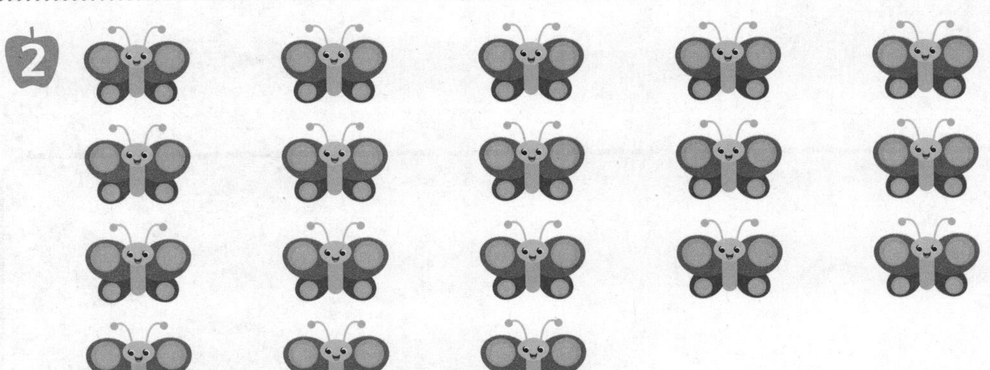

2

3

Directions: 1. How many trains? Count. Write the number to show how many. **2.** How many butterflies? Count. Write the number to show how many. **3.** How many soccer balls? Count. Write the number to show how many.

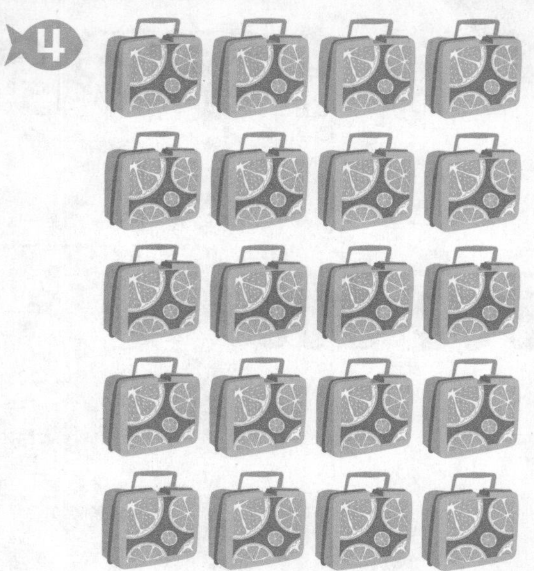

Reflect

Directions: 4. STEM Connection A nutritionist is packing healthy lunches for a class of students. How many did she pack? Count. Write how many. **5. Extend Your Thinking** How can you draw 20 counters?

Reflect: How many? How can you be sure you counted all the objects?

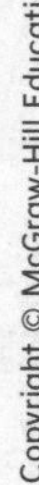

Unit Review

Name ______________________________

Vocabulary Review

1	2	3	4	5	6	7	8	9	10
11	12	13	14	15	16	17	18	19	20
21	22	23	24	25	26	27	28	29	30
31	32	33	34	35	36	37	38	39	40
41	42	43	44	45	46	47	48	49	50
51	52	53	54	55	56	57	58	59	60
61	62	63	64	65	66	67	68	69	70
71	72	73	74	75	76	77	78	79	80
81	82	83	84	85	86	87	88	89	90
91	92	93	94	95	96	97	98	99	100

Directions: 1. How can you count to 100 by 1s? Start at 1. Say each number as you count. **2.** How can you count to 100 by 10s? Start at 10. Color each number yellow as you count.

Review

3

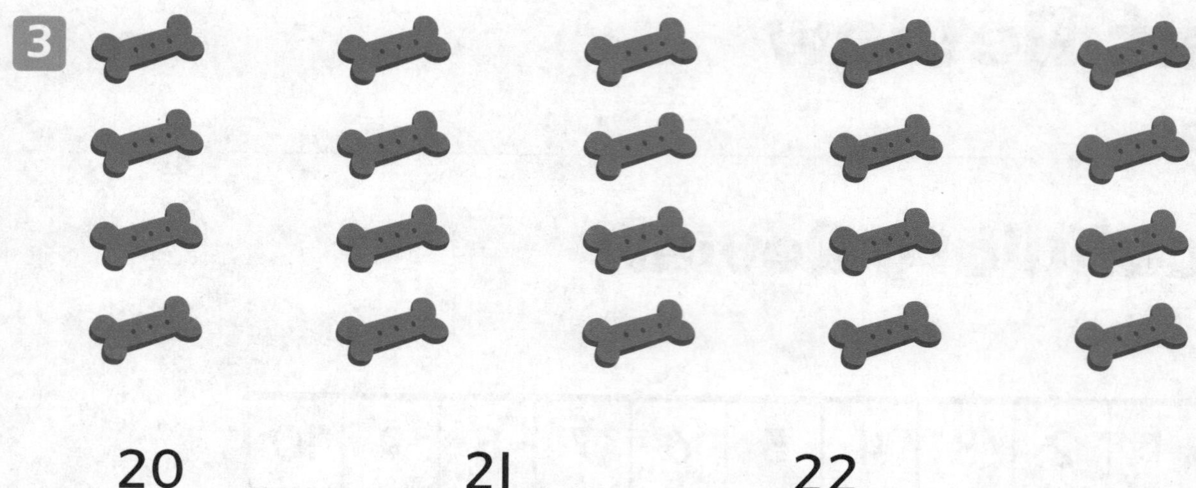

20 21 22

4

33, 34, 35, ______, ______

5

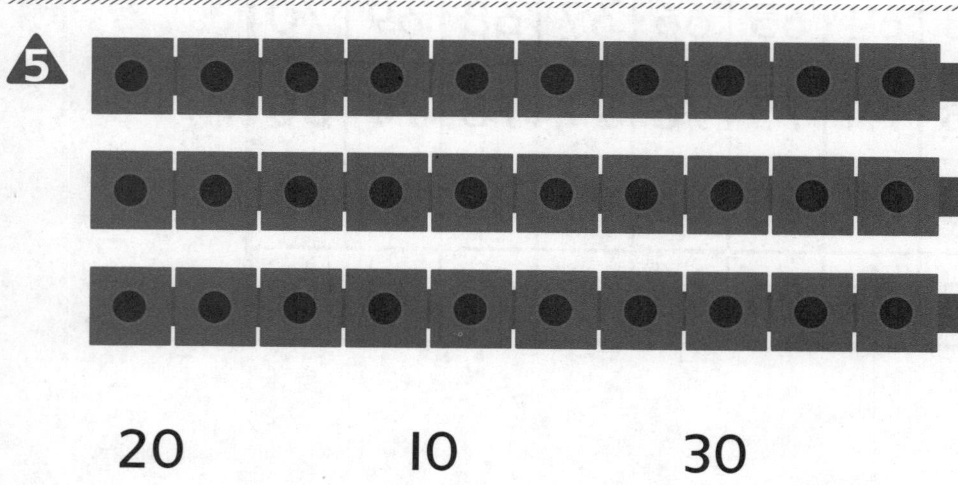

20 10 30

Directions: 3. How many dog treats? Count. Circle the number to show how many. **4.** Which numbers come next? Count. Write the missing numbers. **5.** How many cubes? Count by 10s. Circle the number to show how many.

MATH REPLAY | GO ONLINE

6 57, ____, ____, ____, 61

7 84, 85, ____, ____, ____

8 69, ____, ____, ____, 73

9

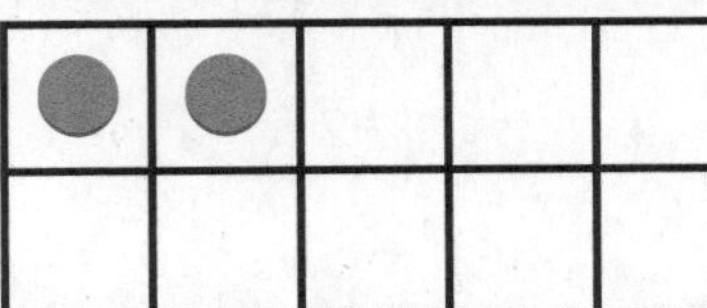

43 42 41

Directions: 6-8. Which numbers are missing? Count. Write the missing numbers. **9.** Which number comes next? Count the counters. Circle the number that comes next.

Performance Task

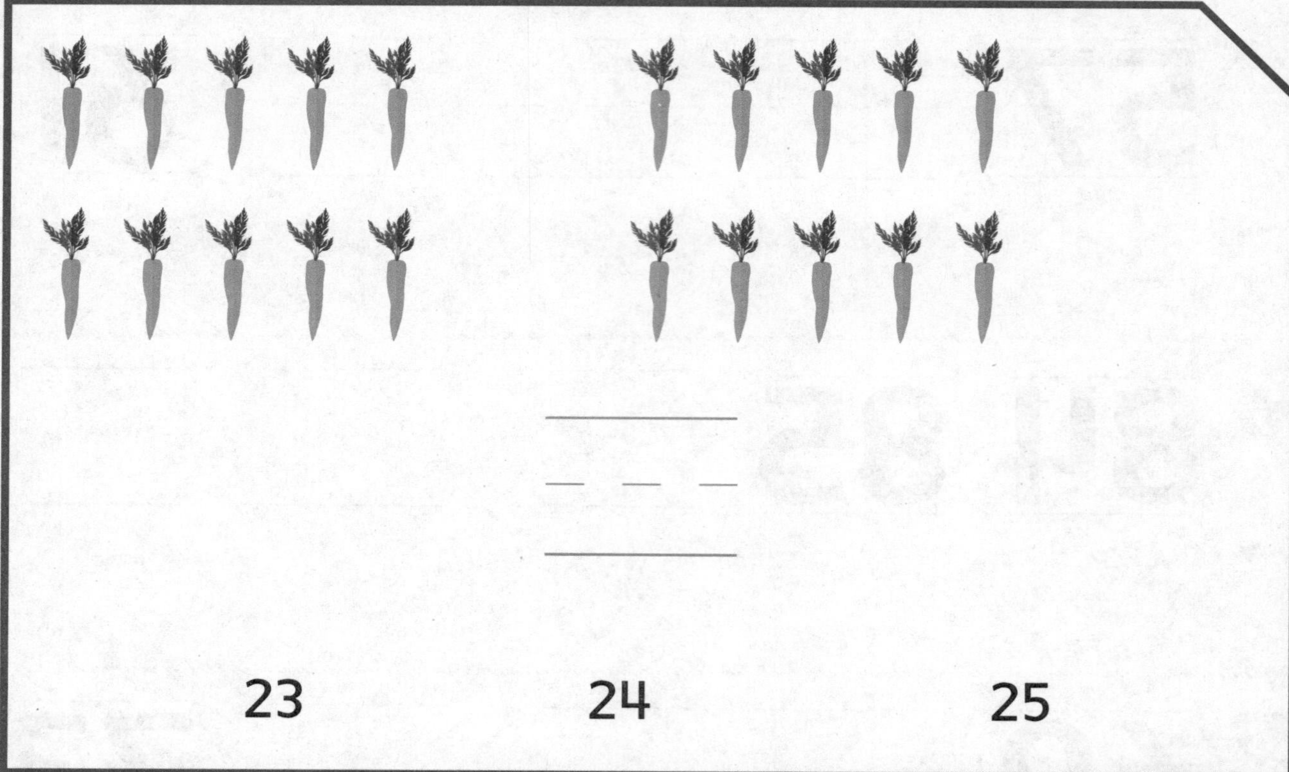

Reflect

Performance Task: A nutritionist counts carrots for a snack. **Part A** How many carrots? Count by 10s to find the number of carrots. Write the number. **Part B** The nutritionist gets 4 more carrots. How many carrots does she have now? Count forward. Circle the number to show how many.

Reflect: How can you count from any number to 100 by 1s and by 10s?

Unit 12

Fluency Practice

Name ____________________

Fluency Strategy

5 − 2 = **3**

1. 3 − 2 = ____

Fluency Flash

2. 2 − 1 = ____

3. 4 − 1 = ____

Directions: Fluency Strategy: Count back to subtract within 5. Count back from the first number as many as the second number. **1.** How can you count back to find 3 − 2? Write the difference.

Fluency Flash: 2. How can you count back to find 2 - 1? Write the difference.
3. How can you count back to find 4 – 1? Write the difference.

Fluency Check

3 − 1 =

2 + 1 =

Fluency Talk

Directions: Fluency Check: 4. How can you count back to find 3 − 1? Write the difference. **5.** How many dots? Write how many. **6.** How can you count on to find 2 + 1? Write the sum. **Fluency Talk:** Look at 3 − 1. How did you find the difference?

Unit 13

Analyze, Compare, and Compose Shapes

Focus Question

How can I tell how shapes are alike and different?

Hi, I'm Erik.

I want to be a video game designer. I'm helping create a game today! The monsters in the game eat 2-dimensional and 3-dimensional shapes.

Name

More Shapes Into Shapes

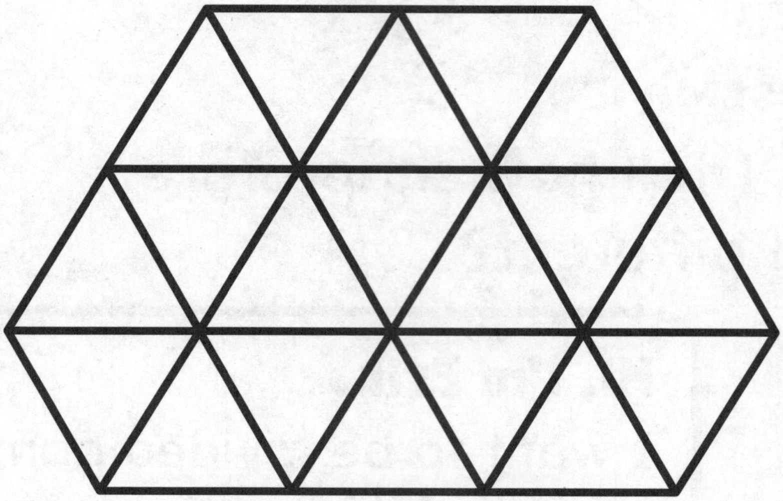

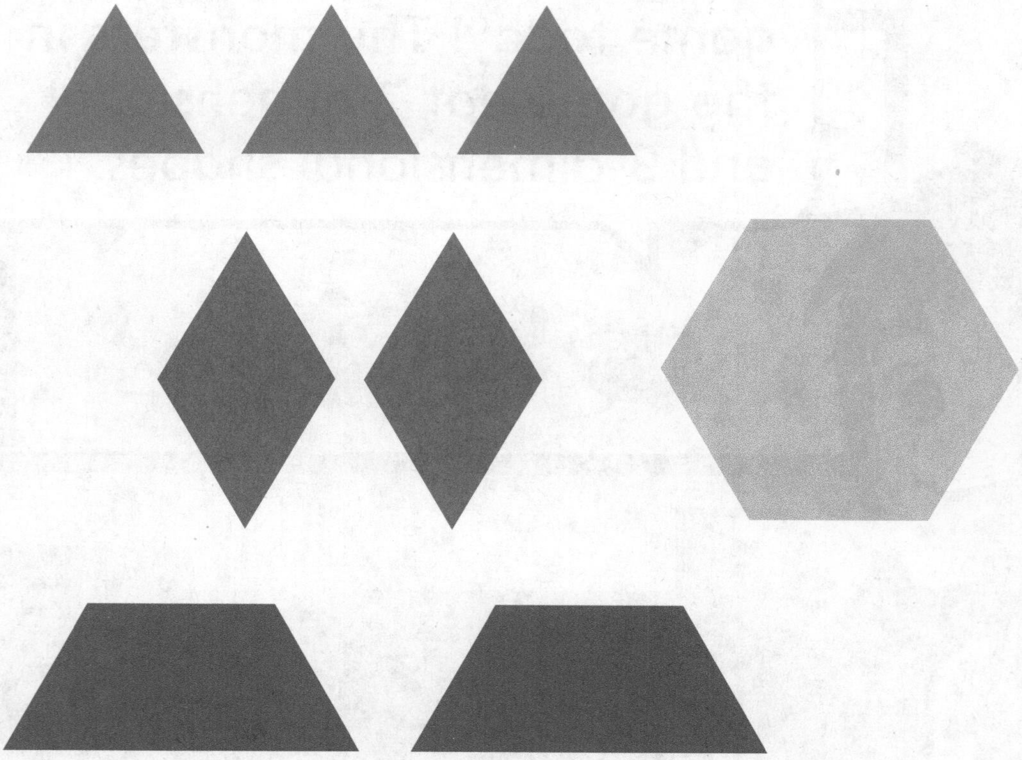

Directions: Use pattern blocks to fill the shape.

Lesson 13-1

Compare and Contrast 2-Dimensional Shapes

Be Curious

Math is... Mindset

Directions:
How are they the same? How are they different?

Learn

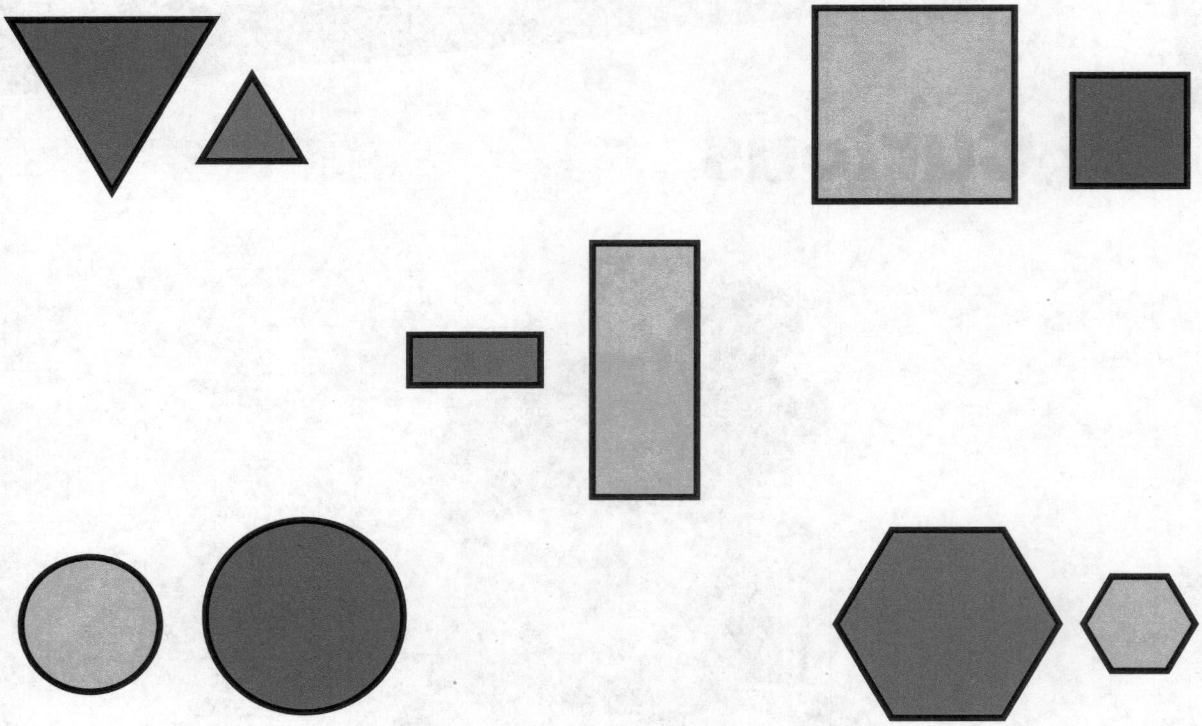

Work Together

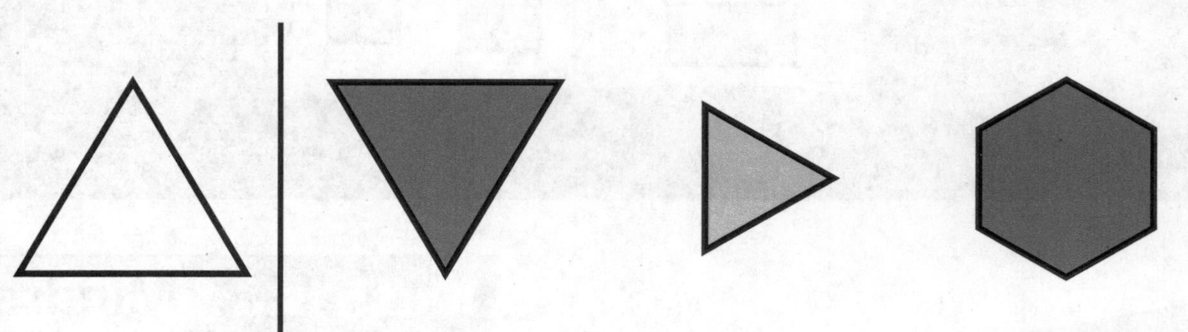

Work Together: How can you compare the shapes? Draw an X on the shape that is different from the first shape.

On My Own

Name ____________________

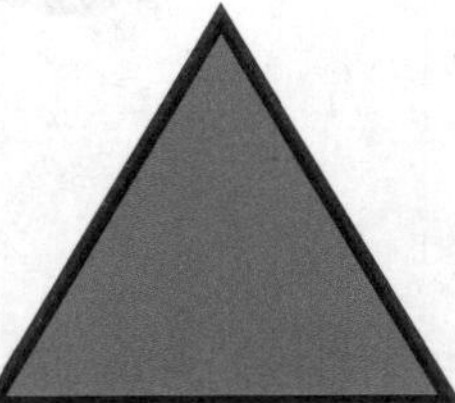

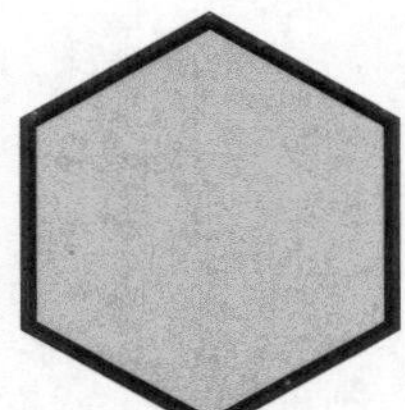

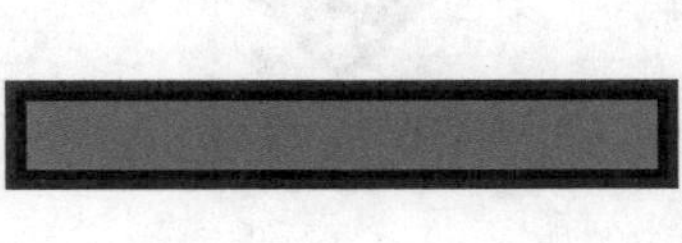

3

Directions: 1. Which shapes are alike? Circle the shapes that are alike. **2.** Which shape is different? Draw an X on the shape that is different. **3.** How can you compare the shapes? Circle the shapes that are like the first shape.

4

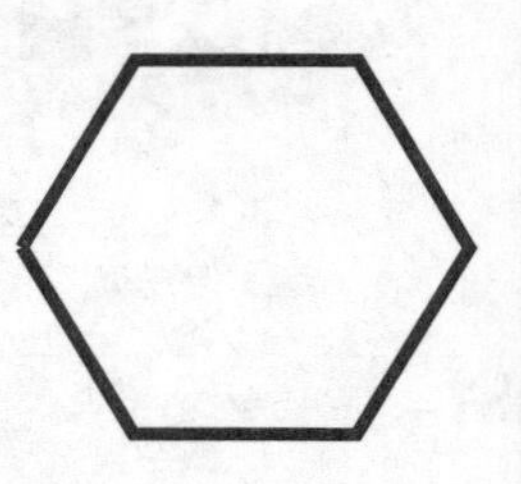

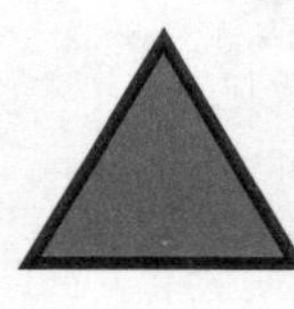

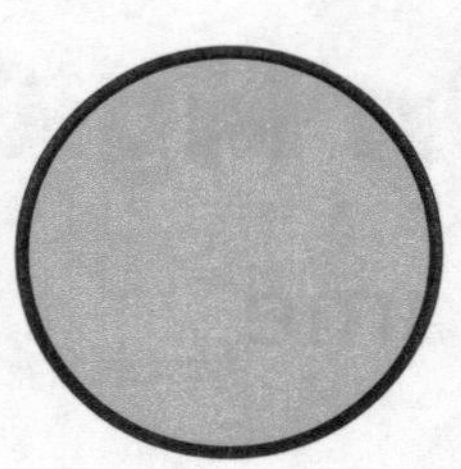

5

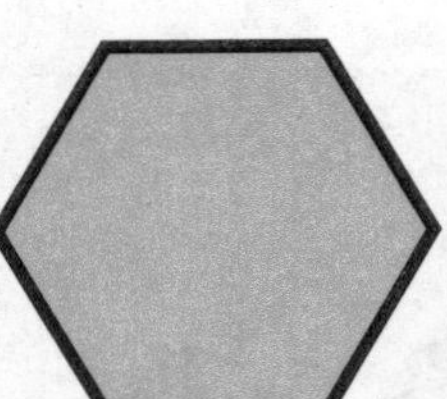

Reflect

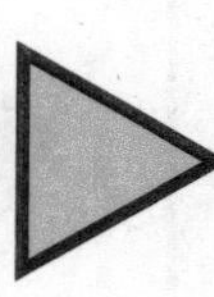

Directions: 4. How can you compare the shapes? Draw an X on the shapes that are different from the first shape. **5. Extend Your Thinking** Which shape has more sides than the others? Circle the shape that has more sides.

Reflect: How can you compare the shapes?

Which Shape Does Not Belong?

Name ____________________

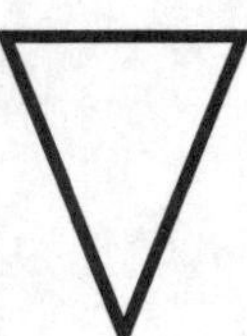

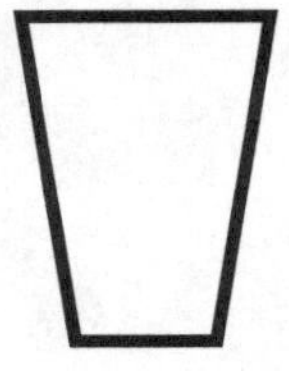

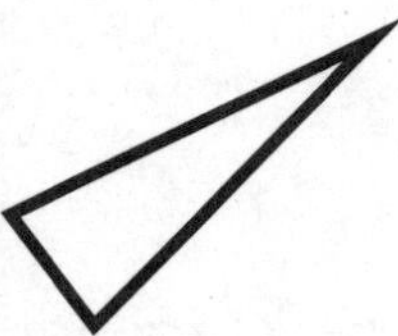

Tell or show why.

Directions: Circle the shape that is not like the others. Tell or show why.

2

Tell or show why.

Reflect On Your Learning

Directions: Circle the shape that is not like the others. Tell or show why.

Reflect On Your Learning: Do you understand? Circle to show your understanding.

Lesson 13-2

Build and Draw 2-Dimensional Shapes

Be Curious

Math is... Mindset

Directions:
Tell me everything you can.

Learn

Work Together

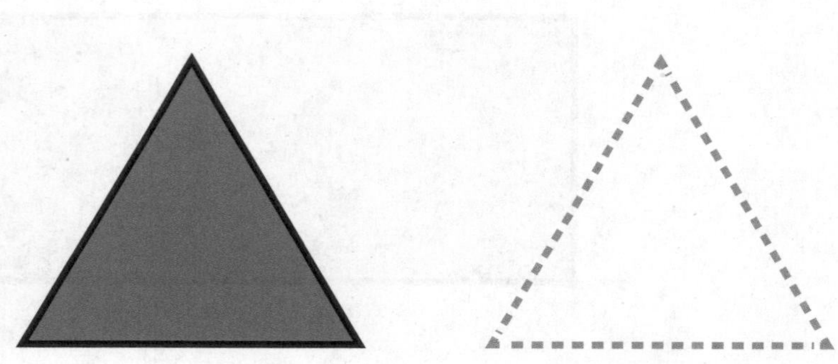

Work Together: How can you draw a triangle? Trace the triangle. Then draw a triangle.

On My Own

Name

1

2

3

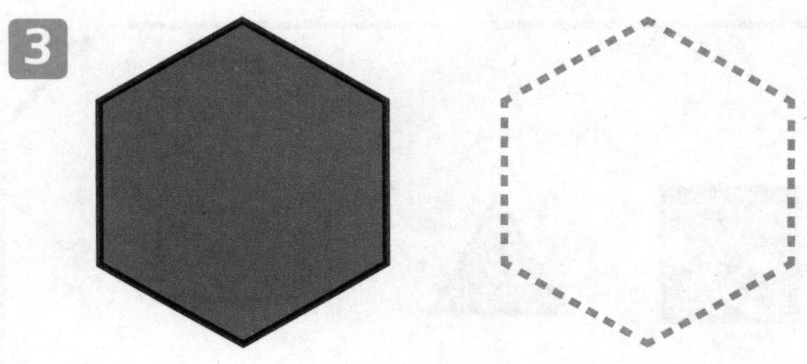

Directions: 1. How can you draw a circle? Trace the circle. Then draw a circle. **2.** How can you draw a square? Trace the square. Then draw a square. **3.** How can you draw a hexagon? Trace the hexagon. Then draw a hexagon.

4

Reflect

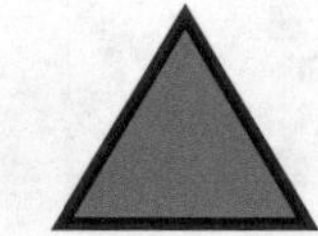

Directions: 4. Error Analysis Josh was asked to draw three triangles. He drew two triangles. Draw a third triangle to help Josh complete his task. **5. Extend Your Thinking** How can you draw a shape with 4 sides? Draw a shape with 4 sides.

Reflect: How can you build and draw 2-dimensional shapes?

Lesson 13-3

Compose 2-Dimensional Shapes

Be Curious

Math is... Mindset

Directions:
What question could you ask?

Learn

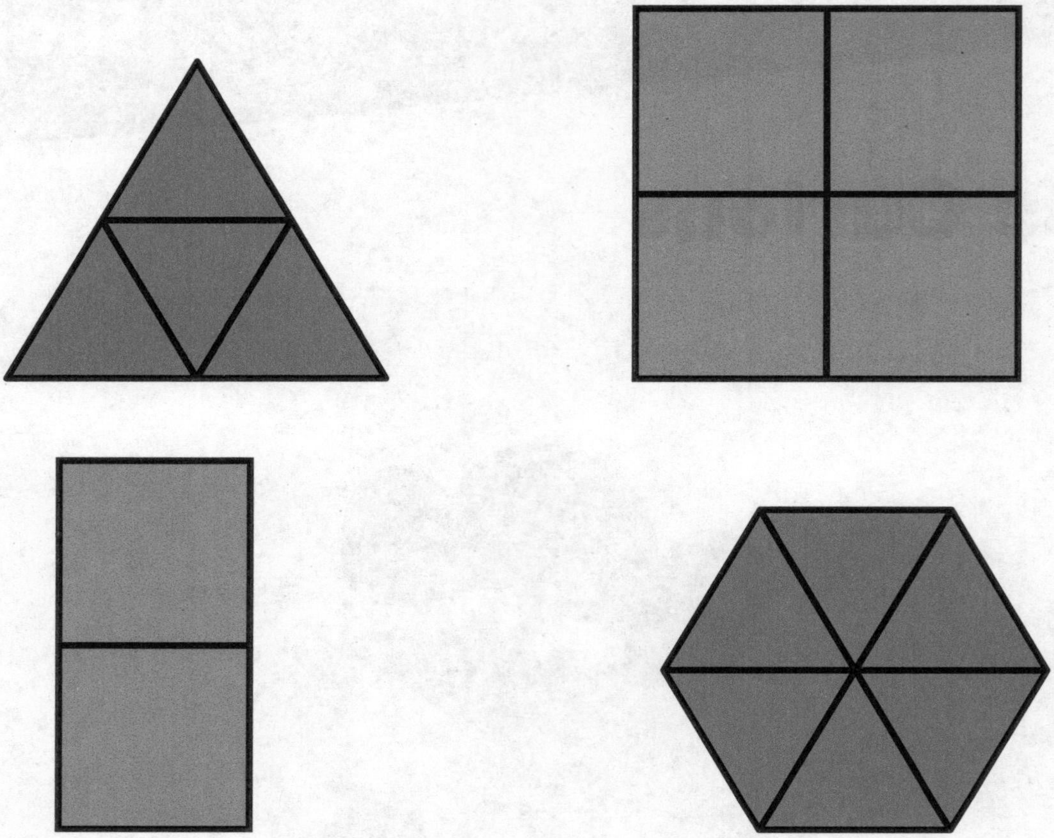

Work Together

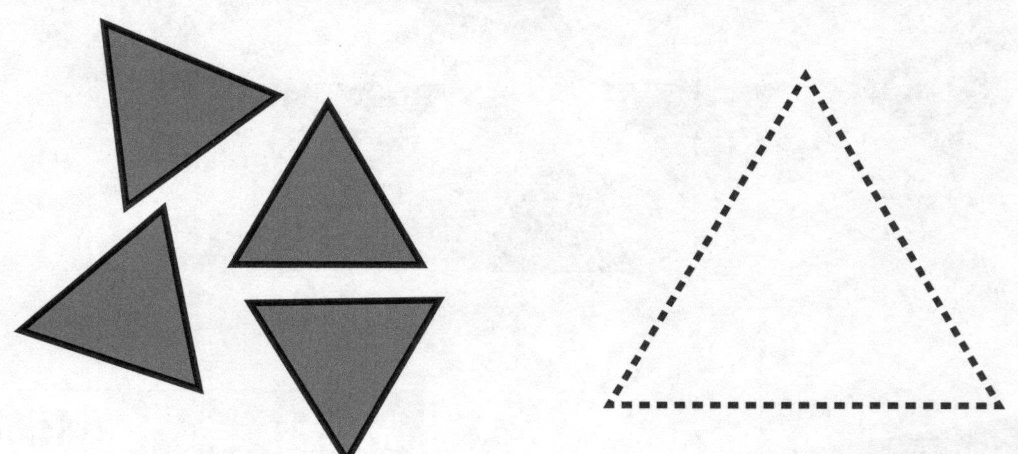

Work Together: How can you use the pattern blocks to make a new shape? Use pattern blocks to fill in the dotted line to make the new shape. Trace the pattern blocks to show the new shape.

On My Own

MATH REPLAY | GO ONLINE

Name ____________________

1

2

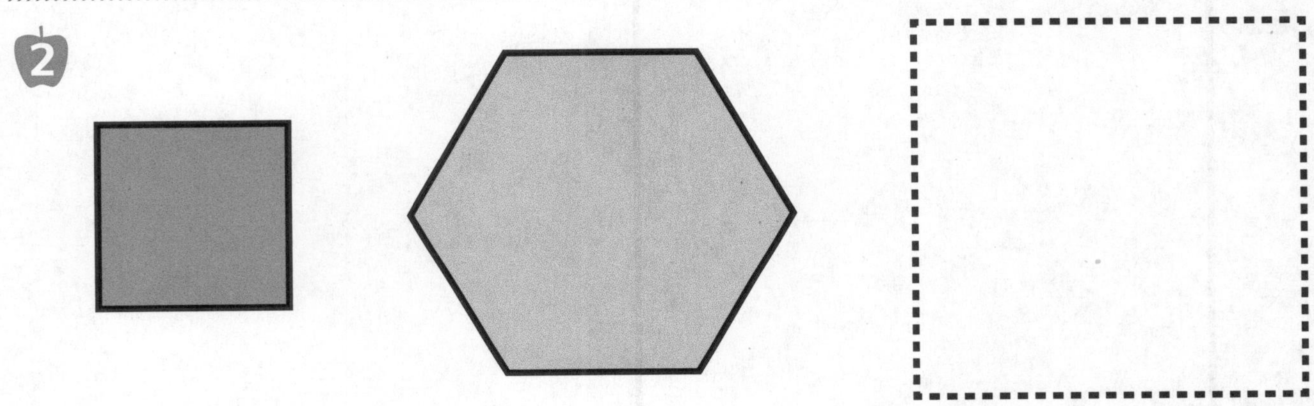

3

Directions: 1. How can you use the pattern blocks to make a new shape? Trace the pattern blocks you used. Name the larger shape. **2–3.** How can you use pattern blocks to make a new shape? Choose one type of pattern block to make the new shape. Trace the pattern blocks you used. Name the new shape.

4

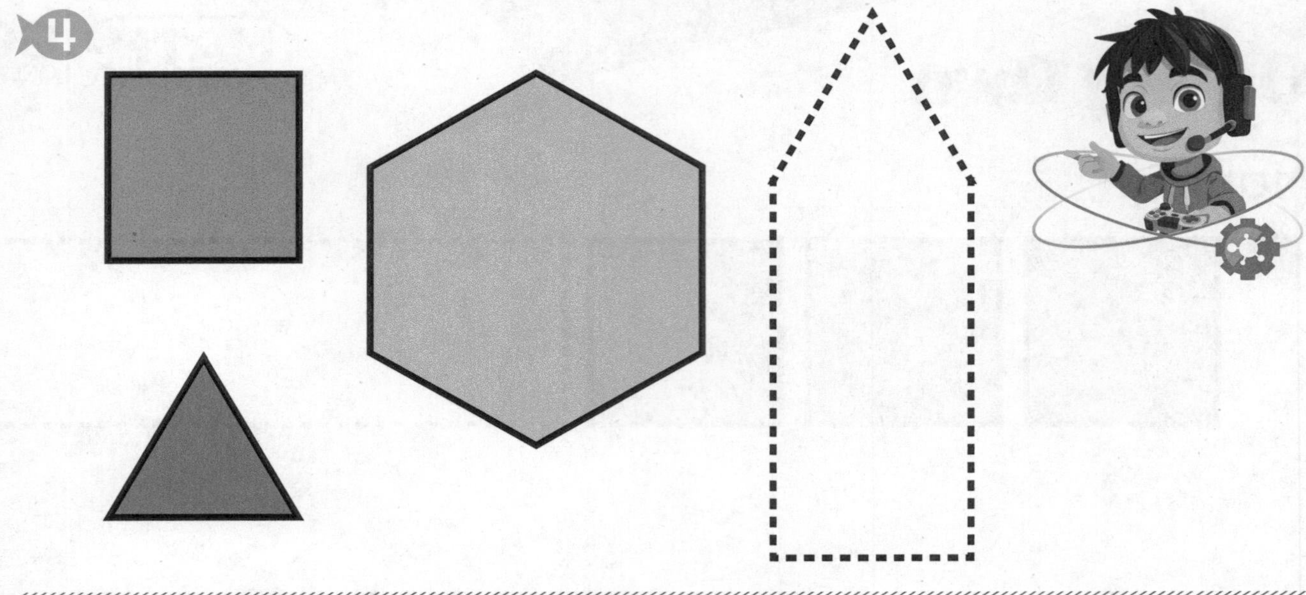

5

Reflect

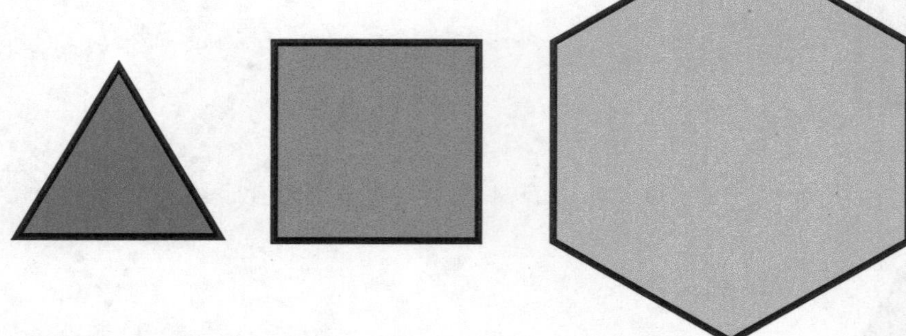

Directions: 4. STEM Connection A video game designer uses shapes to make a building. Choose shapes to use to fill the dotted line and make a building. Trace the pattern blocks you used.
5. Extend Your Thinking How can you use 9 pattern blocks to make a larger square? Trace the pattern blocks you used. **Reflect:** How can you use pattern blocks to make a new shape?

Compare and Contrast 3-Dimensional Shapes

Be Curious

Math is... Mindset

Directions:
How are they the same? How are they different?

Learn

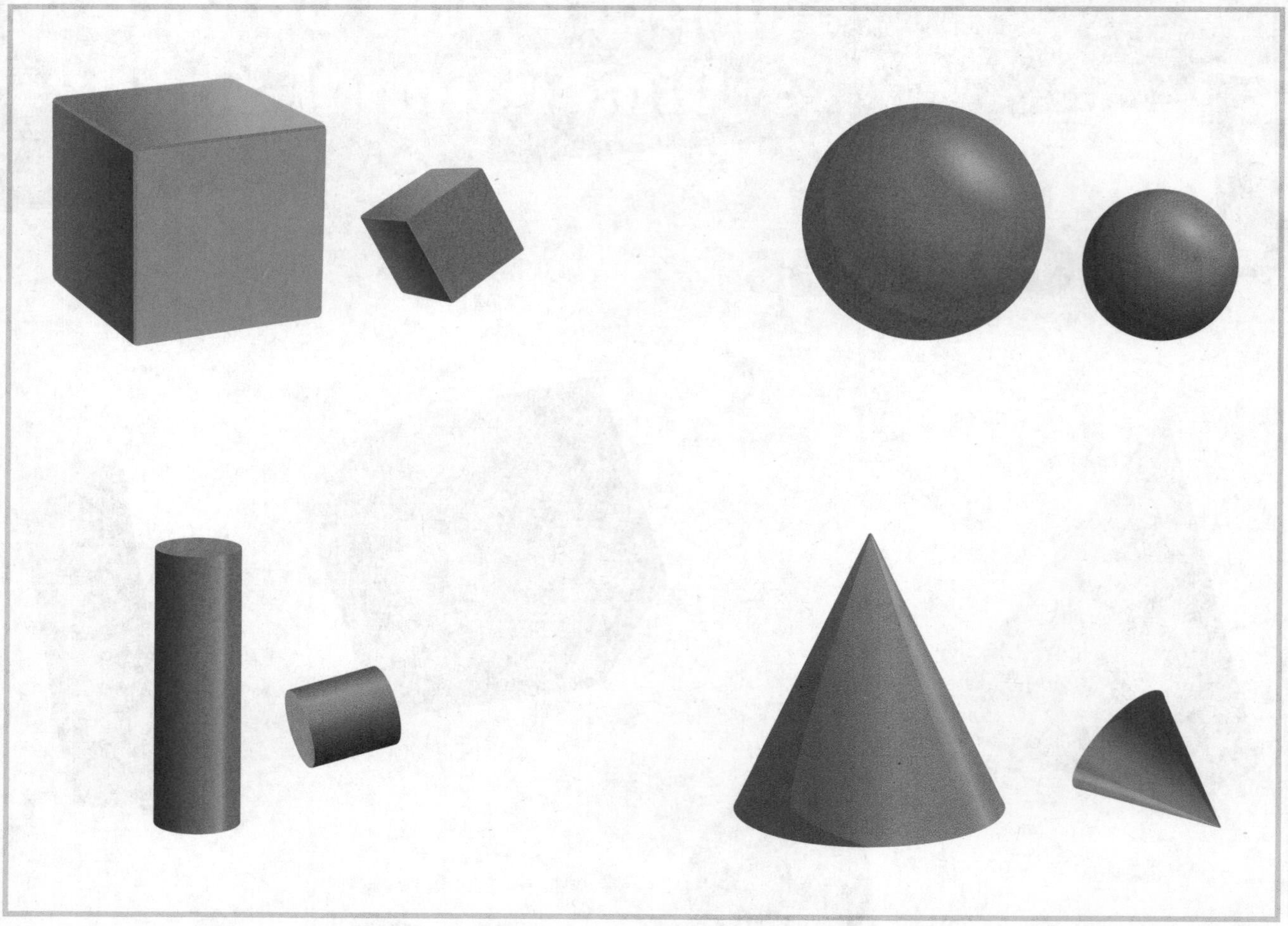

Work Together

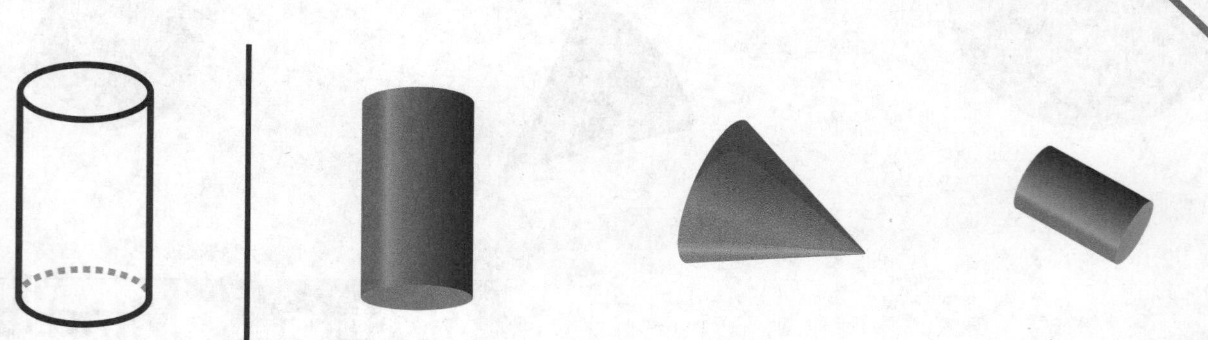

Work Together: How can you compare the shapes? Draw an X on the shape that is different from the first shape.

On My Own

Name ______________________________

3

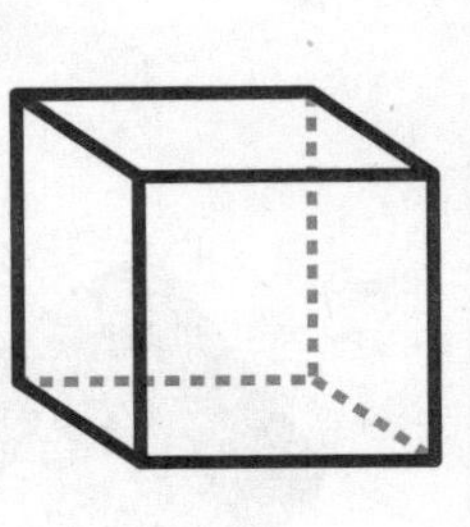

Directions: **1.** Which shapes are alike? Circle the shapes that are alike. **2.** Which shape is different? Draw an X on the shape that is different. **3.** How can you compare the shapes? Circle the shapes that are like the first shape.

4

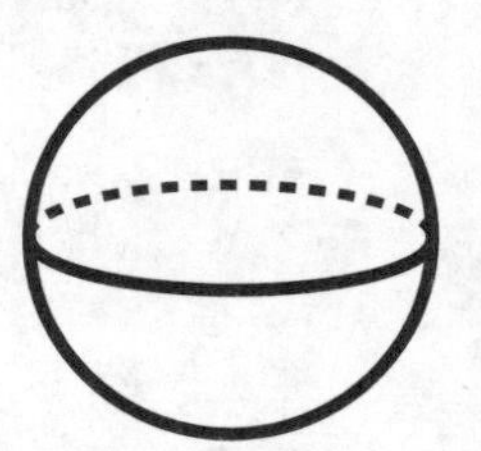

5

Reflect

Directions: 4. How can you compare the shapes? Draw an X on the shape that is different from the first shape. **5. Extend Your Thinking** Draw an X on the shape that is not like the others.

Reflect: How can you compare the shapes?

Lesson 13-5

Build 3-Dimensional Shapes

Be Curious

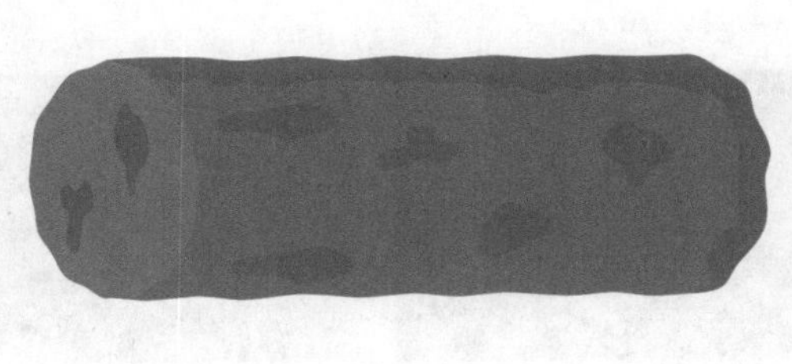

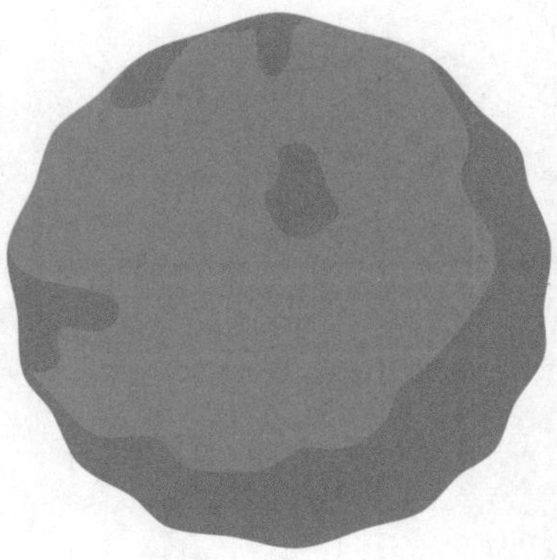

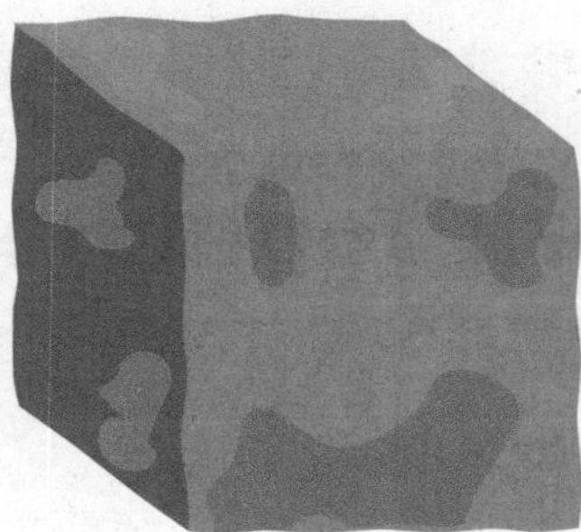

Math is... Mindset

Directions:
Tell me everything you can.

Learn

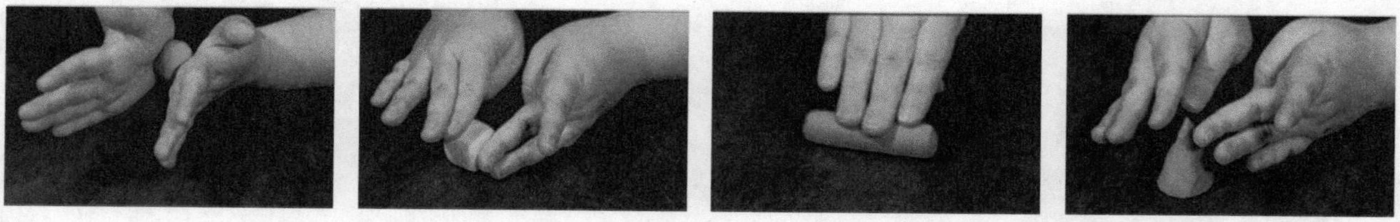

Work Together

Work Together: How can you build a cone? Use clay to build a cone. Circle the 3-dimensional shape you built.

On My Own

Name ______________________________

1

2

3

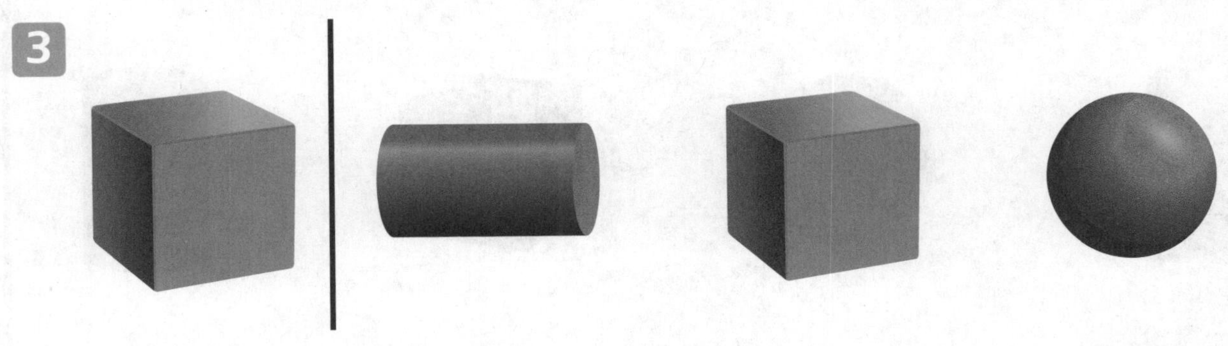

Directions: 1. How can you build a sphere? Use clay to build a sphere. Circle the 3-dimensional shape you built. **2.** How can you build a cylinder? Use clay to build a cylinder. Circle the 3-dimensional shape you built. **3.** How can you build a cube? Use clay to build a cube. Circle the 3-dimensional shape you built.

4

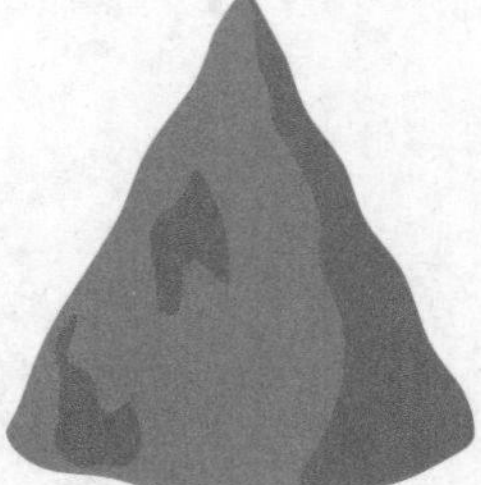

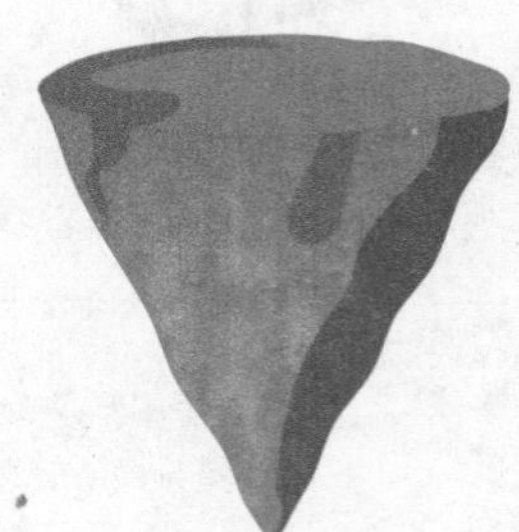

5

Reflect

Directions: 4. Error Analysis Lily was asked to use clay to build three different models of a cone. She built two models correctly. Circle the model that is not correct. **5. Extend Your Thinking** Luke built a shape that is round and can roll. Circle the shape Luke built.

Reflect: How can you build 3-dimensional shapes?

Lesson 13-6

Describe 3-Dimensional Shapes in the World

Be Curious

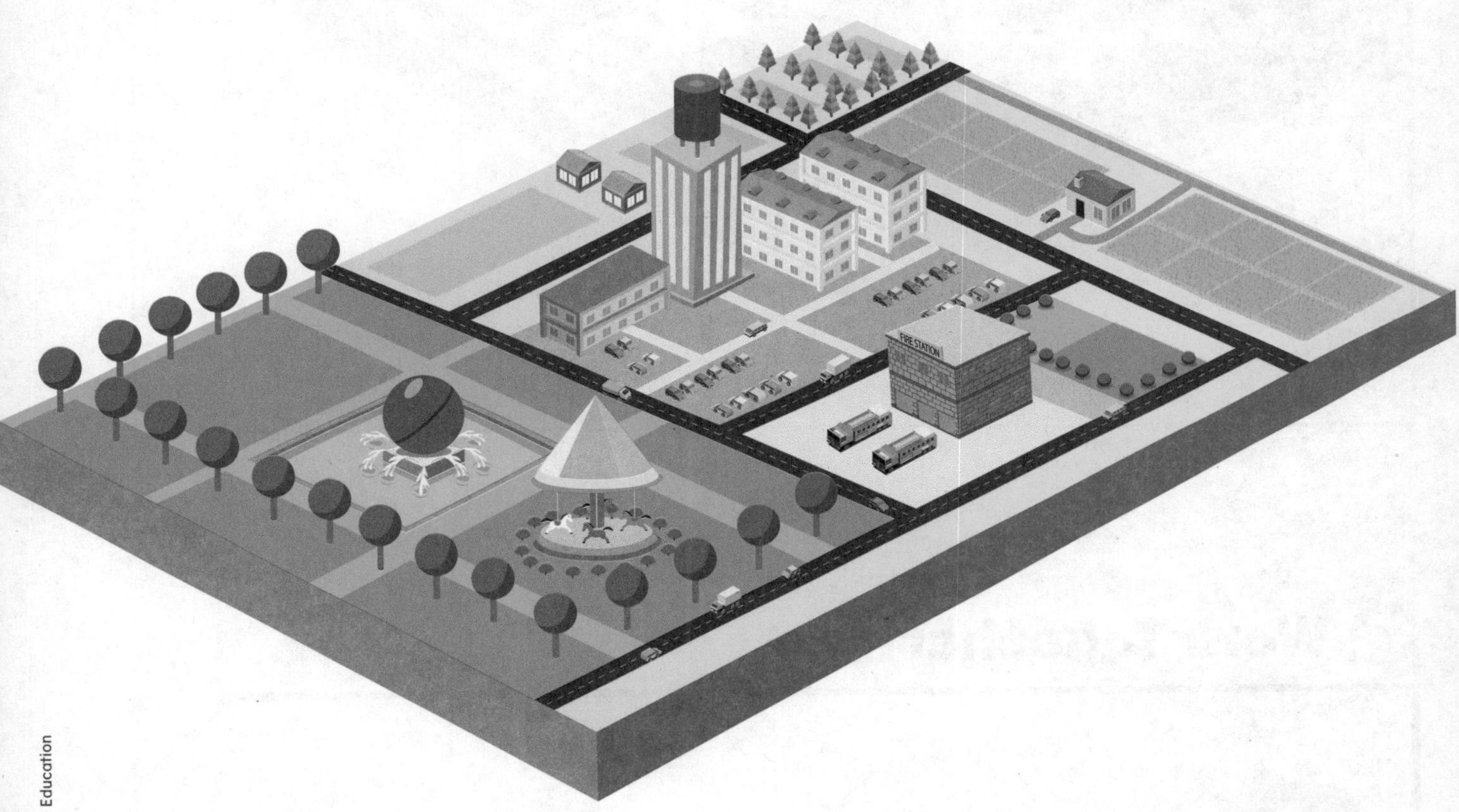

Math is... Mindset

Directions:
Tell me everything you can.

Learn

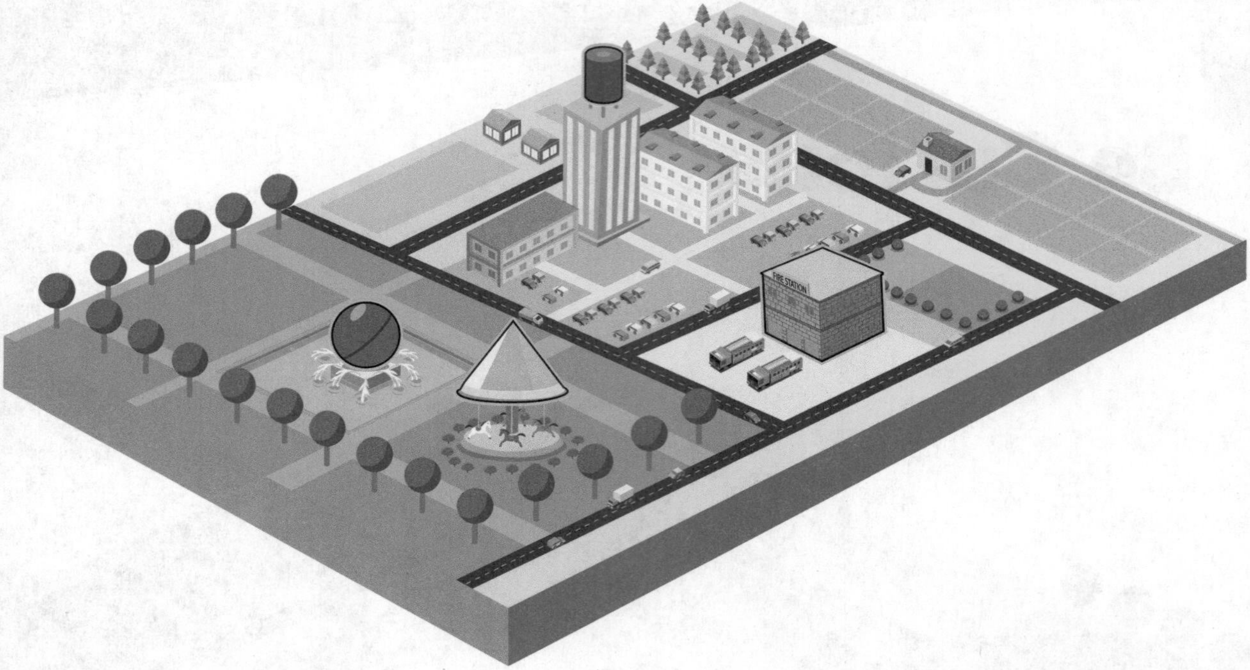

Work Together

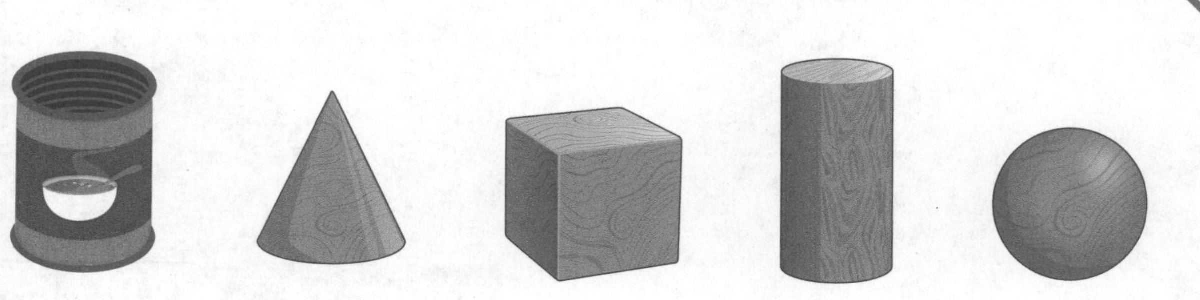

Work Together: What shape does the can of soup look like? Circle the shape. Name the shape.

On My Own

MATH REPLAY | GO ONLINE

Name ______________________________

1

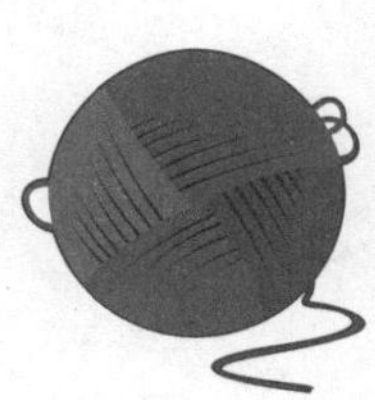

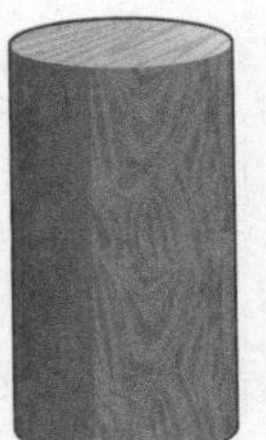
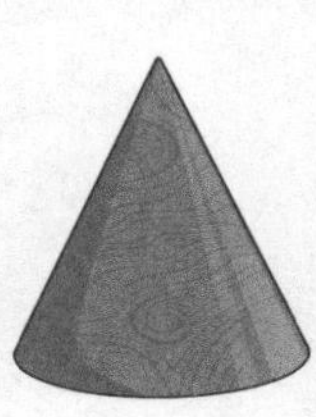

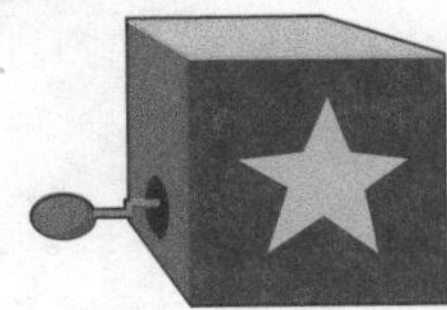

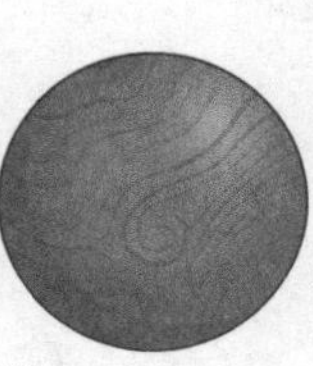

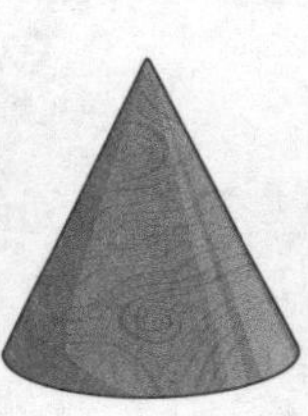

3

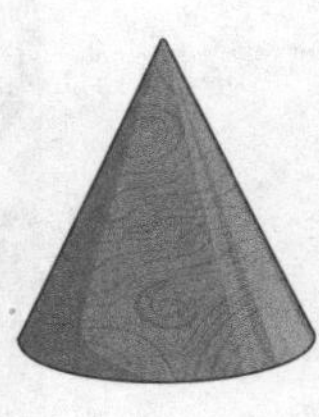

Directions: 1. What shape does the ball of yarn look like? Circle the shape. Name the shape. **2.** What shape does the toy look like? Circle the shape. Name the shape. **3.** What shape does the log look like? Circle the shape. Name the shape.

Reflect

Directions: 4. STEM Connection An animal trainer made a hat for his dog. What shape does the hat look like? Circle the shape. Name the shape. **5. Extend Your Thinking** The tower is made from two different shapes. Circle the two shapes. Name the shapes.

Reflect: What 3-dimensional shapes do you see?

Unit Review

Name ______________________________

Vocabulary Review

1

3

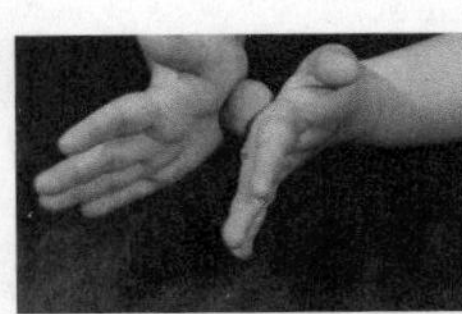
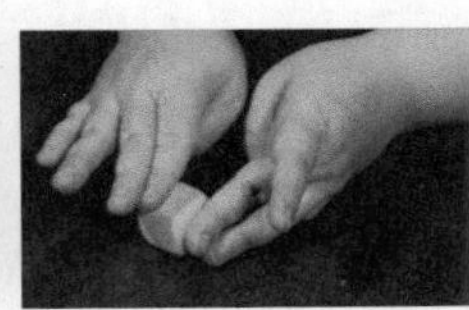
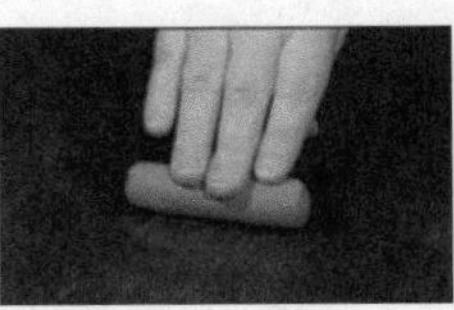
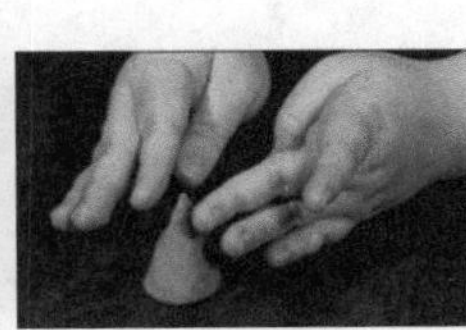

Directions: 1. Which are the 2-dimensional shapes? Circle the 2-dimensional shapes. **2.** Which are the 3-dimensional shapes? Circle the 3-dimensional shapes. **3.** How can you build a sphere? Circle the picture that shows how to build a sphere.

Review

4

5

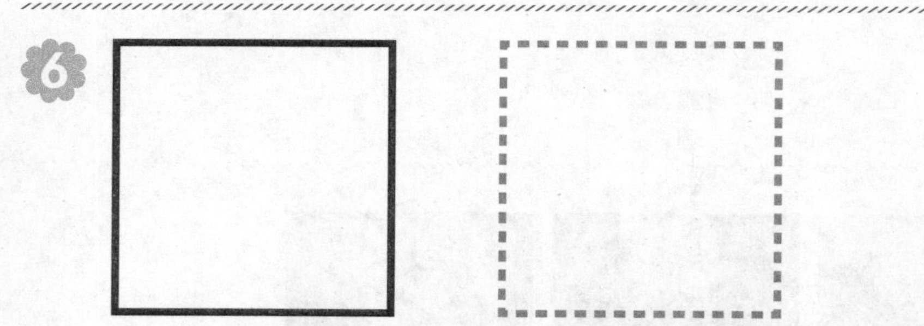

6

Directions: **4.** Which shapes are alike? Circle the shapes that are alike. **5.** How can you compare the shapes? Draw an X on the shape that is different from the first shape. **6.** How can you draw a square? Trace the square. Then draw a square.

MATH REPLAY | GO ONLINE

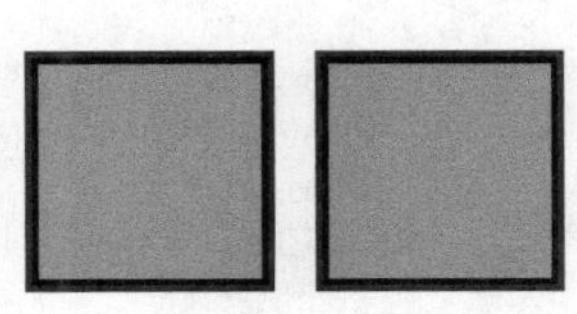

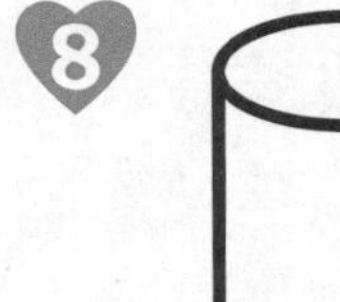

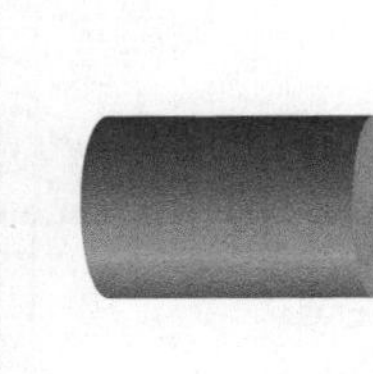

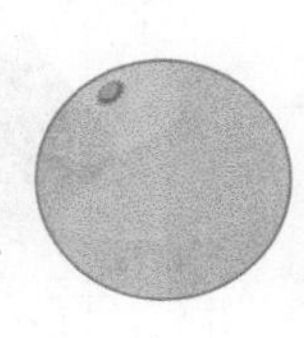

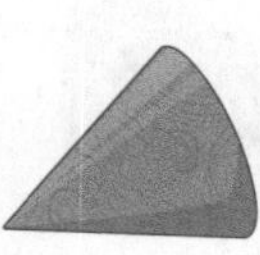

Directions: 7. How can you make a square? Circle the shapes you can use to make a square. **8.** How can you compare the shapes? Draw an X on the shape that is different from the first shape. **9.** Which objects are shaped like a cone? Circle the objects that are shaped like cones.

Performance Task

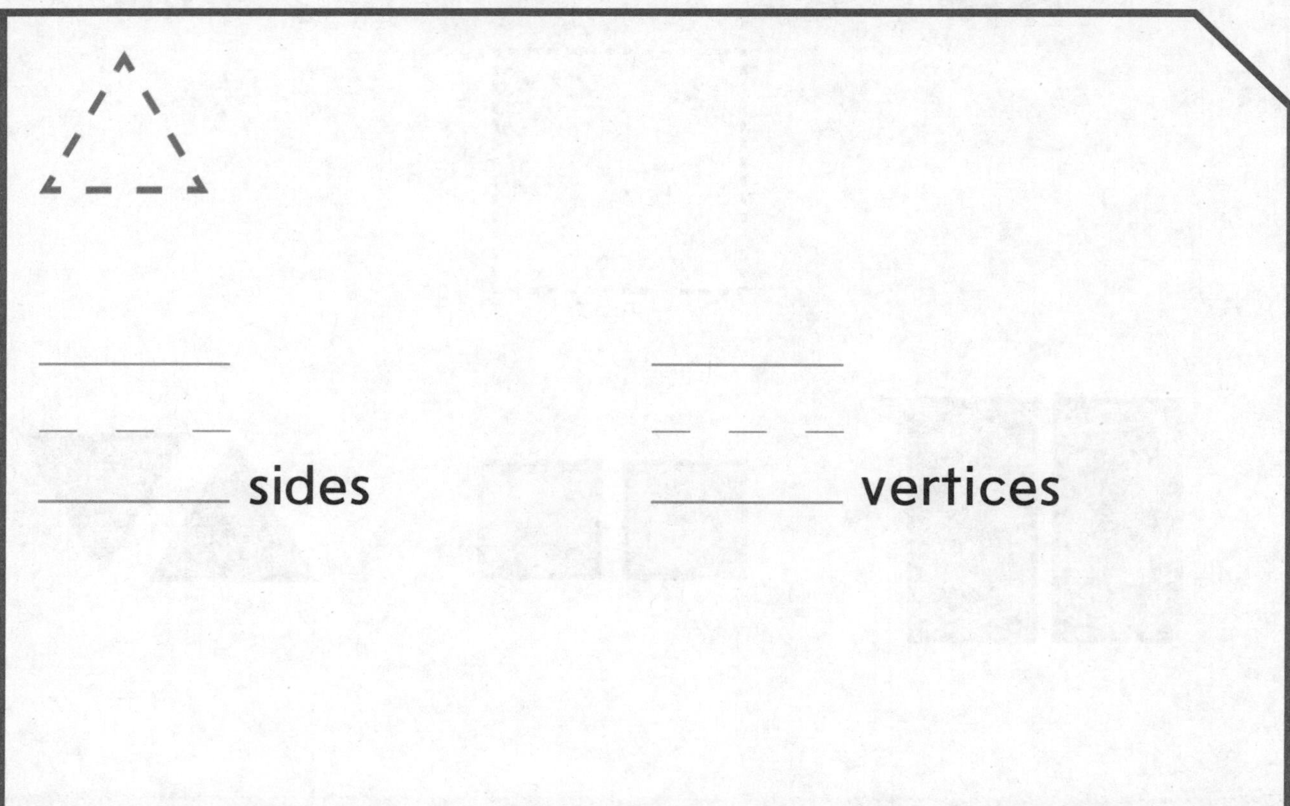

Reflect

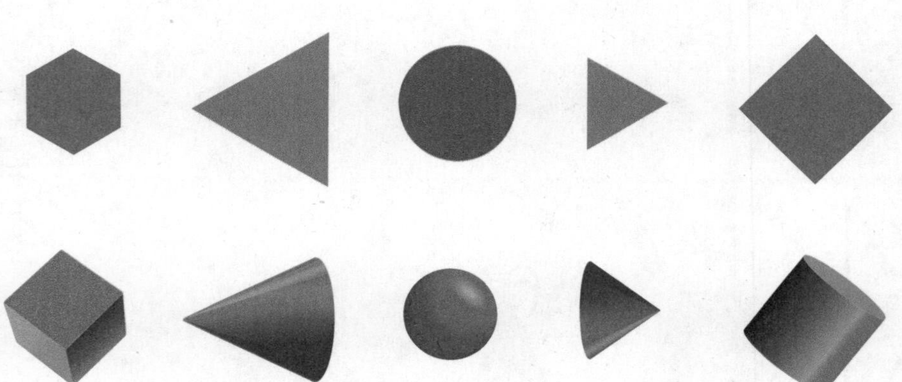

Performance Task: Jenny is drawing shapes for a video game she is designing. **Part A** How can you draw a triangle? Trace Jenny's triangle. Then draw a triangle. **Part B** How many sides did you draw? How many vertices did you draw? **Part C** How can you draw a 2-dimensional shape that is round and has zero vertices?

Reflect: How can you describe the ways shapes are alike and different?

Unit 13

Fluency Practice

Name ______________________________

Fluency Strategy

2 + 2 = 4

1. 3 + 2 = ____

Fluency Flash

2. 4 + 0 = ____

3. 3 + 1 = ____

Directions: Fluency Strategy: Add. Find the sum. **1.** What is the sum of 3 and 2? Count on from 3. Write the sum.
Fluency Flash: 2. What is the sum of 4 and 0? Count on from 4. Write the sum. **3.** What is the sum of 3 and 1? Count on from 3. Write the sum.

Fluency Check

4 − 1 = ____

2 + 1 = ____

3 + 0 = ____

Fluency Talk

Directions: Fluency Check: 4. How can you count back to find 4 − 1? Write the difference. **5.** What is the sum of 2 and 1? Count on from 2. Write the sum. **6.** How can you count on to find 3 + 0? Count on from 3. Write the sum.

Fluency Talk: Look at 2 + 1. How did you find the sum?

Compare Measurable Attributes

Focus Question

How can I describe and compare the length, height, weight, and capacity of objects?

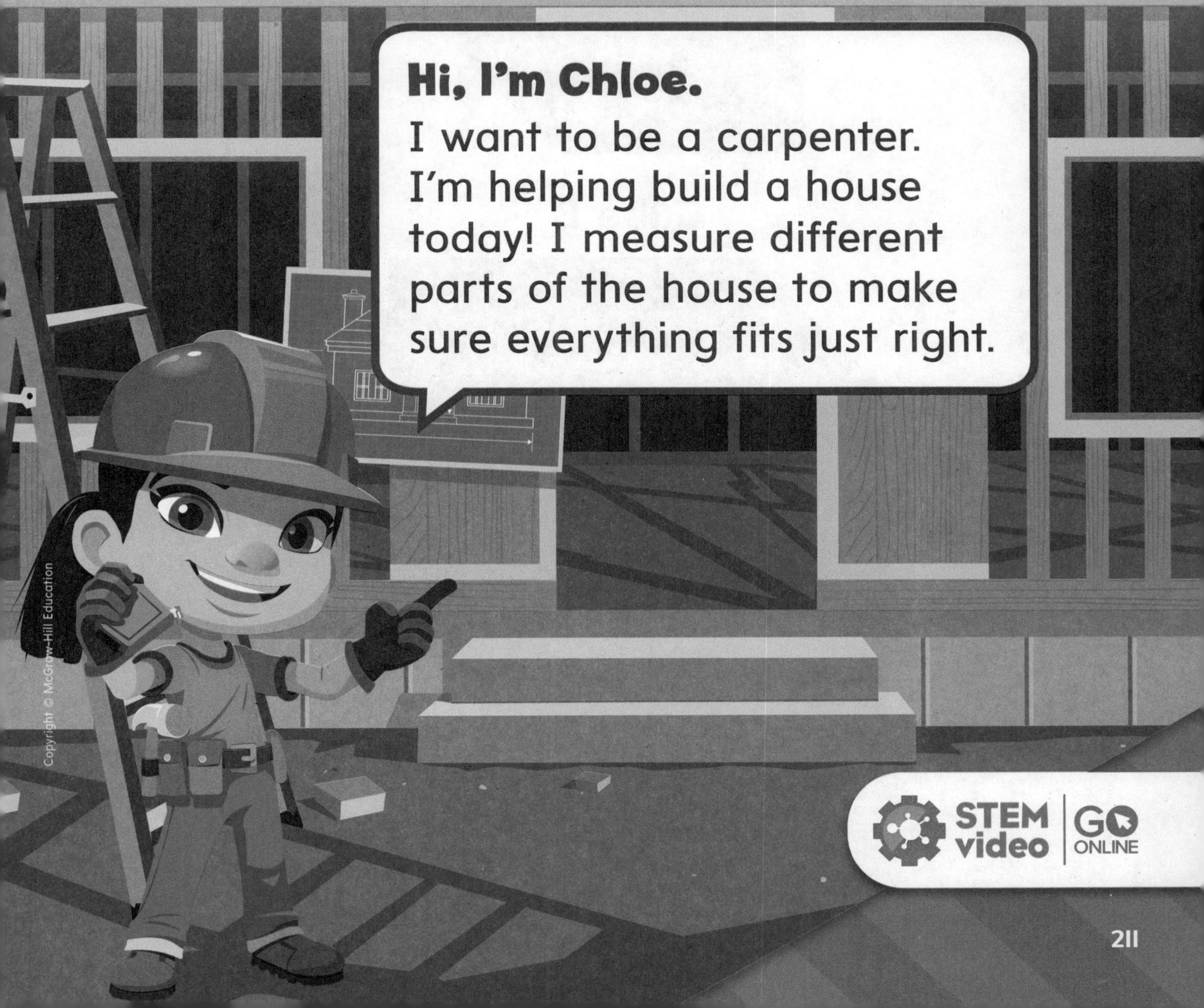

Hi, I'm Chloe.

I want to be a carpenter. I'm helping build a house today! I measure different parts of the house to make sure everything fits just right.

STEM video | GO ONLINE

Name

How Big?

Cube A

Cube B

Directions: Build each cube. Compare them.

Lesson 14-1

Describe Attributes of Objects

Be Curious

Math is... Mindset

Directions:
What do you notice? What do you wonder?

Learn

Work Together

Work Together: How can you describe an object in more than one way? Circle an object. Describe its height and weight.

On My Own

MATH REPLAY | GO ONLINE

Name ______________________________

1

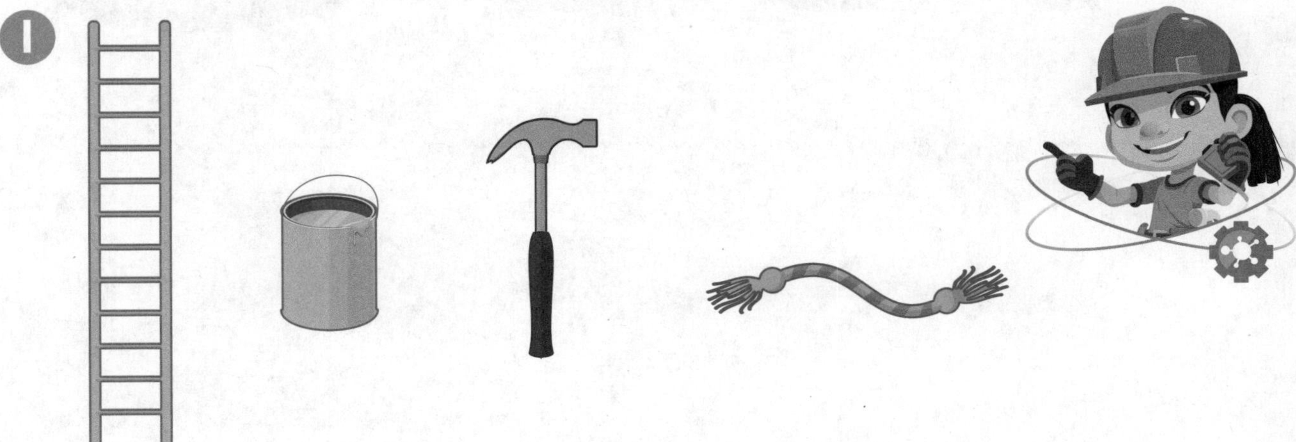

2

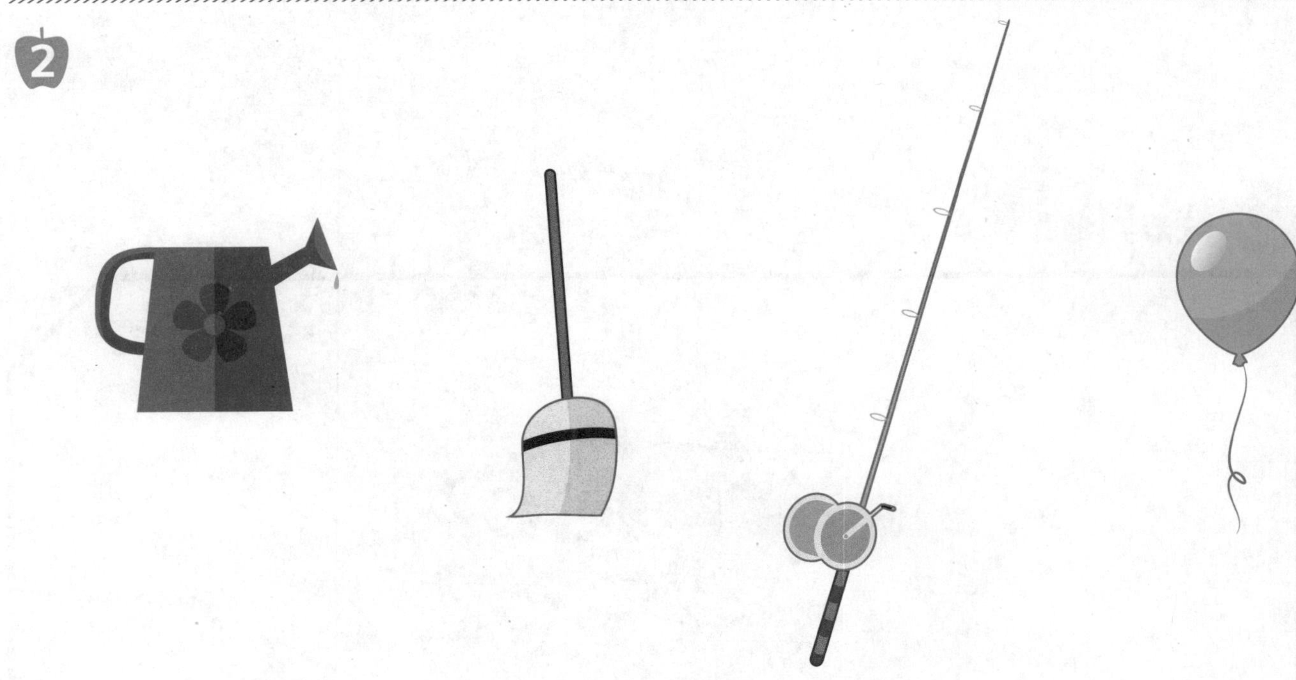

3

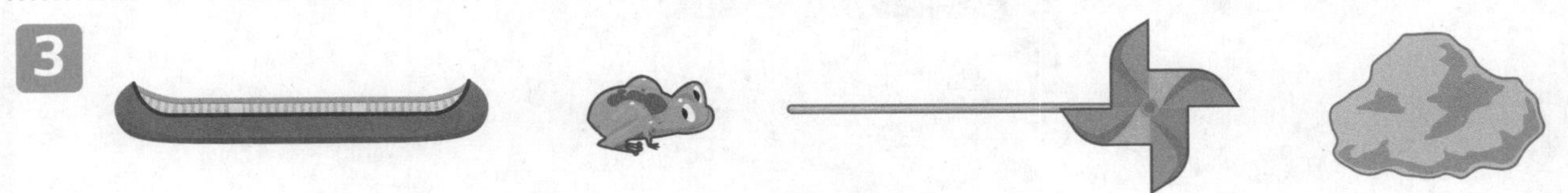

Directions: I. STEM Connection How can you describe an object in more than one way? Circle an object. Describe its length and height. **2.** How can you describe an object in more than one way? Circle an object. Describe its height and weight. **3.** How can you describe an object in more than one way? Circle an object. Describe its weight and length.

Reflect

Directions: 4. How can you describe an object using capacity? Circle an object and describe its capacity. **5. Extend Your Thinking** How can you describe an object in more than one way? Draw an object that is short and heavy.

Reflect: How can you describe the object using length, height, weight, and capacity?

Lesson 14-2

Compare Lengths

Be Curious

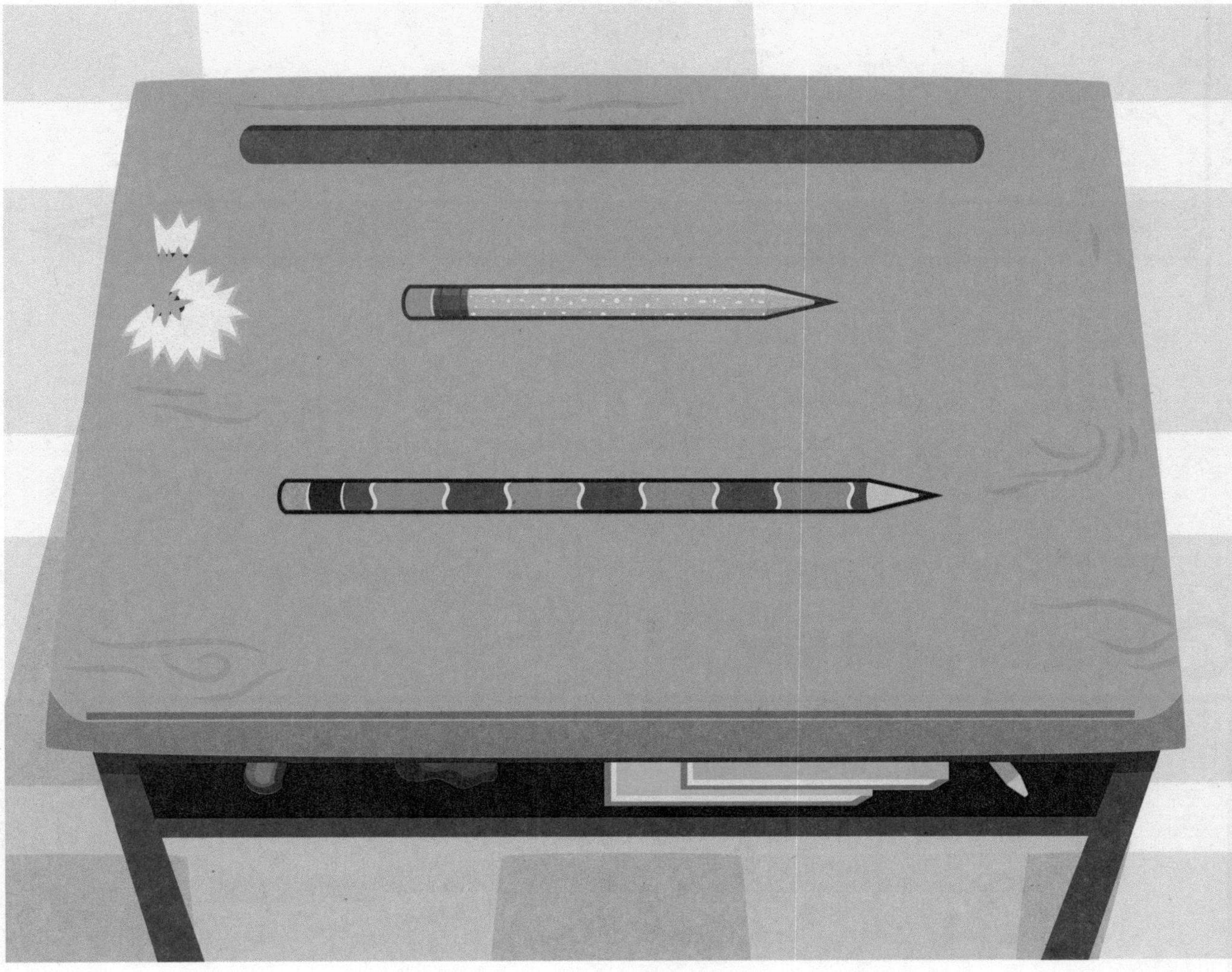

Math is... Mindset

Directions:
How are they the same? How are they different?

Learn

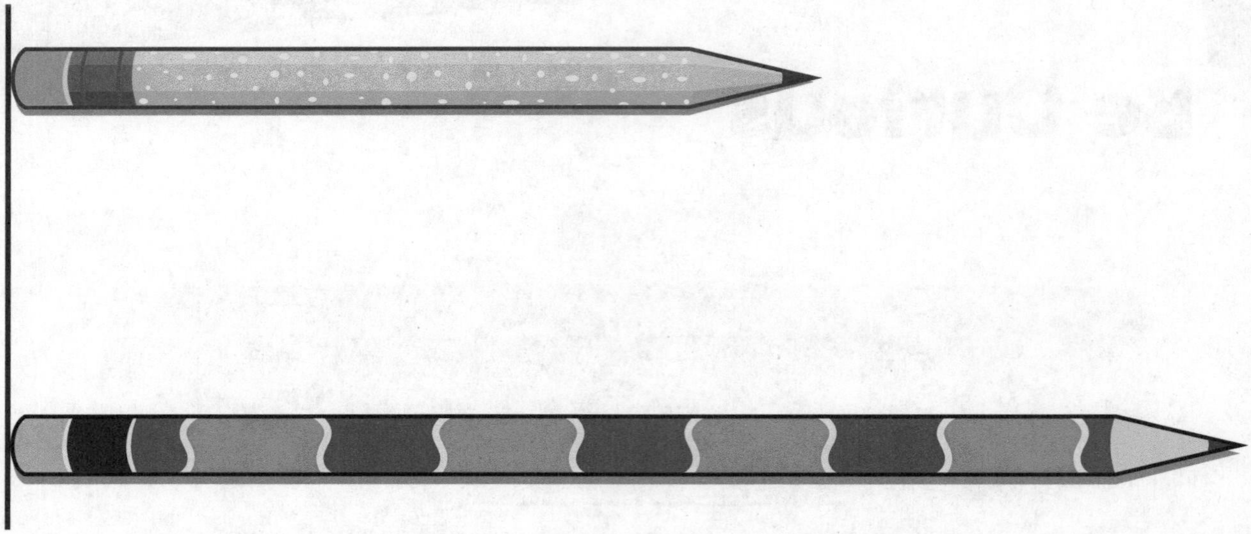

Work Together

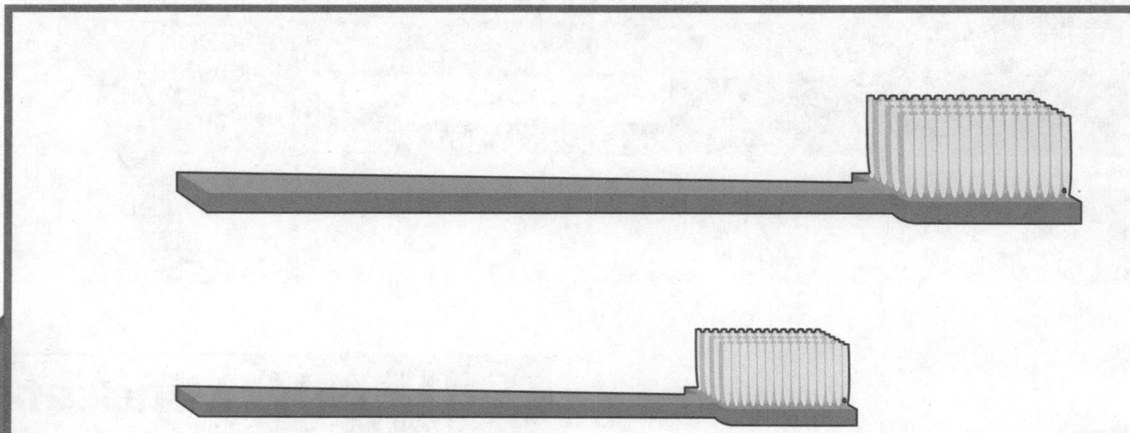

Work Together: Which is longer? Circle the longer object. Underline the objects if they are the same length.

On My Own

MATH REPLAY | GO ONLINE

Name ______________________________

1

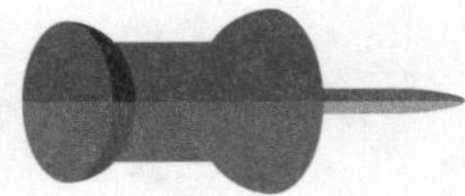

2

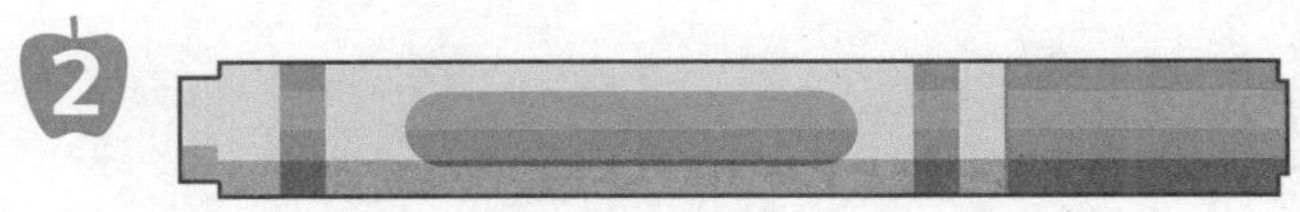

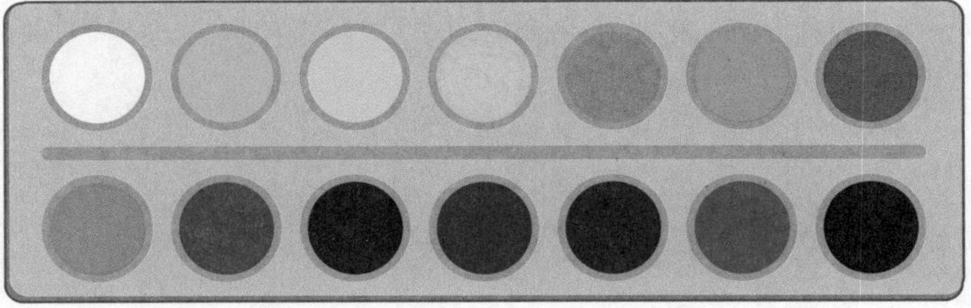

3

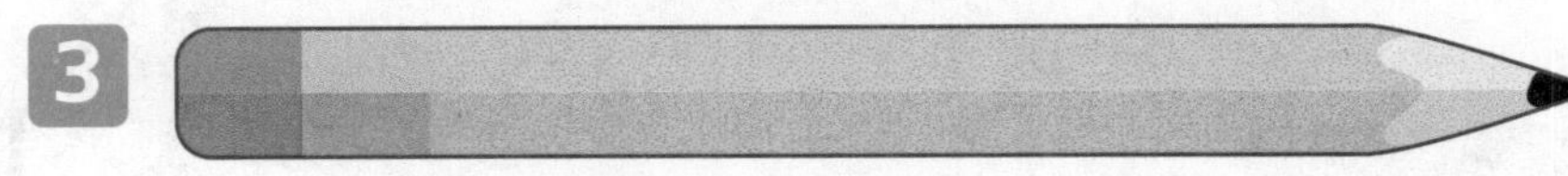

Directions: 1. Which is longer? Circle the longer object. Underline the objects if they are the same length. **2.** Which is shorter? Draw an X on the shorter object. Underline the objects if they are the same length. **3.** Which is longer? Circle the longer object. Underline the objects if they are the same length.

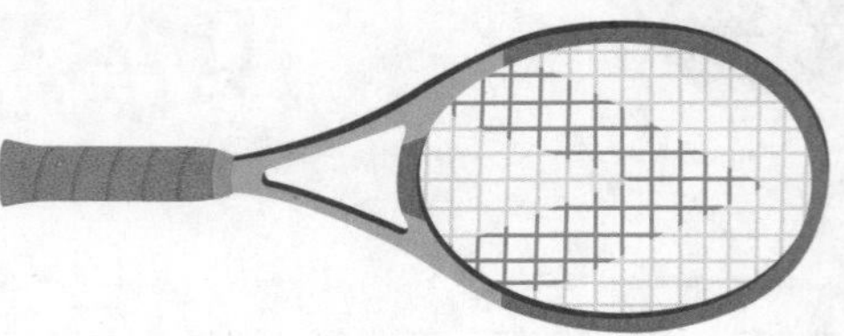

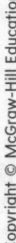

Reflect

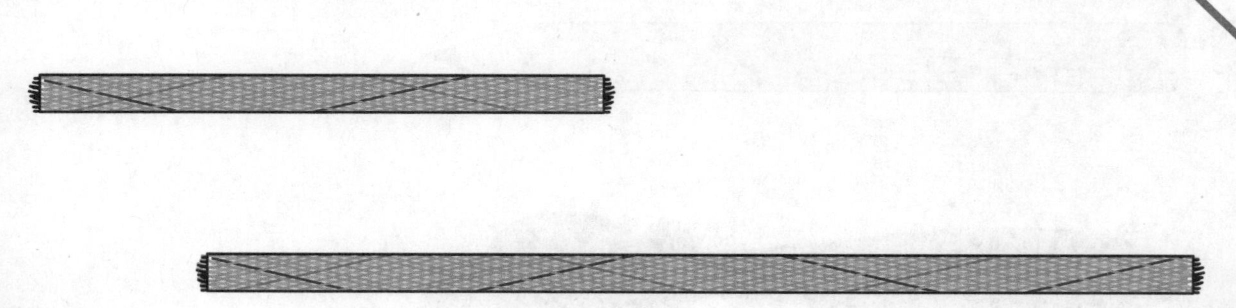

Directions: 4. Error Analysis Amajin says the hockey stick is shorter. Is she correct? Help Amajin by circling the shorter object. **5. Extend Your Thinking** How can you draw an object that is longer? Draw an object that is longer than the boat.

Reflect: How can you compare the lengths of the strings?

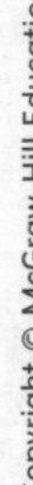

Lesson 14-3

Compare Heights

Be Curious

Math is... Mindset

Directions:
How are they the same? How are they different?

Learn

Work Together

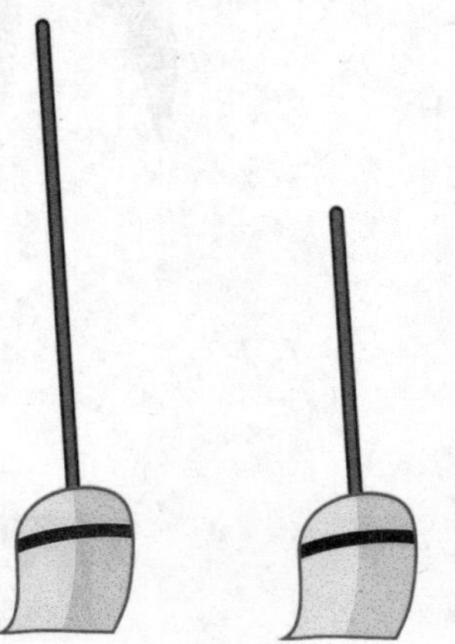

Work Together: Which is taller? Circle the taller object. Underline the objects if they are the same height.

On My Own

MATH REPLAY | GO ONLINE

Name ______________________________

1

Directions: 1. Which is taller? Circle the taller object. Underline the objects if they are the same height. **2.** Which is shorter? Draw an X on the object that is shorter. Underline the objects if they are the same height. **3.** Which is taller? Circle the object that is taller. Underline the objects if they are the same height.

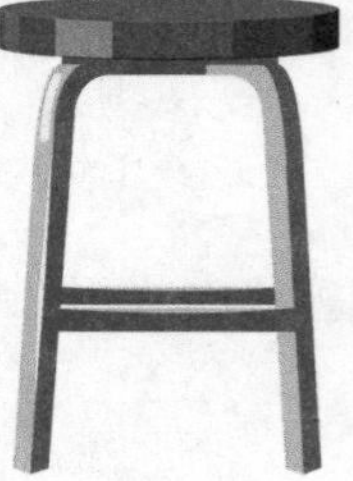

Reflect

Directions: 4. STEM Connection Which is shorter? Draw an X on the shorter object. Underline the objects if they are the same height. **5. Extend Your Thinking** How can you draw an object that is taller? Draw an object that is taller than the stool.

Reflect: How can you compare the heights of the flowers?

Unit 14

Comparing Objects

Name ____________________

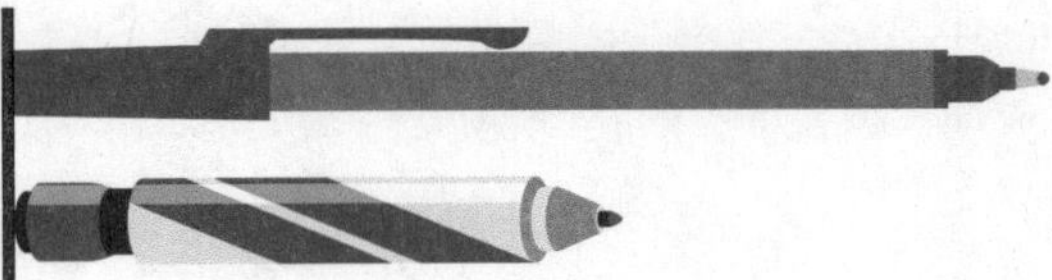

The pen is...

a. shorter

b. longer

c. same length

Tell or show why.

2

The bush is...

a. shorter

b. taller

c. same height

Tell or show why.

Directions: 1-2. How can you compare two objects? Circle the best answer.

3

The cat is...

a. shorter

b. taller

c. same height

Tell or show why.

Reflect On Your Learning

Directions: 3. How can you compare two objects? Circle the best answer.
Reflect On Your Learning: Do you understand? Circle to show your understanding.

Lesson 14-4

Compare Weights

Be Curious

Math is... Mindset

Directions:
What do you notice? What do you wonder?

Learn

Work Together

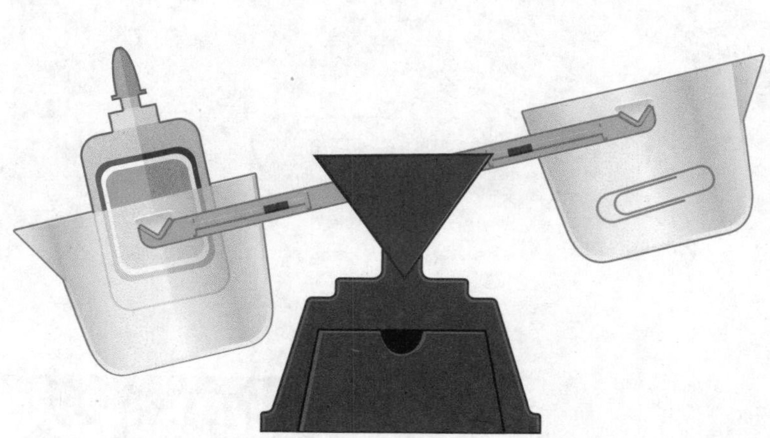

Work Together: Which is heavier? Circle the object that is heavier. Underline the objects if they are the same weight.

On My Own

MATH REPLAY | GO ONLINE

Name ______________________

2

3

Directions: 1. Which is heavier? Circle the object that is heavier. Underline the objects if they are the same weight. **2.** Which is lighter? Draw an X the object that is lighter. Underline the objects if they are the same weight. **3.** Which is heavier? Circle the object that is heavier. Underline the objects if they are the same weight.

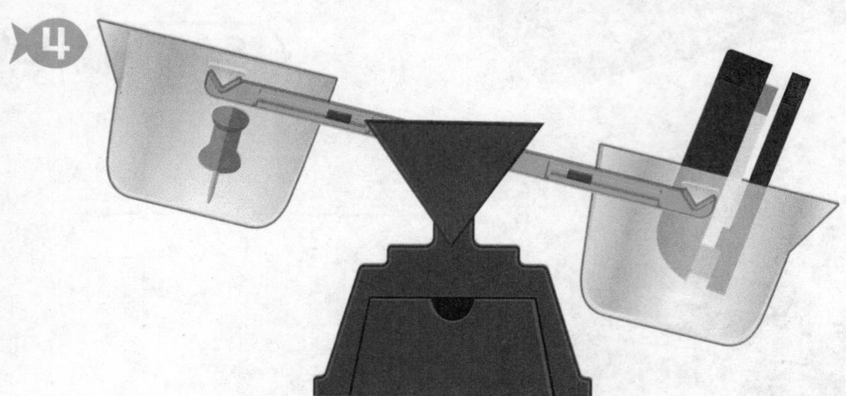

Reflect

Directions: 4. Error Analysis Piper says the stapler is lighter because it is in the lower bucket. Is she correct? Help Piper by circling the object that is lighter. **5. Extend Your Thinking** How can you draw an object that is heavier? Draw an object that is heavier than the tape.

Reflect: How can you compare the weights of the objects?

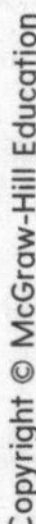

Lesson 14-5

Compare Capacities

Be Curious

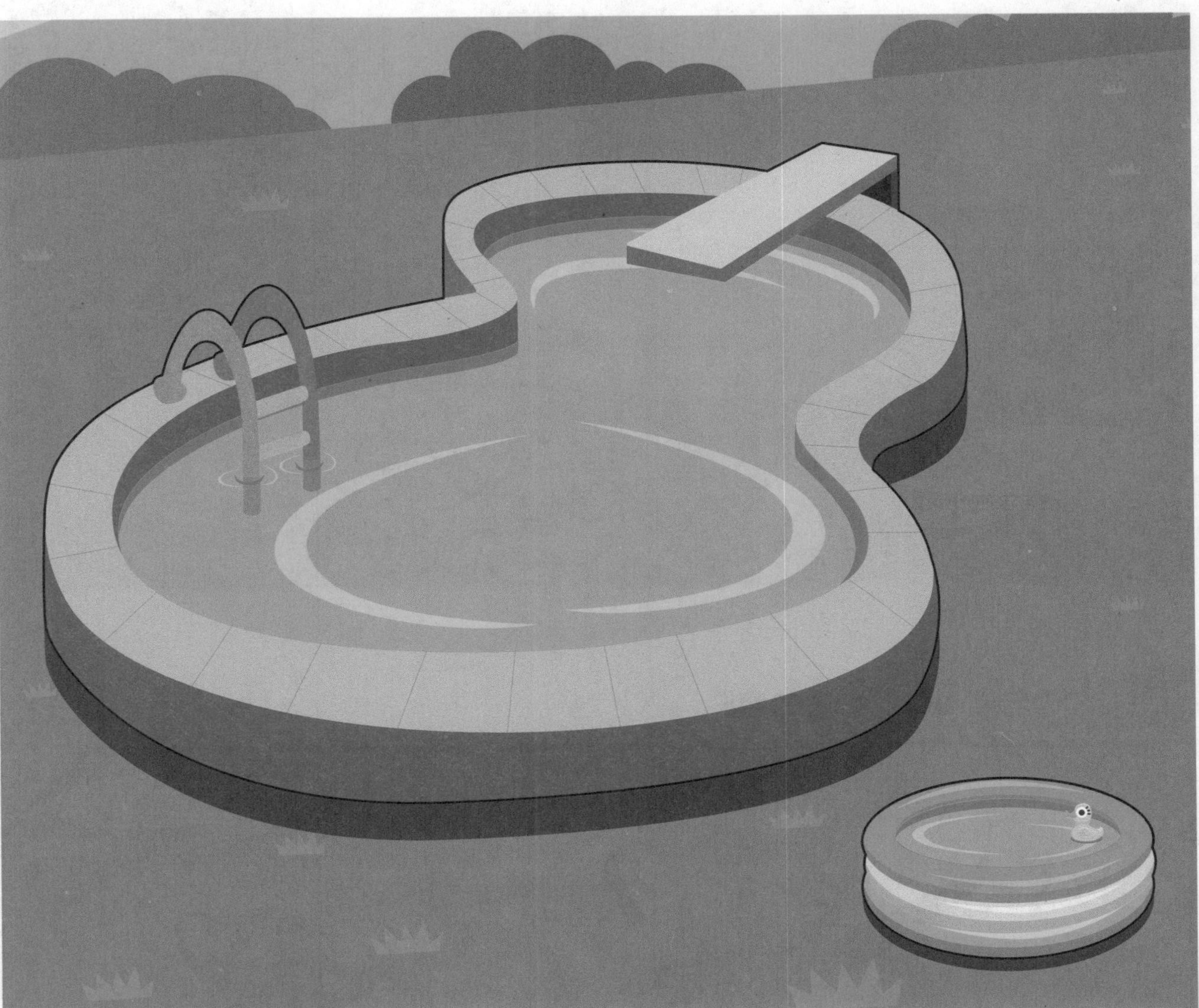

Math is... Mindset

Directions:
What do you notice? What do you wonder?

Learn

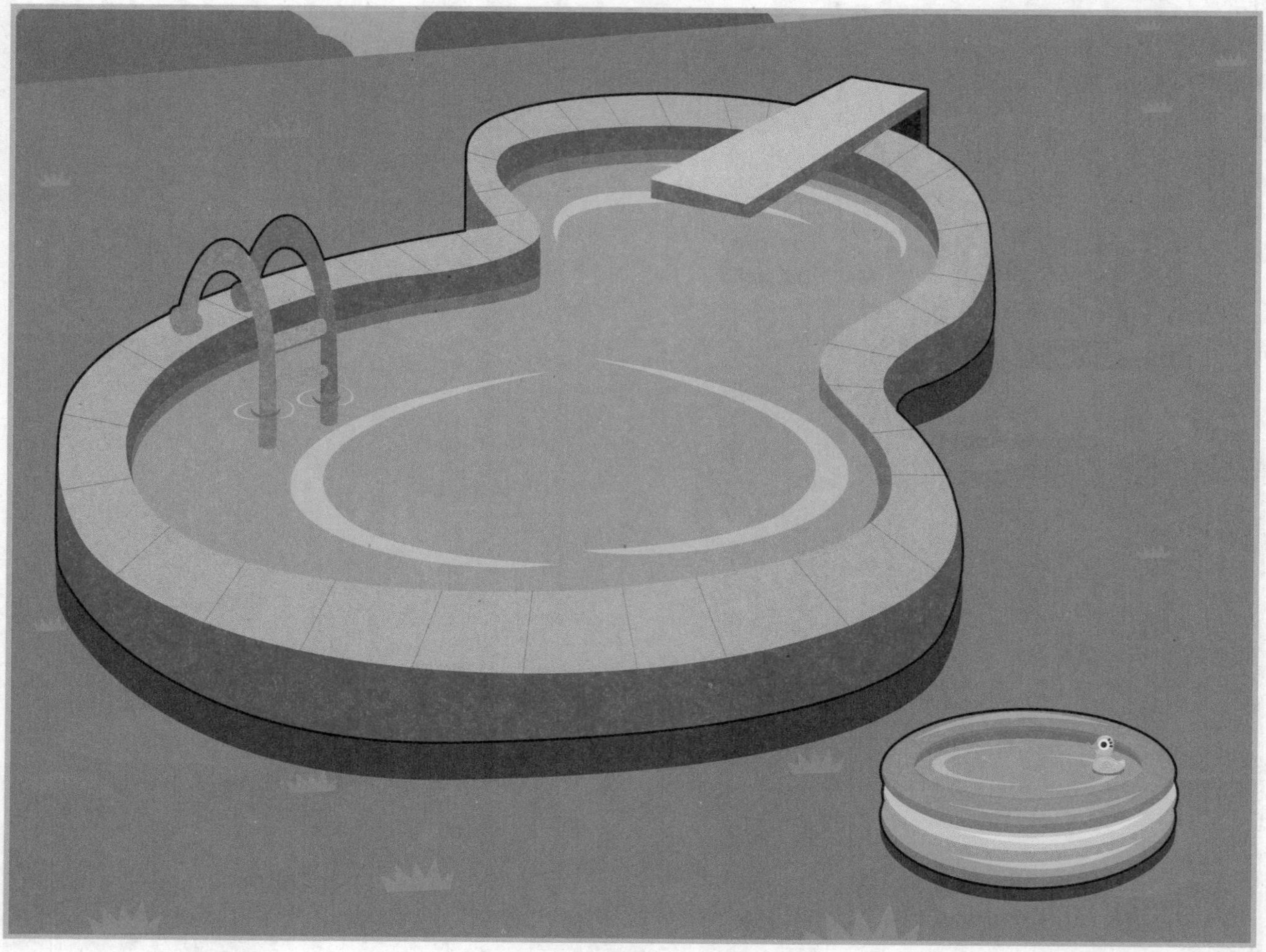

Work Together

Work Together: Which holds more? Circle the object that holds more. Underline the objects if they have the same capacity.

On My Own

Name ______________________________

1

2

3

Directions: 1. Which holds more? Circle the object that holds more. Underline the objects if they have the same capacity. **2.** Which holds less? Draw an X on the object that holds less. Underline the objects if they have the same capacity. **3.** Which holds more? Circle the object that holds more. Underline the objects if they have the same capacity.

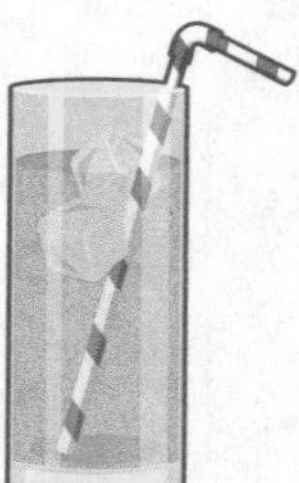

Reflect

Directions: 4. Which holds less? Draw an X on the object that holds less. **5. Extend Your Thinking** How can you draw an object that holds more? Draw an object that holds more than the bucket.

Reflect: How can you compare the capacities of the objects?

Unit Review

Name ______________________________

Vocabulary Review

1

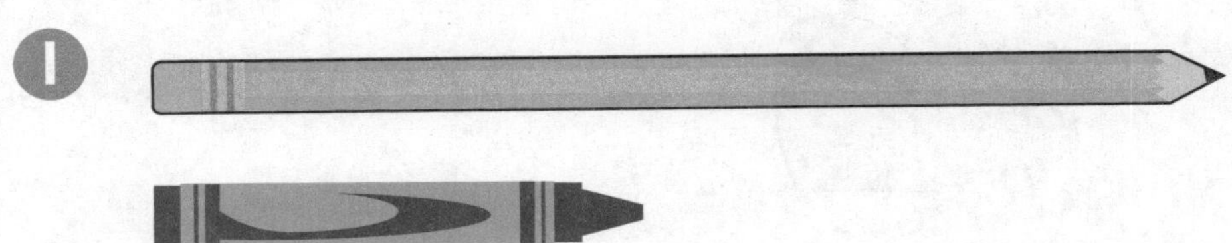

2

3

4

Directions: 1. Circle the object that is longer. Draw an X on the object that is shorter. **2.** Circle the object that is taller. Draw an X on the object that is shorter. **3.** Circle the object that is heavier. Draw an X on the object that is lighter. **4.** Circle the object that holds more. Draw an X on the object that holds less.

Review

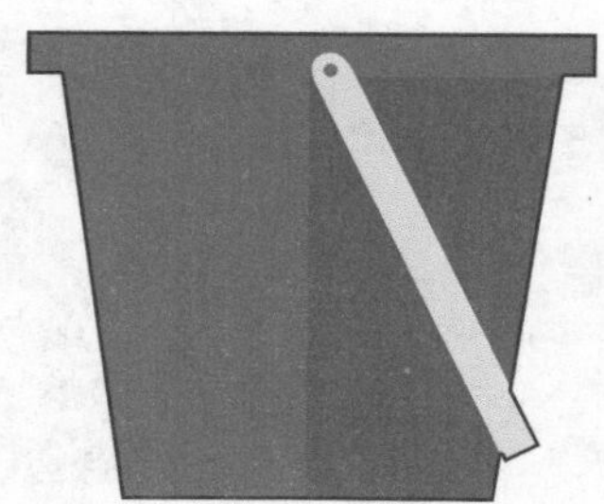

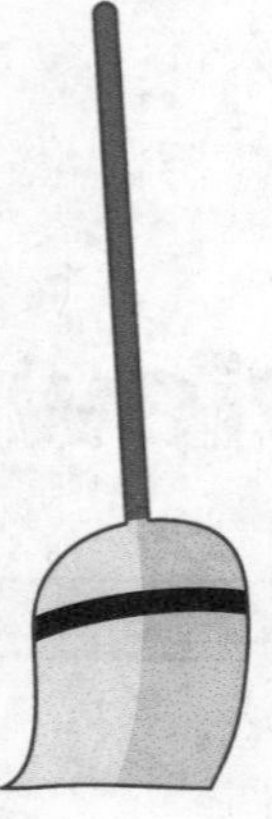

Directions: 5. Which is taller? Circle the taller object. Underline the objects if they are the same height. **6.** Which is longer? Circle the longer object. Underline the objects if they are the same length. **7.** Which holds more? Circle the object that holds more. Underline the objects if they have the same capacity.

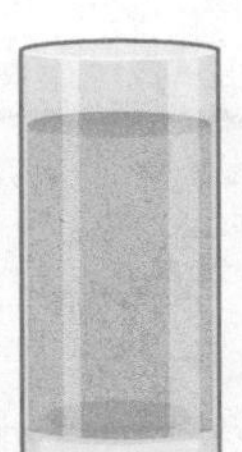

Directions: 8. Which is heavier? Circle the heavier object. Underline the objects if they are the same weight. **9.** Draw an X on the object that holds less. Draw a circle around the object that holds more. Underline the objects if they have the same capacity.

Performance Task

Reflect

Performance Task: Part A A carpenter weighs a hammer and a nail. Draw the objects in the balance scale to show which weighs more and which weighs less. **Part B** A carpenter puts sand in two buckets. Which bucket holds more sand? Circle the bucket that holds more.

Reflect: How can you compare objects? Explain how you can compare the height and capacity of the objects.

Unit 14

Fluency Practice

Name ________________________________

Fluency Strategy

4 − 1 = **3**

1

3 − 2 = ____

Fluency Flash

2

3 − 0 = ____

3

2 − 2 = ____

Directions: Fluency Strategy: Subtract within 5. Find the difference. **1.** What is the difference between 3 and 2? Write the difference.
Fluency Flash: 2. What is the difference between 3 and 0? Write the difference. **3.** What is the difference between 2 and 2? Write the difference.

Fluency Check

5 − 1 = ____

1 + 3 = ____

5 − 2 = ____

Fluency Talk

Directions: Fluency Check: 4. How can you count back to find 5 − 1? Count back from 5. Write the difference. **5.** What is the sum of 1 and 3? Write the sum. **6.** What is the difference between 5 and 2? Write the difference.
Fluency Talk: Look at 5 − 2. How did you find the difference?

Glossary/Glosario

English | **Spanish/Español**

Aa

add

4 + 3 = 7

sumar

4 + 3 = 7

alike

alike different

igual

igual diferente

attribute

color, shape, size

atributo

color, forma, tamaño

Bb

break apart

break apart 6

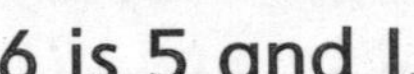

6 is 5 and 1.

descomponer

descomponer 6

6 es 5 y 1.

English	Spanish/Español

Cc

capacity / **capacidad**

holds more

holds less

contiene más

contiene menos

circle / **círculo**

compare / **comparar**

compare	comparar
more	más
fewer	menos

cone / **cono**

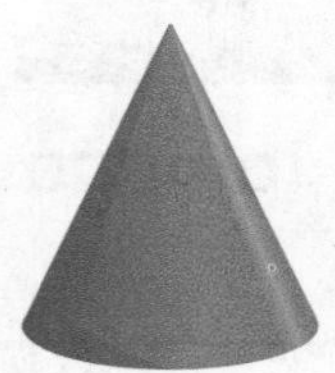

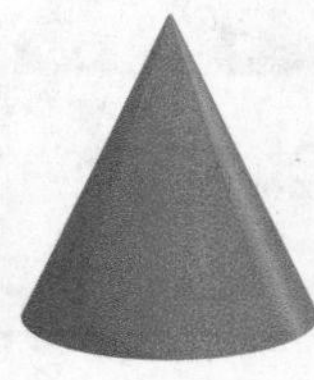

count / **contar**

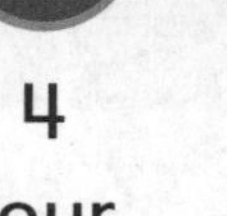
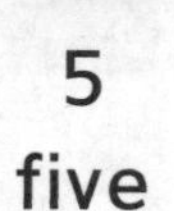

1	2	3	4	5
one	two	three	four	five

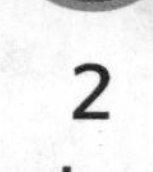

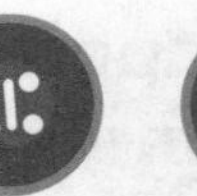
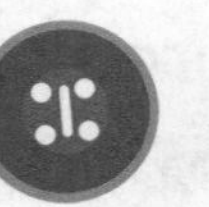

1	2	3	4	5
uno	dos	tres	cuatro	cinco

English	Spanish/Español
cube	cubo

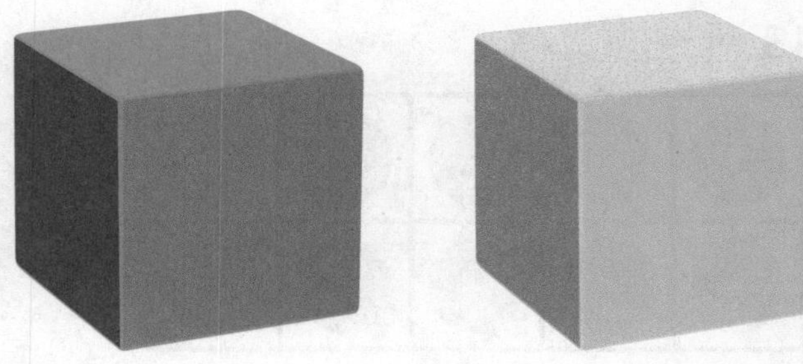

cylinder	cilindro

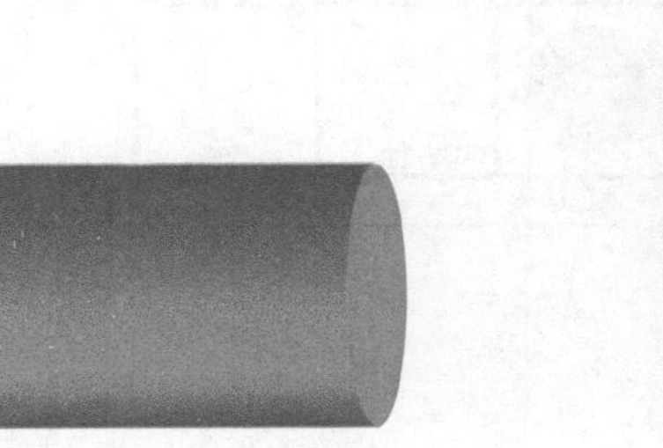

Dd

different	diferente

different alike

diferente igual

Ee

eight	ocho

8

8

English	Spanish/Español

eighteen

18

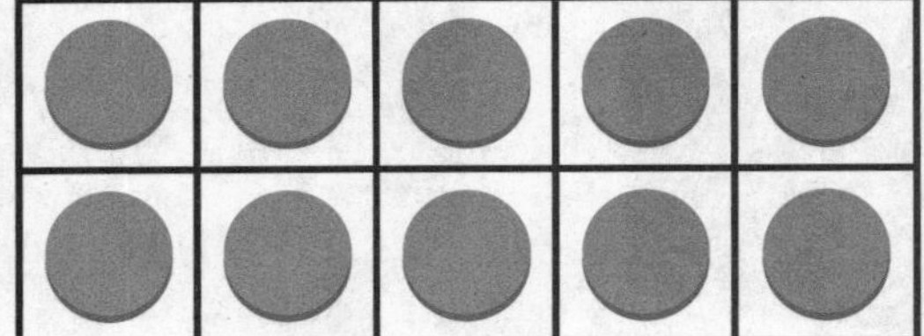
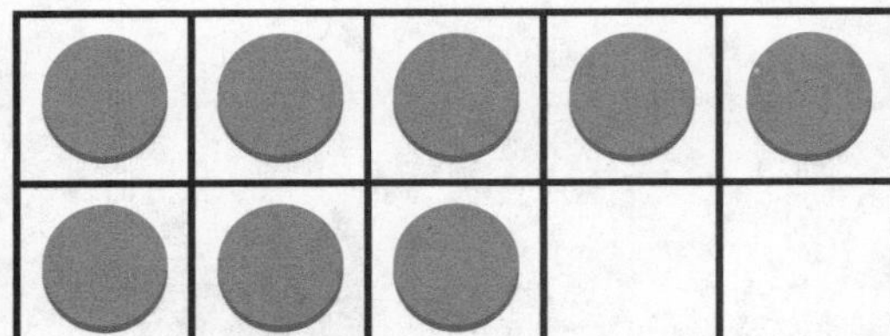

dieciocho

18

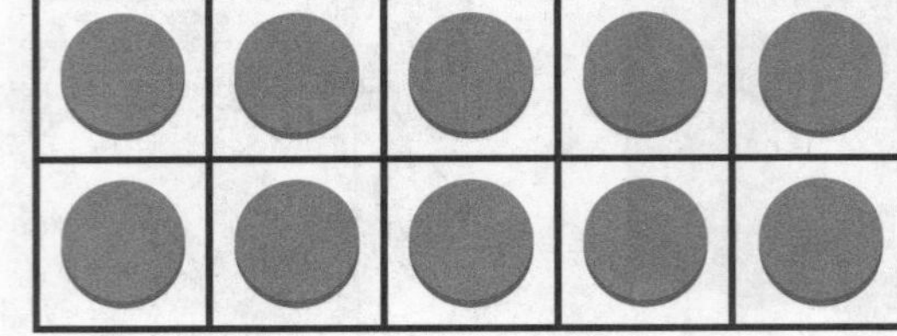
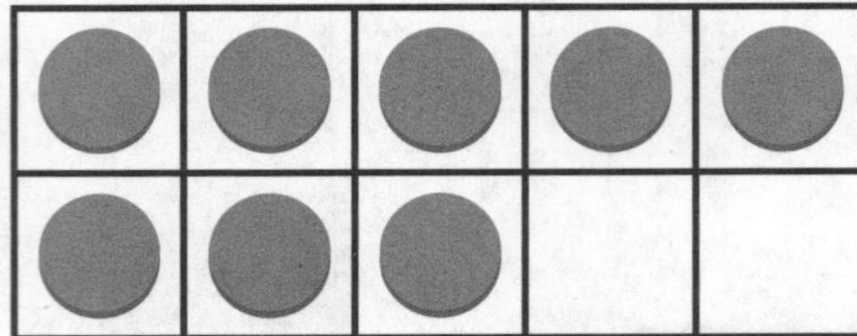

eleven

11

once

11

equal sign (=)

4 + 1 = 5

equals

signo igual (=)

4 + 1 = 5

igual

equal to

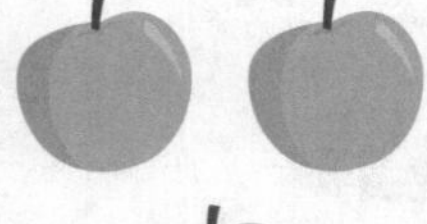
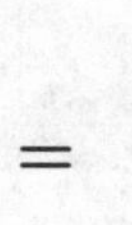
=

igual a

=

English	Spanish/Español
equation	ecuación
$2 + 1 = 3$	$2 + 1 = 3$
$3 - 1 = 2$	$3 - 1 = 2$

Ff

English	Spanish/Español
fewer    fewer	menos   menos
fifteen 15   	quince 15  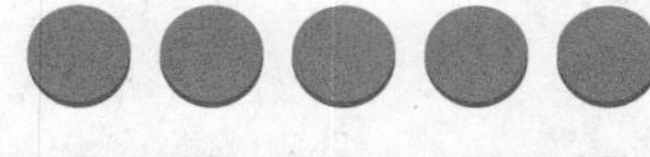 
five 5 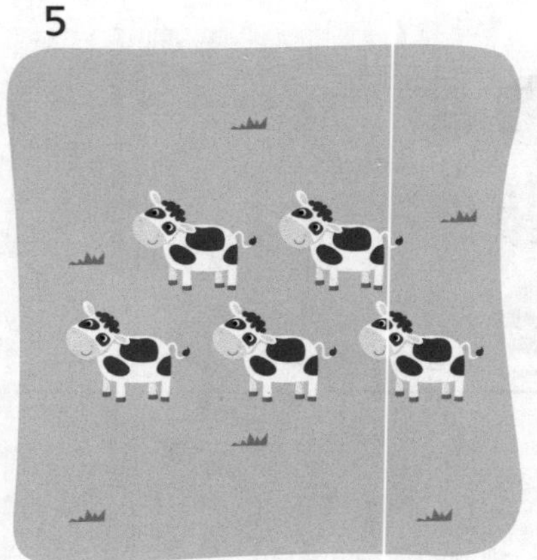	cinco 5 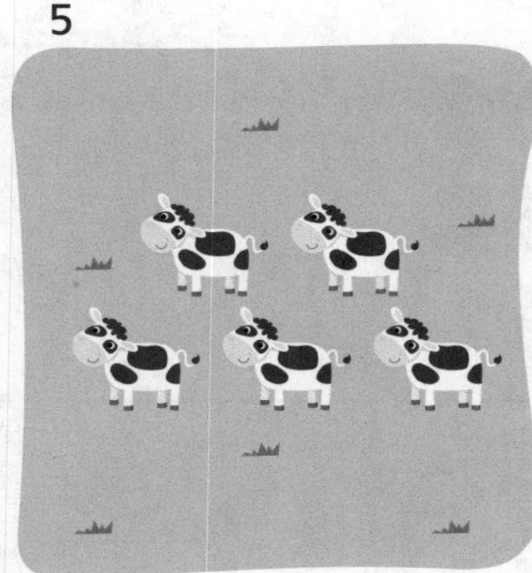

English	Spanish/Español
flat shape	forma plana
	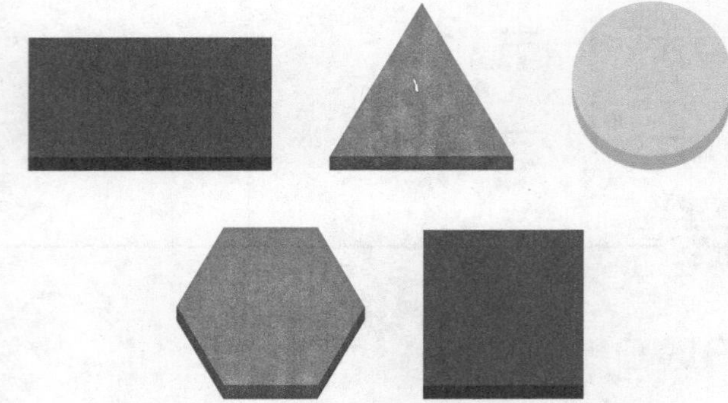
four	cuatro
4 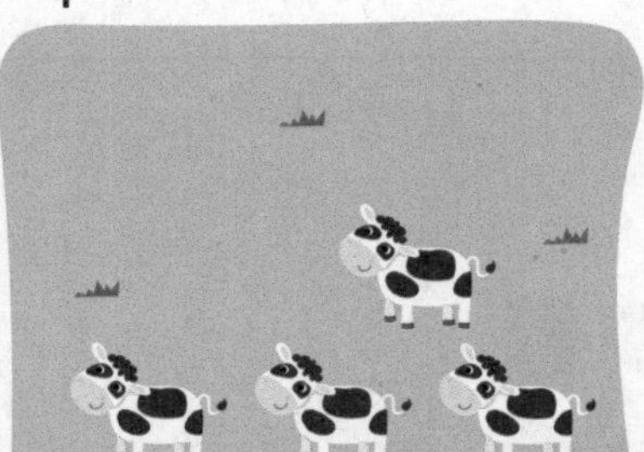	4 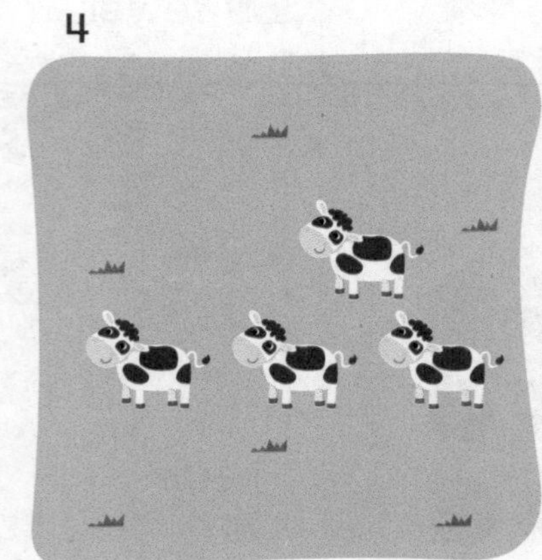
fourteen	catorce
14 	14 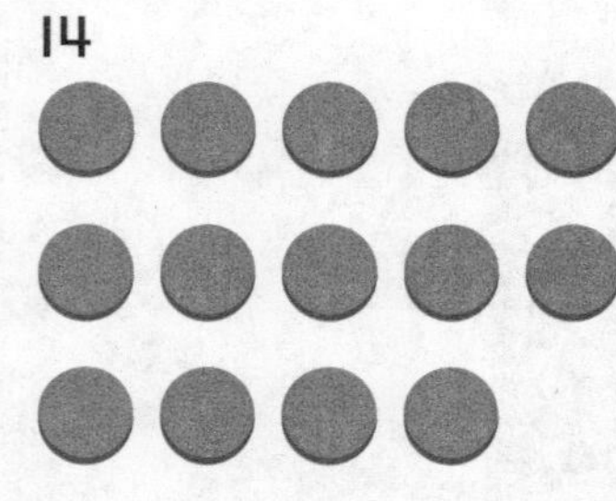

English | Spanish/Español

Gg

greater than

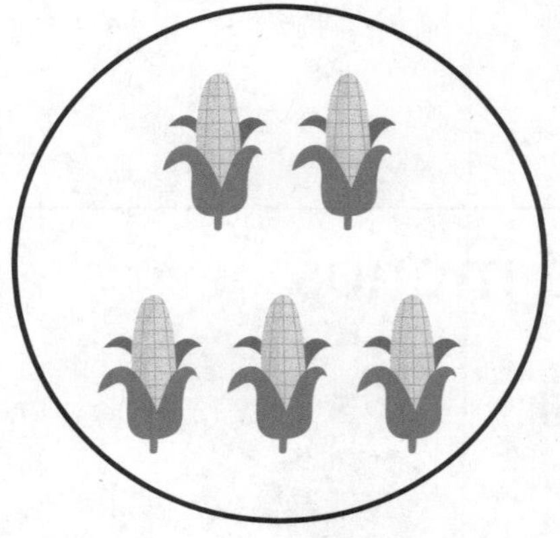

mayor que

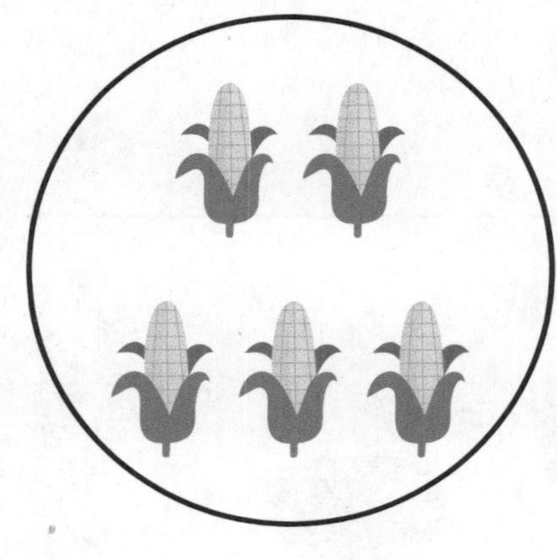

Hh

heavy (heavier)

pesado (más pesado)

height

altura

English	Spanish/Español
hexagon 	hexágono 
holds less  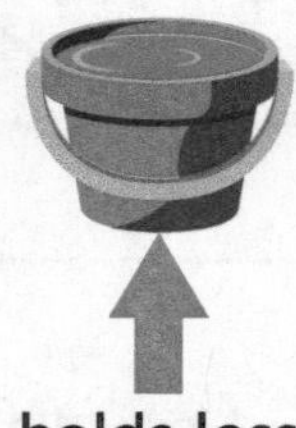 holds less	contiene menos   contiene menos
holds more 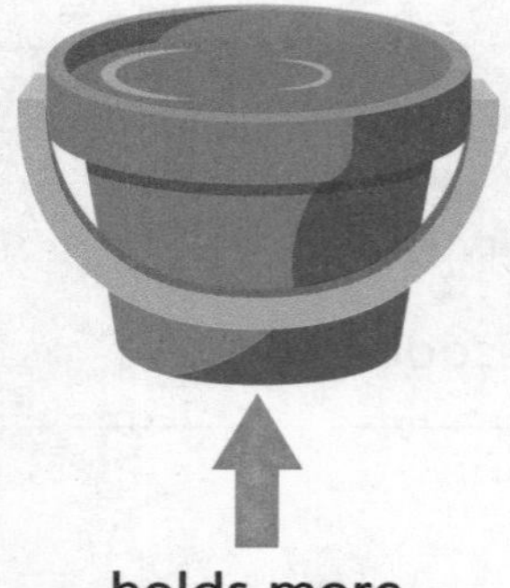  holds more	contiene más   contiene más
how many    1 2 3 3 bears	cuántos   1 2 3 3 osos

English | **Spanish/Español**

Jj

join

3 birds and 2 birds join.

juntar

Hay 3 aves y se les juntan 2 más.

Ll

least

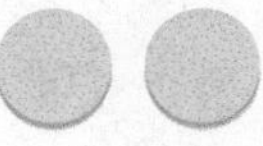

least

menor

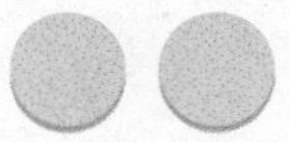

menor

length

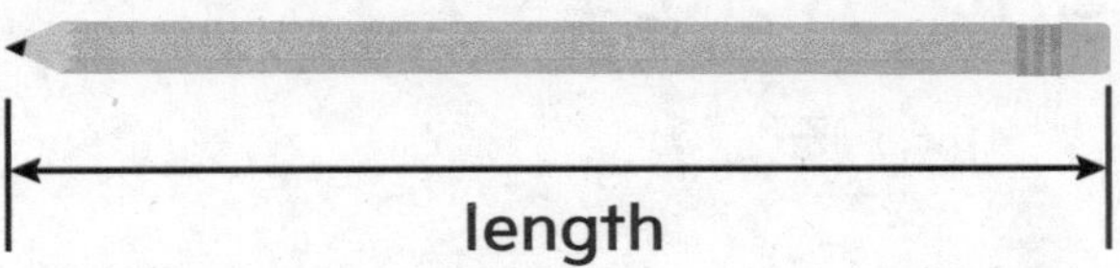

longitud

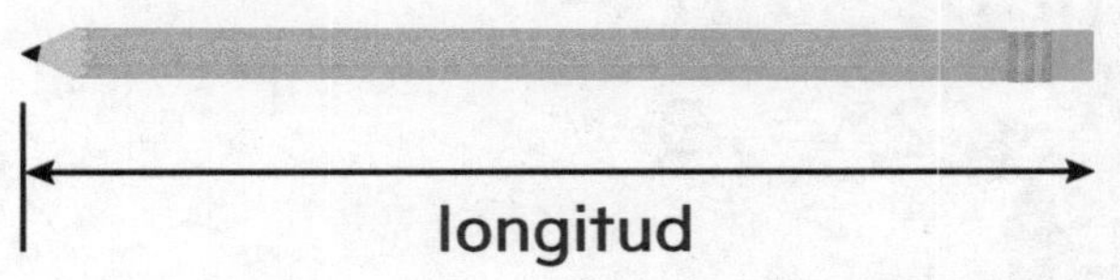

less than

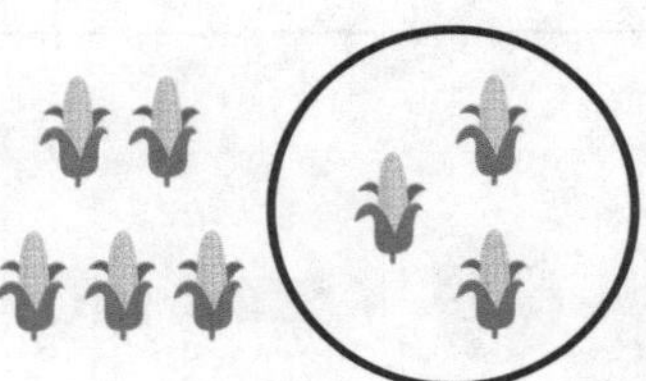

menos que

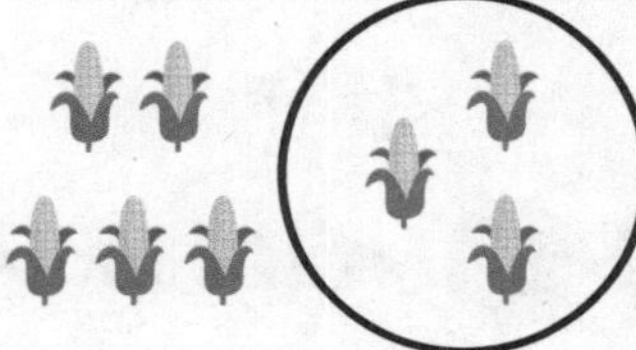

light (lighter)

lighter

liviano (más liviano)

más liviano

English	Spanish/Español
long (longer)	largo (más largo)

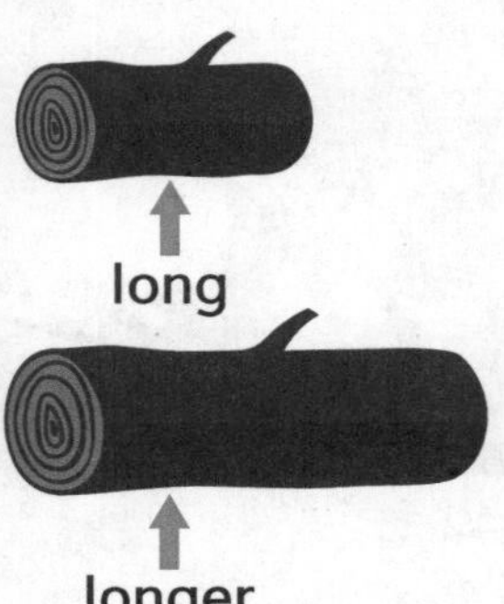

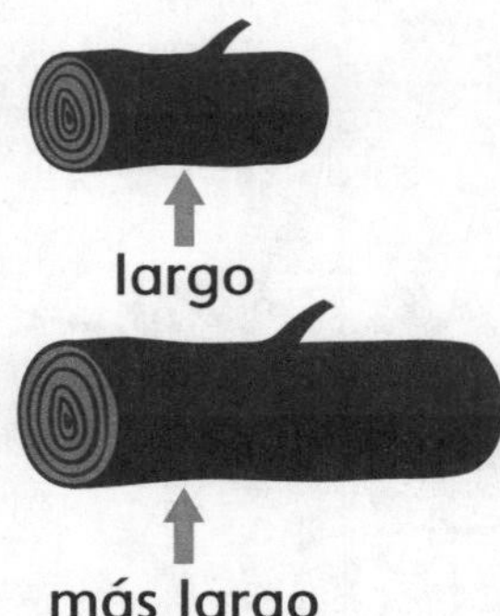

Mm

make

make 5

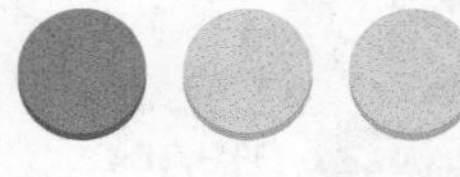

1 and 4 is 5.

formar

formar 5

1 y 4 es 5.

minus sign (–)

5 – 2 = 3

minus

signo menos (–)

5 – 2 = 3

menos

more

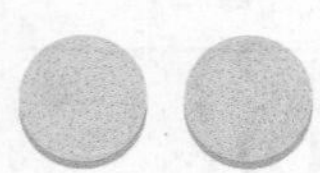

más

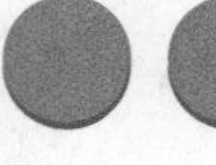
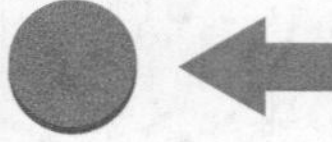

most

mayor

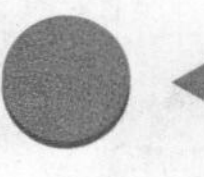

Nn

English	Spanish/Español
nine	nueve

9

9

English	Spanish/Español
nineteen	diecinueve

19

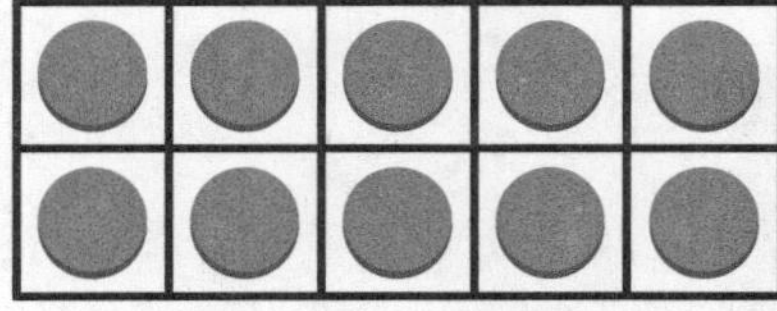

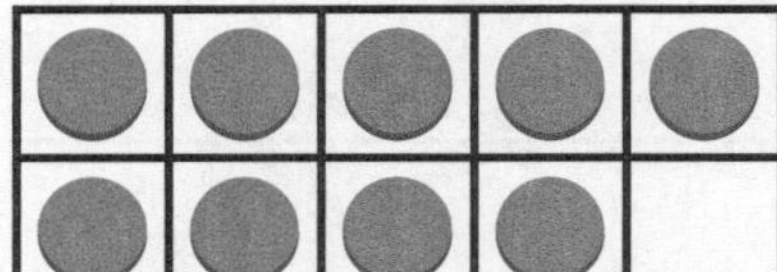

19

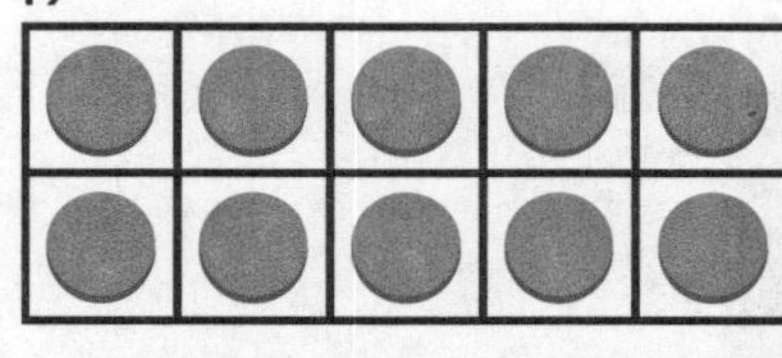

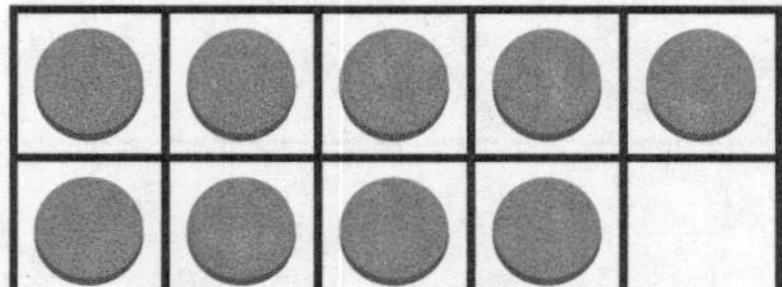

Oo

English	Spanish/Español
one	uno

1

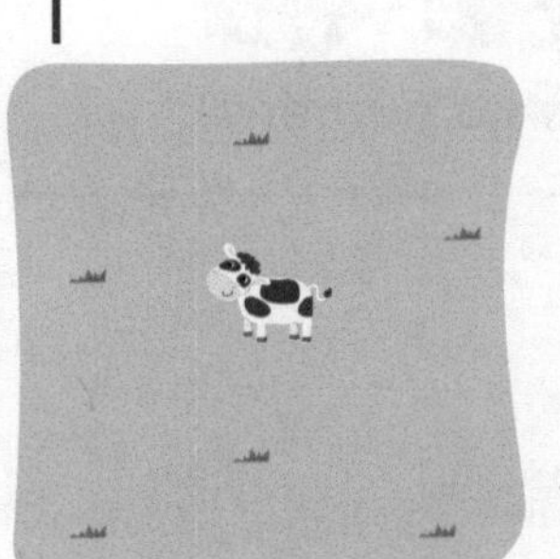

1

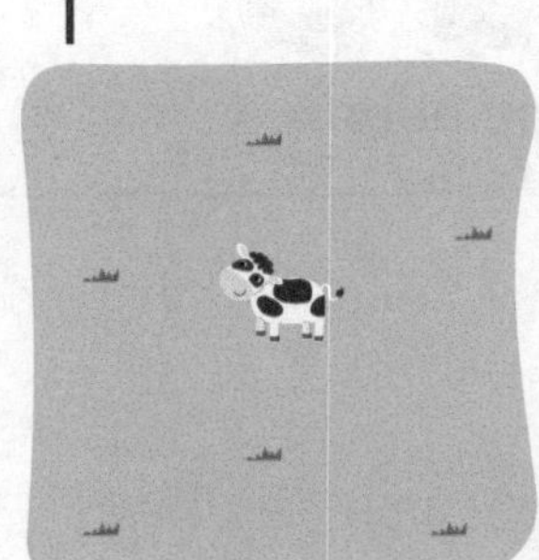

English	Spanish/Español
ones	unidades

10 ones

10 unidades

English | Spanish/Español

Pp

plus sign (+)

5 + 2 = 7

plus

signo más (+)

5 + 2 = 7

más

Rr

rectangle

rectángulo

Ss

same

same color, same number

mismo

el mismo color, el mismo número

seven

7

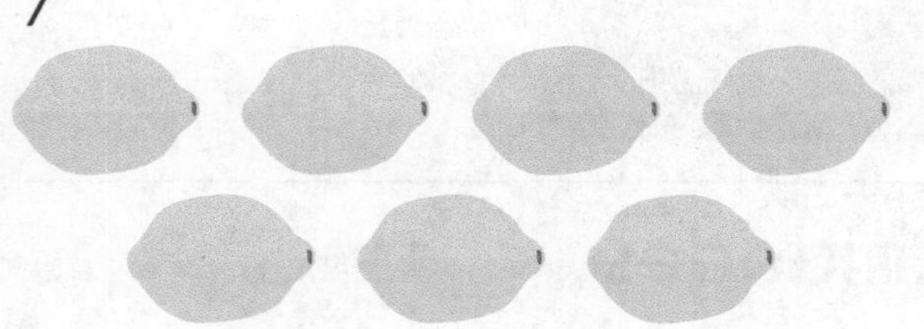

siete

7

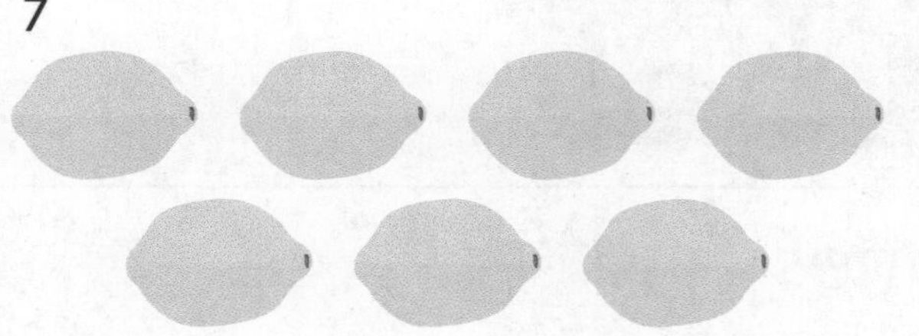

English	Spanish/Español

seventeen

17

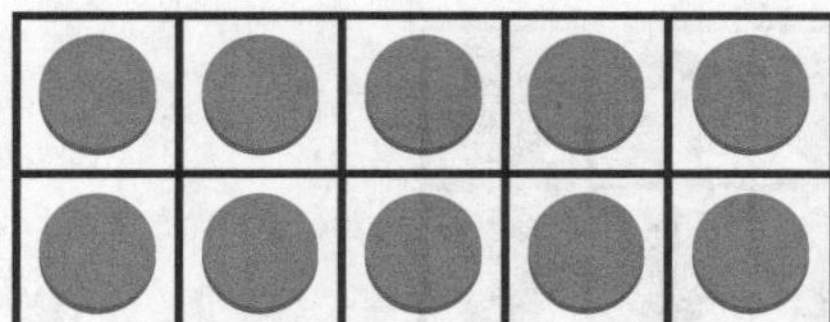
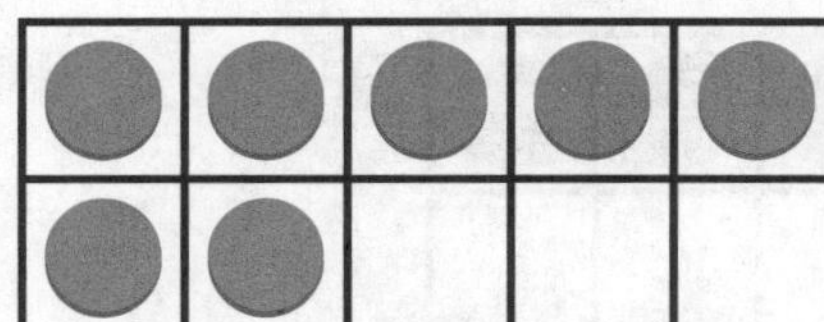

diecisiete

17

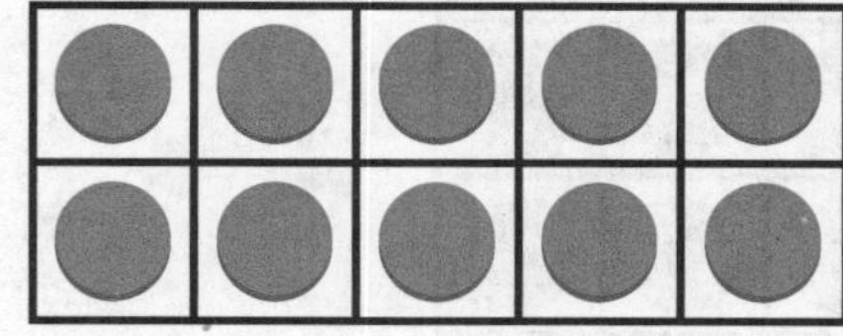
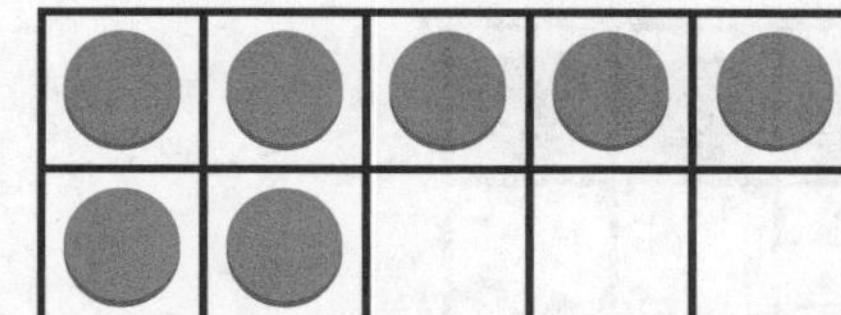

short (shorter)

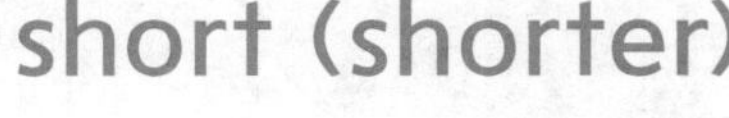
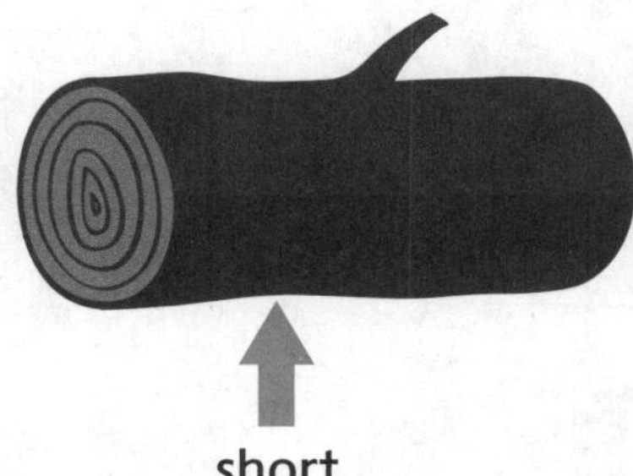

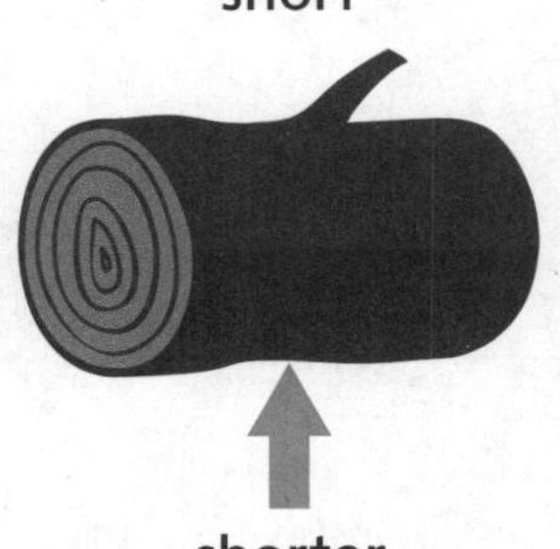

corto (más corto)

six

6

seis

6

English	Spanish/Español
sixteen	dieciséis

16

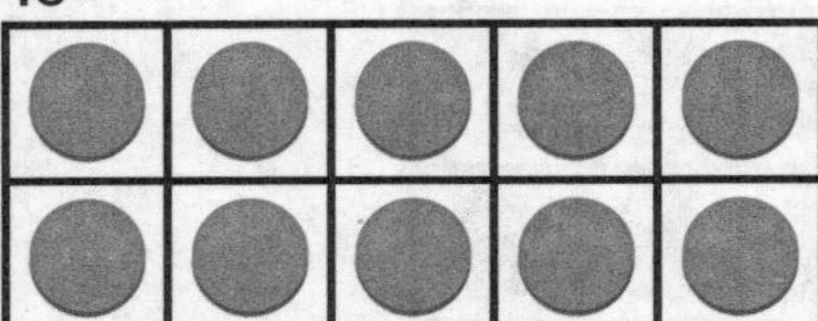
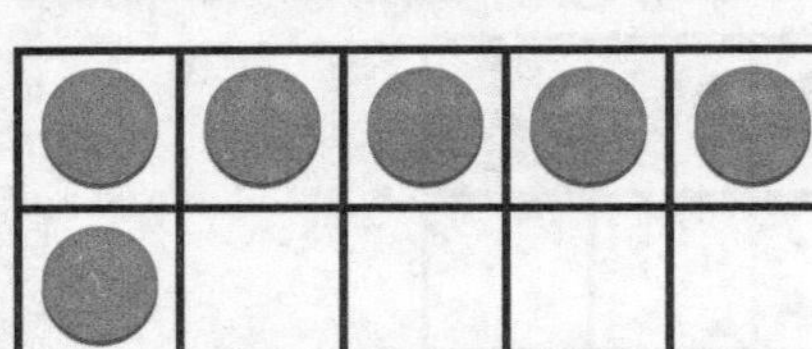

16

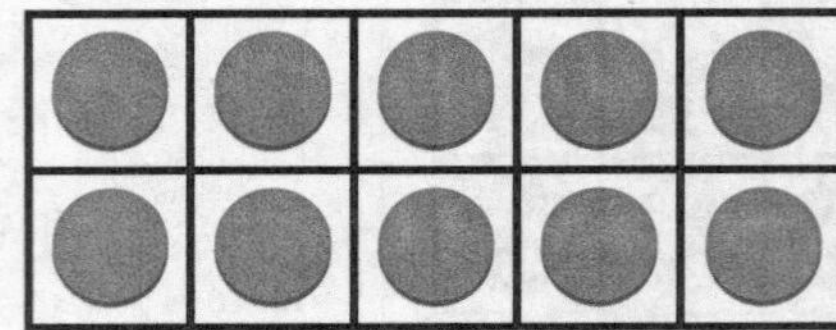
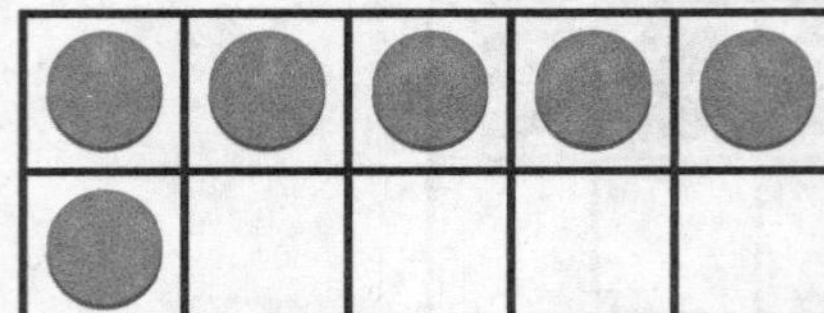

solid shape	forma sólida

sphere	esfera

 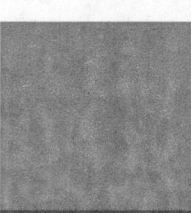

square	cuadrado

English	Spanish/Español
subtract	**restar**
  5 − 2 = 3	  5 − 2 = 3

Tt

English	Spanish/Español
tall (taller)	**alto (más alto)**
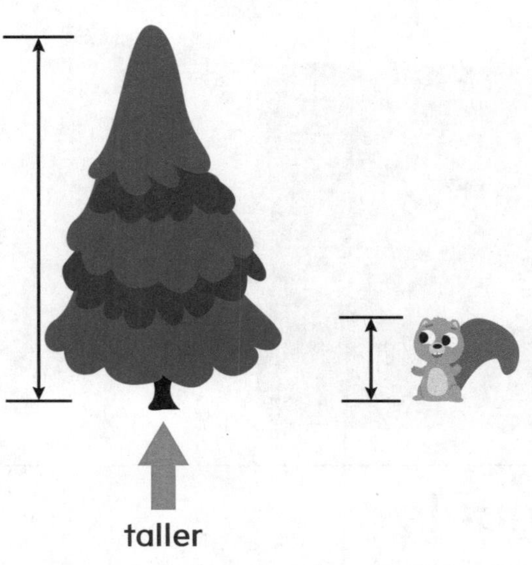	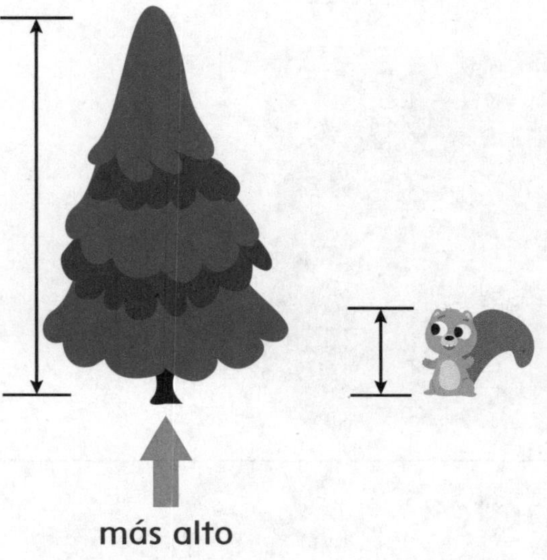
ten	**diez**

English	Spanish/Español
thirteen 13 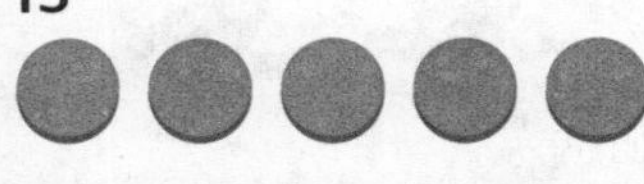  	**trece** 13  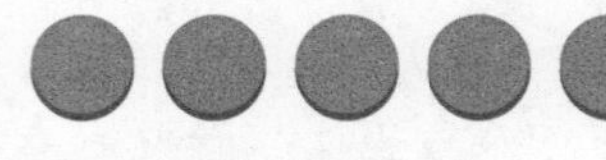 
three 3 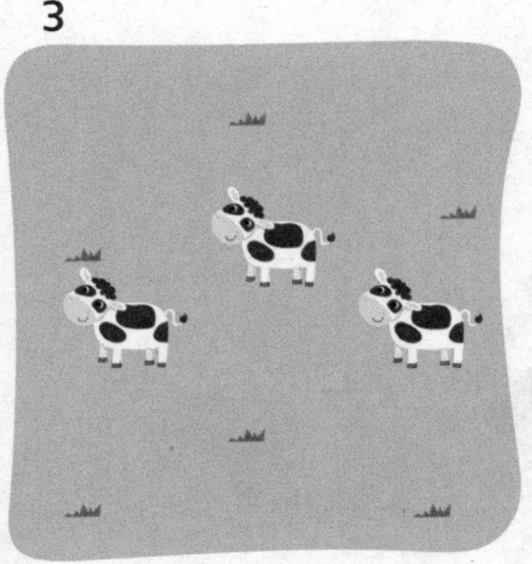	**tres** 3 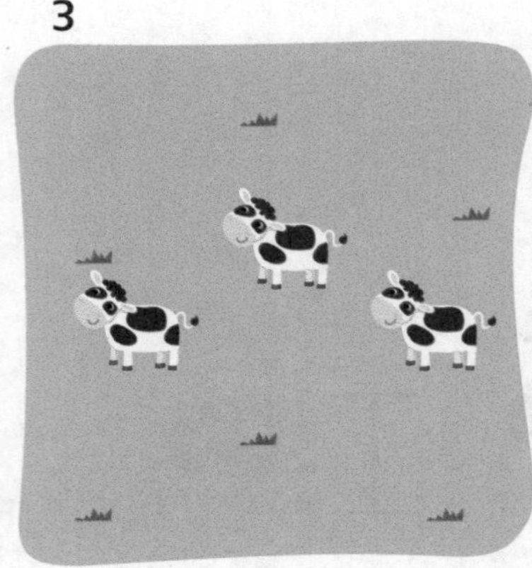
triangle 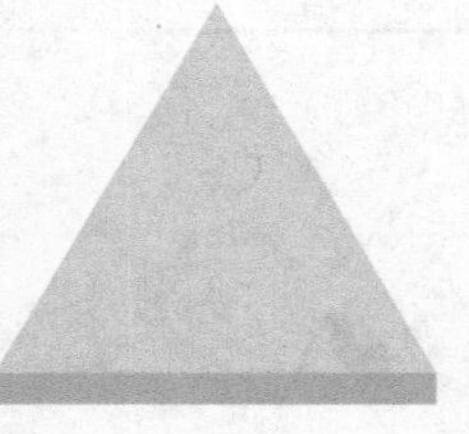	**triángulo** 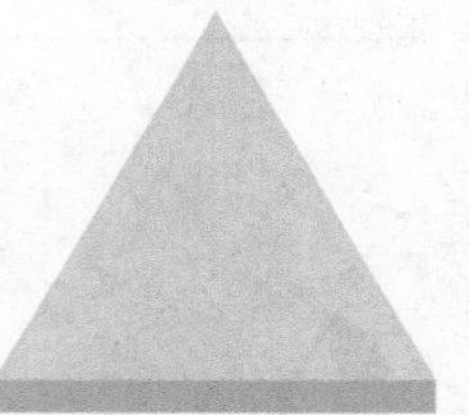
twelve 12   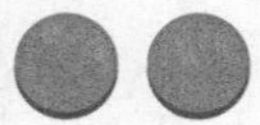	**doce** 12  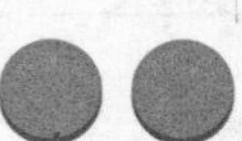

English	Spanish/Español

two

2

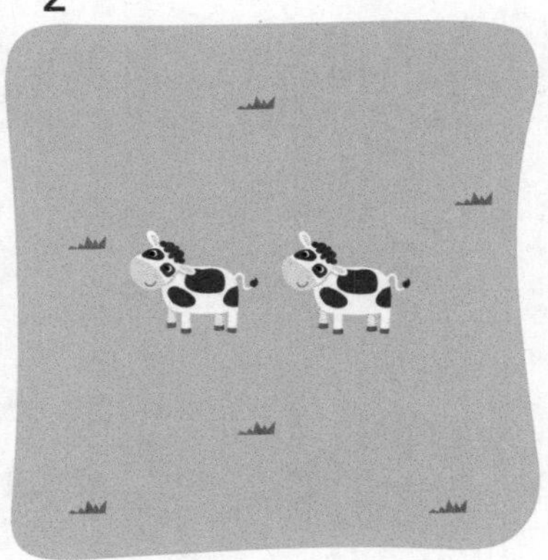

dos

2

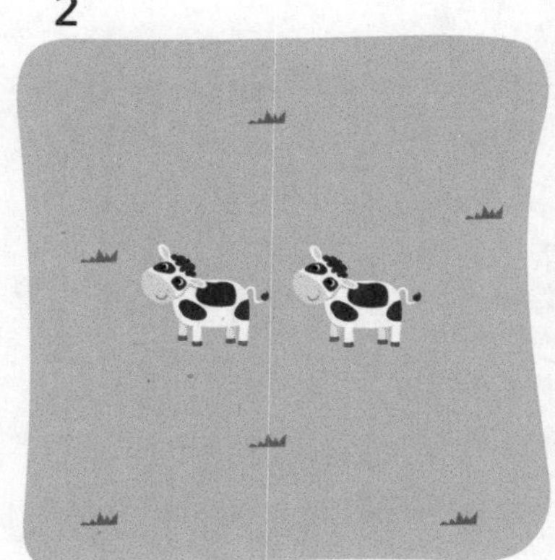

Ww

weight

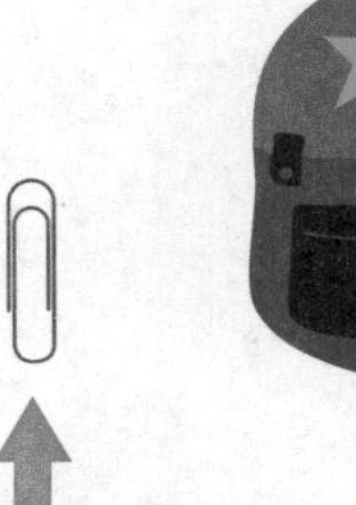

light heavy

peso

liviano pesado

Zz

zero

0

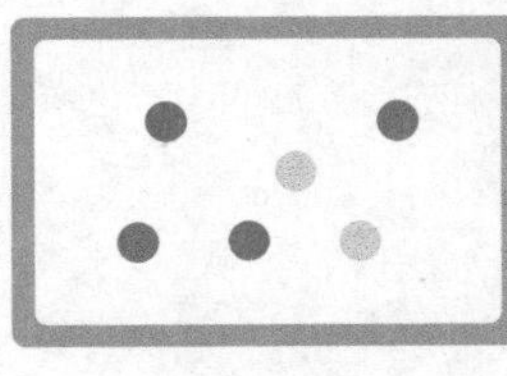

6 0

cero

0

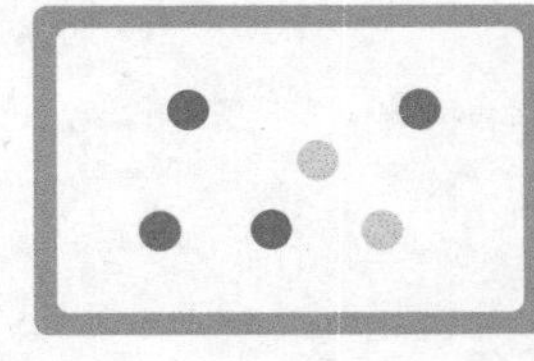

6 0